THE MARCH OF CONQUEST

**GREAT
WAR
STORIES**

THE MARCH OF CONQUEST

THE GERMAN VICTORIES IN WESTERN EUROPE, 1940

by Telford Taylor

 The Nautical & Aviation Publishing Company of America
Baltimore, Maryland

Library of Congress Catalog Card Number: 89-61022

ISBN: 0-933852-94-0

Printed in the United States of America

Library of Congress Cataloging in Publication Data

Taylor, Telford.
THE MARCH OF CONQUEST: THE GERMAN VICTORIES IN WESTERN EUROPE, 1940 / Telford Taylor.
p. cm.

Reprint. Originally published: New York: Simon and Schuster, 1958
Includes bibliographical references and index.
ISBN: 0-933852-94-0
1. World War, 1939-1945 — Campaigns — Western. 2. World War,

1939-1945 — Germany. I. Title.
D756.T3 1990
940.541—dc20

89-61022 CIP

To My Commanding Officers
of the Second World War

CARTER W. CLARKE
BRIGADIER GENERAL USA

and the late
ALFRED McCORMACK
COLONEL AUS

Foreword

ON THE AFTERNOON *of May 21, 1940, a steaming hot day in Washington, my wife and I joined a group of friends for a picnic supper on the rocks overlooking the Potomac rapids. The occasion was a thirtieth birthday celebration, but it was not a gay party. A week earlier the Germans had cracked the French lines on the Meuse, and the news of the day was that the panzers had reached the Channel coast and split the Allied armies.*

The waters of the Potomac danced in the setting sun; someone hopefully recalled the "miracle of the Marne" in World War I. His optimism was not catching. Day by day the newspaper maps had shown the ominous lengthening of the needlelike salient that had started as a tiny bulge at Sedan. Now it had reached Abbéville; only the ocean had stopped the assault that the French were helpless to check.

The world we had known was losing its underpinnings, and we sat silent and stunned. No doubt millions of other Americans sensed impending catastrophe that same evening, even though many clung desperately to a blind faith in the French Army almost until Pétain sued for an armistice. But at some time during the late spring of 1940, every American awoke not only to the fact of French defeat but to a chilling realization that Nazi Germany might well win the war!

It was the end of an American era. In 1814, four thousand British regulars had captured and burned the national Capitol, but in 1940 few Americans and fewer British knew that such a thing had ever happened. A century and a quarter had elapsed since the times when the United States was seriously endangered by foreign military power.

National security was something that Americans took for granted, even after the brief involvement in World War I. Britain and France

vii

were friendly powers; one had the largest Navy and the other "the finest Army" in the world. The United States "had never lost a war," and there seemed to be small chance that it would soon—perhaps ever —have to fight another.

Then these blue horizons were darkened by the ugly cloud of Nazism. At first, Americans found it hard to take Adolf Hitler seriously, with his absurd mustache and strident, extravagant speeches. Soon they came to hate him for sneering at democracy, persecuting Jews, and disturbing the peace. But for the most part Americans did not fear Hitler. He was too queer, too remote.

After Munich, hatred of Nazism was mixed with exasperation at the British and French. Appeasement! Would no one stop this mad adventurer? Next was Poland's turn, and when Britain and France declared war on Germany—shocking as the very idea of war was to a people that had been so lightly touched by its scourge—there was an all but audible sigh of relief from an American public that was overwhelmingly sympathetic to the Allied cause. Sober statesmen predicted a long and terrible war, but American faith in French military prowess was deep-rooted, and who wanted it shaken? The Maginot Line shielded the United States as well as France.

The Wehrmacht struck, and in four weeks' time the French were crushed. Churchill was indomitable, but Britain was in dire straits. Suddenly the entire structure of American military security, which had endured since the turn of the century, collapsed. The agent of its destruction was the Wehrmacht.

A year and a half of uneasy peace remained, while the United States was riven by the isolationist-interventionist debate. But the die was already cast. America could no longer find security in the power of friendly European nations, and a large but antiquated Pacific fleet for insurance against the Japanese. To be sure, the German legions were on the other side of the Atlantic, but what would be America's fate in a world dominated by a Nazi Empire?

France had fallen, Britain must be shored up. But for the United States, security could be regained only by the development of her own vast resources and speedy conversion of the potential to the actual. America must become and remain a great military power. So it has been ever since that spring of 1940, and so it will be as long as can be foreseen today.

Few indeed must be the Americans whose lives were not deeply affected by the events that cast so prophetic a pall over the picnic on the Potomac. The scene of this book is western Europe, but it tells a story of military conquests that turned the course of American history.

TELFORD TAYLOR

New York City
February, 1958

Contents

MAPS

Introduction

ON OCTOBER 6, 1939, Adolf Hitler, fresh from the conquest of Poland, called on the allied French and British governments to put an end to the war. His invitation was declined. On July 19, 1940, Adolf Hitler, master of western Europe from the North Cape to the Pyrenees, arrogantly but hopefully offered his peace to the British. They would have none of it, and their decision to fight on was one of the great turning points of modern history.

This book traces the background and course of the apocalyptic events in the spring and summer of 1940, when the Wehrmacht, like a great scythe, swung from north to south through Scandinavia, the Low Countries, and France. Never in the memory of man had the march of conquest been so swift, or its immediate impact so shattering. In a few weeks France as a great power was done to death, and the world of Versailles was swept into the past.

How were those extraordinary victories accomplished? Not by secret weapons, or "fifth columns," or Hitlerian intuition. Treason and deception played a very minor part in determining the outcome. On the contrary, the issue was drawn and resolved in orthodox military terms. The Germans were better armed and better led. They had an ingenious and flexible plan of attack; the Allies were tied to a rigid and ill-conceived defensive pattern. The Germans had mastered, as the Allies had not, the proper use of armor and air support in the military dimensions of those times. The Wehrmacht, in short, was ready and willing to do battle. The British were not ready, and the French, for the most part, were neither ready nor willing.

1

After the fall of France, Germany's military position seemed impregnable. Her armies, battle-hardened and virtually unscathed, dominated the European continent more completely than ever had even Napoleon's. The Luftwaffe ruled the skies over the mainland and threatened the English in their island fortress with savage, crippling, and perhaps lethal blows.

Still the victor's peace eluded Hitler's grasp. British tenacity in the face of disaster baffled the Fuehrer and frustrated his designs, but it was neither the only nor the primary cause of his failure. Stubborn courage and resourcefulness enable men to do great things with slender means; these admirable qualities stretch and stimulate the sinews of war but they are, alas, no substitute for the sinews themselves. After Dunkirk the British, for all their naval prowess and growing air strength, were virtually powerless on the ground. Had the Wehrmacht succeeded in landing a few divisions on English soil, there would have been small hope of containing them.

But the British were never put to this test. When they spurned Hitler's overtures, the German high command was left wallowing in a morass of indecision. The mighty Wehrmacht stood in its tracks, paralyzed for lack of leadership.

Why were the fruits of these stupendous spring victories allowed to spoil in the summer sun? Throughout the nine months from Warsaw to Compiègne, German grand strategy was as dull as German tactics were brilliant. The Third Reich produced no Great Captain. At times Hitler thought himself one, and Keitel and other military lickspittles often fed the illusion. But Hitler's strategic judgments were uninformed and emotionally distorted, and his personal leadership—by no means devoid of perception and imagination—was nevertheless impulsive and desultory. Halder, Manstein, and a few others could plan campaigns, and the Germans were rich in able field commanders. But none of the generals were able to tell Hitler what campaigns to undertake or how to exploit the victories that they presented to him.

And so it came about that when the Wehrmacht surged across the frontiers of Holland and Belgium and broke through the French lines at the Meuse, its leaders had no sufficient strategic objective. True, they sought to shatter the French Army and improve their own geographical basis for aerial and submarine warfare against Britain. But these goals, however desirable for the prosecution of the war, were not decisive of its issue. Indeed, at no time prior to June 1940 do Hitler or any of the generals appear to have had any idea how the war was to be brought to a successful conclusion, save the hope that the Allies would throw in the sponge once they had suffered serious reverses.

Thus the Germans failed to plan for the very contingency of the overwhelming victory which they so rapidly achieved. They were stunned by their own success, and when the French sued for peace and the British withdrew across the Channel, Hitler did not know what to do next. No more did the generals; they had never envisioned a pursuit of the British or the need to be prepared for amphibious operations.

Nor did anyone on the German side adjust his thinking to the newly emerging shape of things. The outcome of the Battle of France was a foregone conclusion at least by May 26. From then on, the attention of the German high command should have been focused on how their success in France could be turned to decisive advantage in terms of the war as a whole. Instead, the British Expeditionary Force was allowed to escape from Dunkirk, while the full might of the Wehrmacht—at least half again the necessary force—was marshaled to finish off the mortally stricken French. Then, after Compiègne, another month was dissipated in celebration and wishful thinking, while the British licked their wounds and shored up their defenses.

Thereby Hitler and the leaders of the German officer corps—the *ne plus ultra* of military professionalism—violated one of the most familiar and elementary principles of strategy: after a battlefield victory, pursue and destroy the beaten enemy. Hitler the corporal of World War I and Rundstedt and his fellow generals who had then been junior officers were all lost in memories of the Marne and the Somme. Their minds slumbered too long, and when they awoke to the reality of an intransigent Britain, their best opportunity for a quick knockout by invasion was already past.

Perhaps there were other avenues to final victory, via the Mediterranean and the Middle East, or by mobilizing the resources of the entire continent for a war of attrition against the British. However that may be, in the upshot Hitler's instability, the generals' lack of vision, and crucial flaws in the basic structure of the Third Reich stalled the German military machine at the peak of its power and prestige.

In that summer of 1940 Hitler stood on the verge of conquests of such dimensions that his overthrow would have been a desperate undertaking for any combination of nations and could hardly have been accomplished in less than a decade of bloody struggle, unless by the extensive use of nuclear weapons. By those victories in France and

Flanders the generals brought their Fuehrer within sight of an imperium that would have been the envy of a Charlemagne.

Now these events lie eighteen years in the past, among those things that William Butler Yeats called "not old enough to be in the histories or new enough to be in the reader's mind." But they deserve to be remembered and understood. It is well for the world that the British did not flinch, and that Hitler's reach exceeded his grasp.

CHAPTER ONE

The Wehrmacht in 1940

THE GERMAN VICTORIES in the spring of 1940 must be accounted among the most remarkable of modern times. The ensuing years have been so full of martial triumph and disaster, of carnage and atrocity, that memories of the Norwegian landings and the armored dash to Abbéville have been overlaid and obscured. Yet these campaigns, small though they were compared to the long and bloody surge of armed millions on the eastern front and the Allied sweep across western Europe, had a terribly swift and absolute quality which later and bigger battles never matched.

From the standpoint of sheer tactical efficiency, and by the cold-blooded standard of the conqueror, the spring of 1940 was the classic period of the Wehrmacht in the Third Reich. In less than three months Norway, Denmark and the Low Countries were overrun and occupied, France was defeated and knocked out of the war, and the British were swept off the continent and back across the Channel, whipped and stripped of their arms. The world-wide balance of military power was upset, and Germany emerged as the dominant nation-in-arms.

Furthermore, these things were not achieved by overwhelming superiority in men or guns, or at great cost. Planning which was at once imaginative and meticulous, execution which was both spirited and precise, planted the Wehrmacht along the Norwegian coast in the teeth of the Royal Navy and easily accomplished the relatively bloodless but complete overthrow of the vaunted French Army. And before tracing the origin of these plans and the course of these campaigns, it will be useful to survey the Wehrmacht, which was the instrument of these extraordinary conquests, on the eve of their achievement.

Adolf Hitler and the Wehrmacht

At the outbreak of World War II, the relations between Adolf Hitler and the German military leaders were in a state of instability but not of crisis.

Those relations between sword and swastika had fluctuated violently during the six and a half years since Hitler's accession to power. From the outset he had enjoyed the support of the new Minister of Defense, General Werner von Blomberg, and a few other high-ranking officers who were sympathetic to the Nazi movement. But the prevailing attitude among the senior officers was one of considerable suspicion, aroused in large part by the rowdiness, radicalism, and social unacceptability of many of the Nazi party chieftains.

As Chancellor under the venerable President von Hindenburg, Hitler treated the generals with shrewd deference; this and his full support of clandestine rearmament in violation of the Versailles Treaty restrictions quieted many doubts. In June 1934 Hitler reinforced his support in military circles by his ruthless suppression of the *Sturmabteilung* (SA) and the elimination of its chief, Ernst Roehm, who had hoped to transmute the professionalized, semiaristocratic *Reichswehr* into a sort of "people's army" under his own leadership. Even the murderous brutality of this *coup* (in which Hitler's immediate predecessor as Chancellor, General von Schleicher, was killed) awakened few misgivings in the officer corps, for in the clutch Hitler had stood with the Army against what was then the most powerful and hostile component of the Party.

And so when Hindenburg died a month later, and Hitler declared himself Fuehrer of what is known to history as the Third Reich, there was little difficulty in requiring every German soldier to swear an oath of personal allegiance to the dictator. The psychological and moral consequences of this oath were to prove agonizing and stultifying to many officers in time to come. The immediate consequence of Hindenburg's death was that Hitler became not only Chief of State (*Fuehrer und Reichskanzler*), but also the Supreme Commander (*Oberster Befehlshaber*) of the German armed forces, soon to be rechristened the "Wehrmacht."

For the next three years, Hitler and the military leaders co-operated effectively, and for the most part harmoniously, in the serious business of rearmament. Differences there were; Hitler set a faster pace than the top army generals thought wise, and there was a widening gulf of manner and outlook between them and the Nazi-indoctrinated youngsters that were pouring into the expanding Wehrmacht. The remilitarization of the Rhineland in 1936 struck many of the generals as a dangerous gamble, but when it came off successfully they were delighted. There were promotions and big responsibilities for everyone. Even the cautious and high-principled Chief of the General Staff, General Ludwig Beck, was temporarily won over. Open opposition to the Fuehrer was nonexistent; those few who still doubted his leadership held their peace.

This calm was rudely shattered by a bloodless but decisive crisis during the winter of 1937–38. Hitler had concluded that international circumstances would soon be propitious for the annexation of Austria (*Anschluss*) and part or all of Czechoslovakia. But when he disclosed these thoughts to a select few, both Blomberg (by then War Minister and Commander-in-Chief of the Wehrmacht, with the rank of *Generalfeldmarschall*) and Generaloberst Werner von Fritsch (Commander-in-Chief of the Army) reacted very coldly. Two months later Blomberg rendered himself vulnerable by a marriage which, after the lady's past came to light, was regarded by his brother officers as a scandalous *mésalliance*. At about the same time, a dossier was produced from the secret police files purporting to implicate Fritsch in homosexual actions. At the end of January 1938 Blomberg was cashiered and Fritsch was relieved as Commander-in-Chief of the Army. A military court subsequently found Fritsch innocent of the charge and he was given an honorary designation as *Chef* of a regiment, but he was not restored to his post or given any other active command.

The downfall of Blomberg and Fritsch was in large part the work of Hermann Goering and Heinrich Himmler. As Commander-in-Chief of the Air Force (Luftwaffe), the vainglorious Goering had little relish for his military subordination to Blomberg.* Himmler, the leader (*Reichsfuehrer*) of the SS and Chief of the German Police, had replaced Roehm as the arch-antagonist of the officer corps. Essentially it was an ideological conflict, with the allegiance of German youth as the prize. Himmler wished not only to revolutionize the entire army system of training and indoctrination in accordance with the most extreme

---

* Goering, like Fritsch, held the rank of *Generaloberst* and was immediately subordinate to Blomberg, the Commander-in-Chief of the Wehrmacht. In his other official capacities, such as Minister for Air and Plenipotentiary for the Four-Year Plan, Goering was directly responsible to Hitler. Goering was also the successor-designate as Fuehrer in the event of Hitler's death or incapacity, and was thus "second man" in the Third Reich.

Nazi tenets and superstitions but also to establish a separate and elite SS army. On both scores he had fallen afoul of Blomberg and Fritsch, and their ruination was a necessary step to the fulfillment of his aims.

And so Blomberg's marriage and the false police dossier on Fritsch were merely pretexts and devices, serving as tools of Goering's jealousy, Himmler's rivalry, and Hitler's dissatisfaction with these slow-poke generals who threw cold water on his bold plans. With great skill, Hitler made the power struggle appear at first to be merely a matter of personalities. But in breaking Fritsch on a trumped-up charge, Hitler shattered the leadership of the officer corps and established his own personal command and direct control of the Wehrmacht. Blomberg was not replaced, and thenceforth the Commanders-in-Chief of the Army, Navy, and Air Force reported directly to Hitler. Goering was promoted to *Generalfeldmarschall,* and thus became the ranking German officer. The new Commander-in-Chief of the Army, Generaloberst Walter von Brauchitsch, was an able soldier but lacked the prestige and strength of character to reawaken the independent *esprit* of the officer corps, or to maintain the Army's traditional pre-eminence in the structure of the Reich.

The ominous significance of the Blomberg-Fritsch affair was soon obscured in the excitement attending the annexation of Austria in March 1938. It was soon followed, however, by another and even sharper crisis arising out of Hitler's intention to invade Czechoslovakia, which he revealed late in May at a secret conference of top military and diplomatic officials. The Chief of the General Staff, General Beck, was horrified, for he thought that surely the French and British would come to the aid of their Czech allies, and he knew that the Wehrmacht, newly fledged and still far short of full strength, could not successfully undertake a war of such dimensions. Beck immediately embarked on a campaign of quiet but systematic opposition to Hitler's aggressive plans. A number of the generals shared his views, but there was no unanimity. Brauchitsch had misgivings but was pusillanimous and gave Beck no real support. Late in August, about a month before the attack was to be launched, Beck resigned his office, and after Munich he went on the retired list.

His successor as Chief of the General Staff, General Franz Halder, was also strongly opposed to the Czech adventure and went so far as to discuss with a few other generals the possibility of arresting Hitler and overthrowing the Nazi government by a military *coup d'état.* The commander of the German forces on the French border, General Wilhelm Adam, seized his first opportunity to lecture Hitler on the impossibility of holding the French with the resources at his disposal.

But the issue between Hitler and the "opposition generals" was never drawn. Neville Chamberlain flew to Berchtesgaden, and the ensuing negotiations ended in Hitler's triumph at Munich on September 29, 1938. Germany annexed the Sudetenland, and the military power of Czechoslovakia was destroyed. General Adam resigned, and Halder talked no more of resistance. Once again events had played into Hitler's hands and his critics in German military circles were discredited and silenced.

In March of 1939 Hitler swallowed the rest of Czechoslovakia and annexed the Baltic port of Memel. Abroad these events had strong repercussions, and in England the era of "appeasement" came to an end. In Germany, however, these events seemed merely an extension of Hitler's string of triumphs by show of force.

And so when, on April 28, 1939, Hitler denounced the German-Polish nonaggression pact of 1934 and leveled his sights on the Polish "corridor" and Danzig, no one in Germany ventured to dispute his wisdom. A month later Hitler, at a conference of the inner military circle, announced his intention to attack and destroy Poland. He warned his listeners that the Poles would resist, and outlined his plans in the event that Britain and France should come to Poland's assistance. Preparations were to be completed by the end of August.

This time there was no opposition, open or covert, among the leaders of the Wehrmacht. Poland was, after all, an offspring of the hated Versailles Treaty; most of the "corridor" had long been Prussian territory, and throughout the officer corps the geographical separation of East Prussia from the rest of Germany was regarded as intolerable. The Poles were incapable of prolonged resistance, and perhaps the British and French would resign themselves to the inevitable, as they had at Munich. The dire predictions of Beck and Adam had come to nothing, and no one wanted to repeat their mistake.

So the generals turned with alacrity to the task in hand, and by August everything was in readiness. The Army and the Luftwaffe were both much stronger than they had been in 1938, the western fortifications had been improved; Brauchitsch and Halder were sure the western front could be held, in the unlikely event of an immediate Allied attack, until the Poles had been crushed and the bulk of the Army thus released for transfer to the West. The Hitler-Stalin pact, when it was announced late in August, delighted the generals, for it removed the dreaded prospect of a two-front war and was in line with their traditional policy of close relations with the Red Army.

When Hitler gave the order to attack, and Britain and France honored their pledges to Poland by declaring war on Germany, the most unhappy member of the German high command was Gross-admiral Erich Raeder, Commander-in-Chief of the Navy. By the geo-graphical necessity of his calling, Raeder looked toward the West—to the Atlantic Ocean and the mighty Royal Navy. "Today, the war against France and England broke out, the war which, according to the Fuehrer's previous assertions, we had no need to expect before about 1944," Raeder noted for the naval archives, and added the gloomy observation that the Navy was "in no way adequately equipped for the great struggle with Great Britain in the autumn of 1939." But despite his belief that Hitler had prematurely led the Reich to war, Raeder entertained no thoughts of opposition, and his relations with the Fuehrer remained workable and generally serene.

The generals, too, were disturbed to find the Fatherland again at war with the Anglo-French alliance. Indeed, Hitler himself was far from pleased, for he had seriously hoped to isolate the Poles and achieve his immediate ends without a major war. These worries, how-ever, were soon forgotten in the excitement and exhilaration of the Polish campaign. German tanks and planes played havoc with the gallant but obsolete Polish infantry and cavalry formations. Within less than a week the Poles were hopelessly beaten, and by the middle of September the campaign as a whole was over and German troops were already streaming westward to reinforce the front facing the Allies. A few strong points held out until the end of September, but then it was all over, and on October 5 Hitler made a triumphal entry into Warsaw.[1]

No serious clashes between Hitler and the generals occurred during the fighting in Poland. The Fuehrer took a keen interest in operational matters but did not intrude in the sphere of military command. After the victory there were promotions and decorations. Moving pictures of actual combat were combined with others of subsequently "staged" displays, and the resultant concoction, entitled *Feuertaufe* (Baptism of Fire), was widely shown in Germany and neutral capitals.[2]

And so, as the Polish campaign passed into history, Hitler and the Wehrmacht leaders were linked by the bond of a mutually gratifying conquest. But now great strategic issues confronted them. What they had hoped would be a Polish-German war had turned into a major

European conflict. How could Germany bring it to a successful conclusion?

This problem was about to precipitate the third great crisis in the
relations between Hitler and the army generals. The reason for the
crisis was that these relations were, as previously stated, unstable. They
were unstable in that the respective roles of Hitler and the generals in
the taking of strategic decisions were still in a state of flux.

The power of final decision, of course, rested with Hitler as Fuehrer
and Supreme Commander, to whom every officer and man had sworn
personal allegiance and obedience. Furthermore, Hitler had con-
vincingly demonstrated that his military authority was no formality.
He had ridden rough-shod over Blomberg, Fritsch, Beck, and Adam,
swept them off the boards, and established his personal dominion over
the high command. He had carried out the Czechoslovakian adventure
despite the bitter opposition of the leaders of the officer corps and had
drowned his doubters in a tide of bloodless triumphs. And now, at
insignificant cost, the greater part of Poland had been added to the
Greater Reich.

Yet the question whether he would heed the counsels of the military
in the conduct of the war remained unsettled. Kaiser Wilhelm II, too,
had been Supreme War Lord, but his personal authority had dwindled
rapidly during World War I. Every German officer well remembered
the enormous power, transcending the military field, that had fallen
into the hands of Hindenburg and Ludendorff.

War, after all, was a matter for generals, not for ex-corporals, no
matter how dynamic and politically gifted. With the Polish victories
under their belts, the military professionals recovered a measure of the
self-confidence that they had lost as a result of their run-ins with
Hitler in 1938. Furthermore, some of the generals were highly critical
of Hitler's insistence that the Army draw back from the advanced positions in eastern Poland, to the line agreed upon with the Russians in
the secret protocol to the Moscow pact. Halder was especially caustic;
in his diary [3] he described the withdrawal as a "disgrace for German
political leadership." After the campaign was over, he also recorded [4]
Brauchitsch's opinion that the Army's exclusion from the field of foreign political policy had proved "a great drawback" and his conclusion
that: "The high command of the Army must not be left at the mercy
of the vagaries of politics, or else the Army will lose confidence."

On the other hand, the generals in Hitler's immediate entourage
gave almost slavish support to his opinions and policies. There was, in

fact, much division of opinion about the Fuehrer among the military leaders. The army officer corps included many who had been closely allied in viewpoint with Fritsch, Beck, and Adam, and who continued to regard Hitler with considerable misgivings. But there were some who were outspokenly pro-Nazi, and their number increased rapidly among the younger officers. The tank specialists, like General Heinz Guderian, had been favorably impressed by Hitler's support for their bold conceptions of armored tactics. The naval officers generally accepted Hitler's leadership, often with enthusiasm, and in the Luftwaffe, Goering's political stature inevitably imparted a strong Nazi coloration at all levels of command.

In short, it was only among the senior army generals that serious opposition to Hitler's policies was likely to develop. Even in these circles there was, at the outbreak of the war, no disposition to attempt his overthrow; the string of conquests had choked all revolutionary whisperings. But deep resentments lingered, and professional pride was reinvigorated by the victory in Poland. Therefore, any sharp disagreement on crucial military issues between Hitler and the army leaders was bound to precipitate a crisis, as the events of October and November 1939 were about to prove.

The High Command of the Wehrmacht

The relation between Hitler and the army generals was not the only element of instability in the German high command. The other was a problem of military organization which is common to all governments, democratic or totalitarian: how to distribute command among and over the three principal services—land, sea, and air.

Since 1935, when Hitler openly repudiated the arms restrictions of the Versailles Treaty, each service had had its own commander-in-chief and general staff. Each of the three was subordinate to Blomberg as Minister of War and Commander-in-Chief of the Wehrmacht. Interservice planning and co-ordination were handled by the principal department of the Ministry, known as the *Wehrmachtamt,* headed by General Wilhelm Keitel. In 1938 when Blomberg was sacked, Hitler abolished his posts as well, so that the three service commanders-in-chief became his immediate subordinates. At the same time, the Ministry of War was renamed the High Command of the Wehrmacht (*Oberkommando der Wehrmacht*), commonly referred to as OKW.

As Chief (*Chef*) of OKW Hitler chose Keitel. The title is significant,

for Keitel had no power of command over the three services and therefore was not designated as commander-in-chief (*Oberbefehlshaber*). In
substance, the OKW was a military secretariat for Hitler, and Keitel
as its chief could issue orders only in Hitler's name and by his authority. Keitel himself was completely subservient to Hitler. His military
talents were of a low order, and he had no prestige or influence among
his fellow generals, who dubbed him "Lakeitel," a play on the German
word *Lakai*, meaning "lackey."

The OKW * included several departments for special inter-service
activities, of which the largest was the Department for Foreign Intelligence and Security, generally known as the *Abwehr*, under Admiral
Wilhelm Canaris, whose elusive personality and curious role in the
anti-Hitler conspiracy have made a favorite subject of postwar studies.[5]
There were other departments and offices for military economics, inter-
service communications, and administrative matters.

But by far the most important OKW department was called the
Operations Staff (*Fuehrungsstab*) and was concerned with plans and
operations for the Wehrmacht as a whole. Its chief was Generalmajor
Alfred Jodl, an able Bavarian officer who was Hitler's principal military
adviser throughout the war. Jodl's strength of character, unfortunately,
did not match his military capacity. He was not such a door mat as
Keitel and upon occasion would maintain his views despite the
Fuehrer's displeasure. But he was overwhelmed by Hitler's personality
and dazzled by the early successes, and could generally be counted on
to follow the Fuehrer, whom he had come to admire more than the
older generals under whom he had been trained.

The OKW's operational responsibilities were never clearly defined
and in practice fluctuated greatly. Raeder jealously preserved the
Navy's independence, and the arrogant and domineering Goering could
brush past Keitel and Jodl whenever he chose. But the difficulty was
more than one of personalities; it was the fundamental imbalance
among the services. The Army was not only much the largest of the
three but also the tactically dominant component of a Wehrmacht
which had been designed primarily for land warfare on the European
continent.

In the nature of things, therefore, most strategic and operational
problems focused on the Army, and the activities of Jodl's Operations
Staff at OKW overlapped constantly with those of the Army General

---

* See the organization charts of the Wehrmacht and of OKW in Appendix C,
infra, pp. 419–20.

Staff. Friction was inevitable, as the Army leaders had foreseen when the OKW was first established. Soon after his appointment as Commander-in-Chief of the Army, Brauchitsch had submitted a memorandum to Hitler proposing that OKW's functions should be concentrated in the fields of economic mobilization and others pertaining to the "home front" and that the Army Commander-in-Chief should also function as the Fuehrer's Chief of Staff for all military matters. Keitel's reply, no doubt prepared by Jodl,* stressed the need for a single, centralized control over all military plans and operations, apart from and above any and all of the services.

Hitler, characteristically, left the issue unresolved, and the Wehrmacht suffered the natural consequences of such indecision. In preparing the invasion of Norway and Denmark, the OKW for once performed the function of inter-service planning for which it had been designated. With rare exceptions, however, the operational staff of OKW, as Brauchitsch had rightly feared, occupied itself with the review and alteration of the Army's plans and conduct of operations. And throughout the course of the German victories in the West there was strife between "Hitler's generals" at OKW and the Army leadership, as well as recurring disputes between the Navy and the Luftwaffe which the OKW did nothing to resolve.

Beneath this jerry-built and creaky super-command, however, the three branches of the Wehrmacht were each well organized and functioned smoothly in their respective spheres. And two of them—the Army and the Luftwaffe—continued to grow at an impressive rate after the victory in Poland. On the ground and in the air the Wehrmacht of April 1940 was much more massive than it was in the fall of 1939. Also, it was far better trained, as the result of combat experience in Poland and the good use made of the quiet winter months.

The Army

In sheer size, the German field army in the spring of 1940 was about half again as large as it had been at the outbreak of the war, when it numbered some 106 divisions. From September 1939 to April 1940 five new "waves" of recruits and reserves were mobilized in 44 new infantry divisions. With other increments from the armed SS (Waffen-SS),

* It will thus be seen that Keitel and Jodl had both a practical and a doctrinal stake in Hitler's military dominance, for if the Army had swallowed up the OKW Operations Staff, they would surely have lost their positions close to the fount of authority.

there were at least 155 divisional formations when the Battle of France was launched, and close to 3,000,000 men in army uniform.

At the apex of this formidable and wonderfully integrated aggregation was the High Command of the Army (*Oberkommando des Heeres*)—the OKH, headed by Brauchitsch as Commander-in-Chief. The top field commanders-in-chief were directly subordinate to OKH, and in wartime the direction of their operations was its primary activity. But all the paraphernalia of army recruiting, mobilization, training, ordnance, and supply was also part of OKH, and its organization was correspondingly complex.* In wartime, the officers in charge of these supporting functions remained at the main headquarters of OKH on the Bendlerstrasse in Berlin, while the Commander-in-Chief and his operational staff moved to a field headquarters.†

Under Brauchitsch, the principal OKH general was Halder, as Chief of the Army General Staff. Brauchitsch and Halder were an exceedingly competent team but not a happy one. The former had become Commander-in-Chief only by giving moral hostages to Hitler,‡ and he was painfully aware that the Fuehrer could let him out at any time, and for any or no reason. Brauchitsch was not a man of firm enough fiber to hold his own across the table from Hitler and Nazi paladins such as Goering and Himmler, and the result was constant uneasiness and a disposition to yield under the stress of sharp controversy.

This trait was naturally annoying to his Chief of Staff, and especially so inasmuch as Franz Halder was a proud and pedantic staff officer, constantly exasperated by the intervention of Hitler or the OKW generals in matters which Halder regarded as the rightful province of OKH. Professionally gifted, vain, and querulous, Halder was not devoid of decent motives. But his anti-Nazism was continually at war with his own military ambitions, and his occasional contacts with the secret resistance circles never bore fruit in any meaningful action on his part.

Assisting Halder at the forward headquarters of OKH were staff specialists in transportation, communications, supply, intelligence, and other matters closely involved in field operations. By far the most im-

---

* See the organization chart of OKH in Appendix C, *infra*, p. 121.

† From October to May 1940 the OKH field headquarters was at Zossen, about twenty-five miles south of Berlin. For the Battle of France, it was moved westward, close to the German-Belgian border, and after the fall of France it was established at Fontainebleau.

‡ I.e., by retiring certain generals as requested by Hitler and Goering, and by accepting the judgment and assistance of Hitler and Goering in the handling of his own marital affairs.[6]

portant department of the OKH General Staff was responsible for plans and the conduct of operations, under an officer who was designated the *Oberquartiermeister I (O.Qu. I)*. From the outbreak of the war until February 1940 this key assignment was held by General Karl-Heinrich von Stuelpnagel, a close friend of Halder's and a man of greater strength of character, who was subsequently executed for his participation in the military conspiracy to assassinate Hitler and overthrow his government in July 1944.[7] In February 1940 Stuelpnagel fell ill, and Generalmajor Friedrich Mieth, appointed to deputize for him, succeeded to the post in June. Under the *O.Qu. I* was an operations section, headed throughout the western campaign by Oberst Hans von Greiffenberg, and among the members of this section was Oberstleutnant Adolf Heusinger, today the commander of the West German *Bundeswehr*. It was by these officers and their junior colleagues in the operations section that the basic army plans for the Battle of France were drawn.

Under the main headquarters of OKH in Berlin were the departments for personnel, administration, ordnance and weapons development, organization and training, military history and archives, various inspectorates, the War Academy, and other parts of the Army's permanent structure. The commander of this rear echelon, General Friedrich Fromm, bore the imposing title of Chief of Army Equipment and Commander of the Replacement Army (*Chef der Heeresruestung und Befehlshaber des Ersatzheeres*). Fromm never held a wartime field command, but his post (which he held until the summer of 1944, when he was executed for his equivocal conduct during the July conspiracy), was one of vital importance. From an operational standpoint, his major function was to mobilize recruits and reserves, equip and train them, and organize them in combat units, usually of divisional strength, for turning over to the field army.

Fromm was also expected to provide a reserve of trained replacements in order to maintain the field army units at full strength, and to reorganize and re-equip divisions that had been badly mauled or were being converted to new purposes. During the winter of 1939–40, his most important task of this nature was the conversion into panzer divisions of the four light divisions of the peacetime army. These formations, built around motorized rifle regiments and a battalion of tanks, had not been found satisfactory in the Polish campaign, so their armored strength was increased, and in the spring of 1940 they were turned back to the field army as the 6th, 7th, 8th, and 9th Panzer Divisions.

With these, the forty-four new infantry divisions, one cavalry division and one new mountain division, and including three new SS divisions of motorized infantry, the field army's divisional strength in April 1940 compared to September 1939 was as follows:

	Sept. 1939	April 1940
Infantry	88	132
Motorized Infantry	4	7
Mountain	3	4
Light	4	0
Panzer	6	10
Cavalry and Miscellaneous	1	2
	106	155 °

Of these, twenty of the infantry divisions had just been called up and were untrained, while others were composed of over-age personnel suitable only for limited employment. By April, however, there were over one hundred infantry divisions with at least six months of training, and the fifty-odd regular "peacetime" divisions, including the motorized, mountain, and panzer troops, were battle-hardened, fully equipped, and in an excellent state of training and morale. The tanks, indeed, were not so numerous as was supposed at the time on the Allied side; the ten divisions comprised thirty-five tank battalions and about 2500 tanks.[8] Of these, over 500 were the old Mark Is, armed only with machine guns. The basic tank was the twenty-millimeter-gunned Mark II, of which there were nearly a thousand, but there were also some 350 Marks IIIs, armed with thirty-seven-millimeter guns, nearly an equal number of Czech tanks equipped with the same sized gun, and 278 of the new Mark IVs, which mounted a seventy-five-millimeter weapon.

The regular infantry divisions had a strength of over 17,000 and the reserve and conscript divisions of about 15,000 men. The armored divisions varied, but a figure of 11,500 men is reasonably accurate. The entire field army embraced over 2,000,000 mobile effectives, of which the regular peacetime units accounted for about 730,000. In addition, there were 225,000 "static" troops suitable for fortress employment and 425,000 *Bautruppen* (construction troops). Fromm's home army totaled

° An entry in Halder's diary for April 26, 1940, gives the Army a total strength of 157 divisions.

close to a million men. By the spring of 1940, accordingly, the German
Army had some 3,750,000 men on active duty.

Over the divisions were the higher headquarters of the field army—
the "corps" of two or three (rarely four) divisions each, the "armies"
of several corps, and "army groups" of two or more armies. The regimental and other units comprising a division usually stayed together,
but otherwise the command structure was very flexible. Divisions were
frequently shifted from one corps to another, and corps from one army
to another, as operational needs and opportunities dictated. Likewise,
some of the divisions and the corps headquarters were customarily
held in reserve under direct OKH control for allocation to the combat
commands as circumstances required.

Since it was generally undesirable to assign more than three divisions to a corps, the divisional expansion in the winter of 1939–40
required a proportionate increase in the number of corps headquarters.
At the conclusion of the Polish campaign there were twenty-seven
corps;* by the spring of 1940 there were forty-four,† of which five
were still in process of organization and were formally activated during the course of the fighting in France,‡ while eight others were intended for the command of second-line units for training or occupational purposes and were officially designated "higher headquarters for
special purposes" rather than "corps." §

The establishment of the highest army field headquarters—army
groups and armies—was more flexible and was governed by over-all
strategic and tactical requirements rather than by the number of corps
and divisions. In fact, there was no need for an increase. In 1939, two
army groups (North and South) with five armies (the 3rd and 4th in

* The eighteen peacetime corps (I–XVIII), the three new combat corps for the
Polish campaign (XIX, XXI, and XXII), the three former western border commands (XXIII–XXV), the two new corps on the western front (XXVII and XXX),
and the former "Corps Wodrig" from East Prussia (XXVI). In addition to the headquarters staff, a corps usually included signal troops and heavy artillery under its
immediate command.

† The seventeen new corps comprised those numbered XXVIII, XXIX, and
XXXI to XLV inclusive. For some reason no corps XX was established until after
the conclusion of the campaign in the West.

‡ These five were the XXVIIIth, XXIXth, XLIInd, XLIIIrd, and XLIVth Corps.

§ These were the headquarters numbered XXXI to XXXVII inclusive and XLV,
which were originally designated *Hoeheres Kommando z.b.V.* instead of *Armee-
korps,* and were actually administrative headquarters of corps status (in that they
exercised command over divisional formations), usually situated in occupied territory (Poland, and later Norway, Denmark, and France). These lacked the heavy
artillery, antiaircraft, and other "corps troops" allocated to the regular combat corps
headquarters. Sometimes, however, they undertook light combat assignments, as
did H. Kdo. XXXI in Denmark and France.

the north, and the 8th, 10th, and 14th in the south) conducted the Polish campaign, while a third army group (C) with four armies (1st, 5th, 7th, and Army Cadre A) held the western front. In 1940, all three army group headquarters (now designated A, B, and C) were used to command the invasion of France and the Low Countries, still with nine armies (1st, 2nd, 4th, 6th, 7th, 9th, 12th, 16th, and 18th).* No other armies or army groups were constituted at this time.

During the period October 1939 to July 1940 there were four top field headquarters directly subordinate to OKH †—the three army groups on the western front, and the principal military headquarters in Poland, under the Commander-in-Chief, East (*Oberost*). These four commanders and the nine army commanders all bore the title Commander-in-Chief (*Oberbefehlshaber*) and were the senior field generals of the Army.

The three army group commanders, throughout the Polish and western campaigns and in Russia until the end of 1941, were Gerd von Rundstedt, Fedor von Bock, and Wilhelm Ritter von Leeb; in 1939 all held the rank of *Generaloberst*. Rundstedt and Leeb had been retired in 1938; they were in their middle sixties, the oldest of the field commanders-in-chief, none of whom was more than ten years younger. Rundstedt and Bock were Prussian aristocrats, while Leeb was a Bavarian whose title was not inherited but was a perquisite of the *Militaer-Max-Joseph Orden*, a royal Bavarian honor conferred on him during World War I. Leeb was a specialist in defensive "position" warfare, and by 1940 was regarded as somewhat old-fashioned. Bock, then in his sixty-first year but lean and active, was an energetic and experienced commander. However, he was neither brilliant nor reflective, and was often a difficult man to work with. Rundstedt, in contrast, was deeply respected throughout the officer corps, not only for his seniority and impressive bearing but also for his outstanding ability. Despite his years, Rundstedt was resourceful and flexible, and especially he was able to profit by the talents of his staff assistants, to whom he allowed wide scope. But his outlook was almost exclusively tactical.‡

* After the Polish campaign there were no armies ever again numbered 3 or 5. Not until 1943 were subsequent army headquarters given the numbers 8, 10, or 14. The Norwegian invasion was carried out with a reinforced corps headquarters (XXI).

† See the organization charts of the field army in Appendix C, *infra*, pp. 427–31.

‡ The terms *strategy* and *tactics* are used throughout according to the definitions of Clausewitz, *On War* (Jolles trans., Infantry Journal Press, 1950), p. 62: ". . . tactics teaches *the use of the armed forces in engagements*, and strategy *the use of engagements to attain the object of the war.*"

He seldom had much to say about the strategic problems that confronted the high command and was generally cynical or nonchalant
about the political and moral implications of military issues.

The commanders-in-chief of the nine armies, most of whom were
in their middle or late fifties, were all competent and highly trained
professional soldiers. During the Battle of France, the three * who
carried the main burden of the offensive were Sigmund Wilhelm List,
Guenther Hans von Kluge, and Walter von Reichenau, all *Generalobersten*. List, the senior ranking army commander-in-chief, was a specialist
in infantry tactics and an able organizer. A Wuerttemberger and no
aristocrat (his father was a doctor), List was well-disposed toward
Hitler but by no means a yes-man. Kluge and Reichenau, in contrast,
were militaristocrats of the old school. Both were men of great energy
and ambition, but there the resemblance ended. Reichenau was
worldly, articulate, and given to feats of personal athleticism. He was
one of the few senior officers who had openly espoused the Nazi cause
before Hitler came to power, and he had remained in high favor with
Hitler. But his military abilities were not exceptional, whereas Kluge—
familiarly known as *Kluger* † *Hans*—was in the front rank of World
War II field generals. A driving, fearless commander who spent much
of his time at the front, he resembled Rundstedt in his narrow concentration on tactical matters. More than most of his brother generals,
Kluge was troubled by Hitler's headlong course,[9] but during the period
of German victories in the West these doubts were quiescent.

Under the army commanders-in-chief were the forty-and-odd corps
commanding generals (*Kommandierende Generale*), and below them
over 150 divisional commanders (*Kommandeure*). The level of competence was high, but in age and prospects for advancement there
was wide variation among these 200 subordinate field generals. Some
were of comparable ability to the commanders-in-chief and slated for
advancement to higher commands; others had lost favor for political or
personal reasons, or were not regarded as professionally qualified for
major operational responsibility.

The immediate future was especially bright for the "tank generals"
who had scored sensationally in Poland and were again to dominate
the battlefield in France. At the corps level General Heinz Guderian,

---

* The others were Generaloberst Johannes Blaskowitz, Generaloberst Erwin von
Witzleben, and Generals Friedrich Dollmann, Maximilian von Weichs, Georg von
Kuechler, Ernst Busch, and (replacing Blaskowitz) Adolf Strauss. See the rank and
assignment lists in Appendix B, *infra*, pp. 399–408.

† A play on *klug*, meaning "clever," and the "Kluger Hans" of German folklore.

who had nurtured the *Panzerwaffe* from its infancy, was the most prominent member of this group, though he was outranked by General der Kavallerie Ewald von Kleist, scion of a famous Prussian military family, who had been retired at the time of the Blomberg-Fritsch affair but was recalled to active duty at the outbreak of war, and adapted himself with surprising success to mechanized warfare. At the divisional level the only panzer commander destined for great fame was Generalmajor Erwin Rommel, who was now rewarded, for his service as chief of Hitler's military bodyguard, with command of the 7th Panzer Division.

At all levels from army group down to division the commander was assisted by a staff, composed principally of specially trained officers wearing the red trouser stripes of the general staff corps. At the army groups and armies the chiefs of staff were men of proven and exceptional capacity for staff work. Like all staff officers, however, they were expected to alternate between staff and command assignments, and the best of them usually, though not invariably, were equally at home in either role. An almost too perfect example was the dynamic Generalleutnant Fritz Erich von Lewinski *genannt* von Manstein, who served as Rundstedt's chief of staff during the Polish campaign and until February 1940, and in that capacity exerted a decisive influence in shaping the plan of attack in the West. Manstein was then given command of an infantry corps, which he led with distinction in the second phase of the Battle of France, and later in Russia he became an army group commander-in-chief and won wide renown as a field general—a *Feldherr,* as the Germans call a great commander of large forces in the field.

Manstein was exceptional; nevertheless, it is fair to say that few armies have ever had more proficient generals to lead them in battle than did the German Army in the spring of 1940. Especially in the early stages of the war, the caliber of leadership was supported by drawing on the valuable roster of retired generals available for training and administrative assignments and, in a few instances, for combat commands. The small size of the *Reichswehr* during the Weimar and early Hitler years had required a rigorous retirement policy in order to keep the officer corps reasonably fluid at the top. With the expansion of the field army and the wartime proliferation of all sorts of military tasks, most of the retired generals fit for duty were recalled to service. Of these, Rundstedt, Leeb, and Kleist were the only ones to achieve the highest levels of rank and command, but several others—notably

General Hermann Geyer and Generalleutnant Friedrich Koch—served with distinction as corps and divisional commanders.*

In the lower officer ranks, the quality was not so uniformly good. In 1934 the entire corps of officers on active duty numbered only 3700; early in 1939 there were already 100,000, and by the summer of 1940 some 150,000 officers in service. Of these about one quarter were regulars, and about one third were prewar reserve officers, many of whom were unfit for duty in the field army. Several thousand more were former noncommissioned officers, but the ever-increasing needs of the field army had to be met chiefly by young reserve officer candidates.[10] Despite earnest efforts to maintain standards of selection and training, so rapid an expansion of the officer corps was bound to lower its professional caliber.

The loss of homogeneity was not all to the bad. Nazism had many evil features but social snobbery was not among them. The lack of caste feeling among the newer officers, as well as the ideological bonds that Nazism had forged, often resulted in well-ordered but informal relations based on mutual trust between officers and men, quite different from the haughty discipline of the old professional army.

Of course, all this had its ugly side as well. The Army soon was shot through with informers, who ran to the local party headquarters or to the SS with tales of anti-Nazi remarks or attitudes among their comrades or their superiors. Heinrich Himmler was still carrying on the ideological warfare against the old officer corps that had brought about the downfall of Blomberg and Fritsch. Formal religious observance was a traditional feature of German military life; this was a frequent point of friction between Himmler and the generals, but it does not appear to have been a matter of wide concern among the troops.

Another sore subject was the growth of the combat components of the SS—the so-called *Waffen-SS*. The first full division of SS troops was formed shortly after the Polish campaign, and by the spring of 1940 there were three such divisions, all motorized,† as well as the motorized regiment SS-*Leibstandarte Adolf Hitler,* from which Hitler's SS bodyguard was drawn.[11] During the early part of the war the army

---

* See List No. 3 in Appendix B, *infra,* pp. 409–11.

† These were the SS-*Verfuegungs,* SS-*Totenkopf,* and SS-*Polizei* divisions. The military father of the *Waffen-SS* was Paul Hausser, a retired army *Generalleutnant,* who joined Himmler's staff in 1935 to train SS officer cadets. In the western campaign he commanded the SS-*Verfuegungs* Division.

leaders were annoyed by SS recruiting incursions and alarmed by the implications of a separate military organization, but the big expansion of the Waffen-SS did not begin until 1942. In the field the SS units were under army command for operational purposes, but their recruitment, training, and discipline were under the control of Himmler as Reichsfuehrer of the SS.

Despite his unwelcome interest in the ideological side of military service and his pride in the *Waffen-SS*, Himmler made no effort to interfere in the direction of military operations. Neither did any other Nazi bigwig except, of course, Goering. The party philosopher, Alfred Rosenberg, was peripherally involved in the Norwegian adventure, but this was merely a by-product of his prior acquaintance with Vidkun Quisling.

To be sure, Hitler from time to time discussed the conduct of the war with Goebbels, Ribbentrop, and other close civilian associates. But it does not appear that he consulted them on strategic questions, and certainly they were never brought into the military councils. Indeed, as the war lengthened Hitler immersed himself more and more in operational matters and isolated himself from the home front and domestic policy problems, which he left to Himmler, Goebbels, and Martin Bormann. Military matters, in the Fuehrer's view, were to be decided by himself with the assistance of the generals, and this was a professional circle into which party leaders and civilian officials were seldom admitted.

Later in the war, when the Jewish exterminations and other massive planned atrocities were carried out in areas under military control, the officer corps faced a savage and, as it proved, a lethal challenge alike to its prerogatives and its principles, and the conscience and self-respect even of the troops were deeply affected. These terrible events were foreshadowed before the war was a month old by the Nazi occupational regime in Poland, the brutal nature of which soon became widely known among the generals.

But in the spring of 1940 few in the Army's lower ranks had glimpsed the horrors that followed in the wake of German conquests. The German soldier went into Norway, Belgium, or France as the case might be with his head held high, in a state of pride and not of shame. Under the black swastika he fought with the *élan* that was so woefully lacking among the French soldiers called to defend *la patrie*.

Thus, the German Army was strong in its morale as well as in num-

⸢s⸣, weapons, and leadership. It was then the most powerful army in ⸢t⸣he world by far, and it could be counted on to accomplish whatever tasks an army might reasonably be called on to perform for its country.

The Luftwaffe

The Air Force, for all its vaunted might, was not in the same league with the Army. To be sure, there were natural reasons aplenty for this comparative deficiency of the air arm. Because of the Versailles Treaty restrictions, under the Weimar Republic it was nothing but a few shadowy offices hidden in the army and navy establishments, and during the first two years of the Third Reich it remained under cover while the first steps toward its creation were taken. As an independent and acknowledged branch of the Wehrmacht, therefore, the Luftwaffe was only five years old in the spring of 1940. A formidable force had been developed, but flaws and deficiencies of forced growth were inevitable.

But the Luftwaffe's more fundamental limitations were not the consequence of its immaturity but of a deliberate decision, taken in 1937, to design it for short-range operations in support of the Army, rather than for long-range strategic undertakings of its own. The first Chief of the General Staff of the Luftwaffe, General Walther Wever, had been of a different opinion. A regular army officer who was transferred to the Air Ministry in 1933, Wever manifested a keen strategic sense as well as fine administrative ability. He was convinced that any major European war would find Britain ranged against Germany and that, especially with a weak Navy, Germany would need heavy bombers that could attack all parts of the British Isles and participate effectively in the blockade of British shipping. At his behest, the Dornier and Junkers designers were set to work developing a long-range, four-engined bomber.[12]

General Wever was killed in an airplane crash in June 1936, and thereafter the heavy-bomber plans lagged. His successors as Chief of Staff, Generals Albert Kesselring and Hans-Juergen Stumpff, did not follow Wever's thinking or command his influence. Hitler and Goering were thinking in terms of Poland, Czechoslovakia, and France, and the Luftwaffe's development proceeded on the basis that Britain would not be involved. Furthermore, the financial and material cost of heavy bombers was enormous. In 1937 their production was suspended,[13] and the result was that throughout the war Germany had no long-range bomber force, nor was it able to give the Navy much help over the Atlantic. Medium bombers, dive bombers, and fighters were the backbone of the Luftwaffe; they served well for tactical support of the Army in the Polish and western campaigns. But Wever's strategic predictions proved sound, and in the Battle of Britain the Luftwaffe was decisively handicapped by its lack of long-range aircraft, as it was throughout the remainder of the war.

It might fairly be said that in this respect the Versailles Treaty prohibition of German military aviation had precisely the result its framers intended, though the chain of consequence extended far beyond their field of vision in 1919. Despite clandestine expedients, Germany could not possibly keep abreast of the other great powers in the air. German military aircraft design, especially of engines, was seriously handicapped. The Messerschmitt 109, to be sure, was a highly successful fighter, and the Junkers 87 "Stuka" was the best dive bomber of its time, though slow and vulnerable to fighter attack. But there was no adequate heavy bomber, and a number of other types were disappointments under combat conditions. The Luftwaffe leaders could not close the gap in the six peacetime years, and then Hitler plunged into a war to the strategic needs of which it was inadequate.

From the outset, the problem of personnel was crucial. Certainly there were thousands of keen and ardent young Germans, eager to fly for the Fuehrer and the Fatherland. But who was to organize the Luftwaffe, determine its composition, select its aircraft, and train its recruits? Where were the staff officers to be found?

There was a handful of army and navy officers with flying experience in World War I, some of whom had kept in touch as best they could with the progress of military aviation; these officers were transferred to the Air Ministry soon after Hitler came to power. Goering, the Commander-in-Chief to be, had many old associates from the days of the Richthofen "flying circus"—Bruno Loerzer, Ernst Udet, Robert Ritter von Greim, and others who were now called from civil aviation back to uniformed service. But the bulk of the higher staff and command positions in the new Luftwaffe were filled by retired army generals, and by youngish army officers of the general staff (most of them were then in their forties) like Wever, Kesselring, and Stumpff, who were transferred, some willingly and others less so, to the Air Ministry. Most of them had excellent military and administrative qualifications but were totally lacking in aviation experience.

The result of all this was that the Luftwaffe was shaped by aviators who were amateur soldiers, and soldiers who were amateur aviators.

A few of the former army officers, such as Wever and Jeschonnek, won Goering's favor, but generally he preferred those whom he had brought into the Luftwaffe from civil life. No more than Hitler did Goering take kindly to opposition from his subordinates, and those who ventured to cross him usually fared badly at his hands. For example, General Hellmuth Volkmann fell from grace because of disputes with Goering that arose while Volkmann was commanding the "Condor Legion" in Spain.[14] Despite his recognized ability as an air commander, Volkmann was let out of the Luftwaffe shortly before the war and returned to army service.*

Perhaps Hitler was mistaken in entrusting the Luftwaffe to Goering; certainly it was an error of weakness to leave the "Fat One" in charge after his powers of concentration had faded in a mist of self-indulgence. Yet it is hard to see where, after Wever's death, the right leadership could have been found, since the converted army officers, for all their organizing talents, could not be expected to develop seasoned and imaginative concepts of aerial warfare overnight.

The superstructure of the Luftwaffe was unique in that it was both a military headquarters and a civilian ministry.† Goering was both Reich Minister for Aviation (*Reichsminister der Luftfahrt*) and Commander-in-Chief of the Air Force (*Oberbefehlshaber der Luftwaffe*) with the rank of *Generalfeldmarschall*. His deputy and ranking subordinate, Generaloberst Erhard Milch, was State Secretary of the Air Ministry and Inspector-General of the Luftwaffe. Milch, formerly a director of the Lufthansa air lines, was Goering's friend of long standing. He was the administrative genius of the Luftwaffe and rarely participated in operations, although he did take a field command briefly during the Norwegian campaign.

Under Goering and Milch, the Luftwaffe was organized along lines familiar to the ex-army officers who staffed it. At its main headquarters (OKL, for *Oberkommando der Luftwaffe*), Goering was assisted by a general staff, the chief of which, beginning in 1939, was the forty-year-old Generalmajor Hans Jeschonnek, an able and attractive officer but completely under the spell of Hitler and Goering.[15] As at OKH, there were other OKL staff departments for personnel, training, communications, supply, and technical development.

---

* Volkmann commanded the 94th Infantry Division during the Battle of France. He was killed in a motor accident in August 1940.

† See the organization chart of the Luftwaffe in Appendix C, *infra*, p. 422.

Milch and Jeschonnek were two of the triumvirate that dominated OKL. The third was the amiable, colorful, and renowned Ernst Udet— next to Richthofen the leading German fighter pilot of World War I and in peacetime a daring stunt flyer, skilled in aircraft testing and design. Goering had lured Udet into the Luftwaffe as head of the technical department; at the outbreak of war he was a *Generalleutnant* and in charge of supply and procurement, with the title of *Generalluft- zeugmeister*. Udet was witty, fearless, and touched with the genius of a bird, but he was no organizer and even less a politician or strategist. For all his qualities, his weaknesses were a prime cause of the Luft- waffe's malformation. He was too easygoing to resist the overbearing pressure of men like Goering and Milch, and he continued to regard military aviation as a matter of knightly single combat and dive- bomber attacks on enemy troops and supply lines. Thus he was carried away by his penchant for fast, maneuverable aircraft, largely ignored the heavy bombers, and never grasped the independent strategic po- tentialities of air power.

Within the limits of its initial design, the Luftwaffe was approaching its peak in the spring of 1940. During 1938 and 1939 the production rate of new aircraft had increased but slowly, largely because the Luft- waffe was in the course of change-over from old types to the Junkers 88 bombers and Messerschmitt 109 fighters that were to be the staple combat planes throughout the war. By 1940 the German factories were turning out military aircraft at the rate of about 650 per month, of which roughly a quarter were fighters and the balance chiefly bombers, with a scattering of reconnaissance, transport, and naval aircraft.[16]

Against the light losses suffered in Poland, Norway, and France this rate was ample to maintain the Luftwaffe's front-line strength of about 4,000 bombers, dive bombers, fighters, and reconnaissance air- craft.[17] In the spring and summer of 1940 it was the strongest air force in the world, and its lack of range and staying power was not widely recognized. The French had been hopelessly outstripped, and the Rus- sians were far behind. But the British were overhauling the Germans rapidly. The Royal Air Force did not yet match the Luftwaffe in size, but it was far better balanced strategically, and by 1940 the British rate of production exceeded that of the Germans, a statistic which boded ill for the Third Reich.[18]

The basic operational unit of the Luftwaffe was the *Staffel*, with a full strength of about ten planes. Three *Staffeln* comprised a *Gruppe*, and three or sometimes more *Gruppen* a *Geschwader* of 90 to 100 air-craft, all of the same basic type.* *Gruppen* and *Staffeln* could and often did operate independently from widely separated locations.

During the campaign in the West there were a dozen or more *Geschwader*—perhaps one third of the entire combat strength—of level-flight bombers (*Kampfflugzeug*), chiefly Dornier 17 "flying pencils" and Heinkel 111s, but these were being replaced by the greatly supe-rior Junkers 88s. The Junkers 87 dive bombers, known as "Stukas" (from *Sturzkampfflugzeug*), accounted for four *Geschwader*. There were ten or twelve *Geschwader* of fighters, mostly single-engined (*Jagdflugzeug*) Messerschmitt 109s, and twin-engined (*Zerstoerer-flugzeug*) Messerschmitt 110s which did not prove very effective. These formations were the core of the Luftwaffe.

Above the *Geschwader*, the higher headquarters of the Luftwaffe closely paralleled the army pattern. Germany and the occupied areas were divided geographically into air districts (*Luftgaue*), each with an administrative headquarters responsible for supply, transport, con-struction and maintenance of airfields, and other supporting services. The combat headquarters were thus free to concentrate on operational matters, and each of these comprised a commander and his general staff assistants, as in the Army.

The highest field headquarters, each directly subordinate to OKL, were the air fleets (*Luftflotten*). There were four of these until April 1940, when a fifth was established in Norway. Their strength fluctuated according to the necessities of the situation; after the Polish campaign two of them, with only a few subordinate units, were left in the East. The main strength was deployed on the western front, under Kessel-ring's Luftflotte 2, supporting Bock's army group opposite Holland and northern Belgium, and Luftflotte 3, commanded by General der Flieger Hugo Sperrle, with Rundstedt's and Leeb's army groups opposite southern Belgium and France.

Under the *Luftflotten* and directly over the *Geschwader* were the *Fliegerkorps*, each a mixed force of 250 to 500 bombers, fighters, and reconnaissance planes. There were seven of these headquarters in the West, of which two, commanded by World War I naval flyers, were specially intended for coastal and maritime operations such as mine laying. The other commanders included Goering's old friends Von Greim and Loerzer, as well as Generalmajor Wolfram von Richthofen

---

* The commanders of these units were called by the titles *Staffelkapitaen, Gruppenkommandeur,* and *Geschwaderkommodore.*

(a relative of the World War I hero), who had been the last commander of the Condor Legion in Spain and was a specialist in army support tactics.

By 1940 there were well over a million men in the Luftwaffe, but less than half of them were in the air arm proper. Between four and five hundred thousand [19] were antiaircraft (*Flak*, from *Flugabwehrkanone*, air defense gun) troops, an arm that had been subordinated to the Luftwaffe at the time of its unveiling in 1935. In the West, the *Flak* was organized in two corps, one each under Luftflotte 2 and Luftflotte 3, with subordinate divisions, brigades, and regiments down to the basic *Flakbatterie*. Signal communications were especially important to the Luftwaffe, as to any air force, and about 200,000 men were assigned to this branch. More spectacular though not nearly so numerous were Generalmajor Kurt Student's new airborne infantry units, which were to be used for the first time in Norway, Denmark, and Holland.

Antiaircraft and airborne operations varied but did not greatly broaden the strategic scope of the Luftwaffe, for both were primarily army support tasks. In the United States, where the land-based air units were still part of the Army, independent strategic bombardment concepts were in the ascendant (as they were in Britain) and the four-motored B-17 "Flying Fortress" was ready for long-range operational use. But in Germany, where the air arm was independent from the moment of its rebirth and was commanded by the ranking officer of the Wehrmacht and second-ranking political figure of the Third Reich, the Luftwaffe was basically an adjunct of the Army. It added enormously to the power of the Wehrmacht's punch but did not sufficiently lengthen its reach.

As a close-support force, the Luftwaffe's efficacy depended on smooth and speedy co-operation with the Army. This sort of thing was not Goering's long suit, and the relations between OKL and OKH at the top level were never what they should have been. But at the operational and lower staff levels they were generally satisfactory and often excellent, and joint operational methods were highly developed. The Spanish experience gave the Luftwaffe a head start, and in the Polish campaign the complicated inter-service techniques of intelligence, liaison, and communications were further developed.

Each army group, army, and corps had a small air staff (headed by a *Koluft—Kommandeur der Luftwaffe*) to advise the army general on air matters. And each headquarters from the divisional level up had a roving air liaison officer (*Fliegerverbindungsoffizier,* or "Flivo") to

ep the air support formations advised of spot opportunities and emer-
encies, front-line locations, and other operational information. Reconnaissance was as necessary as liaison; each armored division and each
corps and higher army headquarters had attached to it a close reconnaissance *Staffel*. Long-range reconnaissance *Gruppen* of Dornier 17s
and Junkers 88s were operated by Luftwaffe headquarters.

All in all, the Army was well served by the Luftwaffe in Poland and
the West. But at sea it was a different story. During the Norwegian
campaign, to be sure, Germany's airmen gave her sailors decisive support. But over the North Sea and the reaches of the North Atlantic was
where the German Navy needed help in the war on British merchant
shipping. For this task the Luftwaffe was ill equipped, and Goering
did much less than he could have to aid his beleaguered brother Commander-in-Chief, Grossadmiral Erich Raeder, whose slender forces
faced the overwhelming superiority of the Royal Navy.

The Navy

In 1939, German naval planning was based on a new construction program called the "Z plan," under which by 1945 there would have been
a modern high-seas fleet built around eight huge battleships, five battle
cruisers, and two aircraft carriers.[20] This force would still have been
smaller than the British Fleet, but by judicious use and with Italian and
perhaps Japanese help Raeder thought that [21] "the prospect of defeating the British Fleet and cutting off supplies, in other words of settling
the British question conclusively, would have been good."

Two battleship, one carrier, and three cruiser keels were laid and
construction commenced, but upon the outbreak of war the "Z plan" was
scrapped. On October 31, 1939, a new program was adopted which,
except for submarines, contemplated only the construction of eight destroyers and eighteen torpedo boats during the next two years.[22] In
fact not a single German ship larger than a destroyer was launched
during the entire course of the war.

When Raeder received the shattering news of war with Britain, the
two large battleships *Bismarck* and *Tirpitz*, the aircraft carrier *Graf
Zeppelin*, and the heavy cruisers *Prinz Eugen*, *Seydlitz*, and *Luetzow*
had been launched but were not yet completed.* The 32,000-ton battle
cruisers *Gneisenau* and *Scharnhorst* were in commission, but the latter

---

* The *Graf Zeppelin* and *Seydlitz* were never completed, and the *Luetzow* was
sold to the Russians in February 1940, still unfinished.

was not yet "shaken down" for operational use. Of the three 12,000-ton "pocket battleships" (really small battle cruisers), the *Deutschland* and *Admiral Graf Spee* were at sea and ready for action, but the *Admiral Scheer* was in drydock for extensive overhauling. The two heavy cruisers *Bluecher* and *Admiral Hipper* had just been commissioned, and there were six light cruisers—*Nuernberg, Leipzig, Koeln, Karlsruhe, Koenigsberg,* and the old (1925) *Emden.* There were twenty-two destroyers and fifty-seven submarines, but of the latter less than half were large enough for action in the open ocean. There were fifteen large torpedo boats suitable for fleet use, and a considerable number of smaller torpedo boats, patrol boats, mine-sweepers, and auxiliary craft, as well as the pre-World War I battleships *Schlesien* and *Schleswig-Holstein,* which were still serviceable for training and coastal use in the Baltic.[23]

This force was less than half the size of the French and Italian fleets and was dwarfed by the British. Indeed, the German Navy could not venture into the Atlantic *as a fleet* at all. Its potential role in the war was limited to coastal defense, protection of German shipping in the Baltic, preying on enemy merchant shipping, and participation in amphibious operations on nearby coasts.

Only the last two were of strategic importance. On the open ocean, surface raiders could harass the British and draw off their warships, but the only chance to cripple Britain's supply life lines lay with the submarines. At the outbreak of war, however, neither the size of the U-boat fleet nor the rate of construction—about three per month—was sufficient for more than pin-prick operations.[24] This was painfully apparent to Konteradmiral Karl Doenitz, who had been in charge of the submarine arm since 1935. On the first day of war he had sent a memorandum [25] to Raeder recommending that "normal planning and existing naval problems must be put aside, so that the U-boat arm can be brought as soon as possible to such a condition as will enable it to carry out its main task—that is, to defeat England in war." Raeder agreed and pressed these views on Hitler, but the Fuehrer's mind was on other things, and it was not until after the fall of France that the U-boat production schedule was greatly accelerated.[26]

Near the British Isles the airplane, Raeder thought, could join effectively in the antishipping campaign. He wanted his Navy to have its own air arm, but this ambition foundered on the rock of Goering's jealous opposition; only a few hundred reconnaissance and carrier-borne aircraft (the latter for the *Graf Zeppelin* that never sailed) were allowed under naval command.[27] Good inter-service collaboration might have partly compensated for this friction at the top, as it did in Norway. But Raeder and Goering were repeatedly at swords' points due to the latter's failure to commit his forces in support of naval objectives.

Unlike the generals, the naval officers were attuned to strategic thinking. In part this was due to the nature of their calling, and the traditional hostility of continental navies to British sea power. There was also a sociological factor. The generals still reflected the temper of the Junker aristocracy, seeking an expanding destiny on the continent. The Navy was bourgeois, with close ties to German industry and commerce. The officer corps was homogeneous and small, as was the Navy itself; when the war began there were only 8400 officers and about 125,000 men. Most of the senior officers were remote from Nazi party matters, but they responded enthusiastically to Hitler's visions of a *Grossdeutschland* with free access to the Atlantic, far-flung trade, and colonies.

The High Command of the Navy (*Oberkommando der Kriegsmarine*, or OKM) was small and close-knit. Corresponding to a general staff was the Naval War Leadership (*Seekriegsleitung*, or SKL).* The Chief of Staff, Vizeadmiral Otto Schniewind, was Raeder's principal subordinate for plans and operations. The OKM also included staff sections for intelligence, communications and training, and supporting staff departments for personnel, armament, construction, finance, and recruiting.

During the first two years of the war all ocean-going vessels, from battleships to submarines, were under the Chief of the Fleet, called the *Flottenchef*. From October 1939 to July 1940 this officer, who commanded from his flagship when a major force went to sea, was Admiral Wilhelm Marschall, but he was often ill or in disagreement with his superiors, and active command during most of the Norwegian adventure fell to Vizeadmiral Guenther Luetjens, who later went down with the *Bismarck*. Konteradmiral Karl Doenitz and his submarines were nominally subordinate to the *Flottenchef* until 1941, but in practice the U-boat operations in the Atlantic were supervised directly by SKL.

The chain of command from the SKL to the fleet and other opera-

* Raeder himself was *Chef* of the SKL as well as Commander-in-Chief of the Navy, so that the SKL, unlike the general staffs of the Army and Luftwaffe, was an organ of command as well as a staff. See the organization chart of OKM and the Navy in Appendix C, *infra*, p. 423.

tional units was divided geographically. In the Baltic Sea and the Kattegat, command was exercised by the Eastern Group Command (*Marine-Gruppen-Kommando Ost*), under Admiral Rolf Carls. The Skaggerak * and the North Sea were the domain of the Western Group Command (*Marine-Gruppen-Kommando West*), under Generaladmiral Alfred Saalwaechter. Carls and Saalwaechter, who were the senior ranking admirals next to Raeder, reported to SKL. In the open ocean, SKL exercised direct command. Since the *Flottenchef* and the bulk of the ocean-going fleet were usually based at Wilhelmshaven, this meant that its operations were generally under Saalwaechter, except for the submarines and surface raiders that were operating in the Atlantic or more distant waters.

It was the painful irony of Raeder's position that he and his staff saw clearly from the outset of the war that Germany's ultimate strategic objective must be the defeat of Britain, and yet he lacked the resources and influence to lead the Wehrmacht toward that goal. The irony was sharpened by the consequences of the Norwegian adventure, undertaken largely on the initiative of the admirals, which was bold in its tactical conception, skillful in execution, and sensationally successful in its immediate outcome. Yet it proved a Pyrrhic victory, for the German fleet suffered such severe losses and damage in Norwegian waters that it was not merely weak but virtually impotent when, in the summer of 1940, it suddenly dawned on Hitler and the generals that an invasion of Britain might be both a feasible and a necessary step to bring the war to a successful conclusion. Raeder had little enough to work with at the beginning of the war, and most of what he had was expended in pursuit of a secondary objective, so that when the decisive hour struck, Germany had almost no navy at all.

The Wehrmacht As an Instrument of German Policy

From this examination of the individual parts, it is apparent that the Wehrmacht, despite its power and fearsome repute, was an unbalanced and defective force in strategic terms. Armies and navies are built to win wars, not tournaments. It was the German generals' historic mentor, Clausewitz, who formulated the famous apothegms teaching that war is "the continuation of state policy by different means" and that its

* The line between *Ost* and *West* ran from Skagen at the northern tip of Jutland to Goeteborg in Sweden.

end purpose is "to compel our opponent to fulfill our will." As an instrument of the state policy of the Third Reich, the Wehrmacht was
deficient in three major respects—physical, economic, and psychological.

In its sheer physical attributes, the Wehrmacht of 1940 was dominant in Europe and well able to exert such military force as might be
necessary to execute German policy on the continent. But it was not
designed for more distant enterprises. Basically, the Wehrmacht was
the Army. Neither the Luftwaffe nor the Navy was equipped to produce a strategic impact much beyond the practical bounds of army
operations.

Furthermore, the Wehrmacht's staying power was limited by its
narrow economic base. German industry had not been mobilized to produce a flood of aircraft, or submarines, or even tanks. For all the Nazis'
talk of "guns or butter," there was still lots of butter. Goering grew
fatter and was not the man to tighten the nation's belt. Hitler was bent
on ending the war quickly and, as far as possible, painlessly. Shortly
before the invasion of Poland the chief of the OKW section for war
economics, Generalmajor Georg Thomas, strongly urged full mobilization of the nation's productive resources, but Hitler would have none
of it.[28] Much more extraordinary, this almost nonchalant attitude toward the future needs of the Wehrmacht persisted throughout the first
two years of the war. After the war, the United States Strategic Bombing Survey concluded: [29]

The outstanding feature of the German war effort is the surprisingly low
output of armaments in the first three years of the war—surprisingly low as
measured not only by Germany's later achievement but also by the general
expectations of the time and by the level of production of her enemy, Britain.
In aircraft, trucks, tanks, self-propelled guns, and several other types of
armaments, British production was greater than Germany's in 1940, 1941,
and 1942.

. . . The Germans did not plan for a long war, nor were they prepared for
it. Hitler's strategy contemplated a series of separate thrusts and quick victories over enemies that were even less prepared than Germany; he did not
expect to fight a prolonged war against a combination of major world powers.

. . . measured by the standards of other belligerents, there was no "total
mobilization" and no long-term planning to bring the war effort to its attain-
able maximum. The production of civilian goods was restricted only to a
moderate extent; there was no further mobilization of women and no large-
scale transfer of labor from nonessential to essential industries.

Thus the Wehrmacht in 1940 was like a skillful and enormously powerful prize fighter, with a short reach and poor endurance.* It could not conduct anything resembling "global warfare," nor enforce national policies that transcended its continental environs. Even the English Channel and the North Sea loomed as obstacles that would be exceedingly difficult if not impossible to overleap.

Once at war with Britain, how could the Wehrmacht be used to attain victory? This posed the most difficult and complicated problems of military statesmanship—of diplomacy and grand strategy or, in a word, of leadership. And it was here that the Wehrmacht was fatally handicapped by its psychological deficiencies.

There was, as has already been observed, a great dearth of strategic talent. German military thinking was continent-bound; the generals were accustomed to planning for wars with France or the central European countries. They did not much fear the British in Flanders or the Russians west of the Vistula, but the prospect of assailing the island fortress or the Russian heartland did not enter their thinking. So limited, it was natural that the officer corps should concentrate on tactical matters. There were a few exceptions like Wever, and the Navy perforce looked out at the military world as a whole, but by and large the life and training of the Wehrmacht were not fertile soil for the flowering of an imaginative strategy.

Even if by good fortune the officer corps had produced a brilliant strategist, it is more than doubtful that he could have made his views prevail in the shaping of state policy. The decision-making procedures of the Third Reich were erratic, inefficient, and nerve-wracking for the participants. Hitler was a man with a mind of his own, and there was nothing magnanimous about it.

If the vision-gifted general had also been a man of strong and persuasive personality, capable of giving the officer corps real leadership, a clash *à l'outrance* between the Army and the Party would have been almost inevitable. Lacking such dynamic qualities, his counsels would probably have been brushed aside by the Fuehrer. The generals had long since lost the cohesion and loyalty to themselves that might have given corporate weight to the views of the army commander-in-chief. Indeed, the blunder of strategic proportions that the Germans com-

* A French writer (A. Goutard, *1940 La Guerre des Occasions Perdues*, p. 12) has remarked that "One of the most curious characteristics of the memoirs by our generals and the accounts of official and conformist historians is the ignorance in which they leave us concerning the material and moral situation of the German Army in 1939 and 1940."

mitted just before Dunkirk, and which made the large-scale evacuation possible,[30] was just as much the result of Rundstedt's failure to support Brauchitsch as of Hitler's rejection of Brauchitsch's advice.

Then, too, the high command was not a happy family. Mutual confidence was lacking among Brauchitsch, Goering, Raeder, Keitel, and their subordinates. Many of them were deeply disturbed by the consequences of the course that Hitler had steered, and as shocking reports of German conduct in occupied Poland began to spread, some of the generals were assailed by the pangs of conscience. There was a growing awareness that they were in league with something hideously evil, but few ventured to grapple with the moral consequences. The nervous strain of life with a ruthless and impulsive dictator told heavily on the more sensitive officers, and the tension increased when it became clear that generals who incurred the Fuehrer's wrath by openly crossing him were not likely to be promoted. Himmler, rarely seen but always making his power felt, cast a disquieting shadow across the military councils.

And so, when strategic problems arose, the leadership of the Wehrmacht was ill-equipped to cope with them. Hitler and the generals were in complete agreement on the goal of state policy: they wanted to persuade or force the western Allies—and soon after the issue was joined on the battlefield that meant Britain—to give up the struggle and make peace on terms favorable to Germany. But they failed to develop a basic strategy dedicated to that aim and were repeatedly at odds on questions of timing and the selection of immediate objectives.

Before the war was a month old, such a dispute between Hitler and the OKH generals reached the proportions of a state crisis. This conflict of wills was fought out during the strange lull that settled over Europe after the conquest of Poland—a lull which is often referred to as the period of "phony war," and to which this account now turns.

CHAPTER TWO

The Not-So-Phony War

"EVERY GERMAN SOLDIER has the greatest respect for the feats of the French Army. . . . At no time and in no place have I ever acted contrary to British interests." So spoke Adolf Hitler in Berlin on October 6, 1939. His immediate audience was the Reichstag, but the Fuehrer's words were intended primarily for French and British ears. The previous day, Hitler had entered shattered Warsaw. Now he was confronting the western Allies with his Polish conquest as a *fait accompli* and lecturing them on the futility and stupidity of continuing the war. For Hitler, World War II had not yet begun; the speech of October 6 was his notion of an olive branch.

The Fuehrer began his discourse in a triumphal vein. Polish soldiers had fought bravely, but they were led by "irresponsible" officers. Warsaw's stubborn resistance had been worse than stupid. Happily, the German victory had been a cheap one; the Wehrmacht had lost only 10,500 killed and 3400 missing, and suffered 30,000 wounded.

In Hitlerian perspective, the western powers had no reason to deplore what had happened. After all, Poland had never been a "true democracy," and the people had been exploited by "aristocrats and intellectuals." Was it not an English statesman, David Lloyd George, who had long ago condemned the new Polish State as an "unsound" product of Versailles? Furthermore, the Poles had been guilty of unspeakable atrocities against the German minorities. "In 1598 an Englishman—Sir George Carew—wrote in his prophetic reports to the English government that the outstanding features of Polish character were cruelty and lack of moral restraint."

Clearly the researchers of the Wilhelmstrasse had been working overtime to provide the Fuehrer with ammunition for his peace offensive. As usual, however, the results were more offensive than peaceful. Nor was there any hint of concession or compromise so far as the fate of Poland was concerned. "One of the most senseless deeds perpetrated at Versailles is now a thing of the past." For the future there would be a "community of interest" between Germany and Russia. "Long periods in the history of both nations have shown that these two largest states in Europe were never happier than when they lived in friendship with each other." These two, with no interference from the West, would establish "definitive spheres of influence," pacify eastern Europe, and determine the framework for peace. There would be a "residual Polish State" and resettlement of nationality groups.

Then Hitler turned to his major theme. Always he had endeavored to eliminate ill will between Germany and the western powers. If he had failed, it was due to "animosity on the part of certain British statesmen and journalists, which has deeply affected me personally." Continuation of the war would achieve neither the resurrection of Poland nor the destruction of Nazism:

Why should this war in the West be fought? For the restoration of Poland? Poland of the Versailles Treaty will never rise again. . . . The final reorganization of this territory and the question of re-establishment of the Polish State are problems which will not be solved by a war in the West but exclusively by Russia on the one hand and Germany on the other.

But if this war is really to be waged only in order to give Germany a new regime, that is to say, in order to destroy the present Reich once more and thus to create a new Treaty of Versailles, then millions of lives will be sacrificed in vain, for neither will the German Reich go to pieces nor will a second Treaty of Versailles be made. And even should these things come to pass after three, four or even eight years of war, then this second Versailles would once more become the source of fresh conflict in the future.

Abandon the senseless war and follow Hitler down the road to peace! There would be pacification and reconstruction in eastern Europe, international laws to mitigate the horrors of war, the revival of international economic life, an "unconditionally guaranteed peace," and—colonies for Germany. "To achieve these great ends, the leading nations of this continent will one day have to come together to draw up, accept, and guarantee a statute on a comprehensive basis which will ensure for them all a sense of security, of calm—in short, of peace." It would be much better to prepare for this international conference at once and "tackle the solution before millions of men are first sense-lessly sent to death and billions of riches destroyed."

In his own mind, no doubt Hitler equated the men with France and the riches with Britain, and thought his plea cleverly contrived. In his peroration, the pacific and minatory themes were mingled:

> One thing only is certain. In the course of world history, there have never been two victors but very often only losers. This seems to me to have been the case in the last war.
>
> May these peoples and their leaders who are of the same mind now make their reply. And let those who consider war to be the better solution reject my outstretched hand.

Beyond question, Hitler sincerely hoped that this *démarche* would precipitate overtures for peace, or at least discourage the western Allies and divide their counsels, so that the war would degenerate into a halfhearted affair from which an armistice could soon be extracted. But Hitler's "outstretched hand" had too often proved a treacherous and deadly grip. In Paris, Premier Daladier promptly declared that "we must go on with the war that has been imposed on us until victory, which will alone permit the establishment in Europe of a regime of real justice and lasting peace." The British Foreign Office gave out acid comments while reserving final judgment until Hitler's proposals could "be subjected to careful examination."

On October 12, Chamberlain announced in Parliament "the position of His Majesty's Government." The background of the war and Hitler's broken promises—which always seemed to arouse Chamberlain as no other facet of Nazism could—were rehearsed. It was no longer possible to rely on the "unsupported word of the present German government." Furthermore, Hitler's new proposals were "based upon recognition of his conquests and his right to do what he pleases with the conquered." Therefore, peace could be achieved only on the basis of "acts, not words alone." Otherwise, "we must persevere in our duty to the end. It is for Germany to make her choice."

Chamberlain's reply was at once branded as "insolent" by Goebbels' deputy, Otto Dietrich, who also informed the press that the Fuehrer had summoned the generals to prepare for "war in earnest." For once, Goebbels' propaganda machine spoke the truth. The peace offensive had failed within a week, and Hitler was champing at the bit and eager to attack in the West at once. For him, too, World War II had now begun.

But six more months were to intervene before the storm broke in full fury. The cities and towns of Europe were blacked out, but no bombs fell on them. The German and Allied armies were deployed but did not march. Neville Chamberlain described this phase as "twilight war"; in the United States, people spoke of the "phony war."

On the Allied side, the reasons for this "prolonged and oppressive pause" (Churchill's phrase) were plain enough. The French, to be sure, were able to deploy over ninety divisions from the Channel Coast to Switzerland but, after the defeat of Poland, the Germans could out-match this force by half again. By March 1940, Britain had added only ten divisions to the Allied forces in France, and the contemplated increase of the British Expeditionary Force to fifty or fifty-five divisions was expected to take over two years. Quite apart from the French penchant for the defensive, it would have been foolhardy for the Allies to launch a major attack on the western front until their forces had been substantially increased and modernized.

In the air, the fear of reprisals and of adverse world opinion no doubt restrained both sides from commencing a campaign of urban destruction. This was especially true of the French, whose air force was in a sad state of insufficiency. The Royal Air Force, though not yet abreast of the Luftwaffe, was making great strides, but neither side was ready to begin the terrible game which was, in the end, to recoil so heavily upon the Germans.

In fact, however, the war never was "phony" in the dictionary sense of "fake." A "phony war," presumably, is one in which neither side seriously intends to join issue on the field of battle. True, the Germans had hoped to conquer Poland and still postpone a major engagement in the West, but the Allies would not yield. There followed a period of quiet on the western front because the Allies were incapable of attacking and the Germans were divided in their counsels on the method and timing of their assault. This pause did not, however, make the war "phony" in 1939, any more than the period of nearly a year between Pearl Harbor and the Allied landings in North Africa would justify such a description of the opening phase of hostilities between the United States and Germany.

Certainly the war did not seem "phony" to the British merchant seamen and the German U-boat crews; to the 300 men of the British merchant cruiser *Rawalpindi* as their ship sank off Iceland under the guns of the *Scharnhorst;* or to the crews of the *Graf Spee, Exeter, Achilles,* and *Ajax,* as they fought the action off the River Plate. Nor was there anything "phony" about the state of affairs in Poland, where Heinrich Himmler was losing no time in putting his own theories of war to the test of practice.

And if all the misery and death on the high seas and in Poland during the winter of 1939–40 seem in retrospect small compared to what was soon to follow, this was not the fault of Adolf Hitler. Had he had his way, the German and Allied armies would have been locked in battle early in November. That the onslaught was delayed until the following spring was due in part to the weather and in part to fluctuations in the plan of campaign, but also to the opposition of the German generals to any immediate offensive. Beck and Adam had taken their departure a year earlier, but all vestiges of professional independence had not yet deserted the officer corps.

Command Crisis in the West

On September 15, 1939, after the fate of Poland was sealed, Winston Churchill, then First Lord of the Admiralty, addressed himself to Prime Minister Chamberlain: [1]

> It seems to me most unlikely that the Germans will attempt an offensive in the West at this late season. . . . It would seem wise for Hitler to make good his eastern connections and feeding grounds during these winter months, and thus give his people the spectacle of repeated successes, and the assurance of weakening our blockade. I do not, therefore, apprehend that he will attack in the West until he has collected the easy spoils which await him in the East.

Churchill's prediction was correct, but not his reasoning; on this occasion, he diagnosed the mood of the German generals far more accurately than Hitler's. As early as September 10 the Chief of the Army General Staff, Franz Halder, had been contemplating a "change-over to position warfare" at the conclusion of the Polish campaign. A week later, Halder was calling upon his subordinates for "basic data on the organization of troops for position warfare in the West." On September 24 Halder's principal assistant, Heinrich von Stuelpnagel (the *O.Qu. I*), prepared an elaborate memorandum counseling against attacking the French. As late as September 26 Halder and General Otto Gruen (Inspector of Artillery) were discussing the "training of artillery for position warfare." [2]

At about this time, however, it became clear that "position warfare" was the last thing Hitler had in mind for the West. On September 25, Oberst Walter Warlimont (Jodl's deputy at OKW) brought word to Stuelpnagel of "the Fuehrer's plan of attack in the West." On September 27 (the day of Warsaw's surrender) Hitler called a meeting of the principal military leaders and informed them that, if the western powers should insist on continuing the war, he had decided * "to attack in the West as soon as possible, since the Franco-British Army is not yet prepared." The attack would be through Belgium and Holland to the Channel Coast.

The Fuehrer's pronouncements aroused great consternation at OKH. Brauchitsch and Halder hurriedly took counsel, and then sought to convert Keitel and Jodl to a defensive strategy. Early on September 29, Halder was in conference with Generalmajor Thomas of the OKW Economic Department, developing new arguments in opposition to Hitler's plan. Thomas was a willing collaborator; Germany was faced with a monthly steel deficit of 600,000 tons, an offensive in the West would require a cut in aircraft production, and no basic improvement in the situation could be expected short of six to nine months.

Later on the same day Brauchitsch and Halder mapped their tactics for a report to Hitler, arguing strongly against the proposed autumn offensive. The November weather would be unsuitable because the daylight was too short and fog would hinder air support. The techniques of the Polish campaign were "no recipe for the West" and would be "no good against a well-knit army." Much better, therefore, for the German Army to ensure the protection of the Ruhr and "stand opposite the Belgian and Dutch fortifications ready to go out to meet the enemy . . . in the event of a French offensive." In the meantime, Germany could concentrate on naval and air action against British sea power and await a more propitious season and the availability of new arms—heavy tanks, chemical warfare projectors, rockets, and gas.

On September 30, there was another meeting with Hitler, at which the Fuehrer thanked the generals for their achievements in Poland and

---

* The quotation is from a note appended to the OKW War Diary. The meeting also is mentioned but not described in Halder's diary; subsequent entries reflect its general tenor in line with the quotation from the War Diary. See also Westphal, *The German Army in the West* (London, 1951), p. 75: "On September 27, 1939, Hitler ordered the Commanders-in-Chief of the Wehrmacht and their Chiefs of General Staff to attend him in the Reich Chancellery. He informed them that he had decided to attack France, as it was intolerable to wait for the western powers to attack first. . . . The Army was to report back what was the earliest starting date. Hitler made these intentions known without any previous discussion with Brauchitsch or Halder. Both wanted to continue the existing defensive. . . ."

declared himself "prepared for peace" but filled with the "utmost determination" in the event of continued war. That night Brauchitsch and Halder held another "prolonged conference on how we stand on the Fuehrer's plans in the West." A few days later they picked up an ally in a new quarter. Word reached Halder that Goering favored postponement of the offensive until the following spring, because of unfavorable weather, unreadiness of the armored forces, and "political repercussions."

Goering, indeed, had gone much further and was using his Swedish connections to sound out the British on the possibility of peace negotiations. These "feelers" coincided with Hitler's "peace offensive" and were put out with the Fuehrer's approval. But Hitler was not disposed to be patient. If the Allies wanted to talk peace, let them say so at once; otherwise he was determined to attack as soon as the necessary tactical dispositions could be made.

On October 4, Jodl told Halder that a "very severe crisis is in the making" because of the Army's opposition and that Hitler was "bitter because the soldiers do not obey him." And on October 7 (the day after his "peace offer"), when Brauchitsch and Halder presented their unfavorable report on the proposed offensive, they made little or no impression. Hitler countered their arguments by predicting that "the Belgians will call the French to come to their aid. . . . France will do that in the period of autumn fogs." Therefore "we must forestall this with an operation designed to gain a decision, even if we fall short of the original objectives and attain only a line which would afford better protection for the Ruhr."

The dispute had now reached the point where Hitler felt it advisable to assert his authority as Supreme Commander of the Wehrmacht. Without waiting for the official British reaction to his Reichstag speech, on October 9 he issued his "Directive No. 6 for the Conduct of the War": [3]

1. If it should become apparent in the near future that England and, under England's leadership, also France are not willing to make an end of the war, I am determined to take active and aggressive steps without much delay. . . .

3. Therefore I give the following orders for further military operations:

   a. Preparations are to be made for an attacking operation on the northern wing of the western front, through the areas of Luxembourg, Belgium, and Holland. This attack must be carried out with as much strength and at as early a date as possible. . . .

8. I request the Commanders-in-Chief to give me, as soon as possible, detailed reports of their intentions on the basis of this directive and from now on to keep me informed, through OKW, of the state of preparations.

Knowing of the violent opposition to his program, Hitler took the unusual step of supporting this directive * with a lengthy and argumentative but able memorandum [4] for the "eyes only" of Brauchitsch, Goering, Raeder, and Keitel. Therein, Hitler acknowledged "that from the German viewpoint there would be no objection to ending the war immediately," provided that the conquest of Poland were not "jeopardized by the peace treaty." However:

It is not the object of this memorandum to study the possibilities in this direction or even to take them into consideration. In this paper I shall confine myself exclusively to the other case: the necessity to continue the fight, the object of which, as already stressed, consists so far as the enemy is concerned in the dissolution or destruction of the German Reich. In opposition to this, the German war aim is the final military dispatch of the West, that is, destruction of the power and ability of the western powers ever again to be able to oppose the state consolidation and further development of the German people in Europe.

After this intransigent prologue, Hitler devoted himself chiefly to the issue upon which he and the generals were so sharply divided—that of *timing*. First, abroad:

a. The continued neutrality of Russia could not be assured. "The trifling significance of treaties has been proved on all sides in recent years. The greatest safeguard against any Russian attack lies . . . in a prompt demonstration of German strength."

b. "The hope of Italian support for Germany . . . is dependent on the continuation of Fascist influence in that country, and therefore largely in the Duce's remaining alive. Time, here, can therefore under no circumstances be considered as an ally of Germany's."

c. Belgium and Holland "are dependent upon the West in the highest degree. . . . England and France . . . can compel Belgium and Holland to give up their neutrality . . . time is not a factor which promises favorable developments for Germany."

---

* Hitler's basic directives for the conduct of the war were issued in a numbered series beginning with No. 1 of August 31, 1939. The directives for the period August 31, 1939 to August 1, 1940 are listed and summarized in Appendix D, *infra*, pp. 433–36. Some were signed by Keitel under Hitler's authority, and others by Hitler himself.

d. In the United States, too, "time is to be viewed as working against Germany."

Second, at home:

a. In a long war, Germany's "limited food and raw material basis" would endanger the national food supply, jeopardize "the means for carrying on the war," and "the morale, at least of the people, will be adversely affected."

b. Far more important, the vital Ruhr would be subjected to increasing danger from air attacks. "The longer this war lasts, the more difficult will be the preservation of German air superiority." Neutral Belgium and Holland constituted a "protective zone in front of the Ruhr," but at the first opportunity England and France would endeavor to occupy the Low Countries and move up to the German border, the better to strike at the Ruhr.

Third, if the prospect of a long war must be faced, "Germany's military means of waging a lengthier war are, as far as our main enemy is concerned, the Air Force and the U-boat arm." On both scores, possession of the Channel Coast would enormously strengthen the German position:

a. "The weaknesses of German U-boat warfare lie in the great distances to the scene of action. . . . If the war lasts long, increasing difficulty for our U-boats must be reckoned with. . . . The creation of U-boat bases beyond the constricted home bases would lead to an enormous increase in the striking power of this arm."

b. "The Luftwaffe cannot succeed in efficient operations against the industrial center of England and her . . . ports . . . until it is no longer compelled to operate offensively from our present small North Sea coast, by extremely devious routes involving long flights. . . . If we were in possession of Holland, Belgium, or even the Straits of Dover as jumping-off bases for German aircraft, then, without a doubt, Great Britain could be struck a mortal blow. . . ."

Having thus totted up the reasons for an immediate attack, Hitler enlarged upon the present superiority of the German Army and its good prospects for victory, and concluded that "in all circumstances, attack is to be preferred to defense as the decisive war-winning method. *The start, however, cannot take place too early.* The coming months will not lead to any important increase of our offensive strength, but to an important defensive strengthening of our enemies." Finally, the generals were exhorted to "keep firmly fixed in their minds that the destruction of the Anglo-French forces is the main objective, the attainment of which will enable suitable conditions to obtain for later and successful employment of the Luftwaffe. The brutal employment of the Luftwaffe against the heart of the British will-to-resist can and will follow at the given moment."

Except with respect to the timing of the attack, it was a prophetic document. Together with the accompanying "Directive No. 6," it served to crystallize Hitler's strategy and turned the generals' minds to serious planning for the approaching test. But it did not end the bitter disagreement over the timing of the attack. With near unanimity, the generals continued to press for a postponement, at least until the following spring.

The OKW War Diary, for example, reveals that Hitler hoped to launch the offensive by November 10, but the same entry records that "OKH is of the opinion that the preparations of the Army will not be absolutely complete by that time. Frequently the opinion is voiced— by no means shared by the Fuehrer—that an attack in the West is unnecessary, and the war could be satisfactorily ended if we were to wait a little." Jodl, however, was as much under the Fuehrer's spell as ever: [5] "We will win this war, though it may be a hundred times contrary to the doctrines of the General Staff; we will have superior troops, superior equipment, superior armies and a united and methodical leadership." No doubt Jodl's sincere and Keitel's slavish support encouraged Hitler to press forward despite mounting opposition from the other generals.

This next erupted at Frankfurt am Main, from the pen of Generaloberst von Leeb, Commander-in-Chief of Army Group C, facing the French opposite the Rhine and the Maginot Line. His divisions were chiefly composed of over-age troops, and on October 3 he had informed Halder that their morale was largely dependent on the hope that peace would soon come. "It is the generals that push the war," his men were saying.

Soon thereafter Leeb donned the mantle of Beck and composed a long memorandum [6] "on the prospects and effects of an attack on France and England by violating the neutrality of Holland, Belgium, and Luxembourg." His estimate was pessimistic. "Even the first prerequisite of a quick success, operational surprise, does not exist. . . . Even now, during the initial stages of the massing [of troops], Belgium

is bringing up sizable reinforcements in the direction of Liége. . . ."
Leeb was a specialist in defensive warfare,* and now he began to
maneuver the French forces and survey French fortifications as if he
had been in Gamelin's shoes. "Even now, the French have secured and
strengthened their northeastern borders, and they could easily bring
up the bulk of their armies [into Belgium] and Luxembourg on thirteen
double-track trunk railroads. . . . Besides, the French have a very
strong flanking support in their fortified zone. These fortifications, facing Luxembourg and the eastern sector of the Ardennes . . . have
been greatly strengthened."

Leeb recognized that the achievements of the German panzer divisions in Poland "could be advanced as a counter-argument." However,
"such a comparison is dangerous. Apart from the fact that the armored
forces are dependent on the weather to a very great extent, it would be
a mistake to underestimate the French Army and its leadership. . . .
It can hardly be expected that the proven striking power . . . of our
armored forces can attain such a momentum against the western Allies
as was the case in the East, where they raced from one success to
another." Nor would the Luftwaffe swing the balance, opposed as it
was to "the tenacity of the enemy, especially the British" and the
counter-measures which would have to be anticipated.

All this led Leeb to the categorical conclusion that "it is quite certain that a total destruction of the Anglo-French armies, which is the
desired ultimate objective, cannot be achieved." An attack would
simply lead to "trench warfare, either before the French fortifications
or even on Belgian soil." This, reasoned Leeb, was the real answer to
Hitler's argument that time was working for the Allies. "Such reasoning . . . is correct so far as it goes. However, it fails to consider that
an attack costing the attacker more casualties than the defender . . .
would be a disadvantage for us. Trench warfare will be forced upon
us. . . . World War I was sufficient proof that long-drawn-out trench
warfare means tremendous disadvantages for us."

Having covered the military prospects, Leeb turned to "the political
repercussions." A German attack would actually be "a favor" to the
western Allies:

Such an attack would provide England and France immediately with
the one thing they haven't had up to now, i.e., a forceful propaganda slogan,
and this would even be the best one imaginable: to defend the Fatherland—

* His well-known book on the subject was translated and published in the
United States under the title *Defense* in 1943.

even if it is only the Belgian one! No Frenchman will fail to yield to such a slogan; everyone will fight for the homeland as soon as it appears to be threatened by the penetration of German troops into Belgium.

Any violation of Belgium's neutrality is bound to drive that country into the arms of France. France and Belgium will then have one common foe: Germany, which for the second time within twenty-five years assaults neutral Belgium! Germany, whose government solemnly vouched for and promised the preservation of and respect for this neutrality only a few weeks ago! . . .

If Germany, by forcing the issue, should violate the neutrality of Holland, Belgium, and Luxembourg, a neutrality which has been solemnly recognized and vouched for by the German government, this action will necessarily cause even those neutral states which until now have shown some measure of sympathy for the German cause, to reverse their policy. The Reich, which cannot count on Italy's or Russia's military assistance, will also become increasingly isolated economically. Especially North America, whose population easily responds to such propaganda slogans, will become more inclined to submit to England's and France's influence. . . .

The attack would cause our own people to be deeply disappointed. . . . Anybody who experienced our people's enthusiastic attitude on the occasion of our victories in 1914 will become rather doubtful on seeing the apathy of a great proportion of our people during the 1939 campaign in the East. The German people's discipline and its unfailing faith in the Fuehrer's love for peace were the reasons that it was quite willing to carry the burden of the Polish War. At the present juncture, however, after hostilities have ceased, the entire nation is longing for peace as the apogee of its desires. . . . Rumors that are at large to the effect that the Fuehrer wanted peace, and that the generals, on the other hand, were stirring up emotions conducive to launching a war because by doing so they hoped to consolidate the Army's position toward the party, must be rated as symptomatic signs, although they appear to be very inane.

An attack on Belgium, or . . . on France, would mean the continuation of the war. It will fail to rally our people's will and preparedness to fight, and it will cause a cleavage. Any such schisms would only too quickly spread to the armed forces!

What, then, should Germany do? Leeb's answer was to "take a waiting attitude":

If the strength of the German armies necessary for repulsing any attackers should be maintained, and if our armies should remain alerted at the western borders of the Reich, *it would be impossible for anybody* to attack us. Any assault launched by the enemy would cause him grievous losses, and he would never succeed in destroying our preparedness for defense. It would then be impossible for England and France to achieve a *military* victory. . . .

If we wait, this fact will allow us to release both manpower and material for the German economy, which it badly needs to achieve a continuous production program for a war of long duration. The German people will then see that it is only the stubborn attitude on the part of England which forced us to continue the war. It will understand this emergency and prepare itself psychologically and mentally to bear the privations which follow in the wake of such an emergency. In the case of an enemy attack, it will know that the *defense* of the Fatherland is at stake.

Finally, and this is the most salient point I believe, the Reich leadership will retain its armed forces completely intact as the most potent factor for any further negotiations. Nobody could force the government to conclude an unfavorable peace.

Leeb dispatched his memorandum not only to Brauchitsch as Commander-in-Chief of the Army but also directly to Generaloberst von Bock, the Commander-in-Chief of Army Group B on the northern wing of the western front facing Belgium and Holland, where the proposed attack would take place. In his covering letter to Brauchitsch, Leeb declared that "grave anxiety for our future is the reason for surveying our present situation more closely. . . . I am sure that my views are shared by many others who take the trouble to assess the situation."

The Leeb memorandum seems to have had little effect. Halder recorded its receipt at OKH, but without further comment. Quite possibly Hitler never saw it. Furthermore, Leeb did not have wide influence among his fellow officers, many of whom regarded him as overcautious and behind the times, especially in his evaluation of tanks and airplanes in modern warfare. Most of the generals were opposed to an attack in the autumn of 1939, but by no means all of them shared Leeb's discouraging estimate of the success of a properly prepared offensive.

At all events, Hitler was no whit checked. On October 9 Warlimont had told Stuelpnagel that November 25 was the probable date for opening the offensive, although there would be a postponement if the weather were bad for flying. On October 10 Hitler had read his own memorandum to the military leaders, and a long discussion of military plans for the attack ensued. On October 14, following the receipt of Leeb's memorandum and the news of Chamberlain's rejection of Hitler's "peace terms," Brauchitsch and Halder held another "prolonged conference" on the "over-all situation." [7] Brauchitsch now saw three possible courses of action: to attack (Hitler's plan), to "wait and see" (Leeb's plan), and "fundamental changes"—meaning Hitler's overthrow. The Commander-in-Chief and his Chief of Staff were gloomy but indecisive, and Halder recorded that "none of these three possibilities offers prospect of decisive success, least of all the last, since it is essentially negative and tends to render us vulnerable. Quite apart from all this, it is our duty to set forth the military prospects soberly and to promote every possibility to make peace."

Apparently [8] Brauchitsch turned next to Rundstedt and "asked him to talk the Fuehrer out of his plans." Rundstedt was then in command in Poland; if he attempted anything at this time, it was without visible effect. Brauchitsch saw the Fuehrer again on October 17, and later described the meeting's outcome as "hopeless." Hitler, his mind still fixed on England, declared that "the British will be ready to talk only after a beating. We must get at them as quickly as possible." The exact date for the offensive "cannot yet be fixed," but would not be earlier than November 15. A few days later, however, Hitler wanted to attack on Sunday, November 12.

With this target date in view, on October 25 Hitler reviewed the military plans for the offensive at a conference attended not only by Brauchitsch and Halder but also by Bock (as commander of the army group which would carry the main burden of the attack) and his two army commanders, Reichenau and Kluge. Although Hitler's decision to strike had already been pronounced, the generals once again endeavored to persuade him to postpone action until the spring.

Interestingly enough, it was Reichenau, hitherto Hitler's strongest supporter among the generals, who took the lead. He and Bock both stressed the danger of seasonal fog, which could hamper the tactical air support necessary to effect a break-through. Reichenau added that a respite during the approaching winter was necessary to bring the troops to a proper state of training. Hitler countered with the prediction that "one winter night England and France will be on the Maas without firing a shot and without our knowing about it." Reichenau replied that even this hazard was preferable to a premature offensive and was supported by Bock, who emphasized the lack of replacements necessary to sustain an attack.

On October 27 Hitler attempted to inject a harmonious note into the military cacophony by handing out the Knight's Cross of the Iron Cross (*Ritterkreuz*) to fourteen officers, including Keitel, Halder, Guderian, and Jeschonnek. But the tension was not eased. At a conference immediately following the ceremony, Brauchitsch declared that the Army could not be ready before November 26. Hitler pronounced this "much too late" and definitely settled on November 12 for "A-Day." That evening, Halder found Brauchitsch "tired and dejected"; the pair were at their wit's end.

On October 29 a revised military directive for the offensive, which had been given the cover-name *Fall Gelb* (Case Yellow), was issued. At this juncture Leeb spoke up again, his determination perhaps fortified by the unhappy and, as he thought, unnecessary loss of his son in Poland.* To friends he had written that Germany's goal "could have been attained by other means" but that "this war was wanted and was therefore waged" and that "Hitler is drifting toward war in the West as well, which will call for extremely heavy, unimaginable sacrifices. We are living in a sad and violent time! God help our poor people!" On October 31 he dispatched a personal letter to Brauchitsch: [9]

In this fateful time, I feel it urgent to tell you once more how much I appreciate the responsibility which rests upon you. Perhaps the fate of the entire German people depends on you in the next few days. For in the present situation, the Commander-in-Chief of the Army is called upon above all else to advance his views, which are supported by the entire General Staff and all thinking parts of the Army, in every possible way.

I hope that the commanders-in-chief of the other two branches of the Wehrmacht do not close their eyes to this fateful hour.

The military reasons which speak against the plan of the Fuehrer are clear.

We cannot carry it through to the end if only because of the state of our reserves. Even at present, when there are not yet any serious demands for reserves, it is difficult to discharge the enlisted men who are past the age limit. The many officers who are past the age limit . . . cannot be replaced at all.

The sword does not have the edge which the Fuehrer seems to assume. The gaps which we now have, above all the watering down of the officer corps, must necessarily take effect faster and more decisively than was the case in World War I. There are shortcomings everywhere. . . .

I consider the military annihilation of the English, French, and Belgians a goal which cannot be attained at present. And only if they are annihilated by our attack would they be ready for peace.

If the Fuehrer were now to make an end to the present situation, under conditions which were in some measure acceptable, no one would interpret this as a sign of weakness or of yielding; but rather as recognizing the true status of power. The granting of autonomy for Czechoslovakia and allowing the remainder of Poland to stand as a nation would probably meet with the complete understanding of the entire German people. The Fuehrer would then be honored as a Prince of Peace, not only by the entire German people but assuredly also by large parts of the world as well.

I am prepared to stand behind you personally to the fullest extent in the days to come and to bear the consequences. . . .

---

* Leutnant Alfred Leeb, of the 99th Mountain Infantry Regiment, was killed near Lvov the day before the city surrendered, and when Russian forces were already approaching from the East.

Rundstedt, too, was now moved to make his position clear, and sent a personal letter to Brauchitsch bearing the same date as Leeb's.[10] Rundstedt had assumed command of Army Group A on the western front (between Bock's and Leeb's army groups) barely a week earlier but had already concluded that the offensive, as then planned, "cannot have a decisive effect on the war." This, indeed, was the main burden of his letter to Brauchitsch; unlike Leeb, Rundstedt preferred to "pass over all political problems as irrelevant to the sphere of responsibility of a soldier."

Rundstedt pointed out that the attack would have to be "launched frontally from the very narrow area" between the Maginot Line and the Dutch river mouths. There was little chance for surprise, and no room for flanking operations. The Army's reserves were not sufficient to sustain a frontal attack long enough to achieve decisive results; it would come to a stop "possibly at the Somme." An offensive aimed only at the conquest of the Channel Coast might be justified if it would "decisively influence the prospects of the Luftwaffe and Navy in battle against England." However, "with regard to the Navy the World War has already proved the contrary"; there would be no advantage unless the French coast on the open ocean south of the Channel were also captured. The Luftwaffe would benefit by the possession of Holland or Belgium, "but hardly to a decisive degree."

Confronted with these conditions, Rundstedt suggested that the Army fall back on something analogous to the naval concept of the "fleet in being." He opposed allowing "the attacking power of the Army to be consumed for an indecisive and partial objective." In the long run, "*an army capable of attacking* will remain the decisive factor on the continent in the event of a long war." And, with the "unexpected" entry into the war of England and France, "there remains no choice other than to prepare for a long war." Russia's friendship for Germany was based on fear and would wither "as soon as the attacking power of the Army is spent." Therefore, that power must not be dissipated for partial objectives. Much better to harass England from the air, force England and France to take the offensive on land, and thereby shift the onus of violating Belgian neutrality; "our prospects are better if we meet the enemy moving into Belgium against the will of the Belgians, in a mobile engagement," thus "imposing on the French a task which would strain their passive attitude toward the war."

At the time Rundstedt wrote this letter, his army group comprised the Twelfth and Sixteenth Armies. In concluding his letter, Rundstedt related that "the Commander-in-Chief of the Twelfth Army, General-oberst List, approached me several days ago with similar opinions and requested that I put them forward." However, "I did not confide officially in the Commander-in-Chief of the Sixteenth Army" because of reluctance to instill doubts "further down the line." No doubt there were other and unspoken reasons for Rundstedt's reticence in this quarter. The Commander-in-Chief of the newly formed Sixteenth Army was General Ernst Busch, one of the most pro-Nazi among the senior army generals.

Goaded and encouraged by Rundstedt and Leeb, Brauchitsch and Halder spent November 2 and 3 visiting the army group and army headquarters on the northern sector of the front, ostensibly to perfect plans for the attack but chiefly to secure information and support for another *démarche* to Hitler. The moving up of troops was to begin on November 5, but they carefully arranged for "check points" so that the operation could be called off until eight hours before the scheduled time. Halder noted in his diary that "none of the higher headquarters thinks that the offensive . . . has any prospect of success. No decisive success can be expected from ground operations." Everywhere it was reported that the level of training was insufficient, that repairs to equipment had not been completed, and that other deficiencies required postponement of the attack. "At the moment we cannot launch an offensive with a distant objective." Upon their return to Berlin on November 4, further and secret * support was forthcoming from Generalmajor Thomas, who predicted that violation of Belgian neutrality would threaten the flow of iron ore from Sweden and copper from Yugoslavia, and deplete Germany's food supply.

Thus armed with arguments, and with a memorandum in reply to Hitler's document of October 9, Brauchitsch faced Hitler, on November 5, with a demand that the attack be postponed.[11] He paraded the facts which his tour of the front had disclosed, stressing especially the unfavorable weather and the need for more training. The weather Hitler brushed off with the observation that it would also hamper the enemy and that the spring weather might be no better. As for the level of training, "what is argued now would still hold good four weeks from now."

Seeing himself making little headway, Brauchitsch deliberately exaggerated the slackness which had set in during the lull following the Polish campaign and drew a comparison to the period in 1918 when

* Thomas' superior, Keitel, was not told of the conference.

insubordination and even mutiny had broken out among the troops. The result was an explosion of rage from the Fuehrer. Where and in what units had these episodes occurred? He would fly there himself on the morrow. The Army "did not want to fight" and had deliberately lagged in the armaments build-up. How many death sentences for insubordination had been meted out? The unhappy Brauchitsch promised to procure full information. Such a tempestuous scene was little to his liking: "Any sober discussion of these things is impossible."

Brauchitsch, badly shattered, retired from the scene, and the "crisis of mutual confidence" between Hitler and the military deepened. The generals had no more cards to play, and their efforts to forestall Hitler's intended attack came to an end. Rundstedt, for example, called a conference of his subordinate army, corps, and divisional commanders on November 11, to discuss the operational plans for his army group.[12] In opening the meeting, Rundstedt acknowledged that, by reason of its forced growth, the Army was plagued by gaps and shortcomings "which make one wonder whether [it] will be equal to the task it has been given." But, he sternly admonished, these doubts must now be laid aside once and for all. "The period of such thoughts and wonderings is now closed. The Army has been given its task, and it will fulfill that task!"

On November 6 Hitler was working on a "proclamation" for the Belgians and Dutch in justification of the planned invasion, alleging a threatened "French march into Belgium" as the excuse. The next day, however, "after hearing reports on the meteorological and railway transport situations," he ordered that "A-Day" be postponed for three days, and the moving up of troops was halted.[13] And now began a most extraordinary series of alerts and postponements. On November 9, "A-Day" was set for November 19; on November 13, it was put off to November 22; on the sixteenth it was set for the twenty-sixth; on the twentieth for December 3; and on November 27 for December 9. All of these postponements were specified as ordered by Hitler on the basis of the "meteorological situation."

Certainly Hitler had not abandoned his plan to attack as soon as possible; certainly, also, he was furious at the obstacles the generals were putting in his way. And yet there is much to suggest that Hitler was not averse to using the "meteorological situation" as a face-saving device to accommodate himself to the practical situation that the Army faced. For one thing, the tactical plans for the attack were not as yet clearly developed, and Hitler himself was constantly tinkering with them in long conferences with the generals. Even the question whether or not to invade Holland as well as Belgium had not yet been definitely settled. Then, too, new divisions, and old divisions as they completed the refitting which the Polish campaign required, were becoming available week by week. The four "light" divisions were in the process of conversion to panzer divisions. The benefits to be derived from awaiting the full marshaling of this potential strength must have become apparent even to Hitler, as he concerned himself ever more deeply with the military details of the offensive.

Diplomatic and other factors extrinsic to the Army may also have played a part in the postponement. On November 7 the King of the Belgians and the Queen of Holland offered to mediate between Germany and the western Allies. The German Foreign Office treated this move "with sarcasm and sneering" (Halder's phrase), and Otto Dietrich was ordered to "play it down" in the German press. This cold rebuff angered and alarmed the Low Countries; the Belgian Ambassador asked Ernst von Weizsaecker, Undersecretary of the Foreign Office, whether Germany was trying "to pick a quarrel." Hitler may well have decided that this episode both threatened the hoped-for surprise element of the planned attack * and weakened the basis for charging that Belgium and Holland were not truly neutral, and would consent to a Franco-British march-in.

On November 8 Hitler made his customary appearance at the Buergerbau Keller in Munich, for the anniversary celebration of the 1923 "Beerhall *Putsch.*" A few minutes after he left, a bomb planted by the rostrum exploded, killing a few and wounding a number of the old party members gathered for the occasion. At the time, many thought that the affair had been deliberately staged by the Gestapo, perhaps with Hitler's approval.† As far as is now known, however, it was a genuine assassination attempt by one Georg Elser, a fanatically anti-Hitler artisan with Communist ties.

However, Hitler insisted that other forces were responsible, and the Nazi propaganda machine laid the blame on the British secret services. The very next day, apparently on Hitler's personal orders, the SS kid-

---

* See Westphal, *The German Army in the West*, p. 75: "In the end Hitler only withdrew his order to attack on November 12 when it became apparent that the enemy had obtained knowledge of it." In fact, on November 8 the German Ambassador in Brussels reported that King Leopold knew of an impending German attack. See N.D. NG-1726.

† It has also been suggested that the SS contrived the episode without Hitler's knowledge, to arouse his fears and suspicions and thus increase his feeling of dependence on his SS bodyguard.

naped two British intelligence officers, Major R. H. Stevens and Captain S. P. Best, at Venlo in Holland, and carried them across the border to Germany. Agents of the SS had been in contact with Stevens and Best for some weeks in an effort to penetrate the British intelligence service, and there was no evidence of connection between the British officers and Elser. But Hitler clung to the idea of a spectacular trial of all three to arouse public resentment against the British and discredit Dutch neutrality, and he was dissuaded only with difficulty.[14]

Whatever the truth of these murky episodes, they disturbed Hitler's concentration on the controversial western offensive. The upshot of all these circumstances in combination—the weather, the generals' opposition, and extraneous events—was a prolonged state of military alert during which the timing of the offensive, if indeed it were to be undertaken, remained uncertain.

On November 20, this chronic alert was officially embodied in the OKW "Directive No. 8 for the Conduct of the War": [15]

The state of alert, to make possible at any moment continuation of the concentration of troops which has been initiated, must be maintained for the time being. Only this will make it possible to exploit favorable weather conditions immediately.

The various components of the Wehrmacht will make arrangements enabling them to stop the attack even if the order for such action is received by the high command as late as D-1 at 23:00 hours. The keyword "Rhein" (start attack) or "Elbe" (withhold attack) will be passed on to the high commands at the latest by that time.

But although Hitler did not force an immediate attack over the objections of the generals, neither did he forgive their opposition or neglect countermeasures to bring them to heel. During November, Goering and Goebbels both addressed large audiences of high-ranking officers. The Nazi leaders drew comparisons between the spirit and reliability of the Navy and Air Force on the one hand, and of the Army on the other, which were definitely unfavorable to the Army. These disquisitions were followed, on November 23 at noon, by a Hitler lecture to the commanding generals, chiefs of staffs, and other highly placed staff officers. It was the last occasion, so far as the records show, at which Hitler called together all the senior military leaders for an over-all politico-military review of the situation.*

This speech of November 23 was chiefly a pep talk, to discredit the

* Only one record of Hitler's remarks (N.D. 789-PS) has come to light. It is not an exact transcript of his words, but rather a semi-telegraphic précis.

doubters and embolden the halfhearted among his listeners. There was the usual rehearsal of past history, of his own indispensability, and of the arguments favoring an immediate attack. Brauchitsch's strictures on the discipline and valor of the German infantry were much on Hitler's mind:

. . . I am most deeply pained when I hear the opinion that the German Army is not individually as valuable as it should be. The infantry in Poland did not accomplish what one should have expected from it. Lax discipline. I believe that the soldiers must be judged in their relative value in comparison with the opponent. There is no doubt that our armed forces are the best. Every German infantryman is better than the French. Not the exhilaration of patriotism but tough determination. I am told that the troops will only advance if the officers lead the way. In 1914 that was also the case. I am told that we were better trained then. In reality we were only better trained on the drill field, but not for the war. I must pay the present leadership the compliment that it is better than it was in 1914. . . .

. . . I cannot bear it when one says the Army is not in good shape. Everything lies in the hands of the military leader. I can do anything with the German soldier, if he is well led.

Hitler then mentioned the recent attempt on his life at Munich, and the Venlo incident, to undermine the idea that Belgian-Dutch neutrality was sincere or reliable. He reiterated his anxiety about the possibility of a surprise occupation of Belgium and Holland by the Allies and the consequent danger to the vital Ruhr, and then passed to the familiar note of "unalterable determination":

. . . My decision is unchangeable. I shall attack France and England at the most favorable and quickest moment. Breach of the neutrality of Belgium and Holland is meaningless. No one will question that when we have won. We shall not bring about the breach of neutrality as idiotically as it was in 1914. If we do not break the neutrality, then England and France will. Without attack the war is not to be ended victoriously. I consider it as possible to end the war only by means of an attack.

Success, however, depended above all on unity and a determined spirit at the command level: "A prerequisite is that the leadership must give an example of fanatical unity from above. There would not be any failures if the leader always had the courage a rifleman must have. . . . I ask you to pass on the spirit of determination to the lower echelons." All this was capped by a peroration in which Hitler's megalomaniacal demon was uppermost:

. . . As long as I live I shall think only of the victory of my people. I shall shrink from nothing and shall destroy everyone who is opposed to me. I have decided to live my life so that I can stand unshamed if I have to die. I want to destroy the enemy. Behind me stands the German people, whose morale can only grow worse. Only he who struggles with destiny can have a good intuition. In the last years I have experienced many examples of intuition. Even in the present development I see the prophecy.

If we come through this struggle victoriously—and we shall come through victoriously—our time will enter into the history of our people. I shall stand or fall in this struggle. I shall never survive the defeat of my people.

According to some of the participants, Hitler's comments on the lack of spirit in the army leadership were far sharper than anything quoted above.[16] At all events, the noon speech to the senior commanders and staff officers was followed by another to the divisional commanders, the burden of which was, once again, "to arouse enthusiasm for the offensive." In the meantime, Brauchitsch and Halder had returned to the OKH field headquarters at Zossen; early in the evening they were peremptorily summoned back to the Reichschancellery, and Hitler read Brauchitsch a stern lecture on the "spirit of Zossen," meaning the defeatist, obstructive attitude of the OKH and the General Staff. In his diary, Halder referred to November 23 as a "day of crisis."

To some of the generals in Hitler's audience, however, the occasion was genuinely inspirational. For example, General Hermann Hoth, the commander of the XVth Corps and a strong Hitler supporter, made elaborate notes on the Fuehrer's discourse, so that he might relay the words of wisdom to his subordinates.[17] In exhorting the junior officers, Hoth laid emphasis on the unique opportunity for a one-front war afforded by the Hitler-Stalin pact, remarking that "it would be a crime not to exploit it." As for the violation of Belgian neutrality, "success is the supreme judge." The enlisted men were to be encouraged by recollections of victories in Poland and convinced of the inevitability of a "life and death struggle"; it was "either England or we."

But on some of the generals Hitler's speeches had an effect the reverse of what he had intended. Among these were such as Manstein and Guderian, who were confident that a successful offensive could be launched and therefore were in harmony with the Fuehrer's operational thinking, but who were wounded by his aspersions.

Guderian, in particular, was both hurt and puzzled.[18] He and the other "panzer generals," with Hitler's support, had raised the German armored divisions to a high level of efficiency. They had led the Army to impressive victories in Poland. Guderian faced the prospective campaign in the West with energy and enthusiasm and was busily perfecting plans for a decisive break-through. Now he, together with his brother generals, was being admonished by the Fuehrer for lack of spirit and untrustworthiness. His professional pride was touched, and he was not the man to take these strictures in silence.

In this frame of mind Guderian sought out Manstein, at that time Rundstedt's Chief of Staff, who shared Guderian's resentment and had already made complaint to Rundstedt. The latter, however, even after urging by Manstein and Guderian, was not inclined to remonstrate with Hitler. Other senior generals approached by Guderian were equally unwilling to take any steps to counter Hitler's charges. Finally, Guderian went to Reichenau, thinking to capitalize on his "well-known good standing with both Hitler and the party."

Much to his surprise, however, Guderian discovered that Reichenau's stock of good will with the Fuehrer was exhausted. Nazi-minded though Reichenau might be, he was also an aggressive, opinionated man who rated his own military judgment well above Hitler's. His poor opinion of the autumn offensive he had repeatedly stated to the Fuehrer, and he had made no secret of it outside military circles.° As a result, Reichenau informed Guderian: "His relations with Hitler were anything but good . . . he had in fact had serious quarrels with him. Consequently, there would be nothing to be gained by his going to see the Fuehrer. He felt, however, that it was essential Hitler be informed of the sentiments of the corps of generals, and he suggested that I myself undertake this task." Thereupon, Reichenau made an appointment for Guderian to see Hitler in Berlin the very next day.†

The burden of Guderian's statement to Hitler was one of amazement and indignation that the Fuehrer and the Party leaders should openly express distrust of the generals, who had so recently and rapidly defeated Poland. If there were individual generals who did not deserve confidence, they should be dismissed: "The war that lies ahead will be a long one; we cannot afford such a break in our military leadership, and mutual confidence must be restored before a critical situation arises."

° See *The Von Hassell Diaries* (1947), pp. 83, 84, 90, and 94. "It is interesting that it is Reichenau, of all people, who continues to oppose the break-through most sharply; he also says so openly and has submitted a memorandum." (Entry for Dec. 5, 1939.) Halder's diary entry for Nov. 6, 1939, reveals that Reichenau had "received an orientation," presumably a sharp one, from Hitler.

† Guderian does not give the date of his interview with Hitler; apparently it was in late November or early December.

Hitler listened carefully to all this, and then declared simply that it was "a question of the Commander-in-Chief of the Army." Guderian answered that, in such a case, Brauchitsch should be replaced. Hitler asked who should be substituted, and Guderian suggested Reichenau. The result of this proposal, shortsighted as it was in view of what Guderian had already learned, abundantly confirmed Reichenau's fall from grace. "Quite out of the question," declared Hitler.

Guderian next mentioned Rundstedt, and then a series of other names, but none of them met with the Fuehrer's approval. In conclusion, Hitler rehearsed his grievances and suspicions—Blomberg, Fritsch, and Beck had all disappointed him, Brauchitsch had not set his sights high enough on rearmament, and now Brauchitsch and many other generals were obstructing his plans in the West. Guderian achieved nothing in fulfillment of his purpose and returned to his headquarters "deeply depressed by the insight that I had gained."

Thus the "crisis of confidence" persisted undiminished. So far as the proposed attack was concerned, Hitler continued to temporize. Other matters of great importance pressed on him. The Russo-Finnish War broke out on November 30. This aggravated the risk of war in Scandinavia, and early in December Raeder came to him with proposals for a German occupation of Norway. At about the same time, the action off the River Plate occurred, and the fate of the *Graf Spee* claimed his attention.

In addition to all this, the winter of 1939–40 proved severe, and the hoped-for spell of good weather did not materialize. "A-Day" was again put off from December 9 to 11, then to the seventeenth, and then (on December 12) to January 1. Christmas leaves could then be allowed, and a quiet spell ensued.

Hitler still hoped, however, that a period of clear, cold weather, with frozen ground, strong ice, and good flying conditions might eventuate between the middle of January and the middle of February. On December 27, "A-Day" was set for an unspecified date between January 9 and 14. The next day, Jodl learned that Hitler had decided "in the event of bad weather in the middle of January to postpone the attack until the spring."

On January 10, it seemed that Hitler's hopes might materialize. Goering's weather experts came in with a forecast of ten days' to two weeks' "clear winter weather" beginning January 15. "A-Day" was promptly set for January 17, to be preceded by several days of Luftwaffe attacks on Allied airfields and pilot-training schools.

But once again events conspired to favor the generals' desire to postpone hostilities. That very day a German courier airplane carrying two Luftwaffe majors and numerous secret documents pertaining to the plan of attack made a forced landing in Belgium.

What had happened is a striking demonstration of the value of security regulations that often strike the military go-getter as tedious and unnecessary. Major Reinberger, a regular officer of the Luftwaffe and commander of the paratroop school at Stendal, had been detailed to Student's staff to help formulate the plans for airborne operations in Holland and Belgium. Summoned to a conference in Cologne, he was delayed by congested traffic on the railways in the Ruhr area. On the evening of January 9 he found himself at the officers' club in Muenster, where he encountered Major Hoenmanns, a reserve officer and World War I aviator, and commandant of the nearby airfield at Loddenheide. Anxious to combine some flying time with a visit to his wife in Cologne, Hoenmanns offered to fly Reinberger there.

Reinberger was carrying secret maps and orders, and there was a strict prohibition against carrying such documents by air. But he was impatient, and gratefully accepted Hoenmanns' invitation. They took off the following morning; Hoenmanns lost his way in the clouds, and set his course too far to the west. Then he accidentally shut off the fuel supply of the "Taifun," a type of plane which he had but once before flown. The engine conked out, and Hoenmanns crashed the plane near a river which turned out to be not the Rhine but the Meuse. They were about twelve miles north of Maastricht, near the Belgian town of Mechelen-sur-Meuse.

Before Reinberger could complete the destruction of his papers, the two majors were picked up by Belgian soldiers and taken to the regional police headquarters. There Reinberger made another effort to burn the remaining documents, but failed again.* Enough was salvaged by the Belgians to disclose the general outlines of the German plan and the intended location of the airborne landings, and copies of the documents soon were turned over to the British and French.

The immediate result of this extraordinary episode was unbounded confusion on both sides of the front. The Allies did not know whether or not the documents were a deliberate "plant," and the Germans did not know how much the Allies had learned. Hitler, Goering, and Keitel

---

* When the German offensive began on May 10, Reinberger and Hoenmanns were sent to England and then to Canada, where they spent the war years as prisoners.

spent a long evening in Jodl's office poring over files to ascertain what might have been thus disclosed.

Meanwhile there was no temporizing with punishment for the unlucky General Helmuth Felmy, the commander of Luftflotte 2. Although there was no evidence that slackness at his level had contributed to the boner by the subordinate majors, on January 12 Felmy and his chief of staff, Oberst Josef Kammhuber, were, as Kesselring put it,[19] "sent into the wilderness." Kesselring was transferred from Luftflotte 1 to take Felmy's place.

Kammhuber, today the head of the air arm of the new German *Bundeswehr,* was sent to command a bomber group in Bavaria. But Felmy, who had been on bad terms with Goering since 1938 as the result of writing a pessimistic memorandum on the relative potential of German and British air power, was retired to civil life. The cashiered general's summary dismissal aroused sympathetic discussion, and his adolescent sons found themselves drawn into the controversy, to the father's distress. In consequence, as Felmy subsequently related: [20]

In order to bring the whole matter to a head and to avoid differences of opinion, in the autumn of 1940 I reported my entry into the [Nazi] Party. . . . It was, in a certain way, a victory over myself. We officers were brought up to believe that a personal fate has to be subordinated to higher elements, especially in times of crisis. That is what I wanted to show by this step.*

On January 13 the German air attaché in Brussels reported that "the dispatch case was burned for certain." But no one felt really sure, and grave anxiety prevailed. On top of this misfortune, the weather turned for the worse; a current of warm air from the east carried the prospect of fog between the sixteenth and nineteenth of January. Accordingly, another in the long series of postponement orders was issued, setting "A-Day" for January 20. The movement of troops toward the frontier, which had already started, was stopped.

The weather stayed capricious. No sustained clear period could be predicted, and it was reckoned that at least eight days were needed as the Meuse River, where the critical break-through was planned, would not be reached until the fourth day after the attack. Furthermore, the repeated false starts were unsettling to troops and staff alike and were paralyzing the railroads. Finally Hitler concluded that the element of surprise was being vitiated by the way the attacking forces

---

* Felmy was recalled to active duty in May 1941, and thereafter served in Iraq, Greece, and southeastern Russia.

were drawn up ("echeloned in depth"), requiring, as it did, four days to move them to their jumping-off points, and railroad movements which would be a giveaway to Allied aerial reconnaissance.

And so, on January 16, Hitler informed Jodl that he had decided "to put the entire setup of the operation on a new basis," in order to ensure "secrecy and surprise." As developed during the next few days, the new plan was to abandon the whole idea of four-day alerts and deploy the troops so that twenty-four hours' notice would be sufficient. The troops at the frontier would be expected only to clear road blocks and take initial objectives. The heavy battle forces would come up with a sudden rush from their positions farther back.

All this was laid out at a conference called by Hitler on January 20 and attended by Brauchitsch, Goering, Halder, Jeschonnek, Keitel, Jodl, and a few others. The Fuehrer read a stern lecture on military security. He took "the gravest view" and predicted that Germany would lose the war "unless we learn to maintain secrecy." The number of officers and stenographers in the know must be drastically reduced. The new deployment must be such as to enable the Army to "leap from a stand."

Most important of all, neither the enemy nor the German troops must be allowed to know that the system of four-day alerts had been abandoned. Everyone, friend and foe alike, must be kept on edge. This was vital, both to ensure that an unexpected spell of good weather could be exploited and to conceal that the meteorological prospects made unlikely the possibility of an attack before March.

Thus the remainder of January and all of February passed in a state of comparative relaxation. On February 1, Hitler's adjutant, Oberst Rudolf Schmundt, returned from a tour of the front with the report that "tactical mobility is impossible because of the weather." The Army put the time to good use for training, re-equipping, and over-hauling the tactical plans for the offensive. In the middle of February, these discussions led to a fundamental shift in the disposition of forces. The regroupings entailed by these changes were completed during the second week of March, and everything was made ready for an attack during the spring.

Thus came to an end the long-drawn-out struggle between Hitler and the generals to determine the timing of the western offensive. On this occasion the outcome was in accord with the generals' point of view. The many factors that have been traced—meteorological, diplomatic, and others extrinsic to the contest of wills—conspired in support of the professional soldiers. Nor can it be gainsaid that their opinion carried weight in the scales of decision. Hitler's impulsive desire to strike and his rage at their opposition were tempered by a growing realization that they were right. At the end of March, when everything was ready for *der Tag,* he went so far as to congratulate Leeb, Halder, and others [21] on "the good use made by the Wehrmacht of the forced inactivity of the past six months" and "the efficacy of the preparations made, which inspire him with faith in full success."

Yet it can hardly be said that the dispute was resolved by a "victory" of the generals. Brauchitsch was unmercifully berated, and the senior leaders of the Wehrmacht were lectured like schoolboys. Reichenau fell from grace at his first show of opposition. In January, when Hitler for the second time approached the point of decision, there was none of the resistance which had been so vocal in October and November, and it appears to have been a combination of the weather, the forced landing in Belgium, and his own uncertainty that caused Hitler to stay his hand until the spring.

By that time, the issue had been dissolved by the passage of time and changing circumstances. Leeb's cautious and defensive views appeared outmoded, and he himself participated uncomplainingly in the planning and execution of the campaign. The sanguine attitudes of men like Manstein and Guderian more accurately reflected the spirit of the officer corps as a whole. In April, Brauchitsch, so far from looking for excuses to postpone the attack,[22] "put up a strong argument to the Fuehrer that long waiting would not improve the situation."

So the crisis of command passed without a final showdown. The crisis of confidence, however, persisted. The "spirit of Zossen" was a phrase to which Hitler's mind and tongue often recurred when the generals incurred his displeasure. The wounds inflicted were reopened and deepened as time went on. Nor was the argument over the timing of the western offensive the only source of friction and mutual distrust; from Poland came reports of incredible and sinister happenings which deeply disturbed many of the generals, little as they did to check the evil course on which their Fuehrer had embarked.

The Polish Occupation

While Hitler and the generals were wrangling and hesitating in the West, no such temporizing marked the execution of German policy in occupied Poland, where Heinrich Himmler and Hans Frank, the Governor-General, were giving new meaning to the expression "total war." Organized combat had ceased early in October with the liquidation of the Polish Army, and no Polish State survived to negotiate the terms of surrender with the victorious invader. But in no real sense did the war end when the last Polish soldier laid down his gun. For Himmler and Frank, the cessation of hostilities in the classical sense marked the beginning of war in their conception.

To be sure, Poland was only a part of the ideological and racial battlefield. The invasion of Poland, like the conquest of the Sudetenland, darkened the totalitarian hue throughout the Third Reich. For example, on the first day of war, Hitler, despite his absorption in military matters, took time to sign a secret order directing two little-known but powerful civil officials—Philipp Bouhler, Chief of the Nazi Party Chancellery, and Dr. Karl Brandt, Hitler's personal physician—to launch a nation-wide program to accord a "mercy death" to "incurables." [23] Thus was sealed the doom of thousands of "useless eaters" whose elimination, in the interests of the national economy, Himmler and other Nazi fanatics had long urged.

Also on the opening day of war, the screws were tightened in occupied Bohemia and Moravia. A special decree authorized Himmler to take extraordinary measures in the Protectorate for "security and public order," and that very day thousands of prominent Czechs were taken to concentration camps.[24] On October 5 Hitler received Baron Konstantin von Neurath, the "Reich Protector" of Bohemia and Moravia, and laid down a basic policy of Germanization for the entire area, and the crushing of all opposition.[25] The Czech Independence Day (October 28, 1939) precipitated demonstrations in Prague, and student participation on this and later occasions led Hitler to order the closing, for three years, of all Czech universities.[26] Many teachers, students, and other intellectuals were simultaneously arrested, and the last vestiges of Bohemian autonomy were stamped out.

Poland, however, was the prime target of Himmler's racial offensive prior to the invasion of Russia. The broad outlines of German occupation policy in Poland were settled on by Hitler, Himmler, and Reinhard Heydrich (Himmler's deputy) as soon as it became clear that Poland would be crushed and her government destroyed. It was a program compounded of the most extreme tenets of Nazi racial ideology and the most ruthless exploitation of the conquered country by the victor. The Jews were to be concentrated in ghettos in a few large cities, the Polish upper classes (military, religious, and intellectual) were to be wiped out so as to render the Poles a leaderless, subject population, and Polish economic resources were to be systematically looted and exploited for the benefit of the Reich.[27]

Such a program could not possibly be carried out in a country under military occupation without the co-operation, or at least the toleration, of the Army. Hitler and Himmler realized this from the outset and, far from endeavoring to conceal their infernal plans from the generals, they deliberately and repeatedly outlined their policies to the military leaders. Indeed, it is probable that Hitler himself, at a large gathering of Wehrmacht commanders and staff officers at the Obersalzberg just before the invasion of Poland, gave his audience a preview of the ugly shape of things to come,[28] saying that things would happen "which would not be to the taste of German generals" and warning that they "should not interfere in these matters but restrict themselves to their military duties."

Whether or not this account is accurate, it is clear that by September 12 Brauchitsch, Keitel, and other highly placed officers had been informed by Hitler that he meant business and that the Army would have to co-operate or stand aside. On that day Admiral Canaris, chief of the OKW intelligence service, conferred with Keitel on the Fuehrer's military train; according to Canaris' notes, the conversation included the following: [29]

I pointed out to General Keitel that I knew that extensive executions were planned in Poland and that particularly the nobility and the clergy were to be exterminated.

Eventually the world would hold the Wehrmacht responsible for these deeds, under whose eyes such things had happened.

General Keitel answered that the Fuehrer had already decided on this matter. He had made it clear to the Commander-in-Chief of the Army that if the Wehrmacht did not want any part in these occurrences, it would have to accept the SS and Gestapo as rivals. For each military district, therefore, besides the military commander, a civilian commander would also be appointed. The latter would then be in charge of the extermination of folkdom [volkstuemliche Ausrottung].

A week later Heydrich paid a visit to OKH to make sure that the program was well understood at the staff level.* In the OKH general staff, questions of military administration were the province of the

* The Nazi policies in Czechoslovakia were likewise known to the Army from the outset, as clearly appear from a report (N.D. 862-PS) in October 1940 to OKW and OKH from General Erich Friderici, Plenipotentiary of the Wehrmacht in Bohemia and Moravia.

Generalquartiermeister, Generalmajor Eugen Mueller. In conference with Mueller's deputy, Oberst Eduard Wagner, Heydrich described the coming "housecleaning" of "Jews, intelligentsia, clergy, nobility" and emphasized that these "missions must be known to the Army." Wagner promptly reported to Halder, who recorded in his diary the Army's position on this atrocious policy: [30] "Army insists that house-cleaning be deferred until Army has withdrawn and the country has been turned over to civil administration. Early December."

But the SS was not waiting on anyone. The very next day, September 20, Canaris visited List's army headquarters in southern Poland and heard complaints from the staff intelligence officer about "mass shootings, especially of Jews, by an SS 'task force' [*Einsatz Gruppe*]." [31] It was "especially annoying to the troops," the officer declared, "that young men instead of fighting at the front were testing their courage on defenseless people."

That same day Brauchitsch and Halder conferred about the structure of the occupational administration, which was to be a divided regime, with the Army responsible for military security and the SS to be charged with the "housecleaning." The generals were troubled but had no intention of taking a strong stand against the exterminations; rather they wanted to get the ugly prospect out of their field of vision and responsibility as soon as possible. [32] But uncomfortable reminders repeatedly intruded. The next day OKH received a memorandum from Heydrich sketching the procedure by which the "housecleaning" was to be initiated. [33]

A few weeks later, after all Polish resistance had been crushed, Oberst Wagner reported to Halder [34] the gist of a meeting on October 17 between Hitler and Keitel, at which the Fuehrer outlined what Halder described as his "devilish plan" in Poland. The pliant Keitel acknowledged that the Wehrmacht would be happy to be relieved of administrative responsibilities, and then listened to Hitler's description of "the future shape of Polish relations with Germany." According to Keitel's record of the meeting, [35] initialed by Warlimont, the Polish standard of living was to be kept low, and there would be "a hard racial struggle," conducted by "methods which will be incompatible with the principles otherwise adhered to by us." Hitler complained that in Cracow, German officers had been visiting bishops, and that Prince Radziwill was still the owner of his large estates. Jews and Poles were to be cleared from the annexed areas and herded into the Government-General.

In the meantime, the German occupation administration in Poland was taking shape. Hans Frank was installed as Governor-General, with Artur Seyss-Inquart as his deputy. Nazi Gauleiters were appointed to administer the annexed areas. For all practical purposes Poland became the domain of Frank and Himmler.

By now Brauchitsch and Halder were immersed in plans for the western offensive and had neither time nor stomach for Poland. But the Army was still there. On October 23, Generaloberst Johannes Blaskowitz assumed command of all troops in East Prussia and former Polish territory, with the resounding title of Commander-in-Chief, East (*Oberost*).* There were subordinate military commanders in the Government-General, the annexed areas, and East Prussia, and a number of infantry divisions, most of them newly formed, were stationed in Poland for occupational duty and combat training.

Six weeks after the capitulation of Warsaw, Artur Seyss-Inquart, Deputy Governor-General, embarked on a tour of inspection.[36] In Radom, he was informed, "the majority of the intelligentsia have been imprisoned." Indeed, this had caused the local German authorities some concern, especially with respect to public health, and Seyss-Inquart was requested to prevail on the Governor-General to "issue an order that caution and reserve be exercised when arresting doctors." However, when Seyss-Inquart arrived in the Wlodawa region of Lublin Province, he found less concern for such matters. The District Governor, SS Brigadefuehrer Schmidt, pointed out that the region was marshy and insalubrious; therefore, it could well "serve as a reservation for the Jews, a measure which might possibly lead to heavy mortality among the Jews."

Although the Army's occupation responsibility was now limited strictly to military matters, these attitudes and activities of the SS and the civilian occupation authorities inevitably became common knowledge and a topic of lively discussion in the Army, among officers and men alike. The notion, oft-repeated since the end of the war, that the generals knew little of these things, is sheer myth. For example, on November 23, 1939, General der Artillerie Walter Petzel, commander of the newly established Wehrkreis XXI in the Warthegau, sent to Berlin a long report on local conditions and the progress of the "pacification." This document, which was addressed to the Commander of

---

* See the organization chart of the occupational administration in Poland and other countries in Appendix C, *infra*, pp. 421 and 432. "Generalgovernment" was the name adopted for the rump Poland left after the German and Russian annexations.

the Replacement Army (General Fromm) and distributed to several other departments of the OKH general staff, contains the following: [37]

The Warthegau can be regarded as pacified. Repeated rumors of rebellion have not been confirmed in any instance. The reason for this is not a change of heart of the Polish population but realization of the hopelessness of rebellion. . . .

The great work of construction in all spheres is not furthered by the intervention of SS formations who are given special racial political tasks and are not subordinate to the Reich Governor [*Reichsstatthalter*] in this sphere. This tends to interfere in all spheres of administration beyond the framework of these tasks, and to form a "state within the state." *This phenomenon does not fail to have its effect on the troops, who are indignant about the ways the tasks are carried out and thereby generally get into opposition to administration and party.* I shall eliminate the danger of serious differences by strict orders. The fact that this puts a serious strain on the discipline of the troops cannot be dismissed without further ado.

In almost all large towns, public shootings have been carried out by the organizations mentioned. The selection varied enormously and was often incomprehensible; the way it was carried out, frequently unworthy.

In some districts all the Polish estate owners were arrested and interned with their families. *Arrests were almost always accompanied by looting.* . . .

In several towns actions against the Jews were carried out which turned into the most serious excesses. *In Turok on October 10 three SS cars under the leadership of a higher SS leader drove through the streets, while the people in the streets were hit on the heads at random with horse whips and long whips. Among the victims were people of German blood.* Finally a number of Jews were driven into the synagogue, and there had to crawl in between the benches whilst singing, during which time they were continuously whipped by the SS men. They were then forced to take down their trousers in order to be hit on the bare behind. A Jew who out of fright had dirtied his trousers was forced to smear the excrement into the faces of the other Jews. . . .

Whilst the achievements of the Armed Forces were always placed in the foreground by the Reich Governor in speeches and demonstrations, the above [SS] circles, on the other hand, are unmistakably showing a tendency to diminish and denigrate these achievements. A specially crass case in this direction was reported to me from Ostrowo. Reich speaker Bachmann spoke there at a victory celebration on November 5. He never mentioned the Wehrmacht at all, when speaking about the Polish campaign. He only mentioned the Wehrmacht in one sentence, which concerned the war against England. . . .

The impression that this speech, which was heard by the guard of honor which had been provided, made on the soldiers was as might be expected.

Such goings-on aroused the disgust and apprehension of General-oberst Blaskowitz. Shortly before Christmas of 1939 he sent to Berlin a memorandum describing the behavior of the SS,[38] but the outrages continued unchecked. By the middle of January 1940, Blaskowitz was criticizing [39] some of the army officers in Poland for being "too weak" and for failure to "stand up for the unjustly persecuted." On January 19 Halder concluded [40] that there had been a "breakdown of confidence in the East" and that there was need for personnel changes. Soon there was an ugly and open issue at the highest level, and on January 28 Hitler addressed himself "very indignantly" to Keitel "about derogatory remarks made by senior officers concerning measures taken by us in Poland." [41]

Despite his confidence in Hitler's support, Himmler was still disposed to observe superficial amenities in his dealings with the Army. On February 2, at a conference with Brauchitsch,[42] he admitted that carrying out the "ethnical policy" of the Third Reich in Poland was "a difficult mission" and that "mistakes have been made." From Blaskowitz' report, five such "mistakes" had come to his attention. Himmler invited further information from the Army and declared his intention "to carry out his complex task in as considerate a manner as possible and with a minimum of bloodshed." Furthermore, he wanted "good relations with the Army," and nothing was further from his mind than to "set up an [SS] Army beside the Army."

Himmler then proposed that a tank ditch be dug along the entire Polish-Russian frontier, which would constitute a "work project for two and a half million Jews." Brauchitsch agreed "to look into the plan." Increasingly on the offensive, Himmler charged that the Army was supplementing its rations by illegal slaughtering of Polish cattle and that "some officers took their meals with Polish landowners every day." To these accusations Brauchitsch responded only by a request for "details on specific instances."

A month later, the Army was assailed from another quarter. On March 7 Blaskowitz' Chief of Staff, Generalmajor Karl Hollidt, telephoned Halder about "trouble" with Hans Frank.[43] Blaskowitz wished to establish a zone along the Russian border under exclusively military jurisdiction; Frank had declared this an invasion of the Governor-General's prerogatives and threatened "to take steps in Berlin." Three days later Halder was studying a report on "friction" between Frank and Blaskowitz, and the next day he noted a "sudden deterioration" in their relations.

The immediate result of Blaskowitz' efforts to stand up to Himmler and Frank was the blighting of his military career. On March 28

Halder noted in his diary the decision to "take Blaskowitz out." A fundamental reorganization of the German military command structure in Poland was worked out, under which Blaskowitz and his staff were moved to Trier on the western front and became the headquarters of the newly constituted Ninth Army. But Blaskowitz remained as its Commander-in-Chief for only a few weeks. On May 29 Brauchitsch informed him that Hitler had decided to relieve him of his command.[44] From then until the last few months of the war, Blaskowitz held only secondary commands, and he alone of the ten who then held the rank of *Generaloberst* was never promoted to *Generalfeldmarschall.* *

The departure of Blaskowitz from Poland also marked the end of military efforts to check the course and character of the occupational regime. His successor, General Kurt Freiherr von Gienanth (a "retread" who had been retired in 1933), did not long retain the title of *Oberost;* in July it was changed to "Military Commander" (*Militaerbefehlshaber*) of the troops in the Government-General. Gienanth lacked the rank and prestige of Blaskowitz, and made no significant effort to challenge the policies of Himmler and Frank.

As a practical matter, the change from Blaskowitz to Gienanth signified nothing, for the former's remonstrances had accomplished little enough. Beginning early in December 1939, several trains arrived each day in the Government-General loaded with Poles and Jews deported from the formerly Polish areas annexed to the Reich.[45] On January 30, 1940, Heydrich informed a group of SS leaders that 87,000 Poles and Jews had thus far been evacuated to the Government-General.[46] By November 1940 the total had risen above 300,000.[47] The same month witnessed the establishment and enclosure of the Warsaw ghetto.

All of these things—military, racial, and economic—bore a close relation to each other, and these relationships may enable us better to understand the expression "total war" in the twentieth century. Hitler's original decree instituting the Government-General empowered Goering to make arrangements for "the German economic sphere" therein.[48] Goering's basic program was embodied in a memorandum of October 19, 1939, which [49] declared that in the annexed Polish territories a policy of reconstruction and expansion of the economy would be pursued, whereas the Government-General was simply a hunting ground

* Blaskowitz was never given a command on the Russian front. He commanded occupation troops in France after June 1940 and was not again in combat until the Allied landings in France in 1944. Curiously, in view of his fall from grace, Blaskowitz was still on active duty at the end of the war; all the other senior generals except Keitel were by then dead or retired.

from which must be removed "all raw materials, scrap, machines, etc., which are of use for the German war economy." To wield this double-edged economic sword, Goering established a new agency euphemistically dubbed the "Main Eastern Trustee Office" (*Haupttreuhandstelle Ost*). Pursuant to these decrees, German confiscation of the properties of the Polish State, the nobility, the churches, and the Jews proceeded apace.

But it should not be thought that the Reich government alone conducted these confiscations. For example, as soon as hostilities were under way, directors of the huge I. G. Farben chemicals combine were hammering at the door of the Reich Ministry of Economics, armed with detailed information on the Polish chemical plants and urging the designation of a Farben man as "trustee" for the future operation or liquidation of the Polish concerns.[50] These proposals came before Generalmajor Hermann von Hanneken, a regular army officer who had been detailed for several years to the Economics Ministry. Hanneken promptly complied with the suggestion that a Farben nominee, Hermann Schwab, be designated trustee of three plants, and Farben director Carl Wurster then embarked on an inspection trip.

Based upon Wurster's observations, the Farben directors concluded that certain plants should be taken over and operated by Farben, and others dismantled and the useful equipment removed to Germany. To secure government approval of their plans, Farben cultivated and truckled to many of the worst SS leaders and shamelessly exploited the Jewish ownership of some of these properties.

A prominent and respected Jewish dye-stuffs manufacturer named Szpilfogel, ousted from his house and factory by the Farben trustees, was forcibly removed to the Warsaw ghetto in November 1940. Szpilfogel had been well and personally known to the Farben director Georg von Schnitzler, and solicited the latter's aid. But Schnitzler merely passed the letter to the Farben "trustee," Schwab, while carefully refraining from taking any position on the plea. Of course nothing was done; Szpilfogel himself survived, but his son, son-in-law, sister, two brothers, and many other close relatives were murdered by the Germans in the ghetto. Economic spoliation had its vital as well as its financial aspects; total war embraced both.

The nature of the German occupation of Poland did not long pass unnoticed beyond the Polish and German borders. On November 6, 1939, *The New York Times* carried a dispatch on the plight of the

Jews in Poland based on information received by the Polish government-in-exile and Jewish relief organizations. It was stated that
pogroms and confiscation of Jewish property in Lodz and Warsaw
were under way, and that a "specialist" had come from Dachau to set
up Polish concentration camps.

On January 30, 1940, *The New York Times* carried a front-page
story of a report to the Pope by August Cardinal Hlond, Primate of
Poland, comprising a vivid and authoritative description of the shocking conditions in the dioceses of Poznan and Gniezno. Another front-
page news dispatch in the same issue of the *Times* reported Blaskowitz'
objections to the course of events in Poland, a public revelation which
can hardly have improved his standing with Hitler.

The mass extermination camps in Poland, such as Auschwitz,
Maidanek and Treblinka, did not commence operations until the end
of 1940. The camps themselves, however, were much earlier in process
of establishment. On February 21, 1940, SS Oberfuehrer Gluecks, in
charge of concentration camps, reported to Himmler that Auschwitz
(Polish "Oswiecim," near Cracow), a village and former artillery barracks, was a "suitable" site for a camp,[51] and by May it was under
construction. Later that year, when I. G. Farben made plans for a
fourth *buna* factory to be located in eastern Europe, the directors'
choice of a location fell on Auschwitz, in part because of the availability of concentration camp labor to build the plant.[52] Thereafter, the
Wehrmacht's synthetic rubber and Himmler's extermination programs
marched hand in hand at Auschwitz, over the bodies of the inmates.

Such was the face of Poland during and after the "phony war"—
ghettos, deportations, confiscations, concentration camps, and many
other brutalities and atrocities. Perhaps these things are not "war" in
the classic sense. But they were far from "phony," and they were an
integral part of the totality which we have called the Second World
War.

The terrible nature of the German occupational regime in Poland
was not hidden; it could hardly escape the attention of every soldier
and civilian who was stationed in or visited the stricken land. In
November 1939 Major Helmuth Stieff, of the OKH operations staff,
was sent to Warsaw. Stieff, who four years later was hanged for com-
plicity in the July 20 plot, was a close friend of Henning von Tresckow
(one of the leading conspirators) and a confidant of Blaskowitz. The
depth of Stieff's reaction to the Polish scene is poignantly reflected in a

letter to his wife, written on November 21, shortly after his return
from Warsaw: [53]

. . . when one has seen the ruins of Warsaw . . . one feels not like a victor, but as a guilty man! It is not I alone that feel this—the men that are
stationed here feel it themselves. Add to this all that is unthinkable and
beyond the pale, that we must watch with folded arms! The wildest fantasy
of horror propaganda is as nothing to the reality, the organized gangs who
murder, rob and plunder with what is said to be the tolerance of the highest
authorities. There [in Warsaw] one can no longer excuse it as "justifiable
indignation aroused by [Polish] crimes against the *Volksdeutschen*." This
extermination of a whole race, including women and children, is possible
only for subhumans, that no longer deserve the German name.

It shames me to be a German! Unless we stop them soon, this group,
that by murder and arson sullies the German name, will be the misfortune
of the whole German people. Because these doings, as described from competent, on-the-spot sources, must surely arouse an avenging nemesis. Otherwise, someday this mob will turn against us decent people in the same way,
and will terrorize its own people with this pathological rage.

The following morning I spent three quarters of an hour alone with him
[Blaskowitz], during which he . . . unburdened himself about the conditions in the area of his jurisdiction as *Oberost,* and directed me to make use
of the information here [at OKH headquarters], which I am doing.

The corrosive effect of seven Nazi years on Germans of high degree,
civil and military, was by now too deep for hope of change for the
better. Few sought to check Hitler and Himmler, and those few failed
because none joined them. The officer corps, far from rallying to
Blaskowitz' support, left him alone in the face of the Fuehrer's displeasure, and allowed him to be cast aside.

The degenerative process was, perhaps, most sharply manifested by
Georg von Kuechler, an army commander-in-chief who in September
of 1939 had pressed unsuccessfully for the condign punishment of
some SS troops who had massacred Jews.[54] Ten months later, after his
army had taken Paris, and France had capitulated, Kuechler returned
to Poland—a land in which the daily outrages made those of September
1939 pale by comparison. On July 22, 1940, newly promoted by Hitler
to *Generaloberst,* Kuechler distributed the following order to his
troops: [55]

I . . . stress the necessity of ensuring that every soldier of the Army,
particularly every officer, refrain from criticizing the ethnic struggle being
carried out in the Government-General—for instance, the treatment of the

Polish minorities, of the Jews, and of church matters. The final solution or the ethnic struggle, which has been raging on the eastern border for centuries, calls for unique harsh measures.

Certain units of the party and the state have been charged with carrying out this ethnic struggle in the East.

The soldiers must, therefore, keep aloof from these concerns of other units. This also implies that they must not interfere in these matters with criticism.

It is particularly urgent to distribute these instructions to soldiers who have recently been transferred from the West to the East; otherwise, they might be touched with rumors and false information concerning the meaning and purpose of the [ethnic] struggle.

Avert the gaze, still the tongue, and, with due understanding, allow the SS to execute its "ethnic" mission, not only against Poles and Jews but against the church, long cherished in the German military tradition! So spoke Generaloberst Georg von Kuechler to his men, to protect them from "false" information. Such was the lesson taught by an *Oberbefehlshaber* of the German Army, once described by General Wilhelm Groener, Hindenburg's trusted assistant of World War I and Minister of Defense in the last days of the Weimar Republic, as "a center for the physical and moral education of German youth."

The Air and the Sea

If there was any part of the early months of war in the West that can justifiably be described as "phony," it was the war in the air. At sea there were exploits, losses, and deaths from the very outset; on land there was sound reason on both sides to postpone the close-quarters grapple until the spring. But in the air there was little or no war chiefly because neither side could clearly perceive, and both shrank from, the consequences of its commencement. As Churchill put it at Manchester on January 27, 1940,[56] ". . . here is a chapter of war which they [the Nazis] have not chosen to open upon us because they cannot tell what may be written in its final pages." Nor did the British unleash Bomber Command against Germany until after the Nazi conquest of France.

Even against strictly military or naval targets both sides withheld their air power, except for minor forays. Upon the outbreak of war, Goering proposed a mass air attack on the British naval base at Scapa Flow, but Hitler would have none of it.[57] Again, on November 28, Goering urged that aerial warfare against England be intensified, but

Hitler insisted that any such plans await the start of the land offensive in the West.[58]

Indeed, until the summer of 1940, the only offensive operations undertaken by the Luftwaffe over England were a few small raids, including two on October 16 and 17, 1939—the first against cruisers in the Firth of Forth, the second at Scapa Flow. The results were insignificant. At the cost of four bombers lost in the first raid, two cruisers and a destroyer were slightly damaged. The obsolete training battleship *Iron Duke* was damaged by near misses at Scapa Flow and settled on the bottom in shallow water.[59]

The British, for their part, opened the air war with an attack on September 4 by twenty-nine medium bombers (Blenheims and Wellingtons) on the German naval bases at Wilhelmshaven and Brunsbuettel. The *Admiral Scheer* was hit but only slightly damaged by misfused bombs which failed to explode; the *Emden* suffered casualties from a Blenheim which crashed on the deck. This was hardly a high rate of return for seven aircraft lost. At all events, from then on the Royal Air Force restricted itself to leaflet dropping, reconnaissance, and occasional attacks on U-boats and German surface craft, generally unsuccessful.[60]

In March 1940 there was a small flurry; German bombs fell at night in the Orkneys, killing a few civilians. But even the British did not claim that this was deliberate, as the bombs were apparently intended for warships at Scapa Flow. However, three nights later, by way of reprisal, Bomber Command put fifty planes over the German seaplane base on the island of Sylt. Nothing worth while was accomplished.[61]

On neither side, therefore, did the air arm use its bombs for more than experiments to test their value as an adjunct to naval warfare. Indeed, at this time the Luftwaffe made far more effective use of marine mines than of bombs. In September and October of 1939 magnetic mines laid by German aircraft in British harbors became the major worry of the Admiralty. About a dozen merchant ships were sunk as well as two destroyers, while the battleship *Nelson* and the new cruiser *Belfast* were badly damaged. The British countermeasures were ingenious and effective—chiefly electric sweeping, and suppressing the magnetic field of ships' hulls by encircling them with electrically charged cables, a process which became known as "degaussing." The threat was soon eased by the diversion of the Luftwaffe to preparation for the Norwegian attack and the major offensive in the West.[62]

This was not to the liking of Grossadmiral Erich Raeder, whose Navy, from the outbreak of war, faced hopeless odds on the cruel sea. To compensate for the shortage of submarines and the embryonic state of the surface fleet, Raeder demanded full participation by the Luftwaffe against the Royal Navy and British merchant shipping. Goering, however, was un-co-operative, as he always was in inter-service matters, and Hitler gave Raeder no effective support.

The early months of war were a trial of Raeder's patience for other reasons than Goering's "go-it-alone" attitude. Hitler had set his mind on the invasion of France and the Low Countries as the core of German strategy, and naval warfare had to take second place in terms of men, matériel, and the Fuehrer's attention. To be sure, once Hitler had abandoned his peace offensive he readily authorized U-boat attacks against enemy shipping without warning. *Intensification* of the war at sea Hitler was willing to consider sympathetically, and other restrictions on submarine operations were lifted during the winter of 1939–40; on December 30 Raeder's report to the Fuehrer [63] noted that "previous experience has shown that gradual intensification without special proclamation [to avoid stirring up the neutrals] is the best method."

But *expansion* of the naval effort was another matter entirely, and here Raeder's best efforts came to little. His cogent and desperate plea for rapid expansion of the submarine arm fell on deaf ears, as the metals situation was critical and priority was given to the Army's needs. Indeed,[64] "the U-boat construction program was no more extensive in June 1940 than it had been at the beginning of the war," and it was not until early 1941 that a substantial expansion of Doenitz' underseas fleet began to be achieved.[65] This gave the British a welcome respite. Merchant shipping losses declined sharply after the first month of war and did not assume dangerous proportions until the summer of 1940, when German access to U-boat bases and airfields in France and the Low Countries greatly increased the toll.[66]

If the war at sea remained strategically indecisive during the first seven months of the war, tactically it was exciting enough. The *Athenia* and the aircraft carrier *Courageous* were sunk by U-boats during the first three weeks, and on October 14 Guenther Prien's *U-47* penetrated Scapa Flow and sank the *Royal Oak*. The pocket battle cruisers *Graf Spee* and *Deutschland*, accompanied by supply ships, were at large in the South and North Atlantic. The *Deutschland's* record in the North

Atlantic was hardly a glorious one; in October she sank two small ships and took as a prize the American *City of Flint,* which led to diplomatic complications and the eventual release of the ship.

All this time the Fuehrer had been worrying about the *Deutschland* because of her name and pressing for her recall [67] "as her possible loss might be taken as a bad omen by the people." Early in November she started home, and upon safe arrival was renamed *Luetzow.** To cover her withdrawal, the battle cruisers *Scharnhorst* and *Gneisenau* had been sent out on their maiden sorties, and on November 23 the *Scharnhorst* encountered off Iceland the armed merchant cruiser *Rawalpindi,* which heroically engaged the big battle cruiser and was soon sunk, with the loss of 270 seamen. However, this brief encounter exposed the presence of the German ships, and both of them promptly broke off their mission and returned to home waters.

In the South Atlantic, the *Graf Spee* had been living far more adventurously. By October 22 she had sunk five British merchantmen; thereafter she retired to the Indian Ocean off the Mozambique coast for several weeks to throw her pursuers off the trail. Returning to the Atlantic, she was resupplied by her auxiliary, the *Altmark,* and sank three more British ships early in December.† By this time the Royal Navy had organized a number of powerful hunting groups to track down the surface raiders,[68] and Commodore Harwood, commanding one of these, rightly guessed that the *Spee* would head for the Argentine coast to prey on the heavy maritime traffic out of the Plate Estuary.

By a combination of skill and good luck, Harwood's group, comprising the eight-inch-gunned heavy cruiser *Exeter* and the six-inch light cruisers *Ajax* and *Achilles,* managed to sight the *Spee* at dawn on December 13, about 400 miles off Montevideo. In fact, the *Spee* sighted the British ships first, and her commander, Kapitaen zur See Hans Langsdorff, ought to have turned away from the battle, for his mission was to raid merchant shipping rather than to risk damage by engaging enemy warships.[69] Even if the *Spee* were unable to slip away undetected, at long range she would have preserved the full advantage of her eleven-inch main batteries.

Langsdorff, however, at first mistook the *Ajax* and *Achilles* for destroyers and attacked in the hope of destroying the warships quickly

---

* After the Prussian general of Scharnhorst's time, who organized a *Freikorps* to fight against the French and was touted by the Nazis as a precursor of the post-World War I *Freikorpsfuehrer.* The pocket battle cruiser is not to be confused with the unfinished cruiser *Luetzow* that was sold to the Russians.

† In all, the *Spee* sank nine British ships totaling over 50,000 tons.

and then locating the merchant convoy he wrongly assumed them to be escorting. The dramatic encounter that ensued was one of the last major surface engagements in which aircraft played only a minor part.*

Since the British cruisers were outranged by the *Spee*, Harwood rightly strove for close quarters. The *Spee* concentrated her heavy armament on the *Exeter*, and in little more than an hour the latter was seriously crippled and had to break off. In the meantime, however, the *Ajax* and *Achilles* had come up on the *Spee's* starboard quarter, and at close range their six-inch fire was scoring frequently. Their shells were too light to work decisive results but caused sufficient damage so that Langsdorff was obliged to turn his main batteries on the light cruisers. They were badly punished and Harwood had to fall back, but their engines were undamaged, and they stayed on the *Spee's* heels, out of range.

At this juncture the *Spee* could have finished off the *Exeter*, and Langsdorff has been much criticized for not doing so. But the *Spee* was already damaged beyond the possibility of repair at sea, and Langsdorff faced the prospect of an arduous winter passage through the patrolled waters of the North Atlantic to get his ship back to Germany. Rather than risk delay and the likelihood of additional injury if he renewed the battle, Langsdorff decided to head for Montevideo, with the hope of landing his wounded and making quick repairs which would enable him to escape into the South Atlantic before the British could bring up additional forces.

The decision was a gamble, and it proved a bad one. Upon arrival in Montevideo, a survey of the *Spee* indicated that it would take nearly two weeks to make her fit for action and fully seaworthy. The Uruguayan government would not extend her stay beyond the seventy-two hours permitted by international law to a belligerent warship in a neutral port, and in any event a prolonged stop would have given the British time to increase their strength outside the harbor. The heavy cruiser *Cumberland* arrived on the night of December 14, and the British shrewdly spread rumors that other reinforcements had arrived. When one of the *Spee's* gunnery officers reported that from the control tower he had sighted the battle cruiser *Renown* and the aircraft carrier *Ark Royal* (they were in fact off Rio de Janeiro at the time) on

---

* The *Spee* carried an Arado observation plane, but it was inoperable because of a cracked engine block. The *Ajax* put a Seafox spotter into the air during the battle, and the fire of the light cruisers benefited considerably from its reports on the fall of their shot.

the horizon, Langsdorff concluded that the jig was up. On December 16 he reported to SKL that there was "no prospect of breaking out to the open sea and getting through to Germany" and requested instructions on the alternatives of scuttling the *Spee*, submitting to internment, or attempting a break-through to Buenos Aires, where the atmosphere might be more hospitable.

After conferring with Hitler, Raeder ordered Langsdorff to avoid internment, and left it to his discretion whether to scuttle or try to reach Buenos Aires. Langsdorff decided that the latter course was unfeasible and immediately commenced preparations for scuttling.[70]

In a neutral port secrecy was impossible, and so on December 17 a huge crowd of Sunday sight-seers on the shore watched the *Spee* steam out into the Plate Estuary, blow up, and settle on the shallow bottom. Langsdorff thought he had no alternative, as he needed his ammunition to destroy the ship, and he could not count on getting out far enough for deep-sea scuttling. But Hitler was "very angry about the scuttling of the *Graf Spee* without a fight" and gave Raeder some very unpleasant moments, especially over the *Spee's* failure to sink the *Exeter*.[71] The unhappy Langsdorff committed suicide on the night of December 19.

The scuttling of the *Spee* also marked the end of German surface raiding until the spring of 1940.* The *Spee's* sortie had yielded the Germans slender dividends. The 50,000 tons of shipping she had sent to the bottom was a respectable total for three months of raiding but far from sufficient to compensate for her own loss. Furthermore, the basic purpose of the *Spee's* venture was to draw British warships off from other tasks. In this she succeeded admirably as long as she remained afloat, but that was not long enough to be of significant help to the German cause.

The *Spee's* loss was not the only misfortune that befell Raeder's small fleet during the first winter of the war. On December 13, the same day that the *Spee* was engaged by Harwood's force, the British submarine *Salmon* sighted three German light cruisers off Helgoland and succeeded in hitting both the *Leipzig* and the *Nuernberg*. Neither ship sank, and the *Nuernberg* was back in service the following May. But the *Leipzig* was out of action for a full year and even then could

---

* During the spring and early summer of 1940, six German merchantmen converted as commerce raiders took to sea. They met with considerable success in operations which lasted well into 1941.

not be restored to full operational use; she was largely restricted to training and no longer sailed in line of battle.[72]

Additional losses were sustained on the night of February 22, 1940, when two destroyers—the *Leberecht Maass* and *Max Schultz*—were sunk off the Dogger Bank by a German bomber.[73] Raeder promptly cited it to Hitler as an example of the need for unified control by OKM of all sea operations, "regardless of whether it is conducted under, on, or above the sea." Hitler was very angered by the episode: [74] "I would not say anything if the whole Navy were sunk in battle with the enemy, but it is inexcusable if that happens on account of lack of co-ordination." But he did nothing to rectify the matter; Goering and Raeder continued to bicker, and the Luftwaffe declined to put any of its combat units under naval command.

And so, even before the heavy fighting in the West began, Raeder had lost one of his three "pocket" battle cruisers (*Graf Spee*), one of his six light cruisers (*Leipzig*, still afloat but unavailable for combat), and two of his twenty-two destroyers. The new battleships were not yet fitted out, and the *Scheer* was still being overhauled. The other heavy warships—*Gneisenau*, *Scharnhorst*, and *Luetzow* (nee *Deutschland*) remained in home waters throughout the winter.

Caution, however, was not the only reason for the temporary eclipse of the German battle fleet. Preparations were under way for new and far bolder undertakings in northern waters. As the spring of 1940 crept north over Europe, the period of illusory calm drew to a close. The German march of conquest was about to be resumed.

CHAPTER THREE

Weseruebung

T HE GERMAN INVASION of Norway and Denmark in April
1940, by the amphibious operation known as *Weseruebung*
(Weser Exercise), was unique among the Wehrmacht's victories. This
was the only campaign of World War II in which the German Navy,
by far the weakest of the three services, played a leading part. It was
the only large action that called for joint, tightly co-ordinated operations by land, sea, and air. The operational plan was worked out by
an inter-service group under the auspices of OKW, and this was the
only occasion on which that misbegotten agency fulfilled its supposed
responsibility for inter-service planning.

Finally, this was the only major German military undertaking which
was not instigated by Adolf Hitler himself. On the contrary, it originated among the German admirals and was sold to the Fuehrer by
Raeder.

The Admirals' Brain Child

The antecedents of *Weseruebung* were the frustrations of the German
Navy in World War I. The Imperial Navy had a huge battle fleet,
but it never reached the open ocean. German merchant shipping was
swept off the seas. The U-boats and surface raiders of World War I
had to debouch from the few north German ports and traverse the
narrow and dangerous waters of the North Sea, around the narrow
neck of which the British tightened the drawstrings of the blockade.

Small wonder, therefore, that many German naval officers saw the
only salvation for their service in the acquisition of bases somewhere

on the European continent's open ocean shores, so as to escape the restrictions that geography had imposed on the Fatherland. These strategic views had found expression in a book published in 1929 by Vizeadmiral Wolfgang Wegener, which attracted wide attention in naval circles. In *Die Strategie des Weltkrieges* (The Strategy of World War), Wegener argued that the main function of a German Navy must be to keep the sea lanes open for German merchant shipping. But, he wrote, this could never be accomplished from "the dead angle of a dead sea," as he described the German and Danish North Sea coast line: [1]

> The Norwegian position was certainly preferable. England could then no longer maintain the blockade line from the Shetlands to Norway but must withdraw approximately to the line of the Shetlands-Faeroes-Iceland. But this line was a net with very wide meshes. The fresh wind from the ocean then blew from afar into the stifling atmosphere of the hunger block-ade. Moreover, this line was hard for England to defend. In the first place, it lay comparatively near to our bases, but above all . . . we would consid-erably outflank the English strategic position from the north.

In 1939 Raeder had no battle fleet with which to essay a Jutland and could not hope to hold open the channels of German maritime trade. But his U-boats and surface raiders faced the same disad-vantages that Wegener had remarked, and it is reasonable to suppose that as soon as the war began, Raeder and his staff turned their minds to the possibility of extending the Navy's operational basis. Very likely the OKH was asked about the prospects of acquiring bases on the French ocean coast;[2] if so, surely the response in the fall of 1939 would have been that the chances were remote indeed.[3]

The only other possibilities lay in Norway. Wegener's book was well known throughout the naval officer corps, and his views were par-ticularly popular among the younger men. In December 1939 Wege-ner's son Edward, then a *Korvettenkapitaen* and first artillery officer of the *Admiral Hipper*, circulated a memorandum recapitulating his father's teachings.[4] "From Norway," he wrote, "the effectiveness of all categories of our warships would be increased. Our field of strength would extend to Iceland. The possibility of overseas trade would be opened. . . . It is possible, with the Navy's resources, to seize, hold, and build bases in Norway."

However, the initial impetus for the Scandinavian adventure appears to have come from Admiral Rolf Carls, Commander of the Eastern Group Command. The third-ranking active officer, Carls was one of the dominant naval personalities and was known among his colleagues as the "Blue Czar." [5] As the fighting in Poland drew to a close, Carls transmitted to Raeder a letter outlining the military advantages that would accrue to Germany from an occupation of the Norwegian coast.[6] Impressed, Raeder decided that Hitler should "be informed as soon as possible . . . on the possibilities of extending the operational base to the north" and that the Navy should find out "whether it is possible to gain bases in Norway under the combined pressure of Russia and Germany, with the aim of improving fundamentally our strategic and operational position." Accordingly, the SKL was directed to consider which Norwegian and north Danish ports would be most valuable, whether they could be taken without a fight and defended thereafter, and how much development they would require to make them useful as bases.[7]

The reaction at SKL was cautious; the advantages of Norwegian bases were obvious from the standpoint of naval warfare against England, but even clearer were the hazards of expanding the theater of operations in the face of superior British naval power. Doenitz, who was also consulted, thought that only Trondheim and Narvik were suitable as submarine bases, and that of these Trondheim was definitely superior.[8]

On October 10, 1939, in the course of a general report to the Fuehrer, Raeder brought up the Norwegian question. He stressed the value of bases such as Trondheim and suggested the possibility of helpful Russian pressure on the Norwegian government. No conclusion was reached; Hitler asked Raeder to leave his notes on the subject and promised to give it further consideration.[9] And there the matter rested, so far as the German admirals were concerned, for the next two months.

Scandinavia and Finland

While Raeder, Carls, Schniewind, and Doenitz were thus pondering, the Scandinavian peninsula was likewise an area of deep interest to Winston Churchill, then First Lord of the Admiralty. German heavy industry was dependent on large imports of iron ore from northern Sweden, which are normally shipped from the port of Lulea through the Gulf of Bothnia. But in the wintertime Lulea is icebound, and the ore was taken by rail across the neck of the peninsula to the ice-free Norwegian port of Narvik, whence it was shipped south along the Norwegian coast to Germany. Most of this passage could be made within Norwegian territorial waters, which furnished a neutral sanctuary against British interception.

As early as September 19, 1939, Churchill brought this situation to the attention of the British Cabinet, with the recommendation that the German ore traffic be interrupted by laying mines across the three-mile limit to the Norwegian coast south of Narvik. The proposal was tempting, but the Cabinet was reluctant to envisage a violation of Norwegian neutrality and, despite Churchill's repeated urging, no action was taken or authorized at that time.[10]

But this deceptive calm in the lands of the Vikings was soon shattered. Moving rapidly and ruthlessly to exploit the "spheres of influence" marked out for Russia by the Hitler-Stalin pact,[11] the Kremlin's rulers, Hitler-fashion, summoned the emissaries of Estonia, Latvia, and Lithuania and imposed treaties under which the Soviet Union was given the right to occupy, develop, and garrison key bases in all these countries.* But when it came Finland's turn, these tactics proved quite insufficient for the Russian purpose. The Finns were not intransigent, but the territorial concessions they were prepared to make fell far short of Stalin's demands. By the middle of November the negotiations had collapsed; on November 28 Russia denounced the 1934 nonaggression pact with Finland, and the following day diplomatic relations were broken off. On November 30 the Red Army attacked all along the frontier, and Russian planes bombed Helsinki.[12]

None of this brought joy to Hitler. As the price of Soviet peace while he devoured Poland, he had bargained away the Baltic lands to Stalin, but the fulfillment was painful, and, as Germanic refugees came pouring in from the *Balticum* where they had settled and where General Ruediger Graf von der Goltz's *Freikorps* had fought the Bolsheviks twenty years before,[13] it was humiliating. With practically the entire Wehrmacht drawn up along the western front, there was precious little he could do to stem the Russian tide. For the time being, therefore, he put a good face on the Soviet advances and turned a cold shoulder to the Finns.

Elsewhere the reaction was quite different. The unprovoked attack by the Soviet giant on a small, self-reliant neighbor nation conjured up images of David and Goliath and aroused world-wide sympathy for the Finns. The dying League of Nations, in a last courageous gasp,

---

* The three treaties were signed on September 29 (Estonia), October 5 (Latvia), and October 10 (Lithuania), 1939.

condemned Russia as an aggressor and expelled her from membership. Churchill saluted [14] "superb, sublime Finland" and warned that if "the light of freedom which still burns so brightly in the frozen North should finally be quenched, it might well herald a return to the Dark Ages, when every vestige of human progress during two thousand years would be engulfed." His praise was richly deserved by the steely resistance of the Finns, but beneath the Churchillian eloquence there was a strain of enlightened self-interest, for if the Norwegians and Swedes could be persuaded to grant the Allies transit privileges for military aid to Finland through Narvik and Lulea, in all probability the German ore traffic from both these ports could be cut off.

Thus the Russo-Finnish war enormously enhanced the strategic importance of the Scandinavian countries—a fact of which their governments were uncomfortably aware. Fear of Germany and Russia was a stronger influence than sympathy for the Finns, and they clutched their neutrality ever more desperately. But among the Norwegians there were a few who sought to exploit their country's exposed situation for quite different ends, and that is how it came about that Vidkun Quisling appeared in Berlin in December 1939, under the sponsorship of Alfred Rosenberg, the semi-official philosopher of Nazism and chief of the party's Office for Foreign Affairs (*Aussenpolitischesamt*), known as the APA.

Quisling and Rosenberg were not strangers to each other. The former was a reserve officer in the Norwegian Army and from 1931 to 1933 had been Minister of War. Thereafter he had founded a Nazi-type party in Norway; the "Nasjonal Samling" was pan-German, anti-British and anti-Semitic. Quisling visited Rosenberg in 1933, and thereafter their respective organizations maintained contact. In June 1939 Quisling came again to Germany to address a convention of the Nordic Society, a Nazi "front" organization for cultural and trade relations with the Scandinavian countries. He took advantage of the trip to renew his acquaintance with Rosenberg, to whom he spoke alarmingly of the danger of British or Russian occupation of Norway and glowingly of the advantages of a German occupation, in the event of war. As a result of the meeting, twenty-five young Norwegian Nazis were given training by the APA in propaganda and party organization.[15]

For his part, Raeder kept in touch with Norwegian affairs through the German naval attaché, Korvettenkapitaen Richard Schreiber. With the outbreak of the Russo-Finnish war, rumors of planned Allied landings in Norway reached Raeder through Schreiber, and on December 8 Raeder again mentioned Norway during his report to Hitler. Raeder remarked on the active trade between Scandinavia and England, and on the difficulty of preventing it, and then stated: "It is important to occupy Norway." [16]

Consequently, when on December 11 Raeder was informed that Quisling, on Rosenberg's recommendation, was requesting an interview, it was immediately arranged. Quisling was accompanied by his close associate and representative in Germany, a Norwegian businessman named Viljam Hagelin. They told Raeder that Norwegian policy "is controlled by the well-known Jew, Hambro,* a great friend of Hore-Belisha," and that British landings near Stavanger and Christiansand were under consideration. "The Baltic Sea is developing into a theater of war." All Norwegians were gravely concerned over the Russian attack on Finland. Hambro and his followers were counting on Britain to keep Russia out of Scandinavia, but Quisling's party "does not wish to come to blows with Germany because of Britain's gaining a foothold in Norway." On the contrary, the Quisling followers wished "to anticipate any possible British step in this direction by placing the necessary bases at the disposal of the German Armed Forces."

Indeed, steps in furtherance of this treachery had already been taken: "In the whole coastal area men in important positions (railway, post office, communications) have already been bought for this purpose." Negotiations along this line with Rosenberg were getting nowhere, owing to the "incompetency of accredited diplomats." Therefore, Quisling had now come "for the purpose of establishing clear-cut relations with Germany for the future." [17]

Raeder was noncommittal but agreed to lay the project before Hitler. He reported to the Fuehrer the very next day, in the presence of Keitel and Jodl. Quisling, Raeder said, had "made a reliable impression," but of course he was a party leader with an ax to grind. Occupation of Norway by Britain would be disastrous and must be forestalled. Nevertheless, "German occupation of Norwegian coastal bases would naturally occasion strong British countermeasures" and would result in "severe surface warfare off the Norwegian coast" with which "the German Navy is not yet prepared to cope . . . for any length of time." Raeder recommended that OKW proceed to make plans for a Norwegian occupation in collaboration with Quisling. [18]

Hitler agreed that a British occupation of Norway would be "unac-

* Carl Hambro, President of the Storting.

ceptable" but desired to consult Rosenberg and meet Quisling before making up his mind what to do. Rosenberg, it developed, had hurt his foot and was temporarily immobilized, but he drew up a memorandum on Quisling and his party. Raeder consulted Rosenberg at his home on the morning of December 14, and that afternoon took Quisling and Hagelin to Hitler.[19] No record of the meeting has come to light, but afterward Hitler directed that "investigations on how to seize Norway should be conducted by a very restricted staff group" at OKW, and Jodl set the wheels in motion.[20]

Hitler must have been deeply impressed with the importance of the Norwegian situation, for he conferred again with Quisling and Hagelin on December 16 and 18, in the midst of the crisis and emotional tension aroused by the *Graf Spee's* mortal predicament at Montevideo. The Fuehrer was in a cautious mood and emphasized that Scandinavian neutrality was preferable to enlarging the theater of war. But in view of the risk of British action, preparations must now be made, and Hitler promised Quisling financial support for counterpropaganda and to expand his "pan-Germanic" party.[21]

For the next five weeks, the Fuehrer left the further development of the Norwegian situation to the OKW and Rosenberg. An official of the latter's APA, Wilhelm Scheidt, was sent to Oslo, to serve as a channel for financial support to the Quislingites and, in collaboration with Naval Attaché Schreiber, to observe and report on the progress of Quisling's plans for a *coup d'état*, after which the Wehrmacht would be invited to Norway to furnish protection against the English. Hagelin, who had excellent contacts with the Norwegian Navy, moved back and forth between Norway and Germany, bringing information to the German authorities and generally needling them in Quisling's behalf.[22]

In the meantime Keitel and Jodl, in deference to the Fuehrer's instructions that knowledge of the Norwegian matter was to be severely restricted, spoke about it only guardedly to the chiefs of staff of the Air Force (Jeschonnek) and Army (Halder).[23] The Navy, which had instigated the whole thing, prepared a staff memorandum, but the overall planning was carried on by a small group at OKW under Oberst Walter Warlimont. By the middle of January 1940 the OKW had completed a *Studie Nord*, outlining a project for the occupation of Norway, to be developed by a "working staff" headed by a general from the Luftwaffe, with a naval officer as his chief of staff and an operations officer from the Army.

It is not clear to whom this memorandum was distributed. Keitel discussed it on the telephone with Halder on January 10, and a copy reached SKL on January 13.[24] But the proposal, envisaging as it did the joint activity of all three service staffs, did not meet with Hitler's approval. On January 23 he ordered that *Studie Nord* be withdrawn and that all future work be handled by a special staff at OKW.[25]

On January 27 a top-secret OKW directive was issued to the three service commanders, stating that Hitler wished all plans for the Norwegian occupation to be developed under his own "personal and immediate influence" and under Keitel's direct charge. Keitel called on each of the three services to designate an officer skilled in operations and logistics to work with the special staff, and directed that "all further preparations will be conducted under the code name *Weseruebung*." [26] Serious planning for the German occupation of Norway began with the issuance of this order, but still Hitler had not decided whether or when it should be undertaken.

Under Jodl's general supervision, Warlimont remained in immediate charge of the staff,[27] which was now augmented by the three service-designated officers—from the Navy, Kapitaen zur See Theodor Krancke, then the commander of the *Admiral Scheer;* from the Luftwaffe, Oberst Robert Knauss; from the Army, Oberstleutnant Eyk von Tippelskirch, a transportation specialist. On February 5 the staff was formally greeted and given its instructions by Keitel.[28]

In the meantime, the Finns had succeeded in holding off the Russians throughout January. But despite all the sympathy aroused by the little country's gallant stand, effective Allied aid was not forthcoming. A few thousand foreign volunteers and a few score British planes were a drop in the bucket. Churchill's pet project of mining the Narvik harbor entrance was also stalled, and his ardent advocacy failed to overcome the Cabinet's reluctance to risk the breach of neutrality.

The opening on February 1 of the Russian offensive against the "Mannerheim Line" across the Karelian Isthmus again focused Allied attention in the north. When the Supreme War Council met in Paris a few days later, it was agreed that Finland must be saved and that to this end several divisions of reinforcements should be sent in, if possible through Norway and Sweden. Two British divisions due to embark for France were held in Britain to be available for this purpose, but still no systematic effort to win over the Norwegian and Swedish governments was made, nor were alternatives devised for the probable contingency that they might refuse.

In the middle of February, however, there occurred an episode that disturbed the precarious balance of Norwegian neutrality and stimulated Hitler to intensify and expedite German preparations for *Weseruebung*. The scuttled *Graf Spee's* auxiliary supply ship, the *Altmark*, carrying some 300 captive British merchant seamen from the vessels sunk by the pocket battleship, was returning from the South Atlantic to Germany. She succeeded in slipping through the British naval blockade, and on February 14 reached Norwegian territorial waters, where she was soon discovered by a British destroyer flotilla. The Norwegians boarded the *Altmark* but made no search, and informed the British that the ship was unarmed and carried no prisoners.

Knowing the truth to be otherwise, on February 16 Churchill personally ordered the destroyer flotilla commander, Captain Philip Vian, to liberate the prisoners, if necessary by boarding the *Altmark*. That night Vian, on the destroyer *Cossack*, entered Josing Fiord, where the German vessel had taken refuge, and put a boarding party on the *Altmark*. "The Navy's here" was the cry as they rescued the British seamen, who were found locked in storerooms and empty oil tanks. The Norwegian government protested the entry of their territorial waters, an act which the British justified because of "the abuse by German warships of neutral waters." [29]

Whatever the rights or wrongs of the matter under international law, they were of small interest to Hitler in comparison to the military implications of bold British action in Norwegian waters. On February 19 he called for rapid completion of the *Weseruebung* plans, including the selection and fitting out of the ships and forces to carry out the invasion and occupation. Jodl suggested that the commanding general for the operation should be selected and put in charge of the staff, and the next day Hitler summoned to Berlin General Nikolaus von Falkenhorst, Commanding General of the XXIst Corps, stationed at Coblenz and at the time conducting training maneuvers at Grafenwoehr.

Group XXI

Falkenhorst, by then in his middle fifties, was born in Breslau into an old military family, by name von Jastrzembski. He abandoned this unwieldy and un-German moniker * early in his military career, which comprised the usual variety of staff and command assignments of a promising general staff officer. At the end of World War I he had

* His selection of a new name suggests a romantic turn of mind; *Falkenhorst* means "falcon's eyrie."

served as operations officer of von der Goltz's *Ostseedivision* in Finland, and it was this experience which prompted Keitel to suggest his name to Hitler, as an officer having some practical experience in the leadership of combined operations on northern shores.[30]

Falkenhorst reported to Hitler, in the presence of Keitel and Jodl, on the morning of February 21. He described to the Fuehrer his experience in Finland and was entrusted with command of the Norwegian invasion forces. Hitler explained that the action was necessary in order to forestall the British, safeguard the Swedish ore traffic, and open up the northern coasts for German naval operations. Falkenhorst, who undertook the assignment "gladly," [31] was allowed no time for rumination; Hitler stated that five divisions would be put at his disposal and ordered him to return at five o'clock in the afternoon of the same day to outline his plan of campaign.

The new commander purchased a Baedeker of Norway and retired to his hotel room to ponder the problem. Upon his return to the Reich Chancellery at the appointed hour, he was informed by Hitler that the special staff that had been working on the problem proposed to distribute the five divisions one each to Oslo, Stavanger, Bergen, Trondheim, and Narvik. Falkenhorst agreed: [32] "There wasn't much else you could do, because they were the large harbors."

At the conclusion of the conference Hitler enjoined Falkenhorst to work with the utmost secrecy and expedition, and authorized him to bring from Coblenz to Berlin such members of his XXIst Corps staff as "were absolutely necessary for the work." Oberst Erich Buschenhagen (the corps Chief of Staff) and a few others were selected, and Falkenhorst combined them with the Krancke-Knauss-Tippelskirch group into a general staff for his projected task force, now denominated Group (*Gruppe*) XXI. Secluded quarters in the Bendlerstrasse were made available, and detailed operational planning proceeded apace under the direct command of OKW, where Hitler maintained close personal supervision of the project, and Keitel, Jodl, Warlimont, and Oberstleutnant Bernhard von Lossberg participated extensively in its development.

But all the planning in the world would accomplish nothing without troops, and these had to be provided by the Army. When Falkenhorst was appointed, Keitel consulted with General Fromm of the Replacement Army, but the combat-ready divisions were not under Fromm's command, and sooner or later the matter had to be taken up with OKH—i.e., with Brauchitsch and Halder, who had not been favored with Hitler's confidence on his Scandinavian designs. On February 26 Falkenhorst and Buschenhagen visited Halder and requested that some of the Army's crack mountain troops be made available. They found the Chief of the General Staff in an understandably stiff mood. He requested prompt and full information concerning needed strengths and the time and place of their assembly, and exacted a promise from Falkenhorst that OKH would be consulted again before being presented with a formal OKW requisition—a promise which was not kept, as Halder acridly noted in his diary on March 1 when the OKW order arrived.[33]

Halder's pique meant nothing to Hitler. On February 29, when Falkenhorst and staff reported to him with plans calling for two full-strength mountain divisions, the Fuehrer approved, and expressed his gratification with the progress being made. But he had now decided that Copenhagen must also be occupied by "a strong group," and this would require still more staff and troops.

The following day (March 1) Hitler issued the formal military directive for *Weseruebung*: [34]

The development of the situation in Scandinavia requires the making of all preparations for the occupation of Denmark and Norway by a part of the German Armed Forces ("*Fall Weseruebung*"). This operation should prevent British encroachment on Scandinavia and the Baltic; further, it should guarantee our ore base in Sweden and give our Navy and Air Force a wider starting line against Britain. The part which the Navy and the Air Force will have to play, within the limits of their capabilities, is to protect the operation against the interference of British naval and air striking forces.

In view of our military and political power in comparison with that of the Scandinavian States, the force to be employed in the "*Fall Weseruebung*" will be kept as small as possible. The numerical weakness will be balanced by daring actions and surprise execution. On principle, we will do our utmost to make the operation appear as a *peaceful* occupation, the object of which is the military protection of the neutrality of the Scandinavian States. Corresponding demands will be transmitted to their governments at the beginning of the occupation. If necessary, demonstrations by the Navy and Air Force will provide the necessary emphasis. If in spite of this resistance should be met with, all military means will be used to crush it.

The order named Falkenhorst as the commander, under Hitler's direct orders. Denmark and Norway were to be invaded simultaneously and by surprise, the latter (*Weseruebung* North) by sea and air and the former (*Weseruebung* South) by sea and by crossing the Danish-German border in Schleswig.

Together with this directive, OKW presented to OKH its requisition for army units for *Weseruebung*—for Denmark two divisions, a motorized brigade, and another corps headquarters; for Norway, five divisions and various special units. The reaction at OKH, as Jodl described it, was "fury" at the size of the requisitions.[35] As a result they were somewhat scaled down after a conference on March 2 between Keitel and Brauchitsch. The army chiefs were by no means mollified, however, and Halder angrily confided to his diary that [36] "Not a single word has passed between the Fuehrer and ObdH [Brauchitsch] on this matter; this must be put on record for the history of the war." *

But Brauchitsch and Halder were not the only ones whose noses were out of joint. Hermann Goering was in a rage because the OKW directive subordinated to Falkenhorst the Luftwaffe units allocated to *Weseruebung*. He hectored Keitel and flounced off to complain to Hitler, and successfully. On March 4 it was agreed, by Jodl and Jeschonnek for the OKW and the Luftwaffe respectively, that the air units would receive their orders from OKL, to which Falkenhorst would have to address his requests for air support.[37] The idea of unified command of the combined forces thus collapsed at the very outset, and for the usual reason: Goering's vanity, which Hitler was still chary of wounding.

This jurisdictional victory merely whetted the fat one's appetite. Was he not the only active-duty † *Generalfeldmarschall* and ranking officer of the Wehrmacht? Hardly had Jodl finished with Jeschonnek when Goering's shadow, Generalmajor Karl Bodenschatz (liaison officer for Goering at Hitler's headquarters), turned up at OKW to complain that Goering had been slighted and undercut in planning *Weseruebung*; 110 Luftwaffe officers had been consulted by OKW without Goering's prior knowledge or permission. Jodl humbly confessed error.

Next day (March 5), Hitler called a major conference on *Weseruebung*, attended by Goering, Brauchitsch and Raeder, as well as the

---

* Mr. Wheeler-Bennett writes (*The Nemesis of Power*, p. 494): "OKH were appalled at the risks and dangers inherent in the expedition, and, braving their Fuehrer's wrath, they flatly refused to participate in the preliminary preparations." This analysis is contrary to all the evidence I have seen. As abundantly appears from the Halder and Jodl diaries and other contemporary sources, Hitler deliberately excluded OKH from the consultations on *Weseruebung*, to Halder's deep annoyance, reflected in the note quoted above and elsewhere in his diary. Mr. Wheeler-Bennett's misapprehension is accurately diagnosed in Erfurth, *Die Geschichte des Deutschen Generalstabes 1918–1945*, p. 241, n. 27.

† The army rank list still carried the aged and long-retired Generalfeldmarschall August von Mackensen, as well as the Austrian Generalfeldmarschall Freiherr von Boehm-Ermolli of World War I.

OKW and Group XXI leaders—the first occasion on which Hitler had brought either Goering or Brauchitsch into the picture. Jodl recorded in his diary:

Fieldmarshal [Goering] vents his spleen, because he was not consulted beforehand. He dominates the discussion and tries to prove that all previous preparations are good for nothing.

As a result of his expostulations the plans were changed in such a way that even heavier demands were now laid upon both the Navy and the Army. To protect the landing parties, some warships (including the heavy cruiser *Admiral Hipper* or the pocket battle cruiser *Luetzow*) were now expected to remain in the Norwegian ports after landing the troops, instead of immediately running back to German waters to escape the anticipated arrival of the vastly superior British fleet. To ensure speedy occupation, the ground forces were to be strengthened, especially at Narvik; six divisions were to be allocated to Norway, and the equivalent of nine divisions in all to Norway and Denmark. Thus Brauchitsch lost the benefit of the concessions he had wrung from Keitel three days earlier and was faced with requisitions even heavier than those originally presented by OKW. But as usual he did not venture to make an issue of the matter, and on March 7 Hitler signed a revised directive embodying the changes resulting from the March 5 conference.[38]

The inclusion of Denmark in the territory to be occupied appears to have been due to the wishes of the Luftwaffe, naturally eager for advanced fighter bases and extension of its air-warning network.[39] To lead the occupation forces into Denmark (under Falkenhorst's over-all command) the choice fell upon the veteran General Leonhard Kaupisch,* then in charge of the corps headquarters designated Higher Command XXXI, in East Prussia. He and his chief of staff, Generalmajor Kurt Himer, arrived in Berlin on March 5, and joined Falkenhorst's group working at the Bendlerstrasse.

While the German expeditionary force for *Weseruebung* was as-

---

* Kaupisch had been retired from the Army as a *Generalleutnant* at about the time Hitler came into power. He was soon taken into the Luftwaffe, and commanded one of the six air districts, with the rank of *General der Flieger,* until he was again retired at the time of the Blomberg-Fritsch crisis in March 1938. Upon the outbreak of war he was given command of a mixed task force on the Polish border, which crossed the corridor to Danzig. On October 2, 1939, Kaupisch accepted the surrender of the last Polish units holding out on the Hela peninsula. Thereafter he was given command of *Hoeheres Kommando* XXXI, and on April 17, 1940, was retransferred to the army rolls as *General der Artillerie.*

sembling, the Russo-Finnish War approached its climax. The Red Army pounded the Mannerheim line with heavy artillery and tanks, forcing the Finns to a dogged and inching retreat. Bitter as was the fighting, it was waged to the counterpoint of peace feelers and diplomatic offers and counteroffers, transmitted by the good offices of the Swedish government. These were not immediately fruitful, and as the Red tide crept slowly across the Karelian Isthmus, the Finns renewed their pleas for assistance from the western Allies. On March 1, when Soviet troops finally reached Viipuri, the Finnish government inquired whether it would be possible for the Allies immediately to dispatch at least 50,000 troops and 100 bombers with crews.[40]

Without consulting the British, the French government of Daladier (the warmth of whose support for the Finns was due in part to a desire that any fighting take place as far as possible from French soil) offered to send the troops specified.[41] Once again, however, the Swedish and Norwegian governments refused transit for these reinforcements. The French were willing to give assistance despite this obstacle, and on March 8 Daladier reiterated his offer and urged the Finns to fight on. But that very day peace negotiations were resumed in Moscow, and on the twelfth Finland accepted the Soviet terms and the Russo-Finnish War was ended. The Finns' decision was due primarily to Mannerheim's conclusion that foreign aid could not arrive soon enough or in sufficient quantity to save the situation. Furthermore, the Finnish leaders were reluctant to see the Baltic countries become a major battlefield of the great powers, as might well have been the consequence of Allied intervention on a large scale.

With the end of the fighting in Finland, the Allied plans for landings in Scandinavia were shelved. The two divisions [42] "which had been held back in England were now allowed to proceed to France" and British "striking power toward Norway was reduced to eleven battalions." In Germany, however, these events had the opposite result.

As late as February 26 Hitler had been in doubt whether to launch *Weseruebung* before or after the main attack in the west. Two days later Jodl proposed to preserve flexibility in this respect by preparing the two campaigns "in such a manner that they will be quite independent of each other as regards timing and strength," and noted Hitler's agreement to this proposition. Meanwhile, however, the discussions between the Finns and the Allies looking to the dispatch of reinforcements by way of the Scandinavian peninsula were intensified, and Hitler's concern was correspondingly deepened. On March 3 he spoke "very sharply" about the need for "prompt and strong action in Norway," and later the same day he decided to undertake *Weseruebung* before attacking in the West [43]—a decision obviously stimulated if not governed by the increasing possibility of Allied intervention in Finland. Plans for the operation were to be completed by March 10, and the deployment of troops and ships brought to sufficient readiness so that the invasion could be launched on four days' notice.[44]

The conclusion of peace in Finland was greeted with general satisfaction in Germany, as it checked, at least temporarily, the Russian advance in the Baltic region and diminished the hazard of Allied action in those parts. But the changed situation was not without embarrassment for the high command because, as Jodl noted,[45] with the conclusion of peace "the motivation for Falkenhorst's action will be difficult." Hitler, too, was casting about for a new excuse; by March 14 he had "not decided how to justify *Weseruebung*." Indeed, Raeder, the original protagonist of the enterprise, was now "in doubt whether it is still important to play at preventive war in Norway," [46] and some of his subordinates * began to show signs of cold feet.[47]

Hitler's hesitation, however, was only momentary. He left Berlin on March 17 for a meeting the next day with Mussolini at the Brenner Pass, at which he appears to have told the Duce little about his plan of attack in the West and nothing about *Weseruebung*.[48] He spent the following (Easter) week end at the Obersalzberg; returning to Berlin on March 26, he immediately closeted himself with Raeder, Keitel, and Jodl.[49] The Commander-in-Chief of the Navy opined that "the danger of a British landing in Norway is no longer acute at present" but that the enemy would continue to disrupt the ore traffic from Narvik and seek "a pretext for action against Norway." Therefore, "sooner or later Germany will be faced with the necessity of carrying out *Weseruebung*." Overcast, foggy weather and long nights were desirable for the invasion, and with the approach of summer these conditions would disappear. Accordingly, the sooner the better,† and by April 15 at the

---

* There had been considerable disagreement within SKL about the necessity for and wisdom of the Norwegian operation. On January 13, for example, Schniewind had thought that a British occupation of Norway was imminent, but the operations officer, Konteradmiral Kurt Fricke, was of a contrary opinion and preferred to see Norway remain neutral territory. By March 13, Schniewind had come around to the view that there was no imminent risk of a British operation in Norway.

† According to Raeder's War Diary (entry for April 22, 1940), the persistence of "ice conditions in the Baltic" (presumably in the waters off Denmark and the north German coast) prevented the launching of *Weseruebung* during the latter part of March.

latest. On the basis of these recommendations Hitler agreed that the landing operations be scheduled for about April 7, the time of the new moon.

The following day, Hitler told Halder [50] that he wanted to start *Weseruebung* on the ninth or tenth of April. The reasons for the two-day delay past the new moon are not clear, and Raeder strongly opposed the postponement. However, the last few days of March witnessed another eruption of inter-service squabbles * that were not finally resolved until April 2. That afternoon Hitler finally issued the order for the operation to begin, under a naval and air transport schedule that brought the invasion troops to Norwegian shores during the small hours of Tuesday, April 9.

"Wilfred" and "R.4"

In the meantime, Allied strategy vis-à-vis Scandinavia had taken a new turn. The defeat of Finland, which had rendered the old plans obsolete, also toppled the Daladier government. The new French premier, Paul Reynaud, was much more congenial to Mr. Churchill and his designs. Reynaud and his colleagues came to London on March 28 for a meeting of the Supreme War Council, at which Chamberlain at last took up the cudgels for Churchill's long-standing proposal that the Norwegian Leads be mined to cut off the Narvik ore traffic. Reynaud readily agreed, and it was decided to lay the mine fields on April 5. On April 3, however, the British War Cabinet postponed the operation † (known by the cover-name "Wilfred") to April 8.[53]

The probability of German counteraction, far from being overlooked, was consciously anticipated by the British planners. To meet

---

* Raeder wanted the Luftwaffe to lay mines at Scapa Flow and in the major British estuaries to hamper the movements of the British Fleet during the critical period when the *Weseruebung* ships were en route to the Norwegian ports. Goering was insolently unco-operative and preferred more spectacular but ineffective bombing attacks against the fleet at Scapa.[51] Likewise, Raeder wished his ships to quit the Norwegian ports as soon as the troops had landed, so that the safety of home waters might be reached before the vastly superior British Fleet could reach the scene of action. Goering, with Hitler's support, argued that the German warships should remain in the Norwegian ports in order to support the assault.[52]

† The British had proposed at the March 28 meeting that fluvial mines should simultaneously be dropped by aircraft into the Rhine (operation "Royal Marine") to disrupt the river traffic. But on April 3 it was learned that the French War Committee would not agree to "Royal Marine," and "Wilfred" was postponed until the eighth to enable Churchill to fly to Paris and try to overcome French opposition. In this he was unsuccessful.

the contingency that the Germans might land troops to keep the coastal waters open for traffic, "Wilfred" had a military counterpart, designated "Plan R.4." In essence,[54] this was a plan "for a military expedition to take immediate advantage of the somewhat vaguely defined moment when 'the Germans set foot on Norwegian soil, or there is clear evidence that they intend to do so.' " For this purpose, an infantry brigade was put in readiness for the occupation of Narvik, and five battalions for Trondheim, Bergen, and Stavanger. No air support whatsoever was allocated to "R.4," an omission which strikingly exposes its tentative, almost nonchalant, character. Apparently it was expected that the infantry units, once ashore, would be able to hold the ports against German landing attempts, and there was no thought of proceeding with "R.4" in the face of serious Norwegian opposition— rather, it was hoped that British troops would be welcomed as allies against the threat or actuality of a German assault. Viewed in retrospect, and in the light of what the Germans were actually doing, "Wilfred" and "R.4" were, of course, ludicrously inadequate.

And so it came to pass that during the six days that the German invasion fleet was creeping up the Norwegian coast, the British troops earmarked for "R.4" were embarking on transports in the Clyde and cruisers in the Forth, while a force of destroyers, guarded by the battle cruiser *Renown*, was en route to the Norwegian coast near Narvik and Aalesund to lay "Wilfred's" mine fields. The Narvik mines were actually laid at four in the morning of April 8, with simultaneous public announcement and delivery of an explanatory note to the Norwegian government. But British aircraft had sighted large German naval units off the Norwegian coast on the seventh, and it rapidly became apparent that the Germans had undertaken a major naval foray, although its true dimensions were not grasped in London until the evening of the eighth.

As soon as the possibility of large-scale naval engagements was appreciated, the British suspended "Wilfred" and abandoned "R.4." The mine-laying expedition toward Aalesund was recalled before zero hour, and the troops in the Clyde and Forth were rapidly debarked, to free the ships for fleet action. On April 5 Prime Minister Chamberlain had publicly mocked the enemy's failure to "take advantage of his initial superiority to . . . overwhelm us" and complacently declared that Hitler had "missed the bus." Three days later the War Office and Admiralty were floundering desperately in their efforts to retrieve the military situation that had been turned, by the Germans' boldness and ruthlessness, so sharply in their immediate favor. "We have been completely outwitted," declared Winston Churchill on April 10.[55]

"Aggressive" or "Preventive" War

The story of *Weseruebung* is a remarkable case study in international law and morals, and the comparative aggressive potential of democracy and dictatorship. At Nuremberg, the International Military Tribunal held that the German invasion of Norway and Denmark was an "act of aggressive war" and rejected the plea that it was primarily defensive as "preventive" of an Allied occupation. Raeder, Rosenberg, and several others were consequently convicted of planning and waging aggressive warfare against Norway and Denmark.

Yet it is plain enough on the record that Churchill and the British Admiralty were making sheep's eyes at the Norwegian coast almost from the outset of the war. In retrospect Churchill wrote[56] that "the two Admiralties thought with precision along the same lines in correct strategy" and there is little doubt but that, had his counsels sooner prevailed, the Scandinavian peninsula would have been a battlefield months before April of 1940. Was it simply, then, a battle of wits between London and Berlin, beyond the reach of judgment in terms of war guilt?

One may fairly lay to one side the abuse of Norwegian territorial waters as warranting the forceful occupation of the country by either Germany or Britain. True, the merchant shipping of a belligerent power is entitled to cruise in the territorial waters of a neutral. The fact that the Narvik ore traffic was of great importance to the German war effort afforded the British no intrinsic justification for violating Norwegian neutrality by mining the Leads. The Germans, however, had themselves shown no respect for Norwegian waters. They had sunk numerous British and neutral merchantmen within the three-mile limit,[57] and had flagrantly abused its protection in the case of the prisoner-carrying armed naval auxiliary *Altmark*. Furthermore, it is plain from the chronology of the events we have traced that *Weseruebung* was not provoked by the fear of British mines, and had the Germans been bent on protecting the neutrality of Norwegian coastal waters, the last thing to do was destroy that neutrality by belligerent occupation of the mainland.

But what about the danger of a British occupation of Norway as justifying *Weseruebung*? In evaluating this defense it must be remembered that Hitler and Raeder reached the final decision to launch the assault at a time when, in fact and in their estimation, the end of the Russo-Finnish War had greatly diminished the likelihood of Allied military action on the Scandinavian peninsula.[58] Hitler was at a loss for a pretext for *Weseruebung*. Raeder foresaw no "acute" danger of a British landing,* and of "Wilfred" and "R.4" the Germans apparently knew nothing.

Nevertheless, the legality of military action when the stakes are victory or defeat in war cannot be determined by logic-chopping or doctrinaire preconceptions. If "preventive action" on the part of the acting nation would be justified by the enemy's actual intentions and preparations, should we condemn that nation's leaders on the ground that they did not know what the enemy was intending, and acted for aggressive rather than preventive purposes? While it is not unusual in law that guilt or innocence turns upon the accused's state of mind, surely there are grave dangers in applying these refined concepts of motive to the relatively uncharted field of international penal law relating to aggressive war-making. If Hitler and Raeder had been fully informed of all Allied discussions, plans, and decisions relating to Scandinavia— including Churchill's views and the ultimate adoption of "Wilfred" and "R.4"—would *Weseruebung* then have been justifiable as a "preventive" measure? Surely this is a test at once fairer and more favorable to the Germans, but even on this footing it is impossible to support an affirmative answer.

For the most and worst that can be said about Anglo-French strategy in Scandinavia is that the Russo-Finnish War (arousing, as it did, the fears and pro-Finnish sympathies of the other Scandinavian nations) stimulated Allied plans, which might have been carried out but for the Finnish capitulation, to aid the Finns by means which would have brought Norway and Sweden within the Allied ambit; that German violations of Norwegian neutral waters precipitated Allied counteraction, and that the British exploited the situation by mining the Leads in order to obstruct the Narvik ore traffic; and that the British anticipated and assembled a few battalions to meet the possibility that mining the Leads might provoke German landing attempts on the Nor-

---

* The International Military Tribunal at Nuremberg found these circumstances governing, on the basis that "preventive action in foreign territory is justified only in case of an instant and overwhelming necessity for self-defense, leaving no choice of means . . ." whereas the German attack was "not made for the purpose of forestalling an imminent landing, but, at the most" to "prevent an Allied occupation at some future date." [59]

wegian coast. To be sure, Churchill, as First Lord of the Admiralty, advocated a more rapid and drastic course of action, but the War Cabinet would not approve his recommendations, for fear of violating the rights of neutrals and offending world opinion.[60] It is true, of course, that the Allies had a far greater stake in a correct course of conduct than did the Germans, who, after Austria, Czechoslovakia, and Poland, had little to lose in these terms. But this amounts to no more than that a banker has a bigger interest in his good reputation than does a bank robber.

Indeed, the fluctuations of British strategy—two divisions earmarked for Finland in February 1940 but dispatched to France in March; a brigade and four battalions to protect the Norwegian ports embarked on April 7, debarked on the eighth, and partially re-embarked on the eleventh—strongly suggests that it was chiefly open to criticism as pusillanimous rather than aggressive. Finally, it must be borne in mind that at no time, during the Russo-Finnish War or thereafter, did Allied plans envisage landing in Norway in the face of Norwegian opposition,* nor was any action in Denmark ever contemplated.

The contrast is clear enough between these shifting and cautious Allied designs, and the ruthless aggression of *Weseruebung*, the original purpose of which was to lay hands on the Norwegian ports for use as submarine bases, and to stretch the British blockade to the snapping point. From December 1939 to early March 1940, these aims were greatly reinforced by the danger of Allied intervention in the Russo-Finnish War, but the substantial disappearance of this hazard after March 12 [61] wrought no decisive change in Berlin's strategy of aggression. Norwegian resistance was a certainty, but neutral rights counted for nothing with Hitler and Raeder. Denmark was marked as an additional victim for purely tactical reasons, and without the shadow of excuse other than military expediency. And once ashore in Norway the Germans carried out a swift and brutal program of total dominion.

---

* The pitifully small troop allocations and the total lack of air support clearly establish the "friendly" character of "R.4."

CHAPTER FOUR

The Conquest of Denmark and Norway

"THE PREREQUISITES for the success of the operation are surprise and rapid action," Raeder admonished the naval officer corps on the eve of the assault,[1] as he warned that the landing operations were to take place "mainly in an area in which . . . England with her superior naval force is able to exercise control of the sea." Success could be achieved, however, if the Wehrmacht's responsibilities were discharged "with boldness, tenacity, and skill."

These injunctions were fulfilled with devotion and daring, and before nightfall of April 9 Denmark and every major Norwegian port from Oslo to Narvik were in German hands. So unexpected was the assault and so stunning its success that many legends have sprung up around it.

Sabotage, espionage, and treason, it was widely believed at the time, had been crucial factors in the speedy German success.[2] The wires to the mine barrage in the Oslofiord had been cut; German travelers in Norway and Denmark had acted as spies and German residents as a potent "fifth column"; Norwegian officers had traitorously allowed the German invaders to penetrate the ports and had surrendered without offering resistance; Viennese children whom the Norwegians had cared for and saved from starvation in 1920—the *Wiener-barn*—had returned like vipers, as guides among the German invaders of 1940. The reporter Leland Stowe of the Chicago *Daily News* gave wide currency to these sensational stories in a report from Stockholm which he described as "the most important newspaper dispatch I have ever had occasion to write," and which laid the entire success of the German venture at the door of treachery:

Norway's capital and great seaports were not captured by armed force. They were seized with unparalleled speed by means of a gigantic conspiracy. . . . By bribery and extraordinary infiltration on the part of Norwegian civilians and defense officials, the German dictatorship built its Trojan Horse inside Norway. . . .

Postwar investigations revealed that, while there were a few instances of espionage and other assistance to the Germans by local Nazis, the great majority of these tales were quite untrue. It was natural, of course, that the bewildering shock of invasion after so many years of peace would give rise to speculation and rumor. But it is unfortunate that such myths persisted so long that they have warped the memory of those times.

Even as authoritative and distinguished a historian as Winston Churchill has contributed to these misconceptions.* Thus, it was widely reported that seemingly peaceful German freighters, lying in the Norwegian ports for several days before the attack, suddenly disgorged hordes of fully armed soldiers that had lain hidden below the decks. But in the real world of shipping—especially in the small Norwegian coastal cities where every bottom is known and the arrival of every cargo expected—ships do not arrive and lie in port unnoticed by the authorities. The discovery of one such vessel would have given the whole show away.

In any event, no such thing was attempted. On the contrary, the basic plan of *Weseruebung* was that the assault ships should arrive off all the target ports, from Narvik to Copenhagen, at five o'clock in the morning, and that the assault wave should break everywhere within half an hour thereafter. Considering the enormous geographical spread of the operation (it is well over 1000 miles from Narvik to the German-Danish border in Schleswig), the venture required for its success not only the surprise and speed of which Raeder spoke but the utmost precision in planning, and skill and good fortune in execution.

In its opening stages, the naval elements of the operation were, of course, crucial. How could the three divisions which were to make the

---

* "The most daring stroke was at Narvik," Mr. Churchill writes in *The Gathering Storm* (p. 590). "For a week supposedly empty German ore ships returning to that port in the ordinary course had been moving up the corridor [territorial waters] sanctified by Norwegian neutrality, filled with supplies and ammunition." In fact, no such ship reached Narvik. A few merchantmen loaded with military supplies were dispatched to the Norwegian ports in advance of the invasion fleet (*infra*, pp. 105 and 111–12), but most of them were sunk en route and none (except one, which sailed from Murmansk) reached port until after the initial and successful assault on April 9.

initial assault be transported by sea, in the teeth of the British Fleet, to the widely scattered Norwegian harbors, not only safely but with such nice navigation that they would be landed simultaneously in Narvik, Trondheim, Bergen, Christiansand, Oslo, and Copenhagen? Obviously the difficulties varied enormously according to the distance, and the degree and duration of the landing fleet's exposure to British attack. The naval hazards were much greater at Narvik than at Oslo, and generally greater all along the exposed western coast of Norway than in the nearer and more sheltered waters of the Skagerrak and Kattegat, which lay well within the protective radius of the Luftwaffe. A single naval sortie to Narvik might with good luck succeed, though the voyage back to Germany, after the element of surprise had worn thin, would be extremely hazardous; a second expedition so far north, after the British had been fully alerted, would be out of the question. But Oslo could be reached with comparative safety, by sea transport routed from the German Baltic ports through the Danish islands and along the west coast of Sweden to the Oslofiord. There was reasonable hope that a flow of reinforcements and supplies by sea could be maintained at Oslo for as long as necessary.

In broad outline, therefore, *Weseruebung* depended upon the German Navy for one major expedition along the Norwegian coast to land the assault troops and supplies at Narvik, Trondheim, Bergen, Christiansand and Oslo, and thereafter for the establishment and maintenance of permanent sea communications with Oslo. After the landings, some reinforcements could be brought to the west coast ports by air. But the major build-up would be at Oslo, from where the German troops would fan out, establish land communications with the other ports, and complete the conquest of the country. Denmark was to be occupied by simply marching across the border into Jutland and landing troops by air and sea at Copenhagen and a few other key points.

The Danish forces were incapable of serious resistance, and the government's prompt capitulation was confidently anticipated. In Norway the prospects were much more uncertain, but the Germans hoped that, by a combination of ruthless force, threats, and Quisling's connivings, the King might be induced to yield his land to German "protection."

But all these plans and hopes depended on the success of the initial landings. Since speed was of the essence and the Norwegian harbors might be defended, the solution reached was to dispatch the assault troops not on transports under naval convoy but on the naval vessels themselves—on the fast cruisers, destroyers, and torpedo boats of which the German Fleet was principally composed. According to Falkenhorst, this idea "originated with the Fuehrer." [3] By the use of nearly every available ship, it was possible to carry roughly two battalions of troops with light weapons to each of the four major target ports (Oslo, Bergen, Trondheim, and Narvik), and a single battalion to Christiansand —perhaps 9,000 men in all.

As soon as the assault troops went ashore, they would need heavy weapons and equipment for which there was no room on the warships. Furthermore, there would be urgent need for oil, especially at the more distant Norwegian target ports where the destroyers and other light naval craft were to be immediately refueled for the perilous return journey. For these purposes, there were to be an *Ausfuhrstaffel* ("lead-off group") of seven freighters, and four tankers in a *Tankerstaffel;* all but two of these ships were routed to Narvik and Trondheim.* Much slower than the naval ships, these vessels were to sail several days earlier, and it was hoped that they would arrive just before the assault units.

The bulk of the supplies and reinforcements, however, was to come in a series of eight *Seetransportstaffeln* (sea transport groups) that were assembled in the well-protected German Baltic ports. The first of these included five ships for Oslo and ten for Bergen, Christiansand, and Stavanger—none for Trondheim or Narvik, where the hazards would be prohibitive—and was scheduled to arrive hard on the heels of the assault groups, by which time the harbors and harbor defenses would be in German hands. All seven of the following *Seetransport-staffeln* were for the main build-up at Oslo.

During the passage to the target ports, the role of the Luftwaffe was limited to reconnaissance, and spoiling attacks on the British Fleet at Scapa Flow. Once the landings commenced, however, the Luftwaffe assumed the main burden of protecting troops, ships, and the flow of supplies against the anticipated British counterpunch. In Norway, Stavanger and the adjacent Sola airfield were to be captured with parachute and airborne troops. As rapidly as circumstances permitted, German planes were to be based at Norwegian and Danish airfields, to bring the ports and coastal waters under short-range fighter cover and give close support to the ground troops.

The Luftwaffe was also heavily relied on for air transport of troops

---

* One freighter was allotted to Stavanger which (with the adjacent and vital Sola airfield) was to be taken by airborne troops, and one tanker to Oslo.

to Oslo and Christiansand, for the capture of strategic airfields and bridges in both Norway and Denmark, and to meet all kinds of emergency needs that might be expected to arise in the course of the operation. What these might be would depend chiefly on the attitude taken by the Norwegian government and the nature of the British reaction to the assault.

With these general plans implemented by detailed orders to the participating units, on April 1 Hitler called together all the commanding officers for a survey of the plans and preparations. He [4] "talked to each single general and admiral . . . and had him explain exactly what his task was, even to the commanders of the ships, and he . . . went into everything." He described [5] *Weseruebung* as the "most bold and impudent undertaking in the history of warfare" and laid great stress on the need for secrecy. According to Jodl,[6] the Fuehrer got "a very good impression about the thoroughness of the preparations." After a final conference the following afternoon with Raeder, Goering, and Falkenhorst he ordered commencement of the operation, and at two o'clock in the morning of April 3 the first three ships of the *Ausfuhrstaffel* departed from Hamburg for Narvik.[7]

Passage to Norway

During the next three days the preliminary phase of *Weseruebung* went, as Jodl described it,[8] "according to plan." The other lead-off ships and tankers sailed between April 3 and 6,* and on the latter date the ten ships of the first *Seetransportstaffel* assigned to Bergen, Stavanger, and Christiansand left Stettin. Ribbentrop was told what was afoot,[9] and the Fuehrer himself went to work drafting the proclamations that would explain and seek to justify the attack. On April 4 there were conferences with Quisling and Hagelin in which the latter begged [10] that "Quisling should be given an assault group in good time, with the aid of which he could at once seize power and install a new government with the consent of the King." But the request fell on deaf ears; the Germans apparently did not overly trust this precious pair and did not even tell them that the invasion was about to occur.

While the lead-off freighters and tankers were working their way up

* All the freighters and one small tanker left from Hamburg, and two larger tankers from Wilhelmshaven. The big (12,000 BRT) tanker *Jan Wellem,* by special arrangement with the Russians, departed from the Murmansk area for Narvik on April 6.

the Norwegian coast, the assault troops were embarking on cruisers, destroyers, torpedo boats, and mine-sweepers at German harbors on the North Sea (Wilhelmshaven, Cuxhaven, and Wesermuende) and the Baltic (Kiel and Stettin-Swinemuende). General Falkenhorst set up his headquarters at Hamburg, where he was joined by General Kaupisch and Generalleutnant Hans Geissler, the commander of Fliegerkorps X, in which were grouped all the participating air force units. Subject to Raeder's over-all command, naval operations in the North Sea and along the Norwegian west coast were controlled by Generaladmiral Saalwaechter (Naval Group Command West) at Wilhelmshaven, and those in the Baltic and Kattegat by Admiral Carls (Naval Group Command East) at Kiel.*

At midnight on the night of April 6–7 the crucial phase of the operation began, with the departure from Wesermuende and Cuxhaven of the cruiser *Admiral Hipper* and fourteen destroyers loaded with troops for Narvik (Group I) and Trondheim (Group II) under the protection of the battle cruisers *Gneisenau* and *Scharnhorst*. Admiral Marschall was sick, and the entire battle group was under the command of the acting *Flottenchef*, Vizeadmiral Guenther Luetjens, whose flag was on the *Gneisenau*.

At ten o'clock in the evening of April 7 the other major task force (Group V) started from Swinemuende for Oslo; it comprised the heavy cruiser *Bluecher*, the pocket battle cruiser *Luetzow*, the light cruiser *Emden*, three torpedo boats and seven mine-sweepers. Two hours later Group III—the light cruisers *Koeln* and *Koenigsberg*, with the naval auxiliaries *Bremse* and *Karl Peters*, two torpedo boats and seven E-boats—left Wilhelmshaven for Bergen. Early in the morning of April 8 the light cruiser *Karlsruhe* with the auxiliary *Tsingtau*, three torpedo boats and two flotillas of E-boats (comprising Group IV) departed Wesermuende for Christiansand, and four mine-sweepers (Group VI) left Cuxhaven for Egersund, the cable-head to Britain. By this time some twenty-eight U-boats—about two thirds of all those available— had been stationed in the North Sea and off the Norwegian coast for protection of the entire operation.

As Luetjens' battle group stood out from Wesermuende, hundreds of miles to the north the British battle cruiser *Renown* and a large destroyer force was approaching the Norwegian coast to mine the Leads off Bodö. The North Sea itself was clear of major British surface units

---

* Tables of the organization and identity of the major units of the Wehrmacht that took part in *Weseruebung* are set forth in Appendix C, *infra*, pp. 424–26.

but was patrolled by submarines and reconnaissance aircraft. As early as eight o'clock in the morning of April 7, part of the battle group was sighted off the mouth of the Skagerrak by Royal Air Force planes, and as an immediate result it was attacked, without success, by twelve Blenheim bombers early that afternoon.[11] Through these contacts, by late afternoon the Admiralty was aware that a major German naval force was at large, and that evening Admiral Sir Charles Forbes sailed from Scapa in the battleship *Rodney,* with two other capital ships, two cruisers, and ten destroyers, hoping to find and engage the enemy fleet. But the British did not yet appreciate that the Germans planned to land in Norway and were not even sure that they would continue their northward course.*

This question was, however, resolved for the British early the following morning. By this time Luetjens was in the general latitude of Trondheim and perhaps 150 miles off shore. The wind had freshened during the night, and by morning the seas were very high. Considerable military equipment being carried on the destroyers' decks had to be jettisoned, a few soldiers were washed overboard, speed was reduced, and the destroyers were scattered. Ahead of them, the same difficulties were plaguing the British destroyers screening the *Renown.* One of these, the *Glowworm,* sighted two of the Narvik-bound German destroyers at about eight in the morning. The troop-laden German vessels fled, and Luetjens ordered the cruiser *Hipper* to engage and destroy the *Glowworm.*

By ten o'clock this was accomplished, but not before the *Glowworm* had reported by radio her discovery of the German fleet and had then gallantly rammed the *Hipper,* inflicting serious but not disabling damage. The impact, just aft of the anchor on the *Hipper*'s starboard bow, tore away 130 feet of armor belt and the starboard torpedo tubes; the cruiser shipped over 500 tons of water and developed a four-degree list to starboard. The *Glowworm* fell away and blew up a few minutes later with the loss of her captain (Lieutenant Commander G. B. Roope, posthumously awarded the Victoria Cross) and all of her crew but one officer and thirty-seven men, rescued by the *Hipper.*

But despite the *Glowworm*'s reports the British ships did not make contact with Luetjens' force, and April 8 was a day of unfortunate de-

---

* Churchill writes in *The Gathering Storm* (pp. 591–92): "We found it hard at the Admiralty [on the evening of April 7] to believe that this [German naval] force was going to Narvik. In spite of a report from Copenhagen that Hitler meant to seize that port,[12] it was thought by the Naval Staff that the Germans would probably turn back into the Skagerrak."

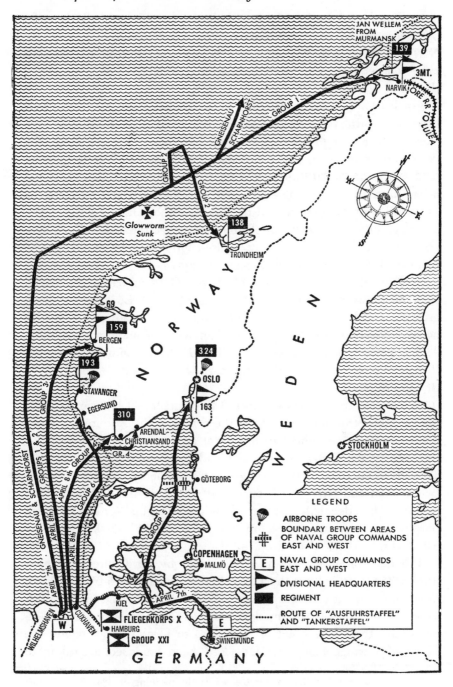

GERMAN INVASION OF NORWAY, APRIL 9, 1940.

cisions for the Admiralty. The British destroyers that had laid the mines off Bodö might have encountered the German force making for Narvik, but immediately after the *Glowworm's* encounter, the Admiralty ordered them to leave the coast and rejoin the *Renown* south of the Lofoten Islands.

For his part, Luetjens released the wounded *Hipper* and the four destroyers earmarked for Trondheim, and sailed on north. By nine o'clock that evening he was close to the entrance to the Westfiord; the destroyers went on in and proceeded unmolested to Narvik, passing west of the newly laid mine field off Bodö, while the *Gneisenau* and *Scharnhorst* moved northwesterly out into the open and very stormy ocean. There they encountered the *Renown* about four o'clock on the morning of the ninth, and a brief running battle ensued. The *Gneisenau* was hit and her main turrets and fire-control system disabled. The *Renown* then lost contact during a snow squall.

And so, as zero hour approached, the German battle groups all stood off the Norwegian harbors according to plan. Luetjens had been greatly aided by the Germans' ability to decipher many of the British naval radio messages,[13] and by the bad weather and poor visibility. All five naval groups entered their allotted harbors unmolested by the British, though the Bergen group narrowly escaped detection by a British cruiser force.

Indeed, as late as noon on April 8 the British still had not grasped the Germans' true intentions.* On the contrary, the Admiralty's viewpoint had remained glued to the naval aspects of the situation, and this is why the British troops that had been embarked for Narvik, Trondheim, Bergen, and Stavanger were hurriedly disembarked between noon and two o'clock on the afternoon of the eighth, for the Admiralty had decided [14] "that every ship was needed for strictly naval purposes and that in any case no expedition should be risked until the naval situation was cleared up."

This decision appears to have been taken by Mr. Churchill as First Lord without consulting the Prime Minister or War Cabinet.[15] Even discounting the advantages of hindsight, it seems astonishingly shortsighted. The fleet was in any case immeasurably superior to the Germans, and the whole point of "R.4" was to forestall and exploit the threat of German landings. Had "R.4" been launched according to

---

* Halder noted in his diary at ten o'clock on the morning of April 8 the report of his chief intelligence officer that apparently "the enemy is not aware of anything as yet."

plan, there would have been promising opportunity of success at Narvik, and even some hope at Trondheim and Bergen.

Ironically, no sooner had the mistake been made than the first real light was shed on the German plan. Even as the debarkation decision was being reached, the Polish submarine *Orzel,* patrolling the Skagerrak, challenged and sank off the Norwegian coast at Lillesand one of the ships of the first *Seetransportstaffel*—the *Rio de Janeiro,* carrying troops, horses, and supplies to Bergen.* Soldiers were picked up by Norwegian fishing boats and, when brought ashore and interrogated, declared that they were en route to "protect" Bergen. When this occurred, Jodl for one assumed that the mask had been torn off,[16] but reception and appreciation of the information at Oslo and London were slow, and no generally effective warning to the British or Norwegian forces resulted.

And so it came about that not only the troop-carrying warships but most of the first *Seetransportstaffel* as well reached their target ports on schedule. The *Ausfuhrstaffel* and the advance tankers, however, did not share in the good fortune. They were delayed during their passage north by the slowness, calculated or not,[17] of the Norwegians † in furnishing pilots for the long passage through the Leads. None of the ships from Germany reached Narvik, and only one arrived, four days late, at Trondheim.‡ Only the big tanker from Murmansk, the *Jan Wellem,* arrived on schedule at Narvik, while the sinking of the other

---

* The *Orzel* was one of two submarines that escaped from Poland to Britain in the first days of the war. In addition to the *Rio de Janeiro,* the smallest of the ships for Oslo (the *Antares*) was sunk by an English submarine. Bergen did not fare well; the *Rio* was the largest of the three ships allocated there, and one of the other two ran aground on the Swedish coast and had to put into Oslo instead; the third reached Bergen safely.

† Raeder thought it due to a "stiffening" of the Norwegian attitude, but it may well be that the lack of pilots was because many Norwegian pilots had been hired by the British and had left Norway. However that may be, Raeder continued to complain that the operation had been seriously disadvantaged by the two-day delay (April 7 to 9) ordered by Hitler. In retrospect, however, the importance of this factor is speculative at most. Better weather on the sixth and seventh than on the eighth and ninth might have greatly assisted British detection and interception of the assault groups.

‡ Of the three freighters for Narvik, the *Rauenfels* was sunk by a British destroyer on April 10 at the entrance of the Narvik fiord; the *Baerenfels* was so delayed en route that she put into Bergen on April 10, where she was unloaded, and was sunk four days later by British aircraft; the *Alster* was captured by an English warship on April 10 in the Westfiord. Of the three for Trondheim, the *São Paolo* was sunk by a mine off Bergen on the tenth; the *Main* was sunk on the ninth off Haugesund by a Norwegian torpedo boat; and the *Levante* made Trondheim safely on April 13. The single ship for Stavanger, the *Roda,* was sunk on the ninth by the Norwegian destroyer *Aeger.*

tanker for Narvik (the *Kattegat*, out of Wilhelmshaven) had, as will be seen,* extremely costly consequences for the Germans.

But in terms of the operation as a whole, these transport losses were insignificant. The landings were successfully accomplished on schedule at every target port, and only at Narvik were the Germans hard-pressed thereafter. Naval losses, however, were very heavy, and this was the main price the Germans paid for the conquest of Norway in a month and Denmark in less than a day.

The Conquest of Denmark

Since the Danish forces were incapable of serious resistance, the crucial question was whether King Christian and the government would accept the fact of occupation and co-operate with the German authorities or would flee the country or engage in some form of passive resistance. To achieve the former was a task for diplomacy as well as arms, and in this instance the collaboration between the Wehrmacht and the Wilhelmstrasse was harmonious and effective.

The chief of staff of the German task force for Denmark, Generalmajor Kurt Himer, had had prewar diplomatic experience as military attaché at Warsaw. On April 6 he was carefully briefed by Weizsaecker and other Foreign Office experts, and on the seventh he took the train to Copenhagen in civilian clothes, accompanied by a Foreign Office functionary carrying the general's uniform as diplomatic baggage, and a top-secret letter for the German Minister in Denmark, Cecil von Renthe-Fink.

For security reasons this letter was not to be delivered to the Minister until eleven o'clock on the evening of April 8. Himer spent the intervening hours reconnoitering the Copenhagen harbor, making sure that there would be an open pier the following morning, and procuring a truck to transport a heavy radio transmitter. In the meantime, the motorship *Hansestadt Danzig* had embarked a battalion of infantry at Travemuende and by the evening of the eighth was approaching Copenhagen harbor.†

When Renthe-Fink opened his letter and learned what was afoot he,

* *Infra*, pp. 126–28. The *Kattegat* scuttled herself off Narvik upon being sighted by the Norwegian naval auxiliary *Nordkap*. Her sister ship *Skagerrak*, headed for Trondheim, was still at sea on April 14, when she was challenged by an English cruiser and was sunk by her own crew.

† The *Hansestadt Danzig* was accompanied by the ice-breaker *Stettin* and two patrol boats. These ships were designated Group VIII of *Weseruebung*.

together with Himer and the air attaché, set to work on the "explanations" and military demands for presentation to the Danish Foreign Minister Munch, with whom an appointment was arranged for four o'clock that morning. At that meeting, Renthe-Fink informed Munch that German troops were already moving into Denmark "to prevent an imminent British attack on Norway and Denmark"; that they were "coming as friends" but that resistance would be ruthlessly broken, and that unless the German demands were accepted at once, the consequences for Denmark would be disastrous.[18]

While Renthe-Fink was pressing this fateful decision on Munch, the *Hansestadt Danzig* was entering Copenhagen harbor. She ran safely past the fort at the harbor entrance,* and by half-past five was tied to a pier and was debarking her troops. Simultaneously, an infantry division and a motorized brigade crossed the Schleswig border and raced northward into Jutland, and another infantry division was landed from German ships at the principal Danish ports and inter-island bridges.† The large airfield at Aalborg in northern Jutland was taken by a platoon of paratroops and secured by a battalion of airborne infantry.

All this was going on in the early morning hours while the Danish King and government considered the German ultimatum. Soon Himer sent word to them that any further delay would cause the bombing of Copenhagen. Still the Danes hesitated, and Himer telephoned to his corps headquarters in Hamburg—the Danes had not yet thought to sever communications with Germany—and called for an aerial demonstration. This call very nearly led to tragedy, as the officer at Hamburg at first misunderstood Himer's request (code words were being used in the conversation) and thought that he was calling for an actual bombing.

Within a few moments German bombers roared over the Danish capital. The battalion of infantry from the *Hansestadt Danzig* had meanwhile made its way to the moated Citadel ‡ and overpowered the

---

* The Danish commandant at Fort Mittelgrund had assumed his post only four days earlier, and this perhaps contributed to the confusion and surprise that led to the passage of the German ships without a shot being fired.

† A transport and mine-sweeper (Group IX) landed one battalion at the Jutland-Fuenen bridge at Middelfart. The landing at Korsoer (western Zeeland) was accomplished from mine-sweepers and trawlers under the protection of the ancient (1906) battleship *Schleswig-Holstein*, all comprising Group VII. Two flotillas of mine-sweepers (Groups X and XI) were sent up the west coast of Jutland to secure the ports of Esbjerg and Tyboroen.

‡ The battalion commander had reconnoitered the approaches during a clandestine trip to Copenhagen in civilian clothes on April 4 and 5.

Royal Bodyguard. The King and government capitulated, and shortly after seven o'clock orders were sent out to the troops to stop the fighting.

After this, Himer's principal problems were to commence the demobilization of the Danish forces, and forestall any possibility of the King's fleeing the country. The Chief of the Danish General Staff, General Goertz, had already been captured in the Citadel, and at ten o'clock in the morning he and his subordinates reported to Himer for their instructions. King Christian made no attempt to escape and soon received Himer and Renthe-Fink. As Himer * described the meeting: [19]

The seventy-year-old King appeared inwardly shattered, although he preserved outward appearances perfectly and maintained absolute dignity during the audience. His whole body trembled. He declared that he and his government would do everything possible to keep peace and order in the country and to eliminate any friction between the German troops and the population. He wished to spare his country further misfortune and misery. General Himer replied that personally he very much regretted coming to the King on such a mission, but that he was only doing his duty as a soldier. It was Denmark's misfortune to be placed between the two great warring powers, Germany and England, and Germany wished to prevent England's plunging the country into war and devastation. We came as friends, etc. When the King then asked whether he might keep his bodyguard, General Himer replied—seconded by Minister von Renthe-Fink—that the Fuehrer would doubtless permit him to retain them. He had no doubt about it. The King was visibly relieved at hearing this. During the course of the audience, which lasted one half hour, the King became more at ease, and at its conclusion he addressed General Himer with the words: "General, may I, as an old soldier, tell you something? As soldier to soldier? You Germans have done the incredible again! One must admit that it is magnificent work!"

Barely five hours had sufficed for the practically bloodless † conquest of Denmark. The following day German planes were already operating from Aalborg, over 200 miles closer to the scene of action in Norway than their home bases in northern Germany. General Kaupisch established in Copenhagen his headquarters as Commander of German Troops in Denmark, in which capacity he was subordinate no longer to Falkenhorst in Norway, but directly to OKH. The orderly governance of the country was uninterrupted, and for the time being no German

* As a *Generalleutnant* and commander of the 46th Infantry Division, Himer was killed on the Russian front in 1942.

† The Danes suffered thirteen killed and twenty-three wounded, and there were some twenty German casualties.

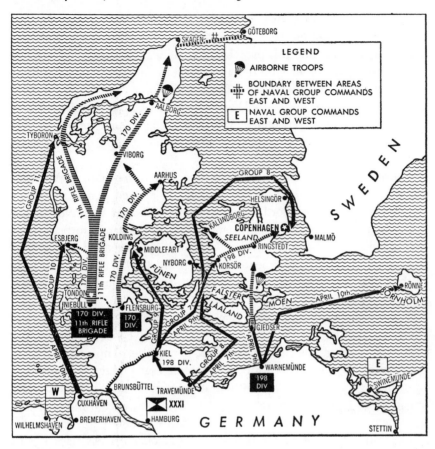

GERMAN INVASION OF DENMARK, APRIL 9, 1940.

civil administration was established. So began the German occupation of Denmark, which was to endure until the very end of the war five years later.

The Capture of Oslo

In Oslo, a quite different reception awaited the Germans. Reports of the northward procession of German men-of-war began to reach the Norwegian capital during the morning of April 8. Early that afternoon the *Rio de Janeiro* was sunk, and shortly after five o'clock the Norwegian Divisional Command at Christiansand reported the ship's military character and apparent destination. Immediately thereafter came a sharp warning from London that a German attack was imminent.

All of this was anxiously discussed at a parliamentary sitting and subsequent Cabinet meeting in Oslo that evening. The coastal fortifications were alerted, and this precaution alone was to cause the Germans heavy losses. But other vital defense measures were lost in a paralysis of surprise, fear, and indecision. The coastal forts were not authorized to lay mines in the fiords and harbor entrances. The decision to mobilize the Army was postponed. Worst of all, as events were to prove, no steps were taken to protect the airfields against capture by airborne troops.

Shortly before midnight the German task force—Group V, commanded by Konteradmiral Oskar Kummetz—arrived at the mouth of the fifty-mile-long Oslofiord, where it was challenged by a Norwegian patrol boat that raised the alarm and rammed a German torpedo boat before being sunk by gunfire. The German ships proceeded up the fiord in single line, the *Bluecher* leading. Fog protected them from the forts in the outer and broader part of the fiord, and the mine field—the key defense of that area—had not been laid.

Some minutes before five o'clock, as dawn was just breaking, the *Bluecher,* followed closely by the *Luetzow* and *Emden,* reached the narrowest part of the fiord at Drobak, some fifteen miles from Oslo, guarded by the Oscarsborg fort of Crimean War vintage. Hoping that the Norwegians would yield without a fight, and under orders to press ahead at all costs, Kummetz decided to risk the passage but was met with heavy and accurate fire from the fort's twenty-eight-centimeter Krupp guns. Fires were started on the *Bluecher*'s decks, laden with army ammunition, aerial bombs, and motor transport with full gasoline tanks. Then she was twice hit by torpedoes launched from the fort, and her engines were knocked out. The stricken cruiser managed to anchor out of range of the Oscarsborg but the fires could not be controlled, and at about half past seven—three hours after she had been due to reach Oslo harbor—the *Bluecher* exploded and capsized. In the icy water covered with flaming oil losses were heavy, but the greater part of the crew and the army "passengers" were able to swim ashore.

The *Bluecher* was not only the flagship of Group V but also carried the staff of the 163rd Infantry Division and its commander, Generalmajor Erwin Engelbrecht, who was to take charge in Oslo pending Falkenhorst's arrival. Both Kummetz and Engelbrecht made shore safely but were in no position to exercise command,* which was tempo-

* The survivors of the *Bluecher* were taken prisoner by the Norwegians but were freed a few hours later when German troops captured the harbor fortifications.

rarily assumed by the *Luetzow's* * commander, Kapitaen zur See August Thiele. Damaged but not disabled by fire from the Oscarsborg, the *Luetzow* withdrew from its range. Rendered cautious by the fear of mines, to which the *Bluecher's* fate was at first attributed, and uncertain of the situation at Oslo, where Group V was now overdue, Thiele turned back a few miles and at about nine o'clock in the morning the German ships were able to land the army troops (about two battalions) on the east bank of the Oslofiord at Sonsbukten, some twenty miles from Oslo. Assault units could then be dispatched to take the Norwegian forts by land, supported by Luftwaffe bombers. The Drobak forts were captured during the evening of April 9, and the following morning the *Luetzow, Emden,* and other vessels of Group V were able to pass through to Oslo.

In that unhappy city, the voice of its approaching fate had been audible in the form of naval gunfire as soon as Group V entered the Oslofiord. Air-raid sirens screamed and the city was blacked out. The Norwegian Cabinet went into midnight session, which was still in progress when the German Minister, Dr. Curt Braeuer, arrived shortly before five o'clock in the morning and presented the German ultimatum to the Norwegian Foreign Minister, Dr. Halvdan Koht.

Dr. Braeuer was a diplomat of the old school and did not relish his assignment. Like Renthe-Fink in Denmark, he had been kept in the dark about his country's intentions until late in the evening of April 8. Earlier that day Falkenhorst's operations officer, Oberstleutnant Pohlman, had come secretly to Oslo carrying Braeuer's instructions. When the seals were broken, Braeuer was all but stunned. Perhaps he did not carry out his mission with the ruthless forcefulness that was expected of him. Certainly this was the judgment of Hitler and Raeder, and Braeuer was to pay dearly for their poor opinion of his performance.

However that may be, the Norwegian Cabinet showed no disposition to capitulate, and after a brief consultation Koht gave answer: "We will not submit voluntarily, and war is already going on." The decision was courageous, but its execution slow and clumsy. Only a partial mobilization of the Army was ordered, and the call-up was by mail rather than radio, so that the men were not expected at their centers until April 11. No doubt the military situation was already beyond redemption, but this was no way to meet a *Blitzkrieg*.

---

* The *Luetzow's* presence in Group V was fortuitous. It had been planned to send her with the *Hipper* to Trondheim (Group II), but because of engine trouble she was given the shorter voyage to Oslo.

Indeed, had the German attack gone according to plan, the entire government and the Royal Family might well have been captured on the morning of April 9. But the Oscarsborg torpedoes that sank the *Bluecher* gave the capital a few hours' reprieve, and at about half past seven the Royal Family, the Cabinet, most members of the Storting, and a group of civil servants fled by train to Hamar, some seventy miles to the north. The government was thus temporarily preserved, but Oslo was left in leaderless confusion and bewilderment.

When this occurred, the only German "forces" in the capital were the naval and air attachés with their tiny staffs, and Oberstleutnant Pohlman. The naval attaché, Korvettenkapitaen Schreiber, had been at the waterfront since early morning, with one of his junior officers out on the water in a small pilot boat, vainly awaiting the ships of Group V. The air attaché, Hauptmann Spiller, was at the Oslo-Fornebu airport awaiting the arrival of German airborne troops. Shortly after seven o'clock Pohlman informed Falkenhorst by radio that Group V had not reached Oslo and that the Norwegian government considered itself at war. Within an hour German planes were over the harbor, and by nine o'clock parachute troops and transport planes loaded with infantry were landing at Fornebu, more than three hours earlier than their planned arrival.

Overpowered and surprised as the Norwegians were, a timely concentration of forces at Fornebu could have made the Germans' capture of the airport a very bloody business. As it was, the Germans lost a few planes to antiaircraft fire, but there was little organized resistance on the ground or in the air. Nineteen Curtiss fighters that the Norwegians had recently received from the United States were still in their crates.

A few German assault units were landed by bombers even before the paratroops, whose planes had been delayed by fog, arrived. Pohlman took command, and by half past nine Fornebu was in German hands. Junkers 52 transports then brought in about six companies of infantry, and at noon Pohlman risked an entry into the city. His forces were still so small that they could easily have been rushed and overwhelmed, but the populace was stunned and leaderless, and the German troops, though green,* behaved with great aplomb. Soon the most important points had been occupied, and the playing of a German military band helped to purvey a feeling of calm confidence.

---

* The 163rd Infantry Division, like the divisions that occupied Denmark, was of the seventh mobilization wave and had been formed only four months earlier.

Braeuer now resumed the diplomatic offensive, with a public appeal to the Norwegian government to reopen negotiations, on the basis that Norway's political and territorial integrity would be respected. At Hamar, where the Storting had reconvened, there was increasing gloom as the events at Narvik, Bergen, Trondheim, and Copenhagen became known. During the afternoon of April 9 the government had moved to Elverum, closer to the Swedish frontier, and before the Storting adjourned it approved the resumption of peace discussions with Braeuer.

Fortunately, it was also decided (on the insistence of the Inspector-General of Infantry, Colonel Ruge, who was appointed Commander-in-Chief the following day) that the road from Hamar to Elverum should be barricaded and defended with the two infantry battalions that were available. For despite Braeuer's overtures, the two companies of German parachute troops that had helped to capture Fornebu had taken off for Hamar in motor buses under the command of the air attaché, Hauptmann Spiller, hoping to raid the Norwegian headquarters and capture the King. In the skirmish at the barricade Spiller was mortally wounded; his force was driven back and returned to Oslo.

Despite this far from reassuring episode, King Haakon and Dr. Koht received Braeuer at Elverum on the following day, April 10. But had there otherwise been any possibility of agreement, it was now shattered by the emergence of Quisling, who had promptly assumed governmental authority in Oslo and had broadcast an order to cancel the mobilization and cease resistance. With that total lack of touch that invariably characterized German efforts to effect a "peaceful" occupation, Berlin thereupon directed Braeuer to insist that the King accept Quisling as the head of his government. This outraged King and Cabinet alike, since Quisling was already regarded as a traitor, and caused the immediate collapse of the negotiations. During his return journey to Oslo that evening, Braeuer was informed by a telephone call from Koht that Quisling could not be accepted and that Norway "would continue to resist so far as possible." [20]

Back in Oslo, Braeuer continued his efforts to find an avenue to peace by conferring with the highly respected Evangelical Bishop of Oslo, Eivind Berggrav, and by emphasizing to Berlin the impossibility of selling Quisling to the Norwegian government. These efforts came to nothing; Hitler and Raeder were furious,* and on April 11 the

---

* In a supplementary note to his war diary, dated April 22, 1940, Raeder wrote: [21] "Seizure of the Norwegian government and political action in general failed completely. . . . the main reason was the fact that the situation was han-

royal headquarters (then at Nybergsund) was savagely but unsuccessfully attacked by the Luftwaffe. Braeuer was recalled and retired from the diplomatic service, and soon he was in army uniform and on his way to the western front.

In the meantime, the Germans' military situation in Oslo was rapidly consolidated and reinforced. Generalmajor Engelbrecht, fresh from his dunking in the Oslofiord, arrived and set up divisional headquarters in the Hotel Continental. On the evening of April 10 General von Falkenhorst flew into Fornebu, accompanied by Admiral Hermann Boehm, who had been given command of all naval operations based on Norway. By April 11 four ships of the first *Seetransportstaffel* had reached Oslo, carrying chiefly ground crews, ammunition, and other supplies for the Luftwaffe. Within the week following the initial assault, the subsequent *Seetransportstaffeln* landed two more divisions, and the Luftwaffe brought in two additional battalions.

These convoys sustained some losses * from Allied submarines, destroyers, and aircraft, but these were wholly insufficient to jeopardize the German build-up at Oslo.[22] The Navy, however, sustained another serious blow when the *Luetzow* was torpedoed and severely damaged by a British submarine early on the morning of April 11 on her return journey. With her propellers and rudder gone, and under heavy air and surface protection, she was towed back to Kiel for repairs which laid her up for the rest of 1940. Oslo was securely in German hands, but Raeder's ships had paid dearly for its capture.

Christiansand, Stavanger, and Bergen

No more than Oslo was Christiansand any picnic for the invaders. It was just to the east of this fortified port (the headquarters of one of the six Norwegian divisional headquarters) that the steamer *Rio de Janeiro* was sunk at about noon on April 8, giving the first clear indication of the Germans' intentions, so that the defenders were on the alert.

---

dled extremely badly on the political side (Minister Braeuer). In such cases the main objective must be to arrest the government at all cost. If energetic steps had been taken it would have been quite possible to do this. . . . Quisling did not obtain the necessary support from General von Falkenhorst and Minister Braeuer. . . . Quisling was suspected [*sic!*] of high treason. . . . The Norwegian population was split into two camps. It remains to be seen whether the appointment of Terboven as Reich Commissioner and the recall of Minister Braeuer will bring any changes."

   * The sinkings in tonnage were less than 10 per cent, and the personnel losses some 2400 men, or about 2 per cent of the troops carried by sea.

Group IV, commanded by Kapitaen zur See Friedrich Rieve of the light cruiser *Karlsruhe*, arrived off the harbor at the appointed hour, but heavy fog made it impossible to enter, and when it began to clear the group was sighted by a Norwegian seaplane, which gave the alarm.

At about half past six o'clock Rieve gave the order to move in. The ships were met by heavy fire from the fortifications and twice driven off, and while taking evasive action the *Karlsruhe* almost went on the rocks. But by midmorning Luftwaffe bombers were over the forts,* and the ships gained access to the harbor.[23] Shock troops were put ashore, and by noon the harbor defenses had been captured, and all resistance overcome. By midafternoon a regimental staff and a battalion of infantry were ashore, and three ships of the first *Seetransportstaffel* arrived safely with supplies and reinforcements. In the meantime the torpedo boat *Greif* had been detached to carry a bicycle troop to the nearby town and cable station of Arendal, which was occupied without resistance.

Early in the evening, his mission accomplished, Rieve led his force out of the harbor to seek the safety of home waters. Less than an hour at sea, the *Karlsruhe* was torpedoed by the British submarine *Truant*. The cruiser was damaged past saving, and her crew were taken on the smaller ships. The *Karlsruhe* was then sunk by torpedoes from the *Greif*, and the rest of the group proceeded safely back to Kiel.

For the Luftwaffe, the big prize in southern Norway was the Sola airfield, a few miles from the ancient fishing community of Stavanger, at the southern end of the Norwegian west coast. Although it was the largest field in Norway, Sola had no permanent antiaircraft protection, and it fell to the Germans almost as easily as Aalborg in Denmark.

At about eight o'clock in the morning six German Messerschmitt 110s appeared over Sola and bombed the machine-gun emplacements that were its main protection. Parachute troops easily captured the field, and during the day transport planes brought in two infantry battalions and a regimental staff, while four ships of the *Seetransportstaffel* arrived on schedule with supplies and the rest of the regiment. In a few hours airfield, town, and harbor were secured; it was almost ridiculously easy. Simultaneously the nearby cable station at Egersund was taken without resistance by a bicycle troop brought in on the four mine-sweepers of Group VI.

Bergen, Norway's second city and port, is about 100 miles north of

* Christiansand lay well within bomber range of the airfields in northwestern Germany.

Stavanger. Compared to Oslo and the Skagerrak ports, Bergen and even Stavanger were more exposed to Allied countermeasures, and accordingly the Germans employed better-trained troops for these ocean-coast landings. The commander of the 69th Infantry Division,* Generalmajor Hermann Tittel, with his staff and some eight companies of infantry, engineers, and marine artillery were brought to Bergen on the two light cruisers and smaller ships of Group III, commanded by Konteradmiral Hubert Schmundt.

Narrowly escaping a British scouting force of cruisers and destroyers off Stavanger, Schmundt brought his group into Bergen on schedule, encountering heavy fire from the harbor fortifications that badly damaged the cruiser *Koenigsberg* and the auxiliary *Bremse*. But the Norwegians were unable to prevent troop landings from the smaller ships, and with the dawn came the Luftwaffe to help reduce the forts. Occupation of the city and the harbor defenses was completed by midmorning, and the Germans at once set to work repairing and readying the guns and fortifications to repel the Allied counterattacks that were feared to be imminent.

Late in the afternoon they came, in the form of an attack on the harbor by twelve British bombers. The German ships escaped damage, however, and an hour later, having ascertained by aerial reconnaissance that the ocean outside the harbor was momentarily clear of the enemy, Schmundt started back to Germany with the cruiser *Koeln* and the two torpedo boats, leaving the E-boats for coastal defense. The *Koenigsberg*, too, remained in the harbor for repairs, as her speed had been reduced by the hits suffered when entering the harbor. But the repairs were never made. Early the next morning fifteen Skuas of the British Fleet Air Arm struck Bergen with a dive-bombing attack that scored three direct hits on the *Koenigsberg*. She burned and sank in a few hours, the first major warship ever destroyed by enemy air attack. The *Koeln* and the torpedo boats were also attacked but reached home waters safely on April 11.

Trondheim and Narvik

Northeasterly from Bergen the Norwegian coast stretches for a thousand miles. Trondheim and Narvik are the only ports of major importance, and these were at once the chief and most hazardous targets of the German assault. Both were valuable as air and submarine

* A second-wave division of reservists, formed in August 1939.

bases, and Narvik for its rail access to the Swedish ore mines. Both were hazardous due to their great distance from home waters and the protective mantle of the Luftwaffe. Because of the rigorous terrain and climate and the prospect of isolation from the main invasion force, the OKW selected for these missions the crack Austrian regulars of the 3rd Mountain Division. It was commanded by one of Hitler's most favored officers, known to him since the old days in Munich and the "Beer-Hall *Putsch*" of 1923 [23a]—the Bavarian Generalmajor Eduard Dietl, who led one of his regiments (the 138th) into Narvik, while the other (the 139th), under Oberst Wilhelm Weiss, went to Trondheim.

After the morning encounter with the *Glowworm* on April 8, Group II—comprising the damaged heavy cruiser *Hipper* and four destroyers—parted company with Group I and steamed northwest and then southeast, to throw the British off the track. The maneuver was successful, and in the afternoon a German aerial reconnaissance found no British ships in the waters off Trondheim. At the zero hour, Kapitaen zur See Hellmuth Heye (skipper of the *Hipper*) brought his group into the fiord and ran past the outer harbor batteries at high speed and without damage. The troops were put ashore at the Trondheim piers, and the city surrendered without resistance, although the forts were not reduced until evening. The all-important Vaernes airfield, sixteen miles inland, resisted and was not captured until noon on April 10, but German seaplanes had already landed in the harbor, and an ice strip was speedily improvised for transport aircraft.

Nevertheless, the Germans' situation in Trondheim was unenviable. None of the ships of the *Ausfuhrstaffel* had arrived,* so that the troops were without heavy weapons and the warships were short of fuel for the return voyage. By scouring the city and commandeering oil from the merchant ships in the harbor, the *Hipper* was enabled to depart on the evening of the tenth, to rendezvous with the *Gneisenau* and *Scharnhorst* off the Shetland Islands. She was followed a day later by two of the destroyers, and all of these ships had returned safely to Wilhelmshaven by the evening of April 12. Trondheim was in German hands, but the invaders were dangerously exposed to Allied counterattacks and entirely dependent on the Luftwaffe for reinforcements and supplies.

If the situation at Trondheim was critical, at Narvik it soon became desperate. The initial assault, to be sure, was highly successful. Nar-

---

* The tanker *Skagerrak* and two of the three freighters for Trondheim were lost en route; the third and smallest freighter made port safely on April 13.

rowly escaping the British destroyers that had been laying mines off Bodö, Kommodore Fritz Bonte led the ten destroyers of Group I on schedule into the thirty-mile-long Ofotfiord, near the head of which lay the town, with its rail head and harbor. It was erroneously supposed (by the British as well as the Germans) that there were coastal batteries at the mouth of the Ofotfiord, and two destroyers, each carrying a company of the mountain troops, were told off to land the soldiers for assaulting these supposed fortifications. A third destroyer was to capture the outlying Norwegian observation posts and watch-boats, patrol the entrance to the fiord, and assist a fourth destroyer that had fallen behind and was making very heavy weather. Further in, Bonte detached three more of his ships, whose troops were to capture the Norwegian regimental depot and military supplies at Elvegaard, a few miles northeast of Narvik on the Herjangsfiord. Bonte himself on the flag destroyer *Wilhelm Heidkamp* (on which Dietl was also traveling), with the remaining two ships, proceeded directly to the Narvik harbor, where they arrived about six o'clock on the morning of April 9.

The principal naval defenses of the harbor were the guns of two old Norwegian ironclads, the *Eidsvold* and the *Norge*. These had been warned by the watch-boats that warships were approaching, but the foul weather made identification difficult and here, as in the other ports, the Norwegians were undone by their newly received orders not to fire on Allied ships. Accordingly, when the destroyers came in sight of the harbor, the *Eidsvold* fired a warning shot and signaled for identification. Bonte stopped and sent an officer in a launch to demand surrender. When the *Eidsvold*'s commander replied that he would resist, the launch fired a warning signal. Without awaiting the parley launch's return, and after a hurried word with Dietl, Bonte ordered the *Wilhelm Heidkamp* into firing position. Her torpedoes blew the *Eidsvold* in two and the ironclad sank at once, with only eight survivors.[*] The *Norge* then opened fire but was immediately torpedoed and sunk, with equally heavy losses, by the destroyer *Bernd von Arnim*.[24]

The three destroyers that had entered the harbor (*Wilhelm Heidkamp, Bernd von Arnim,* and *Georg Thiele*) were now able to de-

---

[*] The propriety of Bonte's and Dietl's conduct has become the subject of bitter controversy. The German defense is, in substance, that necessity knows no law and that, parley or no parley, Bonte could not risk a salvo from the *Eidsvold*. To this Dietl's biographers have added the implausible justification that the slow and unwieldy but heavily gunned ironclad was endeavoring to ram the *Wilhelm Heidkamp*.

bark their troops at the town piers. The town was soon overrun with German soldiers. Dietl himself led a motor caravan through the main streets and soon encountered the town commandant, Colonel Sundlo.[25] This officer was a strong adherent of Quisling, and it did not take him long to decide that Narvik should be surrendered without resistance.* Two companies of Norwegian troops fled down the ore railroad toward the Swedish border; the rest were disarmed. Shortly after eight o'clock in the morning, Bonte was able to inform Wilhelmshaven that Narvik was taken.

For Dietl now the critical problem was supplies, and for Bonte fuel for the long voyage home. None of the ships of the *Ausfuhrstaffel* from Germany had arrived, or ever did. For Dietl's troops, the problem was much eased by the Norwegian weapons and supplies captured at Elvegaard. So too, both Dietl and Bonte were delighted to find waiting for them in Narvik harbor the tanker *Jan Wellem*, which, by special arrangement with the Russians,[26] had come from Murmansk.† But the *Jan Wellem* could refuel only two destroyers at a time, and each pair took seven to eight hours. By midnight only the three destroyers that had first entered the harbor had been refueled, and two of them were still overhauling their engines. In the ocean outside the fiord, the *Gneisenau* and *Scharnhorst* were counting on the destroyers to screen them on the way home.

Accordingly, Bonte held his ready ships at Narvik, planning to depart in greater or full force the following evening, April 10. By then, as events proved, it was too late. The sinking of the other expected tanker, the arrival of which would have doubled the refueling speed, was a fatal mischance for the Germans.

Early on the morning of April 9, five British destroyers under Captain B. A. W. Warburton-Lee had been dispatched to patrol the entrance to the Westfiord, and late that afternoon it was learned that a force of German destroyers had been sighted making for Narvik. The

---

* Sundlo's subsequent justification for his conduct was that "Narvik was not supposed to be defended by infantry," and that once the ironclads were sunk, resistance would have simply caused unnecessary bloodshed. However, he had had ample warning of the German approach, and had he been bent on resistance, would never have allowed himself to be trapped in the town. He could have harassed the German landings, destroyed the supplies at Elvegaard that became invaluable to the isolated Germans, and then, as Dietl himself did later in the face of superior British forces, could have fallen back into the mountains and maintained contact with and a flow of information to the Norwegian divisional command at Harstad (some thirty-five miles to the northwest on the island of Hinnöy).

† More accurately, from an anchorage at Sapadnaia near Murmansk which had been made available to the Germans, who referred to it as "Basis Nord."

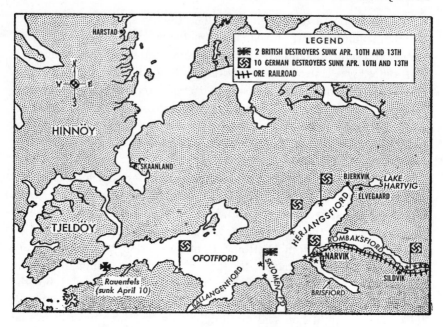

NARVIK AND ENVIRONS.

British Admiralty left to the commander the decision whether to attack at once or await reinforcements. Warburton-Lee chose not to wait, and took his ships into the Ofotfiord shortly after midnight. The bad weather that slowed their approach also prevented their detection, and their appearance in Narvik harbor at half past four o'clock on the morning of April 10 was a complete surprise to the Germans.*

Five of the German destroyers were in the harbor as the British entered. Two were refueling alongside the *Jan Wellem,* two (including the *Wilhelm Heidkamp*) were lying at anchor, and a fifth had entered the harbor just ahead of the British and was steaming toward the piers. The British let fly with a salvo of fifteen torpedoes. The very first one made a shambles of the *Wilhelm Heidkamp* and killed Kommodore Bonte. He was the first German naval officer of flag rank to die in action in World War II. The other anchored destroyer (*Anton Schmidt*) was hit twice and sank at once, and the remaining three were all damaged, one severely.

---

* The U-51, on guard in the outer fiord, had sighted them the previous evening steaming *away* from the entrance, but did not observe their entrance several hours later. The German destroyer that had been on patrol returned to the harbor a few minutes before the British arrived.

The weather was so bad that the Germans at first thought they were under air attack. The British destroyers soon made a second attack, in the course of which all the German freighters in the harbor except the *Jan Wellem* were destroyed. Then, the German force being plainly too large to warrant a landing attempt, they withdrew down the Ofotfiord.

Shortly, however, they encountered the other five German destroyers emerging from the side fiords. The German ships were all larger and heavier-gunned than their opponents, and their fire sank one and forced the beaching of another British destroyer.* But the Germans were all short of fuel and soon had to put back to Narvik. On their way out, the British dealt the Narvik expedition another severe blow by sinking the *Ausfuhrstaffel* freighter *Rauenfels*, which was just entering the Ofotfiord.

Command of Group I now devolved upon Fregatten Kapitaen Erich Bey. Informed of the morning's events, Admiral Saalwaechter of Western Group Command ordered all seaworthy destroyers to refuel at once and depart at dusk. That evening (April 10) Bey set out with two destroyers, but as they emerged from the Ofotfiord the Germans sighted a cruiser and two destroyers patrolling offshore. Regarding a break-through as impossible, Bey put back to Narvik.†

The jig was up and Bey apparently thought as much, for he did not again attempt an escape. Four destroyers were ready by April 11, but Bey informed Saalwaechter that the Allied patrols made any attempt futile. On the evening of the twelfth a U-boat observed searchlights and intense destroyer activity in the Westfiord, and British planes from the aircraft carrier *Furious* attacked Narvik, without notable success.

Early in the morning of April 13 Bey received information from Wilhelmshaven that a large ship and seven or eight destroyers were in the Westfiord. These were in fact the 33,500-ton battleship *Warspite* and nine destroyers, under the command of Vice-Admiral W. J. Whitworth, heading for Narvik. Bey sent two of his ships to the mouth of the fiord, one to scout and the other to hide alongshore for a surprise attack.‡ But these were spotted by the *Warspite*'s scout plane, and

* The beached destroyer was the leader (the *Hardy*), carrying Captain Warburton-Lee, who died of his wounds shortly after he was carried ashore. He was posthumously awarded the Victoria Cross, the first of World War II.

† Saalwaechter ordered that a break-through be attempted at all costs, but the message reached Bey too late for action that night.

‡ This was the *Erich Koellner*, which had been damaged by running aground on April 11 and was no longer readily maneuverable. The other unseaworthy destroyer, *Diether von Roeder*, remained tied to the pier at Narvik.

as the British fleet drove into the fiord shortly after noon the concealed destroyer was easily sunk and the other driven back toward Narvik harbor, from which Bey now emerged with the rest of his squadron.

The *Warspite,* a veteran of Jutland, carried fifteen-inch guns, and the British destroyers outnumbered the Germans three to two. The Germans fought their ships with the courage of desperation but were speedily overwhelmed. One German destroyer was sunk in the Ofot-fiord, another foundered on the rocks in the Herjangsfiord, and a third sank at the quay in Narvik.* The other four fled eastward up the narrow Rombaksfiord. One of these managed to torpedo and sink a pursuing British destroyer, but all were nearly out of ammunition. The Germans then ran their ships on the rocks at the end of the Rombaks-fiord,† and the crews struggled ashore and into the hills, making for the nearby ore railway.

By late afternoon all ten German destroyers had been sunk or totally destroyed. The British ships remained in the fiord overnight picking up survivors from the destroyers they had lost and the crews of British merchantmen that had been caught in the harbor. Admiral Whitworth considered landing, but thought it too risky. The next morning (April 14) he left the fiord, simultaneously informing the Admiralty that the Germans ashore were disorganized and stunned, and that the main British landing force assigned to Narvik [27] should come and occupy the town without delay. In the event, however, the British follow-up was far more cautious than Whitworth's counsel.[28]

So Narvik was taken, at the cost of half Raeder's entire destroyer strength.‡ From the hills surrounding the harbor and the fiords, Dietl and his men had watched with helpless fascination the extraordinary naval drama that unfolded before them. Never in modern times had so heavy a battleship as the *Warspite* ventured a sustained attack in such narrow waters. The thunder of her guns echoed through the mountains for miles around, and when she and her escorting destroyers had finished there was not a German ship afloat in the harbor except the *Jan Wellem,* which miraculously survived both attacks. Her cargo and ship's stores were a major boon to Dietl, whose force was now unex-

---

* These were respectively the *Erich Giese, Hermann Kuenne,* and *Diether von Roeder.* Gunfire from the last-named had earlier damaged and caused temporary grounding of the British destroyer *Cossack,* of *Altmark* fame.

† These were the *Georg Thiele, Hans Luedemann, Bernd von Arnim,* and *Wolfgang Zenker.* Their ruined hulls may still be seen where their crews left them.

‡ Of twenty-two destroyers at the outbreak of the war, two were sunk by a German plane in February 1940, and ten at Narvik.

pectedly doubled by the crews of the sunken German destroyers but who now faced a long and hazardous period of isolation, except by air, from his source of supplies and reinforcements.

Namsos, Aandalsnes, and the Gudbrandsdal

The departure of the *Warspite* from Narvik on April 14 marked both the end of the first phase of the Norwegian campaign and the beginning of the second, for British troops landed the same day at the Norwegian military base at Harstad, some thirty-five miles northwest of Narvik. However, their progress toward Narvik was difficult and slow, and for the next two weeks the principal scene of action shifted southward.

After the German landings had been achieved, the surviving fleet units had returned to home waters, and it had become apparent that the Norwegians would resist and the Allies would intervene, the Wehrmacht faced three principal military tasks in Norway. First, they had to consolidate their position in southern Norway and join their forces in Oslo, Christiansand, Stavanger, and Bergen. Next, they had to effect a rapid build-up of air and ground strength in Oslo, and organize a striking force that could force its way north through Lillehammer and the Gudbrandsdal Valley and link up with Oberst Weiss's regiment in Trondheim. Finally, they had to find means to reinforce Dietl in Narvik, over 400 miles north of Trondheim. And all of this had to be done in the face of whatever resistance the Norwegians could offer and such countermeasures by land, sea, or air as the Allies might undertake.

The first of these tasks was accomplished without great difficulty. After the first day of fighting the British surface fleet did not venture far south of Trondheim, for fear of the Luftwaffe. Their scouting force off Bergen had already been attacked from the air, with some damage to cruisers and the loss of a destroyer. Furthermore, a dive bomber had landed an 1100-pound bomb squarely on the deck of the battleship *Rodney;* the damage and casualties were surprisingly light, but the episode had a very cautioning effect at the Admiralty. Thereafter, offensive missions in the waters off southern Norway and in the Skagerrak were left almost entirely to submarines and airplanes.

Thus deprived of any hope of British aid on the ground,* and in-

* On the morning of April 9 the British chiefs of staff discussed the recapture of Bergen, but the Luftwaffe's attacks on the fleet and the rapid march of events soon convinced them that Bergen was out of the question and that their efforts should be focused on Trondheim and Narvik.

vaded even before full mobilization had been ordered, the Norwegian garrisons in southern Norway could do little to check the German on-rush. By sea and air German reinforcements poured into Oslo, and by April 14 the region east of the city had been overrun and some 3000 Norwegian troops were pushed across the Swedish border. On the next day the Norwegian divisional commander at Christiansand capitulated.* This opened the way for supplies and reinforcements from Oslo to Christiansand and Stavanger, and virtually ended the resistance in southern Norway, except at Bergen.

Here the Norwegian divisional commander, General Steffens, had been able to mobilize a full brigade at his base at Voss, some fifty miles inland in the mountains. With only the two battalions that had been landed by Group III the German commander, Generalmajor Tittel, was temporarily outnumbered. By April 17, however, another German division was arriving in Christiansand and Stavanger to take over occupational and line-of-communications duties. The assault troops that had taken Stavanger could now be sent to reinforce Tittel at Bergen, as were also some units from Denmark. Even so it took the Germans until the end of April to clean up the last Norwegian resistance north and east of Bergen.

In the meantime, Falkenhorst had deployed his forces around Oslo for the northward push toward Trondheim. The main drive was to be launched by Generalleutnant Richard Pellengahr's 196th Division, from east of Oslo through Hamar and Lillehammer up the Gudbrandsdal, and through Elverum up the Oesterdal. Pellengahr's right flank was protected by the Swedish frontier, and his left by Engelbrecht's four-regiment task force, which struck northwesterly from Oslo in the general direction of Bergen.

The sparse roads, narrow valleys, and deep April snows of Norway made it impossible for the Germans to move in more than regimental strength. The terrain favored defensive operations, and the Norwegians, though weak and disorganized, were able to slow Pellengahr's advance by blowing the bridges and blocking the tunnels. By the night of April 19, however, he had taken Hamar and Elverum, and to the west Engelbrecht had made comparable progress. North of Hamar, Pellengahr now confronted far stronger opposition than the Norwegians had yet offered, and the war's first direct encounters between German and British troops were about to take place.

* There were six Norwegian divisional commands: two near Oslo, and one each at Christiansand, Bergen, Trondheim, and Harstad near Narvik.

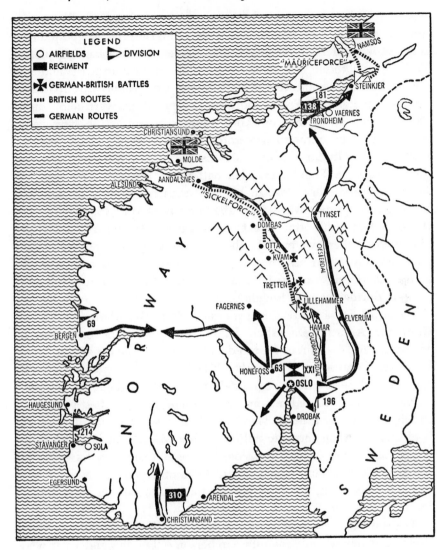

GERMAN ADVANCE THROUGH CENTRAL NORWAY,
APRIL 15–MAY 2, 1940.

On April 9, as soon as the Allies realized that Trondheim and Bergen were in German hands, their military staffs suggested the coastal towns of Namsos and Aandalsnes as possible landing places. The first of these lies some 80 air-line miles northeast and the second 100 miles southwest of Trondheim; the distances by road and rail are much greater. Preparations for these landings were commenced almost immediately, but on April 13 pressure from the Norwegian government, and optimism generated by the *Warspite*'s successful invasion of the Ofotfiord, caused serious consideration to be given to a direct attack on Trondheim. The matter was canvassed for nearly a week and came very close to being attempted. Rightly or wrongly, however, the project was finally abandoned on April 19, largely from the same fear of air attacks that had already restricted Allied fleet activities to northern waters.* In the meantime, advance parties of seamen and Royal Marines had been put ashore at Namsos on April 14 and at Aandalsnes on April 17, and the main landing forces followed these in during the next few days.

By April 20 a British brigade and three battalions of French Chasseurs Alpins were ashore at Namsos under the command of Major General Sir Adrian Carton de Wiart, the whole expedition being known as "Mauriceforce." Another brigade under Brigadier H. de R. Morgan had been landed at Aandalsnes, and was called "Sickleforce."

Namsos and Aandalsnes are both small communities with very rudimentary port facilities. They could not possibly sustain large-scale landings, and their intrinsic military value was almost nil. The Allies hoped, nevertheless, that they could serve as temporary bases for an assault on Trondheim, which was to be captured by a pincers movement. In the event, however, Trondheim was never seriously threatened.

There were many reasons for the failure of these expeditions. Allied strategic planning was woefully cumbersome. London and Paris were stunned by the speed and success of the German invasion; changes of plan were so frequent that it was impossible to aim and co-ordinate solid counterpunches. The troops dispatched to Norway were underequipped to start with and were trans-shipped so frequently that weapons and stores parted company with the men who were supposed to use them. It is a measure of the clumsy Allied improvisation

* On April 17 the cruiser *Suffolk* put inshore off Stavanger to bombard the Sola airfield. She was the immediate recipient of seven hours' attack from the air, in the course of which she suffered a direct hit from an 1100-pound bomb, and arrived badly damaged at Scapa Flow the following morning.

that Lt. General H. R. S. Massy, who on April 22 was appointed to over-all command of the two expeditions, never left London because events so rapidly outstripped his plans. As a consequence Mauriceforce and Sickleforce could communicate with each other only through London.

Had all these disabilities been overcome, it is still doubtful that the Allies could have held their ground in the Trondheim area. The Germans had committed far larger forces to *Weseruebung* than were readily available to the Allies, and their build-up opportunities at Oslo were overwhelmingly superior. Above all, however, it was the air that doomed in advance the British effort. The Norwegian campaign was "perhaps the first real example in history of the impotence of superior naval forces against efficient land-based air forces even when the bombers have to strike several hundred miles from base," writes Asher Lee.[29] An equally significant demonstration was the helplessness of ground forces alone against an opponent enjoying effective air cover and support, a lesson the Germans themselves were later to learn at deadly cost.

Luftwaffe planning for the Norwegian campaign was excellent, both operationally and organizationally. The ground crews were indefatigable, and flexible in adapting themselves to the climatic rigors of the latitude and season. In Denmark, the Aalborg airfield was in use within forty-eight hours of its capture. In less than a week, the Luftwaffe was established at the Oslo, Stavanger, and Christiansand fields, and seaplanes were operating from Trondheim harbor. For the unified command of all Luftwaffe operations in Norway, a new air fleet headquarters—Luftflotte 5—was established on April 12 at Oslo. The commander-in-chief during its first three weeks was the second-ranking officer of the Luftwaffe, Generaloberst Erhard Milch, who apparently felt the itch for a field command after so many years of administrative work. Shortly before the western offensive Milch returned to Germany [30] and was replaced in Norway by General Hans-Juergen Stumpff.

In sharp contrast, the British expedition to Norway ("R.4") was originally planned with no air components whatsoever, on the assumption that the landings would be in a friendly country. When *Weseruebung* pulled the rug from under "R.4," it was too late to remedy the fatal deficiency. A week after the landings at Namsos and Aandalsnes, a single squadron of Gladiators was flown in to operate from a frozen lake some thirty miles inland from Aandalsnes, but within two days the Germans had bombed the lake past usability and destroyed or disabled nearly all of the Gladiators. Apart from this desperate and abortive effort, Mauriceforce and Sickleforce had no air support other than occasional sorties from aircraft carriers and from the Orkney Islands, over 500 miles away.

At Namsos, Mauriceforce totally lacked even field artillery and anti-aircraft guns when it was put ashore on April 17. Nevertheless General Carton de Wiart advanced boldly southward toward Trondheim. That afternoon Steinkjer was reached; by April 19 the British had joined forces with the two battalions of Norwegian troops in the vicinity, and their forward patrols were at the foot of the main Trondheimsfiord, about thirty miles from Trondheim itself. But they did not remain long.

On April 20 Namsos was bombed all day long by German aircraft. The town was set ablaze, and the slender port facilities badly damaged. General Carton de Wiart saw the handwriting on the wall and reported that night to the War Office that he saw "little chance of carrying out decisive or, indeed, any operations, unless enemy air activity is considerably restricted." The bombing continued on the twenty-first, and the next day the Germans finally made serviceable the Vaernes airfield twenty miles east of Trondheim, which greatly improved their situation both for offensive bombing and for the receipt of reinforcements by air.

These, indeed, had begun to reach Trondheim as early as April 18. On the twentieth, Generalmajor Kurt Woytasch of the 181st Infantry Division arrived and took command, and the next day several battalions of his division were brought in. Oberst Weiss's mountain regulars could now be used to strike at the British. On April 21, supported by one each of the destroyers and torpedo boats that had remained in Trondheim, they drove back the British and Norwegian patrols in a series of skirmishes. The Germans were better trained and enjoyed total artillery and air superiority. Steinkjer was heavily bombed, and the following day the town was evacuated and Mauriceforce fell back on Namsos.

Except for patrol actions, that was the end of the ground fighting around Namsos. The "pincers" strategy against Trondheim had obviously and abysmally failed; on April 27 the Supreme War Council in London decided to evacuate both Namsos and Aandalsnes, and orders to this effect reached Carton de Wiart the next day.

Southeast of Aandalsnes, Sickleforce had fought longer, harder,*

---

* The losses (killed, missing, and taken prisoner) of Mauriceforce were 157, and of Sickleforce 1402 men.

and equally unsuccessfully.[31] Brigadier Morgan's initial landing force numbered only 1000 men, but 700 marines and seamen were already at Aandalsnes, and light antiaircraft batteries were provided. Morgan's initial orders were to secure Dombaas, an important road and rail junction 60 miles inland on the Oslo-Trondheim railroad. Once there, Sickleforce was to "operate northward and take offensive action against Germans in the Trondheim area," about 100 miles away.

Alarmed by the first British landing at Namsos and aware of the importance of Dombaas, the Germans had dropped a company of parachute troops there on the evening of April 14. But the Norwegian troops on the spot were alert and took most of the paratroopers prisoner, though a group of about sixty succeeded in blocking the road south to Oslo through the Gudbrandsdal, where Ruge's main Norwegian force was desperately struggling to block Pellengahr's advance.

Landing at Aandalsnes on the night of April 18, Morgan immediately took two companies by rail to Dombaas, and the following morning the last group of German paratroopers was brought to surrender. The route south was thus opened, and Morgan was immediately beseeched to come to Ruge's assistance. After a personal visit to the Norwegian commander's headquarters, Morgan (with War Office approval) ordered his force south from Dombaas. Thus the southern half of the proposed "pincers" against Trondheim was abandoned at the outset, and on April 20 Sickleforce found itself south of Lillehammer and nearly 140 miles from Aandalsnes, facing Pellengahr's determined advance from Hamar.

The German general's battle force comprised three infantry battalions, with supporting companies of engineers, motorized machine-gun troops and artillery, and a few light tanks. Pellengahr was an artillery officer who used his field howitzers with great skill, and his tactical air support was aggressive and effective. On April 21 he attacked in strength, breaking the Allied defenses, and on the morning of the twenty-second his troops were in Lillehammer, with a bag of several hundred British prisoners.

On April 23, two more companies having come from Aandalsnes, the British made another stand at the Tretten gorge. Early that afternoon three German tanks broke through the main British position, and soon a large part of the British force was irretrievably cut off. The remnants of Sickleforce, now reduced to nine officers and 450 men, escaped to the north in motorbuses, leaving the southern and middle reaches of the Gudbrandsdal open to Pellengahr's advance.

A second but very brief phase of the campaign now began. On April 23 and 25 a fresh brigade arrived on the scene with Major General B. G. T. Paget, newly appointed to the command of Sickleforce. Together with the remnants of Morgan's brigade, a new defensive position was established at Kvam, about thirty-five miles south of Dombaas. Barely had the dispositions been made * when the head of Pellengahr's leading column came in sight, and a brisk engagement ensued.[32] This time the British antitank guns were effective, and the Germans were held off throughout the day. The following morning, however, the Germans successfully resorted to their customary outflanking tactics, and on the evening of the twenty-sixth the British fell back a couple of miles to Kjoerem.

They were fighting better now, but General Paget was under no illusions about his prospects. Apart from superiority in numbers and heavy weapons, the Germans' air monopoly was giving them an insuperable advantage. The attempt to fly Gladiators off Lake Lesjaskog had proved a woeful failure. Aandalsnes was badly bombed on April 26. To the east in the Oesterdal, another battle group of Pellengahr's division, led by Oberst Hermann Fischer, had advanced rapidly against weak Norwegian opposition, and by April 26 was sixty miles northeast of Dombaas, threatening the route from Dombaas to Trondheim. That afternoon General Paget asked the War Office for air support, antiaircraft artillery, and a third infantry brigade. Pending their arrival, in his view, Sickleforce could not hold any position longer than two days against a determined German attack and could at best fight a series of delaying actions.

In accordance with this strategy, Kjoerem (which the Germans attacked on the morning of the twenty-seventh) was held only for a day. The next day at Otta, twelve miles back, a battalion of the Green Howards inflicted heavy casualties on the Germans, who made no effort at pursuit when the British withdrew that evening. For the Allies, this was the most successful action of the central Norwegian campaign, and it caused no little consternation in Berlin. The OKW was pressing Falkenhorst to finish his job in Norway with all possible speed, and he countered by demanding more engineer troops and motor transport. Hitler's adjutant, Oberst Schmundt, insisted that Pellengahr give a firm date for the anticipated junction with the Trondheim garrison, but

---

* In retrospect, Pellengahr was highly critical of the British decision to make a stand at Kvam, where, in his opinion, the terrain subjected them to the risk of encirclement, and the newly arrived British troops had no opportunity to accommodate themselves to the rigorous conditions before facing combat.

Pellengahr flatly refused to make any such prediction "in view of the uncertainties of the terrain and combat prospects." [33]

In fact, however, the campaign was all but at an end. On the morning of April 28 orders from London reached both Sickleforce and Maurice-force to prepare for evacuation. This came as a hard blow to General Ruge's Norwegians, who had been counting on greatly increased British support, and confronted General Paget with the difficult task of retreating a hundred miles down a single road and railway, under heavy air attack, and embarking his troops at a port that had been largely destroyed and was by now under almost constant aerial bombardment. If this were to be accomplished without heavy casualties, there was no time to be lost.

Accordingly, when Pellengahr's troops started forward again on April 29 after their battering at Otta the day before, their opponents, who had retreated by road and rail during the night, were already in Dombaas, concealed from air observation and attack. Much hampered by bridge destruction and road blocks, Pellengahr's vanguard approached Dombaas on foot on the afternoon of April 30 and were ambushed, with heavy casualties, by the British rear guard, which escaped by train that night.

This was the last ground action of any consequence. At Aandalsnes the port was a blazing shambles, but cruisers and destroyers from Scapa Flow were able to embark the whole of Sickleforce on the nights of April 30 and May 1, and by two o'clock in the morning of May 2 the last detachment of the rear guard was aboard.*

At sea, Sickleforce suffered no further losses. Mauriceforce was not so fortunate. At Namsos there had been no ground fighting since April 23, and there was no pursuit. Embarkation of the entire force was successfully effected by cruisers, destroyers, and French transports on the night of May 2–3. But by this time the Germans had ample notice of what was afoot (the evacuation of Aandalsnes had already been completed and publicly announced), and the Luftwaffe pursued the ships throughout the day, sinking two destroyers. Thus air power had the last as well as the decisive word in the fighting for central Norway.

The remnants of the Norwegian opposition were rapidly cleaned up. On the evening of April 29 Oberst Fischer's battle group had finally

---

* King Haakon and other members of the Norwegian Royal Family and government were picked up at Molde (twenty-five miles northeast of Aandalsnes) on the night of April 30, and General Ruge the following night. The Norwegians were taken to Tromsoe, about 100 miles north of Narvik.

made contact with the German outposts at Trondheim. Pellengahr's forces reached Aandalsnes on May 2. Two days later Engelbrecht's 163rd Division established direct communications between Oslo and Bergen, and on May 5 organized resistance in central Norway ended with the surrender of Hegra fortress twenty-five miles east of Trondheim, where 300 Norwegians had been besieged for nearly a month.

As Pellengahr's troops moved into Aandalsnes, in Berlin the OKW was drafting a "comprehensive description of the operations in Norway." When Goering saw the draft, he exploded in rage because "the name Pellengahr appears, but not Milch." After his campaign in the Gudbrandsdal, Pellengahr relapsed into the obscurity he had previously enjoyed,* but his mention in dispatches was well deserved. If he had had the decisive advantage of air support in his undertaking, there had been formidable obstacles as well. His troops were green and had to cope with the snow, cold, and mountainous terrain that might have been expected to favor the defensive forces. To push through this country against stiffening opposition, and cover the 300 air-line miles from Oslo to Trondheim in two weeks, was no mean feat.

The psychological fruits of his achievement were likewise notable. Small as the number of troops seems in restrospect, these were the war's first engagements in battalion strength between British and German forces. There was no difficulty in identifying the winners, and neutral nations were duly impressed. Was the Wehrmacht unbeatable? In Britain there was a chorus of anger and disappointment, and a week later, when the Germans launched their main attack on the western front, it was the sorry outcome in central Norway that was chiefly responsible for the fall of the Chamberlain Cabinet and the formation of a National government under Churchill's leadership.

The Fuehrer's "Crisis of Nerves"

Rapid as it was, Pellengahr's progress had not been swift enough to satisfy Adolf Hitler. Berlin, indeed, had been the focus of great excitement and consternation since April 14, when it was realized that Dietl was cut off in Narvik and that all the destroyers of Group I had been lost there. Despite the success of the initial landings, the heavy naval losses and the isolation of Dietl were too much for the Fuehrer's

---

* Pellengahr was promoted from *charakterisiert Generalleutnant* to *Generalleutnant* on June 1, 1940, and was awarded the *Ritterkreuz* a few months later. He was never given another command, and was retired at the age of fifty-nine in 1942.

nerve. The leaders of the Wehrmacht were now to experience a painful foretaste of the even more trying experiences that lay ahead.

Perhaps this first crisis was not devoid of satisfaction to Brauchitsch and Halder, who had been excluded from all participation in *Weseruebung*. When the former saw Hitler at noon on April 14, he was told that all hope of holding Narvik had been "abandoned" because "we have had bad luck." [34] Hitler's first reaction was that Dietl should try to fight his way south to Trondheim, a plan which even the worshipful Jodl described as an "impossible idea." [35] Nevertheless, it lingered in Hitler's mind for the next few days, while he railed at Raeder because the *Scharnhorst* and *Gneisenau* had not engaged the British fleet.[36]

On April 17 the arrival by air of a naval officer from Narvik with a written report from Dietl induced another temperamental outburst on Hitler's part. He declared that Dietl must either march south or be evacuated by air. Jodl reiterated his opposition, pointing out the difficulties and losses inevitably attendant upon so desperate a rescue venture and emphasizing that Dietl could hold out in the mountains for a long time: "A thing should be considered lost only when it is actually lost." In the end these arguments prevailed,* and on April 18 Dietl was ordered to hold out as long as possible †—a directive the execution of which proved easier than might have been expected because the British advance from Harstad (where they had landed on April 15) toward Narvik was cautious, and Dietl was not seriously pressed until the beginning of May.

But in Berlin, one crisis followed another. Hitler was enraged that Minister Braeuer had been unable to bring the Norwegian government to terms, and Goering fed the flames by blaming Falkenhorst for not being "energetic enough" with the civilian population. On April 19

* The sequence of events leading to this order is not entirely clear. The then Oberstleutnant Bernhard von Lossberg (of Warlimont's staff at OKW) has written [37] that on April 18 Hitler signed an order for telegraphic transmission to Dietl, directing him to lead his troops over the Swedish frontier and into internment. In a somewhat melodramatic account, Lossberg describes his own arguments and representations to Keitel, Jodl, and Brauchitsch, as a result of which the message was held up, and Dietl was ordered to hold out. All this is possible, but neither the supposed Hitler order nor any mention of Lossberg's activities in this connection is to be found in the Jodl and Halder diary entries covering the period in question.

† On the same day that the order was issued, Dietl was subordinated directly to the OKW in Berlin instead of Falkenhorst in Oslo. The order was taken to Dietl by an air courier, Hauptmann von Sternburg, who arrived in Narvik harbor on April 22. Dietl was told to tie down enemy forces for as long as possible, and thereafter to make the ore railway unusable by the enemy. When these possibilities were exhausted, he was to "conduct himself so that the honor of the German Wehrmacht would be unsullied."

Josef Terboven, Gauleiter of Essen and a close friend of Goering's, was summoned to Berlin to be "instructed" by Hitler in his forthcoming assignment as head of civil administration in Norway. Keitel and Jodl now fell into unwonted argument with Hitler about the respective spheres of authority of Falkenhorst and Terboven—a controversy so acrimonious that Keitel had to leave the room, and Jodl described the situation as a "chaos of leadership" (*Fuehrungschaos*), since "all details are being overruled from above, and orderly work by the competent military authorities (Raeder and Falkenhorst) is impossible." [38]

The next day was the Fuehrer's fifty-first birthday, a circumstance which seems to have had a soothing effect at the Chancellery. "The tempest has quieted down," Jodl noted, and Keitel was able to have a reasoned discussion with Hitler about the scope of Terboven's authority. The decree appointing Terboven as Reich Commissioner for the occupied Norwegian territories, issued April 24,[39] provided that Falkenhorst as *Wehrmachtbefehlshaber* should retain full power to take all measures necessary for the execution of his orders "insofar as, and as long as, military considerations demand." To be sure, this was scant comfort to the Norwegians, for whom Terboven's coming presaged an occupational nightmare blacker than the Arctic night.

On April 22 events precipitated the third Hitlerian crisis, of which Trondheim was now the subject. The Allied landings at Namsos and Aandalsnes had the Fuehrer "increasingly worried" about "the consequent impossibility of setting up ground communications with Trondheim," and he wanted to send there the big liners *Bremen* and *Europa* loaded with troops and supplies. Raeder was horrified: [40] "They would have to be escorted by the whole fleet. . . . Such operations would entail certain loss of the transports and of the entire fleet. As a result it would also become impossible to escort transports to Oslo." Instead, he suggested that two smaller liners * and some freighters might be sent to Stavanger, and that Trondheim be reinforced only by air and U-boats.

On April 23, after Pellengahr had encountered the British in the Gudbrandsdal, the tension in Berlin increased. Hitler now ordered that the Army's only other division of Austrian mountain troops—the 2nd Mountain Division, commanded by Generalleutnant Valentin Feuerstein—be taken out of the western front and made ready for shipment to Oslo. This was promptly done, but Raeder at length succeeded in

---

* The *Potsdam* and the *Gneisenau*, not to be confused with the battle cruiser of the same name.

talking Hitler out of his notion of sending transports to Trondheim or Bergen. By April 27 Pellengahr's further progress and the favorable reports of staff officers * sent from Berlin to Norway had quieted the Fuehrer's worst fears.

The "crisis of nerves" ended on April 30, when Jodl reported to Hitler the junction between the Trondheim garrison and Oberst Fischer's battle group. "Fuehrer is beside himself with joy," noted Jodl,[41] adding that "at midday I am asked to sit next to him." A more important consequence was that Hitler promptly turned his attention to the western front and ordered that the offensive should be ready for launching by May 5. In the meantime came news of the British evacuation of Namsos and Aandalsnes. Norway rapidly faded from the forefront of Hitler's mind, and the leaders of the Wehrmacht turned their attention to their major undertaking in the West.

Narvik and the Fighting in Northern Norway

Dietl, however, was still in Narvik, and the hardest fighting was yet to come for this comical-faced but tireless and inspirational leader. Despite his isolation, Dietl's material situation had substantially improved during the three weeks that had passed since the landing on April 9. On April 13 a mountain battery was flown in by Junkers 52s, but the planes were wrecked in landing, on the frozen Hartvigsee near Elvegaard, and thereafter air supply came only by seaplane and parachute. The *Jan Wellem*'s supplies were unloaded. By April 16 the Norwegians had been driven away from the ore railroad, and the entire line up to the Swedish frontier was in German hands. The marines and sailors from the sunken destroyers were formed into units and given assignments within their means to accomplish. A few parachute troops were dropped to reinforce the mountain regiment.

Tentative planning and divided command combined to delay the Allied attack on Narvik. When Vice-Admiral Whitworth took the *Warspite* out of Narvik on April 14, he advised an immediate landing. Admiral of the Fleet the Earl of Cork and Orrery, the naval commander of the Narvik expedition that was even then on its way, was eager to follow this bold counsel. However, the army commander, Major General P. J. Mackesy, objected strongly, on the ground that his

---

* Oberstleutnant von Lossberg (to whom Hitler took a strong dislike because of his "schoolmasterly" manner), Oberstleutnant Boehme, and Hitler's adjutant, Oberst Schmundt.

troops were equipped only for an unopposed landing. He proceeded to unload them—three battalions of infantry—at Harstad and deployed them at a respectful distance from Narvik.

On April 20 Lord Cork was placed in full command, but he was reluctant to overrule General Mackesy on army matters, and conditions were plainly unpropitious for a landing under fire in these icy waters and rocky, snow-covered headlands, especially with ill-equipped troops unaccustomed to such conditions. On April 24 the *Warspite,* with two cruisers and a destroyer, went into the fiord to bombard Narvik and its environs. Some damage was done, but the Germans manifested no disposition to surrender, though Dietl now moved his headquarters back ten miles from Narvik to Sildvik, a village on the railway near the foot of the Rombaksfiord.

A few days later the Allied forces were doubled by the arrival of three battalions of Chasseurs Alpins under General Béthouart. In combination with two brigades of Norwegian troops, the Allied forces now considerably outnumbered the Germans, and General Mackesy began a gradual tactic of encirclement. On May 6 two battalions of the French Foreign Legion were brought in, and three days later a four-battalion brigade of Poles under General Bohusz-szyzko. Then on May 11 Lieutenant General C. J. E. Auchinleck arrived to replace General Mackesy as commander (under Lord Cork) of all the air and ground forces (numbering some 25,000 men) of what was now called the North-Western Expeditionary Force, with the mission of capturing Narvik, destroying Dietl's force, and establishing Allied military dominance of northern Norway.

By the time the Allied build-up in Narvik had thus reached its peak, however, its strategic situation had been radically altered by the launching on May 10 of the German offensive in France and the Low Countries. Narvik immediately became a very minor theater and, as the Allied situation in France worsened, the maintenance of so large a force in so remote a place became an increasingly dubious enterprise.

But this was not all, for Cork and Auchinleck now were faced with a new threat in Norway itself, from the forces of Generalleutnant Valentin Feuerstein, advancing northward from Trondheim. His 2nd Mountain Division had originally been moved to Norway on Hitler's personal order, to speed up the advance to Trondheim. On May 4 Feuerstein took command of a battle group at Trondheim comprising his own division, Oberst Weiss's regiment of the 3rd Mountain Division

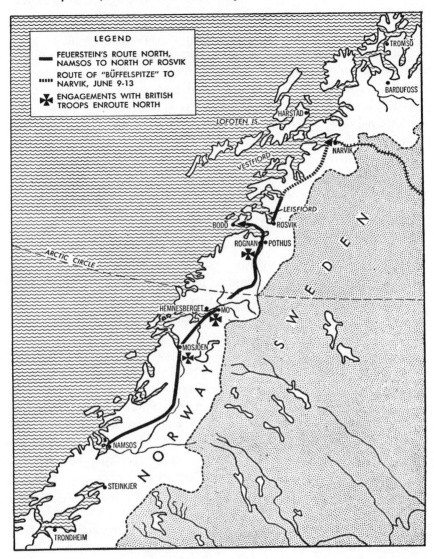

TRONDHEIM TO NARVIK, ROUTE OF SECOND MOUNTAIN DIVISION,
MAY 5–JUNE 9, 1940.

that had originally landed at Trondheim, and some specially attached units of engineers, armor, artillery, and motorcycle troops.*

On May 5 Feuerstein set out on the long and arduous overland route to Narvik, through the little coastal towns of Mosjöen (where the railway from Namsos ended), Mo, and Bodö—an air-line distance of nearly 400 miles. The one road was interrupted by several long ferries, and from Bodö to Narvik there was no road at all. The British had concluded that the route was all but unusable; the Germans soon demonstrated the contrary.

By May 10 they were approaching Mosjöen, where two British "independent companies" had been landed a day earlier to hold the road. After a brief skirmish the British were driven back and retired to Mosjöen, hoping to halt the German advance at the ferry break in the road halfway between Mosjöen and Mo. But the Germans, by an exceedingly daring if small-scale resort to amphibious operations, had already sent a company of mountain infantry by coastal steamer to the *north* end of the ferry at Hemnesberget. With their retreat cut off, the British troops at Mosjöen had to be evacuated by ship and were taken north to Bodö.

At Hemnesberget, Feuerstein was less than 200 air-line miles from Narvik. General Auchinleck now decided to divide his forces and employ all the British troops to halt the German advance from the south, leaving to General Béthouart, who had shown himself expert at mountain winter warfare, the assault on Narvik with the French, Poles, and Norwegians. One British battalion was sent to Mo on May 12, and two more sailed from Harstad to Bodö on the cruiser *Effingham* and the Polish steamer *Chrobry*. Here again German air power asserted itself decisively. The *Chrobry* was bombed and set afire and the *Effingham*, forced to an uncharted route by fear of air attack, ran aground. Both battalions, minus valuable equipment, had to be taken back to Harstad.

Accordingly, the British were heavily outnumbered when the Germans attacked at Stien, a few miles south of Mo, on May 17. The Scots Guards fought well but fell victim to the same outflanking tactics that

---

* At this same time, the end of the campaign in central Norway and the imminence of the western offensive led to a reorganization of the German command structure in Norway. Milch returned to Germany and was replaced by Stumpff as commander of Luftflotte 5. Falkenhorst (with Stumpff and Admiral Boehm) moved the headquarters of Group XXI from Oslo to Trondheim. Dietl, who had been directly subordinated to the OKW since April 15, was now resubordinated to Group XXI, so that all the forces in Norway were again under a single, local command.

Pellengahr had used to good effect in the Gudbrandsdal. Late in the afternoon of May 18 Feuerstein's vanguard was in Mo, and the British were in full retreat up the road toward Bodö.

There were skirmishes on the way north, but the next (and next to last) important ground action in northern Norway was fought on May 25 at Pothus, some fifty miles by road southeast of Bodö, and ten miles south of the ferry break at Rognan. Pothus was manned by a battalion of Irish Guards and four "independent companies," all under Brigadier C. McV. Gubbins. The Germans came up on the morning of May 25, and the bitter engagement lasted three days. Once again German air support and superior mobility were decisive, and late on May 27 the British forces were ferried out of Rognan, protected from immediate pursuit by the four-mile ferry break.

When the battle at Pothus began, the Germans in France had already broken through to the Channel Coast, and Dunkirk loomed. As early as May 20, Mr. Churchill (Prime Minister since May 10) proposed that Narvik be abandoned, reasoning that it was not essential as a naval base, and to hold it would be an intolerable drain on Allied resources. The chiefs of staff agreed, and on May 24 the evacuation order was sent to Cork and Auchinleck. Thus it came about that Narvik was captured after its evacuation had already been decided upon in London.

On May 13 two battalions of the French Foreign Legion had been successfully landed near Elvegaard, and by May 22 Dietl had been pressed back into a narrow strip running from Narvik east along the ore railway to the Swedish frontier. The little military airfield at Bardufoss, fifty miles north of Narvik, was cleared of snow and put into operational use with Gladiators and, later, Hurricanes. The latter arrived on May 26, and the direct assault on Narvik was launched just before midnight on May 27. Under cover of naval bombardment, one battalion of Norwegians and two of the Foreign Legion crossed the Rombaksfiord in small boats, and by noon on May 28 the German garrison was driven out of Narvik. The French invited a Norwegian battalion to make the first "liberation entry" of World War II, a graceful harbinger of Paris in 1944.

Dietl, who had moved his headquarters to the Björnfell mountain just north of the railway, was now confined to a wild, mountainous area of about 100 square miles between the foot of the Rombaksfiord and the Swedish border. During April he had been promoted to

Generalleutnant, and in May he was awarded the *Ritterkreuz,* and he continued to justify this preferment by a sturdy and skillful defense of what little he had left under the most arduous conditions. These, however, were about to be alleviated, and much sooner than he had expected.

For no sooner were the Allies in Narvik than they faced the even more difficult problem of getting out, in accordance with London's orders to evacuate. Demolition of the ore installations proved less of a task than anticipated, because of the extensive destruction of the harbor and its equipment during seven weeks of naval and landing actions and the concomitant heavy bombardments.* Another helpful factor was the air cover that could be provided from Bardufoss. But the evacuation of nearly 25,000 troops from many small points among the fiords was a staggering task, rendered no easier by the angry bewilderment of the Norwegians,† who were desperately eager to drive Dietl over the Swedish border.

The British troops at Bodö were taken to Harstad by destroyers during the last three nights of May. Destroyers were also used to collect the troops from up and down the Ofotfiord and its offshoots, and bring them to Harstad. Fifteen troopships, sent from Britain, came in pairs to Harstad and loaded the troops during the five-day period June 4–8. The cruiser *Devonshire* picked up King Haakon and his government at Tromsö. The Gladiators and Hurricanes at Bardufoss were in action until June 7, when they were flown to the carrier *Glorious*—an exploit the more remarkable in that Hurricanes had never before been landed on a deck. Every effort was made to conceal what was afoot—so successfully that it was not until June 8 that Dietl awoke to the fact of the enemy's departure and re-entered Narvik.

Ignorant of the Allied intentions even after he had reached Bodö at the end of May, Feuerstein, still bent on reinforcing Dietl, faced the problem of the last 100 miles through fiords and trackless ‡ mountain fastnesses. A task force of three light battalions from the 2nd Mountain Division, assembled under the command of Oberstleutnant Ritter von Hengl, was taken by boat to the head of the Leirfiord, and set out for Narvik "through rain, snow, storm, and fog." [42] This expedition, which

---

* After inspection, British engineers estimated that ore could not be exported in appreciable quantities for a year or more.
    † For security reasons, the Norwegian government was not informed of the decision to evacuate until June 1.
    ‡ The road to the north ended at Rösvik, about twenty-five miles north of the Rognan-Langset ferry break.

was given the cover-name *Bueffel*,* was halted by Falkenhorst on June 9, after the British had left Narvik. An officer and about twenty men kept on as a symbolic gesture and reached Narvik on June 13.

So ended the ground fighting in Norway. General Ruge remained to demobilize the Norwegian troops before they were overrun; he negotiated an armistice with Dietl on June 12. Bardufoss and Tromsö were taken by paratroopers without opposition on June 13. From Falkenhorst, the OKW, and the Fuehrer himself came well-earned paeans of praise for Dietl, the *Sieger von Narvik,* for whom more promotions and decorations were in store.[43]

Operation "Juno"

But at sea, the campaign in Norway did not end with the evacuation of Narvik. It was, perhaps, fitting that the German Navy—whose leaders had proposed and planned *Weseruebung,* and whose forces had suffered most at the enemy's hands—should have had the last word as well as the first.

As early as May 14, Raeder's staff had put forward the idea of another sortie by the fleet. A week later he reported to Hitler that the *Gneisenau, Scharnhorst,* and *Hipper* would again be battleworthy by the end of May and might be used to attack British shipping off Harstad and thus relieve the pressure on Narvik. When that time arrived, Dunkirk was in process, and the Germans were emboldened by their astounding success in France. After discussions among Raeder, Schniewind, Saalwaechter, and Marschall † it was decided that the fleet should sail on June 4 with the principal mission of attacking British warships and transports in the Narvik area, and the secondary task of expediting, with supplies and transportation, Feuerstein's progress toward Narvik. The expedition, under Marschall's command and with the cover name "Juno," comprised the flagship *Gneisenau, Scharnhorst, Hipper,* four destroyers, and two torpedo boats.

The preoccupation of the British fleet in home waters (the evacuation of Dunkirk had just finished) and in Narvik (where the evacuation was beginning), plus good fortune, enabled Marschall to reach northern waters and refuel his ships at sea from an auxiliary, unob-

---

* So called as a compliment to Dietl, who, when captain of a mountain company in Munich, used to call his men *Bueffel* (buffaloes) because of their imperviousness to winter weather.

† On April 24 Marschall, who had been ill, returned to his post as *Flottenchef,* which had been temporarily held by Luetjens.

served by the enemy. On June 7 he was north of Trondheim, in the open ocean midway between Norway and Iceland. Luftwaffe reconnaissance had observed an Allied convoy heading toward Scapa Flow, but the Germans, as yet unaware that the British were pulling out, assumed the convoy to be empty ships returning from a supply mission. Marschall's primary goal was Harstad, and that evening he called a conference on the flagship to perfect the plans for an attack there on June 9. But the assembled commanders sensed that Marschall was cool to the project, and his doubts were reinforced by an overheard report from a German reconnaissance plane that only one ship had been observed at Harstad.

Pursuing his hunch,* just after midnight Marschall ordered his fleet to prepare to attack convoys on the next day. His prescience was rewarded the following morning (June 8), when the *Gneisenau* sighted a British tanker and trawler, which were immediately sunk. The *Gneisenau* successfully jammed their radio transmissions, a feat which was repeated later in the morning, when a large but empty transport was sighted and torpedoed.

During the next few hours the hunters had no more luck, and shortly after noon Marschall sent the *Hipper* and the destroyers and torpedo boats off to Trondheim. He was unaware of his own good luck in escaping detection by the British, and equally unaware that Dietl and Feuerstein no longer needed help. So the *Gneisenau* and *Scharnhorst* set their course for Harstad, and it was only by geographical chance that, late in the afternoon, a naval cadet in the foretop of the *Scharnhorst* sighted smoke on the horizon which shortly disclosed the proximity of the British aircraft carrier *Glorious* and two escorting destroyers.[44]

Marschall had struck it rich. It was to the *Glorious* that the Gladiators and Hurricanes had been heroically flown from Bardufoss a few hours earlier. Unwisely, she had raced ahead of the main convoy, despite this overcrowding that fatally hampered her ability to put planes in the air on short notice. She was hopelessly outgunned by the German battle cruisers and was sunk in less than two hours of chase, as were the destroyers *Ardent* and *Acasta*. Some 1500 British officers and men were lost, and there were only forty-three survivors. The *Acasta*,

---

* Marschall signaled to Saalwaechter that the convoys moving westward might indicate the evacuation of Norway. He proceeded on this basis, despite an answer from Saalwaechter urging him to go to Harstad, where he would have found no enemy, since the evacuation was completed on June 8.

however, was able to torpedo the *Scharnhorst,* and this put an end to the achievements of operation "Juno."

The *Gneisenau* and wounded *Scharnhorst* followed the *Hipper* and the smaller ships into Trondheim, where they arrived late on June 9 and learned for the first time that the British had already evacuated Narvik.* The following day the *Gneisenau, Hipper,* and the four de- stroyers put out, hoping to intercept another convoy, but it was too late, and on June 11 they returned to Trondheim, where they remained while temporary repairs were made on the *Scharnhorst.*

Marschall's recurrent disagreements with Schniewind and Saal- waechter aggravated his ill health, and he reported himself sick. On June 20, under the command of Luetjens, the "Juno" expedition set out for Kiel. Escorted by destroyers and torpedo boats, the *Scharnhorst* made her home port, but the *Gneisenau* was torpedoed by the British submarine *Clyde* only a few hours out and had to put back into Trond- heim with her bow all but blown off. In company with the *Hipper,* the light cruiser *Nuernberg,* and four destroyers, she finally returned to Kiel on July 28 and joined the *Scharnhorst* in drydock. "Juno" had cost the British one of their four aircraft carriers, but the laying-up of the *Scharnhorst* and *Gneisenau* until the end of 1940 was, propor- tionately, a much more serious sacrifice of Raeder's slender resources, at a crucial time.

The Norwegian Campaign in Retrospect

It is worth pondering, in strategic terms, the outcome of this, the last action of the Norwegian campaign. Were the Allies more damaged by the loss of *Glorious* than Germany by the disabling of the *Gneisenau* and *Scharnhorst?*

In restrospect it seems clear that the Germans were the heavier los- ers, but this question is but one facet of a much broader problem. What is the meaning of the Norwegian campaign as a whole, in the history of warfare and the story of World War II? The forces involved, compared to those later engaged on the mainland of Europe, were very small. The length of this account of the planning and fighting in the North—necessitated chiefly by the numerous separate actions, each

---

* Not until the morning of the ninth did the British learn that the *Scharnhorst* and *Gneisenau* were at sea and had sunk the *Glorious,* whose signals on being attacked had been jammed. Why the *Ardent* and *Acasta* did not give radio alarm remains a mystery.

of which substantially affected the outcome—may seem disproportion-
ate to the importance of a campaign in which the total casualties on
both sides did not much exceed 12,000 men. But this figure provides no
accurate gauge of the significance of these events.

In the annals of combined operations the Norwegian campaign was,
as already noted,[45] a notable precedent. The campaign was the more
unusual in that the issue was drawn between two great powers competing for control of a third country, geographically extensive but militarily weak, that had been neutral until invaded. In this unique struggle, Germany and Britain each enjoyed marked advantages in divers
ways. The story of the campaign shows plainly enough the two that
decisively influenced the outcome in favor of the Germans, the one
tactical and the other psychological.

Tactically, the decisive factor was air power. The German Navy
was hopelessly outmatched by the Royal Navy and could only function
during brief periods of surprise. On the ground the Germans committed much the larger body of troops, but no more than the Allies could
have dispatched, had they so chosen. It was the German Air Force
that enabled the Germans to capitalize on their assets, that compensated for their disadvantages, and that coped with emergencies. The
Luftwaffe held the Allies out of the waters of the Skaggerak and southern Norway, so that reinforcements could be poured into Oslo. It supplemented the transportation resources at critical times and places,
gave the Germans eyes where the Allies had none, geometrically increased the effective striking power of the ground forces, rendered the
Allied bases at Namsos and Aandalsnes all but unusable, and made it
impossible for the British to gain a foothold for their own air operations. The lesson was repeated with interest and reverse English later
in the war and today is elementary, but it was in Norway that it was
first taught with painful finality.

For all this, the psychological element is of even more fundamental
importance, and it in part explains the British deficiency in air power.
Why did "R.4" make no provision for air support of the ground forces?
The answer is that the British toyed halfheartedly with their problem
until it was too late, while the Germans tackled theirs with foresight
and ruthless vigor months ahead of time. To be sure, the Germans
blundered badly in spots, especially in their stupid attempt to stuff
Quisling down King Haakon's throat. But the British were operating in
a psychological strait jacket. As the official British historian of the
campaign put it in retrospect,[46] ". . . the directives issued from Lon-

don for the conduct of the combined operations in Norway came from an Admiralty which had a greater interest in blockade measures, a War Office all too conscious of its heavy commitments in France, and an Air Ministry whose first concern was the air defense of Great Britain." More generally, the British had not grasped the desperate nature of the challenge that confronted them and tried to handle the strategic problem of Scandinavia with the left hand.

British nonchalance was fully equaled by Norwegian laxity. It is certainly doubtful that alertness would have enabled so small a nation to turn defeat into victory against such overwhelming strength, but it is clear that prompt and full mobilization, better communications, and a well-planned defense of the airfields could have considerably delayed the German incursions, to the great advantage of the British coming to their assistance. These events teach a lesson as old as the art of warfare, but which is more important today than ever before, thanks to the greatly increased striking power of small units in the age of jet and atom.[47]

Within the tactical framework of World War II, *Weseruebung* was a remarkable triumph, which brought the Germans immediate and substantial benefits. As Wegener and Carls had envisaged, the British naval blockade was markedly loosened, and if Germany lacked the sea power fully to exploit this altered circumstance, it nonetheless facilitated blockade-running and naval forays.* More important, it opened a valuable series of new bases for submarine and air operations against Allied shipping, the importance of which increased later in the war, in the time of the Murmansk convoys. In 1942, the mere presence of the *Tirpitz* in Norwegian waters forced the British to concentrate great naval strength that was sorely needed elsewhere, and every convoy to Russia became a major fleet operation.[48]

Here again, however, it was in the realm of war psychology that these events loomed largest. Austria, Czechoslovakia, Poland—and now Norway and Denmark! Was there no stopping the Nazis? By what infernal magic had they snatched this insolent victory from under the very gun muzzles of the mighty British Fleet? If the Allies could give no better account of themselves in a maritime campaign a few hundred miles from Britain, what small neutral would henceforth

* Even the Narvik ore route was not lost to the Germans for as long as the Allies had estimated when they abandoned that port. The first shipment was made in January 1941, and the rate of export rose steadily until 1943, reaching a rate of 1,800,000 tons per annum early that year.

rely on their promises of assistance against the German menace? In the major capitals too—Rome, Tokyo, Washington, and no doubt Moscow—the impact was prodigious, and Allied military prestige suffered a most damaging blow.

In Germany, Hitler's position was greatly strengthened, throughout the Wehrmacht and the civilian population. True, his "crisis of nerves" had been an eye opener to Keitel, Jodl, and the few others who witnessed it, but it had no unhappy immediate consequences. Brauchitsch and Halder might grumble at their exclusion from the councils and the highhanded fashion in which divisions were pulled out of the western front on the eve of the major assault. But these things affected only a small circle in the Army High Command; the average German, in or out of uniform, swelled with pride at the Wehrmacht's latest triumph. Here was no mere victory over a Poland or a Norway—the British had been beaten on land and in the air, and their superior naval power nullified. German soldiers, sailors, and airmen had handled themselves bravely and skillfully,* and commanders had gained valuable experience † and confidence. Co-operation between the three services had been tested and proved at the operational level, although personal jealousies—chiefly between Goering and Raeder—persisted and sometimes produced bad tactical consequences.

In terms of the comparative losses in men and weapons on the ground and in the air, the Norwegian campaign did not significantly affect the course of the war. Casualties, as already remarked, were light on both sides. Losses in planes and pilots were somewhat more serious, especially for the British, but even these had no lasting effect. The Wehrmacht lost 1317 killed, 2375 missing, and 1604 wounded,

* The troops employed in the conquest of Norway for the most part remained there on occupational duty or were used in Finland after the outbreak of war with Russia.

† However, few of them had notable records after the Norwegian campaign. Falkenhorst remained as military commander in Norway until his retirement at the end of 1944. He also served briefly as commander in Finland but was replaced in this assignment by Dietl, who remained there until his death in an airplane crash in 1944. Feuerstein had a corps command in southern Norway until 1943, when he was given a corps in Italy and commanded at Cassino. Pellengahr and Woytasch retired in 1942. Engelbrecht was the occupational commander in Trondheim throughout most of the war, and Tittel succeeded Feuerstein in command at Oslo. Buschenhagen (Falkenhorst's chief of staff) became a corps commander on the eastern front, was captured in 1944, and joined Paulus' National Free Germany Committee. Stumpff stayed in Norway as Commander-in-Chief of Luftflotte 5 until 1944, when he returned to take charge of the air defense of Germany. On the naval side, Marschall succeeded Saalwaechter as commander in the West. Boehm remained in Norway until 1943. Luetjens went down on the *Bismarck* in 1941, and Bey was lost in the North Sea in 1943.

making a total casualty list of 5296. British, French, and Norwegian casualties on land were under 5000. The British lost much more equipment than the Germans, chiefly because of their several evacuations. The twenty fighter aircraft and 1515 lives lost in the sinking of the *Glorious* and her two escort destroyers were a serious blow at a time when it could be ill afforded. The Germans lost many more planes than the British—the estimates vary from 117 to 242—but not a large proportion of the air strength committed in Norway.[49]

At sea, however, the Germans suffered much more severely than the Allies in both absolute and comparative terms. The British lost the carrier *Glorious,* one cruiser, and seven destroyers, and the French and Poles one destroyer each. But the Germans sacrificed ten destroyers—half of their entire strength—and three of their eight ready cruisers. In addition, both of their heavy battle cruisers and one of their two remaining pocket battle cruisers were put out of action for many months. The losses were never made up, and the disablings occurred at a very critical time. In retrospect, the destruction of virtually half of Germany's strength in cruisers and destroyers and the wounds suffered by *Scharnhorst, Gneisenau,* and *Luetzow* appear to have been the most important strategic results of the campaign. In this ultimate sense, *Weseruebung* cost the Wehrmacht more than the victory was worth.

At that stage of the war, for Germany its successful conclusion meant finishing off Britain. To achieve a successful landing in England, the expenditure of the entire German Fleet would not have been too heavy a price to pay. But when the moment came, that payment could not be made, because the fleet had already been shattered off Norway.

If Hitler had not attacked Norway, in all probability the western offensive would have been launched nearly a month earlier.* There is no reason to think that it would not have progressed as rapidly in April as it in fact did in May, or that the defeat of France might not thus have been brought about in May rather than June. Hitler would then have had the entire summer and fall before him, with the German Fleet intact, to deal with Britain. The hazards of an assault across the Channel would still have been great, but there is no gainsaying that the availability of the *Scharnhorst, Gneisenau, Luetzow, Bluecher, Karlsruhe, Koenigsberg,* and twenty destroyers—to say nothing of an

---

* On April 14 Brauchitsch strongly counseled against further delay in the West.[50] It was the involvement of the Luftwaffe in Norway that made it impossible to attack in the West until May.

additional month of good weather—would have greatly increased the prospects of success. Instead, as Mr. Churchill observes: [51]

. . . at the end of June 1940, a momentous date, the effective German Fleet consisted of no more than *one eight-inch cruiser, two light cruisers, and four destroyers.* . . . The German Navy was no factor in the supreme issue of the invasion of Britain.

Conversely, the advantages gained by the Germans from the occupation of Norway and Denmark shrank markedly in the relative scale after the conquest of France and the Low Countries. Raeder and Doenitz would not have gambled so heavily for submarine pens at Trondheim had they known that Cherbourg, Brest, and the other French Atlantic ports were about to become available. The Aalborg and Sola airfields played no significant part in the Battle of Britain, for by then the Luftwaffe could take off from bases in Flanders and northern France, only a few miles from England.

Even the danger that the Allies might themselves occupy Norway was substantially eliminated by the collapse of France and the military isolation of a badly battered Britain. Not until 1943 at the earliest could the Allies have spared the means for a Scandinavian operation, and it is highly unlikely that they would then have jeopardized their moral position by a violation of neutrality. Having once taken Norway and Denmark, however, the Wehrmacht was obliged to garrison them throughout the rest of the war. At the outset this was no problem, but after the entire continent became a theater of war and the Germans had met with resistance and reverses that stretched their man power to the breaking point, the occupation of Norway drained off men and weapons that were sorely needed elsewhere.

In the final analysis, therefore, it must be concluded that, for the Reich, *Weseruebung* was a strategic error.[52] But this conclusion emerges only in retrospect, and in the light of the situation created by the Wehrmacht's sweeping victory in the Battle of France. Memories of the Gudbrandsdal and Narvik were soon obscured by a sequence of dazzling military triumphs—Eben Emael, Sedan, Dunkirk, the Somme—of a magnitude that dwarfed the fighting in the North. These were the victories that laid western Europe at Hitler's feet and opened the prospect of a farflung and enduring German empire.

CHAPTER FIVE

Fall Gelb: The Plan of Campaign in the West

THE GREAT ISSUE of whether and when to attack the Allies on the western front rocked the German high command during the fall of 1939–40 and caused a bitter cleavage between Hitler and the generals. Brauchitsch, Halder, Rundstedt, Bock, Leeb, List, and Reichenau were united in vehement and open opposition to Hitler's desires and orders for an immediate offensive in the West, and the dispute precipitated what I have called the "crisis of confidence," which left enduring scars and was ultimately resolved only by the passage of time and changing circumstances. Came the spring of 1940, with good weather for the panzers and the Luftwaffe; the Army was stronger, hopes for another Munich had ebbed, and the generals were reconciled to or even enthusiastic about the long-postponed *Westfeldzug*.

Throughout these winter months, and concurrently with the question of *whether* and *when* to launch the assault, ran a quite separate argument about *where* and *how*. This was not an issue between Hitler and the generals as a group, for the professional soldiers themselves were sharply divided. It was, however, a matter of great historic interest in which the relations among the military leaders, and their differing tactical conceptions, decisively affected the plan of campaign.

Jealousy, vanity, and simple forgetfulness have sadly distorted the accounts of the shaping of this plan that have since been given out by or in behalf of those who participated in the process. Rundstedt, Manstein, Halder, and Guderian have given their versions in books by or about them, and the development of the plan has also been discussed in works by Liddell Hart, J.F.C. Fuller, Walter Goerlitz, and others.[1]

155

Perhaps the most prevalent misconception is that Brauchitsch, Halder, and their staff at OKH produced an unimaginative copy of the pre-World War I Schlieffen plan [2] which Manstein, in a swift stroke of genius, transmuted into the ultimate and highly successful plan for an armored thrust through the Ardennes and Sedan to the Channel Coast at Abbéville. But in fact the original OKH plan bore only the most superficial resemblance to Schlieffen's and, while Manstein's role is not to be minimized, the final plan was no *coup d'oeil*, but the product of a long evolution to which several others besides Manstein—including Hitler himself—contributed importantly.

By now most if not all of the returns are in, and with the aid of these and the contemporary documents it is possible to trace the development of the plan—masterful in conception and execution—in true sequence, causation, and proportion.

The OKH Plan

The initial plan, of course, had to be based on the forces available for an offensive. During the Polish campaign the West had been held chiefly by reserve and over-age units, and as soon as victory in Poland was assured, Brauchitsch's first concern was to reinforce the West, especially in the Rhineland. Even before Warsaw fell, Reichenau, Kluge, and List, with their headquarters and most of the troops comprising their three armies, were pulled out of Poland and sent west for rest and refitting. Early in October they took up positions along the borders of Luxembourg, Belgium, and southern Holland opposite the Ruhr.* In the middle of October they were joined by Blaskowitz' and Kuechler's armies, although these commanders were immediately replaced by Generals Maximilian von Weichs and Ernst Busch respectively.†

With seven armies thus drawn up along the western front, more army group headquarters were needed. Leeb's Army Group C remained opposite the Maginot Line, with command over Dollmann's

---

* They replaced Liebmann's Fifth Army headquarters (transferred to Poland for occupational duty) and Hammerstein's Army Cadre A (disbanded). Reichenau's Tenth and List's Twelfth Army headquarters were renumbered as the Sixth and Fourteenth respectively; Kluge's retained its designation as the Fourth Army.

† Kuechler stayed on occupational duty in the East until November, when he came to the West to take a new army command, while Blaskowitz succeeded Rundstedt as commander-in-chief in the East (*Oberost*), where he remained until May 1940. In the West, Kuechler's Third Army was renumbered the Sixteenth, and Blaskowitz' Eighth Army the Second.

Seventh Army along the Rhine and Witzleben's First along the southern border of the Rhineland from Karlsruhe to Luxembourg. Bock's army group headquarters was taken out of northern Poland in September, and on October 10, redesignated Army Group B, it took over the entire frontier bordering on the Low Countries.[3] Ten days later Rundstedt came west with his staff, and on October 24 established the headquarters of Army Group A at Coblenz, between Bock on the north and Leeb on the south. Initially the Twelfth (List) and Sixteenth (Busch) armies were subordinated to Rundstedt and deployed along the border of Luxembourg, while the Second (Weichs), Sixth (Reichenau), and Fourth (Kluge) were assigned to Bock and covered the Belgian and southern Dutch frontiers. The Dutch frontier north of the Rhine was merely "observed," as no possibility of attack was anticipated there.

These were the forces and the alignment on the basis of which the first plan of attack was drawn up by the staff of OKH. It may be noted that neither this nor any later plan envisaged an initial attack on the Maginot Line. Leeb's role remained purely defensive, except for feinting operations to hold French forces in the line and prevent their being used as reinforcements elsewhere. From the outset the Germans planned to strike through the Low Countries, despite their neutrality, using the forces that comprised the army groups of Bock and Rundstedt.

Military plans are not composed for the intrinsic beauty of their pattern, like a Bach fugue; they are shaped to achieve specific objectives. It is especially important to bear this in mind when analyzing the original German plan of attack in the West, for only in this way can one understand the much criticized limitations of the plan that the highly competent staff of OKH produced in October of 1939.

At that time, as has been seen, Brauchitsch and Halder did not want to attack *at all*. The entire initiative came from Hitler. So the staff of OKH did not attempt to draw up a plan that would achieve a decisive victory, which they did not then believe feasible. Indeed, their minds and energies were focused not so much on the offensive as on how to prevent its being launched. The original plan—*Fall Gelb*—was improvised hastily and reluctantly under the pressure of Hitler's order, and to achieve the purposes that he had stated in support of his decision to attack before the winter. Accordingly, it is to those purposes that we must look in order to understand the shape that *Gelb* first took.

The bitter argument between Hitler and the generals about whether or not to attack forced Hitler to specify his objectives with great particularity, both orally and in directives and memoranda, as we have already seen.[4] And it is interesting indeed that the primary reason for Hitler's impatience to attack in the West was precisely the same as the one that later helped to bring about his decision to occupy Norway—*fear that the Allies would get there first.* "How situation would turn out if France-England marches into Belgium-Holland is constantly the concern of the Fuehrer" is the notation in the OKW war diary for October 6.[5] The same theme recurs again and again in Hitler's expressions throughout October,[6] culminating in the altercation with the generals on October 25, when Bock and Reichenau joined the chorus of opposition to the offensive.[7] Hitler overbore their arguments for its postponement with the warning that "the enemy gains strength, and one winter night England and France will be on the Maas without firing a shot and without our knowing about it."

Why did Hitler attach such importance to the Low Countries? In part it was concern for the safety of the Ruhr, the heart of Germany's war potential, which lay along the Rhine just behind the southern Dutch border. But his motivation was not purely defensive; on the contrary, he repeatedly stressed the advantages for the war at sea and in the air that would flow from German occupation of the Channel Coast. His war directive [8] of October 9 reflects both these aims, for it specified as the territorial purpose of the offensive the winning of "as large an area as possible in Holland, Belgium, and northern France as a base for conducting a promising air and sea war against England and as a protective area [*Vorfeld*] for the Ruhr."

Finally, there were political considerations. Hitler did not want a long war and still hoped to avoid a finish fight with the English. But they had rebuffed his overtures after the conquest of Poland and needed to be taught a lesson. Perhaps the sting of defeat would bring them to their senses. "The British will be ready to talk only after a beating," he told Brauchitsch on October 17,[9] and so: "We must get at them as quickly as possible."

These were the purposes that Brauchitsch was ordered to fulfill, and which governed the OKH officers as they reluctantly sat down to shape the offensive of which they so strongly disapproved. Accordingly, the plan that emerged on October 19 as the original version of *Gelb* [10] was designed to inflict a sharp defeat on the Allies but was not expected to knock the French out of the war or drive the British off the continent. It was designed to overrun the Low Countries and gain the Channel

Coast. The very first available record [11] of Hitler's purpose in launching the offensive, dating from late (probably the twenty-seventh) in September, specifies as the object of the attack: "to gain the Channel Coast." It had no larger or more decisive objectives. Strategically it was Hitler's plan, and all that OKH did was to give it a tactical military formulation.

By October 15 the broad outlines of the first *Gelb* had been worked out. As Halder described it to Jodl,[12] the main armored thrust would be in Belgium and southern Holland, just north of Liége. About seventy-five divisions would be used for the assault, with mountain troops in the Ardennes and motorized troops on the north wing. The OKH "deployment directive" (*Aufmarschanweisung*), issued to the field forces on October 19, was merely an elaboration of this general scheme.

The attack was to be launched from the Rhineland by Army Groups A and B, and from the Muenster area north of the Rhine by "Army Cadre North"—a force of corps strength directly subordinate to OKH. Apparently this headquarters was never separately established.* Its intended mission was to overrun the Netherlands north of the Rhine and take Utrecht, Amsterdam, and Rotterdam, while light forces occupied the northernmost Dutch province of Groningen.

Bock's Army Group B, comprising three armies and thirty-seven divisions, was to strike the big blow. In the northern tip of the Rhineland, Weichs's Second Army was to cross the Maas just south of Nijmegen and move southwesterly across Holland and into northern Belgium. In so doing it was to screen the right flank of Reichenau's Sixth Army, which was to deliver the main attack north of Liége. Most of the panzer divisions were allocated to the Sixth and Kluge's Fourth Army, which was to cross the Meuse between Liége and Namur. By-passing Liége, the Sixth and Fourth would come together in the Brussels area. Here the main encounter with the Allied forces, moving in to aid the Belgians, was expected, and from here Bock was to continue his attack due west through Ghent and Bruges to the Channel Coast at Ostend, Dunkirk, and Calais.

The mission of Rundstedt's smaller Army Group A was to protect Bock's left flank against a French attack from the southwest. To accomplish this, List's Twelfth Army was to advance west through the Ardennes and cross the Meuse south of Namur, and Busch's Sixteenth

---

* The force was to comprise only three divisions in the Xth Corps, commanded by Generalleutnant Christian Hansen, and perhaps it was intended to enlarge Hansen's corps headquarters into the "army cadre" headquarters.

Army was to occupy Luxembourg and the southeastern tip of Belgium.

The combined strength of Army Groups B and A and Army Cadre North was sixty-seven divisions, with nine more in reserve. Felmy's Luftflotte 2 and Sperrle's Luftflotte 3 were to support Bock's and Rundstedt's army groups. The main obstacles anticipated were the network of rivers and canals characteristic of the Low Countries and the fortifications with which the natural defenses had been supplemented. With this in mind, Brauchitsch reminded the army groups that speed was of the essence, and that enemy strong points should be by-passed by the assault waves and reduced later by following forces.

This original Gelb had a short life. Even its creators were highly critical. Halder, for example, saw no purpose to the proposed operation in Holland north of the Rhine and doubted that Army Cadre North would be able to continue its advance if the Dutch flooded the approaches to Amsterdam. The plan did not make clear whether the focal point of the attack (Schwerpunkt) lay with Reichenau north or Kluge south of Liége, and it was doubted whether Reichenau had been given enough motorized troops to exploit an initial success.

All these problems were discussed at a meeting of Hitler, the OKW (Keitel and Jodl), the OKH (Brauchitsch and Halder), and Army Group B (Bock, Reichenau and Kluge) on October 25. Elimination of the attack on Holland and concentration south of Liége were favorably considered, but no final decisions were reached. Brauchitsch and Halder were with the Fuehrer again on October 27 and 28, and from these conferences emerged the second edition of Gelb, embodied in Brauchitsch's directive of October 29.[13]

The principal change in the plan was the elimination of Army Cadre North and a general southerly shift in the center of gravity. Holland was to be left untouched except for the "Maastricht appendix"—the narrow strip of Limburg between Belgium and Germany on the east bank of the Maas northwest of Aachen, which was to be crossed by the German forces attacking north of Liége.

Bock's Army Group B was enlarged to forty-three (including nine panzer and four motorized) divisions in four armies, one of which was to be a newly formed Eighteenth Army under Kuechler.[14] However, under the revised plan neither the Eighteenth nor Weichs's Second Army was to take part in the initial assault, for which only the Sixth Army to the north and the Fourth to the south of Liége would be used. The Eighteenth was to be deployed behind the Sixth, and the Second behind the Fourth, ready to follow and reinforce the attack.

The Sixth Army was to be deployed opposite the Maastricht appendix, and to advance due west, by-passing Liége on the north, and carrying the first attack all the way to Brussels and Antwerp. The Fourth Army was also to take a more direct westerly course than under the original plan, crossing the Meuse on both sides of Namur and pressing the assault beyond Charleroi.

In Army Group A, the defensive role of the Sixteenth Army remained unchanged. List's Twelfth Army, however, after pushing through the Ardennes, was to turn toward the southwest and endeavor to break through the French border fortifications, cross the Meuse north of Sedan, and advance toward Laon. This feature appears to have been the result of Hitler's suggestion at the conference on October 25 of a break-through "in the direction Reims-Amiens." For this ambitious program, however, no armor was furnished, and Rundstedt's army group was even weaker under the revised than under the original plan.[*]

Despite such differences in tactical detail, the strategic bases of both these early *Gelb* plans were similar: to inflict a defeat on the enemy ground forces and reach the Channel Coast. That was what Hitler had said he wanted, and that was what Brauchitsch and Halder were guided by in drafting the OKH orders to Bock and Rundstedt.

For all its simplicity, the OKH plan has been grossly and almost universally misdescribed in the postwar accounts. "The Army High Command, spurred on by Hitler, was intending to use, once again, the so-called 'Schlieffen plan' of 1914," writes Guderian,[15] adding the comment that "this had the advantage of simplicity, though hardly the charm of novelty." The order "was an unimaginative replica of the Schlieffen plan," exclaims Halder [16] of his own handiwork. Their junior colleagues, Guenther Blumentritt and Siegfried Westphal, have expressed themselves to the same effect.[17] Indeed, this misappreciation of the OKH plan has now acquired the authority of general repetition and has been accepted by Liddell Hart, Chester Wilmot, Walter Goerlitz, Adolf Galland, Alan Bullock, and other historians and commentators.[18]

Now, the only excuse for this prevalent misunderstanding is that there are two points of resemblance between the Schlieffen plan and the OKH *Gelb* order of 1939. Both envisaged an advance through Belgium, and both placed the *Schwerpunkt* of the attack in the right

[*] It was reduced from twenty-seven to twenty-two divisions, and lost the one panzer and two motorized divisions previously assigned to it.

wing of the German forces. But these similarities are superficial, as Manstein realized at the time and has plainly demonstrated in his memoirs.[19]

Schlieffen developed his famous plan after the Franco-Russian alliance of 1893 had confronted Germany with the prospect of a two-front war.[20] Thus threatened with a superior coalition—especially if Britain should come to the aid of France—Schlieffen sought a solution by planning for the total destruction of the French Army in a single operation upon the outbreak of hostilities, so that the bulk of the German forces could thereafter be transferred to the eastern front. Above all, therefore, the vital engagement in the West had to be *decisive* and knock the French out of the war. To this end, Schlieffen devised his gigantic wheeling movement through Belgium and northern France, pivoting on Metz. The right wing was to be so strong that it could sustain a month-long advance from Aachen to the Somme, and thereafter cross the Seine and turn eastward against the French rear. Thus the enemy forces would be encircled and broken against their own fortifications north of the Swiss frontier.

The mere statement is enough to show how small a part of this gigantic conception was embodied in the *Gelb* plan of 1939. By his pact with Stalin, Hitler had temporarily neutralized Russia and avoided the two-front war. He had no expectation in 1939 of eliminating the French at one blow; he sought only to gain the Channel Coast and the military and psychological advantages that would flow from this limited achievement. And if this simple analysis has since escaped some of his generals, it was clear enough not only to Manstein but also to Hitler himself. In the OKW minutes on the initial *Gelb* conference of September 27 it is reported [21] that: "From the very beginning it is the Fuehrer's idea not to repeat the Schlieffen plan but to attack . . . through Belgium and Luxembourg under strong protection of the southern flank, and to gain the Channel Coast."

The Manstein Variant

Whatever the historical antecedents of the 1939 plan *Gelb*, no one was satisfied with it. The OKH generals, who had drafted it under compulsion, did not like it because they were violently opposed to any offensive whatsoever at that time. Hitler, whose brain child it was, started tinkering with the plan within twenty-four hours of its distribution to the army groups. The more aggressive generals such as Guderian and Manstein, who believed in the necessity and probable success of an offensive although they favored its postponement until the following spring, thought the OKH plan deficient because it promised no decisive results.

Even the Navy and the Luftwaffe, for whose benefit the occupation of the Channel Coast was largely intended, found little to commend in the limited goals of the campaign. The Luftwaffe was especially displeased with the revisions of October 29 that had eliminated Holland from the proposed area of conquest. The very next day Goering sent his Chief of Staff, Jeschonnek, to see Hitler and raise "the objection that, if no Dutch territory is occupied, the English will take possession of the Dutch airports." [22]

As for the Navy, Hitler had repeatedly cited in support of his plan the advantages of using the Channel ports as U-boat bases. On November 10, when Raeder came in for a general discussion of naval operations, Hitler asked him "whether the Navy has any particular wishes in connection with bases on the Dutch-Belgian coast." Raeder's reply was discouragingly negative, because "the bases lie too close to the coast of England and are therefore impracticable as submarine bases." [23]

As matters turned out, it was the Luftwaffe's objections that caused the first major modification in the *Gelb* directive of October 29. To be sure, Jeschonnek's first attempt was fruitless, for Hitler directed that "at present no changes will be made." But on November 11 Jeschonnek was back again at OKW [24] insisting that "Holland must be occupied, because England will violate Holland's air sovereignty and then we will not be able to protect the Ruhr area." This time he was more successful; on November 14 Hitler issued an order through OKW warning: [25] "In case Germany should march through the southern tip of Holland or fly over Holland with huge units, we must reckon anew with the possibility that our opponents . . . may no longer respect the neutrality of Holland and may fly over Dutch territory with assault units, or may even set foot on Fortress Holland. . . . For the air defense of western Germany, especially of the Ruhr region and the North Sea harbors, it thus becomes necessary to gain a broader *Vorfeld* for our air defense by occupying as much Dutch territory as possible."

Thus Holland, like Denmark, [26] was included in the German program of conquest on the principal initiative of the Luftwaffe. Initially, the Army (Army Group B) was to move in only upon special orders from OKH, and the extent of the occupation was left indeterminate. [27]

Bock assigned Hansen's Xth Corps to the task of seizing the territory between the German border and the Dutch fortifications. Groningen and the Frisian Islands were to be taken by light forces and with the Navy's assistance.

But the Luftwaffe was far from satisfied with this "halfway solution." [28] As a result of continued pressure from the air generals,* the new "Directive No. 8 for the Conduct of the War," issued on November 20,[29] provided that: "Contrary to previously issued instructions, all actions intended against Holland may be carried out without special order when the general attack starts." At the end of January 1940, revised *Gelb* directives issued by OKH [30] provided for the speedy occupation of Holland in its entirety, and Kuechler's Eighteenth Army was given this assignment.

In the meantime, however, a much more important change in the basic conception of *Gelb* was under intensive and often acrimonious study. On October 21, while passing through Berlin on his way from Poland to Coblenz (where the headquarters of Army Group A was being set up), Manstein visited the OKH headquarters at Zossen and picked up a copy of the October 19 directive.[31] In his diary he wrote, "*Begleitmusik* [accompaniment] Halder, Stuelpnagel, Greiffenberg," † meaning that Hitler was calling the tune, and OKH filling in the harmony. From conversations with Halder and his staff, Manstein soon grasped the negative attitude of the OKH and their lack of faith in the plan.

The revisions of October 29 did nothing to dispel Manstein's unfavorable view of *Gelb*. Its fundamental shortcoming, as Manstein saw it,[32] was that it would lead to a frontal encounter between the German and Allied forces in Belgium. True, the Germans might be able to push the enemy back, but the Allies could simply retreat toward the Somme in northern France. Sooner or later the German attack would peter out, leaving the Allied forces intact on a line from Sedan to the Channel Coast, much as in World War I. The plan seemed to offer no possibility of cutting off and annihilating any substantial segment of the enemy forces. Furthermore, if the French showed any disposition to take the initiative, they would have a good opportunity to

* So eager was the Luftwaffe for the Dutch bases that later Jeschonnek suggested that *only* Holland, Norway, and Denmark be occupied and that Belgian neutrality be guaranteed "for the duration of the war." (J.D., Feb. 6, 1940.) This idea, politically and militarily naïve, came to nothing.

† Stuelpnagel was the *O.Qu. I* and Greiffenberg the Chief of the Operations Section of the General Staff, both of which positions Manstein had held between 1935 and 1938.

counterattack northeastward from Lorraine into the weak hinge of the German line and perhaps bottle up the German forces in Belgium.

Upon his arrival at Coblenz Manstein, as Chief of Staff of Army Group A, raised these questions with his commander-in-chief, Rundstedt. The latter saw the problem in much the same light. The upshot was that, when Rundstedt transmitted to Brauchitsch his personal letter of October 31 advising against any immediate offensive,[33] he sent with it a memorandum of the same date [34] embodying the rudiments of the plan of attack eventually adopted.

"The success of the whole operation," wrote Rundstedt, does not depend on an initial success in Belgium but "on whether it will be possible completely to defeat and *annihilate* the enemy forces fighting in Belgium and north of the Somme, not merely to push back their front line." To this end, he declared, the *Schwerpunkt* of the assault should be in the south instead of the north wing. Only then would it be possible to push the mechanized spearhead right through northern France to the Channel Coast, and thus to cut off the Allied forces that would have been drawn into Belgium to check Bock's push past Liége. Defensively, too, this plan would be superior, as a strong south wing would be better able to repel the anticipated French counterattack in Lorraine. "Both the danger and the chance of great success lie with Army Group A," Rundstedt concluded.

When Rundstedt's two-pronged *démarche* reached OKH, Halder noted deprecatingly that it lacked "positive aspects." [35] Apparently Brauchitsch never mentioned Rundstedt's memoranda to Hitler, or even to OKW.* It is not difficult to infer the reason for this lack of enthusiasm, quite apart from whatever part professional jealousy or Halder's ill-concealed dislike of Manstein [36] may have played. Brauchitsch was then resorting to every conceivable device to dissuade Hitler from launching the offensive that fall, and it would hardly have served this purpose to come up with a plan that promised better results than the one then in effect. Indulging inference a bit further, it may be noted that, if reaching the Channel Coast was in fact the primary objective, the OKH plan was superior to the Rundstedt-Manstein proposal.† Only if the encirclement and destruction of the Anglo-French

---

* Jodl's diary contains no reference to the Rundstedt papers, and Halder's diary reflects a note of caution about showing them to OKW.

† From Aachen (Reichenau's starting point) to Ostend is about 150 miles, and the Germans could expect to cover half this distance before encountering the Anglo-French forces. From Luxembourg to Abbéville or Boulogne is over 200 miles, and the Germans would have to pass through the Ardennes and breach the French fortified line at the Meuse.

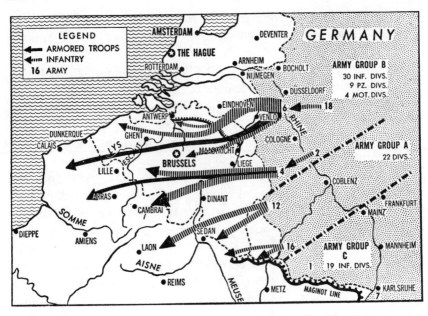

ORIGINAL OKH PLAN "GELB," AS MODIFIED OCTOBER 29, 1939.

armies in northern France were the first goal, did the new conception hold greater promise. If things went badly the Channel Coast might not be reached at all, an outcome which Hitler and Goering would be sure to view with the sharpest disfavor.

But by remarkable coincidence Hitler, ignorant as he was of the Rundstedt-Manstein proposal, was fumbling with a notion of his own that was not altogether dissimilar. "Fuehrer comes with new idea about having one armored and one motorized division attack Sedan via Arlon," Jodl noted in his diary on October 30. This "new idea," to be sure, was only the merest glimmer of the Army Group A conception; Hitler had not thought through the problem with the precise clarity of a Manstein or a Rundstedt. But surely Hitler's little brain child predisposed him to favor the Army Group A proposals when they eventually reached him.

For the time being, however, the issue lay between Army Group A and OKH. On November 3 Brauchitsch and Halder visited Rundstedt's headquarters. Much of the time was spent bemoaning Hitler's obstinate insistence on attacking in the fall, but Rundstedt took the occasion to press his tactical views on Brauchitsch. In this he had little success;

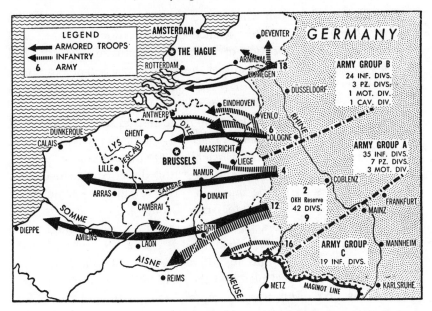

MANSTEIN PLAN "GELB," AS MODIFIED BY OKH IN FEBRUARY 1940.

Brauchitsch was not disposed to shift the weight of the attack from Bock to Rundstedt, and the latter's demands for another army headquarters and strong armored troops were countered with the excuse that these were not available. At length Rundstedt persuaded Brauchitsch to take from the OKH reserve the one panzer division that had not been allocated to Bock and put it, with some motorized units, at Rundstedt's disposal. This upshot, it may be noted, was not unlike Hitler's "new idea" of October 30.

Upon his return to Berlin, Brauchitsch engaged Hitler in the discussion of November 5 that terminated so unpleasantly,[37] and the planning came to a temporary standstill. But on November 9 Hitler was back again with his "new idea" for an armored strike through Arlon and Tintigny toward Sedan.[38] His wish was now given effect; Guderian's XIXth Corps headquarters, which had been resting near Berlin, was to be sent to Coblenz and used as the nucleus for an armored striking force in Rundstedt's army group.

The order accomplishing this, issued by OKH on November 11,[39] assigned to Guderian two panzer divisions, and one division and two independent regiments of motorized infantry. The corps was to be put in "either on the south wing of the Twelfth or in the sector of the Sixteenth Army" and was to advance through Arlon, Tintigny, and Florenville * "in the direction of Sedan and eastward." Its specified mission was to gain the west bank of the Meuse near Sedan and create favorable conditions for the progress of the offensive, especially in the event that Bock's mechanized groups were stalled in Belgium.

This idea that the *Schwerpunkt* might be shifted south if the initial success there were greater than in the north was stated more clearly in the new "Directive No. 8" of November 20. In addition to putting Holland back into the scheme of things,[40] this directive provided that: "All arrangements are to be made in order to shift the main effort quickly from Army Group B to Army Group A in case faster and greater success should be achieved at A than at B, as one might well anticipate from the present distribution of enemy forces."

Thus Rundstedt and Manstein, with a strong assist from Hitler, had seriously shaken the OKH plan, but they had not made their own prevail, and the first result was an unpromising mixture of two different concepts. The XIXth Corps might be able to break the French line at Sedan, but it was not nearly strong enough to exploit its own success by pushing on to the Channel.† The main focus of the attack remained with Bock in Belgium; only if he ran into difficulties was the weight to be shifted south to Rundstedt.

Naturally, therefore, these changes were very far from satisfying Army Group A. Manstein had now acquired an aggressive and outspoken ally in Guderian, who was completely won over to Manstein's ideas and added the weight of his own expert judgment as a tank specialist that the wooded hills and narrow roads of the Ardennes would not prove an insuperable obstacle to the German panzers.[41] On November 21 Brauchitsch and Halder came to Coblenz for a conference with all the army group and army commanders, and Manstein equipped Rundstedt with a memorandum recapitulating the arguments for strengthening the south wing by adding a third army to Rundstedt's army group.[42] But the OKH and Army Group B generals were pre-

---

* This route, following the general course of the Semoy River in the southeastern tip of Belgium, lay across the boundary between the Twelfth and Sixteenth armies. General Busch, the Sixteenth Army commander and a strong supporter of Hitler, had been to see the Fuehrer on November 10, and may have requested that the new armored force be subordinated to the Sixteenth Army.

† In Manstein's view (*Verlorene Siege*, p. 107) Hitler's purpose in ordering the armored thrust to Sedan was purely tactical, in that it was not intended to be followed up and was expected only to ease the task of Army Group B in its big push beyond Liége.

occupied with details of the offensive, then scheduled to begin on December 3, and Rundstedt made no progress.

On November 27 Rundstedt, accompanied by Busch and Guderian, conferred with Hitler. No record of the discussion has come to light, but on the journey back to Coblenz, Busch (who had seen the Fuehrer alone on November 10) remarked that Hitler had shown great sympathy for the views put forward by Army Group A.[43] Perhaps Busch or Guderian (who also saw Hitler privately at about that time)[44] had spoken to the Fuehrer about the Manstein plan, or maybe Hitler's adjutant Schmundt had gotten word of it.* Whether or not this be so, Rundstedt and Manstein began to feel that they might win Hitler over to their views, if opportunity presented itself. They made no effort to by-pass Brauchitsch but continued to bombard OKH with memoranda, despite repeated rebuffs from Brauchitsch and Halder.

Thus on November 30 Rundstedt sent a memorandum[45] to Brauchitsch repeating his request for an additional army. He pointed out that if Guderian's XIXth Corps were successful in crossing the Meuse near Sedan, that very circumstance would tend to pull the Twelfth Army west and south, away from the Fourth Army in Belgium, and therefore: "If unnecessary loss of time during the operation is to be avoided and if the line of communications is to function smoothly, preparations must immediately be made to insert a new army headquarters." This document was followed by a much more elaborate memorandum of December 6[46] from Manstein to Halder, recapitulating the entire analysis and arguing that: "The postponement of the offensive makes it possible to re-examine the structure and deployment of the army group. . . . It appears certain that the emphasis of the German offensive must be on the *south* wing. . . . The *decision* will be reached by a strong advance across South Belgium toward the Somme estuary, thereby accomplishing the encirclement of the Franco-British troops in Belgium."

To these Halder returned noncommittal replies.[47] Rundstedt thereupon scheduled a conference in Berlin with Brauchitsch, hoping that thereafter a meeting with Hitler might be arranged. The discussion with Brauchitsch took place on December 22,[48] without decisive results. No conference with the Fuehrer ensued, but from some source Jodl and, through him, Hitler were again made aware of the issue be-

---

* According to the OKW staff officer Von Lossberg (*Im Wehrmachtfuehrungsstab*, p. 55) Schmundt saw Manstein's plan while on a visit to the headquarters of Army Group A.

tween OKH and Army Group A.[49] Shifting the *Schwerpunkt* from Bock to Rundstedt, of course, would involve the Luftwaffe as well as the Army and was therefore a matter of legitimate concern to OKW.

During the next two weeks Halder and Stuelpnagel recanvassed the competing plans,[50] but the existing directives were allowed to stand. On January 10, encouraged by the prospect of clear weather, Hitler ordered preparations to launch the attack on the seventeenth. Then, as we have seen,[51] the changeable forecasts and the loss of secret documents in the forced landing of a German airplane in Belgium caused postponement of the offensive until the spring.

In the meantime Rundstedt had sent Brauchitsch another memorandum, dated January 12,[52] together with a personal letter [53] which flatly requested that the memorandum be submitted to Hitler, inasmuch as "the Fuehrer has reserved to himself the right to determine the point of concentration in executing the operation—meaning that OKH is not free to make operational decisions. . . ." This sharp if not insulting demand Brauchitsch promptly rejected,[54] saying that Hitler was involved only in order to effect the necessary co-ordination with the Luftwaffe and would act "upon my recommendation." But the constant pressure from Rundstedt was beginning to take effect, for Brauchitsch now explained that the OKW *Gelb* plan was only "the basis for the first act of the attack" and that "provision has been made" to commit an additional army under Army Group A in the course of the operation.

Throughout January, Army Group A continued to batter OKH, verbally and in memoranda,[55] and on February 7 these efforts were finally rewarded. On that day an elaborate "war game" or "map maneuver," attended by Halder and the principal officers of Army Group A and Luftflotte 3, was held at Coblenz.[56] Busch, *in loco* Gamelin, distributed hypothetical orders to the "Red" (enemy) forces; the other German commanders issued orders to their own "Blue" forces in general accordance with OKH plan *Gelb*.

The probable results were then worked out in consultation around the maps, and it was agreed that Guderian's armored spearhead might reach the Meuse at Sedan within three or four days. Guderian wanted to continue the attack westward immediately and without waiting for the infantry to catch up. Halder disagreed violently and envisaged a "concerted" attack across the Meuse with armor and infantry on the ninth or tenth day. Apart from this argument, however, it became clearly apparent—as Army Group A had long contended—that the armored force should be strengthened and closely followed by motorized infantry. At the conclusion, Manstein got the impression that Halder was beginning to fall in with the army group's conception of the attack.

A week later another war game, also attended by Halder, was staged at List's Twelfth Army headquarters. Manstein was not present; he had left Coblenz on February 9 to take command of a new infantry corps.[57] If present he would surely have been pleased to see how plainly the maneuver bore out—even to Halder's satisfaction—his oft-repeated contention that the attack across the Meuse would tend to split the German advance, and that another army was needed to fill the gap.[58] But the same disagreement about the timing of the thrust beyond Sedan developed again. Guderian and General Gustav von Wietersheim, whose motorized XIVth Corps was to follow Guderian's armor, displayed a total lack of confidence in the leadership of the operation—an attitude in which they were not supported by Rundstedt and which resulted in a very tense atmosphere.[59] The issue was again left unresolved, but in Berlin the events were even then taking place that would determine the outcome.

Once again the initiative came from Hitler himself, who had earlier requested a detailed recapitulation of the Army's intended dispositions, by battalions, batteries, and tanks. This survey was presented to him on February 13, and the Fuehrer immediately reopened the question of the center of gravity of the assault.[60] He now questioned the wisdom of using so many tanks in the "barricaded and fortified" terrain around Liége. They would be stopped at the Maas, Hitler predicted, and could be much better employed at Sedan, where the enemy would least expect them.* Jodl injected a note of caution, warning that "the thrust against Sedan is a tactical gamble, where one can be surprised by the God of War," and advocated a concentration just south of Liége. At the end of the day Greiffenberg and Heusinger † were summoned from OKH to discuss the question, and thereafter to follow up Hitler's ideas with a detailed study.

And so, when Halder returned to Berlin from the inconclusive war game at List's headquarters, the entire plan of campaign was in a fluid condition. Once again the long arm of coincidence played its part. On

---

* In this connection, Hitler referred to the documents that had fallen into Belgian hands from the forced landing on January 10, and which reflected the OKH plan for a drive through Belgium to the Channel.

† Both were subordinates of Stuelpnagel, the *O.Qu. I* of the OKH staff, who had become ill. Generalmajor Friedrich Mieth, Chief of Staff to Witzleben, was called to Berlin to deputize for the ailing Stuelpnagel, and eventually succeeded him as *O.Qu. I.*

the evening of February 17, Hitler received at dinner five newly appointed corps commanders, including Manstein.* After the meal, Manstein seized the opportunity to expound his views on the planning of the offensive. His presentation followed the lines worked out at Army Group A during the preceding months: the need for a decisive assault which would cut off and destroy the Allied forces advancing into Belgium; consequently, *Schwerpunkt* in Army Group A, which would need another army in addition to the Twelfth and Sixteenth; strengthening of Guderian's XIXth Corps spearhead with the close support of Wietersheim's XIVth—"in the south we must have strong armor or none at all, since what is in the rear cannot reach the battlefield in time"; rapid exploitation of the Sedan break-through by pushing on to the Somme estuary at the Channel Coast to complete the encirclement of Belgium and the Allied forces there.[61] At the end, according to Manstein, "the Fuehrer approved this exposition." [62]

It has often been said or suggested that this encounter between Hitler and Manstein was the decisive factor in reshaping the plan of attack.[63] This is a gross exaggeration of its importance. Halder, who was not present, appeared before the Fuehrer at noon the next day with an outline of the new plan. It was, in fact, the product of many circumstances: the pressure from Rundstedt and Manstein during the preceding months; Hitler's restless curiosity and considerable inventiveness; Brauchitsch's and Halder's lack of enthusiasm for their own plan; and its disclosure to the enemy by accident of the forced landing. All these influences culminated in the events of the ten-day period February 7 to 17—from the war game at Coblenz to the Fuehrer's reception in Berlin—which gave the *coup de grâce* to the OKH plan and demonstrated the soundness of Manstein's conception.

The immediate result was a revision of *Gelb* that was *far more drastic than anything Manstein had ever proposed.* The plan brought to Hitler by Halder on February 18 (developed by Halder's staff following the Greiffenberg-Heusinger-Jodl discussion on February 13) proposed to shift the line between Army Groups A and B northward and transfer Kluge's Fourth Army from Bock to Rundstedt. Bock was also to lose a large part of his armor, which was now to be concentrated in Army Group A for a massive assault across the Meuse north

* These were Manstein (XXXVIII), Generalleutnant Rudolf Schmidt (XXXIX), Generalleutnant Georg Stumme (XL), Generalleutnant Georg-Hans Reinhardt (XLI), and Generalleutnant Leo Geyr von Schweppenburg (XXIV). Rommel, who had just been given command of the 7th Panzer Division, was also present.

of Sedan.[64] The Second Army of Weichs was also to be deployed in the sector of Army Group A ready for insertion as soon as the front was broadened.

Thus the previous ratio between Rundstedt's and Bock's army groups was completely reversed. Under the new plan Rundstedt would have four armies with some forty-four divisions and three quarters of the mechanized troops; Bock was left with two armies, comprising about twenty-eight divisions, of which only three were armored.

Explaining the plan to Hitler, Halder tried to make out that it was really a reversion to the original OKH concepts.* This, of course, was disingenuous face-saving, and Halder was now obliged to pick up the very arguments that he had been resisting when advanced by Manstein. "Our plan," he now told Hitler, "must be to get behind the fortified line in northern France at the very start."

During the next few days Halder worked busily drafting the new orders for *Gelb*, his task complicated by the troop demands for *Weseruebung* that were simultaneously emanating from OKW and Falkenhorst.[65] On February 24 the army group and army commanders were summoned to Berlin to discuss the new plan, and the final *Gelb* orders were issued at the conclusion of the conference.[66] Redeployment of the forces at the front was to be completed by March 7.

Ironically, at the very time that Army Group A's plans prevailed, Rundstedt got "cold feet" about using armor as the spearhead of the attack. But Rundstedt's doubts, reflected in Halder's diary entries for February 21 and 24, did not affect the plan or the eventual outcome. They appear to have been precipitated by a memorandum, dated February 16, by Oberst Guenther Blumentritt (operations officer of Army Group A) warning that the barricades and fortifications under construction in Belgium and Luxembourg, and the enormous length of the German armored columns on narrow roads, might cause the armor to get "stuck" and suggesting that the infantry lead the attack and the armor follow. Blumentritt's views were shared by Sodenstern (Manstein's successor as chief of staff to Rundstedt), who embodied them in a letter to Halder early in March. But Halder replied that the methods of World

---

* H. D., February 18, 1940: "Original plan was to break through the enemy front between Liége and the Maginot Line. Drawback was constriction between 'Fortress Belgium' and Maginot Line. Extension of the attack north of Liége area was envisaged so as to obtain wider frontage. The central feature of that plan was to concentrate the main weight in the south and to use Antwerp instead of Liége as the pivot of the great wheeling movement. Now we have reverted to the original scheme."

War I must be laid aside and that it was a time for new ideas and the taking of risks commensurate with the magnitude of the operation.[67] In the end the fears of Rundstedt and his staff were overcome by Guderian's fiery advocacy of armor as the major instrument of the assault.

An important question of command remained to be worked out. The "armored wedge" that was to attack through Sedan was now to include not only Guderian's XIXth armored and Wietersheim's XIVth motorized corps but Reinhardt's newly formed XLIst armored corps as well. It seemed apparent that this large concentration of mechanized troops—unprecedented at that time—needed a co-ordinating over-all command of its own, apart from the army and army group head-quarters that would be concerned with a multitude of other matters.

Who should command the armored wedge? Guderian was an obvi-ous candidate, but he was outranked by Wietersheim, who had been in disfavor with Hitler ever since an altercation between them in August 1938. Manstein was also considered but he was even farther down the rank list than Guderian; furthermore, he had had no com-mand experience with armor and had become a somewhat controversial figure as a result of his intransigent opposition to the OKH plan. Weichs had the necessary seniority and knew tanks (he had been the first commander of the 1st Panzer Division) but was already in command of the Second Army. The only corps commander senior to Wietersheim who had handled armor * was Kleist, and eventually the choice fell on him. No doubt the rank problem could have been handled by a promotion or by transferring Wietersheim, and the selec-tion of Kleist was a surprising one both politically † and because he was regarded as "old-school" in tactical matters. But apparently Brauchitsch and Halder thought that he would be more tractable and less likely to take the bit in his teeth than Guderian or Manstein, and on February 29 Hitler agreed to his designation as commander of "Panzer Group Kleist," [68] comprising the three corps of Guderian, Wietersheim, and Reinhardt.

And so, during the first part of March, the troops and headquarters of the German Army redeployed and reorganized themselves in accord-ance with the new dispensation. On March 13 Brauchitsch and Halder

* Kleist's XXIInd Corps in southern Poland had included one panzer and one light division.
† Kleist, of an old Prussian military family and a close friend of the Hinden-burgs, had been retired from active duty at the time of the Blomberg-Fritsch affair.

went to the front to review the results with the field commanders. On March 15 the principal generals from Army Group A and its armies and armored corps came to Berlin to outline their dispositions and intentions to Hitler, and the following day came the leaders from Army Group B.[69] Bock, not unnaturally, displayed some dissatisfaction over the weakening of his forces, an anxiety which the Luftwaffe (Kesselring) shared, inasmuch as a rapid advance into Holland and Belgium was particularly necessary from the standpoint of the airborne troops that were to be dropped at critical points behind the enemy lines. Nevertheless, the following day Halder recorded his impression that [70] "The Fuehrer now approves the preparations and is manifestly confident of success."

One basic question, however, remained unsettled: if and when the "armored wedge" crossed the Meuse and broke through the French lines at Sedan, what should be done next? This was the very question on which Guderian and Halder had differed so violently at the February war games, and Hitler put it squarely to Guderian during the Army Group A conference on March 15. As Guderian recounts the discussion: [71]

> Hitler asked: "And then what are you going to do?" He was the first person who had thought to ask me this vital question.* I replied: "Unless I receive orders to the contrary, I intend on the next day to continue my advance westward. The supreme leadership must decide whether my objective is to be Amiens or Paris. In my opinion the correct course is to drive past Amiens to the English Channel." Hitler nodded and said nothing more. Only General Busch, who commanded the Sixteenth Army on my left, cried out: "Well, I don't think you'll cross the river in the first place!" Hitler, the tension visible in his face, looked at me to see what I would reply. I said: "There's no need for you to do so [i.e., make the crossing], in any case." Hitler made no comment.

Following the conference, Halder noted [72] as one of its "interesting points" the fact that Hitler had "reserved decision on further moves after the crossing of the Meuse." As will be seen, this uncertainty had awkward though not decisive consequences when the anticipated contingency actually arose during the campaign.[73]

With the preparations for *Gelb* as well as *Weseruebung* virtually complete, Hitler went off to the Brenner Pass to meet with Mussolini, and then to the Obersalzberg. Upon his return, attention centered on

---

* This comment, of course, is nonsense, as the question had been repeatedly and heatedly debated.

the Scandinavian adventure, which was to be undertaken before *Gelb*. At OKH and on the western front during the intervening weeks, the generals were occupied with special features of their program—the airborne landings planned for Holland and Belgium, Leeb's feint attacks to hold French troops in the Maginot Line, and numerous details of logistics and communications.

The only major planning activities during this waiting period concerned the front along the Rhine and Maginot Line, held by Leeb's Army Group C. Its role in *Gelb* was purely defensive, but some consideration had been given to a subsequent attack (given the cover-name *"Gruen"*) on the Maginot Line in the Saar area, if *Gelb* were successful and the French were thereby badly weakened.[74]

On March 21 a new element was injected into this picture by a letter from OKW to OKH stating that: "Fuehrer requests that C-in-C Army Group C be directed to draw up a plan for an offensive operation from the Upper Rhine in the direction of the Plateau de Langres." It was to be assumed that thirty to thirty-five divisions would be available, that parts of the French Army had already been beaten, and that its reserves were fully committed on the main front.[75] Subsequent discussion with OKW revealed that an uncertain number of Italian divisions might be available for this operation, to which the name *"Braun"* was applied. No doubt it was a by-product of the meeting at the Brenner Pass, from which Hitler had returned on March 19.[76]

On March 27 Leeb came to Berlin, accompanied by his chief of staff and army commanders,* for a conference with Hitler, Brauchitsch, and Halder.[77] After the commanders had reported on the army group's general situation, Hitler discussed Italy and Mussolini, explaining "that Italy is too weak to come in before France has been dealt a heavy blow." Leeb and his subordinates then departed, but Hitler continued the discussion with Brauchitsch and Halder. If *Gelb* were successful and the Germans reached the Seine, what next? Perhaps an attack just north of Basel, through the so-called "Belfort gap" toward Dijon, would bottle up the entire Allied Army in northeastern France. This was the strategic basis of *Braun,* and:

> For this offensive we may reckon with about twenty Italian divisions. At the outset [of *Gelb*], Italy will be requested to get ready. Italy will need two weeks for mobilization. During those two weeks it will become clear

* The army commanders were Witzleben (1st) and Dollmann (7th), and the chief of staff was Generalleutnant Hans Felber. Leeb's former chief of staff, Generalleutnant Georg von Sodenstern, had replaced Manstein at Army Group A.

whether or not we have any prospects of a major success. If the prospects are good, Italy is sure to march. It will take the Italians twenty days to get their troops over to us, so that if everything goes according to plan we should be able to strike on the Upper Rhine about six weeks after X-Day [i.e., the first day of *Gelb*]. Prior to X-Day, only theoretical preparations.

A few days later Halder went to Frankfurt for further analysis of *Braun*. Leeb was planning for twelve assault crossings of the Rhine by forty-two divisions, with the main effort south of Strasbourg, and the concentration opposite Mulhouse-Belfort. Throughout April and early May, while Norway was being conquered, OKH and Army Group C made paper preparations for this offensive.[78] General Heinrich von Stuelpnagel, who on April 6 returned to duty after an illness, was put in charge of the staff for liaison with the Italians.*

However, there was little serious intention behind *Braun*. Mussolini would not come into the war until the French were half beaten; at that point would there be any real need to bring Italian troops to the upper Rhine? Someone suggested the opposite notion that *Braun* might be resorted to if *Gelb* proved indecisive. Halder had "no sympathy at all for this scheme, which is reminiscent of Ludendorff's policy of unceasing attacks in 1918 . . . the strategy of attrition, a policy that is sterile of success."

The Italian general staff was no more enthusiastic than the German,[79] and spoke interestedly of the Balkans, foreshadowing the ignominious Greek campaign that Mussolini was to launch in October. On April 29, Stuelpnagel reported to Halder[80] that Italian preparations had "made no progress." In the end nothing came of *Braun;* during the second phase of the Battle of France the Germans went over the Rhine alone, and the Italians made little more than a gesture in Savoy.

And so, on May 10, the German attack was launched in substantial conformity with the plan—which I have called the "Manstein variant"— formulated on February 24 and finally approved on March 15 and 16. I have given it Manstein's name because he, more than any other one person, was responsible for its conception and adoption. I describe it as a variant because it was a tactical modification of the OKH plan rather than a new strategic concept. Manstein himself has been careful to point out[80a] that his plan did not contemplate the defeat of the Allied armies in a single operation, but rather the destruction of the

---

* Mieth continued to deputize as *O.Qu. I,* and formally succeeded Stuelpnagel in that office in June.

Allies' northern wing, so that, thus weakened, the enemy forces could be knocked out by a second offensive.

Today, others are anxious to seize the military credit. Halder's post-war booklet does not even mention Manstein's name in this connection and pictures the plan as an OKH product.[81] Under interrogation in December 1947, Halder claimed it as his own, and egregiously mis-described Manstein's plan as embodying an intention to turn south rather than west after breaking through at Sedan, in order to pin part of the French Army against the northern end of the Maginot Line.[82] As we have seen, there is not the slightest basis for this perversion of the facts.*

Even more preposterous is the contention, advanced by Goerlitz, that Manstein's plan was designed to avoid the violation of Belgian neutrality [83]—a notion never espoused by Manstein, and which would surely provoke his own wry smile. For Manstein proposed to launch the major push through Luxembourg and southeastern Belgium, an area just as neutral as northern Belgium. And he proposed to weaken, but not abandon, Bock's advance across the Meuse at Liége, in order to draw the Allies into Belgium, where they would be encircled by the German drive to the Somme estuary. Manstein sought victory and was no more troubled about Belgian neutrality than were his brother generals.

The Manstein plan entailed risks which, against a more evenly matched foe, might well have proved fatal to its success. According to Heusinger,[84] Bock delivered himself in April of an emphatic warning to Halder. Bock, to be sure, had personal reasons to dislike the new plan, which deprived his army group of the primary mission. But his misgivings were reasonable enough. Had the French been able to main-tain and maneuver a strong reserve behind the northern end of the Maginot Line, Rundstedt's left flank would have been an inviting and vulnerable target for a counteroffensive. But Halder now regarded the plan as his own and defended it strongly against Bock's criticisms. The OKH counted heavily on surprise, French caution, and the diversionary effect of Bock's own offensive north of Liége, and in the upshot this optimism was fully vindicated.

---

* It is true that Manstein warned against a French counterattack in Lorraine and wanted to spoil it by advancing south as far as the Aisne. But, beginning with the very first memorandum of October 31, 1939 (*supra*, p. 165), the Army Group A plan envisaged pushing west to the Somme estuary, in order to cut off the Allied forces in Belgium. Halder did not fear the supposed counterattack, and in this respect events bore him out.

Manstein's transfer to a corps command from his post as Rundstedt's chief of staff has been commonly pictured as an act of revenge by OKH because of his vigorous and outspoken opposition to the original *Gelb* plan.[85] In this there is a modicum of fact and much exaggeration. It is clear enough that Halder resented Manstein's manner and distrusted his willingness to follow orders; certainly Bock was annoyed by the diminution of his role in the offensive. No doubt the OKH generals wanted to get Manstein out of their hair, and it is very possible that, even if Manstein had had the rank and field experience to warrant giving him command of a panzer corps, Halder might have found means to prevent it. Under interrogation in 1947, Halder declared that he brought about Manstein's transfer from Rundstedt's army group, and opposed giving him command of the armored wedge, because he feared that Manstein would follow his own ideas and disregard orders from OKH.

Nevertheless, Manstein's transfer from army group chief of staff to corps commander was no demotion, but a promotion in strict accordance with standard German military personnel practice. His promising brother officers of approximately equal rank—Christian Hansen, Vietinghoff, Stumme, Rudolf Schmidt, Reinhardt, Brockdorff-Ahlefeldt—were given corps commands at about the same time. Except for a brief period as a divisional commander in 1938–39, Manstein had been on staff duty since early in 1934, and he was long overdue for a field assignment.

On his record, however, he had no legitimate claim to command a panzer corps, much less the three-corps panzer group. Each of the armored and motorized corps was already commanded by a general of senior or nearly equal rank and proven ability, and with field experience in the command of mechanized forces,* which Manstein entirely lacked. Later in the war he was to emerge as one of the ablest *Feldherrn,* but on the eve of the Battle of France Manstein was a *Generalleutnant* who had made his mark as a brilliant staff officer. There was not the slightest reason to prefer him to any of those who then held armored corps commands.

There is, accordingly, no warrant for gilding Manstein's record with an aura of martyrdom. His was the role of staff planner, and he fulfilled it with distinction. The German attack in the West was one of the most shrewdly and skillfully contrived plans in the annals of modern war-

* These were Wietersheim (XIVth), Hoth (XVth), Erich Hoepner (XVIth), Guderian (XIXth), Rudolf Schmidt (XXXIXth) and Reinhardt (XLIst).

fare. In its conception and formulation Manstein had the greatest individual share but no monopoly. His commander, Rundstedt, and his staff subordinates, Blumentritt and Henning von Tresckow, as well as Guderian, all contributed importantly to the development of the plan and in demonstrating its practicability and promise. Halder, for all his initial hostility to the army group's proposals, greatly strengthened the plan when he finally grasped its potentialities.

Finally, the participation of Hitler should not be minimized. Amateur that he was in military matters, he had sense enough to be dissatisfied with the original *Gelb* plan, to cast about for a better one, and to recognize the merit of Manstein's ideas. This was an occasion—one of relatively few—when Hitler and the generals teamed effectively if not harmoniously, and their collaboration laid the basis for a military triumph of breathtaking speed and dimensions.

The Final Dispositions

Late in the afternoon of May 9, Adolf Hitler and his entourage set off from Berlin in his special train. Those not in the know, such as his press chief, Otto Dietrich, were told that the Fuehrer was going to inspect shipyards at Hamburg.[86] But the train soon turned southwest toward Cologne, and before dawn on May 10 the passengers disembarked at Euskirchen, from where they proceeded by automobile to Hitler's headquarters—which that incurable romantic called the *Felsennest* ("Eyrie")—near Muenstereifel, some twenty miles southwest of Bonn. Fifty-five miles due west of the *Felsennest* lay Liége, toward which Bock was even then launching the attack on which all eyes were riveted this opening day of the great western offensive.

As Hitler fidgeted nervously in front of his bunker, OKW staff officers under Jodl's direction were laying out maps showing the German and enemy dispositions, on which the progress of the campaign would be plotted for the Fuehrer's benefit.* They covered a front of nearly 400 miles, from the Ems estuary between Holland and Germany on the North Sea coast to the Swiss-Franco-German corner near Basel.

The German high command had a reasonably accurate picture of what forces lay on the other side of this long front. In Holland some ten divisions, and in Belgium about twice that number, waited nervously behind their defenses. The Dutch relied heavily on their

* Tables of the organization and identity of the major German units on the western front are set forth in Appendix C, *infra*, pp. 427–29.

numerous canals and flooding devices to seal off from the Germans their western stronghold—"Fortress Holland," including Amsterdam, Rotterdam, and The Hague. The Belgians had built fortifications, including the famous Fort Eben Emael, along the Meuse and the Albert Canal. In France 103 divisions (including ten British) were deployed in three army groups between the Channel and Switzerland.

The 135 French, British, Belgian, and Dutch divisions matched the Germans in numbers of men and tanks. But they were an aggregation, not a force. For fear of provoking the Germans, the Dutch and Belgians had refrained from staff consultations with their more powerful potential allies, the French and British. The French armor was not concentrated in powerful formations, like the German, but was scattered along the front.

The Allied high command was waiting and guessing where the blow would fall. It rightly assumed that the Germans would come through Belgium, but it had no counterplan other than to advance toward the Scheldt or perhaps the Meuse and help the Belgians stem the German tide. This intention the Germans divined; the Allies' northward advance into Belgium was, indeed, the key to the success of the Manstein plan.

On the entire western front, the Germans marshaled a total of 136 divisions.* Of these, some nineteen were assigned to Leeb's Army Group C, to stand fast opposite the Rhine and Maginot Line, and feint an attack in the Saar area. The bulk of Leeb's forces was concentrated in Witzleben's First Army west of the Rhine; on the river itself, Dollmann's weak Seventh Army would have to depend on "static" divisions and defensive artillery, in the unlikely event of a French assault.

For *Gelb*, accordingly, the Germans were able to assemble about 117 divisions, of which at least forty-two were held in OKH reserve for subsequent commitment depending on the development of the battle. The initial assault, therefore, was made in a strength of seventy-five divisions, grouped in twenty-two corps. Thirty divisions were in Bock's Army Group B, and forty-five in Rundstedt's Army Group A. This vast force was deployed along a front (from Luxembourg to Nijmegen) only 165 miles long. It was correspondingly "deep," and some of the attacking units had to march many miles in Germany before reaching the frontier.

At the northern end of the battle front, Kuechler's Eighteenth Army

* About twenty other divisions were in Norway, Denmark, East Prussia, and Poland.

(one of Bock's two) was to overcome the Dutch defenses and occupy Holland. This operation was not really an integral or necessary part of *Gelb;* as we have seen,[87] it was only because of the Luftwaffe's insistence that the Netherlands was included in the scope of the offensive. It was appropriate, therefore, that Goering's airborne troops should play a leading part in the reduction of "Fortress Holland," by capturing and holding strategic points for the advancing ground forces. These latter were grouped in three corps, and included six second-string infantry divisions, an augmented division of motorized SS infantry, a cavalry division (the only one in the German Army), and one of the ten panzer divisions.

Bock's other army—the Sixth, under Reichenau—was far more powerful, comprising seventeen infantry divisions in five corps, and Hoepner's mechanized XVIth Corps with one motorized infantry and two panzer divisions. The army was deployed north of Liége and was to strike in a southwesterly direction toward Ostend and Calais. If all went according to plan, the Allies would throw their left wing northward, and Reichenau would clash with them in Belgium west of the Meuse.

Between Liége and Luxembourg, the main blow was to be delivered by Rundstedt's Army Group A. In numbers it was half again as large as Bock's, and it included seven of the ten German panzer divisions. Kluge's Fourth Army, with nine infantry divisions in three corps and Hoth's XVth Corps of two panzer divisions, was to drive across southern Belgium, crossing the Meuse in the Dinant-Namur area and the French border near Maubeuge. Kleist's three-corps panzer group was the Sunday punch; its five panzer and three motorized infantry divisions were to race through the Ardennes of southern Belgium and northern Luxembourg and break through the French lines near Sedan. This "armored wedge" was to be followed, and protected against a flanking counterattack from the southwest, by List's Twelfth and Busch's Sixteenth armies, jointly comprising six corps with twenty-five infantry divisions.

Some of the forty-odd infantry divisions of the OKH reserve were already marshaled behind the assault wave, while others were scattered at garrisons and training grounds all over Germany. Behind Rundstedt's lines, Weichs's Second Army stood ready to take command of a sector between List and Kluge, as the German advance broadened the front. Still farther back, the Ninth Army (initially under Blaskowitz) was in the process of formation as another reserve army headquarters. Half a dozen corps headquarters, including the newly formed XXXVIIIth (Manstein), XLth (Georg Stumme), XLIInd (Walter Kuntze) and XLIIIrd (Hermann Ritter von Speck), waited in the rear for commitment to battle after the initial assault.

On the airfields of northeastern Germany, Goering's Luftwaffe massed some 3500 aircraft to support the ground assault. The German Air Force was at or near "the peak of its operational efficiency as an offensive air force," [88] with the experience of the Spanish, Polish, and Norwegian campaigns, a flexible and smoothly functioning field organization to meet the vicissitudes of battle, and an attitude of exuberant confidence. Among the fighter pilots were those still obscure lieutenants and captains—Werner Moelders, Adolf Galland, Wilhelm Balthasar, and Helmut Wick—who were about to emerge into fame as aerial gladiators.

For *Gelb*, the German air units on the western front were divided between Kesselring's Luftflotte 2 and Sperrle's Luftflotte 3. The former was to support Bock's army group and the latter Rundstedt's. Within the *Luftflotten* the bombers and fighters that were to give direct support to the ground troops were grouped in five *Fliegerkorps* of about 750 planes each. In Luftflotte 2, Richthofen's Fliegerkorps VIII was to work closely with Reichenau's Sixth Army and especially Hoepner's armored XVIth Corps, while General Alfred Keller's Fliegerkorps IV was to concentrate on long-range objectives, such as enemy airfields and rear-area depots. Under Sperrle were General Ulrich Grauert's Fliegerkorps I, Von Greim's Fliegerkorps V, and Bruno Loerzer's Fliegerkorps II, which was to operate in conjunction with Kleist's armored wedge.

The primary missions of the Luftwaffe were to attack and, so far as possible, destroy the Allied air forces, and to give tactical support to the Army. But these were by no means its only battle functions. The antiaircraft units were grouped in two *Flakkorps* of three *Flakregiments* each. To Sperrle's *Luftflotte* was allocated Flakkorps I under General der Flakartillerie Hubert Weise, and to Kesselring's, Flakkorps II under Generalleutnant Otto Dessloch. Kesselring also had the responsibility for naval air operations, and to his *Luftflotte* was assigned the newly formed Fliegerkorps IX under Generalleutnant Joachim Coeler, which was being trained for mine-laying and other maritime missions.

Finally, there were the special and spectacular tasks of General Kurt Student's 7th Fliegerdivision for airborne troops, which was also subor-

MAJOR GERMAN AND ALLIED DISPOSITIONS, MAY 9, 1940.

dinated to Kesselring. Under the original *Gelb* plan, it had been intended to use Student's forces in Belgium near Ghent, to expedite Bock's advance to the coast.[89] The removal of the bulk of the armor from Bock's army group under the revised plan, however, made it unlikely that Ghent could be reached on the ground soon enough to warrant an air landing there, and the reinsertion of Holland within the scope of the offensive on Goering's insistence dictated Student's employment there to capture bridges and airfields.

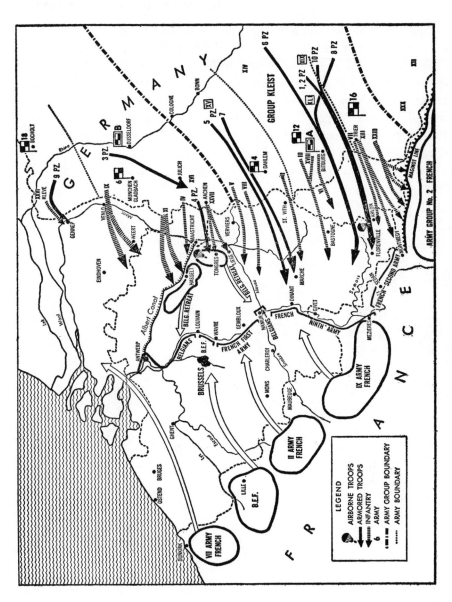

GERMAN DISPOSITIONS FOR THE BATTLE OF FRANCE (GELB), MAY 10–11, 1940.

And what of the German Navy in these great plans? It was the Franco-Prussian War all over again;[90] Raeder had little to do, and, especially after the losses sustained in Norway, little to do it with. A few sorties by U-boats in the English Channel and E-boats along the Dutch coast, the occupation of some of the West Frisian Islands—that was all. On May 7, just three days before the offensive was launched, Raeder conferred with Hitler about Norway, mine-laying, and other naval matters, but *Gelb* was not even mentioned.[91]

Victory in the West was to be the victory of panzer and Stuka.

CHAPTER SIX

Holland:
The Five-Day War

A T DAWN on May 10 the Wehrmacht hurled itself across the borders of Holland, Belgium, and Luxembourg, launching the great campaign that had been so carefully planned during the quiet winter months. Strategically it was a single offensive, and at the time the fighting during the first few days appeared to be all one battle, albeit of wide geographical range.

From a tactical standpoint, however, the German invasion of Holland was quite separate from the major attack through Belgium and Luxembourg. Indeed, it was not even a necessary part of the Battle of France. In this and other respects there is a striking resemblance between the German operations in Scandinavia and Holland, for neither was vital to the main German design in the West. With the possible exception of the narrow Maastricht "appendix" of Holland between Germany and northern Belgium (and even this might have been skirted, as it was in 1914), the basic plan *Gelb* for defeating the Allied armies and gaining the Channel Coast could have been carried out without any incursion on Dutch soil.

In both Scandinavia and the Netherlands, the Germans' purposes were primarily related to future air and sea warfare against Britain or, more accurately, both air and sea in the case of Norway, air only in Denmark and Holland. So, too, in both instances the fear of being anticipated by the English was a major factor. Even if the Dutch could be cajoled or frightened into tolerating the passage of German troops through the Maastricht area into Belgium, the Germans were by no means sure that London would passively accept this condition of affairs. To the Luftwaffe especially, it appeared far preferable to seize the Dutch airfields rather than worry about their falling into British hands.

If the fighting in Holland was, in a military sense, a sideshow, it was one of great interest and variety, in which the old and the new were strangely mixed. German soldiers crossed the Dutch frontier in airplanes, tanks, trucks, boats, railroad trains, on foot, and in the north on horseback. As in Norway, the Wehrmacht relied heavily on surprise, speed, and deception. In both operations a handful of second-line divisions was stiffened with a division of Austrian regulars. A few parachute and air-landing units had been employed to good effect at Oslo, Stavanger, and a few other key points in Norway and Denmark. In Holland a much larger contingent of airborne troops—nearly two divisions—played the decisive part in the rapid success of the assault.

As in the other western democracies overrun by the Germans in 1940, the invasion of Holland was accompanied by a host of rumors of treason and espionage. German parachutists were said to be descending disguised as policemen, farmers, priests, and even as nuns. "Fifth columnists" were reported to be sniping at Dutch troops from windows in The Hague and Rotterdam, and there was a story that in Amsterdam's Hotel de l'Europe "magnesium bombs" had been found which were intended for signaling to German aircraft.

True or false, these rumors were harmful to the Dutch cause. Public confidence was badly shattered, and much time and energy were wasted in wild-goose chases. In fact, the stories were mostly unfounded. A few resident Germans and Dutch Nazis aided the invaders, and at the Maas bridges the Germans tried a number of deceptive stratagems, involving the use of Dutch uniforms. But most of these tricks misfired, and careful investigations since the war have abundantly proved that in Holland, as in Norway, the reports of subversion and sabotage were uniformly exaggerated and often utterly groundless.[1]

Although the Netherlands is a small country, her common frontier with Germany is over 200 miles long. The defense of so extensive a front was plainly impossible with Holland's slender military resources, and it was manned only for reconnaissance and to screen the destruction of bridges over the Maas and Yssel and other watercourses near the border. The Maas and Yssel themselves were lightly fortified as a first delaying position, but even this line (from Maastricht to Kampen on the Ysselmeer, more familiarly known to Americans as the Zuider

Zee) is 125 miles in length and was far beyond the Dutch defensive capacities.

The first of the two main defense positions, known as the "Grebbe-Peel Line," extended from the south shore of the Ysselmeer near Amersfoort south and slightly east to the Belgian frontier near Weert. It was not much over eighty miles long and exploited the natural defenses of the Geld Valley (much of which could be flooded), the Maas, the Peel marshes (whence the name "Peel" for the southern part of the line), and the Noorder Canal to the Belgian border. North of the Rhine the natural strength of the "Grebbe" part of the line had been augmented by extensive field fortifications, with casemates, bunkers, and antitank obstacles.

The last-ditch defense line surrounded "Fortress Holland" *—the area (including Rotterdam, Amsterdam, The Hague, Utrecht, and Leyden) from Den Helder to the Holland Deep. It was protected on the south by the Rhine-Maas estuary, and on the east by the Ysselmeer and the extensive inundations that could be effected along the so-called "East Front," between Muiden and the estuary. This "Front" was covered with permanent and extensive fortifications, but they were not so modern as those of the Grebbe Line.

To man these defenses, the Dutch Army had four corps of two infantry divisions each, a light division of cyclists and motorcyclists, and an assortment of independent brigades, artillery regiments, and frontier battalions. Three of the corps and the light division were deployed along the Grebbe-Peel Line, with the fourth corps in reserve in Fortress Holland. The Army was pitifully weak in modern artillery of all kinds, especially antitank and antiaircraft weapons. The Air Force comprised but four fighter squadrons, and one each of bombers and reconnaissance aircraft. The invasion of Norway made the Dutch aware of the danger of airborne troop landings on airfields, but they were unable in four weeks to take effective countermeasures.[2]

The Germans calculated with nicety the forces that would be required to overcome Dutch resistance in a few days. General Georg von Kuechler's Eighteenth Army—the smallest of the German armies engaged in the West—did not outnumber the Dutch ground forces but was vastly superior in mobility and fire power. Even more important,

---

* Although "Holland" and "Netherlands" are used interchangeably in English, the former name correctly applies only to the provinces of North and South Holland, lying west of the Ysselmeer and north of the Rhine-Maas estuary.

the Germans enjoyed total superiority in the air, and their striking power was greatly augmented by the airborne troops of Student's 7th Fliegerdivision that immediately penetrated Fortress Holland to seize bridges, tie down the Dutch reserves, and spread confusion behind the lines.

The Airborne Assault

Across North Brabant, and in Rotterdam and The Hague, the citizenry was awakened early in the morning of May 10 by the heavy drone of airplanes. For a time it was thought that perhaps they were on their way to England, but the delusion was short-lived. The first large-scale airborne invasion in military history was under way.

Paratroop training was still in an elementary stage, and Student had available only two regiments (about 4500 men) of qualified jumpers (*Fallschirmjaeger*).[3] The bulk of the airborne troops was "borrowed" from the Army and was to be landed by Junkers transport planes. The three regiments of the 22nd Infantry Division and one from the 46th had been specially trained for air-landing (*Luftlande*) operations. Under the command of Generalleutnant Hans Graf von Sponeck, these constituted the bulk of the troops landed near Rotterdam and The Hague.

Among those roused by the air armada's thunder was Foreign Minister Eelco van Kleffens, at his home in The Hague.[4] Shortly before four o'clock he was informed by telephone that the principal Dutch airdromes were being bombed. Swarms of German planes then appeared over The Hague itself, bombing the nearby airfields and barracks. Van Kleffens dispatched urgent appeals for aid to London and Paris, and hurried off to an emergency Cabinet meeting at the Prime Minister's residence. At about six o'clock he was told that the German Minister, Count von Zech-Burkersroda, was urgently requesting an interview.

Van Kleffens drove at once to the Foreign Ministry. On the way he was obliged to take cover from three low-flying German planes, strafing the streets with machine-gun fire and throwing out leaflets demanding Holland's immediate surrender under threat of heavy destruction. When he reached his office, the German Minister—son-in-law to Von Bethmann-Holweg of "scrap-of-paper" fame—read an ultimatum calling for the cessation of all resistance to the German forces. As justification, Count von Zech charged, on Berlin's instructions, that the Nether-

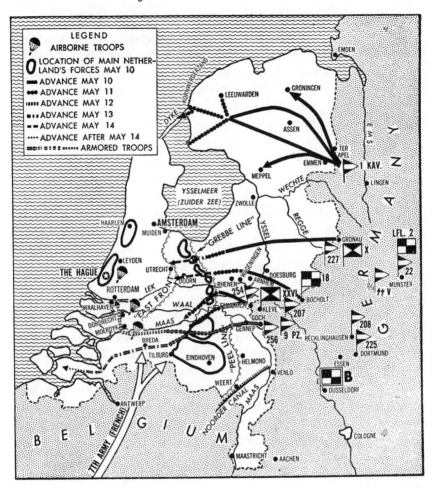

THE GERMAN CONQUEST OF THE NETHERLANDS, MAY 10–15, 1940.

lands and Belgian governments were conniving at an imminent Anglo-French invasion of their countries. Even as he spoke, in Berlin Ribbentrop was handing to the Dutch Minister a crudely concocted dossier in support of these accusations. The Dutch promptly and indignantly denied them, and van Kleffens informed Count von Zech that Germany's unprovoked attack had brought about a state of war.

The war, indeed, was already raging, not only at Holland's threshold but at her very hearth. The first wave of German planes had bombed the barracks, hangars, and defensive emplacements at the Dutch airfields. The bombers were followed by Junkers 52 transports, which

disgorged parachute troops near the Dordrecht and Moerdijk bridges and around the edges of the airfields of The Hague and Rotterdam.*
The *Fallschirmjaeger* at once assaulted the dazed and decimated defenders, many of whom had been caught in their barracks and slaughtered by the bombs, as was to happen again at Pearl Harbor's Hickam Field on a later "day of infamy." Hard on the tails of the paratroop transports came others that landed on the runways (carefully spared by the bombers), and from these poured the heavily armed airborne infantry of Sponeck's 22nd Luftlande Division.

The largest force of parachute and airborne troops—including two regiments of the 22nd Division, led by Sponeck in person—was put down near The Hague and the neighboring cities of Leyden and Delft. Their purpose was to capture the nearby airfields (Valkenburg, Ockenburg, and Ypenburg), tie down the Dutch reserves, invest The Hague, paralyze the government, and forestall any British efforts to reinforce the Dutch † on the ground or in the air.

These objectives were only partly achieved. The three airfields were all captured in the first assault, and most of Sponeck's troops were safely landed. But the Dutch reacted energetically; infantry reserve units were brought up to counterattack with artillery support, and by evening all three fields had been recaptured. The Germans then fell back into the nearby villages and established defensive positions from which the Dutch were unable to dislodge them. In this way Sponeck's force tied down the Dutch reserves in considerable numbers, at a moment when they were sorely needed elsewhere.

The German plans to capture the Queen and a number of high officials, and thereby to disrupt the machinery of government in The Hague, did not succeed. They did, however, spawn some fantastic and widely believed *mythes de guerre*. One which has gained respectable currency [6] is that Sponeck's plane was shot down, and that he and his white horse were killed in the crash. Documents are said to have been found on his body showing that he was under orders to capture The Hague on the first day of the invasion and that the horse and the general's dress uniform had been put aboard the plane so that he would be suitably accoutred for a triumphal entry.

---

* Other airfields, at Schiphol (Amsterdam), Hilversum, and elsewhere, were bombed without efforts to capture them.

† The British did in fact send one battalion to the Hook of Holland on May 11, but the situation was so confused that it merely held its position there and encountered no enemy troops. The battalion was re-embarked and withdrawn to England on May 14, when it became clear that Dutch resistance was collapsing.[5]

In fact, Sponeck lived to fight another day,* and of course there was no such horse. This tale finds its origin in the fact that orders signed by Sponeck were found on the body of a German soldier near the Valkenburg airfield. These were based on accompanying reports from German agents in The Hague, and maps with arrows indicating the air-raid shelter of the Royal Family and the dwellings of the Premier and other civil and military dignitaries. Clearly, the Germans had planned to send advance detachments from the captured airfields into The Hague (mounted not on white horses but on motorcycles) to capture these personages and throw the Dutch leadership into chaos. But these schemes had to be abandoned because of the strong Dutch resistance and their speedy recapture of the fields.

More immediately important to the success of the invasion were the landings farther east. Student himself jumped with his paratroops near Rotterdam, despite the strong disapproval of his immediate superior, Kesselring, who thought that Student should have commanded from the rear until co-ordinated operations on the ground became possible. But Student enjoyed direct contact with Hitler and Goering, both of whom participated personally in planning the airborne assault, and Kesselring was unable to check the paratroop general's flair for the spectacular.[7]

The primary targets of the operation at Rotterdam were the bridges over the Nieuwe Maas giving access to the city from the south. The greater part of the city lies on the northern shore of the Nieuwe Maas. There is an island in the river at this point, so that there are bridges over both the northern and southern arms of the river. These were initially secured by a company of airborne infantry daringly landed on the river in old hydroplanes. In the meantime the main body of the troops was landed a few miles southwest of the city at Waalhaven airport, which was captured by the usual sequence of bombing and paratroop assault, prior to the arrival of the airborne infantry in Junkers transports.†

* He was awarded the *Ritterkreuz* for his exploits in Holland and was later given a corps command in Russia. However, he was never promoted and during the winter of 1941–42 he incurred Hitler's violent displeasure for what the Fuehrer regarded as disobedience. Sponeck was stripped of his rank and imprisoned. Shortly after the July 1944 plot against Hitler, Sponeck was executed although apparently he was not involved in the conspiracy.

† The fighting in Rotterdam is graphically described in *Soldat unter Soldaten* (1951), by Dietrich von Choltitz, then an *Oberstleutnant* in the 16th Regiment of the 22nd Division. This was the first German regiment adapted for air-landing operations, and it had been given especially rigorous training in preparation for the Rotterdam undertaking. Interestingly enough it was discovered that the noise of

As soon as Waalhaven was in hand, infantry and paratroops raced to the bridges, to relieve the water-landed company. The Dutch counterattacked with determination but were unable to shake the Germans' grip on the bridges. Meanwhile German reinforcements were pouring into Waalhaven, including field guns and a mountain battery. On May 11 Dutch artillery fire and air bombing, in which British planes participated,[8] rendered Waalhaven unusable, but the Germans by then were landing their transports at a large parking space (Feyenoord) southeast of Rotterdam, and their hold on the bridges, though tenuous, could not be broken.

The approaches to Rotterdam were protected, not only by the Nieuwe Maas but also by the more southerly branches of the Rhine-Maas estuary, the Oude Maas, and Holland Deep. The former was spanned at Dordrecht, and the latter by two great bridges, road and rail, at Moerdijk. It was by this route that Kuechler planned to break into Fortress Holland, and the Moerdijk bridges were essential to this purpose.

They were, of course, wired for destruction, but the Dutch were reluctant to blow them up because they were part of the speediest route for sending reserves from Holland to the Peel line in North Brabant, and the only route by which Allied ground troops from Belgium could reach Holland. Exploiting this hesitancy, the German paratroops were able to take the Dutch guards by surprise and overpower them before they could destroy the bridges. The same was done at Dordrecht, and thus all the bridges giving access from North Brabant to Rotterdam and Fortress Holland fell at once into German hands.

Because of the great width (more than a mile) of the Holland Deep, the loss of the Moerdijk bridges was an especially severe blow to the defenders. But it was impossible to send reinforcements from Holland, because the Germans also held the bridges south of Rotterdam. Dutch artillery of ancient vintage shelled the Moerdijk bridges from the west, but the structures were too strong and the distance too great. On May 11 units of the French Seventh Army reached North Brabant and a mechanized group approached Moerdijk, but it was driven off by heavy Stuka attacks. The Dutch forces south of the estuary were already breaking before the German advance from the frontier and were

---

the transports' engines was one of the greatest obstacles to success, as the men were deafened as they emerged from the planes, exposed to concealed enemy fire. The paratroops landed in relative quiet and could take immediate cover; the air-landed troops could succeed only by immediately getting away from the planes and off the field, and attacking the defenders.

unable to intervene effectively. And so the Moerdijk bridges were still held by Student's *Fallschirmjaeger* when the German armored spearhead reached them on the morning of May 12.

The Fighting on the Ground

During the evening of May 9, the Dutch government had received clear warning that the German attack was impending on the morrow. Very disquieting reports had, indeed, reached both Brussels and The Hague as early as May 5, from their military attachés in Berlin and the Papal Nuncio in Brussels. When, on May 9, these and other sources warned the Dutch government that the invasion would be launched in a matter of hours, the roar of motors and other ominous sounds across the German border took on unmistakable meaning.[9]

For the initial assault at the border,* Kuechler's army was divided into two corps of approximately four divisions each. North of the Rhine, Generalleutnant Christian Hansen's Xth Corps, poised for the invasion of the northern Dutch provinces, comprised a cavalry division and two *Landwehr* (over-age) infantry divisions, each strengthened with an SS motorized regiment. South of the Rhine, in the area of Cleve and Goch, General Albert Wodrig's XXVIth Corps, with two divisions of reservists, the 9th Panzer Division, and part of the SS motorized *Verfuegungsdivision*, was to launch the principal assault through North Brabant, link with the airborne troops dropped south of Rotterdam, and thus penetrate Fortress Holland from the south. In army reserve, Kuechler held two more *Landwehr* divisions and the newly formed XXXIXth Corps headquarters, commanded by Generalleutnant Rudolf Schmidt.[10]

The fighting north of the Rhine was of secondary importance and brief duration. The Dutch plains east of the Yssel (comprising the provinces of Overyssel, Drente, Groningen, and Friesland) were held only by a few frontier battalions. The entire area was overrun by Generalmajor Kurt Feldt's 1st Cavalry Division † in less than forty-eight

---

* The attack across southern Limburg (from Helmond in the north to Maastricht in the south), carried out by Reichenau's Sixth Army, was really part of the campaign in Belgium, and is dealt with *infra*, pp. 213–14.

† The 1st Cavalry Division, formed during the winter of 1939–40, comprised four *Reiter* (cavalry) regiments, a bicycle regiment, and a few tanks. It subsequently fought in France and Russia, and in 1942 was reorganized as the 24th Panzer Division. The only other German cavalry divisions of World War II were the 8th SS Cavalry Division *Florian Geyer* and the 1st Cossack Division, both of which were formed later in the war for use in southern Russia and the Balkans.

hours, and by the evening of May 11 his vanguard had reached the Ysselmeer at the northwestern end of the dike across to Den Helder. There was heavy local fighting here from May 12 to 14, but the Dutch-fortified position at the northeastern end of the dike was still holding out at the time of the capitulation.

On the Yssel itself the Dutch blew all the bridges, but these destructions and the frontier battalions delayed the German advance for only a few hours. Generalmajor Friedrich Zickwolff's 227th Division, supported by the motorized SS Regiment *LAH* (commanded by Obergruppenfuehrer Josef "Sepp" Dietrich, long the chief of Hitler's personal bodyguard), forced a crossing at Zutphen. Generalleutnant Karl von Tiedemann's 207th Division, with a motorized regiment detached from the SS *Verfuegungsdivision,* went across near Arnheim. In the meantime the main body of Dutch troops had been deployed along the Grebbe line. Despite sharp attacks by the Germans just north of the Rhine (Wageningen-Rhenen) the Dutch held this position until the night of May 13. They then retired to the defenses on the east front of Fortress Holland, which they still occupied when the capitulation was signed late on May 14.

Following closely the retreating Dutch troops, a regiment of the 207th Division overran Doorn, where the aged ex-Kaiser still resided. The regimental commander, Oberst Fritz Neidholdt, posted a guard of honor, and Wilhelm II was saluted by German soldiers for the first time since his abdication in 1918. But when Hitler got wind of these suspiciously monarchist doings, he ordered the guard of honor withdrawn, and Doorn was declared out-of-bounds to all members of the Wehrmacht.[11]

In the meantime, the main German attack was launched south of the Rhine by Wodrig's XXVIth Corps. The tanks that so rapidly penetrated to the Moerdijk bridges belonged to the 9th Panzer Division, the personnel of which was largely Austrian, as was its commander, Generalleutnant Dr. Alfred Ritter von Hubicki. The division had crossed the Maas into North Brabant on the morning of May 11 over the railway bridge at Gennep—the only bridge near the Dutch frontier that had not been destroyed before the initial German assault.

The German high command had made very special preparations for the capture intact of the Maas bridges at Nijmegen and Gennep, and near Maastricht. In the spring of 1939, Admiral Canaris, chief of the intelligence and special operations branch of OKW, had established a combat battalion * of troops with linguistic and technical skills. In anticipation of the assault on Holland a unit of about eighty Dutch-speaking Germans and thirty Dutch Nazis ("Mussert-men," so called after the Dutch "Fuehrer" Anton Mussert) was put under the command of Leutnant Wilhelm Walther and supplied with Dutch military police uniforms. Their mission at the Maas bridges was prepared with the utmost secrecy under the fitting cover-name "Trojan Horse."

Along the Maas and Waal near the German-Dutch frontier these undertakings generally failed because the Dutch took advantage of their brief advance warning to destroy the bridges before the attack was launched. Even at Nijmegen, where a group of Walther's men reached the bridge hidden in barges before the zero hour, the defenders succeeded in exploding the bridge.

At Gennep, however, Walther had better luck. Two Dutch Nazis and one German in Dutch uniforms took the guards at the east end of the bridge by surprise at about four o'clock in the morning, and Walther himself † with only eleven men in all succeeded in crossing and holding the west end while the main German attacking force covered the few miles from the border to the bridge.[12]

With the Maas as an obstacle all along his front, Wodrig held back his armor on the first day and attacked with his two infantry divisions. The 254th, commanded by Generalleutnant Friedrich Koch, went in just south of Nijmegen and soon forced a crossing of the Mass-Waal Canal at Hatert, where the bridge destruction was incomplete. The 256th, under Generalmajor Gerhard Kauffmann, promptly exploited the Gennep railway bridge by sending across an armored train and a freight train loaded with infantry, which succeeded in penetrating some ten miles beyond the bridge and straight through the Peel line west of Mill. The infantry poured from the train and immediately attacked the Dutch fortifications from the rear.

By noon the Germans had forced their way across the Maas at several points in the Nijmegen-Gennep area, and the Dutch withdrew to the Peel line, where some of the casemates were already in the hands of the German infantry that had come in on the train. Heavy fighting developed near Mill, where the Germans brought artillery and Stukas

---

* It was called Bau-Lehr-Battalion z.b.V. 800 and was later expanded to regimental (Lehr-Regiment Brandenburg z.b.V. 800) and then divisional status as the "Brandenburg Division."

† Walther, who received the *Ritterkreuz* for his exploit, survived the war and testified at the trial of Mussert in 1946 which resulted in the latter's execution.

into the action. The pressure was more than the Dutch could withstand, and during the night of May 10–11 they withdrew from the Peel line. Part of them crossed northward over the Maas and Waal to join the forces on the Grebbe line, and the rest retired westward, making such defensive use as they could of the canals and rivers of North Brabant.

On the morning of May 11, Wodrig sent the 9th Panzer Division across the Gennep bridge, followed by the motorized infantry of the SS *Verfuegungsdivision,* commanded by Gruppenfuehrer Paul Hausser. The Dutch had practically no antitank weapons and were constantly exposed to air attack. Their front in North Brabant speedily collapsed. German tanks and troop-laden trucks sped westward, encountering little opposition. West of the Peel line, Hubicki divided his forces, sending one armored column toward Moerdijk, while the other veered southwest toward Tilburg. Hausser's SS division followed the southern column, and Sepp Dietrich's SS regiment *LAH,* transferred from north of the Rhine, supported the advance to the Moerdijk bridges.

The only hope of holding the German armor away from Moerdijk now lay with General Henri Giraud's Seventh Army, coming from the south. French motorized units reached Tilburg on the afternoon of May 11 and made an effort to hold a line. But the French were no better off for air support than the Dutch and had no armored concentrations to match Hubicki's. Late that afternoon they fell back on Breda, thus opening the Germans' path to Moerdijk, where the northern armored column arrived on the morning of May 12 and at once started across the bridges that had been held by the *Fallschirmjaeger.* The Germans pushed rapidly northward, crossed the Dordrecht bridge, and early that afternoon made contact with the airborne troops south of Rotterdam.

Thus were the southern defenses of Fortess Holland paralyzed from the air and punctured on the ground within little more than forty-eight hours. In the meantime, Dutch resistance in North Brabant had practically ended. The French clung to Breda but were hard pressed by the German southern armored column, which had reached Tilburg, and on the evening of May 12 the entire civilian population of Breda (some 40,000 persons) was evacuated into Belgium. Behind the armored columns, the infantry was mopping up in the area of 's Hertogenbosch.

The German forces deployed in North Brabant were now faced with the distinct tasks of driving the French out of the Netherlands in the south and completing the conquest of Fortress Holland north of the Rhine-Maas estuary by taking Rotterdam and The Hague. Accordingly, Generalleutnant Rudolf Schmidt's XXXIXth Corps headquarters was sent forward on May 13 to take charge of the attack on Rotterdam, using the 9th Panzer and 254th Infantry Divisions, the SS Regiment *LAH,* and the airborne troops.

The rest of the infantry and the SS *Verfuegungsdivision* remained under Wodrig's command for the operations in the southwestern corner of the Netherlands. Their task was not difficult. Things were already going badly for the Allies in the Battle of France; on May 13 German tanks crossed the Meuse near Dinant and Sedan. Under these circumstances, the French had little stomach to continue their desperate and losing effort to aid the Dutch. On May 13 they were forced to fall back on Rosendaal, and on May 14 they withdrew from the Netherlands to Antwerp. The remnants of the Dutch forces south of the estuary retired into Zeeland.

At Rotterdam, however, the Germans did not find the going so easy. The Dutch had had ample time to seal off the bridgehead into the city and were in strong defensive positions. There was little opportunity for the Germans to deploy their tanks, and the deadlock at the bridges remained unbroken throughout May 12 and 13.

And so the morning of May 14 found the Dutch still defending Rotterdam and maintaining an as yet unbroken line along the east front of Fortress Holland. Had the issue been drawn exclusively on the ground, they might well have held out at least several days longer. This prospect was not at all to the Germans' liking, as they wanted to move the 9th Panzer Division and the SS motorized troops to France as soon as possible, to help exploit the break-through at the Meuse. Early on May 14 Halder noted in his diary: "The important thing now is to have Army Group B liquidate Holland speedily." To this end, Hitler and Goering now decided to send Stukas, against which the Dutch were practically defenseless, to attack the Dutch forces in the heart of Rotterdam.

The Dutch were acutely aware of this peril and of the terrible choice that was confronting them. The French had failed to assist them on the ground, and the British could give them no hope of protection in the air. On May 13 Queen Wilhelmina and the government had left The Hague aboard two British destroyers and had been taken to London, leaving the Dutch commander-in-chief, General Winkelmann, in full authority. Events were moving rapidly and inexorably toward a

capitulation, in the course of which occurred one of the most controversial episodes of World War II—the bombing of Rotterdam.

The Capitulation and the Bombing of Rotterdam

The senior German army officer at the Rotterdam bridges was Oberstleutnant Dietrich von Choltitz, commander of a battalion of the 16th
Regiment of the 22nd Division. He is known to military history chiefly
in connection with capitulations, on both ends of that type of transac-
tion, for he was on the scene and deeply involved in the Dutch surrender at Rotterdam, and four years later (as a *General der Infanterie*)
he was the military commandant of Paris at the time of the liberation.

According to Choltitz' account,[13] on May 13 he had, on his own responsibility, sent two Dutchmen (a priest and a merchant) to the
Dutch commander in Rotterdam, to urge that the city capitulate. The
curt reply was that civilians had no proper part in such negotiations,
and there were no further contacts until the following day. In the
meantime, arrangements were made for the Stuka attack on the Dutch
strong points surrounding the bridgehead, to be followed by a tank
attack.

At about eight o'clock on the morning of May 14, a general staff
officer from Schmidt's XXXIXth Corps headquarters came to the
bridges and told Choltitz that he had orders to cross into Rotterdam
and demand a surrender, under threat of an air attack on the city.
Choltitz urged him to lose no time, and the officer went across under
white flag with a typewritten ultimatum.[14] The Dutch commandant,
Colonel Scharroo, was suspicious of a ruse and a stickler for etiquette;
he sent back a note pointing out that the German message contained
neither the name, rank, nor signature of the sender. Nevertheless,
shortly after noon a Dutch officer, Captain Bakker, came under white
flag to Choltitz to negotiate a surrender. Choltitz sent him to Schmidt's
headquarters, where Bakker remained for about an hour and then
started back with Schmidt's terms. He crossed the bridge to Rotterdam,
and the Germans sent up red flares. Simultaneously bombers appeared
and loosed their cargo, with terrible results. The heart of the city was
leveled, over 800 persons were killed, and some 78,000 were rendered
homeless.[15]

Wherein lay the blame for this tragic and unnecessary destruction
and slaughter? In behalf of the Germans, it must be recognized that
Rotterdam was not an undefended city. Dutch troops were deployed

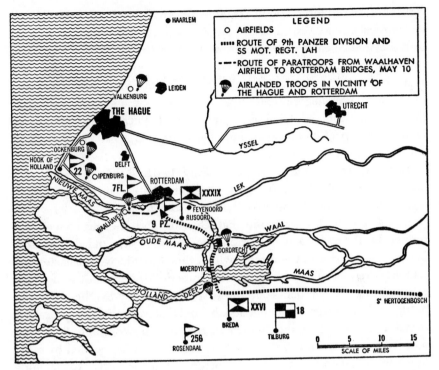

BATTLE SITUATION NEAR ROTTERDAM AND THE HAGUE, MAY 14, 1940.

in strength around the bridgehead, successfully blocking Schmidt's advance.*

Furthermore, the Dutch had not yet capitulated at the time of the attack. After the bombardment, Schmidt and Choltitz went on to the bridge, where they met Colonel Scharroo. Surrender terms were not finally accepted until about six in the evening.

No doubt, too, the destruction and loss of life in Rotterdam were far greater than had been expected, largely because the fire department was rendered helpless. The situation was aggravated by the flaming oil spread from a margarine factory that was hit by a bomb.

Were Goering and Kesselring aware that negotiations were in prog-

---

* See the Dutch account in Van Blokland, "The Five Days of Holland," in *The Fortnightly* (London, October 1940), p. 337: "Artillery was brought up right into the center of Rotterdam to blast the enemy out of his position on the other side of the river. A destroyer steamed up the narrow winding river and went into action in the middle of the city shelling the southern river bank at point-blank range."

ress when the bombers were dispatched? At Nuremberg, both denied it vigorously. There is no direct proof to the contrary, but the burden of the evidence casts grave doubt on their testimony.[16] The war diary of Schmidt's XXXIXth Corps records that Student * sent a radio message at about noon stating "bombing attack Rotterdam postponed owing to surrender negotiations," and that this message was received at the headquarters of Generalmajor Richard Putzier, to whom the bomber group (*Kampfgeschwader* 54, equipped with Heinkel 111s) was immediately subordinate.

Furthermore, on the morning of May 14 the OKW had issued a new general directive calling for the immediate crushing of Dutch resistance, and specifying that the Luftwaffe should be used for that purpose. It is highly probable that Goering and Kesselring were informed by Putzier that negotiations were under way, and deliberately decided not to cancel the attack, which they thought would hasten the Dutch surrender. The red flares were intended by Schmidt as a signal to warn off the bombers, but these were obscured by the smoke of battle and were seen and heeded by only one of the two attacking formations. The other one, which carried out the bombing, was even ordered to fly a second sortie over Rotterdam, but was recalled by radio in midflight, when Schmidt and Scharroo met at the bridge to conclude the capitulation.

However the matter might be judged under the laws of war † if all the facts were clear, the bombing of Rotterdam was plainly the result of callous ruthlessness on the part of the Luftwaffe leaders. They were engaged in an unprovoked attack against a small, neutral country. They well knew that Dutch resistance was rapidly disintegrating. The only motive for the bombing was to finish matters off rapidly so that the German mechanized forces in the Netherlands could be moved to France. For this tactical gain, they brought fire and death to Rotterdam, and to a people that wished only to be left alone.

It is clear enough from Kesselring's labored apologia that even he had serious compunctions about the projected attack, for he speaks [17] of "hours of heated conversation" with Goering "as to how the attacks . . . were to be carried out, if at all." After the bombs had fallen and the city was ablaze, Schmidt sent word to Scharroo that he deeply

---

* Kesselring (*A Soldier's Record*, p. 56) offers the excuse that Student had been wounded, but Choltitz, who was on the spot, states explicitly (*Soldat unter Soldaten*, p. 70) that Student was wounded several hours later.

† None of the defendants at the Nuremberg trials was convicted of criminal guilt in connection with the Rotterdam bombing.

"deplored" * the bombardment [18]—a gesture of a sort that does not come easily to generals.

But these individual qualms, such as they were, do nothing to mitigate the brutality of the attack. The bombing of Rotterdam was part of the German pattern of conquest—a pattern woven by Hitler and the Wehrmacht. A Luftwaffe whose pilots would strafe the streets of The Hague in the first hour of the assault was a Luftwaffe whose leaders would not boggle at the destruction of Rotterdam as the capstone of aggression. Even as the bombs fell, the German radio was loudly predicting that Utrecht would soon receive the same treatment.

Such threats were in fact unnecessary, for General Winkelmann was under no illusions about the fate his nation faced and was making preparations for the inevitable. All Dutch naval vessels were sent off to Britain, and early in the afternoon of May 14 the naval commander and staff departed. The forces in Zeeland were transferred to Allied command, so that they would not be covered by the capitulation. There was little more that could be done, and late in the afternoon General Winkelmann issued a proclamation [19] of military capitulation, an order to all Dutch forces under his command "to suspend operations," and an appeal to the civilian population "to secure the respect of the enemy by the maintenance of a worthy, earnest, and peaceful attitude during the occupation which is in prospect."

But in Rotterdam the sounds of war still echoed. As darkness fell on the stricken city, the Dutch troops were threading their way through the blazing ruins back to their command posts and barracks, where they were to deposit their arms in accordance with the surrender terms. Simultaneously, a column of the German air-landed troops that had captured the bridges entered the city. Student and Choltitz proceeded to the Dutch military headquarters (*Kommandantur*), which Student took over as his temporary command post. Just outside the *Kommandantur*, several hundred Dutch troops assembled to check in the arms they were surrendering.

Suddenly there was a great roar of tanks and trucks. It was Sepp Dietrich's SS motorized regiment *LAH*, racing northward through the city toward The Hague, to make contact with Sponeck's still-isolated forces. Trigger-happy and perhaps unaware of the surrender terms, the SS men were alarmed to see armed Dutch soldiers and cut loose at them with machine guns. Student and Choltitz ran to the window of the *Kommandantur* to see what was going on. A bullet clipped Student

* *"Der Herr Generalleutnant Schmidt bedauere das Bombardement sehr."*

in the head, and he fell against Choltitz, seriously wounded and bleeding profusely.

His uniform covered with Student's blood, Choltitz rushed out of the building to stop the shooting. The situation was very ugly, for Choltitz' own troops were confused by the firing, and suspicious that the Dutch had led them into a trap. The gory appearance of their commander did nothing to calm their nerves. With considerable presence of mind, Choltitz ordered the Dutch into a nearby church, out of harm's way, and averted the grave risk of renewed fighting in the heart of Rotterdam.

Elsewhere the capitulation was effected without untoward incidents of any magnitude. In Zeeland, on the islands of Walcheren and South Beveland, a few Dutch and French battalions held out until May 17, when they were overcome by a battle group of mixed German infantry and SS motorized troops under Hausser, strongly supported by the Luftwaffe.

So ended the fighting in the Netherlands. The five days of hopeless battle left the Netherlands badly scarred, but this was as nothing to what that unhappy country was to suffer in the five years of German occupation that now ensued.

From a military standpoint, the German conquest of the Netherlands repeated the lesson of the Norwegian campaign that it so strikingly resembled.[20] Once again, decisively superior air power carried the day. Writing in retrospect, Winston Churchill deprecated the military utility of the Dutch water defenses: [21] "The Germans broke through at every point, bridging the canals or seizing the locks and water controls. In a single day all the outer line of the Dutch defenses was mastered." But this is inaccurate in both detail and perspective.

In fact, the water defenses accomplished about what was expected of them. The Maas-Yssel and Peel lines were only delaying positions, and delay the Germans they did. The Grebbe line was broken with great difficulty at one point, but this might well have been mended had not the airborne troops tied up the Dutch reserves. The east front of Fortress Holland, though never tested, remained intact. It was the airborne troops that opened the way for the panzers over the bridges to the heart of Holland, but this was due to no failure of the water defenses. They accomplished their essential purpose of holding back the Germans until Allied aid arrived. But when it did arrive, the story of Namsos and Aandalsnes was told again. Without air support, the

French were no more able than the Dutch to check the German onslaught.

Throughout the operation, speed was the Germans' watchword. Even before Zeeland was mopped up, Schmidt's XXXIXth Corps and the 9th Panzer Division were whisked off to augment Hoth's armored force in northern France. A few days later most of the SS motorized troops departed to the same destination. As early as May 14, when the French withdrew from Breda into Belgium, Wodrig's XXVIth Corps turned south and advanced toward Antwerp. Kuechler's Eighteenth Army thus abandoned its independent role in the Netherlands and became the right wing of Bock's attack through northern Belgium. Barely a division was left in the Netherlands,* as the world's attention was fixed on the fateful struggle in Belgium and northern France.

* The *Fallschirmjaeger* and the airborne infantry, having suffered heavy losses, were withdrawn to their home garrisons in Germany for rest and refitting. Student was hospitalized for some time as the result of the head wound sustained in Rotterdam but recovered and subsequently led the airborne attack on Crete.

CHAPTER SEVEN

The Battle of France

THE DECISIVE BATTLES of the victorious German campaign in the West were fought in the northwest corner of the European peninsula. This was the dawn of modern, mobile warfare, with tanks, motorized columns of infantry, and tactical air power, but the crucial area was no larger than in the days of horse and foot. From Ostend to Maastricht on the north and Abbéville to Luxembourg on the south side, the rhomboidlike area was but two hundred miles long and eighty miles wide.

For centuries, these close cities and narrow fields have been the stage of famous battles and have witnessed the ebb and flow of military power in Europe. Winston Churchill's great ancestor, Marlborough, won his victories over the armies of Louis XIV at Ramillies near Namur, and at Oudenaarde. Waterloo lies but a few miles southwest of Wavre. Through these same towns Reichenau's Sixth Army drove back the Belgians and British in 1940, and finally broke the Belgian front near Passchendaele, the scene of Douglas Haig's costly offensive in 1917. The Third Empire met its death when McMahon was routed by Moltke in 1870 at Sedan, where Guderian shattered the armies of Corap and Huntziger seventy years later. Ludendorff first won fame in 1914 at Liége, which fell so rapidly to Student's airborne troops and Waeger's infantry in 1940. Kleist's armored wedge drove westward through St. Quentin, and Rommel first encountered the British near Arras, among other storied battlefields of World War I.

Marlborough, Napoleon, Wellington, Moltke, and Ludendorff would all have found the terrain of the Battle of France familiar, but the scope and instruments of combat had developed beyond their furthest

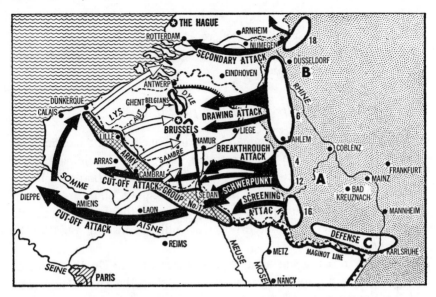

ELEMENTS OF THE GERMAN OFFENSIVE IN THE WEST, MAY 10, 1940.

imaginings. The tank, the motor truck, and the airplane enabled the leaders of the Wehrmacht in 1940 to treat the entire area as a single battlefield and to feint, concentrate, shift, and strike with a flexibility and power that worked a revolution in the tactics of land warfare.

Despite the vast scale of the German offensive, the essential structure was simplicity itself. An initial blow at Liége to crack the outer Belgian defenses and draw the Allies into Flanders; a second and far stronger attack through the Ardennes to destroy the French forces on the Meuse; a rapid drive from the Meuse to the Channel Coast to divide the Allied forces; the subsequent destruction of the Allied armies cut off in Flanders—these were the elements of the grand design that had emerged from the combined and sometimes heated counsels of Hitler, Brauchitsch, Halder, Rundstedt, Manstein, and Guderian.

In the Netherlands, the cutting edge of the German sword flashed through the air; in the Battle of France it ripped through the wooded hills and ravines of the Ardennes, and across the fields of Picardy and Artois. So sharp was the blade and so swift its thrust that the Allies were not fully aware of its approach until the very moment when it pierced the vitals of their defenses. For the precedent of 1914, which the Germans had discarded, still gripped the minds of the Allied strategists. While Guderian's tanks pressed relentlessly toward Sedan, the French and British forces plunged recklessly into Flanders and Brabant, aiming to stem what their leaders imagined to be the main German attack, in Belgium.

The Allied Battle Plans

Although the Allied high command thus misconceived the location and direction of the decisive German thrust, they rightly anticipated that the Germans would attack through Belgium and perhaps Holland, rather than attempt to smash through the Maginot Line directly into France. The Belgians, too, were acutely aware of the danger that their country might once again find itself, willy-nilly, furnishing a battlefield for the great powers.

The Belgian Army was about twice as large as the Dutch and comprised some twenty-two divisions. No more than the Dutch, however, did the Belgians cherish any hope of holding off the Germans with their own military resources. Nor, except for the heavily fortified area around Liége, did they plan to offer determined resistance at the frontier. The outer defenses along the Meuse and the Albert Canal were intended only to delay the German advance until Allied reinforcements could be brought up.

Nevertheless, the rigid neutrality to which Belgium was wedded had precluded joint staff planning with the British or French. This policy has since been sharply criticized, by Winston Churchill and others, as inflexible and shortsighted.[1] But it is by no means clear in restrospect that Belgium would have benefited much from such joint military arrangements, and her government was perhaps wise to maintain its moral position of strict neutrality.* In the event, as we shall

---

* Churchill (*Their Finest Hour*, pp. 34–35) speaks glowingly of the offensive and defensive advantages which would have ensued had Belgium agreed to the creation of an Allied front along the Meuse and the Albert Canal. As previously remarked (*supra*, pp. 50–52), such a move would have well suited most of the German commanders—notably Rundstedt, Leeb, Bock, Reichenau and Halder—because the Germans could have then met the Allies on their way into Belgium and would have been spared the onus of violating Belgian neutrality. Of course, if prior to the war the Allies and Belgians had extended the Maginot Line northward along the Belgian frontier, the Germans would have been confronted with quite a different problem, but Franco-British sentiment was no more prepared for such a step than was Belgian, as Munich witnessed. Furthermore, it is hard to see how Belgium's open adherence to the Allied cause could have prevented the break-through from Sedan to the French coast, which was the key to the German victory.

see, the Allied plan to come to Belgium's assistance was executed with smooth dispatch but led to most unhappy consequences.

Two alternative plans to meet the German assault had been formulated by the Allied high command. "Plan E" called for an advance of the Allied left wing to the Escaut (Scheldt) River. The more daring "Plan D" envisaged a great swing by all the Allied forces west of the Meuse to the main Belgian defense line on the Dyle and Meuse rivers (Antwerp-Louvain-Namur-Givet-Mézières). In essence, the latter was the Allied counterpart of the original OKH plan, and if both had been carried out the opposing forces would have encountered each other in strength in the heart of Belgium. It was to avoid this, and to cut off the Allies in Belgium, that Manstein had proposed shifting the German *Schwerpunkt* to Sedan for the drive to the Channel.

But of this the Allies and the Belgians knew nothing. General Gamelin and the Belgians talked secretly in November 1939, and it was agreed that the Dyle-Meuse line would be strengthened with all speed. This, of course, assumed the adoption of "Plan D," a decision which was put to and approved by the British at a meeting of the Allied Supreme Council on November 17. At about the same time it was agreed that, if Holland were also attacked, General Giraud's Seventh Army, on the seaward flank, would rush up the Channel Coast and join the Dutch north of Antwerp.[2]

Like the Dutch, the Belgians had advance, though brief, warning, that the Germans were about to strike.[3] On May 7 King Leopold's aide-de-camp, General van Overstraeten, had concluded that "the decisive day was approaching." When the Wehrmacht hurtled across the borders of the Low Countries, the Belgian forces were on the alert.

The French and English, however, seem to have had no definite [*] warning of the German attack. London was in the throes of the Cabinet crisis that resulted, later that same day, in Chamberlain's replacement as Prime Minister by Churchill. As late as May 7 and 8 the Allies were discounting the alarming reports current in Brussels and The Hague.[4] At the British Expeditionary Force (B.E.F.) Headquarters at Arras[5] "the stillness of a spring night was rudely broken just before daybreak

[*] Sir Edward Spears (*Prelude to Dunkirk*, p. 143) quotes a postwar report that on April 30 the French military attaché in Berne had learned "from a reliable source" that the Germans would attack between May 8 and 10, "the main effort to be made at Sedan," and that this information was made available to Gamelin on May 3. If all this be fact, the intelligence appears to have been either disbelieved or overlooked.

on the morning of the tenth of May, when German aircraft roared over the city and bombed the neighboring airfields."

Earlier that morning the Belgians had appealed for aid, and shortly after six o'clock the French high command ordered the immediate execution of "Plan D." Along the coast, Giraud's Seventh Army started its dash to Holland. Under the command of Lord Gort, the B.E.F. advanced rapidly toward the Dyle River and took its position between Louvain and Wavre. To the north, from Louvain to Antwerp, the line was to be held by the Belgian forces retiring from the Albert Canal. To the south, between Wavre and Namur, the French First Army of General G. M. J. Blanchard moved in to protect the so-called "Gembloux Gap" in the Belgian watercourse defense between the Dyle at Wavre and the Meuse at Namur. The fortress of Namur was already garrisoned by Belgians. South from Namur, through Dinant and Mézières, the Meuse line was occupied by General André-Georges Corap's Ninth Army. From Mézières to Sedan and the northern end of the Maginot Line at Montmédy, General Charles Huntziger's Second Army held its prepared positions along the Franco-Belgian frontier.

This great wheeling movement was largely accomplished within forty-eight hours and before there were any serious clashes with the Germans advancing from the east. But it is one thing to reach a position and quite another to fortify it and deploy to meet a heavy attack. Furthermore, the Allies were still unaware of Kleist's armored wedge pushing through the Ardennes, intended and destined to strike with tremendous force where they were weakest.

Considering the size of the forces committed on both sides, the issue was drawn and the die cast with remarkable speed and surprisingly little bloodshed. We will now examine how this was accomplished by the Wehrmacht,* taking the front from the north, where the immediate developments were most sensational, to the south, where the course of events soon proved terribly decisive.

Belgium: Fort Eben Emael and the Dyle Line

The Belgian forces were alerted for an imminent German attack at midnight on May 9, and within three hours the troops guarding the eastern frontiers were on the *qui vive*. The principal border defenses included three modern forts (Neufchâteau, Battice, and Pepinster)

* See the charts of the order of battle of Army Groups A and B in Appendix C, *infra*, pp. 428–29.

guarding the eastern approaches to Liége, and the newest and strongest fort of all at Eben Emael, a few miles south of Maastricht, near the junction of the Meuse and the Albert Canal. These waterways comprised the Belgians' first prepared line of defense, and in the area of Liége and Maastricht they hugged the Dutch border so closely that defense in depth was impossible. Hence the powerful fixed fortifications which, it was hoped, would stop the Germans dead in their tracks and hold up their advance for a week or more, as in 1914.

With the first glimmer of dawn on May 10, aircraft appeared in the eastern sky over Eben Emael, descending rapidly and silently, as if crippled. Troop-carrying gliders they were, and the Germans had chosen well this first occasion of their use in battle, for paratroops would have landed too slowly, widely scattered, and lightly armed for the tasks in hand.

The gliders came to earth in four groups of nine or ten each. Three of the groups landed on the west bank of the Albert Canal, each near one of the three bridges carrying the main highways from Maastricht west and south into Belgium. The fourth landed on top of Fort Eben Emael.[6]

Each of the gliders [7] disgorged nine men, heavily armed with grenades, machine guns and flame-throwers. At the Canal, they at once attacked the shelters housing the machinery by which the bridges were to be destroyed in the event of an attack from the east. At Canne, barely a mile north of Fort Eben Emael, the attack miscarried and the bridge was blown from a switch inside the fort. But at Vroenhoven and Veldwezelt the speed and violence of the assault overwhelmed the defenders, and the emplacements were captured before the guards could touch off the explosives. These two bridges thus fell intact into German hands within a few minutes after the gliders had first appeared overhead. Furthermore, the bridge at Briegden, carrying the north-south road west of Maastricht, though not immediately attacked, failed to explode.

The glider-borne invaders were now reinforced by parachutists. In fact these numbered only some 500, but they appeared far more numerous because the German planes also ejected dummies suspended on parachutes and wired for sound so that they gave off explosive noises upon landing. Stukas supported the action by bombing the Belgian artillery emplacements, headquarters, and command posts. Field communications were disrupted, and the Belgian officer in charge of bridge destruction was killed by a bomb in the casern at Lannaeken.

In the meantime, even more remarkable events were in progress at
Fort Eben Emael itself. At the time, much mystery surrounded the
Germans' speedy conquest of this great installation, and there were
dark rumors of new and secret weapons such as "nerve gases." But the
crucial weapons were simply gliders, special explosives, and imaginative planning coupled with bold and speedy execution.

The plans and means for the capture of the fort and the Albert Canal
bridges had been in course of development for over six months. In
November 1939 a special assault detachment of about 400 men had
been assembled at Hildesheim, under the command of Hauptmann
Walter Koch. Dummies of the Belgian fortifications were erected and
the men were trained intensively in glider landing and assault tactics.
Three groups were assigned to the bridges. The fourth, comprising
about eighty-five men under Oberleutnant Rudolf Witzig, was to deal
with Fort Eben Emael.

The assault was timed for twenty-five minutes after five, to give the
attackers five minutes of "surprise time" before the general advance
across the German border. At half past four, about forty Junkers 52s,
each towing a glider, took off from two airfields near Cologne. They
rose to a height of 7000 feet and released the gliders over Aachen,
some twenty miles from their destinations.

Witzig's glider broke its tow rope south of Cologne, and another
came down in Holland. Nine gliders with 80 men landed on the roof
of the fort, and Feldwebel (Sergeant) Wenzel took charge in the ab-
sence of Witzig, who took off again from Cologne and reached the fort
a few hours later. But by that time the fate of Eben Emael was already sealed.

Witzig's men were equipped with powerful "hollow charge" explosives (Hohlladungssprengskoerper) that directed their force down-
ward, blowing holes in the fort's armored turrets and spreading flame
and gas within.* Flame-throwers were used at the gunports and other
openings, and the attackers were soon able to penetrate the fort's
upper galleries. Within less than an hour Eben Emael was operationally blind, and large parts were out of action.†

The Belgian infantry deployed west of the fort counterattacked desperately, seeking to sweep the invaders off the battlements, but German

---

* According to Kesselring,[8] "the use of 'hollow-mines' . . . was Hitler's own
idea."
† Both Koch and Witzig were awarded the *Ritterkreuz* for their exploits on
May 10.

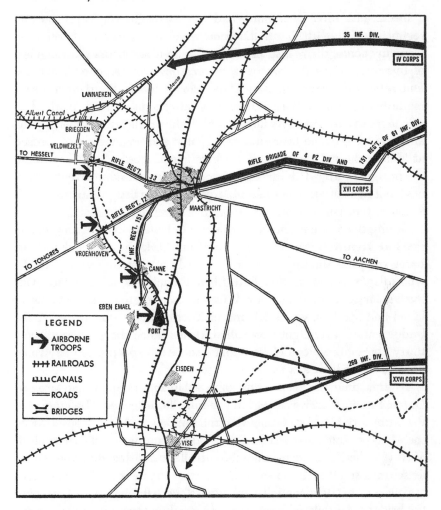

THE ASSAULT AT EBEN EMAEL AND THE ALBERT CANAL BRIDGES,
MAY 10, 1940.

parachute reinforcements and Stuka attacks brought these efforts to
nothing. A gallant and determined Belgian stand at Briegden was
more successful, and the bridge was destroyed on the morning
of May 11. But at the Vroenhoven and Veldwezelt bridges the Germans
were firmly established, and repulsed all counterattacks.

While Student's airborne troops were thus desperately clinging to
the Albert Canal bridges and the superstructure of Fort Eben Emael,

a special task force of infantry and combat engineers * and the rifle regiments of the 4th Panzer Division were racing to their relief from Germany across the Maastricht appendix. In a few hours the vanguard of this force reached Maastricht, where they were stopped when the Dutch blew the Maas bridges. The Germans forced the river in pneumatic boats, and by the middle of the afternoon on May 10 the first rifle units reached the Vroenhoven and Veldwezelt bridges held by the airborne troops. The task force of infantry and engineers also crossed at Maastricht and then set off southwest to Canne, where they found the bridge destroyed. A few units forced the canal under cover of darkness, but not until the morning of May 11 did the first group cross close to the fort and make contact with Witzig's men.†

During the morning the fort was surrounded and came under deadly pressure from the ground as well as from Stuka attacks and the airborne troops in the upper galleries. Shortly after noon on May 11 the white flag was shown, and Fort Eben Emael was surrendered, with twelve hundred prisoners. Of Witzig's assault group, six men were killed and nineteen wounded, and of Koch's other detachments at the bridges, only thirty-eight were killed. It had taken the Germans barely thirty hours to reduce defenses that had been expected to deny them passage for at least a week.

By this time the main body of Reichenau's infantry had crossed Dutch Limburg and was pushing rapidly into northern Belgium. On the Army's right wing, General Hermann Geyer's IXth Corps crossed the Maas at Venlo and reached the Belgian frontier on the evening of May 11. The XIth Corps, under Generalleutnant Joachim von Kortzfleisch, crossed the Maas near Roermond, at the neck of the Maastricht appendix. The Belgians fell back across the Albert Canal, destroying the bridges; Kortzfleisch's infantry appeared on the opposite bank near Hasselt at about noon on May 11. General Viktor von Schwedler's IVth Corps went over the Maas just north of Maastricht and started to attack across the Albert Canal on the afternoon of May 11.

However, the critical point of Reichenau's offensive was on his left wing, where General Alfred Waeger's XXVIIth Corps drove in behind the Melzer-Mikosch task force, opposite the Liége forts and Eben Emael. The Belgian screening forces east of Liége fell back rapidly,

* It comprised a reinforced regiment of infantry under Oberstleutnant Walther Melzer, and a battalion of engineers under Oberstleutnant Hans Mikosch, who received the *Ritterkreuz*.
† The first crossing to the fort was made by a boatload of engineers led by Oberfeldwebel Josef Portsteffen, who was awarded the *Ritterkreuz*.

while the forts held out as islands in the German tidal wave. German infantry invested Liége, and the engineers soon had pontoon bridges across the Maas at Maastricht and Visé.

Now General Erich Hoepner's XVIth armored corps was ready to roll. The panzers poured across the bridges, and by noon on May 11 had driven to Tongres, strongly supported by Stukas. The tiny Belgian Air Force sent nine planes to bomb the bridges, but they had no success, and seven were shot down.

With tanks racing through the gap west of Maastricht, the Meuse-Albert Canal defense line was no longer tenable. On the evening of May 11 the Belgian high command ordered a general withdrawal to the Dyle line. To delay the German advance, the British finally (on the morning of May 12) sent a suicide group of five obsolete Fairey Battles to bomb the Vroenhoven and Veldwezelt bridges. The latter was temporarily knocked out,* and other British air attacks later that day at Maastricht, Hasselt, and Tongres gave the Germans some difficulty. But the British losses in planes and crews were staggering,† and the damage to roads and bridges was soon repaired.

While the Royal Air Force was making these gallant but costly and largely futile efforts to check the flow of German reinforcements and supplies through the Maastricht gap, the Belgian Army effected in good order its retreat to the Dyle, and its allotted sector (Antwerp-Louvain) of the Allied front in central Belgium. The infantry of Reichenau's right wing crossed the Albert Canal northwest of Antwerp on May 12, but their advance toward Antwerp and Louvain was delayed by Belgian screening forces along the Gette River, and there was heavy fighting near Diest. On the Sixth Army's left wing, Waeger left an infantry division to deal with the defenders of Liége and pushed on with the bulk of his forces toward Namur, in the wake of Hoepner's armor.

On May 13 the principal action was northeast of Namur, between

---

* Four of the Battles were shot down over the targets, and the fifth crashed on the return flight. The Germans who captured the British airmen that survived their crashes were baffled by the timing of the attack, and an officer at Veldwezelt was reported as saying: [9] "You British are mad. We capture the bridge early Friday morning. You give us all Friday and Saturday to get our *flak* guns up in circles all round the bridge and then on Sunday, when all is ready, you come along with three aircraft and try and blow the thing up." Flying Officer D. E. Garland and his observer, Sergeant T. Gray, who crashed and died after knocking out the Veldwezelt bridge, were posthumously awarded the Victoria Cross, the first of the war to members of the Royal Air Force.

† The British bombers (Blenheims and Battles) of the Advanced Air Striking Force numbered 135 serviceable on May 10, and seventy-two at the end of the day May 12.[10]

Tirlemont and Huy, where Hoepner's two armored divisions * encountered two French light divisions with tanks. The French fought
well, and Halder noted in his diary that evening: "Left wing of Army
Group B makes only slight headway against partly mechanized French
forces north of Namur." But the French tanks were only screening the
First French Army, taking its position in the Gembloux Gap, and on
the morning of May 14 they retired behind the Wavre-Namur Line.

By this time the Belgian, English, and French forces were in position along the Dyle line from Antwerp to Namur, awaiting the German
assault. From the Scheldt estuary north of Antwerp to Louvain on
the Dyle, the Belgians had eight divisions in the line and about five in
reserve. In the seventeen miles of front from Louvain to Wavre, the
British Expeditionary Force put three divisions into the line (including at Louvain the 3rd Division, commanded by the then Major
General B. L. Montgomery) and held six in reserve. In the Gembloux
Gap, General Blanchard's First Army numbered eight infantry and two
"light" armored divisions. In the Namur fortifications were one French
and two Belgian divisions, so that the Allied force opposing Reichenau
comprised some thirty-six divisions in all, including the entire British
Expeditionary Force.†

These forces, under the command of the French general P. Billotte,
steeled themselves to stem what they thought to be the main German
assault. Actually, of course, it was not. The Allied forces north of
Namur outnumbered the attacking Germans, but this was not a strategically significant advantage, for Bock's Army Group B had already
fulfilled its initial mission. The Netherlands had been overrun by
Kuechler's Eighteenth Army, and had capitulated. The Albert Canal
defenses had been carried, and Reichenau's Sixth Army had overrun
northeastern Belgium. Far more important, however, Reichenau's assault had drawn the flower of the Allied armies into Belgium, just as
Manstein had envisaged. Thus the essential conditions had been established for the success of Rundstedt's massive thrust south of Namur,
on the Meuse. On the evening of May 13, Halder jotted in his diary an
accurate and shrewd estimate of the situation: [11]

In the area north of Namur we are now confronted with a completed
build-up, comprising approximately twenty-four British and French and

---

* The 4th Panzer Division, under Generalmajor Joachim Stever, which had been
the spearhead of the thrust through the Maastricht gap, and the 3rd Panzer Division, commanded by Generalmajor Horst Stumpff.

† Exclusive of one division which had been sent to the Saar front.

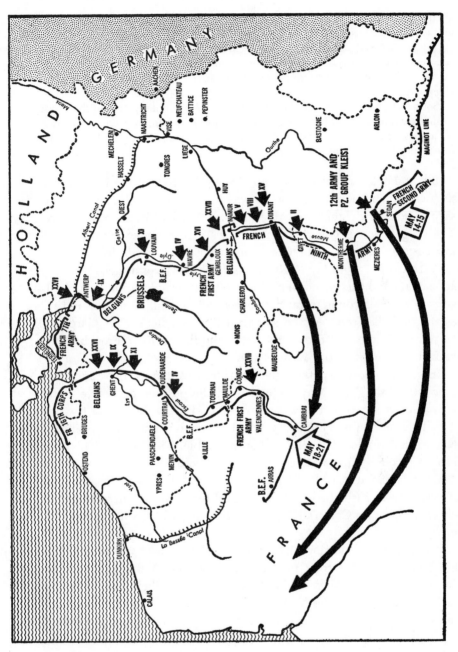

GERMAN ADVANCE AND ALLIED RETREAT FROM THE DYLE-MEUSE LINE TO
THE ESCAUT, MAY 14–21, 1940.

about fifteen Belgian divisions. Against these we can put up fifteen divisions in line and six divisions in reserve . . . which if necessary can be reinforced from the Eighteenth Army. . . . We are strong enough to fight off any enemy attack. No need to bring up any more forces. An offensive mounted by us now would not produce anything apart from gaining ground for Hoepner.

South of Namur we are faced with a weaker enemy, about half our strength. Outcome of Meuse drive will decide if, when, and where we will be able to exploit this superiority. The enemy has no substantial mobile forces in the rear of this front.

But if Bock's offensive was now relegated to a secondary role in the over-all strategy, by no means was it abandoned, for it was necessary to hold in Belgium the Allied armies that had been drawn there. The Belgian forces covering Antwerp were kept under pressure from the east by Geyer's IXth Corps, and from the north by Wodrig's XXVIth Corps.* On May 15 Kortzfleisch's XIth Corps attacked sharply at Louvain and succeeded in pushing to the railroad station, but Montgomery's troops counterattacked successfully in the afternoon and reestablished the front. At the same time, Schwedler's IVth Corps attacked at Wavre and forced the left wing of the First French Army back a few miles to the Lasne River.

In general, however, the Allied line from Antwerp to Namur held very well throughout May 15, and even the position at Wavre could have been restored by throwing in reserves. But by the end of the day it had become apparent to the Allied command that events south of Namur had rendered the Dyle line untenable. The French had been broken through on the Meuse near Dinant and Sedan, and the entire Allied position north of Namur was in danger of being outflanked. Reserves were rushed south from behind the Dyle line in a desperate effort to shore up Corap's Ninth French Army, which was rapidly disintegrating.

And so, on the evening of May 15 the order was given to abandon the Dyle line and retreat to the Escaut (Scheldt) River.† Thus the course of battle in the Netherlands was repeated, albeit on a far larger scale, in Belgium. In the Netherlands north of the Waal the main defense line of Fortress Holland was not carried frontally but was turned

---

* From Kuechler's Eighteenth Army which, after the capitulation of the Dutch forces on May 14, was converted into the right wing of the German offensive in Belgium.

† This was the line to which the French and British would have initially advanced under the more cautious "Plan E."

by the armored and airborne troops that penetrated the fortress from the south. So, too, the Dyle line, while still strongly manned and successfully resisting Reichenau's assault, was turned by the French collapse on the Meuse.

For the Belgian Army this was an especially bitter pill. Antwerp, Brussels, and Namur had to be abandoned to enemy occupation. A number of the forts at Namur and Liége still held out, and Belgians and British alike continued to offer strong resistance to Reichenau's slow but steady advance toward the sea. The disheartening retreat to the Escaut was successfully executed, and the new line was held until May 21.

By that time, however, Reichenau's army had ceased to be the principal threat to the Allied forces in Belgium. On May 17, his armor (Hoepner's XVIth and Schmidt's XXXIXth Corps) had been sent south to augment Rundstedt's drive to the Channel.[12] On May 20 German armored spearheads reached the Channel at Abbéville, and the Belgian Army, the British Expeditionary Force, and the French First and parts of the Seventh and Ninth armies were cut off from the main body of French forces south of the Somme. The campaign in Belgium thus lost its separate tactical identity and melted into the Battle of France.

The Break-through on the Meuse

In all the long history of French arms, no proper name strikes the ear so mournfully as does Sedan, a town of some 13,000 inhabitants on the north bank of the Meuse at the edge of the Ardennes forests, about five miles from the Belgian frontier. Here in 1870 McMahon's army crumbled under Moltke's blows, and Napoleon III ordered the white flag run up over the fortress and surrendered his own person into captivity, spelling the end of Imperial France. During the First World War the town was again overrun and occupied by the Germans until its liberation by American forces in the closing weeks of the conflict. Came the spring of 1940, and the defense of Sedan disintegrated under a rain of death from Stukas, enabling Guderian's armor to cross the Meuse and tear a mortal breach in the French lines. Again the name of Sedan was on every tongue, a threnody of the "finest army in the world."

Indeed, the disaster at Sedan on May 13, 1940, has been magnified somewhat beyond its true significance in the events of that day. The terrible impact of Guderian's thrust there cannot be gainsaid, but it

was not unique, for the Meuse was crossed elsewhere at about the
same time, and other German commanders gave as good an account of
themselves that day as did Guderian. In fact, the French position on
the Meuse was shattered all the way from Dinant to Sedan, and it
was in large part the width of the German penetration that enabled
the Wehrmacht to strike so swiftly to the Channel.

South of Liége, Rundstedt confronted a terrain very different from
that with which Bock had to cope in the north. All along the Dutch and
North Belgian frontiers, the Germans were faced with water obstacles
such as the Meuse and Albert Canal, as well as the heavy fortifications
at Liége, so that Bock's initial assault had to be made with infantry
and combat engineers, in conjunction with airborne troops. His armor
could not move forward until the watercourses had been carried and
bridged.

In southeastern Belgium and Luxembourg, in contrast, there were
no major river obstacles. True, the terrain of the Ardennes is rugged
and heavily wooded, and the roads narrow and winding. It was for
these very reasons that the Allies anticipated no large-scale armored
attack in this area. But in fact there were no impassable obstacles for
armored vehicles, and the panzer divisions led the advance. It should
not, of course, be thought that these divisions consisted solely of tanks,
for each included a brigade of motorized infantry, including a battalion
of motorcycle troops, supporting the panzers.

Rundstedt's Army Group A, as already noted, comprised Kluge's
Fourth Army on the right wing, at the Belgian frontier south of Liége;
List's Twelfth Army opposite northern Luxembourg; and Busch's Sixteenth Army opposite southern Luxembourg and in the northern part
of the Saar. Kluge, with Hoth's XVth armored corps, was to strike
toward the Meuse at Dinant. List, with Kleist's panzer group, was to
hit the Meuse farther south, between Givet and Sedan. Busch's army,
devoid of armor, was to advance into northern Lorraine and protect
the southern flank of the armored thrust.

Kluge's initial advance into Belgium was not difficult. On account
of the marshes in eastern Belgium between Eupen and Stavelot, his
attack was concentrated in the region of St. Vith and Vielsalm, just
north of Luxembourg. It was opposed only by the Belgian *Chasseurs
Ardennais,* who fought delaying actions and fell back rapidly toward
the Meuse.

Hoth's XVth Corps, comprising the 5th and 7th Panzer Divisions,

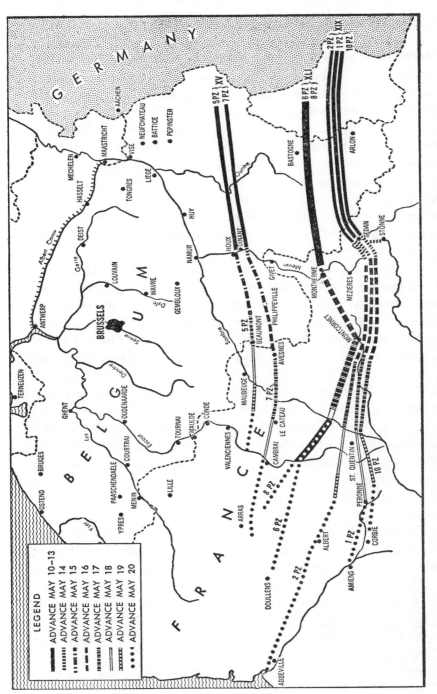

GERMAN ARMORED BREAKTHROUGH FROM THE MEUSE TO THE CHANNEL
COAST, MAY 13–20, 1940.

commanded respectively by Generalleutnant Maximilian von Hartlieb *genannt* Walsporn and Generalmajor Erwin Rommel, led the attack. The armored assault was followed up by three infantry corps—from north to south, the Vth Corps under General Richard Ruoff, the VIIIth under General Walter Heitz, and the IInd under General Adolf Strauss. Air support was furnished by General Ulrich Grauert's Fliegerkorps I.

Rommel's 7th Panzer Division made the first crossing of the Meuse, and we have the benefit of his personal account [13] of the assault. Barricades and mine craters were the main obstacle to his initial advance, but they were for the most part undefended by the retreating Belgians. Cavalry and a few tanks from General Corap's Ninth French Army were easily brushed back behind the Meuse, which Rommel reached in the afternoon of May 12 just north of Dinant. Walsporn's 5th Panzer Division came up on his right wing, closer to Namur.*

The French destroyed the bridges over the Meuse at Dinant and Houx just as Rommel's vanguard reached the river, and his plan for an immediate crossing with tanks was frustrated. Early on the morning of May 13, accordingly, his rifle regiments started across in rubber boats, under the cover of the divisional artillery. The French † fought tenaciously and soon brought the crossings to a temporary halt after a few small units of infantry and motorcycle troops had crossed. On both banks the Germans were pinned down by small-arms fire from French positions too well concealed for observation by the German artillery on the east bank. Rommel took personal command of a rifle battalion and brought up more tanks to hold the west bank under close and heavy fire; under this cover the crossings were resumed in rubber boats and bridge pontoons. Gradually the west bank was cleared of French, and after dark it was possible to ferry tanks across the Meuse on pontoons.

Early the following morning Oberst Georg von Bismarck (commander of the 7th Rifle Regiment) reached the village of Onhaye, three miles west of Dinant, and Rommel immediately sent thirty tanks

---

* It is perhaps revealing of a self-centered personality that Rommel's published papers on the Battle of France never mention Walsporn, nor his air support commander, and only rarely refer to any of his colleagues of equal or superior rank. In this respect, Guderian's account (*Panzer Leader*) of his own campaign is in sharp contrast.

† *Not* the Belgians, as is erroneously stated in Brigadier Desmond Young's biography *Rommel the Desert Fox* (1950), p. 49. The Belgian screening forces in this area had been withdrawn behind the Meuse after Corap's Ninth Army took its position along the river from Namur to Mézières. The French 18th Division held the west bank of the Meuse at Dinant at the time of Rommel's attack.

under Oberst Karl Rothenburg (commander of the 25th Panzer Regiment) to exploit the breach.* French artillery and antitank fire inflicted heavy casualties and hit several tanks, including those in which Rothenburg and Rommel were riding. Rommel himself was wounded in the face by a shell splinter, but he was not incapacitated and continued to drive home the attack. By nightfall he had cleared enough space west of the Meuse to assemble his division for a major thrust on the next day, May 15.

A morning Stuka attack on the French positions paved the way for Rommel's advance, led by Rothenburg's panzer regiment. Rommel rode in Rothenburg's tank, and soon they penetrated to Philippeville, encountering only sporadic resistance from Corap's dazed and battered French troops. On the morning of May 16 Kluge (who shared Rommel's taste for exercising command at the front line) [14] appeared at the divisional headquarters and approved Rommel's plans for the day's drive across the French frontier at Avesnes.

By this time Walsporn's 5th Panzer Division had crossed the Meuse in Rommel's wake and was coming up on his right, toward Beaumont. Following the armored advance, Heitz's VIIIth and Strauss's IInd infantry corps were mopping up both banks of the Meuse. Thanks to Rommel's determined assault at Dinant on May 13, Kluge's Fourth Army had cracked the Meuse line in four days and stood poised for the sweep to the Channel. And in these first few days of his career as a field general, Rommel had established the pattern of personal command at the front that was to be his hallmark in France and North Africa and was to win him fame and a field marshal's baton. In his notes written in the field, Rommel observed: [15]

A tight combat control west of the Meuse and flexibility to meet the changing situation were only made possible by the fact that the divisional commander [Rommel] with his signals troop kept on the move and was able to give his orders direct to the regiment commanders in the forward line. Wireless alone—due to the necessity for encoding—would have taken far too long, first to get the situation reports back to Division and then for Division to issue its orders. Continuous wireless contact was maintained with the division's operations staff, which remained in the rear, and a detailed exchange of views took place early each morning and each afternoon between the divisional commander and his Ia [operations officer]. This method of command proved extremely effective.

* Bismarck and Rothenburg were both awarded the *Ritterkreuz*. The former died in Africa two years later, and the latter in Russia a few days after the invasion, in June 1941.

In the meantime, List's Twelfth Army had achieved equally spectacular successes, and on a larger scale. Here it was Guderian's XIXth
Corps of three panzer divisions that played the leading role.

Considering the size (six corps, comprising seventeen divisions)
and enormous power of List's army, the sector of the German frontier
from which his forces debouched was extremely narrow—some thirty
miles along the border between Germany and northern Luxembourg.
Four infantry divisions from General Curt Haase's IIIrd and General
Otto Foerster's VIth Corps held this line. There was no room at the
front for General Eugen Beyer's XVIIIth Corps of one mountain and
two infantry divisions, which was deployed thirty miles behind the
frontier near Hillesheim and Gerolstein. It was planned that, as the
advance into Belgium and France broadened the front, the XVIIIth
Corps would overtake the IIIrd on its right and thus extend List's
right wing and cement the contact between the Twelfth and Fourth
armies.

The panzer and motorized divisions of Panzer Group Kleist could
not be deployed within the confines of the Twelfth Army's sector; they
spilled over into Busch's Sixteenth Army sector to the south, and to
the east beyond the Rhine. Guderian's XIXth Corps alone was deployed close to the frontier west of Bitburg, with the 2nd Panzer Division (Generalleutnant Rudolf Veiel) on the north in the Twelfth
Army sector, and the 1st (Generalleutnant Friedrich Kirchner) and
10th (Generalleutnant Ferdinand Schaal) Panzer Divisions in the center and south, within the Sixteenth Army area. Generalleutnant Georg-
Hans Reinhardt's newly formed XLIst Corps, with the 6th (Generalmajor Werner Kempf) and 8th (Generalleutnant Adolf Kuntzen)
Panzer Divisions was deployed well to the rear. General Wietersheim's
XIVth Corps of three motorized infantry divisions was in the same
general area, near Wetzlar. It was anticipated that as the front opened
out, Reinhardt would move up on Guderian's right flank to broaden
the armored thrust, and Wietersheim would follow close behind, to
hold the ground won by the tanks and enable them to maintain a rapid
rate of advance.

At the insistence of Goering,[16] a battalion of infantry from the independent Regiment *Grossdeutschland* * was landed in Fieseler-Storch
planes near Martelange, a few miles west of the Belgian-Luxembourg

* This was an elite regiment of four battalions from which Hitler's military
bodyguard (*Fuehrerbegleitbataillon*, commanded by Rommel in 1938 and 1939)
was furnished on a rotating basis. At this time the regiment was attached to
Guderian's XIXth Corps.

border. This operation proved militarily insignificant,* but it fixed Martelange as Guderian's first objective. With the 1st Panzer Division in the van, Guderian crossed the frontier at the zero hour and traversed Luxembourg unopposed, reaching the Belgian frontier late in the day. Contact was made with the airborne troops that evening, but the roadblocks, demolitions and mine fields along the Belgian border proved more of an obstacle to Guderian in the mountainous Ardennes than they had to Hoth farther north.

On the morning of May 11 the border obstructions were cleared, and Guderian's entire corps surged across the southeastern corner of Belgium toward the French frontier, encountering only slight resistance from Belgian *Chasseurs Ardennais* and French cavalry. The advance continued on the following day, and by evening the 1st and 10th Panzer Divisions had captured Sedan and occupied the north bank of the Meuse in that area. Veiel's 2nd Panzer Division was delayed crossing the Semois River and had not yet reached the Meuse; nevertheless General Kleist immediately ordered Guderian to prepare to attack across the river at four o'clock in the afternoon on May 13.

Guderian readily agreed to this, but he and Kleist then became embroiled in a heated argument concerning the nature of the air support which the Luftwaffe was to furnish for the crossing. Guderian had arranged with Generalmajor Wolf von Stutterheim (commander of the Stukas supporting his advance) and Generalleutnant Bruno Loerzer (commander of Fliegerkorps II, of which Stutterheim's units were a component) that there should be no massed air attack preceding the crossing, but that the bombers and dive bombers, in accordance with a precise time schedule, should constantly attack the French emplacements while the crossings were in progress, in order to pin down the enemy gunners.[18] However, when Guderian conferred with Kleist on the afternoon of May 12, he discovered that the latter had come to a contrary understanding with Loerzer's immediate superior, General Hugo Sperrle (commander of Luftflotte 3), under which a heavy air and artillery attack on the French positions would be made just before the crossings were undertaken. Guderian was unable to persuade Kleist to alter these plans, and the former returned, highly disgruntled, to his corps headquarters to prepare the orders for the scheduled attack.

* It was intended to cause confusion among the Belgian frontier forces and thereby speed Guderian's advance toward Sedan. In actuality the Belgians retreated rapidly according to plan, and there was little for the German airborne troops to do.[17] Fieseler-Storchs were small, unarmed liaison planes that could be landed only in undefended terrain.

During the night of May 12–13, Reinhardt's XLIst Corps came up according to plan on Guderian's right, ready to attack simultaneously across the Meuse between Charleville and Monthermé. Wietersheim's motorized infantry of the XIVth Corps was assembling in Belgium behind Guderian's corps, ready to move forward according to the development of the battle.

During the morning and early afternoon of May 13, the rifle and motorcycle troops of the panzer divisions took up their ready positions, and the French positions were hammered by artillery fire. At the scheduled hour of four in the afternoon the Stukas appeared. To Guderian's huge delight, they followed the tactics he had settled on with Loerzer and Stutterheim,* and maintained a constant and heavy bombardment while the troops were crossing in rubber boats. The concrete emplacements along the south bank of the Meuse were destroyed and the French machine-gunners driven to cover.

The first crossing in strength was made just west of Sedan by one of the 1st Panzer Division's rifle regiments under a very energetic and able commander, Oberstleutnant Hermann Balck,† and by the Regiment *Grossdeutschland*. Guderian himself crossed early in the evening and remained on the south bank until nearly midnight, by which time the entire rifle brigade was across and was assaulting the main French defenses two to three miles south of the Meuse.

To the east at Sedan, two rifle battalions of the 10th Panzer Division succeeded in crossing and establishing a small bridgehead, but were unable to make further progress on May 13 because of French heavy artillery fire from the western end of the Maginot Line near Carignan.‡ To the west, the 2nd Panzer Division had not yet reached the Meuse in strength, and its advance elements were not at first able to cross the river. To the north, beyond the northward bend in the

---

* According to Guderian (*Panzer Leader*, p. 104), Loerzer (with whom he spoke by telephone that night) did not receive Sperrle's order for an earlier mass attack until it was too late to change the original plan. This lends authenticity to his account. Another German author, however, states that the Luftwaffe attacked at noon, "using up to a thousand aircraft in dense formations." See F. W. von Mellenthin, *Panzer Battles* (1956), pp. 14–15. Mellenthin, however, was not an eye-witness, and his estimate of the number of aircraft is improbably high. The official British account speaks of two hundred Stukas. (Richards, *Royal Air Force*, Vol. I, p. 119.)

† Later in the war a *Generaloberst* and army group commander-in-chief.

‡ The Maginot Line "proper" ended in the general vicinity of Montmédy-Carignan. The so-called "extension" westward along the Meuse consisted mainly of field fortifications.

Meuse at Mézières-Charleville, rifle troops of Reinhardt's XLIst armored corps succeeded in crossing. Here the French fought well, and Reinhardt was unable to enlarge his bridgehead and secure room for maneuver.[19]

And so, although Panzer Group Kleist secured three bridgeheads on the evening of May 13,* it was Balck's that proved immediately decisive. His riflemen pushed southward throughout the night of May 13–14, and by morning he was at Chemery, over ten miles south of the Meuse. Meanwhile Guderian had returned to the river to hasten the construction of a pontoon bridge, so that tanks could cross.

The bridge was completed by dawn on May 14, the decisive day on the Meuse. Guderian poured the tanks of the 1st and 2nd Panzer Divisions across the bridge, while hundreds of British and French aircraft attacked bridge and bridgehead in a desperate attempt to check the flow. French tanks attacked the bridgehead from the south. But the bridge escaped destruction, while the Allied bombers suffered prohibitive losses from *Flak* and Messerschmitt 109s. Of seventy-one Battles and Blenheims that made a late afternoon attack, forty were lost. Kirchner's and Veiel's armor destroyed seventy French tanks and stopped the attack dead in its tracks. Stukas continued to hammer the French positions, and their resistance weakened. Soon the Germans had thousands of prisoners at the Meuse, and the French defenses rapidly disintegrated. Guderian immediately ordered the 1st and 2nd Panzer Divisions to turn sharply to the right and strike westward across the Ardennes Canal. By nightfall on May 14 the bridgehead was some fifteen miles deep and thirty miles wide.

Guderian's blow had shattered the extreme left wing of Huntziger's Second French Army, near its point of junction with Corap's Ninth Army, driving a great breach between the two. Corap's own line had been breached by Reinhardt at Monthermé and Rommel at Dinant, and his forces were outnumbered, outgunned, and outclassed by the attacking Germans. On the evening of May 14 he ordered a general retreat † to a new defensive position along a railroad parallel to the Meuse and about ten miles to the west.[20] It was a futile move, for

---

* Rommel had crossed the Meuse at Dinant earlier the same day, so that there were four German bridgeheads in all.

† The order is sharply criticized by Liddell Hart in his notes to *The Rommel Papers*, p. 14. Catastrophe ensued, but probably would have no matter what Corap had attempted. Had there been any hope of reinforcement perhaps he would have endeavored to stand firm, but in fact there was no strategic reserve.

Rommel penetrated the new line the following morning before it was even manned. Farther south, the retreat opened up the country around Reinhardt's little bridgehead at Monthermé and enabled him to bridge the Meuse, get his tanks across, and start his westward armored thrust. The consequence was that Corap's forces lost all unity of action and command.*

Thus the French line of the Meuse was shattered all the way from Namur to Sedan. Meanwhile, Busch's Sixteenth Army, pivoting on its own left wing, had swung across southern Luxembourg and the southeastern tip of Belgium and confronted the Maginot Line and its western extension, from the Meuse near Sedan to the Franco-German border east of the Moselle.

With the French Second and Ninth armies decisively beaten, and with the French First and Seventh armies and the British Expeditionary Force heavily engaged by Bock in Belgium, the only threat to the German units beyond the Meuse was the possibility of a French attack from the south. On May 14 Luftwaffe reconnaissance brought reports [22] of rail and motor movements from Soissons, Metz, and Verdun toward Sedan. Schaal's 10th Panzer Division was heavily attacked at Stonne, some twenty miles south of Sedan.

Concern for the protection of his southern flank, accordingly, was very much in Guderian's mind as he started his westward thrust. Early on the morning of May 15 General Wietersheim arrived at Guderian's headquarters to discuss the procedure and timing for the deployment of the XIVth Corps' motorized infantry, which had now reached the Meuse. It was agreed that the 10th Panzer Division and the Regiment *Grossdeutschland* would pass temporarily to Wietersheim's command and remain near Stonne to hold the southern flank until the motorized infantry could take over the sector. Having made these arrangements, Guderian went off to direct the westward thrust of the 1st and 2nd Panzer Divisions.

While Wietersheim and Guderian were conferring near Sedan, in London Winston Churchill, still in bed, was taking an agonized telephone call from Paul Reynaud in Paris.[23] "We have been defeated," said Reynaud. "We are beaten; we have lost the battle." Churchill endeavored to reassure the French Premier, but without much success.

* Corap was relieved of his command and replaced by General Giraud, who, shortly thereafter, was captured by the Germans. At the time Corap was much blamed for the debacle, and Premier Reynaud accused him of failing to destroy the Meuse bridges. This charge was unfounded, and Corap was cleared at the Riom trials. He died on August 17, 1953, at his home in Fontainebleau.[21]

Indeed, Reynaud was tragically right, for the Allied cause in France was already lost beyond redemption.

The Thrust to the Channel

"Our break-through wedge is developing in a positively classic manner." On this note of professional satisfaction General Franz Halder began his diary entries for May 16, 1940, adding that "west of the Meuse our advance is sweeping on, smashing tank counterattacks in its path. Superb marching performance of infantry (5th Division, 1st Mountain Division)." [24] The course of events rapidly justified Halder's encomiums, although the infantry had more marching than fighting to do, and the armored divisions were plagued more by disagreements in the German high command than by any Allied countermoves.

For example, as Guderian was about to strike west from his bridgehead at Sedan on the night of May 15–16, he received a message from Kleist which [25] "ordered a halt to any further advance and to any extension of the bridgehead." Guderian expostulated violently on the telephone with Kleist and his chief of staff (Oberst Kurt Zeitzler, later chief of staff of OKH) and finally extracted permission for another twenty-four hours' advance. On May 16 the 1st and 2nd Panzer Divisions penetrated beyond Montcornet, where they joined forces with Kempf's 6th Panzer Division of Reinhardt's XLIst Corps, which had broken out of the bridgehead at Monthermé.

South of Sedan, Wietersheim's motorized infantry took over the defense of the southern flank, and the 10th Panzer Division rejoined Guderian's XIXth Corps. By nightfall, Guderian's and Reinhardt's spearheads were over fifty miles west of Sedan. Meanwhile Rommel, forty miles north, led his 7th Panzer Division across the French border and through the fortifications near Avesnes, a few miles south of Maubeuge. Plunging daringly and, indeed, recklessly through French infantry defenses and hordes of refugees on the roads, he finally stopped just short of Le Cateau at about six o'clock on the morning of May 17.

Despite or, perhaps, because of these sensational advances, a paralysis of nerves and indecision gripped the German high command on May 17. Early in the morning Guderian, poised and itching to push forward, received a second order from Kleist's headquarters to halt at once. Kleist himself soon appeared on the scene and administered so scorching a dressing-down that Guderian asked to be relieved of his command. Matters went so far that Guderian summoned his senior divisional general, Veiel, to take over the corps, and reported his intentions to the army group headquarters. Rundstedt thereupon sent forward the Twelfth Army commander, List, to settle the argument. List explained to Guderian that the stop-order was not Kleist's but emanated from OKH. He directed Guderian not to move his corps headquarters, but authorized him to conduct "reconnaissance in force." Guderian promptly made shift to exploit this limited permission by laying miles of telephone wire forward from his corps headquarters, so that his communications could not be monitored by the radio intercept units of OKH and OKW, and prepared to resume his advance. Earlier that day, and before the stop-order had been relayed to the divisions, Kirchner's 1st Panzer Division had reached the Oise just east of St. Quentin, and that evening the river was successfully crossed.

These alarms at higher headquarters were partly, but not entirely, the fault of Adolf Hitler, who gave Brauchitsch and Halder a very bad time on May 17. The reports of French troop movements toward the southern flank of the armored wedge appear to have caused both the Fuehrer and Rundstedt great concern.

Hitler met with Brauchitsch at noon on May 17. According to Halder,[26] there was "little mutual understanding." Hitler insisted that the "main threat is from south." Halder saw "no threat at all at present" and no reason to stop the armored advance; the southern flank could be adequately protected by bringing up the infantry. Nevertheless Hitler insisted on going to Rundstedt's headquarters at Bastogne to review the situation. There the Fuehrer found his own anxieties shared by Rundstedt and the army group staff,[27] who "now awaited a great surprise counteroffensive by strong French forces from the Verdun and Châlons-sur-Marne area, northward . . . against the ever-lengthening left flank of the armies pressing toward the west."

As Halder correctly judged, the French were unable to mount any such offensive. Strangely enough, however, there were other uncertainties in Halder's own mind. Guderian, as we have seen,[28] had always planned to exploit the break-through at Sedan by striking west to the Channel, but this intention never had been formally approved by the high command. There were alternative possibilities that Halder had not eliminated from his calculations, and on the morning of May 17 he was still considering an attack in a southwesterly direction toward Compiègne, "with the possibility of subsequently wheeling . . . in a southeastern direction past Paris" in order to take the main Maginot Line in the rear.[29] "A great decision must be taken now!"

After numerous telephone calls and conferences, however, the decision was to let the armored divisions continue west to the Channel *
and protect the south flank with List's infantry, which was already
pouring through the breach at Sedan. Thus the Manstein-Guderian
plan was pursued after only a brief pause. Nevertheless, as Halder
noted in his diary late on the evening of May 17, it had been a "rather
unpleasant day." Hitler, he wrote, was terribly nervous: "Frightened
by his own successes, he is afraid to take any chance and so would
rather pull the reins on us. Puts forward the excuse that it is all because of his concern for the left flank! Keitel's telephone calls to the
army groups, on behalf of the Fuehrer, and Fuehrer's personal visit
to army groups have caused only bewilderment and doubts."

The next day witnessed no improvement in the situation at higher
headquarters. Halder was still promoting his pet idea of attacking
southwest across the Somme. Hitler was more excitable than ever: [31]
"The Fuehrer unaccountably keeps worrying about the south flank.
He rages and screams that we are on the best way to ruin the whole
campaign and that we are leading up to a defeat. He won't have any
part of continuing the operation in westward direction, let alone
southwest, and still clings to the plan of a northwestern drive. This
is the subject of a most unpleasant discussion at Fuehrer headquarters
between the Fuehrer on the one side and Brauchitsch and myself on
the other." At OKW the other military diarist, Jodl, described [32] May
18 as a "day of great tension," because the army leaders had failed to
build up a new flanking position to the south: "The Commander-in-
Chief of the Army and General Halder are called immediately and
ordered peremptorily to adopt the necessary measures immediately."

According to Tolstoy,[33] Napoleon did not direct the course of the
Battle of Borodino, "for none of his orders was executed and during
the battle he did not know what was going on before him." Philosophizing about battle in the Second Epilogue to *War and Peace*, Tolstoy remarked that: "Every order executed is always one of an immense number unexecuted. All the impossible orders inconsistent with the course
of events remain unexecuted. Only the possible ones get linked up
with a consecutive series of commands corresponding to a series of
events, and are executed."

Tolstoy wrote of battle at a time when communications and trans-

---

* On May 15, Rundstedt had flatly declared [30] that he could not take the responsibility for turning List's Twelfth Army to the south, after initially pointing
west. "Hopeless chaos would result."

port were so slow and uncertain that precise command and rapid maneuver of large armed forces were impossible. All the more interesting it is that his observations fit so nicely the German high command in the middle of May 1940, with all the liaison paraphernalia—radio communications, motorcycle couriers, Fieseler Storchs, and what-not else—then available. For all this bitter disputation among Hitler, Keitel, Jodl, Brauchitsch, Halder, and the army groups had little or no effect on the battlefield. The uncertainties and alternatives about which they wrangled did not much trouble Guderian, Reinhardt, or Rommel. While OKW and OKH argued, the panzers rolled on west and reached the Channel almost before the high command knew what was happening.

On May 18, under the guise of "reconnaissance in force," the 1st and 2nd Panzer Divisions of Guderian's corps overran St. Quentin and advanced toward Péronne. Reinhardt's XLIst Corps approached Cambrai. To the north Rommel had spent May 17 consolidating his position near Le Cateau, but by the afternoon of May 18 he was able to resume his advance, and that evening one of his tank battalions reached and captured Cambrai.

Thus, by the morning of May 19 the three armored corps of Guderian, Reinhardt, and Hoth formed a solid wedge of seven panzer divisions. At St. Quentin, Veiel's 2nd Panzer Division was only fifty miles from the Channel at Abbéville. Plainly, there was no reason to delay the final westward advance, to cut off the Allied armies in Belgium, and Guderian was now released from his "reconnaissance in force" restriction by an order from Brauchitsch [34] which authorized "further advance by Panzer Group Kleist."

Rommel did not participate in the last push to the west, for Hoth's XVth Corps remained at Cambrai to await infantry reinforcements and protect the northern flank of the wedge. Guderian's troops again led the way. Early on May 19 Kirchner's 1st Panzer Division captured Péronne, and the German advance continued along the north shore of the Somme, across the old battlefields of the First World War. Guderian was temporarily threatened by De Gaulle's 4th Armored Division, but the French tanks were unable to check the Germans. At midnight on May 19 Guderian ordered Kirchner to strike for Amiens and Veiel for Abbéville. Outstripping Reinhardt's XLIst Corps, the 1st Panzer Division captured Amiens the next day at noon, and Veiel's 2nd Panzer Division took Albert at about the same time. Here Veiel proposed to stop, claiming to be out of fuel, but Guderian ordered him on, and by evening on May 20 the 2nd Panzer Division was in Abbéville.

"On the evening of this remarkable day," writes Guderian,[35] "we did not know in what direction our advance should continue; nor had Panzer Group Kleist received any instructions concerning the further prosecution of our offensive." This was small wonder, for OKW and OKH were quite unprepared to find their troops at the Channel Coast so soon. On May 19 Jodl was worried that the Allied forces in Belgium might escape to the south,[36] and as late as the morning of May 20 Halder was concerned [37] lest Bock's pressure on the Allies in Belgium might result in "driving the game away, as it were, past Kleist. In view of Bock's ambition to dash out in front such a development seems entirely possible." But the Allied units on the Escaut in Belgium held, and Guderian's arrival at the coast cut off their line of retreat to the south. When the news of Guderian's capture of Abbéville reached OKW, Jodl recorded in his diary:

Fuehrer is beside himself with joy. Talks in words of highest appreciation of the German Army and its leadership. Is working on the peace treaty, which shall express the tenor: return of territory robbed over the past 400 years from the German people, and of other values.

First negotiations in the forest of Compiègne as in 1918.

Britishers can get a separate peace any time after restitution of colonies.

A special memorandum by the Chief of OKW [Keitel] is in the files, containing the emotion-choked words of the Fuehrer when receiving the telephone report from the Commander-in-Chief of the Army about the capture of Abbéville.

In addition to setting the Fuehrer off on an emotional jag, Guderian's exploit shaped the immediately ensuing course of German strategy. Halder, to be sure, could not refrain from noting in his diary, after a conference with Brauchitsch on the afternoon of May 20: "What I have been preaching for the past three days has finally been adopted. The operation in southwestern direction will be conducted in the following order . . . [as detailed by Halder]." But this was narcissistic face-saving. The Germans had always planned to strike south into the heart of France *after* the encirclement and elimination of the Allied forces in Belgium. It was not until two weeks later—after Dunkirk and a general regrouping of the German Army along the Somme and Aisne—that Halder's "operation in southwestern direction" was undertaken.

For the moment, the Germans had their hands full in Belgium and northwestern France. Guderian had simply driven a narrow armored prong across Picardy. Behind him the countryside was a chaos of refugees and wandering enemy units, some of considerable strength. Communications and transport had to be organized, and supplies and reinforcements brought up with the utmost speed. North of the armored wedge, which dwindled to a point at Abbéville, some forty Allied divisions, including the most battleworthy, were still intact though hard-pressed. Their only chance of avoiding annihilation or evacuation by sea lay in breaking through the German wedge and forming a common front with the French forces south of the Somme. To frustrate such an effort was now the main task of List's Twelfth and Kluge's Fourth armies.

The attempted break-through was not long delayed. By May 20, as we have seen,[38] the Allies in Belgium were drawn up along the Escaut, with the Belgian Army in the north covering Ghent, and the British Expeditionary Force in the south, with its right flank at the French border near Tournai. The French First Army, which had originally held the "Gembloux Gap" north of Namur, had been forced back into France, past Valenciennes; its left wing joined the British near Tournai, and its right rested on Douai. South of Douai, defending Arras, there was a single division (the 23rd) of half-trained British Territorials. It was through the twenty-five-mile gap between Arras and Péronne that Guderian's and Reinhardt's armor pushed through to the Channel, and it was at Arras (where the B.E.F. had maintained its headquarters during the "phony war") that Lord Gort, commanding the B.E.F., decided to strike south.

It was a desperate enough venture at best, for Gort was already under severe pressure from Reichenau's Sixth Army on the Escaut. Furthermore, the British attack was the product of great confusion and misunderstanding at the high command level. General Gamelin's last general order, issued on May 19, directed the Allied forces in Belgium to fight their way south to the Somme. But that same day Gamelin was relieved by Weygand, whose first act was to cancel the order, pending his personal consultation with the Allied commanders in Belgium. He flew to Calais on May 21 and conferred at Ypres with King Leopold and the French field commander, General Billotte. But Lord Gort was delayed en route to the meeting and did not arrive until Weygand had departed. Billotte was fatally injured in a motor accident on the way back to his headquarters. Communications and plan-

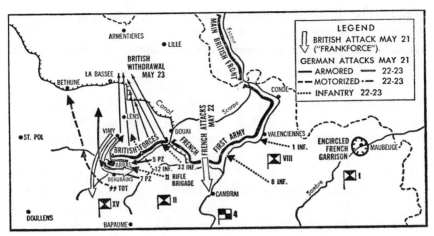

ACTIONS NEAR ARRAS, MAY 21–23, 1940.

ning between the Allied forces in Belgium and the Allied high command rapidly became chaotic.

Nevertheless, Gort was still under orders from London (issued on May 19) to force his way southward to the Somme. On May 20 he had directed Major General H. E. Franklyn, commanding a mixed force of infantry and tanks, to reinforce Arras and block the east-west roads to the south. Simultaneously he had arranged with General Billotte that two divisions from the French First Army would attack toward Cambrai. In London and Paris it was hoped that the French would also advance northward from the Somme and thus pinch off the German salient to the Channel and enable the Allies to re-establish an unbroken front. But the attack from the south never materialized, and the French two-divisional move toward Cambrai was delayed. French tanks from Blanchard's First Army reached the outskirts of Cambrai on May 22, but retreated when heavily bombed by Stukas.[39]

General Franklyn's operation at Arras on May 21 was conducted with components of two British infantry divisions and one tank brigade, supported west of Arras by part of a French division. With so modest a force, Franklyn could hope for nothing more than a local success at Arras; the prospect of a break-through to the Somme was out of the question.

For all that, Franklyn did well and might have done better but for the long arm of coincidence. Rommel's 7th Panzer Division had paused to rest and reorganize at Cambrai, which it had captured on

May 18. The XVth Corps commander, Hoth, came to Rommel's head-
quarters late in the afternoon of May 19 and cautioned against renew-
ing the offensive until the troops had thoroughly recuperated. But
Rommel persuaded Hoth that a night attack would be less costly,[40]
and very early in the morning on May 20 he led a tank advance toward
Arras, which penetrated to a point some three miles south of the city.
During the day Rommel brought up his motorized rifle troops, while
Walsporn's 5th Panzer Division came up on his right flank and the
SS motorized division *Totenkopf* * on his left.

On the afternoon of May 21, Rommel resumed his westerly advance
from his spearhead position south of Arras. At almost the same hour,
General Franklyn commenced his operation to block the roads in that
area. So far as appears, neither commander knew of the other's intentions, and Rommel would not have been there at all had Hoth's views
prevailed at their conference on May 19. Thus it transpired that Franklyn † soon found himself up against a far stronger force than he had
expected, and that the brunt of the Allied attack fell upon the 7th
Panzer and SS *Totenkopf* Divisions.

The German tanks drove westward without encountering the British,
and on this occasion Rommel was in the rear, needling his infantry and
artillery to follow the tanks more closely. It was these units, as well
as the SS motorized infantry, that first clashed with the advancing
British columns of tanks, field artillery, and infantry. The British attack penetrated several miles south of Arras and inflicted serious casualties on the Germans, whose antitank guns were too light to stop
the slow, heavily armored "Matilda" tanks. But the British had only
sixteen of these among seventy-four tanks in all. They soon suffered
heavy losses from the German field and antiaircraft artillery which
Rommel personally deployed to stop the British tanks, as well as from
timely and accurate Luftwaffe attacks.

Franklyn simply did not have the resources to follow up his first advance, which ground to a halt late in the afternoon. Rommel now ordered his tanks, which had stopped to wait for the supporting infantry,
to turn back and take the British in the rear. The result was a sharp
tank battle early in the evening, in which both sides suffered severely.
By this time it was clear to the British that they would be unable to

* This newly organized SS Division, commanded by Gruppenfuehrer Theodor
Eicke, had been in reserve near Kassel. It was among the infantry reinforcements
that were being rushed forward to hold the salient created by the armored advance.
† Major General G. LeQ. Martel was in immediate command of the assault
troops.

hold, much less extend, their area of penetration, and that night they withdrew to Arras.[41]

Rommel had found his first encounter with the British no picnic. His divisional losses on May 21—nine medium tanks, a number of light tanks and other combat vehicles, and some 400 killed, wounded, and missing—were by far the heaviest he had yet sustained.

Furthermore, Rommel's failure to capture Arras had a profound psychological effect on the German high command. By late afternoon on May 21, Halder was exhorting Reichenau's Sixth Army to push ahead hard on its left (near Tournai in Belgium) "in order to help along the Fourth Army. The decision will fall on the high ground of Arras." At midnight Halder was on the telephone with Bock: "In the end he gets the idea why left wing of Sixth Army must not get stalled and promises to take action accordingly." Brauchitsch had been forward to visit Rundstedt, List, and Kleist during the day and had concluded that "the big battle is in full swing." All efforts were now in order to move the infantry in behind the advancing armor: "Only when we have seized the high ground of Arras shall we have won the battle." [42]

And now there developed a most curious situation, again reminiscent of Tolstoy's commentary on Borodino. London and Paris knew nothing of the outcome of Franklyn's one-day counteroffensive at Arras. On May 24 Churchill and the Imperial General Staff in London, and Reynaud and Weygand in Paris, were still reposing faith in the so-called "Weygand Plan" to break through the German salient by simultaneous attacks from north and south, which would meet near Bapaume.[43] As late as May 26 Weygand telegraphed Lord Gort that he and General Blanchard (who had replaced Billotte) should attack toward the south "with confidence and the energy of a tiger," and assured him that the French advance from the south "is in very good shape." [44]

All this was empty fantasy. Gort was never able to renew the offensive from Arras and was hard-pressed even to hold that city, which was under constant and heavy bombardment by the Luftwaffe. Hoth sent his infantry and the 5th Panzer Division to attack Arras frontally from the south and the east, while Rommel advanced northward on the west, to outflank the British position. The garrison held out until late in the evening of May 23, when Gort ordered General Franklyn to withdraw northward some eighteen miles to the line of the canal at Béthune. It was a move of obvious wisdom in view of the increasing German pressure on all sides of the Allies' front in Belgium and the growing hazard that they might be cut off even from escape by sea. Nevertheless, it was the cause of bitter recriminations on the part of Reynaud and Weygand, and it exposed the folly of continued reliance on the "Weygand Plan."

By May 24 the Allies had been pressed back into a triangular area, with its base on the Channel Coast between Gravelines and Terneuzen and its point in the vicinity of Valenciennes. On the next day Gort and Blanchard agreed that the "Weygand Plan" no longer made the slightest sense and prepared to withdraw toward the coast. Dunkirk loomed.

Meanwhile the OKH had been pouring into the salient almost every unit on which it could lay hands. These came not only from the OKH reserve formations in Germany but also from an extensive shifting of divisions and corps headquarters from Bock's Army Group B to Rundstedt's Army Group A. The manner in which this enormous maneuver was carried out markedly affected the course and upshot of the entire Battle of France.

Fearing as he did an attack on the south flank of his advancing armor, Rundstedt's first concern was to line that flank with infantry divisions in defensive posture. Busch's Sixteenth Army, as already noted, formed the eastern wing of this line. As the panzer divisions moved west along the Aisne and Somme, they were periodically relieved by the immediately following motorized infantry of Wietersheim's XIVth Corps, and these in turn were replaced by the slower foot infantry divisions. Thus the three infantry corps (VIth, IIIrd, and XVIIIth) of List's Twelfth Army swung into place on Busch's right and held a line along the Aisne River from south of Sedan to west of Laon. Next came a single corps (Vth) from Kluge's Fourth Army (the rest of which was on the north flank of the salient) in the vicinity of St. Quentin, and from there to the coast at Abbéville the line of the Somme was held by Wietersheim's XIVth Corps.

The north flank of the salient was, of course, much shorter, for Bock had already pushed the Allies back to the Escaut. For the most part, this flank was held by the panzer formations that had created the salient, with Guderian on the coast, Hoth at Arras, and Reinhardt in between. Between Maubeuge and Arras, however, they were supported by the other two infantry corps (IInd and VIIIth) of Kluge's Fourth Army.

Such was the course and disposition by May 24 of the divisions initially committed to Rundstedt's offensive. For the most part, the foot infantry on the southern flank of the salient had a rather easy time, and their casualties were very light.* Busch's Sixteenth Army had some heavy fighting on its right wing southeast of Sedan after the mechanized troops departed toward the west, and subsequently there were sharp engagements near Laon and Vouzières. But the French, as we have seen, were unable to mount a sustained counteroffensive from the south, and the Aisne front lay quiet from May 20 until the second German offensive early in June.

The reserve infantry divisions that followed the front-line troops had an even less adventurous passage. Some came by rail and truck, others on foot. The general movement of the OKH reserves toward the front began as soon as the armor reached the Meuse. The divisions coming from north Germany had to traverse the rear of Reichenau's Sixth Army sector, while those from the south passed behind Busch's front.[46] Weichs's Second Army headquarters was moved forward near List's west of the Meuse, to serve as a sort of transit higher command post for the new units coming into the salient.[47] By May 24, twenty or more additional infantry divisions were moving westward along the southern flank. Five new corps headquarters had also been brought in, as well as Blaskowitz' Ninth Army headquarters, which had been activated on May 14. Among the new corps were Manstein's XXXVIIIth and Stumme's XLth Corps, which were sent with fresh infantry divisions all the way to the coast, to replace Wietersheim's motorized infantry along the Somme and hold the bridgeheads on the south bank that had been established at Amiens and Abbéville. Life was a little livelier at the coastal end of the southern front, and Manstein, exercising his first combat command, had to cope with a sharp British armored attack at Abbéville on May 29.[48]

All these new armies, corps, and divisions from OKH reserve were sent to Rundstedt's southern flank; none went to Bock. On the contrary, Bock's army group was stripped of all its armored and motorized

* The experience of the 1st Mountain Division (of Beyer's XVIIIth Corps) is illustrative. Because of lack of room at the frontier on May 10, this crack division of regulars (commanded by Generalleutnant Ludwig Kuebler) started from Bad Neuenahr, forty miles behind the Luxembourg border, crossed the Meuse at Monthermé in the wake of Reinhardt's panzers, and passed Hirson, where, on May 17, the division suffered its first (and light) combat casualties. It then proceeded to the front north of Soissons at Coucy-le-Château on the Oise-Aisne Canal, which was reached on May 21 after a march of over 200 miles in ten days. Here the front remained generally quiet for the next two weeks, after which the Germans renewed their offensive.[45]

troops, much of its tactical air support, and even of its infantry reserves, in order to augment Rundstedt's drive. Army Group B dwindled
to twenty-one infantry divisions in six corps.

Army Group A, in contrast, by May 24 was swollen to over seventy
divisions (including all the mechanized units), grouped in five armies
and twenty-two corps. The salient became a congested jumble * of
headquarters, supply points, and moving columns. Problems of routing,
transport, and communications were multiplied and complicated, and
Halder noted [49] that "the developments of the past few days show that
Army Group A is indeed experiencing considerable difficulties in man-
aging this unwieldy mass of seventy-one divisions. I have a good idea
its staff has not been energetic and active enough."

The original purpose of transferring Bock's mechanized divisions to
Rundstedt was to give added punch to the latter's cut-off drive to the
Channel, after the Allied forces had been drawn north to meet Bock's
vigorous initial push.[50] But by the time these troops arrived in Rundstedt's sector, Guderian had already reached the Channel Coast. Consequently, the transferred armor was used to strengthen the Germans'
northerly thrust against the southern side of the Allied position, between Valenciennes and the coast.

Thus, the armored and motorized divisions released from Holland
—Hubicki's 9th Panzer Division, Hausser's SS *Verfuegungsdivision*,
and Sepp Dietrich's SS Regiment *LAH*—were all sent to reinforce
Kleist's Panzer Group on and near the Channel Coast. From Reichenau's front in Belgium was lifted Hoepner's XVIth Corps (3rd and
4th Panzer and 20th Motorized Divisions), which moved around to
join Kluge's Fourth Army west of Arras. Hoth's XVth Corps headquarters was now upgraded to a panzer group (like Kleist's) with command over Hoepner's XVIth and Rudolf Schmidt's XXXIXth Corps,
transferred from Holland. Finally, the only motorized units in the
OKH reserve, consisting of the new SS *Totenkopfdivision* and the Eleventh Rifle Brigade,† were also sent to Hoth's group.

The result was that by about May 23 every armored and motorized
unit in the German Army was in the narrow end of the salient between

* The congestion became painfully apparent during a telephone conversation
between Rundstedt and Halder on May 22, reported in the latter's diary: "Vth
Corps moved into Péronne area, since everything farther north is congested with
motorized troops. One division of XLth Corps is directed toward St. Quentin.
Nothing else can be gotten through. Ist Corps slated to go to Le Cateau—will take
time, as all roads are taken up by 20th Motorized Division."

† This was the independent motorized brigade which had invaded Jutland in
Denmark on April 9. *Supra,* pp. 113–15.

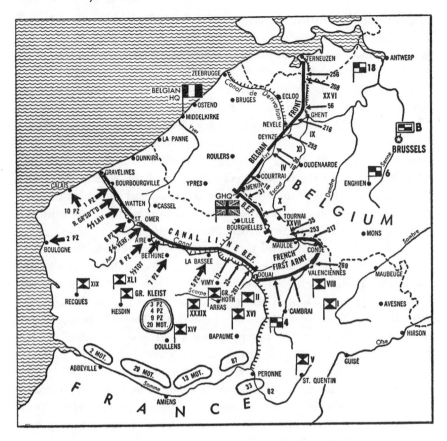

BATTLE SITUATION AT TIME OF GERMAN "STOP-ORDER" OF
MAY 24, 1940.

Cambrai-Péronne and the Channel Coast, in position to strike with crushing force against the Allies' southern front. Both Kleist's and Hoth's panzer groups were now subordinated to Kluge's Fourth Army near Cambrai, while List's Twelfth Army remained near the eastern end of the battle front to control the flow of infantry along the southern flank of the salient.

Despite this enormous concentration, the German high command continued to worry about the situation near Arras and the ability of the British garrison to hold on there. Kleist became nervous and required Guderian and Reinhardt to leave some of their forces in defensive positions near Abbéville and west of Arras, thus weakening their northerly attack toward the Channel ports.[51] Halder was also disposed to slow down the armor until Arras had been cleared up.[52] Then, too, the French First Army, albeit hemmed into a pocket southwest of Lille, was fighting well. A French garrison held out at Maubeuge, and a French tank attack on May 22 nearly reached Cambrai.

For all these reasons, the OKH became desperately anxious to bring strong infantry forces to bear on the situation. On the morning of May 22, 1940, Halder noted in his diary: "Above all it is important for the infantry to get to Arras and westward as quickly as possible." Those nearest were Strauss's IInd and Heitz's VIIIth Corps of Kluge's Fourth Army, which had followed behind Hoth's panzers. These two infantry corps, comprising well-trained regulars, had had much rougher going than those that followed Kleist and were now lining the southern flank of the salient along the Aisne and Somme.

For example, Rommel had simply smashed through the French border fortifications at Avesnes, and on May 17 and 18 Strauss's IInd Corps had to fight a bloody battle to widen the breach and advance westward.[53] While Kleist's panzers had been able to break through into virtually undefended country far behind the French lines, Hoth's thrust ran right along the so-called "extended Maginot Line" on the Franco-Belgian border and continued to meet resistance from the French First Army and the B.E.F. It became apparent that the Fourth Army's two infantry corps * were not strong enough, and so Reichenau's forces were again drawn on by sending Generalleutnant Hans-Kuno von Both's Ist Corps with two crack infantry divisions † to augment Kluge's infantry near Arras.

The British attack at Arras resulted in an emergency call for Strauss's IInd Corps and the 11th Rifle Brigade; on May 23 the former attacked northward on the city's eastern side, while the latter assaulted it directly from the south.[54] When Arras was evacuated that night, Strauss advanced to the Canal du Nord, some twenty miles south of Lille. The VIIIth and Ist Corps were mopping up the Maubeuge fortress and pushing the French First Army out of Valenciennes and Douai. The fighting was bitter and the German losses heavy.‡

Meanwhile, Guderian had been moving northward along the Chan-

---

* The other infantry corps of the Fourth Army (Ruoff's Vth) had wound up on the southern front near St. Quentin.

† The Ist Corps had been in reserve behind Reichenau's Sixth Army. With it went the 1st and 11th Divisions.

‡ The former Crown Prince's eldest son, Prince Wilhelm of Prussia, serving as a company commander in the 11th Infantry Division, was mortally wounded near Douai. He was buried at Potsdam on May 29; the Crown Prince and Princess and the venerable Mackensen attended the funeral.[55]

The *Admiral Graf Spee*, anchored in the Plate estuary off Montevideo, is blown up by her own crew at sundown on December 17, 1939. *British Information Services*

Narvik harbor on April 10, 1940, soon after the attack by British destroyers. At the pier are the German destroyers *Hans Luedemann* (left) and the badly damaged *Diether von Roeder*. Behind the latter is one of the German merchantmen sunk by the British destroyers. *British Information Services*

German troops entering Oslo. *United Press*

General der Flieger Leonhard Kaupisch, commander of the German forces that occupied Denmark, inspects an infantry battalion in the citadel of Copenhagen. At left is his chief of staff, Generalmajor Kurt Himer. The general in the center is probably the commander of the 198th Infantry Division, Generalmajor Otto Roetig, whose headquarters was in the citadel. *Ullstein*

1. Grossadmiral Erich Raeder, Commander-in-Chief of the German Navy. *Wide World*

2. Generaloberst Nikolaus von Falkenhorst. In April 1940, he commanded the German Army forces that invaded Norway and Denmark. *Wide World*

2.

3. Vizeadmiral (later General-admiral) Rolf Carls. In October 1939, Carls wrote a letter to Raeder which initiated German planning for the invasion of Norway.

4. Generalleutnant Richard Pellengahr, commander of the 196th Infantry Division, wearing the *Ritterkreuz* awarded to him for his conquest of central Norway and defeat of the British forces that landed at Aandalsnes. *Ullstein*

5. Kommodore Friedrich Bonte, commander of the German destroyers that carried Dietl and his troops to Narvik. Bonte was killed during the British destroyer attack on April 10, 1940. *Wide World*

4.
6.

6. General der Gebirgstruppen Eduard Dietl, commander of the Third Mountain Division, acclaimed as the "Hero of Narvik."

World War II, new style: German parachute troops in action near the Hague on May 10, 1940. *Ullstein*

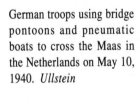

World War II, old style: German troops fording a Dutch stream. The exact locale of this picture, so reminiscent of World War I, is unknown, perhaps these are components of the First Cavalry Division invading the northern Netherlands. *Ullstein*

German troops using bridge pontoons and pneumatic boats to cross the Maas in the Netherlands on May 10, 1940. *Ullstein*

Generaloberst Kurt Student. In May 1940 he commanded the airlanding operations in the Netherlands and Belgium. *Ullstein*

Bridge destruction on the Maas does not stop the German advance at Maastricht. *Wide World*

Oberstleutnant Dietrich von Choltitz, commander of an airborne battalion at Rotterdam. *Ullstein*

The ruins of Rotterdam along the Nieuwe Maas, some eight months after the German bombing on May 14, 1940. *Ullstein*

1. Generaloberst Heinz Guderian, commander of the armored corps that broke through from Sedan to Abbeville.

2. Generaloberst Ewald von Kleist, commander of the panzer group that smashed the French line on the Meuse above Sedan.

3. Oberst Hermann Balck, who commanded a rifle regiment of the 1st Panzer Division. *Ullstein*

4. Generalmajor Wolf von Stutterheim, commander of the close-support bombers that operated with Kleist's panzer group at Sedan. Died of wounds suffered shortly thereafter. *Ullstein*

5. Generalleutnant Erich von Lewinski *genannt* von Manstein. As chief of staff to Rundstedt, Manstein contributed decisively to the German plan of attack in the west. *Ullstein*

6. Generalleutnant Hermann Ritter von Speck, an infantry corps commander and the only German Army general killed in action during the battle of France. *Ullstein*

1.

2.

3.

4.

5.

6.

German airborne troops at Eben Emael relax after the surrender. *Ullstein*

An assault force under Oberfeldwebel Josef Portsteffen makes the first crossing of the Albert Canal just north of Fort Eben Emael. A gun-flash from the Fort is visible near the center of the picture. *Ullstein*

Hitler awards the *Ritterkreuz* to Oberfeldwebel Portsteffen and Oberstleutnant Hans Mikosch, commander of the combat engineer battalion that completed the capture of Fort Eben Emael.

In May 1939 Adolf Hitler inspects the German defenses on the Rhine south of Karlsruhe. In the foreground is General Kurt Waeger, then commander of the border troops on the Upper Rhine. *Ullstein*

Dunkirk: Waiting on the beach.
United Press

Dunkirk: A "human chain" from shore to ship. *British Information Services*

Dunkirk: An evacuation ship departing for England. *British Information Services*

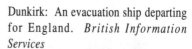

British and French troops from Dunkirk arriving at an English port. *British Information Services*

A wounded Tommy, rescued at Dunkirk, is helped ashore in England. *British Information Services*

For these there was no miracle: French and British prisoners at Dunkirk.

Generalfeldmarschall Gerd von Rundstedt, Commander-in-Chief of Army Group A. *Wide World*

Generalfeldmarschall Walter von Brauchitsch, Commander-in-Chief of the German Army. *Wide World*

Generalfeldmarschall Fedor von Bock, Commander-in-Chief of Army Group B. *Wide World*

Generaloberst Franz Halder, Chief of the General Staff of the German Army.

General der Artillerie Georg von Kuechler, Commander-in-Chief of the 18th Army.

Generalfeldmarschall Guenther von Kluge, Commander-in-Chief of the 4th Army.

German mechanized troops in action in France.

A light tank of Walsporn's 5th Panzer Division in Rouen, about June 9, 1940.

German bombers (Heinkel llls) over Paris early in June 1940.

German infantry marching through the Arc de Triomphe in Paris, about June 14, 1940. *Wide World*

Hitler skips with joy at his headquarters, on receiving news of Pétain government's request for an armistice. *Wide World*

A section of the military balcony at the Kroll Opera House on July 19, 1940.

In the front row (l. to r.) are Kluge, Bock, Rundstedt, Leeb, List, Blaskowitz, Witzleben and Kuechler. Behind Bock is Bockelberg, and to his right in the second row are Gienanth, Kleist (standing to acknowledge his promotion), Fromm, Halder and Heitz. Behind Fromm is Strauss, and to his right are Kienitz, Hoth and Foerster. Ruoff is behind Strauss and to the right is Hoepner. Emil Leeb is behind Foerster and to the right is Streccius (bearded). In the row next to the top the Army officers are Olbricht, Haase, Reinhardt, Schmidt, Vietinghoff and (finger to nose) Manstein.

At Compiégne, near the statue of Foch, Hitler chats with (left to right) Hess, Raeder, Brauchitsch, Goering, an unidentified official, and Keitel.

The Luftwaffe *Generalfeldmarschaelle* with Hitler and Goering: (left to right) Milch, Sperrle, and Kesselring.

"ON EV'RY SIDE FIELD MARSHALS GLEAM'D"

The Army *Generalfeldmarschaelle* with Hitler and Goering: (left to right) Keitel, Rundstedt, Bock, Brauchitsch, Leeb, List, Kluger, Witzleben, and Reichenau.

nel Coast, his progress considerably slowed by the restraints put on him by Kleist with the approval of Rundstedt and Halder. After reaching Abbéville on May 20, Guderian had planned to send the 2nd Panzer Division to Boulogne, the 1st to Calais, and the 10th toward Dunkirk. But Kleist removed the 10th from Guderian's command and ordered that it remain near Abbéville for possible defensive use. Parts of the 1st and 2nd also had to be left behind to hold the Somme bridgeheads pending the arrival of Wietersheim's motorized infantry.

With the bulk of these two divisions, Guderian started north on the morning of May 22.* Resistance was strong, and now the Germans began to suffer painfully from air attacks, for the Luftwaffe bases were far in the rear, while the British fields in England were close at hand. On the morning of May 24, Halder noted that "for the first time, enemy air superiority has been reported by Kleist." Nevertheless, the 2nd Panzer Division reached the outskirts of Boulogne, and the 1st approached Calais. Boulogne was entered on May 23 by curiously archaic means—point-blank artillery fire and scaling ladders over the old city wall—and the Allied garrison was evacuated by sea that night.

Calais, however, was strongly defended by several battalions of regular British infantry with a tank regiment, which had been dispatched from England soon after Guderian had reached Abbéville. On May 23 the British tanks made sallies toward St. Omer and Dunkirk, but were driven back by the 1st Panzer Division. The British commander, Brigadier C. N. Nicolson, began at once to organize a perimeter defense around the city. Guderian, who had regained command of the 10th Panzer Division the same day, gave it the task of capturing Calais, and sent Kirchner's 1st Panzer Division on toward Dunkirk.

On May 24 Kirchner reached and established several bridgeheads over the Aa Canal, which opens into the Channel at Gravelines, about twenty miles west of Dunkirk. Farther inland Reinhardt was across the Aa at St. Omer. Arras had just been evacuated, and Hoth's armor was attacking toward Lille; the Germans no longer had cause for concern in that sector. Kleist's armor was massed and poised for a thrust to Dunkirk and beyond, which would cut off the entire Allied force in Belgium from escape by sea, and ensure its annihilation. And it was on this same day that the famous and much-debated order was given that stopped Kleist dead in his tracks at the Aa Canal, and left the *coup*

* At OKH Halder, worried about Arras, where Franklyn had attacked the previous day, was under the impression that Guderian's advance had been halted by orders from Rundstedt. In fact, the only effect of the order was a few hours' delay in Guderian's attack on Boulogne.

de grâce to be administered by Bock's depleted army group and Goering's Luftwaffe.

The origin, purpose, and effect of this order will presently be examined as part of the story of Dunkirk. But first it is necessary to recur to the fighting in Belgium and trace the events that led to the surrender of the Belgian Army.

King Leopold's Capitulation

During the night of May 15–16 the Allies in Belgium had been obliged to abandon the Dyle line, where their major stand had been planned.[56] In the north, the Belgian Army fell back in good order and on May 19 took up positions on the Terneuzen Canal and the Escaut, with their left wing at Terneuzen in Zeeland, a bridgehead on the eastern bank of the Escaut to protect the city of Ghent, and their right wing extending along the river to Oudenaarde. From there through Tournai to the French border at Maulde, the Escaut was held by the British Expeditionary Force, and south of the frontier to and beyond Valenciennes by the French First Army. There was also a French infantry corps (a relic of the Seventh Army's brief adventure in Holland) under General M. Fagalde in Zeeland west of Terneuzen, to guard against a possible German attack from Walcheren. Altogether the Allies disposed of some thirty-five battleworthy divisions—approximately fifteen Belgian, nine British, and ten French.

Opposing these forces was Bock's Army Group B, depleted by the withdrawal of all his mechanized troops and the Ist Infantry Corps. Bock did not drive the Allies from the Dyle to the Escaut; rather, he followed hard on the heels of their tactical retreat, forced on them by Rundstedt's sweep across France to the Channel. Thus Brussels and Antwerp fell into Bock's hands, and he did not again encounter a determined defense until he arrived before the Terneuzen-Escaut line on May 20, the same day that Guderian reached the Channel at Abbéville.

Bock came up to the Allies' new defense line with Kuechler's Eighteenth Army constituting his right and Reichenau's Sixth Army his left wings. Their mutual boundary was drawn just south of Ghent. Kuechler's army comprised only two corps of three divisions each; Wodrig's XXVIth Corps was deployed along the Terneuzen Canal north of Ghent, and Geyer's IXth Corps * prepared to attack the Ghent bridge-

---

* Transferred from Reichenau to Kuechler after the latter's army had completed its task in Holland and was shifted to the northern front in Belgium.

head. Reichenau's front lay along the Escaut from south of Ghent to Valenciennes, with three corps comprising eleven divisions in or near the line and a fourth corps * in reserve. Kortzfleisch's XIth Corps was immediately south of the Ghent bridgehead, Schwedler's IVth opposite the B.E.F. from Oudenaarde to Tournai, and Waeger's XXVIIth opposite the French in the area of Maulde and Valenciennes.

On May 20 Bock's forces assaulted the Ghent bridgehead and the Belgians on the Escaut south of the city, without significant success. The next morning Reichenau launched an attack in force against the B.E.F. at Oudenaarde and Tournai. Late that afternoon he reported to Halder: [57] "[Sixth] Army has come up against solid front. Would like to shift main effort to right wing, which is believed to afford better tactical opportunities." But Halder would have none of this proposal: "I [Halder] make it very plain . . . that the important thing is to keep going on the left wing in order to help along the Fourth Army. The decision will fall on the high ground of Arras. . . . If left wing of Sixth Army lags behind, Fourth Army will be compelled to tie up forces at Valenciennes." The British counterattack at Arras had taken place the same day, the French were holding stoutly at Valenciennes and Maubeuge,[58] and these developments sharpened Halder's insistence that Reichenau concentrate his efforts on the left (southern) wing of his army, near his point of junction with Kluge's Fourth Army.

At midnight Halder continued his prodding in a telephone conversation with Bock: "In the end he gets the idea why left wing of Sixth Army must not get stalled and promises to take action accordingly." But in fact matters were not adjusted to Halder's liking, for the *Schwerpunkt* of the German attack in Belgium was directed at Oudenaarde near the junction of the British and Belgian armies, where Bock and Reichenau apparently believed the prospects of success to be better.[59] Near Oudenaarde, Reichenau on May 21 succeeded in establishing a bridgehead which the British were unable to eliminate, but their resistance was stubborn, and on May 23 Halder was grumbling [60] that Waeger's XXVIIth Corps on the left (opposite the French Army near Condé) was advancing too slowly, whereas "Reichenau is still fighting his private battle in the area of Oudenaarde, which probably will cause bloody losses without corresponding operational gains."

Except on the Terneuzen Canal north of Ghent, there was heavy fighting all along the Belgian front on May 21. The Germans were out-

* This was Christian Hansen's Xth Corps which, after occupying northern Holland, was transferred from Kuechler to Reichenau.

numbered by the Allies but had the attacker's advantage of planned concentration and total air superiority. Nevertheless the Allied lines held firm, except at Oudenaarde. Once again it was the course of events in the south that dislodged them, and these events were reflected in the decisions reached at the Ypres conference on May 21, attended by King Leopold, Weygand, Billotte, and (after Weygand's departure) Gort.

It was at this meeting that General Weygand had put forward his plan for a dual attack (north from the Somme and south from Belgium) to pinch off the German armored salient. This posed especially grave problems for the Belgians. It was one thing if the plan envisaged the re-establishment of a common front, to reunite the separated Allied forces. It was quite another if the true purpose were simply to effect a temporary break-through, so that the Allied armies in Belgium could escape to the south and thus live to fight another day south of the Somme. Such an outcome would leave all Belgium to the mercy of German occupation and would face the Belgian Army with the alternatives of destruction or surrender in Belgium, or flight to the south. Furthermore, in either event the mounting of an offensive against Rundstedt's salient must inevitably draw off troops from the defense of the Escaut line, which was even then being held with the greatest difficulty. Indeed, for this very purpose, Weygand wished to abandon the Escaut line, and fall back to the Yser. To do this would involve the evacuation of nearly all Belgian territory still in Allied hands, including Ghent, Bruges, Ostend, and Ypres.

Small wonder that such a course of action was little to King Leopold's liking. His army had already been obliged to abandon the Dyle line, not in defeat, but because of the French collapse on the Meuse. The Belgian troops had fought gallantly and effectively; another retreat on orders from above might be ruinous to their morale. Furthermore, neither Billotte nor Gort was optimistic about the prospects of the Weygand plan, or their ability, under the growing pressure from Bock, to disengage enough troops for a worth-while attack toward the Somme. All of the Allied commanders in Belgium were agreed that the principal effort to break the German salient would have to come from south of the Somme.[61]

The upshot was a compromise. Leopold refused to withdraw to the Yser but agreed to retreat from the Escaut to the Lys, and extend the front held by his army to the French border at Menin. This enabled the British to shorten their line by falling back to their original positions (from which they had advanced to the Dyle on May 10) along the French border between Menin and Bourghelles. The intended purpose of this maneuver was to free British forces for a renewed attack south of Arras, but as matters worked out the divisions thus freed were soon needed for defensive employment elsewhere.

And so when Reichenau renewed his attack south of Oudenaarde on the morning of May 22, the British were already preparing to withdraw from the Escaut to the French border, a maneuver which was completed that night.[62] Meanwhile the front to the north was reasonably quiet, and the Belgians were able to withdraw their right wing in good order and extend it along the Lys to Menin.[63] This extension, however, required a thinning of the Belgian forces from Ghent to Terneuzen, which had unfortunate results. The Belgian First Division at Ghent had to be moved south of Courtrai, and Ghent was left nearly empty of troops during the afternoon and evening of May 22, pending the intended arrival of their replacements. The disappearance of the troops lent credence to the false rumor that the city was to be abandoned, and the confusion was aggravated by showers of German leaflets urging surrender. And so, when the relief units entered Ghent on the morning of May 23, they discovered that German *parlementaires* were already at the city hall, negotiating a surrender with the municipal officials. It was too late to retrieve the situation, and Ghent fell without further fighting.

And now, after two weeks of heroic resistance, the entire Belgian front began to disintegrate. The British and French (except for Fagalde's corps on the coast) had been driven out, and Leopold's forces were undertaking to defend the entire sixty-mile front in Belgium, from the Escaut estuary to the French border. It was a task beyond their strength.

On May 23 Wodrig's XXVIth Corps attacked across the Terneuzen Canal north of Ghent, with heavy air and artillery support.* Bridgeheads were soon established, and the Belgian position on the canal became untenable. That evening, Leopold's headquarters ordered a general withdrawal from the Ghent-Terneuzen line, and the formation

---

* Halder disapproved of this attack, noting in his diary (May 23) that it served "no operational purpose." And in view of the hopeless situation of the Allied armies, it is indeed hard to see what the Germans stood to gain by this action, which simply drove the Belgians back toward the Channel ports, where they might have been used to cover an evacuation by sea.

of a new front along the so-called Lys Canal de Dérivation, covering
Bruges and Zeebrugge.

On May 24 the main blow fell at the south end of the Belgian
front. Artillery and Stukas bombarded the defensive positions around
Courtrai all morning. In the afternoon, Schwedler's IVth and Kortzfleisch's XIth Corps attacked the Lys line with four divisions of regular
infantry. Serious breaches were made both north and south of Courtrai,
which the Belgians were able to check east of Roulers only by throwing
in their last available reserves.

The following day, Bock increased his pressure all along the Lys.
In the north, Kuechler's Eighteenth Army had again made contact with
the Belgians, and Geyer's IXth Corps established a bridgehead across
the Canal de Dérivation north of Deynze. The main German effort,
however, still lay with Reichenau, who now inserted Christian Hansen's Xth Corps and a fresh infantry division between Schwedler and
Waeger.* The previous day's penetrations near Courtrai were deepened, and a dangerous gap appeared between the Belgian right wing,
forced back from Menin, and the British left wing.

From the Allied standpoint it was vital that this gap be closed, for
if Bock were able to drive a wedge between the Belgian and British
forces and get behind their line, he would then be able to swing southward and cut off the B.E.F. and the French First Army by effecting a
junction west of Lille with Hoth's panzer group and Strauss's IInd
Corps, which were advancing toward Lille from the south.

By the evening of May 25 the gravity of this threat had become
apparent to Lord Gort. In addition to battle reports from Belgian headquarters, Gort had the benefit of documents captured that day from
the staff car of Oberstleutnant Eberhardt Kinzel, liaison officer between
OKH and Bock's Army Group B (who escaped capture when his car
was attacked and set on fire by a British patrol), containing the plans
for the German attack toward and south of Ypres.[64] He came to an
immediate decision which saved the Allied armies from encirclement.
On his own responsibility, Gort called off his projected attack toward
the south (which, as part of the Weygand plan, was still the "official"
Allied plan), and sent the two British divisions then in reserve for that

---

* After the retreat to the Lys, the Belgian southern front ran from southwest to
northeast, while the Anglo-French front turned from it almost at right angles and
ran roughly north-northwest to south-southeast. Thus, as Waeger's XXVIIth Corps
advanced against the British and French it tended to be drawn slightly south,
while the rest of Reichenau's army was pulled north. The Xth Corps was put in
to fill this gap and increase the weight of Reichenau's push toward Ypres.

attack (the 5th and 50th, which had been at Arras) north to restore the line between the British and Belgian armies.

Thus the maneuver of May 22 was now done in reverse. The Belgians had thinned and extended their line to enable Gort to shorten his front and create a reserve; the Belgian thinning enabled the Germans to break through; now the British had to recommit their reserves and extend their own line to retrieve the situation. It was the death blow to any lingering Allied hopes of holding out in Flanders and Artois, and on the next day the British and French forces east of Lille started to withdraw toward the coast.[65]

If Gort's decision saved the Anglo-French forces from encirclement, it did not wholly restore the common front with the Belgians. The British simply extended their line down the Yser to Ypres. But because of the ninety-degree angle in the Lys front at the French border, the retreat of the Belgian right wing inevitably swung away from the British and the Yser. On the night of May 25–26 the Belgians made a desperate effort to keep contact by lining the Ypres-Roulers railroad with an unbroken line of cars as a barrier. But when British troops arrived at Ypres on May 26, the nearest Belgian troops were eight miles to the northeast, near Passchendaele, where the flower of the British Army had been slaughtered in Haig's bloody and futile offensive of 1917.

Throughout May 26 Bock's infantry and Kesselring's Stukas battered the Belgian lines. From Nevele to the south the Belgians were pushed five to twenty miles west of the Lys. In the north, Wodrig's XXVIth Corps crossed the Canal de Dérivation near Ecloo. At noon, Belgian headquarters informed the French that "the Belgian Army is in a serious situation" and "has nearly reached the limits of its endurance," but that it was intended to carry on the fight as long as resources permitted.[66] Leopold moved his general headquarters to Middelkerke, on the Channel just south of Ostend. The end was very near.

May 27 was the Belgian Army's last day of fighting. Zeeland was evacuated. Great holes were torn in the line west of Deynze, and the road to Bruges lay open to the German advance. Between Ypres and Roulers there was a determined effort to keep contact with the British forces, now pouring back toward the coast, but the gap east of Ypres widened as the Belgians fell back to the northeast. Behind the Belgian lines, communications and transport were in chaos, as the result of Stuka attacks and the press of refugees. The Belgian forces were disintegrating, and planned maneuver became impossible. Shortly after midday Leopold informed Gort that capitulation was imminent, and the French liaison officers at the Belgian headquarters were given a similar warning.

And so, at five o'clock in the afternoon of May 27, Leopold sent Major General Derousseaux, Deputy Chief of the Belgian General Staff, to Reichenau's Sixth Army headquarters near Courtrai, to negotiate a surrender. He returned that evening with Hitler's answer: [67] "The Fuehrer demands that arms be laid down unconditionally [Bedingungslos]." Shortly before midnight Leopold accepted these terms, and early in the morning of May 28 firing ceased along the entire Belgian front. Far behind the German lines, the great fort Pepinster east of Liége held off the Germans until May 29, when the commander, Captain Devos, received official word of the ending of hostilities.[68]

The Protocol of Surrender, signed by Reichenau and Derousseaux on May 28, provided that all members of the Belgian Army should regard themselves as prisoners of war, and that all Belgian territory should pass at once under German occupation. Belgian officers were permitted to keep their weapons, and the palace at Laeken was to remain available to Leopold as a royal residence. That unhappy monarch, despite British urgings,[69] decided to remain in Belgium as a prisoner of war.* A government-in-exile was established in London by M. Paul Henri Spaak and other Cabinet ministers who had fled the country.

Leopold's action in surrendering his army was immediately and violently denounced by Premier Paul Reynaud as a betrayal of the Allied cause and "a deed without precedent in history." The criticism was echoed by M. Pierlot (the Belgian Prime Minister in exile) and, in highly intemperate language, by David Lloyd George. Winston Churchill at first declined to pass judgment on the King, but on June 4, after opportunity for reflection, he joined the ranks of the critics by telling the House of Commons: [71]

Suddenly, without prior consultation, with the least possible notice, without the advice of his ministers and upon his own personal act, he sent a plenipotentiary to the German Command, surrendered his army, and exposed our whole flank and means of retreat.

When he spoke, Churchill was under pressure from both the French and the Belgian government-in-exile to condemn Leopold. Further-

* In surrendering the Army, Leopold acted not as King or Chief of State but only as military Commander-in-Chief.[70]

more, he was under the strain of Dunkirk and the incipient renewal of the Battle of France on the Somme. On the other hand, Churchill retracted nothing in his description of the Belgian surrender in his postwar memoirs. Under the circumstances of the time his expressions are understandable, but in retrospect the criticisms do not appear justified.

There was no lack of notice to the Allies that the Belgians would soon have to give up. At noon on May 26 the French mission at Leopold's headquarters was given plain warning, and on May 27 Gort was told in the clearest terms that capitulation was imminent. It may be that Leopold did not consult his cabinet, but it must be borne in mind that he was acting as Commander-in-Chief, not as King; furthermore, Spaak, Pierlot, and other leading ministers had left Belgium two days earlier.[72] There is no evidence that Leopold failed to consult with his military staff, or that the staff opposed his decision to send General Derousseaux to seek an armistice.

Churchill's complaint that the Belgian surrender exposed the Allied flank and endangered the line of retreat is true more in appearance than actuality. Two days before the surrender, the Belgian right wing had been torn loose from its junction with the British and all but pulverized under the weight of the German attack. The Belgian command immediately told the British that there were no reserves available to extend their line and renew the common front.[73] On the morning of May 27, when Gort met with the French commanders to plan the withdrawal to Dunkirk and establish a defense perimeter, the participants did not include the Belgian Army in their plans "as its situation was obscure." [74]

It is clear that after May 26 there was little the Belgians could do to protect the British left flank, and that Gort and the French were well aware that they would have to fend for themselves. The Belgian surrender did, however, enable Kuechler's Eighteenth Army to advance through West Flanders and reach the Channel Coast on Reichenau's right, near Nieuport. But Kuechler's troops did not arrive there in strength until late in the afternoon of May 28, and the British were able to hold them off while the Dunkirk defense perimeter was being manned.

However history may ultimately judge King Leopold, the verdict on the Belgian Army must certainly be "well done." The Belgians were painfully surprised at Eben Emael and the nearby Albert Canal bridges, but the shock gave way not to desperate confusion but to a most determined and well-directed defense. The successive retreats forced upon the Belgians by the French catastrophe were skillfully carried out. The forts and defensive positions were tenaciously held, and the Belgian artillery proved itself exceptionally effective, despite a murderous rain of bombs from a strong enemy air force enjoying complete mastery of the skies.

This laudatory judgment of the Belgians is not universally shared. A very adverse opinion is expressed in the diary [75] of General Sir Alan Brooke (later Field Marshal Lord Alanbrooke and Chief of the Imperial General Staff), who commanded the British IInd Corps on the left wing of the B.E.F. front. Brooke, who seems to have had unfavorable preconceptions about the Belgians, was constantly nervous about his left flank, which adjoined the Belgian front. These worries were reflected in Brooke's diary by a stream of critical references, from which one would conclude that the Belgian staffs were totally incompetent and the troops wholly lacking in "fighting spirit." [76]

But Brooke did not support his harsh comments with any specific instances of poor Belgian performance in combat. If he was worried about his left flank, it was always because of French failures on the right that he was compelled repeatedly to retreat. In fact, the Belgians never broke, and Brooke's left flank remained firmly anchored, until the very end, after the Belgians had lengthened and thinned their own front in response to the pleas of the British and French.

Whatever Brooke may have thought of the Belgian soldiers, the Germans became most respectful. "It was astonishing to see that the Belgians fought with increasing tenacity the nearer the end approached," wrote one able and subsequently distinguished German staff officer who went into Belgium with Kuechler's army.[77]

For eighteen days Leopold's army held on against the German tide, fighting gallantly long after the course of the larger battle had spelled Belgium's doom. If the quality of the Belgian performance had been duplicated in other lands, the German march of conquest might have been shorter.

Dunkirk: The Reprieve

The British decision to attempt an evacuation by sea was a painful and desperate one. Not unnaturally, awareness and preparation at the lower levels of command preceded open acknowledgment above. The Anglo-French high command had reacted to the German assault on May 10 in the firm expectation that the crucial clash would be in Flanders,

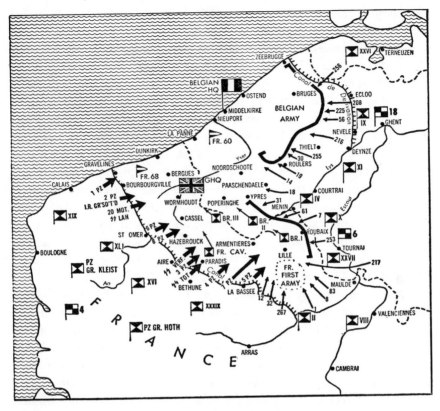

BATTLE SITUATION ON MAY 27, 1940 AT THE TIME OF THE BELGIAN
SURRENDER.

on the Dyle and Meuse or the Escaut. After the French collapse on the
Meuse south of Namur, there ensued the Gamelin order and the Weygand plan—born in the hope of severing Kleist's armored salient and
re-establishing a north-south front from the Somme to Belgium, and
dying in the realization that the Allied armies in Belgium were hopelessly cut off.

On May 19, when Guderian's vanguard reached St. Quentin, Gort's
chief of staff (Lieutenant-General H. R. Pownall) telephoned to the
War Office in London and pointed out that, if the French were unable
to check the German drive, the B.E.F. would be cut off from France,
and Gort might be obliged to withdraw toward the coast. The War
Office immediately opened discussions with the Admiralty on the contingency of an evacuation from Dunkirk, and the very next day the

British naval commander at Dover (Vice-Admiral Sir Bertram Ramsay) began to assemble shipping for the purpose.[78]

And so, while Franklyn's attack at Arras and the other moves in furtherance of the Weygand plan were under way at the front, at Dunkirk and the other Channel ports still in Allied hands the evacuation to England of all noncombatant personnel and other "useless mouths" was already in process.[79] Meanwhile the battle picture went from desperate to hopeless. Arras was evacuated on May 23. The Belgian front at Courtrai was broken on May 25, Gort had to send his reserves toward Ypres to protect his line of retreat toward the coast,[80] and "all hope of escape to the southward vanished."[81] In Paris, Reynaud and Weygand discussed a retreat to the Channel ports with Churchill's personal representative, Major General Sir Edward Spears.[82]

The following morning, May 26, Gort and Blanchard met and agreed on a program for the retreat of the B.E.F. and the French First Army to a defensive bridgehead around Dunkirk.[83] Blanchard regarded this move as retirement into a fortress and had no thought of evacuation by sea. But there was no such confusion in the minds of the British. Gort was notified by the War Office to make all preparations for embarkation at the Channel ports.[84] Churchill informed Reynaud that "the policy was to evacuate the British Expeditionary Force" and asked that the French issue "corresponding orders."[85] A few minutes before seven in the evening (May 26) the Admiralty issued orders to Admiral Ramsay to commence "Operation Dynamo,"[86] that being the naval cover-name for the projected evacuation. By that time, the Navy had already brought 27,936 "useless mouths" back to England, under the policy of partial evacuation adopted on May 21.[87]

This final, fateful decision, envisaged throughout the preceding week, was triggered by Reichenau's break-through at Courtrai and the imminent collapse of the Belgian front. But in fact the greater danger loomed on the Channel Coast itself, where Kleist's panzers had started northward on May 21. It was to stem their advance toward Dunkirk that British reinforcements, including heavy tanks, had been sent to Calais on May 22. But they were hopelessly outnumbered by Guderian's armored corps. By May 24 Calais was besieged by Schaal's 10th Panzer Division, and Kirchner's 1st Panzer Division had secured four bridgeheads across the Aa Canal, of which one (at Bourbourg-ville) was barely fifteen miles from Dunkirk. Farther inland Reinhardt held another bridgehead near St. Omer, while in the vicinity of Arras (evacuated by the British the previous night) Hoth's armor and the infantry of Strauss's IInd Corps were pushing north toward Armentières and Lille.

To meet this growing pressure on their south flank, the British had endeavored to establish the "Canal Line," along the Aa, Aire, and La Bassée canals, through Gravelines, St. Omer, Béthune, and La Bassée. But their main strength was heavily engaged on the front facing Bock, and the Canal Line had to be manned with improvised and, for the most part, ill-equipped task forces. On the Channel Coast, the line was held by a French division from Fagalde's corps; here the defense was considerably aided by the terrain, which was interlaced with ditches and small canals, and much of which could be flooded. It was definitely not good tank country, but all along the Canal Line from St. Omer to the Channel the German superiority in men and weapons was so crushing that a determined attack could not long have been withstood, especially since the Germans already held several bridge-heads across the Aa.

Such was the situation on the evening of May 24 when OKH, on Hitler's insistence and over Brauchitsch's violent objections, issued an order halting the attack of the armored forces against the Canal Line and prohibiting any further advance on their part. For two days the Germans stood motionless along the Canal Line. It was a welcome and crucial reprieve for the Allies, for it was during this period of quiet on the Canal Line that Reichenau broke through the Belgian front at Courtrai, precipitating Gort's decision to withdraw to the coast. Had the Canal Line simultaneously been heavily engaged, it is extremely doubtful that Gort would have had two divisions available to send north toward Ypres to fend off Reichenau. The stop-order enabled Gort to redeploy his forces, and plan and commence the retreat to Dunkirk, without confronting a heavy attack on his south flank, the results of which would surely have been desperate and quite possibly disastrous for the entire evacuation project.

It is small wonder, therefore, that the origin and basis of this order has become one of the most controversial questions in the history of World War II. It is equally unremarkable that after the war was over and this matter entered the arena of public discussion, the German generals announced *una voce* that the responsibility for the stop-order was solely Hitler's, or Hitler's and Goering's, and that its issuance was a horrible example of the ill effects of interference by those amateurs in military matters which were beyond their ken and competence.[88] Then in 1949 Winston Churchill published the second volume of *The Second World War,* in which he declared [89] (based on entries in the war diaries of Rundstedt's Army Group A and Kluge's Fourth Army) that the stop-order was issued "on the initiative not of Hitler but of Rundstedt." The debate thus precipitated * still thrives, and more generals and other German writers have rallied to the defense of Rundstedt against the charge of military shortsightedness or worse.[90]

As is not infrequent in the discussion of competing propositions, the protagonists of each have overlooked the possibility that they are not mutually exclusive. Such, indeed, is the key to clear understanding of this particular episode, for the materials now available make it clear that both Hitler and Rundstedt took decisive initiative to bring the armored advance on Dunkirk to a temporary halt. Nor were these two the only persons who were importantly involved in the stop-order's origination.

The stop-order was not long premeditated, and therefore the circumstances immediately surrounding its issuance are the best guide to its *raison d'être.* As the Allied lines in Flanders contracted and the ground they held dwindled to a bridgehead, there was a corresponding pressure and crush of German headquarters and formations on the shrinking front. The separate campaigns that Bock and Rundstedt's army groups had waged tended to fuse as both hammered concentrically at the Allied pocket. There was increasing need for co-ordination of Rundstedt's and Bock's operations, now that their tasks were identical and their sectors so tightly meshed.

This co-ordination of command might have been undertaken by OKH itself, and indeed this was the course advocated by Halder. But Brauchitsch thought otherwise, and decided to give Bock over-all command of the final encirclement operation. Halder's comments were caustic indeed: [91]

The stated desire of ObdH [Brauchitsch] to unify direction of operations under Army Group B [Bock] for the last phase of the encircling battle will

---

* In 1952 the late Chester Wilmot, in his widely read and justly praised *The Struggle for Europe,* took issue (pp. 18–21) with Mr. Churchill and laid the blame for the stop-order exclusively on Hitler, describing it as the Fuehrer's "first great military mistake." A year later the formidably documented official British history by Major L. F. Ellis—*The War in France and Flanders 1939–1940*—was published, and this account furnishes the details (pp. 138–39, 150, 347–52, 383–84, and 397–98) in support of Mr. Churchill's viewpoint that Rundstedt initiated, and Hitler merely confirmed, the stop-order.

get us into serious trouble owing to the personalities of the Commander-in-Chief of Army Group B and his staff,* and the difficulties for Bock to get through to all commanders at a point of the battle when to do so would be difficult even with well-established communications.

ObdH's insistence of unification of command looks to me like a device to side-step responsibility. He keeps arguing that he has no choice but co-ordinate the efforts of the various elements converging on the pocket under his own command or under that of Bock. The first alternative, which I should think he would accept as the logical and manly one, he feels unsure about. He seems glad to let someone else take the responsibility. But with that he also foregoes the honors of victory.

The distribution of credit and honors, and insistence on his own ample share, was a matter never long absent from Halder's mind. But in this case he was right; the order putting Bock in sole command was a bad one. It was Rundstedt and his army and panzer group and corps commanders—Kluge, Kleist, Hoth, Guderian, and Reinhardt—that had thrown the successful "Sunday punch" at the Allies. Indeed, Bock had even been stripped of his mobile forces and his reserves to strengthen Rundstedt's hand.[92] By now all the armored and motorized troops lay on the southern flank of the Allied salient. Bock had none left and had been totally out of touch with the fighting in northern France.

Nevertheless, Brauchitsch's order was issued on the evening of May 23 (although Halder withheld his signature "to signify my disapproval of the order and its timing"), and the following morning Brauchitsch went forward to Reichenau's Sixth Army, which was launching its assault at Courtrai.[93] Hitler chose the same morning to pay a visit (accompanied by Jodl and Schmundt) to Rundstedt's headquarters at Charleville. The Fuehrer arrived in a good mood, but it soon vanished when he was informed of Brauchitsch's order transferring Kluge's Fourth Army to Bock's army group. According to Jodl's account:[94]

Fuehrer is very much displeased and thinks this order is a mistake, not only militarily but also psychologically. Commander-in-Chief [Brauchitsch] is ordered to report, and shifting of the army group boundary is rescinded. New crisis of confidence. . . .

* Bock's chief of staff, Generalleutnant Hans von Salmuth, was not a favorite of Halder's, whose diary entry for June 26, 1940, mentions a long talk between the two "which at times becomes very warm." Halder then concluded that Salmuth was "the trouble-maker in Army Group B," and added: "It was just like him to tell Bock that our regrouping plans [after the fall of France] were an insult to him [Bock] as C-in-C, and that he had better go on furlough and let the army group veterinary take over his job."

And so Brauchitsch returned from the Belgian front to confront a very irritated Hitler. They conferred early that evening, with results described by Halder: [95]

ObdH returns from OKW: Apparently again a very unpleasant interview with Fuehrer. At 20:20 [8:20 P.M.] a new order is issued canceling yesterday's order and directing encirclement to be effected in area Dunkirk . . . Lille . . . Ostend. Our left wing, consisting of armor and motorized forces, which has no enemy before it,* will thus be stopped dead in its tracks upon direct orders of the Fuehrer! Finishing off the encircled enemy army is to be left to the Air Force!!

Jodl, too, recorded the issuance of the stop-order on the evening of May 24, and his account confirms that it was insisted on by Hitler.[96] In the light of these contemporaneous accounts, it is clear that the stop-order was issued from Supreme Headquarters on the evening of May 24, and at Hitler's personal direction over the strong objections of Brauchitsch.

Nevertheless, Hitler's decision was stimulated, at least in part, by his visit to Rundstedt's headquarters, and herein lies the portion of truth in the Churchill-Ellis version of the affair. For the Fuehrer had found Rundstedt in a cautious frame of mind, induced perhaps by a like attitude on the part of Kleist and Kluge. Kleist had been very anxious ever since the British attack at Arras, and bemoaned his high tank losses in the stiffer fighting on the Channel Coast.[97] Kluge telephoned Rundstedt late in the afternoon on May 23 to report on the situation and commented that "the troops would welcome an opportunity to close up tomorrow." [98] With Rundstedt's approval, Kluge then telephoned to the headquarters of Kleist and Hoth and told their respective chiefs of staff that on the morrow the Fourth Army (including Panzer Groups Kleist and Hoth) would not advance but would hold its positions so that the rearward troops could close up to the front.[99]

It is on the basis of these entries that Major Ellis argues that the decision to hold the German armor on the Canal Line was actually made by Rundstedt on May 23, and that Hitler merely confirmed it on May 24.[100] But this will not do. In the first place, the records of these conversations on May 23 contain no reference to the line on which the armored halt was subsequently ordered. In the second place, the

* This was not wholly true (*supra*, p. 255), as the British had improvised task forces along the "Canal Line."

conversations did not constitute binding orders, nor were they so regarded by the field commanders. The best proof is that the German
armor *did not halt* at that time. On the contrary, Guderian and Reinhardt resumed their advance on the morning of May 24, and it was
on that day that Kirchner's 1st Panzer Division captured the bridgeheads on the Aa Canal nearest to Dunkirk, while Reinhardt fought to
enlarge his bridgehead at St. Omer.[101]

But the caution reflected in the Kluge-Rundstedt conversation was
projected in the Rundstedt-Hitler meeting the following morning.[102]
Rundstedt proposed that the infantry continue to attack east of Arras
but that the armor be halted on the Canal Line. Hitler not only agreed
but stated emphatically that the armor should be conserved for future
operations (referring to the coming offensive south of the Somme) and
observed that "any further compression of the ring encircling the
enemy could only have the highly undesirable result of restricting the
activities of the Luftwaffe." This last comment, albeit disclosing a vast
misconception of aerial warfare on the Fuehrer's part, suggests that
Goering had already been talking to him about the Luftwaffe's role
in the annihilation of the encircled Allied armies.

Thus Hitler and Rundstedt found themselves in total agreement,
and apparently an order temporarily stopping the armored attack along
the Canal Line was at once sent out from Rundstedt's headquarters.*
At the same time, the transfer of Kluge's Fourth Army from Rundstedt
to Bock was suspended, pending Hitler's conference with Brauchitsch,
who was told to report to the Fuehrer that evening at Supreme Headquarters.

From this evening meeting issued the OKH order establishing the
Canal Line as the limit of the armored advance, and it is a probable
inference that the climate which Hitler had imbibed at Charleville
influenced him to resist Brauchitsch's expostulations, and insist that
the armor be spared. No doubt, too, a well-founded exasperation with
Brauchitsch over the foolish order transferring the Fourth Army made
the Fuehrer the more willing to override the Army Commander-in-
Chief. And finally, another influence had certainly by now been
brought to bear in the person of Hermann Goering, who, as Jodl's
diary reveals,[103] had complained to Hitler that Brauchitsch was not
pushing Bock's advance hard enough.

* Mr. Churchill records (*The Gathering Storm*, p. 76) that the British intercepted an uncoded German radio message at 11:42 A.M. on May 24 (a time at
which Rundstedt and Hitler were actually in conference at Charleville) ordering
that the attack on the Canal Line be discontinued for the time being.

It now became apparent that Hitler and Goering, who had undertaken that his Luftwaffe would "finish off" the encircled Allies, wanted
the last act to be staged not in Belgium but in northern France. In the
posture of things on May 24, this could be accomplished only by stopping the armored advance from the south (which already threatened
to push the Allies out of Dunkirk and across the Belgian border) and
maintaining Bock's pressure in the north, so as to drive the Allies out
of Belgium and toward Dunkirk. This desire [104] is clear from Halder's
account of another meeting of Hitler and Brauchitsch on the morning
of May 25: [105]

The day starts off with one of those painful wrangles between ObdH
and the Fuehrer on the next moves in the encircling battle. The battle plan I
had drafted called for AGp. B, by heavy frontal attacks, merely to hold the
enemy, who is making a planned withdrawal, while AGp. A, dealing with
an enemy already whipped, cuts into his rear and delivers the decisive blow.
This was to be accomplished by our armor. Now political command has
formed the fixed idea that the battle of decision must not be fought on
Flemish soil, but rather in northern France. To camouflage this political
move, the assertion is made that Flanders, crisscrossed by a multitude of
waterways, is unsuited for tank warfare. Accordingly, all tank and mot.
troops will have to be brought up short on reaching the line St. Omer–
Béthune.

This is a complete reversal of the elements of the plan. I wanted to make
AGp. A the hammer and AGp. B the anvil in this operation. Now B will be
the hammer and A the anvil. As AGp. B is confronted with a consolidated
front, progress will be slow and casualties high. The Air Force, on which
all hopes are pinned, is dependent on the weather.

This divergence of views results in a tug-of-war which costs more nerves
than does the actual conduct of the operations. However, the battle will be
won, this way or that.

The result of the "tug-of-war" was that Hitler, although opposed to
Brauchitsch's desire to resume the armored advance, left the decision
up to Rundstedt.* And so, when on May 25 Rundstedt received authority from OKH to renew the attack, Oberst Guenther Blumentritt
(operations officer of Army Group A) was able to write on the OKH
directive: [106] "By order of the Commander-in-Chief [Rundstedt] and
Chief of Staff [Sodenstern], *not* passed on to the Fourth Army, as the

---

* J. D., May 25: "In the morning the Commander-in-Chief of the Army arrives
and asks permission for mechanized divisions to push forward from the high terrain Vimy-St. Omer-Gravelines toward the west into the level terrain. Fuehrer is
against it, leaves decision to Army Group A. They decline for the time being because tanks should rest a while to be ready for tasks in the south."

Fuehrer has delegated control to the Commander-in-Chief of the Army Group." The war diary of the army group also recorded Rundstedt's opinion that, even if a resumption of the armored advance were highly desirable, it was first and urgently necessary that the motorized infantry close up behind the armor.

And so the stop-order lasted through May 25 by Hitler's preference and Rundstedt's decision. The latter, indeed, apparently had little enthusiasm for further fighting in the north; the army group war diary entry for May 25 concludes with the observation:[107] "The task of the army group can be considered to be in the main completed." And in the light of all this it is as absurd to contend (as do the German generals in their postwar apologia) that Rundstedt had no responsibility for the stop-order[108] as to argue (as does Major Ellis) that Rundstedt had already acted on May 23 and that Hitler merely "endorsed" Rundstedt's decision. As the records now available amply demonstrate, Hitler, Goering, and Rundstedt all played important roles in the decision to halt the armor on the Canal Line.

The morning of May 26 dawned with the stop-order still in effect, and Brauchitsch and Halder in a very bad mood. The latter noted in his diary that the German tanks had "stopped as if paralyzed . . . and must not attack." If things went on in this fashion, "cleaning out the pocket may take weeks, much to the detriment of our prestige and our future plans." As for Brauchitsch:[109]

> All through the morning, ObdH is very nervous. I can fully sympathize with him, for these orders from the top just make no sense. In one area they call for a head-on attack against a front retiring in orderly fashion and still possessing its striking power, and elsewhere they freeze the troops to the spot when the enemy rear could be cut into any time you wanted to attack. Von Rundstedt, too, apparently could not stand it any longer * and went up front to Hoth and Kleist, to get the lay of the land for the next moves of his armor.

But the leash was about to be removed. At about noon on May 26, OKH was informed[110] that Hitler would now permit the extreme left wing (Guderian's XIXth Corps) to advance within artillery range of Dunkirk "in order to cut off, from the land side, the continuous flow of transport (evacuations and arrivals)." Then Hitler sent for Brau-

---

* An interesting entry. Either Halder was unaware that Rundstedt had favored the stop-order, or else by May 26 the latter felt that the pause had accomplished its purpose of closing up the infantry support behind the tanks, and that the advance should be resumed.

chitsch and agreed that, in view of Bock's slow progress in Belgium,[111] the armor could resume its advance toward Dunkirk and Cassel. According to Jodl,[112] this action was taken in part because the British and French were not attacking along the Canal Line but were digging into defensive positions.* At all events, Brauchitsch returned "beaming" to OKH, and Halder happily noted: "At last the Fuehrer has given permission to move on Dunkirk in order to prevent further evacuations." Other attacks along the Canal Line, toward Ypres and Lille, were also authorized, in order to link up with Bock and break the Allied pocket into fragments.

Thus ended the episode that so sharply divided the German counsels. We have traced the chain of responsibility for the order. What were the true reasons for its issuance?

So far as Rundstedt was concerned, they were tactical and temporary. He was somewhat cautious in his conception of mechanized warfare;[113] the astonishingly rapid advance across France had been followed by heavy tank losses at Arras and on the Channel Coast.[114] His subordinate commanders, Kleist and Kluge, were in a mood to slow down and bring up the infantry before moving on. The terrain close to Dunkirk was difficult for armor, as Guderian † was to discover a few days later when the ban was lifted. However, by then the Allies had had an opportunity to retreat into the Dunkirk area and establish a defense perimeter. At the time the stop-order was issued the Germans would have encountered far less opposition.

But Rundstedt sensed no urgency about the elimination of the Allied pocket. He knew that another major offensive, against the French south of the Somme, was soon to commence, and that the armor would be needed again. So he preferred to spare his own troops and was by no

---

* An Allied attack from the Canal Line would have tended to pull their forces out of Belgium and into France—an outcome which, as we have seen, Hitler and Goering desired. But since they did not attack, and Bock was making slow progress, Hitler decided to increase the pressure on the Allies by again throwing in the armor.

† A French writer (Jacques Mordal, *Guderian sur l'Aa ou le véritable miracle de Dunkerque*, in the *Revue de Défense Nationale*, Aug.-Sept. 1955, pp. 196–210) contends that Guderian was chiefly responsible for the B.E.F.'s escape at Dunkirk, because he could have gone there immediately after he reached Abbéville and could easily have taken the port, which was not yet prepared for defense. Calais and Boulogne, it is argued, should have been by-passed, as they would be hopelessly cut off once Dunkirk was in German hands. In this there is much force, but it seems hardly fair to blame Guderian, who had planned to send the 10th Panzer Division to Dunkirk but was frustrated by Kleist's order (*supra,* p. 243) removing it from his command and holding it at Abbéville. It was, after all, the responsibility of Guderian's superiors, with the benefit of air reconnaissance and an over-all appreciation of the battle, to spot such opportunities.

means unwilling to leave to Bock the difficult and bloody task of cleaning up Dunkirk.

Goering's motivation appears to have been vanity pure and simple. Crucially important as was the work of the Luftwaffe while the airborne troops smothered the key defenses in Holland and Belgium and the panzers swept across France, the air arm had achieved no victory all its own. Both Kesselring and Jeschonnek had grave misgivings about the Luftwaffe's ability to dispose of the encircled Allied armies singlehanded, but Goering overruled their objections [115] and made an illadvised and reckless commitment which Hitler took at face value.

With Hitler, the situation was somewhat more complicated. During both the Norwegian campaign and the earlier stages of the Battle of France he had shown a tendency to over-caution, or even to panic, in the clutch. Thus Rundstedt's cautious advice fell on willing ears, at a moment when Brauchitsch's stock was low, and Goering offered what looked like an easy way out. Quite possibly, too, Hitler had no desire to see the army generals, for whom he had little love, reap the full glory of the triumph. As a Nazi politician, no doubt he preferred to see Goering's brow crowned with the laurels of victory.[116]

The story that Hitler wanted to let the British down easily, in the hope that they might more willingly make peace, has attained wide currency. It seems to be based on little more than gossip and is quite incredible in view of the Germans' violent efforts to block the Dunkirk evacuation, once it was under way. Guderian has written that "neither then or at any later period did I hear anything to substantiate this suggestion." The story seems to have originated in postwar comments by members of Rundstedt's staff, who no doubt were eager to cover up their share of responsibility for the stop-order.[117]

But political motives do seem to have played a part in the decision to annihilate the encircled Allied forces in northern France rather than Belgium. Why? France had declared war on Germany; Belgium had not and had been invaded in a manner painfully reminiscent of 1914. If the final act of destruction was to be accomplished by Luftwaffe bombs in a crowded coastal area, it might sit much better with world opinion if the terrible scene were set in France rather than Flanders. Furthermore, Hitler had been dreaming about the Nazification of the Flemish and turning all or part of Belgium into a national-socialist *Gau* of the Greater Reich. An annihilating hail of bombs would not be an auspicious beginning for such a project.[118]

But all this leaves unsolved the basic question: Why did the Germans miscalculate so badly? Granting some substance to the tactical and political factors that prompted the stop-order, they were far outweighed strategically by the possibility of cutting off the Allies from their retreat by sea and destroying the B.E.F. How could an experienced and able commander like Rundstedt, or ruthless conquerors like Hitler and Goering, throw away such an opportunity?

The answer is that it had not crossed their minds that a large-scale evacuation from Dunkirk was possible. This is not so surprising as it might seem at first blush. According to Mr. Churchill, when "Operation Dynamo" was set in motion the British themselves did not hope to hold Dunkirk for more than two days and thought they would do well to get out 45,000 men.[119] If the seafaring British were so pessimistic, it is easy to understand that to the continental minds of the Germans and French, a mass evacuation by sea was inconceivable.

The French, indeed, made precisely the same mistake as the Germans. General Sir Edward Spears has vividly described his difficulties in conveying the "Dunkirk idea" to Premier Reynaud and General Weygand:[120]

I suddenly realized with a clarity that had never before been vouchsafed me in all the long years I had worked with the French Army that to them the sea was much the same thing as an abyss of boiling pitch and brimstone, an insurmountable obstacle no army could venture over. . . .

To fall back to Dunkirk represented retiring into a fortress, which might be supplied by sea, but from which there was no retreat. . . . I explained that . . . behind the harbors lay God's own highway, the greatest, widest highway in the world, one that led everywhere. If the troops could get on to ships they would soon be in the line elsewhere. This statement was received in glum silence.

In Belgium, the French Commander-in-Chief (General Blanchard) was similarly afflicted with the landlubber's narrow outlook. He was "horrified" when the idea of evacuation by sea was first put to him,[121] and the consequent laggardly French withdrawal to the coast was to cost them dear.[122]

The Germans suffered from the same blindness. There is no mention of the possibility of evacuation in Halder's diary until May 26 and no mention whatever in Jodl's diary, which comes to an end on that date. There is no indication of awareness on Halder's part that a mass evacuation was under way until May 30,[123] by which time the British had brought out over 100,000 men.

And so, while the British were preparing and commencing the

greatest naval rescue operation in recorded history, Hitler and the generals wrangled about the stop-order and busied themselves with plans for the approaching offensive on the Somme-Aisne front. The stop-order would not have been issued but for their failure to grasp the urgency of cutting the Allies off from the coast before the resourceful might of British sea power could be brought to bear in a huge salvage operation. The reprieve of the stop-order was the prelude to "the deliverance of Dunkirk." [124]

Dunkirk: The Miracle

The stop-order was lifted during the afternoon of May 26, a few hours before the Dunkirk evacuation—Operation Dynamo—was ordered by the Admiralty. During the night of May 26–27, just as the British and French were commencing their general retreat toward the coast, the German armor resumed its attack all along the Canal Line. But by this time the British had been able to deploy three regular infantry divisions along the line, and the Germans made slow progress.

Guderian, on the coast, had a particularly difficult time in the flooded country around Gravelines, which was defended by one of Fagalde's French divisions, and it took two days for him to take Gravelines, Bourbourgville, and Wormhoudt. Reinhardt, meanwhile, broke out of his St. Omer bridgehead toward Cassel and Hazebrouck, and Hoepner attacked * across the canal near Béthune. None of them was able to break through the British front, in order to cut off the Allied line of retreat to Dunkirk.

The right wing of Hoth's armored group, however, had better success. Rommel's 7th Panzer Division got over the canal between Béthune and La Bassée on the night of May 26–27 and put a bridge across the next day. Here the Germans were in better tank country, and by the morning of May 28 Rommel was astride the road running west from Lille, between that city and Armentières. This advance was the de-

---

* In the course of this attack, a company of the SS *Totenkopf* Division (of Hoepner's XVIth Corps) showed that the Waffen-SS was capable of perpetrating atrocities in France as well as in Poland. About 100 men of the Royal Norfolk Regiment were overrun and surrounded at Paradis on the night of May 26 and surrendered the following morning. After being searched, the men were paraded past a barn wall in single file and mowed down by machine-gun fire, on the orders of the SS company commander, one Fritz Knochlein. This episode, sadly anticipatory of the "Malmédy massacre" of American troops in December 1944, is known as the "Paradis massacre." Knochlein was apprehended after the war and was sentenced to death by a British military tribunal in 1948.[125]

cisive step in trapping a large part of the French First Army near Lille.

Throughout May 27, the Allies stubbornly held off the Germans and simultaneously prepared for a general withdrawal that night to a defense perimeter around Dunkirk. By the morning of May 28 all of the British forces from Lille and two corps of the French First Army were beyond Armentières and heading rapidly for the coast. The rest of the First Army, however, was still near Lille, its line of retreat gravely threatened by Rommel's advance to the Lille-Armentières road. King Leopold had surrendered the Belgian Army, and it had become a matter of desperate urgency to hasten the Allied withdrawal.

The more extraordinary it was, therefore, that when Lord Gort met with General Blanchard late in the morning on May 28, the French officer exhibited no inclination to bestir his troops and get away.[126] His orders from Paris went no further than to retreat to the Lys, and he "declared that an evacuation from the beach was impossible." A liaison officer from General Prioux (commanding the First Army) then arrived, and reported that Prioux planned to withdraw no farther that day. The British generals pleaded in vain; the French would not be budged.

They paid a heavy price for their shortsightedness, for the subsequent attempts to break out of Lille toward the coast were largely unavailing. On May 29 Hoth's armor and Waeger's XXVIIth Infantry Corps (of Reichenau's Sixth Army) met near Armentières and closed the trap on some five French divisions—nearly half the First Army. After two more days of desperate resistance, these encircled remnants surrendered, swelling by some 50,000 the German haul of prisoners.

The British and the rest of the French continued with all speed their retreat to Dunkirk. May 28 was an especially critical day, for after the Belgian surrender Reichenau lunged forward to the Yser River northwest of Ypres, and Kuechler's Eighteenth Army marched straight through West Flanders, captured Ostend, and approached Nieuport, about seventeen miles from Dunkirk. Here they were held by an improvised task force of French and British troops, while the major Allied units poured into the coastal area. During the night of May 29 the retreating forces reached the line Poperinghe-Noordschote, and by noon on May 30 practically all of them were within the defense perimeter that had been organized to protect the embarkation. The evacuation was now in full swing, and nearly 100,000 men had been brought to England.

The Dunkirk defense perimeter extended some twenty-two miles

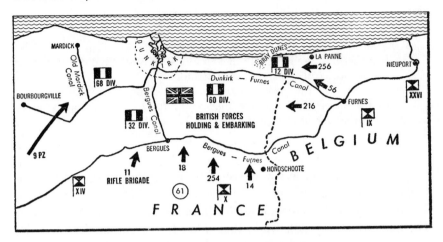

BATTLE SITUATION AT DUNKIRK, JUNE 1, 1940.

along the coast, so that the troops could be embarked not only from
Dunkirk harbor but from the beaches between that city and Nieuport.
The French held the area between Dunkirk and Mardick, five miles
to the west, and the British the much longer sector to the east. Inland,
the perimeter was bounded by the canal running through Bergues,
Furnes, and Nieuport, so that the defense area was about six miles
deep near Dunkirk and thinned to two miles at Nieuport. Much of it
was flooded, and nearly all was so cut up by ditches and small canals
as to be nearly impassable for tanks and heavy artillery.

As the Allies folded back into the bridgehead, the Germans reduced
and radically altered the composition of the forces surrounding it. The
panzer generals who had waxed wroth at the stop-order now turned
decidedly cool to the further use of their tanks. For this change of heart
there was, to be sure, good reason, quite apart from the difficult terrain.
The new offensive on the Somme was to start in about ten days, and
the armored divisions badly needed an opportunity to rest and refit.
Furthermore, the Belgian surrender had brought Kuechler's Eighteenth
Army up to the bridgehead, so that infantry divisions were now available for the final assault. All these reasons are manifest in a report
made by Guderian, just back from a visit to his first line, to Zeitzler
(Kleist's chief of staff) on the evening of May 28: [127]

(1) Now that the Belgians have capitulated, continuation of operations
here is . . . costing unnecessary sacrifices. The armored divisions have only

50 per cent of their armored strength left, and their equipment is in urgent need of repair if the Corps is soon to be ready for other operations.

(2) A tank attack in this marshy, rain-soaked country is pointless. The troops hold the high ground south of Dunkirk . . . and have good artillery positions from which they can fire on Dunkirk.

Furthermore, the Eighteenth Army is approaching . . . from the east, with infantry forces more suitable than tanks for fighting in this kind of country, and the task of closing the gap on the coast can therefore be left to them.

That very night, orders were issued for the withdrawal of the XIXth Corps, and its replacement at the bridgehead by Wietersheim's XIVth Corps, which had been trailing Guderian all over northern France.[128] The next day (May 29), while the Allied forces gathered within the defense perimeter, Reinhardt's XLIst Corps was also sent back to rest. A few infantry divisions remained in the Lille area, but by May 30 nearly all units of Kluge's Fourth Army had been withdrawn from combat, and a general movement toward the Somme front was soon under way.

These transfers left a plethora of higher headquarters—Army Groups A and B, the Fourth, Sixth, and Eighteenth armies, and Panzer Group Kleist—still responsible for the elimination of the Dunkirk bridgehead. Naturally, they were fairly tumbling over one another, for the defense perimeter was but thirty miles in length, and only ten German divisions were engaged. The chain of command from Army Group A down through the Fourth Army and Panzer Group Kleist had under its orders at the front (west of Dunkirk, opposite the French) only Wietersheim's XIVth Corps, with one armored and the equivalent of two motorized divisions. Along the Bergues-Furnes Canal, Christian Hansen's Xth Corps of Reichenau's Sixth Army deployed four infantry divisions. From Furnes to Nieuport was the sector of Kuechler's Eighteenth Army, with two corps (Geyer's IXth and Wodrig's XXVIth) but only three infantry divisions.

This extraordinary division of command did not lend itself to a vigorous and well co-ordinated assault on the bridgehead. Partly because of OKH's preoccupation with the coming Somme offensive, and partly owing to Rundstedt's hesitant field tactics, the German high command was slow to appreciate the astonishing progress of the evacuation and to reorganize the chain of command so as to centralize responsibility for the bridgehead's elimination.

The lower field headquarters took a much more realistic view. As early as May 27, Zeitzler reported to the Fourth Army [129] that the British were embarking in large numbers, commenting that "it is very bitter for our men to see this." Later that day Blumentritt informed Kluge's chief of staff (Generalmajor Kurt Brennecke) that Dunkirk was being attacked by the Luftwaffe, on Goering's orders, "in such a manner that further embarkations are reported to be impossible." But Brennecke quickly disillusioned Blumentritt: "The situation in the Channel ports is as follows: big ships come alongside the quays, planks are run up, and the men hurry aboard. All equipment is left behind. We do not want to find these men, freshly equipped, in front of us again later."

Not until May 30 did the OKH generals realize that, for all their victories, the B.E.F. was slipping through their fingers. Halder's awakening was sudden indeed. His diary entry for that day opens with the complacent comment that "disintegration of the bottled-up enemy forces is continuing," with some British units still fighting, while others were "streaming back to the sea and trying to get across in anything that floats." In an allusion to Zola's novel on the Franco-Prussian War, Halder described this situation as "Le Débacle." But a few hours later, in conference with Brauchitsch, Halder's tune turned glum: [130]

He [Brauchitsch] is angry, and the reason is that the effects of the blunders forced upon us by OKW (detour in direction of Laon and holding back the tanks at St. Omer) are beginning to be felt now. We lost time and so the pocket with the French and British in it was sealed later than it could have been. Worse, the pocket would have been closed at the coast if only our armor had not been held back. As it is, the bad weather has grounded our Air Force, and now we must stand by and watch countless thousands of the enemy get away to England right under our noses.

As a result of this high-level dissatisfaction, pressure was now brought to bear on the field headquarters to clean up the bridgehead. This "needling" and its frustration by both the Allies' stubborn defense and the overcomplicated German chain of command are vividly reflected in the communications that day between the operations officer of the Fourth Army (Oberstleutnant Rolf Wuthmann) and Zeitzler (Kleist's chief of staff).[131]

Early in the afternoon of May 30 Wuthmann transmitted orders to Zeitzler directing that Wietersheim's XIVth Corps should close in on Dunkirk so that the town could be shelled with ten-centimeter guns. Wuthmann complained that Fourth Army headquarters had the impression "that nothing is going on today, that no one is now interested

in Dunkirk." He urged that the town be bombarded, so as to spread
panic and stop the evacuation. There ensued some messages between
Rundstedt's and Kluge's headquarters, indicating that Kluge, Reichenau, and Richthofen (commanding Fliegerkorps VIII) were all
thoroughly confused as to each other's plans. Then Wuthmann again
directed Zeitzler to press the attack on both sides of Dunkirk right up
to the coast. Zeitzler replied that Kleist's forces were not overly suitable for this mission, since tanks could not be used in that area. Wuthmann rejoined with the information that higher headquarters were
insisting that "an end must finally be made of the embarkation at
Dunkirk." Kluge added his personal authority to this mandate. "The
situation at Abbéville is untenable," * he informed Zeitzler, and therefore: "All your forces must immediately attack along the coast east of
Dunkirk. The divisional commander † should be told that he must
without fail reach the coast today!" Subsequently, Kleist's headquarters
reported that the 20th Division was advancing toward the coast, but
that the group's left wing was stuck in front of Gravelines and Bergues,
and could make no progress.

In fact, May 30 was a very unsuccessful day for the German forces
surrounding Dunkirk. Kuechler's heavy attacks at the eastern end of
the bridgehead got over the canal but were beaten back. Wietersheim
did no better. Unified command was badly needed, and measures to
that end were taken at the end of the day. Kuechler's Eighteenth
Army (which remained subordinate to Bock's Army Group B) was
given command of the entire operation, utilizing the four corps headquarters and ten divisions already at the defense perimeter. Rundstedt's Army Group A (together with Kluge's Fourth Army and Panzer
Group Kleist) and Reichenau's Sixth Army relinquished their command
responsibilities at Dunkirk and went off to the south, to prepare for
the Somme offensive.

Kuechler, on taking over command, was the recipient of some "personal suggestions" from Brauchitsch and Hitler. These comprised: [133]

(a) The landing of troop units from the sea, in the rear of the English
forces.

* A reference to the sharp Franco-British attacks against the German bridgehead on the south bank of the Somme at Abbéville (then held by Manstein's
XXXVIIIth Corps), which were in progress from May 27 to May 30. The bridgehead was held, but on May 29 the vigor of the Allied assault had caused the Germans considerable anxiety.[132]
† The reference is to the Austrian, Generalleutnant Mauriz Wiktorin zu Hain-
burg, commanding the 20th Motorized Infantry Division.

(b) Withdrawal of advanced infantry units from the bank of the canal [at the edge of the defense perimeter] so as to allow unhindered and effective air support.

(c) Use of antiaircraft shells with time fuses to compensate for the reduced effectiveness of artillery in the sand dunes (a suggestion of the Fuehrer and Supreme Commander).

Such a message leaves little room for the theory that Hitler was deliberately allowing the Allies to escape. But the suggestions from on high did not help much; neither did the change in command bear immediate fruit, because of the delay in rearranging the communications network. There was fighting all along the defense perimeter on May 31, but the Germans had no significant success, and that evening Halder recorded that: [134]

Lacking unified leadership (Army HQ 18 could not establish contact with all [subordinate] HQs soon enough), our attack resolved itself into individual local actions against an enemy stubbornly defending himself behind the canals, and therefore achieved only small local successes. An intercepted radio signal indicates that the enemy will continue evacuation operations during the night. It will be difficult to stop him. We are now paying the penalty for our failure, due to interference from above, to cut off the coast.

In fact, May 31 was the peak evacuation day of Operation Dynamo, with 68,000 men returned to England. That night the British withdrew from the Belgian portion of the bridgehead at its eastern end around Furnes and Nieuport, and by the morning of June 1 the total of troops taken out had risen to 194,000, or more than four times the initial British estimate of what was possible. On the British government's firm orders, Lord Gort and his staff departed, and Major General Harold Alexander was left in command of the remaining British troops.

On June 1 the Germans finally succeeded in crossing the Bergues-Furnes Canal, but the flooded land and stubborn defense held them away from the harbor and the beach to the east of Dunkirk. Evacuation went on throughout the day and night, and over 64,000 more troops were taken across to England. By morning there were only a few thousand British left. But there were still nearly 100,000 French under Admiral Abrial, and evacuation operations continued during the nights of June 2 and 3, in the course of which General Alexander and the British rear guard, and some 60,000 French, were rescued from the harbor. The French fought off the Germans with great gallantry during the last two days, and Dunkirk (with some 40,000 French soldiers) did not fall to Kuechler's troops until the morning of June 4. Operation Dynamo by then had carried some 350,000 Allied soldiers across the Channel.

Such was the course of battle on the ground. But the real "miracle of Dunkirk" transpired on the sea and in the air.

Hermann Goering's promise that the Luftwaffe would annihilate the encircled enemy proved an empty boast. The failure was not, however, due to any lack of energy or bravery on the part of the German flyers and their commanders. Kesselring and Sperrle threw into the operation practically all the fighters and tactical bombers of their respective *Luftflotten*, and their attacks on the bridgehead and the evacuation shipping were pressed home with great determination.

Indeed, it appeared at first that the Luftwaffe might vindicate Goering's vanity. On May 27—the first day of Operation Dynamo—the town and harbor of Dunkirk were so destructively bombed that all British troops were moved out, and the local naval commander reported that the harbor was unusable, so that the troops would have to be lifted from the beaches.[135] Incoming ships that night were diverted from the harbor to the beaches; this gave rise to a false rumor that Dunkirk had fallen to the Germans, so that some ships turned back to England without embarking any troops. By midnight only 7669 men had been evacuated, and the future of Operation Dynamo was most unpromising.

But on further inspection the Dunkirk harbor proved still usable, and the next day (May 28) six destroyers came in to take men from the mole, while other craft went to the beaches. At the bridgehead there was less air activity, for most of the German bombers were employed farther inland against the retreating troops. The weather was worse, and the harbor gained a measure of protection under the thick clouds of smoke from the stores of fuel and matériel that had been set afire.[136] A few ships were sunk by bombs, but the pace of the evacuation was greatly accelerated.

On May 29 the Luftwaffe commanders, desperately aware that the British were getting away in hordes, turned the full force of their attack against the evacuation fleet.[137] But the German flyers were now encountering the Royal Air Force on something like even terms for the first time, for the aerial battlefields were about midway between the English and German bases, and the British were going all out. They were heavily outnumbered, but not outflown, and Spitfires proved a match for Messerschmitts. The Boulton-Paul Defiant—a two-man fighter with rear turret—had its brief hour of glory, for it was lethal to the German bombers, and its vulnerability to faster fighters had not yet been exposed.

Twice, however, the Germans appeared in force when there was no British air cover. Much of the RAF's activity was not visible to the men in the harbor and on the beaches, and there were ugly scenes at Dover and the other Thames ports when the battle-strained troops debarked and insulted men in RAF uniforms.[138] Five ships were sunk in the harbor; again there were reports that Dunkirk was blocked, and incoming craft were diverted to the beaches. But with great effort the harbor was partially cleared, and the rate of evacuation reached its peak during the next four days.

May 30 brought the Luftwaffe the frustration, and the Allies the blessed respite, of bad weather. The German bombers were grounded, the German generals fumed, and British craft of all types and sizes plied back and forth across the Channel, laden with troops. The following day turned fine after an early morning haze, and that afternoon the Luftwaffe launched three heavy attacks on the shipping. But the luck of timing was with the RAF fighter patrols; the attacking squadrons were harassed and disrupted, and most of the bombs missed their targets, as Operation Dynamo enjoyed its biggest day.

The climax of the air battles over Dunkirk came on June 1, when the RAF and Luftwaffe each lost some thirty planes. "Throughout the day," so ran the German Air Ministry account,[139] "waves of aircraft attacked troops assembled for embarkation, the harbor of Dunkirk, and warships and merchant vessels off the coast and in the sea area between Dunkirk and England." Bombing the beaches proved surprisingly ineffective, for the sand tended to smother the explosions.[140] But the Germans pushed home two heavy attacks during intervals between the RAF patrol flights and sank three destroyers and numerous lesser craft. It was Goering's last chance, for the evacuation was nearing completion, but despite the Luftwaffe's greatest efforts and the extensive damage it caused, nearly as many troops were lifted as on the previous day.

The bridgehead was now suffering such punishment both from the air and from approaching German artillery that daytime evacuation had to be stopped. Night bombing was in its infancy and was not seriously attempted, and the RAF was able to concentrate its patrols in the hours of dusk and dawn when the ships were approaching and leaving the bridgehead. In the closing phases of the evacuation the weather again turned bad. As a result of all this, the Luftwaffe was unable to interfere seriously with Operation Dynamo during its last days, when the French were being brought out. It was not the Luftwaffe but ammunition shortage and the encircling pressure of Kuechler's infantry that brought the evacuation to a finish on June 4.

And so, for all of Goering's vainglory, the Luftwaffe was unable more than to nick the British at Dunkirk—to nick them painfully, to be sure, but, in strategic terms, insignificantly. As Kesselring and Jeschonnek had foreseen, the German air arm was unequal to this sort of mission. It had been designed primarily to work hand-in-hand with the Army. For the massive bombardment of shipping and harbor installations, the German aircraft were neither numerous nor heavy enough, especially when confronted for the first time with a determined and skillful enemy air force. As General Galland has remarked,[141] "Dunkirk should have been an emphatic warning for the leaders of the Luftwaffe," as it foreshadowed its greater failure in the Battle of Britain.

The Luftwaffe was the Wehrmacht's primary arm at Dunkirk. For the British, and despite the fine performance of the RAF, Dunkirk was a naval affair. It was a marvelous feat of naval organization and improvisation, but it was not alone the Admiralty's glory. Winston Churchill has eloquently pictured "the spontaneous movement which swept the seafaring population of our south and southeastern shores": [142]

Everyone who had a boat of any kind, steam or sail, put out for Dunkirk, and the preparations . . . were now aided by the brilliant improvisation of volunteers on an amazing scale. The numbers arriving on May 29 were small, but they were the forerunners of nearly four hundred small craft which from the thirty-first were destined to play a vital part by ferrying from the beaches to the off-lying ships almost a hundred thousand men.

And where, at this crucial moment of sea power, was the German Navy? Submarines sank two British destroyers on May 29, and E-boats scored a few kills around the harbor and beaches. These pinpricks were all that Raeder could achieve. Half of his destroyer force already lay on the bottom or the beaches near Narvik. The major fleet units in home ports were about to return to northern waters for "Operation Juno." [143] There was little left for Dunkirk.

Interestingly, the German Naval War Staff had foreseen the use that the British might make of small craft, though they failed to anticipate the success of the evacuation as a whole. On May 26 Admiral Schniewind (Chief of the Naval War Staff) opined: [144] "Evacuation of troops without equipment . . . is conceivable by means of large numbers of smaller vessels, coastal and ferry steamers, fishing trawlers, drifters, and other small craft, in good weather, even from the open coast."

Schniewind went on to acknowledge that the German Navy could take no effective part in the Dunkirk fighting "with the means at its disposal." Later he reported that artillery and air bombardment, coupled with mine-laying and "the nightly successful appearance of German speedboats," were causing the British "great difficulties," but simultaneously and accurately predicted "that the western powers, by ruthless use of naval forces and transport vessels, will succeed in getting a considerable part of their troops over to England, even though in complete disorder and without heavy arms or equipment." The German admirals were, in fact, little more than bystanders at Dunkirk, and when Raeder met with Hitler on June 4, just as the city fell to Kuechler and Operation Dynamo ended, they did not even mention the evacuation,[145] pregnant as it was with ominous significance for the Wehrmacht.

But the dire consequences of their failure to cut off the Allies from the sea were not to be visited upon the Germans until later in the war. The men of the British Expeditionary Force had been saved, but it was an unarmed and unorganized horde, and not an army, that returned to England. For the moment, the British Army was *hors de combat,* and the stricken, decimated French Army now confronted a far more powerful and supremely confident Wehrmacht. The fall of France was imminent.

CHAPTER EIGHT

The Fall of France

THE SECOND PHASE of the Battle of France began in the early morning of June 5, 1940, less than twenty-four hours after the last British ship left Dunkirk. Within two weeks the French were beaten to their knees, and on June 25—one day less than three weeks after the offensive was launched—the cease-fire orders became effective, and the battle ended.

In terms of ultimate strategy, the second phase of the campaign in the West was more remarkable for what the Germans did not do than for what they did do. The Wehrmacht did not follow up the beaten British, well-nigh defenseless as they were after Dunkirk. The German leaders did not even begin to plan or prepare for an invasion of England, or any other stroke that might yield decisive results against their principal foe.

Instead, the entire resources of the Wehrmacht were devoted to annihilating the remnants of the French Army. The reorganization and regrouping of the German field forces for the drive to the south across the Somme and Aisne was a brilliant tactical achievement, and an impressive demonstration of German military techniques. Strategically, however, it was like using a steamhammer to drive home the last coffin nail.*

Few of the fluctuations and sharp disagreements that had marked the development of plan *Gelb* for the opening offensive recurred during preparations for the second phase, which was given the name *Rot.*

---

* On June 1 Generalleutnant Moriz von Faber du Faur, then attached to Kuechler's Eighteenth Army, wrote (*Macht und Ohnmacht*, p. 255): "The French cover Paris with a Weygand Line near Amiens, but the fact is that this campaign will soon be over."

It had been assumed from the outset that, even if *Gelb* were fully successful, there would have to be a second offensive to complete the conquest of France. The operations staff at OKH had been working on plans for the second phase even while the first was in its opening stages, and by May 20—the day that Guderian reached the coast—they were ready for presentation to Hitler.

The jump-off line for *Rot* had been traced by the left wing of Kleist's Panzer Group as it drove through northern France, and was nailed down by the infantry divisions that followed the armor and deployed themselves defensively along the front, to guard the southern flank of the armored salient. The line followed generally the Somme and Aisne rivers, from the bridgeheads on the Somme at Abbéville and Amiens, past Noyon, Soissons and Rethel, to Montmédy at the western end of the Maginot Line. This was a span of some 200 miles and, since Leeb's Army Group C along the Maginot Line and the Rhine was also to participate in the second phase, the entire front for *Rot* was about 400 miles long.

The tactical problems which the German planners faced on this occasion were far simpler than those they had confronted at the outset. The Allied armies had been reduced by over a quarter in numbers and more than that in strength, since the bulk of the French mechanized forces had been trapped in Flanders. There was little cause to worry about Allied attacks, and neither need nor opportunity to lure forward and cut off part of the enemy forces by subtle deceptions such as Manstein had developed for *Gelb*. The front was broad, and west of the Maginot Line there were no strong points like Eben Emael or prepared fortifications as in Belgium and Holland. The Germans already held several bridgeheads over the Somme, and beyond the Somme and Aisne the country was open and well suited to armored warfare.

The Germans Regroup

Nevertheless, there were two questions upon which there was division of opinion within the high command: whether to launch the main thrust on the east or the west side of Paris, and whether or not to attempt a secondary offensive across the upper Rhine, toward the Belfort Gap—the valley between the Vosges and the Jura, joining the basins of the Rhine and Rhone, and a traditional military and commercial route between southern Germany and central France.

The Rhine project had been under study for some time, and staff discussions with the Italians had envisaged the participation of some twenty Italian divisions in a joint offensive ("*Braun*").[1] General Heinrich von Stuelpnagel had been in charge of formulating the plans for this operation, but Mussolini was reluctant to declare war until France's defeat was assured, and *Braun* never went beyond the paper stage. On May 20 Stuelpnagel was directed to drop the matter,[2] and the Italians were encouraged to make preparations for an offensive on the Franco-Italian frontier south of the Alps.

The abandonment of *Braun* did not, however, eliminate the idea of an upper Rhine operation. Halder's first plan, which Brauchitsch approved on May 20, called for an offensive with fifteen German infantry divisions on the upper Rhine, and a supplemental attack with eight more divisions against the Maginot Line near Saarbruecken. These were to follow by several days the main assault on the Somme-Aisne front. Halder proposed to concentrate nearly all of the armor west of Paris under Bock, while Rundstedt, with three infantry armies, would attack on the east side, all with the object of enveloping the French forces southwest of Paris in the Plateau de Langres.[3]

The OKH plan was presented to Hitler on the morning of May 21, and the Fuehrer gave his approval.[4] But Hitler had ideas of his own on the subject,* and that same afternoon he called in Keitel and Jodl to say that he had "changed his mind." He declared that "it is wrong to employ all armored and motorized divisions west of Paris, and it would be better to direct the main thrust, including the bulk of armored forces, so as to by-pass Paris on the east." Jodl transmitted the Fuehrer's desires to OKH that evening. It may be assumed that they were not joyfully received in that quarter, but at this point OKW and OKH both became very much preoccupied with the British attack at Arras and the controversy over the stop-order.

Halder again turned his attention to *Rot* on May 25, when he spent the entire day at "work on the regrouping of our forces for the next phase of the campaign." That evening the results of the labors were presented to Hitler, who, as Halder's diary records, "as usual" received the Chief of Staff "in a cool, almost hostile manner." Halder's plan, however, was approved without major changes. The proposed deployment envisaged the main thrust east of Paris, as Hitler had desired. However, a strong force, including armor, was to attack from the

* On the morning of May 20, before receiving the OKH plan, Hitler had proposed that the main assault be launched southwesterly through Rheims, with another heavy attack west of Paris and a supplementary push in the Saar region against the Maginot Line.[5]

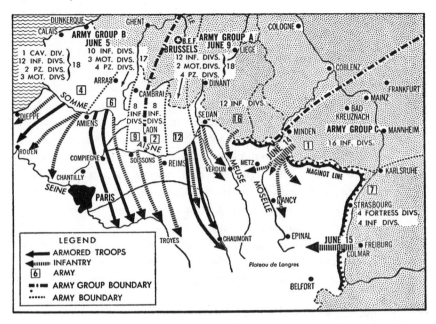

ESSENTIALS OF GERMAN PLAN "ROT" FOR SECOND PHASE OF
BATTLE OF FRANCE.

Somme west of Paris and penetrate to the Seine as fast as possible. Where it should go thereafter—whether south to the Bay of Biscay in order to seal off the coast or southeast to link with the forces from east of Paris and surround the French armies—was left for later decision as the course of the battle might dictate.

The Fuehrer was much concerned about Paris, from a political as well as a military standpoint.[6] If the city was strongly defended, he wished to disengage rather than press the attack. But he was apprehensive of revolutionary developments attendant upon a French defeat and directed that "a strong armored force must be held in readiness for a quick thrust into Paris in the event of internal disorder."

On May 27 Halder visited Rundstedt's headquarters at Charleville, to expound and receive comments on the *Rot* plan. The army group staff proposed a change of no great consequence in the alignment of armies in the western sector. Generaloberst Blaskowitz, commanding the newly created Ninth Army, was reported as "worried" about a possible French offensive in the central sector between the Somme and Oise rivers. Rundstedt and Halder did not share Blaskowitz' apprehensions, and the conference disclosed no other problems or disagreements of any importance.

The following day (May 28), the final changes in the plan were made by Hitler in conference with Brauchitsch and the OKW generals.[7] The Fuehrer's idea of holding an armored force in readiness to occupy Paris was abandoned; instead, the city was to be encircled and then captured with infantry forces. The upper Rhine offensive was to be deferred until the main advance southwest through Rheims had approached the Moselle River near Toul. This drive was to be the *Schwerpunkt* of the entire operation and was to be spearheaded by Guderian's armor. Amusingly characteristic of Halder is his description of this decision: "At long last my idea has penetrated that for this operation we must concentrate our armor in front of our left wing." Eight days earlier, when the *Rot* plan as initially approved by Brauchitsch placed the bulk of the armor on the *right* wing, Halder had written: "What I have been preaching for the past three days has finally been adopted."

This meeting was productive of changes in command as well as plan, to the benefit of Guderian and the misfortune of Blaskowitz. The former's huge success in the drive from Sedan to Abbéville was now to be recognized by giving him, like Kleist, command of a panzer group of two armored corps. Since there were only five such corps, this meant that Hoth, who had been given panzer group status in the course of *Gelb* when Schmidt's and Hoepner's corps were transferred to Rundstedt's army group,[8] was relegated to the command of his XVth Corps.[*]

As for Blaskowitz, that unhappy officer had been falling increasingly into the Fuehrer's disfavor since the start of the war. His small Eighth Army, assigned a secondary role in Poland, had suffered a temporary but annoying reverse.[9] Then in the spring of 1940 he was relieved as military commander in Poland (*Oberost*) because of friction between him and the civilian occupation authorities.[10] Perhaps Blaskowitz' unshared fears about a French attack, if reported to Hitler, were the last straw. However that may be, Hitler decided to relieve Blaskowitz as Commander-in-Chief of the Ninth Army, and on May 29 Brauchitsch had the unpleasant task of relaying "the Fuehrer's decision to relieve him of his command." [†] Blaskowitz was replaced by General Adolf

[*] Hoth was not, however, subordinated to either Kleist or Guderian, but was placed directly under Kluge, whose Fourth Army was to conduct the attack west of Paris.

[†] Blaskowitz was shortly appointed Military Commander (*Militaerbefehlshaber*) in northern France.

Strauss, who had led the IInd Corps with distinction both in Poland and in the fighting near Arras, while General Heinrich von Stuelpnagel, whose duties in connection with *Braun* had just come to an end, re-placed Strauss as commander of the IInd Corps.

On May 29 Brauchitsch, Halder, and the commanders-in-chief of Army Groups A and B and of the component armies met at Charleville for a final review of the coming operation. Two days later there was a similar meeting at Bad Schwalbach with the Army Group C com-manders-in-chief.[11] Halder had been worried about Leeb's inability "to free himself from the concepts of position warfare in 1918," and special steps had been taken to ensure that "Leeb and the men around him assimilate the lessons of the drive across the Meuse." [12] But the confer-ence on May 31 was uneventful. On the planning side everything was now in readiness, and June 5 was specified as the target date for launch-ing the new offensive.

The plan in its final form [13] called for an offensive in three main waves, rolling along the front from west to east.* Bock's Army Group B, covering the front from the Channel Coast to the Aisne north of Rheims, was to attack on June 5 and make for the Seine on both sides of Paris. Rundstedt's Army Group A, in the central sector from the Aisne to the Franco-German border southeast of Luxembourg, was to jump off on June 9. Leeb's Army Group C was to assault the Maginot Line and the upper Rhine front about a week later. If all went according to plan, the German forces would converge south of Paris and bottle up the main French forces in the Maginot Line and the Plateau de Langres.

In this second phase of the Battle of France, Bock had the most com-plex initial task of the three army group commanders, and the largest force, comprising some fifty divisions. Kluge's Fourth Army, deployed along the Somme from the Channel Coast to Amiens, was responsible for the drive west of Paris to the Seine, with Hoth's XVth Corps of ar-mored and motorized troops as the spearhead. Reichenau's Sixth Army, the largest in the army group, was to cross the Somme and Aisne rivers between Amiens and Soissons and then turn slightly to the east, in or-der to by-pass Paris and reach the Seine near Troyes. Panzer Group Kleist, with two mechanized corps, provided the punch for this attack. Bock's left wing was Strauss's small Ninth Army, the infantry of which was to protect the army group's left flank against French counterat-tacks. Far behind the front, Kuechler's Eighteenth Army was still mop-

* See the charts of the order of battle of the German forces in the second phase of the French campaign in Appendix C, *infra,* pp. 430–31.

ping up at Dunkirk and was to be held in reserve to command the infantry forces that would occupy Paris in the event of the city's surrender, or of revolutionary outbreaks.

Rundstedt's Army Group A numbered about forty-five divisions. Weichs's Second Army was on the right wing next to the Ninth Army, to which it was similar in size, composition, and mission.* The army group's offensive strength was concentrated in List's Twelfth Army. Its field of attack lay between Châlons and the Argonne Forest; the infantry was to establish bridgeheads on the south bank of the Aisne, and from there the two mechanized corps of Guderian's new panzer group were to drive southward to the Plateau de Langres. Rundstedt's left wing was Busch's Sixteenth Army of thirteen infantry divisions. Those east of Montmédy confronted the Maginot Line and were to sit tight, but between Montmédy and Le Chesne (south of Sedan) General Eugen Ritter von Schobert's VIIth Corps was to advance on List's left, to guard against a possible French flanking sally from behind the Maginot Line.

Along the Franco-German border from Luxembourg to Switzerland, Leeb's Army Group C deployed twenty-four infantry divisions, of which two thirds were in Generaloberst Erwin von Witzleben's First Army between Luxembourg and the Rhine, and the remainder in General Friedrich Dollmann's Seventh Army along the Rhine. The original OKH plan for a major attack across the upper Rhine was abandoned, and Leeb's principal assault was to be launched on June 15 against the Maginot Line in the Saarbruecken area. Dollmann's Seventh Army, strengthened by the addition of Waeger's XXVIIth Corps with four fresh divisions, was to carry out a secondary assault across the Rhine toward Colmar. Leeb's attacks, if successful, were intended to converge with Rundstedt's major offensive and encircle the French in Alsace, Lorraine and the Plateau de Langres.

The three German army groups thus disposed of some 120 divisions, and twenty-three more were held in the OKH general reserve.† The Luftwaffe, with Kesselring's Luftflotte 2 supporting Bock and Sperrle's Luftflotte 3 behind Rundstedt and Leeb, had sustained some losses

---

* Both comprised eight infantry divisions and had the mission of guarding the flank of their respective army groups (Bock's left and Rundstedt's right) that would be exposed by an advance in the center. Bock's right flank was on the Channel Coast, and Rundstedt's left extended along the Maginot Line.

† It is a measure of the Germans' confidence that nothing was to be feared from the Russians that only seven divisions of second-rate troops were left on the eastern frontier. There were also seven divisions in Norway.

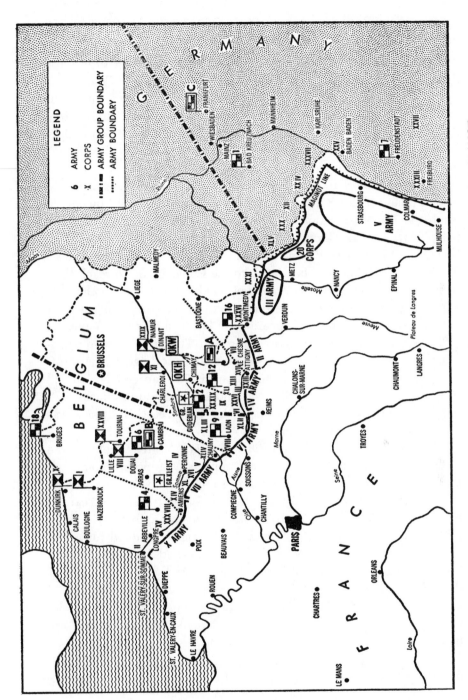

GERMAN DISPOSITIONS FOR THE SECOND PHASE OF THE BATTLE OF FRANCE,
JUNE 5, 1940.

over Dunkirk but was about as strong as it had been at the outset of the Battle of France.

Against this formidable array the French could muster little more than sixty-five divisions, and the British only one.* The French had practically no air force left, there were only a few British squadrons south of the Somme, and the RAF home bases were too distant from the scene of operations to enable British air power to bear significantly on the coming battle. The outcome, however gallantly the French might fight, was a foregone conclusion.

Indeed, the most remarkable German military achievement in the second phase of the Battle of France was not so much its success in combat as the organizational efficiency and flexibility displayed in the redeployment of the German forces. The 1st and 2nd Panzer Divisions, for example, had covered some 300 miles in their sweep across northern France to Abbéville and then north to the Canal Line. To reach their sector for *Rot* they had to reverse their field and traverse another 200 miles. "Signs of extreme fatigue on the part of the troops and of wear to their vehicles began to be apparent," [14] but in short order they were sufficiently rested and re-equipped for *Rot*. The other armored divisions had covered almost equally long distances and had likewise suffered heavy losses. Rommel wrote [15] that his 7th Panzer Division had "lost a lot of equipment on the road and in enemy tank attacks, and this must be put right as soon as possible." In a week his division was across the Somme and heading for Rouen.

The pause between *Gelb* and *Rot* was a time of great strain for the technical branches of the Wehrmacht, especially transport, communications, and supplies. Ammunition and supply dumps had to be relocated, headquarters and hospitals and air bases transferred, careful routings and timetables for troop movements prescribed, wire lines relaid and radio networks reorganized. The entire armored force had to wheel around and deploy on the new front, and for Guderian's divisions, moving east, this entailed cutting across the line of march of the infantry reinforcements coming westward into line. On June 3 Halder recorded that "movements of foot troops and motorized elements are crisscrossing pretty badly, and road jams and delays are unavoidable."

* This was the 51st, which had been in the Saar sector but was then moved to the Channel Coast. There was also a portion of the 1st Armored Division refitting south of the Seine, and an *ad hoc* formation of odd units known as "Beauman Force." Other British units landed in France during *Rot*, but of these only one brigade saw action before the final collapse.

But German efficiency prevailed over these formidable logistic obstacles. Kesselring's retrospective admiration for the Army's accomplishment was well warranted: [16] "Anyone who watched from the air and on the ground, as I did, von Kleist's and Guderian's panzers swing round from the northern maneuver toward the Channel and drive south and southeast to the Somme and the Aisne, could not repress a surge of pride at the flexibility and skill of the German Army Command and the state of training of the troops. Nevertheless, that these movements could be carried out without a hitch in daylight is attributable only to our air superiority."

The interlude was also a time for decorations and for the Fuehrer to bestow the favor of his smile. The *Ritterkreuz* [17] was pinned on Rommel on May 26, and on June 3 a number of other panzer generals—Rudolf Schmidt, Kuntzen, Kempf, and Veiel—were similarly honored, as were Oberst Rothenburg (the commander of one of Rommel's panzer regiments) and Oberstleutnant Hermann Balck, commander of the rifle regiment that had first crossed the Meuse at Sedan. Several Luftwaffe generals and ace pilots were awarded the medal during the air battle at Dunkirk.

On June 1 Hitler visited Bock's army group "to express his thanks and appreciation," and the next day he was at Rundstedt's headquarters for the same purpose.[18] To many of the officers, these were great occasions. Rommel, for example, wrote ecstatically to his wife: [19]

The Fuehrer's visit was wonderful. He greeted me with the words "Rommel, we were very worried about you during the attack." His whole face was radiant and I had to accompany him afterward. I was the only division commander who did.

At OKH, too, these were halcyon days, and much of the bitterness of past weeks subsided. Halder spent June 2 awarding Iron Crosses of lesser degree to members of his staff. The next day he moved to the new OKH headquarters near the Franco-Belgian border northwest of Sedan. Hitler and the OKW also moved forward to new headquarters —which the Fuehrer called *Wolfsschlucht* (Wolf's Glen)—at Brûly-de-Pesche in southern Belgium.

On the evening of June 4,[20] a few hours before the start of the new offensive, Halder joined Brauchitsch "for a glass of wine at his country estate billet." The successful completion of the plans and redeployment for *Rot* was conducive to euphoria. "Wonderful eventide peace! Harmonious atmosphere!" It was, after all, a fine war.

The Somme-Aisne Offensive

The French Army was like a prize fighter on his last legs. Powerless to attack, and with barely enough strength left to fend off or absorb for a few days the blows that were about to fall, the French stood dogged and dazed along the Somme and the Aisne, awaiting the assault. It came in two savage blows—a right and a left—that sent the French reeling back to the Seine and the Marne. In ten days the Germans were in Paris.

During the first few days of June, before the Army started its offensive, the Luftwaffe launched a series of bombing attacks on the French railways, in order to impede troop and supply movements behind the lines. Then on June 3 and 4 several hundred bombers attacked the airfields and aircraft factories near Paris. "Operation Paula," as this early example of strategic bombing was called, appears not to have been an unmixed success. Kesselring declares that over 100 French aircraft were shot down and several hundred destroyed on the ground. The reports that Halder received were equally rosy: "Defensive was weak. A big success . . . like parade formation flying at the Nuremberg Party Rally." But the famous German ace Adolf Galland, who flew fighter cover, says that the "success of this undertaking was debatable . . . twenty-five to thirty German planes were lost." [21]

At dawn on June 5 Bock attacked along his entire front. On his right wing, between Amiens and the sea, Kluge's Fourth Army embarked on a highly successful campaign of which Rouen and the Seine west of Paris were the immediate objectives. Kluge, himself one of the ablest army commanders, had plenty of talent among his subordinate generals—Hoth commanding the XVth Armored Corps, which still comprised Walsporn's 5th and the redoubtable Rommel's 7th Panzer Divisions, and Manstein undertaking his first offensive assignment as a corps commander.

Kluge's task was aided by the consequences of the fruitless attacks which the Allies had been making during late May and early June, in an effort to eliminate the Abbéville bridgehead. The British armored units had sustained serious losses, and all the troops of General Ihler's IXth Corps [22] (opposite Kluge) had suffered heavy casualties and were exhausted when *Rot* commenced. Furthermore, these ill-calculated offensive efforts had caused the French to neglect the destruction of the railway bridges over the Somme near Longpré, midway between Amiens and Abbéville.

This was just where Hoth launched his armored assault, and the bridges greatly accelerated Rommel's initial advance, for he was able to remove the rails and drive his tanks right across the Somme, instead of waiting for pontoon bridges to be built.[23] By nightfall he was already eight miles south of the Somme, and the rest of Hoth's corps was likewise making good progress.

On Kluge's left wing, Manstein's XXXVIIIth Corps had put strong elements across the Somme before dawn in pneumatic rafts. They encountered stubborn resistance from the Alsatian * and French African defenders but were able to win enough ground on the south bank during the day so that they could bridge the river and bring the artillery across during the evening.[24]

And so on the morning of June 6 both Hoth and Manstein were across the Somme and ready to drive for the Seine. Hoth made it in three days; by the end of June 8 Rommel was on the Seine just east of Rouen, and Walsporn's 5th Panzer Division, which on this occasion matched Rommel's progress, was at the city's northern gates. They encountered little opposition until they neared Rouen, and Rommel escaped getting mired in the hordes of refugees that were choking the roads by avoiding roads and villages and moving his division straight across country,† in a manner graphically described in his contemporaneous account: [25]

The attack began 10:00 hours [A.M.]. . . . The division, in extended order, over a 2000-yard front and a depth of twelve miles, moved as if on an exercise. In this formation we advanced up hill and down dale, over highways and byways straight across country. The vehicles stood up to it well, even those which were not meant for cross-country work. With the tanks clashing every so often with enemy forces, the attack moved forward slowly enough for the [motorized] infantry to follow up and maintain close contact.

---

* In his postwar memoirs (*Verlorene Siege*, pp. 134–35), Manstein commented sadly on the Alsatians: "It was really tragic to encounter these young Germans as enemies. Many of the prisoners related, not without pride, that their fathers had served in the German Army, the Guard, or the Imperial Navy. I recalled the many Alsatian recruits that I myself had trained in the 3rd Regiment of Guards, and what good soldiers most of them made. . . ."

† Colored and inaccurate accounts of Rommel's advance to the Seine persisted until the publication of his papers. For example, a widely circulated book [26] has it that: "The division moved at night, and as the tanks rumbled and clanked through the silent villages, the French peasants, thinking them British, turned out to wish the crews *bonne chance*." In fact, the division moved mostly in the daytime and avoided villages, and French peasants are quite capable of telling north from south.

This was a very different method from the one Rommel had pursued in northern France, where his tanks dashed far out in front and then waited for the riflemen to catch up. Only on the night of June 8–9, when he was racing to capture the Seine bridges at Elbeuf, did Rommel take to the roads and resume his ghostly nocturnal tactics. For all his speed that night, the French were not caught unaware and blew the bridges as Rommel was preparing to attack them, to his great chagrin.[27]

Meanwhile, Manstein's XXXVIIIth Corps had been doing some superb marching, and the vanguard reached the Seine only a few hours later than Rommel.* The corps had had to fight sharp engagements south of Poix on June 7 and 8, but after the enemy had been routed by a combination of artillery and Stuka bombardment followed up by infantry, Manstein concluded that the French were no longer able to offer sustained resistance. On this assumption, he sent his motorized reconnaissance units ahead † and ordered the main body of artillery and infantry to make all speed in their wake, in order to reach the Seine on June 9 and establish bridgeheads on the south bank before the French had time to organize their defenses. Two of his divisions were on the Seine that afternoon, and by the morning of June 10 the 46th Division had strong positions on the south bank at Vernon.

Less spectacular than the achievements of Hoth and Manstein was the role of Stuelpnagel's IInd Corps on Kluge's right wing. This corps already held the bridgeheads over the Somme at St. Valéry-sur-Somme and Abbéville that General Ihler's IXth Corps had been vainly trying to reduce. Suddenly the attackers found themselves attacked. British and French alike gave ground grudgingly, but by nightfall they had been forced to fall back some ten miles toward the Bresle River, where

---

* The 6th Division (Generalmajor Arnold Freiherr von Biegeleben) reached Les Andelys on the Seine shortly before noon on June 9, about twelve hours after Rommel's 25th Panzer Regiment arrived at the river near Rouen. Rivalry persists on this score. Manstein's biographer (Paget, *Manstein*, p. 26) erroneously claims that "Manstein's corps then raced Rommel's panzers and was the first corps to reach the Seine," and Manstein himself (*Verlorene Siege*, p. 140) indulges that erroneous implication. But it is true that Manstein was the first to *cross* the Seine, as Hoth's corps turned west to the sea after reaching Rouen.

† This may be the basis of Liddell Hart's rather exaggerated comment that Manstein was "handling his infantry like mobile troops." Both Hart and Paget also state that Manstein made the breach in the Somme line through which Rommel's tanks advanced.[28] For this there seems to be no factual basis, although no doubt Manstein's rapid advance on Hoth's left flank was excellent protection for the armored advance. Manstein's infantry covered the seventy-five-odd miles from the Somme to the Seine in less than five days, which was certainly a remarkable achievement.

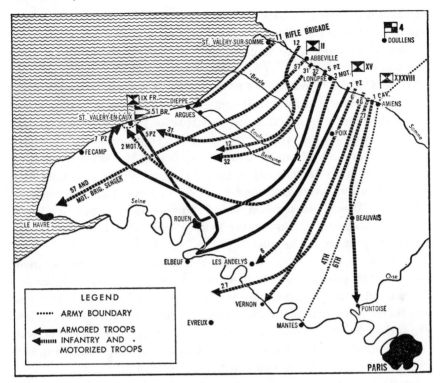

THE ADVANCE OF KLUGE'S 4TH ARMY FROM THE SOMME TO THE
SEINE, JUNE 5–12, 1940.

the Allies planned to make their stand. Then the German pressure
diminished, and for the next three days the Bresle front was relatively
quiet. It was a false security, however, for as Hoth's panzers neared
Rouen, Ihler's line of retreat southward was gravely threatened.

According to Churchill,[29] the British had made "urgent representations" to the French that Ihler's corps should fall back to Rouen, but
Weygand refused and insisted on holding the Bresle line. However that
may be, Weygand did not authorize a retreat until the afternoon of
June 8. By then it was too late, for Rommel reached the Seine that
night and Walsporn took Rouen on June 9. Hoth was now ordered to
turn west and make for the sea. Previously, Bock had intended to turn
Kluge's forces east, to pinch the French between Kluge and Reichenau
north of Paris.[30] Apparently, however, when Hoth neared Rouen with
Ihler still on the Bresle, the obvious wisdom of turning Hoth west to

cut Ihler off from Le Havre caused the change of plan. Early on the morning of June 10 his corps was on its way, and that same afternoon Rommel, after racing his tanks along the roads at speeds up to forty miles an hour, hit the coast between Fécamp and St. Valéry-en-Caux.

General Ihler's forces were now hopelessly cut off.[31] Their retreat had begun June 9, and when it was learned that Rouen (which Weygand had blindly specified as their destination) was in enemy hands, Le Havre was chosen as the evacuation port. To guard that port, which was only forty miles from the Germans at Rouen, two brigades of British infantry were detached from Major General Victor Fortune's 51st Division on the Bresle front and sent off to Le Havre on the night of June 9–10. These units reached their destination safely, but when Rommel cut across to the coast on the tenth, the bulk of Ihler's corps had retired only as far as Dieppe.

Stuelpnagel's IInd Corps had been rather slow in following up their withdrawal,* but this possible negligence did not prove costly to the Germans. An Allied evacuation from Le Havre was now out of the question, Dieppe was untenable, and Ihler was left with nowhere to go but the little port of St. Valéry-en-Caux, where a defense perimeter was hastily established late on June 10 just as Hoth's corps came up and brought the town under bombardment.

With great difficulty, the IXth Corps was able to hold out in St. Valéry on June 11, in the hope of evacuation by sea that night. But when darkness came, a heavy fog made impossible what in any event would have been a desperate venture, as Rommel had gained the western cliffs overlooking the harbor and its approaches. About 3300 men were taken off a beach a few miles east of the town, but in St. Valéry the troops waited vainly throughout the night of June 11–12 for the naval rescue ships, lying fogbound off the coast.

The next morning German tanks penetrated to the harbor, and the jig was up. Ihler, Fortune, and ten other French and British generals surrendered to a delighted Rommel in the market place of St. Valéry,[32] and thousands more Allied soldiers passed into German captivity.

To the south, the British Navy successfully evacuated some 11,000 troops from Le Havre, which then fell to the Germans without a fight on June 13. Kluge's Fourth Army now lay along the Seine from the sea

---

* See Ellis, *The War in France and Flanders*, p. 283. Stuelpnagel's field generalship was commented on adversely at higher headquarters (Halder diary, June 9), and after the fall of France he was returned to staff duties on the Armistice Commission.

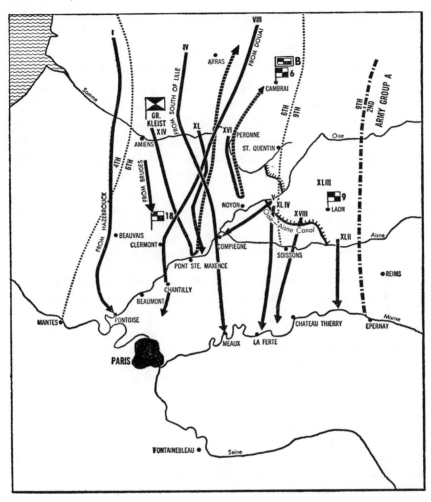

GERMAN ADVANCE FROM THE SOMME-AISNE TO PARIS AND THE
MARNE, JUNE 5–12, 1940.

to Vernon, had thus achieved its immediate goal under *Rot*, and its
advance came to a temporary pause.

While Kluge was advancing with dispatch on the west wing of
Bock's army group, the center and the east wing met with varying de-
grees of success. In the center, Reichenau's Sixth Army launched
separate armored attacks from the Amiens and Péronne bridgeheads
south of the Somme. To the east, the infantry corps of the Sixth Army

and of Strauss's Ninth Army jumped off from positions north of the Aisne.

At first, Kleist's panzer group made good progress. Late in the afternoon of June 6, Bock's chief of staff, Von Salmuth, reported to Halder [33] that "the success of XIVth Corps [Wietersheim's, debouching from the Amiens bridgehead] . . . represents a major victory" and that "the enemy fronting XVIth Corps [Hoepner's, south of Péronne] has been smashed." But the next day, when Brauchitsch went forward to see for himself, he found these claims unwarranted. On his return to OKH that evening (June 7) he informed Halder: [34]

Their attacks make slow progress. At times they seem to be short of ammunition. In XVIth Corps 30 per cent of the tanks are reported total losses. Rifle and motorcycle elements of the armored divisions seem to be much weakened by combat losses. All are begging for replacements.

Kleist's difficulties became the subject of anxious discussion at an afternoon conference with Hitler on June 8, as recorded by Halder,[35] who was in one of his not infrequent didactic moods:

First, I outline the principles of employment of armor. Tanks are operational assets only where they have open country to maneuver in. In slow-moving battles they only burn themselves out. Such fighting is the department of the infantry, with which we are amply supplied.

As for Kleist's situation:

The tanks have been in frontal attacks too long. But since Bock has just committed them again, nothing can be done about it now.

The conclave agreed, however, that something should soon be done about it. This was nothing less than the withdrawal of Kleist's panzer group and its reinsertion in the front at a more advantageous location farther east. For the infantry on the left wing of Bock's army group had meanwhile met with excellent success. In Reichenau's easternmost corps (Generalleutnant Friedrich Koch's XLIVth), the crack 1st Mountain Division (Generalleutnant Ludwig Kuebler) had crossed the Oise-Aisne Canal on June 5, reached the Aisne just west of Soissons on June 6, and established a bridgehead on the south bank that night.[36] East of Soissons, units of Strauss's Ninth Army had also reached the Aisne, and by June 8 the prospects of a rapid advance to the Marne near Château-Thierry appeared very favorable. In addition, the offen-

sive of Rundstedt's Army Group A toward Rheims and Châlons-sur-
Marne was scheduled to jump off the following day, June 9.

In the light of this promising situation, it was decided at the Fuehrer
conference on June 8 to pull Kleist out of the sector north of Paris and
transfer his entire force to the eastern end of Bock's front, in order to
exploit the infantry's success on the Aisne. It was a bitter pill for
Reichenau and his Sixth Army staff,[37] who now, just as in Belgium,[38]
saw their armor transferred to another sector. Furthermore, while
Hoepner's XVIth Corps was still heavily engaged west of Noyon,
Wietersheim's XIVth was now advancing much more rapidly. On June
8, some thirty miles south of Amiens, Wietersheim started to swing
toward the east to by-pass Paris. On June 9 he took Clermont, and on
June 10 a bridgehead over the Oise at Pont Sainte Maxence, about
thirty miles north-northeast of Paris.[39] By that time, however, Hoepner's corps had already been withdrawn. Brauchitsch decided that it
was pointless to send Wietersheim's corps, by then much weakened,
on alone against stiffening opposition, and it was disengaged and
moved rearward on June 10.

What was the explanation of this check to Kleist's panzers, at a
time when the Germans enjoyed overwhelming general superiority in
the field? In post mortem a German general, contrasting Kleist's tactics
with those of Guderian (whose subsequent attack from the Aisne was
a complete success), has written: [40]

> The success of Guderian and the failure of Von Kleist were the result
> of a difference in methods. The attacks of the latter from the Amiens and
> Péronne bridgeheads demonstrate that it is quite useless to throw armor
> against well-prepared defensive positions, manned by an enemy who expects
> an attack and is determined to repulse it. In contrast Guderian's tanks were
> not committed until the infantry had made a substantial penetration across
> the Aisne.

This passage is a good example of the myths that flower from half-
truths. In fact, as will shortly be seen,[41] Guderian vainly requested that
his armored divisions be allowed to capture their own bridgeheads,
and ultimately attacked from a very shallow infantry penetration on
the south bank of the Aisne.[42] His preference was only natural, as on
the Meuse rifle regiments of the German armored divisions had
broken the French defenses, and the tanks had thus been able to cross
the river before the infantry divisions came up.[43] Furthermore, Wietersheim successfully broke out of the Amiens bridgehead, and even
Hoepner made some headway south of Péronne.

Kleist's progress suffered chiefly by comparison with the truly sensational results of other German panzer attacks. That his gains on this occasion were more modest appears to have been due, not to any difference in method, but to the sharper and better-organized resistance he encountered. The French regarded Kleist's sector, almost due north of Paris, as crucially important. The Commander-in-Chief of the French ground forces, General Alphonse Georges, had had opportunity here to organize a sort of defense in depth, so that Kleist's tanks had to penetrate much farther before breaking into the open behind the lines. Especially south of Péronne, the French infantry resisted fiercely, inflicting serious losses on Hoepner's panzers and suffering very heavy casualties before retreating.[44] This was a far more intransigent foe than Guderian had encountered at Sedan, or Rommel on the lower Seine.[45]

Even before Kleist's group was withdrawn, on June 7, a stretching and thinning of the German front line had begun to show up near Beauvais, as a result of Kluge's southwesterly course toward Rouen and Reichenau's south-southeasterly advance toward the east side of Paris. To fill this gap, Bock now requested that Kuechler's Eighteenth Army—then in reserve near Lille—be prepared for commitment between Kluge's and Reichenau's armies.[46] Two days later General Hans-Kuno von Both's Ist Corps, from the army group reserve, was brought into the "thin" area near Beauvais. Then, after Kleist's two armored corps departed on June 11, the Eighteenth Army was brought into the line immediately north of Paris, with command of the Ist and General Walter Heitz's VIIIth Corps (also from army group reserve) and the westernmost corps, General Georg Stumme's XLth, from Reichenau's army.* At the time of the new army's insertion, its forward units were astride the Oise from Pontoise to Chantilly, barely twenty miles from Paris.

While these changes in deployment were taking place north of Paris, Rundstedt's Army Group A had opened its offensive on the Aisne. It was launched at dawn on June 9, in strength of about fifteen infantry divisions, by Weichs's Second Army north of Rheims and List's Twelfth Army in the area of Rethel and Attigny. The first reports at OKH were rosy; Halder wrote that [47] "all along the front our troops have crossed the Aisne in the first bound. A superb achievement, in which

---

* In this way five fresh divisions from reserve came into line and were combined with one division (the 1st Cavalry) from Kluge's and three from Reichenau's armies, so that Kuechler's army comprised nine divisions in all.

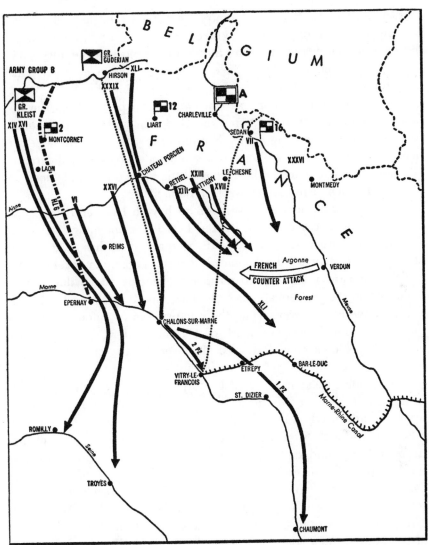

RUNDSTEDT'S ADVANCE FROM THE AISNE TO THE MARNE AND
SEINE, JUNE 9–14, 1940.

the exemplary work of the general staff officers in this army group has
a substantial share."

But all had not gone as smoothly as the early reports indicated. The
infantry was supposed to establish bridgeheads, and the engineers
were then to build bridges over which the mechanized troops would

cross and attack through the infantry front. Guderian had asked List
to designate crossing points to be taken by the panzer divisions, as he
did not like the idea of attacking through road-blocking infantry divisions. List turned him down, in order to save the panzer divisions
from the casualties likely to be suffered in crossing the Aisne.[48] But
at Rethel, where the armor was concentrated in preparation, the infantry failed to get over the Aisne, and Guderian started casting about
for other possible crossing points. Not until the afternoon did he learn
that the 17th Division of Bavarians, commanded by Generalleutnant
Herbert Loch, had gained a bridgehead little more than a mile deep at
Château-Porcien, a few miles west of Rethel.[49]

The impatient Guderian dashed off to have a look, and then told
the XXXIXth Corps and 1st Panzer Division commanders, Rudolf
Schmidt and Kirchner, to start the division across at dusk. Later that
afternoon two other small bridgeheads gained in the same area enabled
Veiel's 2nd Panzer Division to put some elements across during the
night. When the panzers attacked the next day, they found the going
hard, for the French were using the same system of defense in depth
that had troubled Hoepner south of Péronne and were also able to
launch strong tank counterattacks. However, by the end of June 11
Schmidt had penetrated nearly twenty miles south of the Aisne.

Meanwhile, Reinhardt's XLIst Corps, with Kempf's 6th and
Kuntzen's 8th Panzer Divisions, came across the Aisne in Schmidt's
wake and advanced on his left. The XLIst Corps immediately ran into
a fierce battle with French armored forces which debouched from the
Argonne Forest and kept Reinhardt heavily engaged south of Attigny
through June 13. Schmidt, however, profited by the protection Reinhardt gave his left flank. Veiel's 2nd Panzer Division reached Châlons-
sur-Marne on June 12 and started to cross the bridge, but the French
exploded it before the Germans gained a foothold on the south bank
of the Marne. Veiel continued along the north bank, and on June 13
both the 2nd and 1st Panzer Divisions reached the Rhine-Marne Canal,
the former near Vitry-le-François and the latter at Étrépy. Here the
indefatigable Oberstleutnant Balck, despite Schmidt's orders to halt,
captured the bridge over the canal, a piece of disobedience which
Guderian highly approved when he arrived at the scene. His panzer
group was now fairly in the clear and ready to set sail southward to the
Plateau de Langres.

By this time the entire French front on the Aisne had collapsed. On
Reichenau's left wing, Koch's XLIVth Corps crossed the Marne at La

Ferté-sous-Jouarre and Château-Thierry on June 12. The same day Hoepner's XVIth Corps was reinserted at the front between the Sixth and Ninth armies and crossed the Marne at Château-Thierry. The Ninth Army itself was across at Épernay, and the Second Army was well south of Rheims. The Twelfth Army infantry was treading hard on Guderian's heels, and Schobert's VIIth Corps, on the west end of Busch's Sixteenth Army beyond the end of the Maginot Line, was swinging south to maintain contact with List. The infantry advance south of the Aisne had, indeed, gained such speed that it was overtaking the panzers, to Guderian's considerable irritation: [50]

Our progress was made more difficult through confusion that arose from the impetuous advance of the infantry following behind us. The infantry units . . . in some cases . . . caught up with the panzer units which were fighting their way forward. Divisional boundaries had not been drawn with sufficient clarity and units overlapped. A request was made to [Twelfth] Army headquarters that this be sorted out, but in vain. At points along the Suippes there were a number of animated scenes. Both arms of the service wanted to lead the advance.

And so, in victorious confusion, the German Army surged across France like a tidal wave, from the Somme to the Seine, and from the Aisne to the Marne. The French government fled Paris on June 10, the same day that Mussolini declared war on Britain and France. On June 12 Paris was declared an open city. The French front was dropped to the south of Paris on June 13, leaving the city open and defenseless to Kuechler's Eighteenth Army. Operation *Rot* had required nine days to accomplish its ends. The "Weygand Line" was smashed from end to end, the French Army was in rout, and the Battle of France was almost at an end.

Debacle

"A great day in the history of the German Army!" exulted Franz Halder.[51] "German troops have been marching into Paris since nine o'clock this morning." The troops were infantry from Generalleutnant Rudolf Koch-Erpach's 8th Division of regulars, a component of Heitz's VIIIth corps and Kuechler's Eighteenth Army. The date was June 14, 1940, and it marks, perhaps better than any other, the end of France's Battle and the beginning of her Fall.

Kuechler's entry into Paris was bloodless and orderly, and its significance was symbolic rather than military. But June 14 also signalized

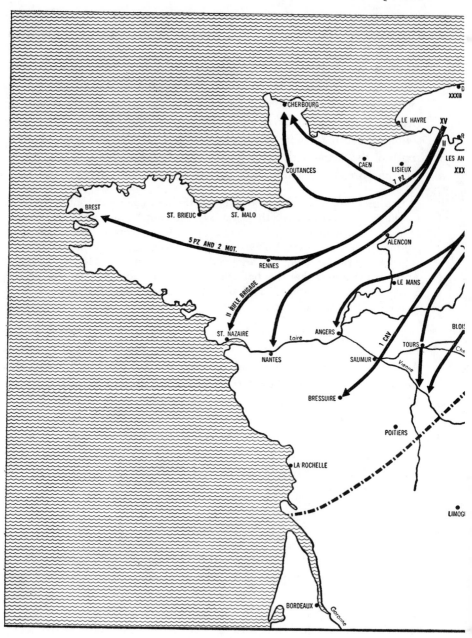

FINAL PHASE OF THE BATT

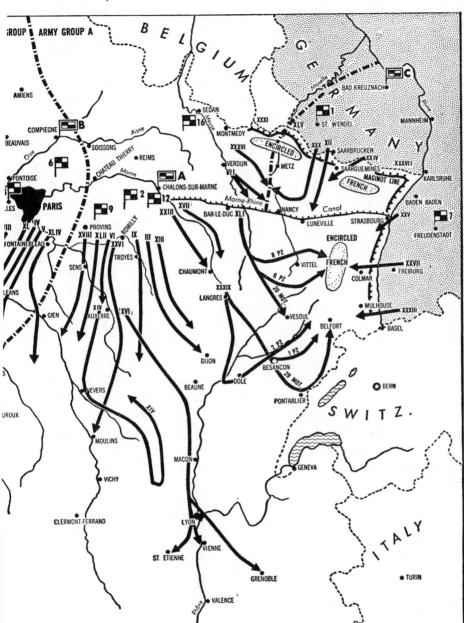

FRANCE, JUNE 14–22, 1940.

the opening of the third and final phase of *Rot*—Leeb's frontal attack on the Maginot Line in the Saarbruecken area, immediately followed (June 15) by the Upper Rhine offensive opposite Colmar. And on that same June 14 General Sir Alan Brooke (commanding the B.E.F.), after meeting with Generals Weygand and Georges, informed London that the Allied cause in France was hopeless. After a telephone conversation between Churchill and Brooke that night, orders were given for the immediate evacuation by sea of all British troops.[52]

Finally, it was on June 14 that the German high command, aware of the French collapse, issued new directives for the windup of the campaign.[53] The French Army was already defeated, and the orders of June 14 called for the "pursuit" and "annihilation" of the enemy. Essentially, they envisaged a fanning-out of the German advance south of the Seine-Marne line.*

Bock's Army Group B (now comprising the Fourth, Eighteenth, and Sixth armies) was to attack in a southwesterly direction. Kluge was to send his motorized forces westward to occupy the Normandy and Brittany peninsulas, and his infantry toward the Biscay coast at La Rochelle and Bordeaux. Kuechler and Reichenau were to advance in a more southerly direction, toward Tours and Bourges.

Rundstedt's Army Group A, to which the Ninth Army was now attached, was to send its right wing (Strauss and Weichs with Kleist's armor) southward into Burgundy. Guderian's panzer group was to cross the Plateau de Langres and make for Besançon and the Swiss border, in order to cut off the French line of retreat from Alsace and Lorraine. Behind him, List and Busch were to swing their infantry southeasterly into the rear of the French forces holding the Maginot Line and the Rhine.

Leeb's Army Group C was now given an offensive mission for the first time since the start of the war. Witzleben's First Army was to go through the Maginot Line and into Lorraine, making a pincer with Busch. Dollmann's Seventh Army was to cross the Rhine and help List and Guderian bottle up the French in Alsace.

The greater part of this huge operation was more pursuit than battle. There were, to be sure, numerous sharp engagements in localities

---

* From the very beginning of *Rot*, Halder had been advocating that the entire army swing southwesterly after crossing the Seine and Marne. On June 7 he heard "rumors" that OKW was considering his plan "with the modification of having Army Group B attack in southwestern and Army Group A in southeastern direction." Halder's comment was that this idea was "very dangerous," but in fact this is about what happened under the June 14 directives.[54]

where the French will to resist persisted. But the French Army as an
entity no longer existed. Weygand had no reserves and, in general, no
transport or organized channels of command. There was little he could
do but report to the Cabinet, at first desperately and soon hopelessly,
on the progress of the German advance.

At a Cabinet meeting on the evening of June 12 at Cangé, near
Tours, Weygand had demanded that the government request an immediate armistice, and Pétain vehemently supported him. Reynaud,
Mandel and other ministers would have none of this proposal, at least
without British consent, but when the government reassembled in
Bordeaux on June 14 it soon became apparent that Pétain and Weygand had the upper hand. On June 16 Pétain replaced Reynaud as
Prime Minister, and the next day the French request for an armistice
was transmitted to Hitler via Spanish diplomatic channels. However,
the armistice was not signed until six days later, and in the interim the
Germans drove on into the heart of France, encountering local but
considerable pockets of resistance.

In this confused and tragic campaign of pursuit, Kluge's Fourth
Army had the most varied objectives. On June 12 Manstein's XXXVIIIth
Corps resumed its advance from its bridgeheads on the south bank of
the Seine near Vernon. Stuelpnagel's IInd Corps simultaneously crossed
the Seine in the Rouen area and moved up on Manstein's right. The
French fell back rapidly, and there was little fighting. By June 17 the
infantry of these two corps was halfway from the Seine to the Loire,
toward which the French were withdrawing.

The way was now clear for Hoth's mechanized forces to strike west-
ward along the Normandy and Brittany peninsulas. Rommel, his 7th
Panzer Division strengthened with the independent motorized Brigade
Senger,* was dispatched to Normandy, with the mission of capturing
Cherbourg. The rest of Hoth's corps (the 5th Panzer and 2nd Motor-
ized Infantry Divisions and the 11th Rifle Brigade) struck out from
Alençon into Brittany, heading for Brest.

Hoth's advance into Brittany was relatively uneventful. The Allies
had discussed a plan to hold the peninsula as a permanent "fortress
bridgehead," but by the time so desperate a step seemed desirable it
was already impossible, for lack of troops to man the 100-mile front
that the project would have required. It was over 200 miles from
Alençon to Brest, and Hoth did not reach the port until June 19. By
the time the Germans arrived, the British Navy had evacuated over

---

* So called after its commander, Oberst Fridolin von Senger und Etterlin.

30,000 troops, the French warships had sailed, the harbor installations had been demolished, and the city was empty of Allied forces.[55]

Rommel, however, had a last, brisk brush with the enemy at Cherbourg. It was here that the British had been disembarking two fresh divisions from England. After General Brooke's telephone conversation with Churchill on June 14, the process was reversed. The bulk of the troops was evacuated on June 16 and 17, but the last transports were still loading on the afternoon of June 18, when Rommel arrived at the city's outskirts. He was heavily outnumbered by the French garrison, but it made no sortie. The defenders cut loose with a heavy artillery barrage from the fortifications, in which the British warships joined. Rommel was forced to draw up outside the port, and the last British ships sailed that evening. There was more fighting the following morning, but after negotiations the French surrendered late in the afternoon of June 19.[56]

Between Hoth's corps on the Atlantic Coast and Kleist's and Guderian's panzer groups in Champagne, there was no German armor. Here the infantry of Kluge's, Kuechler's, Reichenau's, Strauss's, and Weichs's armies advanced almost in a solid wall toward the Loire. The French had neither time, resources, nor, after Pétain's request for an armistice, much inclination to organize a defensive line along this great river of central France. A number of German units reached or crossed it on June 19 and 20—Stuelpnagel's IInd Corps at the port of Nantes, Manstein's XXXVIIIth near Angers, Feldt's 1st Cavalry Division at Saumur, Heitz's VIIIth Corps at Tours, General Viktor von Schwedler's IVth and General Richard Ruoff's Vth near Orléans. The hard-marching 1st Mountain Division sent motorized units far ahead which reached the river at Gien on June 18.[57] Wodrig's XXVIth Corps also advanced with remarkable speed and by June 19 was at Moulins, some twenty miles south of the Loire.

Infantry and armor alike pushed ahead of them a horde of refugees, fleeing from northern France toward the desperate hope of safety in the south.[58] The north-south highways were jammed. Communications and maneuver became all but impossible for the French forces, badly disorganized as they already were, and even the German advance was seriously hampered.[59] Perhaps in an effort to clear the roads, perhaps to terrorize the population and the government, perhaps because many of the German pilots found nothing better to do, the Luftwaffe roared along the columns of refugees, with machine guns blazing, and sometimes dive-bombing the tangled mass of humanity below.[60] On this score there is no need to rely exclusively on the testimony of Allied witnesses. On June 18 Oberst Wilhelm Ritter von Thoma, then attached to OKH as staff specialist for mechanized forces,[61] related to Halder [62] "appalling details of the effect of dive-bombing attacks on refugee columns on the lower Seine, between Les Andelys and Pontoise."

A staff officer with one of the divisions of the XXVIth Corps has written that after the bitter fighting on the Aisne organized French resistance practically ceased: [63] "From then on it was really only a question of marching, marching, marching, in order to stick to the heels of the enemy. . . ." No doubt this extraordinary marching was partly at the behest of infantry generals eager to share in the glory of conquest, which hitherto had been almost monopolized by the tank generals.* There were still Frenchmen who would fight, and ambitious impetuosity cost one German general his life.

Generalleutnant Hermann Ritter von Speck was a brave and ardent Bavarian whose division (the 33rd) had been stationed on the western front during the Polish campaign. Thereafter he was given command of the newly constituted XLIIIrd Corps but early in June was designated acting commander of the XVIIIth Corps *vice* General Eugen Beyer, who had been taken ill.† Speck led the XVIIIth with great dash, and Halder noted [64] reports of "the inspiration given his troops by Von Speck . . . who is constantly in the front line." On June 14, as the leading elements of his corps approached the Yonne River, Speck and his chief of staff, Oberst Hubert Lanz, flew forward in a Storch liaison plane to locate the French strong points. They landed close to the French lines, and both officers joined the assault troops. It was nineteenth-century generalship, an old and heady wine. The next day at Pont-sur-Yonne they were again at the front, but Ritter von Speck's

---

* Most of the fame, both at the time and subsequently, went to the armored group and corps commanders. With the single and notable exception of Rommel, none of the ten armored division commanders was destined for great prominence in later stages of the war. Stever and Walsporn never advanced beyond the rank of *Generalleutnant* or the divisional level of command. The others all attained the rank of *General der Panzertruppen* and all but Stumpff became corps commanders. Schaal served briefly in 1943 as commander of the headquarters cadre of the Eighth Army in Russia, and Kirchner proved an exceptionally able armored corps commander and in 1945 was awarded a high order of the *Ritterkreuz*. But Rommel alone reached the top level of rank and field command, and won renown beyond German military circles.

† Beyer had been the senior officer of the Austrian *Bundesheer* before the *Anschluss*. He was fatally ill, and died in Salzburg not long after he left the field.

luck did not hold. He was mortally wounded and died within a few hours, the only German army general of World War II who fell during the Battle of France.[65]

While the German infantry overran central France to the Loire, Kleist and Guderian drove southeast and cut the French Army in two. On June 15 Guderian was in Langres, and the next day Hoepner's XVIth Corps reached Dijon, Schmidt's XXXIXth took Besançon, and Reinhardt's XLIst passed through Vesoul. On June 17 Generalmajor Freiherr von Langermann und Erlencamp's 29th Motorized Division of the XXXIXth Corps reached the Swiss border at Pontarlier, and Guderian now turned his armored group to the northeast toward the Vosges, striking at the rear of the French forces along the Rhine. Kleist kept on southward to Lyons, where his advance was halted by the armistice.

During these closing days of the Battle of France, there was little heavy fighting except in Alsace and Lorraine, along the Maginot Line and in the Vosges. Even in these areas, however, French resistance was a matter of isolated pockets rather than an organized system of defense. The Line itself was never subjected to a real test of its efficacy, for the French reserves had long since been drawn away, the fortifications were manned chiefly with "static" troops, and soon they were attacked from the rear. The French will to resist was likewise sapped by Pétain's plea for armistice, and it is chiefly remarkable that some of their units held out so long.

Leeb's Army Group C, therefore, had but a brief moment of prominence, and a lack-luster victory. Witzleben's First Army attacked the Maginot Line between St.-Avold and Sarreguemines on June 14 in strength of six divisions. Many of the fortified areas held out, but the Germans were able to penetrate between them, and the French had no defense in depth. Once past the main fortifications the German infantry fanned out, leaving the French pockets to be reduced at leisure.

Meanwhile the right wing of Busch's Sixteenth Army had been pushing south through the Argonne Forest. On June 14 Schobert's VIIth Corps captured Verdun, giving Halder another pleasurable thrill when he awoke the following morning: [66] "Another important day in military history! Verdun, scene of the heroic struggle in World War I, is in our hands." The German high command had set great store by the capture of Verdun and had proposed to detach a mechanized task force from Guderian's panzer group to take the city, but Schobert's advance made this unnecessary.

By June 17 Schobert was approaching the Rhine-Marne Canal east of

Bar-le-Duc, and the next day Busch's and Witzleben's armies met near Nancy, encircling the French in the line from the Saar to Montmédy. Many of the fortress garrisons held out until after the armistice, and some last-ditch defenders did not surrender until June 30.[67]

On June 15, one day after Witzleben launched his attack from the Saar, Dollmann's Seventh Army put three divisions across the Rhine opposite Colmar. They were under the command of General Alfred Waeger's XXVIIth Corps, which had had successful experience with river and canal crossings in Belgium.[68] The German assault boats took off in midmorning; they profited by the French custom of relaxing their state of alert after dawn, and some of the defenders were caught asleep in the bunkers.[69] The French forces were rapidly forced back into the Vosges. Guderian was already approaching from the south; Kirchner's 1st Panzer Division took Belfort on June 18 and made contact with Waeger's infantry the next day, completing the encirclement of the Vosges pocket. The French fought stubbornly in the heavily wooded highlands,[70] but capitulated on June 22, the day the armistice was signed.

Since it was contemplated that most of southern France would remain free from German occupation, the general advance was halted on the Loire and Cher rivers. But a strip along the Atlantic Coast to the Spanish border was to be occupied, and for this purpose Wietersheim's XIVth Corps and Kleist's panzer group headquarters were moved westward to Kluge's sector,[71] where Stuelpnagel's IInd Corps had gone down the coast only a little beyond Nantes and St. Nazaire. The British Navy had lifted thousands of troops from Nantes, St. Nazaire, and La Rochelle before the Germans arrived, and evacuation operations continued at Bordeaux and St.-Jean-de-Luz until June 25. Shortly thereafter Wietersheim's motorized troops reached the Spanish border, completing the geographical conquest.

Low Tragicomedy in the Maritime Alps

As France crumbled under the impact of the Wehrmacht, Benito Mussolini anxiously gauged the moment when it would be safe to come in on the kill. On June 1 Hitler told Brauchitsch [72] that Italy would enter the war "within coming weeks." This news caused something less than a sensation in the German high command. The Italian declaration of war on June 10 was likewise received with considerable indifference, especially since the Italian forces on the French frontier did little or nothing to signalize the Duce's grandiloquent announcement from his Roman balcony. The Italian army command was realistic and far from ardent for *gloria*. On June 13 the Italian military attaché in Berlin told Halder that [73] "Italy intends starting operations on the Alpine front only if we [the Germans] open it up from the rear."

The stricken French were equally unenthusiastic about embarking on hostilities in that quarter. On June 14 an enterprising French naval squadron bombarded factories and oil tanks and refineries near Genoa; Admiral Darlan promptly forbade any further offensive operations against Italy.[74] The Royal Air Force had comparable troubles; on June 11 the French drove trucks onto a Marseilles airfield [75] to prevent British Wellington bombers from taking off for a night raid over northern Italy. The British succeeded in putting a few bombers over Turin and Genoa on June 11 and 16, but the results were negligible. Pétain's request for an armistice put an end to these first Allied efforts to strike at Italy from the air.

When Pétain requested an armistice, however, the Duce grew fearful that unless he achieved some sort of military success on French soil he would come empty-handed and impotent to the armistice negotiations. On June 18, with Ciano, he hied himself to Munich to discuss the armistice terms with Hitler and Ribbentrop. Mussolini chafed visibly at his own secondary role and found Hitler anything but reassuring in his attitude toward Italian territorial claims. The Fuehrer's shrewder side was uppermost, and he had no intention of imposing such harsh terms as might provoke the French to continue the struggle from Africa, or drive the French fleet into British hands.[76]

Hitler returned to his military headquarters on June 19 and promptly administered a stiff dressing-down to a surprised and pained Brauchitsch, because the French pockets of resistance in Alsace and Lorraine had not yet been mopped up. The Fuehrer also brought word that "the Italians are going to start their offensive on the Alpine front in two or three days." Furthermore, he had undertaken to assist the Italian attack by pushing some of Rundstedt's forces southward into Savoy, so as to take the French Alpine defenses in the rear.[77]

This was hardly the sort of mission to enthrall Brauchitsch and Halder. Nevertheless, they dutifully issued orders on the morning of June 20 for the assemblage of a special task force under List's command, comprising Hoepner's XVIth Corps, which had already reached Lyon, several improvised units of motorized troops, and part of the 1st Mountain Division, temporarily motorized. These orders sat ill with

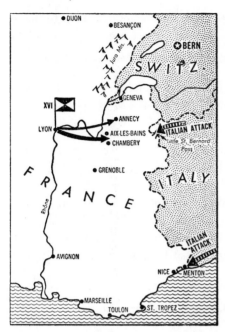

LOCALE OF ITALIAN ATTACKS AND SUPPORTING GERMAN ADVANCE, JUNE 19-25, 1940.

Rundstedt, who, as Army Group Commander, thought that the selection and organization of the task force should be left to him. Halder went to bed that night with burning ears, after recording in his diary:

A very disagreeable telephone talk with Generaloberst von Rundstedt, who regards OKH orders of 20 June [i.e., those issued by Brauchitsch and Halder that morning] as an interference in his command functions. He uses language which one would not think possible between German generals.

Despite Rundstedt's irritation, the List Group was assembled near Lyon, in line with the OKH orders. But the Germans were in no hurry to help clear the road for the Italians, and there was considerable dragging of feet. The French armistice delegation reached Compiègne on June 21, and List's operation was held in abeyance pending the outcome of the negotiations.[78]

This was little to the liking of the Italians. It had been agreed by the two dictators at Munich that there would be no immediate Italian annexation of French soil, for fear that such demands might blow up the armistice. Instead, the French were to be required to demilitarize a zone fifty kilometers wide, opposite the line held by Italian forces at the moment of peace. But the Italian Army made no progress, and the unhappy Duce was obliged to console himself with the reflection that equipment was lacking, and that "even Michelangelo had to have marble to make statues." On June 21, Galeazzo Ciano sadly noted in his diary: [79]

> Mussolini is much humiliated because our troops have not moved a single step forward: again today we had no success, and are stopped at the frontier by the first French fortifications.

Simultaneously, Halder was recording scornful doubts that the Italians would make any headway. He had been told by them that they would mount an attack at the Little St. Bernard Pass, but the weather was bad, and Halder thought it "safe to assume that these attacks will be limited to some patrol activities." During the day the Italians asked that List's push to Grenoble and Chambéry (in French Savoy west of the Little St. Bernard Pass) be started on June 22, but Halder would have none of it: [80]

> We are not going to do this. List's Group will not be ready before June 23. Apart from this, we must first see whether this so-called attack of the Italians will be anything more than a patrol skirmish.

The armistice negotiations at Compiègne were still in progress during the morning of June 22. With Hitler's approval, Brauchitsch and Halder continued to cold-shoulder frantic pleas from the Italian General Staff for List's immediate intervention in the French rear. Late in the afternoon the French delegates finally signed, but the cease-fire was not to become effective until six hours after the conclusion of a Franco-Italian armistice, so the Italians still had a day or two to endeavor to improve their position. With some condescension, the Germans now told the Italians that List's group would advance toward Grenoble and Chambéry the following morning.[81]

By noon of June 23 List had reached Annécy and the area of Aix-les-Bains.[82] But as they approached the Alps, the Germans encountered French "defense positions armed with antitank guns and manned by mountain troops." Should German soldiers die to win ground for the Italians? Hardly, thought Brauchitsch and Halder, and Rundstedt was informed that "any increase in pressure involving major German casualties would not be in line with the intentions of OKH."

The Italians, for their part, commenced an attack on the Riviera, directed at Nice. It soon came to a stop in the suburbs of Menton, just across the French frontier.[83] The Little St. Bernard offensive met with no greater success. Achille Starace, returning from the front, reported his impressions to Ciano: [84]

. . . the attack in the Alps has demonstrated the utter lack of preparation for the undertaking: total deficiency of offensive means, and complete inadequacy of command. These men have been sent to a useless death two days before the armistice. . . . If the war in Libya and Ethiopia is going to be conducted in this fashion, the future will indeed be bitter.

On the evening of June 23 the French armistice delegation arrived in Italy. The fighting was bound to end in a day or two, and the Italians still had nothing to show for their pains. A stratagem worthy of Falstaff was now concocted in Rome, which enlivened Halder's opening diary entry on June 24: [85]

Morning reports show a piquant note. The Italians have been stalled by the French fortifications and cannot make any headway. But as they want to present themselves at the armistice negotiations with as large a chunk of French territory as they could occupy in a hurry, they have approached us with a scheme to transport Italian battalions behind List's front, part by air via Munich, part directly to the Lyon area, so as to get them to the points which include the area for which they want to make occupation claims.

Halder's pen fairly quivered with righteous indignation:

The whole thing is the cheapest kind of fraud. I have made it plain I will not have my name connected with that sort of trickery.

Before the morning was over, the scheme fell apart:

In the end the whole thing turns out to have been a plan hatched by Roatta [Deputy Chief of Staff of the Army], and disapproved by Marshal Badoglio [Chief of the Staff of the Supreme Command]. The people at OKW will have to swallow it that they allowed themselves to be taken in by a device proposed by a subordinate, which the responsible Italian Marshal (who seems to be the only respectable soldier in the lot) has rejected as dishonorable.

On this shabby note the Battle of France faded into history. The Franco-Italian armistice was signed early in the evening of June 24, and at thirty-five minutes after one o'clock the following morning, the fighting ceased.

The Fall of France in Retrospect

The causes of the French collapse in 1940 have been often rehearsed. Some commentators find it an easy problem. For General J. F. C.

THE MARCH OF CONQUEST

Fuller, for example, France was the victim of treason and moral rot: [86] "The German [morale] was fantastically good, the French fantastically bad—'there was treachery in the French Army from top to bottom.' * The people and the Army alike had been completely demoralized by the Blum Popular Front and rotted by Communist propaganda."

Treason there may have been, but soberer observers [87] than General Fuller have stressed less startling if equally depressing reasons for the French failure. Widely circulated reports that the Meuse bridges at Sedan were traitorously left intact to speed the German crossing were quite false, and few if any of the rumors of "fifth-column activity" have been substantiated by postwar investigations. In retrospect, it has become apparent that treason did not play much of a part in the French collapse, or in determining the outcome of the campaign, at once one of the briefest and most decisive in military history.[88] The late Antoine de Saint-Exupéry, then a pilot in the French Air Force, was impressed rather with the fact of French resistance after Dunkirk in the face of hopeless odds than with the prevalent talk of traitors: [89]

We stand to the enemy in the relation of one man to three. One plane to twenty. After Dunkerque, one tank to one hundred. . . .
I was later to hear foreigners reproach France with the few bridges that were not blown up, the handful of villages we did not burn, the men who failed to die. But here on the scene, it is the contrary that strikes me so powerfully. It is our desperate struggle against self-evident fact. We know that nothing can do any good, yet we blow up bridges nevertheless, in order to play the game. . . .

Defeatism there was, however, with all its ugly concomitants. After viewing the debris in Paris and northern France, William L. Shirer concluded simply that [90] "France did not fight." In the sense that there was no synthesis of national will to victory, this is true. Yet many Frenchmen fought—Prioux's First Army at Lille, De Gaulle's armored division, Fagalde's XVIth Corps at Dunkirk, Frère's Seventh Army at the Péronne bridgehead, even the center and northern wing of Corap's ill-fated Ninth Army, at Monthermé and Dinant. The trouble was that those who fought were woefully hampered by those who did not, and fatally handicapped by those who had failed to prepare.

* As authority for the quoted charge, General Fuller cites William L. Shirer's *Berlin Diary* (N. Y., 1941), p. 432. But Mr. Shirer, in the passage quoted, merely reported the inference of an anonymous informant in Paris. If such use of sources is hardly refined scholarship, it is undeniably an easy way for General Fuller to draw a sensational conclusion.

This is a story of German conquest, not of the socio-political background of French military decay. Whatever the historical causes, the result was an ill-balanced, obsolescent military establishment. Much has been made of the "Maginot mentality," but, as General Fuller rightly points out,[91] the fault did not lie in the Line itself, which "was a shield, it wanted a sword" whereas "the French field army was a broomstick." French (and British)* officers, with rare exceptions, had simply failed to concentrate on the problem of how to win ground with tanks and planes. Not knowing how to do it, they had little notion how to stop it.

Lack of know-how was matched by lack of means, most strikingly exemplified by the total disintegration of French air power. Unprepared and ill-equipped for what the Germans called *Bewegungskrieg* (mobile warfare), later known popularly as *Blitzkrieg* (lightning warfare), it is doubtful that the Allies, even under inspiring and imaginative leadership, could have decisively stemmed the Wehrmacht's onslaught. But the Germans would have had a far more difficult time, and perhaps won a less complete victory over the French,† but for Gamelin's initial and costly blunder, and Weygand's utter failure to grasp and face its consequences.

Gamelin had all but sealed the fate of France even before the Germans attacked, by failing to assemble forces in reserve. This error at once dissipated the very benefits that he might have reaped from the Maginot Line, for the true purpose of those elaborate and expensive fortifications was to eliminate the Franco-German frontier as a suitable area for a German attack, and thereby economize man power and mobile equipment, which could thus be reserved either for a planned Allied offensive or for defensive purposes to counter German thrusts.

Instead, under "Plan D" Gamelin threw the bulk of his maneuverable forces northward to establish an extended defensive line along the Meuse and Dyle rivers. The result was a front over 350 miles long, of which the northern 100 miles was but sketchily fortified, and the lack

---

* Major General Sir Francis de Guingand, Military Assistant to the Secretary of State for War (the Right Honorable Leslie Hore-Belisha) during the early months of the war and later General Montgomery's chief of staff, has graphically described the failure of the British Army and the Royal Air Force to grasp the crucial importance of tactical air support:[92] "We . . . never gave sufficient thought to the whole problem. We never grasped the lessons that were there to be learned during the Spanish Civil War."

† Projects such as a withdrawal to Africa or the maintenance of an Allied bridgehead in Brittany might have more likely been attempted had the Allied losses in equipment and prisoners in Belgium and northern France not been so catastrophic.

of a substantial group of ready reserves for defensive emergencies or opportunities for counterattack. Winston Churchill has vividly described [93] his last meeting with Gamelin on May 16, two days after the German break-through on the Meuse, and the shattering effect of Gamelin's one-word reply—"*Aucune*"—when Churchill asked, "Where is the strategic reserve? *Où est la masse de maneuvre?*"

It was the end of Gamelin as Commander-in-Chief, and his legacy to Weygand was certain defeat and probable disaster. The Allies' only chance lay in the instantaneous disengagement of their forces in Belgium, a swift retreat toward the Somme, and the energetic and imaginative improvisation of some sort of defense in depth to prevent the German armored columns from racing almost at will through the countryside behind the French lines.

All this would have offered at best a forlorn hope. In the event, Weygand was not the man of the hour; he showed great personal energy but failed to grasp the rapidly unfolding pattern of German victory, or galvanize the lethargic and routinized French military bureaucracy into the resourceful action which the desperate situation required. Inevitably, this stodgy and defeatist atmosphere was communicated to the troops, and toward the end, as General Spears has written: [94]

The troops, weary supers, had ceased to take any part in a play they felt they had been brought into under false pretenses, and were moving off stage. It was to have been a war fought behind unassailable defenses, active only in the verbal exchange of insults over the radio; and now they were being chased across their own country, with no one giving any indication of how soon the end would come. So they trudged on, throwing away as they went their inadequate weapons, the symbols of the outmoded war theories of their chiefs.

But the fall of France was the result not only of Allied weakness but also of German strength. True, it was in large part the product of Allied "inferiority of numbers, inferiority of equipment, inferiority of method," as Gamelin put it,[95] but there is no inferiority on one side without superiority on the other. Rapid and total victory is rarely achieved in war between evenly matched forces; it is usually the result of relative shortcomings of preparation, power, or leadership, which the victor is able to exploit.

The extraordinary proportions of the Germans' victory were due, above all, to their ability to anticipate and detect Allied flaws of preparation and deployment, and bring their own superior strength promptly to bear at decisive points. It is this quality of the Battle of France that warrants its description as a "classic" victory—that is to say, a military triumph gained not by mere margin of power but by rightly controlled power, and a strategic conquest achieved with economy of means and without crippling losses.

German casualties in the Battle of France were, in fact, extraordinarily light. The official figures, which have been generally accepted as accurate,[96] reported 27,074 dead, 18,384 missing, and 111,034 wounded —far less than the casualties in many single battles of World War I. This amounted to only some 350 men lost, and 1150 total casualties, for each German division deployed. Of course, those that were heavily and frequently engaged suffered more severely; Rommel's 7th Panzer Division, for example, lost 682 men killed, 296 missing, and 1646 wounded.[97]

The Wehrmacht's officer casualties were correspondingly light and can hardly have exceeded 5 per cent of the total. I have seen no overall breakdown as between officers and enlisted men. The officer casualties in Rommel's division were about 6 per cent of the divisional total. The 12th Infantry Division of the IInd Corps, which was heavily engaged near Arras and on the Somme, had twenty-two officers and 414 men killed, fifty-two officers and 1236 men wounded.[98] The German generals certainly did not shrink from personal exposure to hazard on the ground or in the air, yet only two lost their lives. Ritter von Speck, as has been told,[99] was killed at the front a few days before the fighting ended. In the Luftwaffe, Generalmajor Wolf von Stutterheim, commander of the dive bombers that supported Guderian's break-through at Sedan, was later shot down by a French Morane fighter and mortally wounded in the crash.*

Allied losses were, of course, much heavier than those of the Germans. The British, for example, with but ten divisions committed in the first phase of the battle and two in the second phase, suffered over 68,000 casualties. Yet even among the vanquished the bloodshed was amazingly low, considering the size of the forces engaged. No doubt

---

* Stutterheim is a dashing figure in German military annals. As a young Guards-officer in World War I he won the *Pour le Mérite* and was saluted as "the bravest officer of the Guards" by his commanding general. He was often and severely wounded, and retired from the Army in 1918 after suffering terrible injuries in a fall from a horse. Between the wars he was a *Forstmeister* in the Harz Mountains and trained young men in glider-flying. During the 1936 Olympiad, he crashed in a glider in the Black Forest, breaking both legs. His injuries from the forced landing in France caused an embolism, from which he died on December 3, 1940. He is buried in the Berlin Invaliden-Friedhof.[100]

this was in part due to the poor fighting spirit of some French units, but the primary cause was the German tactics of rapid encirclement, which compelled the surrender of literally millions of French troops, many of whom never saw combat.

For the same reason, the Allies lost huge quantities of weapons and other military equipment. From the British standpoint, indeed, this was the most serious consequence of the Dunkirk evacuation, confronted as they were with the threat of invasion.[101] German losses of tanks and planes were by no means trivial, but in strategic terms they were inconsequential, since the Wehrmacht had ample time to re-equip its legions.

But the strategic consequences of the Battle of France cannot be measured in comparative statistics of killed and wounded, prisoners, and booty. The Germans had conquered France and the Low Countries and the suction of their victorious surge had drawn Italy into the fray as their co-belligerent. They had defeated the British Expeditionary Force and swept it off the continent. But they had not conquered Britain.

Did Hitler and the German generals neglect to pluck all the fruits that these triumphs brought within their reach? That question will be examined in the concluding chapters.

Whatever the answer, the dimensions of the German victories in the West were staggering. Within three months all of western Europe except Switzerland and the Iberian peninsula had been brought under German occupation or domination. Britain was battered and isolated, bereft of allies. The Wehrmacht had been tested and tempered in battle at small cost and was not even yet at peak strength. Many strategic opportunities were opened up by Germany's control of the Atlantic Coast, and vast economic gains might be reaped by skillful exploitation of the newly occupied territories.

Hitler and the generals had shown that they knew how to conquer neighboring lands. It remained to be seen whether they understood how to profit by their victory.

CHAPTER NINE

Sieg Heil!

FRIDAY THE TENTH of May 1940 dawned bright and blue in the old city of Luxembourg. At 56 Rue Michel Walter the doorbell rang frantically, and the Schuler-Wagner family awoke to the cry in the street, *"D'preise sin hei."* * Mme. Margarit Schuler-Wagner, a bookkeeper, dressed and hurried to her office at a men's clothing factory to urge the Jewish proprietor, M. Oppenheim, to flee at once to France. But her employer was not to be budged; he was needed at his business, and he was old and the Germans surely would not harm him.†

For all M. Oppenheim's calm, few Letzeburgers worked that morning. They gathered on the streets in little groups, watching the German troops pass through and speculating on when the French would arrive. The Schuler-Wagners lunched at home as usual, but curiosity was getting the better of discretion, and early that afternoon Mme. Schuler-Wagner, with her daughter, a younger brother, and a neighbor, set out to the center of town to see what was going on. M. Schuler-Wagner, after cautioning his wife to keep out of trouble, took himself off to his favorite café *comme d'habitude* for coffee, tobacco, and talk.

The quartet of sight-seers strolled up the Avenue de la Liberté, across the Pont Adolphe, along the Boulevard Royal, and turned down the Grand'rue to the heart of the city. German troops were everywhere, and Mme. Schuler-Wagner did not find them good to look upon. The

---

* "The Prussians are here" in Letzeburgesch.

† M. Oppenheim's trust was misplaced. He was immediately reported as a Jew by his German factory manager, one Oster, whose family M. Oppenheim had generously supported when Oster was conscripted during the First World War. In consequence, M. Oppenheim was forced out of his business long before the other Jews of Luxembourg were touched. He and his wife died in a concentration camp in Poland.

315

little party turned off the Grand'rue on to the Rue du Charbon and approached the Place d'Armes. Here they came upon a German officer who was amiably passing the time of day with *une jeune habitante.* Mme. Schuler-Wagner's reaction was swift and unexpected to all concerned. She spat full in the face of the Rittmeister Freiherr von und zu Otto.

The *Rittmeister* was a man of quiet action. Not a word was exchanged while he and his chauffeur hustled Mme. Schuler-Wagner and her daughter into his staff car and drove to the French Embassy, which the Germans had already appropriated to their uses. The complaint was lodged, the *Rittmeister* disappeared, presumably in the direction of France, and the daughter was sent home. Mme. Schuler-Wagner was put into solitary confinement in the Luxembourg prison, the first civilian in western Europe to pay the price of resistance to the all-conquering Wehrmacht.

By any standards, and certainly in comparison to what would have been done to her in later years of the German occupation, Mme. Schuler-Wagner got off very lightly.* She was imprisoned for three months for insulting the German Wehrmacht *"indem sie ohne jede Veranlassung einem deutschen Offizier . . . ins Gesicht und auf den Waffenrock spuckte"* (in that without cause she spat in the face and on the tunic of a German officer). It might well have been a heavier sentence, considering that Mme. Schuler-Wagner adamantly refused to apologize or even plead the excuse of impulsive action.

In fact, the German administration in France, Belgium, and Luxembourg was at first mild and conciliatory, and the troops generally behaved correctly and even with courtesy.[2] But this restraint on the conqueror's part was short-lived, as the course of events in the little Duchy of Luxembourg soon revealed.

The Grand Duchess and her government had escaped to England, and the administration of the country was undertaken by an improvised "Commission" of civil officials. The Germans did not at first set up any

---

* But later in the war the family was less fortunate. M. Schuler-Wagner met his death in the *résistance,* while his wife and daughter suffered three years of forced labor in Bohemia. In retrospect, Mme. Schuler-Wagner wrote to her daughter, now married to an American and living in New York City:[1] "You may believe it or not, it seems always to me as a present or what may I call it, if somebody is interested in those things. Not that I count gather late 'Lorbeeren' for my behaviour or for whatever we did, I mean, you and your father and our friends. But may be one day or the other the story, I do not say 'History' will paint a real picture of all those events, not a picture with 'Hurra-Patriotisme' not a picture with medals and Glory, but just something we had into our selves, something in which we believed, something for which we lived and for which people like your father died."

special civil occupational agency for Luxembourg, and enforced military authority through a district headquarters * (*Oberfeldkommandantur*) under direct army command.

But the military regime lasted little more than a month, for Luxembourg was marked for absorption into the "Greater Reich." Early in August 1940 Gustav Simon, the Gauleiter of "Moselland" (the Coblenz-Trier region), was designated Chief of the Civil Administration of Luxembourg, responsible directly to Hitler. Before the end of the year the Constitution was "repealed," the parliament was dissolved, and the Nazi racial laws were introduced.[3] In February 1941 Luxembourg was declared to be part of the "Gau Moselland."

The treatment of Luxembourg illustrates, in miniature and brief compass, the transition of German occupational policy from the initial and light yoke of authority exercised only for purposes of military security, to virtual annexation and a systematic campaign of Nazification. Much the same thing happened in Alsace and Lorraine, and in Norway and Holland, where Nazi party officials were put in charge, a severe occupational regime was rapidly inaugurated.

But the pattern was by no means uniform. Belgium and Denmark at first fared much better than Norway and Holland. In France, where the stakes of victory were much the highest, the picture was confused and complicated both by the division of the country into occupied and unoccupied zones, and by overlapping and sometimes conflicting occupational authorities.

A survey of the initial shaping and evolution of German occupational policies, in the weeks immediately following the military conquest of western Europe, sheds much light on German strategy and its abysmal shortcomings in the moment of victory. These defects were the result of both lack of vision and conflict of views among the German leaders—military, political, and industrial—who seized, grasped at, or let slip the opportunities laid open by the Wehrmacht's triumphs.

Especially portentous was the failure of the generals to formulate a program or to stake out and defend an area of military responsibility and influence. They were the architects of victory in France; they faced the challenge of an intransigent Britain. By right and reason it was to them that the Fuehrer should have turned in developing an over-all

* The first district commander for Luxembourg was Generalmajor Otto Gullmann, a Bavarian and one of the numerous police officers taken into the army in 1935. By the fortunes of war Gullmann became something of a specialist in the affairs of small occupied countries, since he subsequently served as German Plenipotentiary-General in Albania.

strategy which would destroy Britain's power or will to resist. But the leaders of the Wehrmacht did not assert themselves decisively and, within a few weeks, Hitler shrewdly contrived to drape the garlands of victory on his own shoulders, and once again to undermine the prestige of the officer corps and the authority of its leaders.

In the final chapter, attention will be given to what the Germans *did not* do, and what they might have done, to exploit their victory on the continent and move toward a successful conclusion of the war. This chapter is concerned with what the Germans *did* do during the crucial weeks of June and July that witnessed and immediately followed the conquest of western Europe.

Compiègne, 1940

When the French armistice loomed the Germans confronted a new occupational problem. Poland, Denmark, Norway, and the Low Countries had been completely overrun. All of France lay within reach of the German grasp, but Hitler did not wish to drive the French government to North Africa, or the French fleet into British hands. Besides, France had exacted an armistice from Germany at Compiègne in 1918, and if there was anything that Hitler loved it was to cause history to repeat itself in reverse.

On June 17 it became known that the new French government of Marshal Pétain, through Spanish diplomatic channels, had approached Germany with a request for an armistice. This intelligence reached Hitler at his headquarters *Wolfsschlucht* at Brûly-de-Pesche near the Franco-Belgian border. The Fuehrer was not a gay man or at all given to dancing, but the report so excited him that then and there he executed a victor's jig, preserved for posterity by the photographer's art.[4] His facial expression is almost articulate: "I've really done it! And how remarkably easy it has all been! Now I'm a real conqueror!"

The French request came as no surprise to the German generals, for any military man could have foreseen for at least a week past that the French were done for. Brauchitsch and Halder discussed the conditions for an armistice on June 16, and later that day Halder and Generalleutnant Friedrich Mieth (*O.Qu. I*), who was ticketed for a place on the armistice commission, went into the details. It was agreed that the entire coast line of France should be occupied, and that most of the French Army was to be demobilized and a complete inventory of all *matériel de guerre* be turned over to the Wehrmacht. Mieth was then designated the "armistice specialist" for OKH, and the next day Halder remarked that "work on this subject, which is a little unfamiliar to us soldiers, is going rather slowly." But if the soldiers were slow, they were equally grasping, for the next day Halder proposed to OKW a demarcation line that would have permitted the Germans to occupy not only the coast to the Spanish border but the entire Rhone valley as well.[5]

Armed with this advice when the French request for an armistice was received, Hitler and Ribbentrop flew off to Munich to confer with Mussolini and Ciano. The Italian dictator was desperately eager to exploit his last-minute declaration of war; he and Ciano talked about the annexation of Nice, Corsica, Tunis, and French Somaliland, and the Duce was particularly insistent on seizing the French Fleet.[6]

But on this occasion success tempered Hitler's inner demon, and he gave the Italians little encouragement. On his return to Brûly-de-Pesche on June 19 he had OKW issue a directive forbidding the Army to advance south of the Cher River, except on the Atlantic Coast and in the region of Lyon.[7] On this general basis the armistice terms were prepared for presentation to the French.

Arrangements were then made for the French armistice delegation to cross the German lines between Poitiers and Tours during the evening of June 20, and Halder sent his chief intelligence officer, Generalmajor Kurt von Tippelskirch, to meet them at the front. The plan was to offer them the armistice terms the following morning at Compiègne, but transportation difficulties caused delay, and the occasion had to be postponed until the afternoon of June 21.[8]

Whoever first suggested that Foch's famous *wagon-lit* of 1918 should be the scene of the 1940 armistice, the idea and the manner of its execution bore an unmistakable Hitlerian stamp. The historic railroad car was taken out of the museum where it had been on display and moved to the exact spot that it had occupied twenty-two years before. At a little after three o'clock Hitler arrived with Goering, Keitel, Raeder, Brauchitsch, Ribbentrop, and Hess. Their attention was immediately attracted by a granite memorial bearing the inscription: "Here on the eleventh of November 1918 succumbed the criminal pride of the German Empire . . . vanquished by the free peoples which it tried to enslave." What ensued has been vividly described by William L. Shirer, an eyewitness:[9]

Hitler reads it and Goering reads it. They all read it, standing there in the June sun and the silence. I look for the expression on Hitler's face. I am but fifty yards from him and see him through my glasses as though he were directly in front of me. I have seen that face many times at the great moments of his life. But today! It is afire with scorn, anger, hate, revenge, triumph. He steps off the monument and contrives to make even this gesture a masterpiece of contempt. He glances back at it, contemptuous, angry—angry, you almost feel, because he cannot wipe out the awful provoking lettering with one sweep of his high Prussian boot. He glances slowly around the clearing, and now, as his eyes meet ours, you grasp the depth of his hatred. But there is triumph there too—revengeful, triumphant hate. Suddenly, as though his face were not giving quite complete expression to his feelings, he throws his whole body into harmony with his mood. He swiftly snaps his hands on his hips, arches his shoulders, plants his feet wide apart. It is a magnificent gesture of defiance, of burning contempt for this place now and all that it has stood for in the twenty-two years since it witnessed the humbling of the German Empire.

Hitler and his party then entered the *wagon-lit,* and the Fuehrer sat down, exactly where Foch had sat, to await the French, who arrived within a few minutes. The delegation consisted of General Charles Huntziger (who had commanded the Second Army at Sedan), General Parisot, General Bergeret of the Air Force, Vice-Admiral Le Luc, and M. Léon Noël, the former Ambassador to Poland. They had been given no warning of the *mise-en-scène,* and its impact was not lost on them. At the door of the car they were met by Tippelskirch and Oberst Kurt Thomas, who had succeeded Rommel as commandant of Hitler's military escort. After an interchange of salutes they entered the car, took seats, and Keitel commenced reading the German terms.

After a few minutes Hitler and most of his party departed, leaving Keitel to preside over the negotiations. On his return to OKH headquarters that evening, Brauchitsch described the events of the day to Halder: [10]

ObdH [Brauchitsch] returns from Compiègne. He is deeply stirred. The French (the most likable of whom was the Army representative) had no warning that they would be handed the terms at the very site of the negotiations in 1918. They were apparently shaken by this arrangement and at first inclined to be sullen.

The Fuehrer and ObdH were present only at the reading of the preamble. In the following negotiations, presided over by Keitel, there seems to have been a great deal of wrangling and ObdH is worried that the French might not accept.

I don't understand his apprehension. The French must accept, and with

Pétain at the helm will do so. Moreover, our terms are so moderate that sheer common sense ought to make them accept.

French attempts to have our terms bracketed with those of the Italians, and to make acceptance of our terms contingent on what the Italians demand, has of course been rejected by us. They have been given until tomorrow noon to accept. Aerial assault of Bordeaux has been authorized.

Brauchitsch's fears were groundless, and Bordeaux was not bombed. The negotiations on technical points were protracted and the French representatives consulted by telephone with Weygand in Bordeaux,[11] but as Halder had observed, the French had no choice, and the document was finally signed late in the afternoon on June 22.

The French were taken in German planes to Rome on the next day and received the Italian terms from Ciano, Marshal Badoglio, and other principal officers. Huntziger asked for time to communicate with Bordeaux, and further negotiations were then left in Badoglio's hands.[12] The French signed during the evening of June 24, and six hours later both the German and Italian armistices became effective.[13]

Their terms were harsh, but coming from Hitler and Mussolini might well have been far worse. As Huntziger had put it to Weygand,[14] "*Les conditions sont dures, mais il n'y a rien contre l'honneur.*" Geographically, the Franco-German armistice followed out the original suggestions of Halder and Mieth, except that the Rhone Valley was allowed to remain unoccupied. In the occupied area, the French local authorities were to take orders from the German military commanders. German hopes for an early end to the war were reflected in the stipulation that "after ending hostilities with England" the French Atlantic Coast would be occupied only "to the extent absolutely necessary."

All French armed forces were to be demobilized and disarmed, except those needed for the "maintenance of domestic order"; the exact size of this force was to be fixed subsequently. French units in the occupied area were to put all their weapons at the Germans' disposal. In the unoccupied area, all military equipment was to be stored under German or Italian control. The French Navy, except for those vessels needed "for protection of French interests in its colonial empire," was to be laid up and demobilized, and was the subject of special German pledges:

> The German government solemnly declares to the French government that it does not intend to use the French war fleet which is in harbors under German control for its purposes in war, with the exception of units necessary for guarding the coast and sweeping mines.

It further solemnly and expressly declares that it does not intend to bring up any demands respecting the French war fleet at the conclusion of a peace.

All German prisoners in French custody were to be freed at once, but French troops in German hands were to "remain prisoners until conclusion of a peace." This stipulation was especially distasteful to the French, and of course gave the Germans enormous leverage for the future, as the millions of French prisoners became virtual hostages. The French also undertook to deliver up "all Germans named by the German government in France" and in the colonies, a provision which boded no good for Jews and other Germans who had fled the Nazi regime and settled in France.

Under the Franco-Italian armistice, the Italians occupied only the areas they had taken, and this meant Menton on the Mediterranean coast and a few small bits along the border in the Alps. The French were required to demilitarize a fifty-mile zone opposite the Italian "front" and other zones in the African colonies. The other provisions of the Italian armistice largely paralleled the German.

The Germans and Italians each appointed a "commission" to supervise the execution of the armistices. The German commission (*Waffenstillstandkommission*) was established in Wiesbaden, and General Karl-Heinrich von Stuelpnagel was designated as its president. General Huntziger remained as head of the French delegation to the armistice commissions.

Severe though it was, the armistice of June 1940 was a far from unreasonable act of international statesmanship, and the Germans might have used it as the basis for a policy of conciliation and *rapprochement* with the Vichy government of France. Hitler had checked Mussolini's annexationist rapacity and, could he have but governed his own appetite, the French might soon have been in the hollow of his hand. The anti-British temper of Pétain, Darlan, Laval, and other Vichy leaders was propitious for Germany, especially after the British naval action against the French warships at Oran on July 3, 1940. A liberal German policy in France, with the return of prisoners and the establishment of the French government in Paris, would have cut the ground from under De Gaulle and fostered noninterventionist sentiment in the United States, and might ultimately have locked Britain in isolation.

Despite its profound importance for the future prosecution of the war, occupation policy was a matter of indifference to most of the generals. This was not true of Stuelpnagel and his staff at Wiesbaden, or of the more conscientious staff officers of OKH. At OKW and the top levels of field command, however, attention was focused on other matters. In fact, Hitler and the leaders of the Wehrmacht never sat down together to analyze the strategic implications of the occupation or to work out a broad policy that would aid in achieving the final victory.

With the fighting over, the German troops in France put their binoculars to new uses, more fitting to the pleasant surroundings. The headquarters of OKH was established at Fontainebleau, while Rundstedt's Army Group A settled down at the Hotel Henri IV in St. Germain, just outside Paris.

"Settled into the plush" might be a more apt phrase, for Compiègne ushered in a period of relaxation and pleasure for the German troops stationed in France. It was early summer, and Paris beckoned. Fearing that the end of combat might unleash too many impulses, the military authorities first put the City of Light "off limits." Generalleutnant Kurt von Briesen,* an exceedingly severe disciplinarian, was installed as Commandant of Paris, and passes to enter the city were issued only for official purposes. But the troops behaved excellently, "incidents" were few and far between, and soon these restrictions were greatly relaxed. The hope of peace was in the air and occupation life was good, especially for staff officers with broad-minded commanders such as Rundstedt.[15]

Adolf Hitler permitted himself no such sybaritic interlude, for which, in fact, he had neither the taste nor the capacity. The day after the armistice was signed at Compiègne, the Fuehrer and a small entourage (including the Party-favored architects Albert Speer and Hermann Giesler) paid a brief visit to Paris. He toured the city, went up the Eiffel Tower, and examined the Paris Opera House from top to bottom, with all the fervor of the frustrated architect that he was.

But the climax was at the Invalides, where he indulged in a long reverie, gazing down at Napoleon's tomb.[16] "That," he announced to his acolyte and photographer Heinrich Hoffmann, "was the greatest and finest moment of my life."

Then the Fuehrer went off to his new headquarters, "Tannenberg," in the Black Forest near Freudenstadt. Hitler had his terpsichorean thrill of victory at *Wolfsschlucht,* drained the cup of triumph at Compiègne,

---

* As commander of the 30th Infantry Division, von Briesen was wounded during the Polish campaign and at its conclusion received the *Ritterkreuz.* As a corps commander, he was killed in action in Russia in 1941.

and had his rendezvous with history at the Invalides. After that, France
had nothing more to offer.

"The New Order for Western Europe"

Considering that Hitler was bent on conquest and that the Wehrmacht
was used to fulfill that aim, there was an amazing dearth of prewar
political planning in Berlin for the eventuality of success in the field.
Poland was invaded without first deciding whether or not an independent "rump" state would be tolerated after Polish resistance had
been crushed, and it was Stalin, not Hitler, who first answered that
question in the negative.[17]

The campaigns in the West were launched with the same lack of
political forethought. In the small nations—Denmark, Norway, and the
Low Countries—Hitler hoped to capture the royal families and leading
ministers, or to overwhelm them with threats, so as to throttle opposition and preserve the appearance of a "peaceful" occupation. Resistance was to be "ruthlessly crushed." That was as far as the German
field of political vision extended.

In the event of victory, were these lands to be sovereign once more?
What strategic criteria should be applied to questions of annexation,
spheres of influence, and to the general structure of Europe in the
wake of German victory? These questions were left unanswered before
the onslaught, and most of them remained so even after the military
conquest was completed.

In this almost nonchalant condition of political unpreparedness, there
was a high degree of improvisation in the occupational regimes that
the Germans established. As matters worked out, the western countries
overrun by the Wehrmacht were subjected to three reasonably distinct
types of occupational control: *

(1) Belgium and the occupied portion of France, which might
continue to be the scene of large-scale military operations against
Britain, remained under direct army control, exercised through generals
who were immediately responsible to OKH. Denmark was also within
the purview of OKH, but there the German commander had authority
only over the German troops stationed in Denmark, and civil authority
continued to be exercised by the Danish government.

(2) In Norway and Holland, primary authority passed into the

---

* See the chart of German military and civil authority in the occupied territories, Appendix C, *infra*, p. 432.

hands of the Nazi "pro-consuls" Josef Terboven and Artur Seyss-In-quart, who, like Hans Frank in Poland, were answerable only to Hitler himself. The OKH was divested even of military authority in Norway and Holland, where the German commanders were subordinated to the OKW.

(3) The Belgian border areas of Eupen and Malmédy were annexed outright, and Luxembourg was treated for all practical purposes as part of the Reich. As will shortly be described, the same fate was in store for Alsace and Lorraine.

Despite these political and military differences, there was an underlying uniformity of economic occupation policy. The generals might not have any clear notion of what use should be made of the western victories, but the German industrialists of the Rhine and Ruhr were in no such state of foggy indifference. Furthermore, Goering, who still had the chief role in state administration of the German economy, was more decisive in that field than was Hitler in the resolution of the big problems of statecraft.

Perhaps this was merely because the basis of German economic occupation policy was simple and stark. The resources of the occupied countries were to be exploited immediately and intensively for the benefit of the Wehrmacht and the German war potential. This policy contrasted sharply with the partial and superficial mobilization of the Reich's domestic economy.[18] Indeed, it was almost as if Goering, having decided to leave the belt as loose on German home consumption as on his own ample person, had determined to compensate for this slackness by squeezing the occupied countries to the bone. I have seen no contemporary German document in which this comparison is spelled out, but in the upshot that is just what happened, at least until 1943.

Throughout the period under consideration, the Germans were still hoping for a speedy end of the war, with Britain throwing in the sponge. Insofar as there were long-term objectives, they were to render the occupied countries increasingly dependent upon and partly assimilated into the German economy, and to inseminate them with Nazi ideology. Thereby western Europe would become a sort of appanage of the Greater Reich. The propaganda cliché "New Order" (*Neuordnung*)—by which, of course, was meant a German Order—well characterizes the German occupational design.

Much of this was foreshadowed months before the fighting in the West began. On January 30, 1940, for example, Goering received at

Karinhall Generalleutnant Georg Thomas, Chief of the Economic and Armament Department of OKW, and informed him: [19]

> The Fuehrer is firmly convinced that he will succeed in reaching a decision in the war in 1940 by a big attack in the West. He believes that Belgium, Holland, and northern France will come into our possession, and that the industrial areas of Douai, Lens, Luxembourg, Longwy and Briey could replace the raw material supplies now received from Sweden. . . . The decision follows to exploit every thing of ours to the utmost in 1940, and to exploit the raw material reserves at their [i.e., France, Belgium, and Holland] expense in later years.

To carry out these policies, special military economic staffs and field units were established by both OKW and OKH. Primarily, however, this was the province of OKW, and promptly on the outbreak of war in 1939 Thomas' department sent economic liaison officers to each army headquarters. For the campaign in the West "economic teams" (*Wirtschaftstruppen*), each comprising a few specialist officers assisted by enlisted clerks and drivers, were established by OKW and attached to the army groups. At the same time OKH borrowed a high official, Dr. Hans Posse, from the Economics Ministry, and gave him charge of a special economics staff attached to the *Generalquartiermeister* of the General Staff.[20]

The economic teams were instructed [21] "to reconnoiter quickly and completely in the newly occupied territories the raw materials (scarce and rationed) most important for the war effort and essential war production machinery, to catalogue and seize them for the Reich, and, with the permission of the Commander-in-Chief of the Army, to prepare for their eventual shipment to the Reich." Rubber, hides, asbestos, industrial diamonds, industrial oils, and a variety of ferrous and non-ferrous metals and semi-manufactured metal products were listed in an appendix to the instructions, and the teams were admonished [22] that "trainload after trainload" must be sent "to finishing plants in the occupied territories and in the Reich, according to the requirements of manufacturing programs."

Goering and other high Nazi officials were not the only ones who viewed the occupied territories as a promised land. The directors of the I. G. Farben chemicals combine and of the great Ruhr steel and coal trusts were following the Wehrmacht's advance with eager interest, and there was no mystery about what they wanted. For weeks past they had been studying maps and lists of industrial concerns in the conquered areas, with an eye to annexations and confiscations from which they might benefit.

So avid were the tycoons that Goering and Walter Funk (Minister of Economics), neither of them overly fastidious in international business ethics, thought best to caution them against overreaching. Just as the Somme-Aisne offensive began, Funk met at Duesseldorf with a select circle of steel magnates—Friedrich Flick, Paul Kloeckner, Ernst Poensgen, Wilhelm Zangen, and others—to discuss the future ownership and operation of various enterprises in the newly occupied areas. The Economics Minister [23] "referred to the fact that he had given considerable assistance to business, particularly as regards the problem of taxation, and he now asked in return that he should receive assistance by a reasonable attitude in the future, and that care be taken that no excesses occur which might give an opening to the opponents of private enterprise to make accusations against business; particularly one should seek to repress all desire for annexation, etc." What Funk put thus tactfully, Goering stated in much sterner fashion on June 19: [24] "The endeavor of German industry to take over enterprises in the occupied territory must be rejected in the sharpest manner."

Early in August, however, Goering was singing a different tune and instructing the occupation authorities in Norway, Holland, and Belgium that economic "penetration" by "German circles" was to be encouraged in every possible way.[25] Perhaps the previous admonitions were intended merely to preserve appearances until France had signed the armistice. At all events, they fell on deaf ears. Even before the armistice, Friedrich Flick was declaring [26] "that the industry of Lorraine and Luxembourg and, probably, that of the Briey basin as well will one day return to Germany."

Such was the general viewpoint of the German steel and coal magnates, all of whom were staking claims to enterprises which they had owned in the days before World War I when Lorraine was in German hands, or which they regarded as otherwise "suitable" for their purposes. These demands were put before Generalleutnant Hermann von Hanneken, a regular army officer who had specialized in economics and was then serving as Plenipotentiary-General for Iron and Steel Allocation in the Ministry of Economics. After the victory in the West, Hanneken had a very active and touchy time sorting out and adjusting the various and often conflicting claims, of which Goering was the supreme arbiter when compromise proved impossible.[27]

Apart from territories such as Lorraine which were marked for annexation, some formula had to be found to give color of propriety to the economic "penetration" of the occupied countries. This was the real purpose of the phrase "New Order for Europe," on which Funk expatiated in a speech on July 25, 1940, and which was subsequently written into the Tripartite Pact.* Tricked out with verbal finery borrowed from Briand, Zeeland, the Pan-European Union, and other prewar liberal sources, the New Order envisaged international division of labor, controlled rates of exchange, and European self-sufficiency in raw materials.

But from a non-German standpoint, the New Order was strictly spurious, for upon analysis it became apparent that the exports of the other countries were to be carefully regulated or even eliminated, so as to protect German markets, and that their economies would be partially deindustrialized for the same purpose and to increase European agricultural output.[28] Indeed, Funk was blunt about the New Order's true aims: "The coming peacetime economy must guarantee for Greater Germany a maximum of economic security and for the German nation a maximum consumption of goods to raise the level of the nation's well-being. The European economy must be adapted to achieve this aim."

Inevitably, so harsh an economic policy tended to determine the political character of the occupation as well. If the Germans were determined to sap the resources of the conquered countries and subject large enterprises to the control of the Ruhr and Rhine industrialists, they could not at the same time rule with a velvet touch and pursue a political policy of conciliation. If there were those in high places who favored more moderate policies, they were easily silenced.

Holland was the first (as it was to be among the last †) of the western European countries to feel the impact of Nazism. The initial stage of the German occupation of the Netherlands generated considerable friction between Hitler and the OKH generals, who wanted a purely military administration. Before the invasion began, Bock and the OKH were working out a plan for "centralized administration of occupied territory under OKH" and had earmarked General Alexander von Falkenhausen as the future occupational commander.[29]

---

* In this pact (signed September 27, 1940), Japan recognized "the leadership of Germany and Italy in the establishment of a new order in Europe," and Germany and Italy similarly acknowledged Japan's "new order in Asia."

† The Netherlands north of the Rhine-Maas Estuary and Norway (and Denmark, where conditions were not equally bad) were the last western countries to be liberated from the German occupation.

In line with these policies, as soon as the Dutch forces capitulated General von Kuechler issued a preliminary occupational directive naming Generalleutnant Christian Hansen (Commander of the Xth Corps, in northern Holland) as military commander for the entire country, with his divisional generals as regional commandants.[30] But a few days later Hansen was supplanted by Falkenhausen, who established a military occupational headquarters with several high-ranking German civil servants as his assistants for civil administration.[31]

By May 20 the greater part of Belgium, including Brussels and Antwerp, was in German hands, and Falkenhausen was formally designated *Militaerbefehlshaber* * for both Belgium and Holland. In his early sixties at the time of his appointment, Falkenhausen had an unusual breadth of experience in foreign lands. During World War I he had served with the Turkish Army in Palestine, and after his retirement from the *Reichswehr* in 1930 he went to China, where he succeeded Seeckt as chief of the advisory staff of retired German officers assembled by Chiang Kai-shek at Nanking.[32] He returned to Germany in 1938 when the German group was dissolved as a result of the growing German-Japanese affinity, and upon the outbreak of war was recalled to active duty as Commander of Wehrkreis IV in Dresden, where he served until summoned to his new occupational command.

Despite Falkenhausen's outstanding qualifications, his tenure as commander in Holland lasted only a week, for Hitler had very different ideas from those of Brauchitsch and Halder about the future administration of that country. Once again the remarkable parallelism of German policies in Norway and Holland was manifested. On May 17 Keitel, speaking for the Fuehrer, told Brauchitsch that the "setup" in Holland would be the same as in Norway.[33] This was hardly pleasant news to Brauchitsch, for the OKH had been from the inception of *Weseruebung* totally excluded from authority in Norway.[34] Accordingly, as Keitel put it, there would be no need for OKH to have any "elaborate administrative machinery" in Holland, for Seyss-Inquart was to be "put in charge" there, just as Terboven had been in Norway.

Brauchitsch expostulated, and insisted that there be a forthright definition of jurisdiction for military and civilian officials in Holland. But he made no progress with Keitel, and Halder commented gloomily in his diary[35] that the whole affair "has demonstrated once again the

---

* The title given to German military commanders of important occupied areas, whose authority did not cover locally stationed air and naval units, and who were responsible to OKH rather than OKW.

utter dishonesty of our top leaders in relation to OKH." And right he was, for the upshot of the dispute was that Holland was taken entirely out of the jurisdiction of OKH.

On May 18 Hitler issued a decree designating Dr. Artur Seyss-Inquart "Reich Commissioner [*Reichskommissar*] for the Occupied Netherlands Territories" and vesting him with "supreme civil authority," subject only to the Fuehrer himself.[36] A week later Seyss-Inquart, the Austrian Nazi who had been serving as Deputy Governor-General in Poland under Hans Frank, announced his assumption of "supreme governmental authority within the civil domain." On May 29 he declared himself to be possessed of "all powers, privileges, and rights heretofore vested in the King and government" under the Netherlands constitution.[37]

Hitler's decree did, to be sure, leave "supreme military authority" in the Netherlands to the military commander. But the orders of the military commander, insofar as they affected civilian life, had to be carried out through the *Reichskommissar*, and it was plain that this stipulation, together with the commissioner's direct responsibility to Hitler, would inevitably reduce the military commander to a secondary role, little to the taste of a strong personality. Perhaps Falkenhausen was more pleased than offended when, on May 28, he was relieved of his responsibilities in Holland. The initiative for this move is not clear; Halder's diary entry for May 27 suggests that the Dutch Nazi leader, Anton Mussert, did not want the German Army to have authority in Holland.

Falkenhausen's successor, General der Flieger Friedrich Christiansen, was cut from a very different cloth. A merchant mariner by original bent, he joined the Navy during World War I and became a daring and expert pilot of seaplanes. He collaborated closely with the aircraft manufacturer Ernst Heinkel during the postwar years, joined the Nazi party and made friends with Goering, and eventually was commissioned in the Luftwaffe and appointed Chief of the NSFK (National Socialist Flying Corps).[38]

Christiansen was an adventurous and colorful character, but he was not the man to offer much opposition to Nazi occupational policies. His appointment was no doubt a sop to Goering, and as an air general the choice was superficially logical, in that Holland had been occupied largely for the benefit of the Luftwaffe,[39] and was not expected to be a theater of great importance to the Army. At all events, he was thoroughly insulated from OKH influence by his background and his appointment as *Wehrmachtbefehlshaber*,* responsible directly to the OKW.

Having assumed the royal and governmental powers when he took office as *Reichskommissar*, Seyss-Inquart dissolved the Dutch legislature a few weeks later. The administrative heads of the government departments he then formed into a sort of cabinet, subordinated to his personal authority. In rapid succession there followed decrees for the dismissal of civil servants at the Reich Commissioner's pleasure, banning private entry into or exit from Dutch territory and authorizing confiscation of the property of those "of whom it is to be assumed that they will assist anti-German activities." Well versed in such matters by virtue of his experiences in Austria and Poland, Seyss-Inquart promptly dismissed all Jews from the Dutch civil service, and soon banned them from commerce and "Aryanized" their enterprises.[40]

In the Netherlands the Dutch Nazis never attained much importance, apparently because they were internally divided, and their leadership was mediocre.[41] Seyss-Inquart described the Dutch "Fuehrer" Anton Mussert as a man whose "political qualities are not as great as those of an average Gauleiter in the Reich."

In this respect the course of events differed in Norway, where the Germans made a systematic and ultimately successful effort to utilize Quisling as their puppet. However, Quisling's initial effort to establish a government at the time of the invasion foundered within a few days on the rock of violent Norwegian opposition, and during the early months of the occupation he remained in the background.

Throughout the summer of 1940 the Germans continued to hope that the Norwegians would disavow King Haakon and collaborate in the occupational administration, and for this reason Terboven moved more slowly than Seyss-Inquart in the introduction of Nazi policies. But there was never any doubt that Norway was Terboven's province, and Falkenhorst, as *Wehrmachtbefehlshaber*, confined himself to military matters. After the summer of 1940 Nazification proceeded apace, and the harshness of the Terboven regime soon aroused a most active and courageous resistance movement under the leadership of patriots such as Paal Berg and Bishop Eivind Berggrav.[42]

For the time being Belgium fared better than Norway and Holland, except for the annexation of Eupen and Malmédy.[43] Partly this was

* This was the same title as had been given to Falkenhorst in Norway, and carried with it command of all Army, Navy, and Air Force units in the area, together with subordination to OKW rather than OKH.

because Belgium, like northern France, lay in close proximity to England, and the consequent possibility of renewed military operations on Belgian and French soil enabled OKH to maintain its authority.

Military administration under the decently inclined General von Falkenhausen was far less onerous than the Nazi regimes of Terboven and Seyss-Inquart. The Belgian civil service was not at first much disturbed, and King Leopold's decision to remain in Belgium checked the growth of the resistance movement. Germanic Flemings were more susceptible than French-speaking Walloons to Nazi blandishments, and the occupation authorities played one group against the other. At the outset, the Germans' interest in Belgium was chiefly military and economic, and it was growing public awareness that Belgian resources were being ruthlessly exploited that eventually aroused the hostility of the population.[44]

In France, of course, the occupational stakes were much higher and the political issues far more complex. It was not merely a matter of pacification and exploitation, for despite their defeat the French still held some cards—the fleet, the colonies, and the army units abroad, especially in North Africa. Part of France was unoccupied, part was a springboard for a possible invasion of Britain, and part was a highway to Spain, Gibraltar, and Morocco. There were the competing interests of France, Italy, and Spain in the Mediterranean, and the Italian claims on the Riviera. In short, France—in the persons of Pétain, Laval, Huntziger, Noël, Darlan, and others—had to be dealt with, as the smaller countries did not, and German policy in France was much more subject to extraneous events and pressures than it was in the other conquered countries.

After Dunkirk Blaskowitz, who had been left jobless upon his removal as Commander-in-Chief of the Ninth Army,[45] was appointed *Militaerbefehlshaber* in northern France, comprising the departments Nord and Pas-de-Calais.[46] Following the German entry into Paris, General Alfred von Vollard Bockelberg was given the same title in the French capital.

Immediately after the armistice, however, there was a complete rearrangement of the German occupational administration in France. Again the ax fell on Blaskowitz.* The two northern departments were, for occupational purposes, joined to Belgium, and Falkenhausen was

* Blaskowitz was left idle for four months, and then was appointed Commander-in-Chief of the First Army in succession to Witzleben, who was advanced to an army group command.

given the title *Militaerbefehlshaber Belgien-Nordfrankreich.* Bockel-berg was let out at the same time,* to clear the decks for an over-all military administration in occupied France (except Nord and Pas-de-Calais) for which Halder had been laying plans.

"The problem of organizing the administration in France is causing quite a headache," Halder noted on June 23. He did not like the title *Militaerbefehlshaber,* on the ground that it connoted too great a power of command. Instead, he proposed a "Chief of Military Administration" (*Chef der Militaerverwaltung*) who "would act on behalf and under the authority of" the Commander-in-Chief of the Army. Halder's theory apparently was that, just as Keitel as *Chef* of OKW could issue no orders in his own right but only by Hitler's authority, so the *Chef* of military administration would have to act in the name of the Army Commander-in-Chief, and this would give OKH immediate control of all his doings.

Halder succeeded in persuading Hitler of the merits of his proposal, and on June 26 General Alfred Streccius, another "retread" who had been retired in 1931, was appointed Chief of Military Administration in France, with Oberstleutnant Hans Speidel as his Chief of Staff.† In authority and prestige his position was inferior to that of Falkenhausen, not only because of his less resplendent title, but also because occupied France remained the seat of the principal army field headquarters and abounded with generals who outranked Streccius.

Halder's hopes of a unified administration of occupied France under OKH were not fulfilled. From the outset, the situation was complicated by the overlapping and proliferating lines of authority in the German occupational machinery. Execution of the armistice was entrusted to the Armistice Commission, which was responsible to OKW, but even within this sphere economic problems were removed from Stuelpnagel's purview and entrusted to Minister Hans Hemmen, who looked to

---

* This was the end of active service for Bockelberg, who had been recalled from retirement on the outbreak of war to serve as Commander of Wehrkreis I in East Prussia. He was taken away from Berlin by the Russians in 1945 and has not been heard of since. It was Bockelberg who had represented the German Army at Moscow in June 1933, when the Red Army and the *Reichswehr* broke off the close relations they had enjoyed for the past ten years.[47]

† Early in June, according to Halder's diary (June 6), Speidel had been attached to Bock's army group "for special tasks in Paris." Generalleutnant Faber du Faur, writing at Rambouillet on June 20 (*Macht und Ohnmacht,* p. 255) was somewhat cynical about the "experts . . . Abetz, Speidel, and their entourage" that were "swarming" in Paris, who "see all France through German spectacles" and who "know the French as little as the Prussians do the Bavarians." Faber du Faur presciently concluded that: "Only a total victory can help us now; otherwise it will be total defeat."

Goering and Funk for authoritative guidance.[48] The German combat units in occupied France remained under the army groups and armies of the field army, while the military district commanders reported to OKH through Streccius as Chief of Military Administration.

For political matters, Otto Abetz was designated as "Ambassador" in Paris; he was attached to OKH, but took orders from Ribbentrop as Foreign Minister. Some time later there was also a "Representative of the German Wehrmacht" at Vichy—Generalmajor Alexander Freiherr Neubronn von Eisenburg—who was responsible to OKH.[49] The French were not slow to perceive and exploit this division of authority, and had they not themselves been so riven, would have been even more successful than they were in playing the German organizations one against the other.[50]

In such an administrative morass, it would have been difficult enough to pursue a purposeful occupation policy, had there been one. But there was none, for the German counsels were divided at the highest level. Goering and Ribbentrop favored a "hard" program; the OKH and Abetz were somewhat more flexible in their inclinations. Hitler blew hot and cold, and had no patience for difficult problems that seemed to him tedious details. He and the high command were increasingly preoccupied with Britain, Spain, Gibraltar, Russia, the Italian campaign in North Africa, and other questions of major strategy. As a result of all this, basic issues of occupation policy remained unresolved. At times the Germans talked of winning the French to their side by decent treatment, but more often they seemed oblivious or indifferent to the disastrous effect of their exploitation of the French economy, and their annexationist measures in Alsace and Lorraine.

Opportunities for a Franco-German *rapprochement* were not lacking. After the British naval action against the French Fleet at Oran, the French broke off diplomatic relations with Britain. Shortly thereafter, the French delegation to the Armistice Commission suggested "a more intimate co-operation between Germany and France." The proposal was laid before Hitler, but he could not make up his mind:[51] "A decision . . . is dependent on how much France can contribute to the war effort and therefore further time to think it over is required." In the same document, Hitler directed that "goods vital for the war and raw materials must be taken out of the unoccupied territory," a policy little likely to cultivate good will. Even so, the French made new approaches. In September, General Huntziger proposed to Stuelpnagel that their countries enter into an "alliance." Hitler directed a reply that the idea was "under very serious consideration," but once again there was no follow-up.[52]

Indeed, everything the Germans did belied their sometimes fair words. The occupation costs assessed against the French were astronomical. In addition to their economic measures, the Germans' refusal to release the French prisoners of war—which, to be sure, was within their rights under the armistice terms—aroused deep hostility.

During the early months of the occupation, however, the bitterest pill for the French was the "Germanization" of Alsace and Lorraine. A few days before the armistice, Goering declared at a small planning conference that Hitler had decided to incorporate both provinces into the Reich.[53] No such intention was publicly announced, but in July the Germans began expelling "Francophiles" and Jews from Alsace and Lorraine into unoccupied France [54] and preventing French refugees from returning.[55]

As in the case of Luxembourg, there was never any declaration of annexation by Germany. But in August a decree was promulgated attaching Alsace and Lorraine to the *Reichsgaue* Moselland and Westmark, respectively. Josef Buerckel, Gauleiter of the Saarland, was designated Chief of Civil Administration for Lorraine, and Robert Wagner, Gauleiter of Baden, was given the same title in Alsace.[56] Wagner promptly issued an order for the "Reintroduction of the Mother Tongue" in Alsace, requiring the populace to use "exclusively the German language" and directing all persons with French Christian names having no German equivalent to apply for a change of name so as to "show their attachment to Germanism." [57]

The French were outraged. During the armistice negotiations, Ambassador Noël had elicited a verbal commitment from Keitel that the French administrative and judicial officials in occupied France, including Alsace and Lorraine, would continue to discharge their usual functions.[58] Now they were being ousted by the German "civil administration," and Huntziger promptly reproached Stuelpnagel with breaking the agreement.[59]

Thus the restraint by which Hitler had been measurably governed when the terms of the French armistice were laid down deserted him almost before the ink on that document was dry. For lack of a basic strategy the Germans muffed chance after chance to win the French to their side. As conquerors, they had no conception of the relative value of different and often conflicting objectives. In the scales of fate, the annexation or "Germanization" of Luxembourg, Alsace, and Lorraine counted for nothing as against a victorious conclusion of the war. It called for no eye of genius to see this; a dash of common sense should have sufficed.

After the fall of France the Germans confronted two great obstacles to their final victory: Britain, and the gathering force of public opinion in the western world, especially in the United States. In the long run, Britain's hopes depended not on her own unaided power but on accessions of strength from the Empire and the other still-neutral western democracies. A German occupation policy of moderation in France and the other defeated countries would have gone far to allay the fear and hostility that the march of conquest had aroused.

No doubt it is too much to expect that Hitler should have acted as the enlightened man which he was not. But in domestic political matters he had, more often than not, been diabolically shrewd, as he had also been during the days of the *Blumenkriege* in Austria and Czechoslovakia.[60] Now even this lower faculty seemed lost to him. He could not keep the claws sheathed until the prey was lured within reach. The appointments of Nazi Gauleiters to rule in Norway and Holland; the annexations of strategically unimportant but symbolically resonant lands on Germany's western borders; the grasping exploitation of the occupied countries' resources—all these things confirmed the fears which so rapidly flowered in the Grand Alliance that spelled defeat for the Third Reich.

Such were the results of Conquest in the West. Except for the annexations and "incorporations" in the fringe areas, none of the German and Italian plans for territorial revision in western Europe was ever consummated. But before passing on to other matters it may be enlightening to pause for a moment on "might-have-beens," even though their study takes us a few months beyond the chronological ending of the main part of this account.

Pax Germanica

On May 28 Churchill told his Cabinet that:[61] "Of course, whatever happens at Dunkirk, we shall fight on." After the fall of France, he proclaimed with fierce eloquence Britain's determination to win the coming battle for "the survival of Christian civilization."[62] But suppose the Empire's leaders had been men of weaker mold? There is no doubt that Hitler and the generals hoped and half expected the British to sue for peace in the summer of 1940. If they had, what would have been the immediate fate of western Europe under a victorious German dispensation?

As far as is known, a definitive blueprint of conquest was never made. But this was a subject to which Hitler and some of the military leaders gave no little thought during that agreeable summer of 1940, when the glint of victory shone on their horizon. And the surviving records, patchy though they are, give a sufficient picture of the sort of terms which Hitler might have dictated had the British laid down their arms and suffered a *Pax Germanica* to settle over Europe.

Hitler appears to have said little about peace terms until July 13, 1940. The occasion was a military conference at the Berghof at which Halder and others reported on the progress of planning for an invasion of Britain. Before the gathering broke up, however, Hitler held forth on the "political situation from a military angle." The Fuehrer revealed that he and the Duce had been canvassing the African situation, and that Italy's prime interests lay in the "hinterland," especially a corridor to connect Libya with Abyssinia and establish a geographically unified African dominion. Hitler was proposing that Germany take both French and Belgian Congo and divide the French North African possessions with Spain, as bait "to draw Spain into the game in order to build up a front against Britain extending from the North Cape to Morocco." [63]

No doubt Hitler enjoyed these dreams of colonial empire, but his serious aims remained focused in Europe. It is clear that he had ideas of annexing a considerable part of France in addition to Alsace-Lorraine, for he tried to prevent the war refugees from returning to the north provinces (Nord and Pas-de-Calais) and eastern Burgundy. To this end an unannounced "Black Line" or "Fuehrer Line" was drawn along the Somme and southeastward to the Swiss border. The occupation forces were supposed to keep the refugees south of this line, but the order was difficult to enforce, and except in Alsace and Lorraine it was evaded without much difficulty. The French, however, soon grasped the purport of the "Black Line," and another obstacle to Franco-German collaboration thus arose.[64]

During the summer of 1940, Hitler and Raeder several times exchanged views on how best to reap the harvest of victory. The naval Commander-in-Chief was customarily foresighted, though not always wise, on strategic matters. His senior staff officers were encouraged to submit their views, which generally reflected the German naval officers' traditional vexation with the narrow confines of German coastal waters, and a deep desire for ports and bases on the open ocean—the same motives that had found outlet in *Weseruebung*.[65]

In keeping with this practice, on June 3, 1940, the Chief of the Operations Sections of the Naval War Staff, Konteradmiral Kurt Fricke, prepared a memorandum entitled "Questions of Territorial Expansion and Bases." [66] What was the intended or actual use of the memorandum remains obscure,* but it foreshadowed views which were soon being expressed at a higher level:

I. These problems are pre-eminently of a political character and comprise an abundance of questions of a political type, which it is not the Navy's province to answer, but they also materially affect the strategic possibilities open—according to the way in which this question is answered—for the subsequent mission and operation of the Navy.

It is too well known to need further mention that Germany's present position in the narrows of the Helgoland Bight, and in the Baltic—bordered as it is by a whole series of states, and under their influence—is an impossible one for the future of Greater Germany. If, over and above this, one extends these strategic possibilities to the point that Germany shall not continue to be cut off for all time from overseas by natural geographical facts, the need is clear that somehow or other an end shall be put to this state of affairs at the end of the war.

The solution could perhaps be found among the following possibilities:

1. The territories of Denmark, Norway, and northern France acquired during the course of the war continue to be so occupied and organized that they can in future be considered as German possessions.

This solution will recommend itself for areas where the severity of the decision tells, and should tell, on the enemy, and where a gradual "Germanizing" of the territory appears practicable.

2. The taking over and holding of areas which have no direct connection with Germany's main body, and which, like the Russian solution in Hangö, remain permanently as an enclave in the hostile state. Such areas might be considered possibly around Brest and Trondheim.

This type of solution can only be discouraged.† It is fraught with every conceivable weakness to which a bridgehead in a hostile country and national body, difficult of access, far removed from the homeland and thrown

---

* At Nuremberg, counsel for Raeder, through the testimony of Admiral Gerhard Wagner (Fricke's immediate subordinate at the time the memorandum was written), attempted to portray the document as a "fantastic" personal effusion of Fricke's, which was never transmitted outside the operations section.[67] Fricke himself cannot be asked, for he has been "missing" since the Russian occupation of Berlin in 1945.[68] But the opening sentence of the memorandum suggests that it was written on invitation, and Fricke signed it as "1. Skl." (Section 1, *Seekriegsleitung*, the section of which he was chief), so it was plainly a regular staff memorandum. Furthermore, it bears the pencil annotations of some reader who agreed with much of it but thought it did not go far enough with respect to Trondheim.

† Marginal pencil notation: "But this isn't at all the case with Trondheim."

back on its own resources, is subject. On the face of it the thought of having made provision for the outbreak of a fresh war is a right one. As, however, it assumes the possibility of a war breaking out in the near or distant future, it is basically wrong and ineffectual.

3. The power of Greater Germany in the strategic areas acquired in this war should result in the existing population of these areas feeling themselves politically, economically, and militarily to be completely dependent on Germany.* If the following results are achieved: that expansion is undertaken (on a scale I shall describe later) by means of the military measures for occupation taken during the war—that French powers of resistance (popular unity, mineral resources, industry, armed forces) are so broken that a revival must be considered out of the question—that the smaller states, such as the Netherlands, Denmark, and Norway are forced into a dependence on us which will enable us in any circumstances and at any time, easily to occupy these countries again †—then in practice the same, but psychologically much more, will be achieved.

The solution given above, therefore, appears to be the proper one, that is, to crush France, to occupy Belgium, part of North and East France, to allow the Netherlands, Denmark, and Norway to exist on the basis indicated above. To straighten out relations with Switzerland.

The possession of Iceland would mean material strategic expansion for Germany. ‡

II. I would advise against the creation of bases in North and South America, Asia, or Australia. On the other hand, contiguous possessions in Central Africa are considered extremely desirable—possessions which are made up of the area between Senegal and the Congo and stretch east as far as German East Africa—that is, they comprise: the French possessions, say, south of the line of latitude running through the mouth of the Senegal, the former German colonies of Central Africa and the Belgian Congo. For the purpose of rounding off this area, German Southwest Africa could be considered as exchange territory for British or Portuguese possessions.§

The acquisition of one or more bases on the groups of islands off Africa would be of the greatest importance, and besides this the possession of Madagascar and the French groups of islands in the Indian Ocean.

Time will show how far the outcome of the war with England will make an extension of these demands possible.

At his first conference with Hitler following the French request for an armistice,[69] Raeder remarked on the importance, from a naval standpoint, of obtaining bases on the Atlantic Coast of Africa, "for example, Dakar." Hitler's rejoinder, if any, was not recorded, but he did declare

---

* Marginal pencil notation: "What does this mean in Norway's case?"

† Marginal pencil notation: "No, I can't agree there as far as Trondheim is concerned. If we clear right out of Trondheim the British could make difficulties again one fine day. We must have Trondheim!"

‡ Marginal pencil notation: "Yes."

§ Marginal pencil notation: "Yes."

his intention "to use Madagascar for settling Jews under French supervision." Raeder was unimpressed and countered with the suggestion
that Madagascar be turned over to Portugal in exchange for "the northeastern portion of Portuguese Angola," to strengthen Germany's position in the Atlantic.

Early in July, Hitler and Raeder were again peering into the
future.[70] The *Grossadmiral*, in line with the views in the pencil notes
on Fricke's memorandum, had decided that Trondheim was his for
keeps: "The Navy has begun planning the naval base; it requests to
be put in charge of base installations, since the over-all plan will have
to be co-ordinated." Hitler reacted in a characteristically rhapsodic
vein:

The Fuehrer wishes to make Trondheim a base with extensive defenses
against both land and sea attack. . . . There must be facilities for construct-
ing the largest ships. . . . A beautiful German city is to be built on the fiord,
separate from Trondheim. . . . The Fuehrer agrees that private firms may
be commissioned to build the shipyard. A super-highway is to be built via
Luebeck, Fehmarn bridge, Zeeland, Helsingoer bridge, Sweden, Trondheim.

Possibly the railway to Narvik could be given to Sweden in exchange for
the extraterritorial use of Swedish soil. The Trondheim-Kirkenes road will be
widened and improved; parts of it will have to be blasted out of rock, entail-
ing ten to fifteen years' work.

Later in the same meeting Raeder again stressed the Navy's need
for Dakar and pooh-poohed Madagascar as "of less importance, since
the Atlantic remains the main theater of war." Hitler then came up
with a new idea; French Morocco was to be turned over to Spain, in
return for which Germany would "acquire one of the Canary Islands
from Spain," the Navy to select the most suitable for its purposes.

Meanwhile, Hitler and Goering had been shaping the new Greater
Reich's continental design. Luxembourg and Norway were both to be
incorporated in the Reich, according to Goering's report to a gathering
at his headquarters on June 19, 1940.[71] Alsace and Lorraine were of
course to be annexed; furthermore, independent states were to be
established in Brittany and Burgundy. The future of Belgium was unclear.

Breton and Burgundian independence were fantastic and short-lived
ideas. Early in August enforcement of the "Black Line" ban was relaxed, and the line itself was moved east from Burgundy toward
Belfort.[72] The Battle of Britain and plans for *Sea Lion* (the German
cover-name for the projected invasion of Britain) then pushed annexa-

tionist thoughts into the background until September, when it became plain that Britain would not capitulate and that no end to the war was in sight.

On September 6 Raeder seized an opportunity [73] to ask what sort of program Hitler had in mind, and returned to his favorite African theme: "the extreme importance of Dakar for Germany in this war." Again Hitler responded with talk of the Canary Islands; matters were right back where they had been two months earlier. Raeder then inquired about "the Fuehrer's plan regarding treatment of the occupied northern areas, and Sweden and Finland," with the following result:

> The Fuehrer conceives a north Germanic union in which the individual members have a certain sovereignty (diplomatic representation, etc.) and have armed forces trained and equipped by them but organized on the pattern of the German Wehrmacht. Otherwise, however, they should be both politically and economically closely connected with Germany. These are the views of Quisling, whose standpoint the Fuehrer recognizes to be the correct one as opposed to that of Terboven, the Foreign Office, and Von Falkenhorst; the Navy alone, moreover, held these views, quite rightly, from the very first.

The parallel between these observations and the recommendations in paragraph I(3) of Fricke's memorandum is readily apparent.

Later that month, as the prospect of undertaking *Sea Lion* became increasingly remote, Hitler's mind turned toward Gibraltar as the only remaining spot on the continent where he could strike directly at British power. But this project depended on Franco's collaboration, and El Caudillo was sure to demand a substantial *quid pro quo*. Italian and Spanish (to say nothing of German) goals in the Mediterranean and Africa could be satisfied only at the expense of France, and this drew Hitler's attention back to the possibility of a dictated "settlement" in western Europe. On September 16 Halder learned [74] that Spain would be offered "concessions" in French Morocco and French West and Equatorial Africa. Otto Abetz had "been instructed to bring about the formation of a French Cabinet that would accept a harsh peace," but that wily envoy was not optimistic that this could be accomplished.

Two weeks later Brauchitsch returned to Fontainebleau after a visit to Berlin and informed Halder [75] that "Germany's demands on France are not by any means fixed yet." However:

> It seems that annexation of Alsace-Lorraine and portions of Burgundy is a foregone conclusion. On the question of the departments in northern

France [Pas-de-Calais and Nord], however, there seems to be still some wa-
vering. In any event, the issue of the northeastern frontier is going to be impressed so emphatically on the minds of the French people that in the end
they will deem themselves lucky to get off with a whole skin at least in that
corner. In addition, Germany puts forward a claim to the Azores, the Canary
Islands, and Dakar (to be obtained by exchange, if necessary), as well as to
that often-discussed strip of Africa from the west coast across the continent
to the east coast.*

With such thoughts running through his head, Hitler went off to
the Brenner Pass on October 4 to confer with Mussolini. Before his
departure, the Fuehrer was realistic and cynical enough to observe
privately that the reconciliation of conflicting French, Italian, and
Spanish interests in Africa would be possible "only by a gigantic
fraud." [76] Truer words were never spoken, for Hitler's only hope of
winning over the French lay in resisting the temptation to gouge them,
while Italy and Spain could be satisfied only at French expense. This
emerged clearly enough from the settlement terms discussed at the
Brenner Pass, as subsequently reported to Halder by his friend Hasso
von Etzdorf † of the Foreign Office: [77]

Duce: Demands 8,000 square kilometers; 1,000 in Nice area and 7,000
in Corsica, Tunisia, and Djibouti.
Fuehrer: German demands. Alsace-Lorraine with certain corrections to
round out territory. Colonial bases on West African coast. Return of old colonies with certain corrections. . . . Trondheim as permanent German naval
base. Might accept one of the Canary Islands instead of Agadir or some
other base on the coast of Northwest Africa.
Spanish demands: Gibraltar, Morocco, Oran. If France hears that she
will cease defending her colonies and play them into British hands. . . .
The question now is to find a suitable compromise between Spain and
France.
Duce: . . . is in general agreement with the ideas developed by the
Fuehrer. Wants to know the size of France's future population.
Fuehrer: Perhaps 38, possibly even 40 million. Germany wants Alsace-
Lorraine. Also the iron ore basin of Briey and a border corridor south of
Belfort. Claims to northern France are contingent on the development of our
relations with Holland and Belgium. The Netherlands, with which we have
only loose ties, are to be left independent, mainly on account of their colo-
nial possessions. Belgium on the other hand would have to change her am-
biguous position and come out squarely for Germany. If she does, she might

* That is, from former German West Africa to German East Africa.
† Etzdorf, who held the rank of Legation Councilor, was the liaison officer between the Foreign Office and OKH. His account of this meeting is more detailed
than, but tallies generally with, that of Ciano.[78]

be allowed to remain a sovereign state; in any event, Germany would have to keep bases on the coast.

Hitler also revealed that he planned to confer separately with Franco and Pétain later in the month, and the conversation then turned to military matters. The Hitler-Franco meeting took place at Hendaye on the Hispano-French frontier on October 23; it was a most trying experience for the Fuehrer, and no agreements were reached. Next day he received Pétain in his railway car at Montoire. The old Marshal was dignified and circumspect and Hitler was favorably impressed. He explained to Pétain that "someone has to pay for the loss of war" and that it would be the French * unless they helped bring Britain to terms. But everything was left up in the air and Hitler returned to Germany in a great state of dissatisfaction.⁷⁹ His temper was not improved when he learned that Italy was about to invade Greece, a move of which Mussolini had given no inkling at the Brenner barely three weeks earlier.

That was virtually the end of the Axis plans to redraw the map of western Europe and Africa. Within a short time Italy was mired in Greece and retreating in Libya, and nine months later the Germans were engaged in Russia, the Balkans, Greece, Crete, and North Africa.

Thus the "New Order for Western Europe" degenerated rapidly into *Festung Europa*. As Arnold Toynbee has remarked,⁸⁰ "Direct annexations were the only changes in the political conditions of Hitler's Europe in which Hitler himself showed an interest." He lacked the first faculty of the successful conqueror; he could only smash and grab and was quite incapable of putting anything back together. And of all the highly skilled generals and admirals who led the Wehrmacht to victory from the North Cape to the Pyrenees, there was none with the clarity of vision and strength of will to guide the Fuehrer toward a more prudent course of action.

It is the remarkable fact that these dazzling triumphs brought the generals little popular acclaim and no new or revived power or influence in the Fatherland. In World War I the names of Hindenburg and Ludendorff were on every tongue; they outshone and eventually dominated even the Kaiser, "Supreme Warlord" though he was.

But Adolf Hitler was taking no chances on anything of that kind. Whatever his shortcomings as a conqueror, he was still more than a

---

* That same day Brauchitsch told Halder (H. D., Oct. 24, 1940) that Pétain had been told that "France will have to cede territory in the Nice area (not the city itself), Corsica, Tunisia down to Lake Chad [*sic*], and Djibouti."

match for the generals at political in-fighting and domestic public relations. These faculties were strikingly demonstrated on July 19, 1940, at the Kroll Opera House victory celebration where the Fuehrer, ostensibly honoring the generals, wove tighter the web of isolated subservience in which they were enmeshed.

"On Ev'ry Side Field Marshals Gleam'd"

While paying his respects to the Little Corporal at the Invalides, the Fuehrer was also pondering how best to celebrate the victory that had brought him there. He had been attracted by the idea of a gigantic "Paris Victory Parade," and Halder's staff was already busy making arrangements for the spectacle.[81]

Hitler then went off to Leeb's front, to view the operations that had breached the Maginot Line. He was in high spirits, and Albert Speer, then his pet architect, was summoned to the new headquarters in the Black Forest to review the public building plans for Berlin in the light of what Hitler had seen in Paris.[82]

Early in July [83] Hitler returned to Berlin, where all government ministers and high party officials were bidden to the Anhalter Station to receive the great man. Even Hjalmar Schacht was on hand for the occasion, and Hitler could not resist twitting him with the query: "Well, Herr Schacht, what do you say now?" For once the stiff-necked "old wizard" said the right thing—simply "May God protect you." [84]

But the Fuehrer felt no such need. He was now planning a triumphal Reichstag session, to be attended by all corps, army, and army group commanders and a few special heroes of lower rank. This was to be the occasion not only for a shower of promotions but also for a major speech in which Hitler would magnanimously hold out the olive branch to the British and demonstrate the folly of their continuing the war. After one postponement in the expectation of a "reshuffle of the British cabinet," [85] the date was set for Friday, July 19, 1940.

Meanwhile, elaborate rehearsals for the Paris parade were in process. Guderian and the staff of his panzer group were sent in, with a great number of the largest and newest tanks, the Mark IIIs and IVs. On July 9 *Paris-Soir,* then being published in Marseilles, carried reports that the Avenue de la Grande Armée and the Avenue Foch were the scene of military calisthenic displays and massed motorcycle maneuvers, and that the Place de la Concorde was decorated with fasces and Nazi flags, and the Étoile with blue hortensias.

The French reporter inferred that the parade would take place on Bastille Day, but the Germans were not quite that insensitive. In fact, the whole idea was under the cloud of second thoughts. There were disturbing rumors that the Royal Air Force might not let such an occasion pass unnoticed.[86] On July 16 Halder noted that "the decision on the Paris parade is still hanging fire"; the situation had grown "intolerable," especially since the tanks held in Paris could not be shopped for repairs. In the end the parade did not take place at all, and on July 20 Halder's staff was told to break up and reassign the parade units.[87]

Berlin had its parade on July 18, when the locally conscripted 218th Infantry Division marched through the Brandenburger Tor. It was rather a tame affair; Hitler did not attend, and the troops were received by Goebbels and General Fromm, Commander of the Home Army.[88] However, the hotels were soon overflowing with generals summoned for the morrow's big show in the Kroll Opera House.

According to William Shirer, an eyewitness reporter of that evening's doings,[89] Hitler was at the top of his form, "so wonderful an actor, so magnificent a handler of the German mind, that he mixed superbly the full confidence of the conqueror with the humbleness which always goes down so well with the masses when they know a man is on top." Arrogant and impossible as the "peace offer" sounded in British ears, it was a masterpiece of domestic political propaganda. Ciano, Quisling, and a number of Balkan emissaries were in attendance, and their servile behavior in the diplomatic box left no doubt who was the master of Europe.

Row on row, the generals and a sprinkling of admirals sat in the first balcony, a solid mass glittering with gold epaulets and decorations, including many a spanking new *Ritterkreuz*. The officer corps was there to be honored, but even as Hitler spoke its stature dwindled. This was no mere chief of state, graciously and gratefully applauding the exploits of a Wellington or Nelson, a Foch or Pershing. This was the very Author of Victory—this was Napoleon or Frederick the Great, pausing to acknowledge that his assistants had indeed been of service, and favoring them with a smile and a new spangle for the breast or shoulder.

How had the downfall of France been so rapidly and cheaply encompassed? The French and British were planning to occupy the Low Countries and thereafter the Ruhr. "I advised the German forces of the possibility of such a development and gave them the necessary detailed orders." Early in May the enemy was about to carry out his nefarious plan.° "I therefore gave orders for an immediate attack. . . . Contrary to the Schlieffen plan of 1914, I arranged for the operation to bear mainly on the left wing of the front, where the break-through was to be made. . . . As a second operation I planned to aim for the Seine and Loire rivers and also to get a position on the Somme and the Aisne from which the third attack could be made."

Small wonder that the observant Shirer thought Halder the "saddest figure" in that martial assemblage, as Hitler calmly assumed parenthood of all the General Staff's brain children of the recent weeks of triumph. And yet one cannot altogether blame Hitler for his egoism, for he had indeed contributed to the planning, and some of the generals had flattered him shamelessly. Keitel, observing the triumphant jig when the French sued for peace, had declaimed: [90] "My Fuehrer, you are the greatest military captain of all time!" And now this subservience was rewarded, for Hitler, after mentioning the principal army commanders, picked out Keitel and Jodl for the highest praise; it was they who "played the chief part in the realization of my plans and ideas."

Then came the promotions, as from a cornucopia: [91] "As the name of each promoted officer was called he arose and saluted Hitler with raised right arm. And when he sat down he had to shake hands with all his colleagues in the immediate vicinity, and there was much slapping of backs and smiling among the officers."

The process must have taken some time. A full dozen marshals' batons were handed out, and a thirteenth, jumbo-size, for Goering, who received the newly created rank of *Reichsmarschall des Grossdeutschen Reiches*. There were also nineteen promotions to *Generaloberst*, one to *Generaladmiral*, and seven to *General*.

This was no mere burst of Hitlerian generosity. It was a deliberate and highly successful maneuver to debase the coinage of military rank. Throughout World War I, the Kaiser had named only five *Generalfeldmarschaelle* from the officer corps;† now there were twelve before World War II was a year old. No doubt each was gratified to attain the highest rank, but even the least sensitive among them must have perceived that the batons were sadly cheapened by their profusion.[92]

° Shirer wrote (*Berlin Diary*, p. 454): "I noticed again, too, that he can tell a lie with as straight a face as any man."

† Hindenburg, Buelow, Mackensen, Woyrsch, and Eichhorn. In addition, field marshal's rank was conferred on six members (variously dukes, princes, and kings) of the royal houses of Saxony, Wuerttemberg, Bavaria, and Austria, on three allied monarchs, and on the Austrian Chief of Staff, Graf Conrad von Hoetzendorf.

The result was a perfect illustration of W. S. Gilbert's apothegm: "When ev'ryone is somebodee, then no one's anybody." *

Hermann Goering, however, had no reason to be plagued by these sour doubts. Ensconced above the multitude in the Speaker's chair, he watched the proceedings in high glee. When Hitler handed him a box containing the new baton, the proud recipient "could not deny himself a sneaking glance under the cover of the lid." [93] The promotional citation hailed him as "the creator of the Luftwaffe," and he was awarded the Grand Cross of the Iron Cross.† There was to be a brand-new uniform, with gold crossed batons on one collar tab and a golden Reich eagle on the other. This gave rise to some hilarity, but *unser Hermann* could not have been more pleased with his new baubles,[94] and in the all-time German military rank list the name of Reichsmarschall Hermann Goering, like Abou ben Adhem's, leads all the rest.

The army promotions reflected both traditional German seniority practice and political favoritism. Ten officers held the rank of *Generaloberst;* all were promoted to *Generalfeldmarschall* except the ever-unlucky Blaskowitz, who thus became, and remained throughout the war, the senior *Generaloberst.* Among the new marshals Brauchitsch was given seniority, but Keitel was moved ahead of Rundstedt, Bock, and Leeb,‡ much to the disgust of the older members of the officer corps, who regarded Keitel as a mere clerk to the Fuehrer.

The fourteen new Army *Generalobersten* were headed by Halder, § and included the five *Generale* (Dollmann, Weichs, Busch, Kuechler, and Strauss) who had commanded armies and the three (Kleist,

---

* On ev'ry side Field Marshals gleam'd,
Small beer were Lords Lieutenant deem'd,
With Admirals the Ocean teem'd
Around his wide dominions. . . .

In short, whoever you may be,
To this conclusion you'll agree,
When ev'ry one is somebodee,
Then no one's anybody.
    —*The Gondoliers,* Act II

† The only such award in World War II. The five previous recipients were Hindenburg, Ludendorff, Mackensen, Prince Leopold of Bavaria, and Kaiser Wilhelm II himself.[95]

‡ The seniority order of the field marshals was Brauchitsch, Keitel, Rundstedt, Bock, Leeb, List, Kluge, Witzleben, and Reichenau.

§ Shirer (*Berlin Diary,* p. 457) writes that younger generals were promoted over Halder to *Generalfeldmarschall,* but in fact all the army officers promoted to that rank except Reichenau were older than and had always outranked Halder. Reichenau was the same age and had outranked Halder since 1935.

Guderian, and Hoth) panzer group commanders. The other five were Falkenhorst of Norway, Fromm of the Home Army, and three corps commanders: Schobert, Haase, and Hoepner. The elevation of the pro-Nazi Schobert was arrant favoritism, as his corps had not been prominent until the taking of Verdun in the last phase of the campaign, when the French were already beaten.[96] A number of senior corps commanders were passed over, including Wietersheim, who had led a mechanized corps with great success, but had been under a cloud of displeasure since August 1938, when he contradicted Hitler at the Obersalzberg.[97]

Two army officers of lesser rank were signally honored at the Kroll Opera House. One was Jodl, who was given a double jump from *Generalmajor* to *General der Artillerie*. The other was Dietl, who had been made a *Generalleutnant* only three months earlier and was now promoted to *General der Gebirgstruppen*. This doughty Bavarian mountaineer was, next to Goering, the lion of the hour. He was photographed with the Fuehrer, who hailed him as *der Held von Narvik* and presented to him the *Ritterkreuz* with Oak Leaves (*Eichenlaub*)—the highest order of the Iron Cross awarded for heroism up to that time. All this was in tune with Hitler's policy that special public acclaim should attend only those generals whose exploits took place far from the homeland, a preference from which Rommel was soon to profit in Africa.

Dietl was honored for his role in the Norwegian campaign, and that venture had been primarily a Navy show. But this was not the Navy's night. "A full appreciation of the achievements of the German Navy and its leaders cannot be given before the end of the war," Hitler declared. Perhaps he feared that the story, however guardedly told, might reveal the crippling losses which the Navy had suffered and thus put heart into the British at the very time that he was trying to frighten them into suing for peace. Whatever the reason, the only admiral who rose to salute and be promoted was Rolf Carls, the "Blue Czar," whose memorandum had touched off *Weseruebung* [98] and who was now advanced to the rank of *Generaladmiral.**

The Luftwaffe had no such cause for complaint. In addition to Goering's unprecedented elevation, three of his subordinates were

---

* Raeder was already a *Grossadmiral*, and the next ranking officer, Saalwaechter, had been promoted to *Generaladmiral* on January 1, 1940. It appears to have been the policy that only the Commander-in-Chief of the Navy should hold the rank of *Grossadmiral*, which was thus conferred on Doenitz when he succeeded Raeder as Commander-in-Chief in 1943.

made *Generalfeldmarschaelle*—Milch, who was already a *Generaloberst,* and Kesselring * and Sperrle, the two *Luftflotte* commanders of the Battle of France, who were double-jumped from their previous rank of *General der Flieger.* There were five promotions to *Generaloberst* (Stumpff, Grauert, Keller, Weise, and Udet) and five to *General der Flieger,* including the young Chief of Staff, Jeschonnek, who (like Jodl) was double-jumped from *Generalmajor.* The other four were Geissler, Loerzer, Greim, and Richthofen.

This gala evening ended with *Deutschland ueber Alles* and the *Horst Wessel* song. The army leaders then went off on leave or returned to their headquarters and the congratulations of their staffs, while the Luftwaffe generals repaired to Goering's Karinhall to celebrate.

The promotions announced at the Kroll Opera House were not, of course, the only ones given out following the victory in the West. In the Army, for example, during the summer of 1940 there were twenty-six additional promotions to *General* (junior corps commanders such as Manstein, Schmidt, and Reinhardt, and senior staff officers such as Sodenstern), twenty-seven to *Generalleutnant,* and thirty-three to *Generalmajor.* The result was that, although the Army was much the same size in August that it had been in May, there were half again as many generals of the top three grades, and almost two and a half times as many of the top two.†

"In my capacity as Fuehrer and Chief of State," Hitler once declared,[100] "I am obliged to stand out clearly from amongst all the people around me. If my close associates glitter with decorations, I can distinguish myself from them only by wearing none at all." ‡ Berlin wits had it that Goering deliberately fattened himself so that he would have space for more medals than anyone else.

The contrast bespeaks Hitler's immeasurable superiority to Goering in political acumen and grasp of the true elements of power. He was above rank, and he knew that the best way to prevent any of the generals from exploiting victory for political purposes was to render them indistinguishable one from another. "They're cheaper by the dozen" was the sardonic comment of many [101] on the new *Generalfeld-*

---

* Kesselring, at least, would have preferred the rank of *Luftmarschall,* after the British practice. But Goering said he preferred *Generalfeldmarschall* to ensure full equality with the army field marshals.[99]

† In May there were no *Generalfeldmarschaelle,* ten *Generalobersten,* and thirty-six *Generale,* for a total of forty-six. After August 1 the comparable figures were nine, fifteen, and forty-seven, for a total of seventy-one. See the rank and assignment lists Appendix B, *infra,* pp. 399–408.

‡ It was, however, Hitler's habit to wear his World War I Iron Cross.

marschaelle of the Kroll Opera House festival. At the same time, the generals' thirst for higher rank was slaked. They were "fattened on titles, decorations, and gifts," [102] and there was small chance for any malcontent to win a following.

To be sure, there were few enough generals with potential political individuality, and victory in the West had stilled the whisperings of opposition that had been barely audible before Munich and during the late fall of 1939.[103] Nevertheless, the very magnitude of the Army's achievement was a reminder of old traditions and past glories.

Brauchitsch and Halder, at least, glimpsed a hope that the officer corps might regain its once proud niche in the structure of the Reich. In August they conferred at length [104] on the "future tasks" of the General Staff, with a view to re-establishing its leadership in the field of military education. The recognized tendency to "one-sidedness" was especially to be combatted, so that the officer corps might acquire "the cultural background required for its leadership function."

Brauchitsch also sought to establish himself as a public personality. After all, he was Commander-in-Chief and ranking *Generalfeldmarschall* of the mightiest and most successful German Army since the Franco-Prussian War. If anyone was in a position to don the mantle of Moltke, it was he. But his aspirations, however seriously entertained, came to nothing. Early in September,[105] Halder found him "very bitter about the obstacles put in his way whenever he wants to reach the public." The two military men concluded that "the Fuehrer obviously is jealous." Jealous or not, Hitler certainly gave Brauchitsch no chance to spread his wings.*

"The Army fights anonymously as far as its leadership goes," wrote von Hassell [107] at the time of Dunkirk. "One can clearly see what this will lead to: the destruction of everything that remains of the old tradition." Little enough remained even then. The *rocher de bronze* which had so remarkably endured the defeat of 1918 and the death of the imperial regime was already and hopelessly corroded by the vitriol of Nazism.

In 1938—the year of the *Blumenkriege* and the Blomberg-Fritsch crisis—Hitler shattered the leadership of the German officer corps and bent the generals to his will.[108] In 1940, by shrewd tactics of which

---

* Halder, it may be noted, was equally unreceptive to Rommel's publicity-seeking and declined to approve the public release of the many photographs of the 7th Panzer Division in action, which Rommel had had taken and assembled for publication.[106]

the Kroll Opera House celebration is the prime example, Hitler converted the generals' stunning victories to his own uses, and thus perpetuated his own domination of the officer corps. He made them pay dearly for their batons and stars and medals. The price was a powerless anonymity, and it is chiefly remarkable that so few of the generals sensed the cost, and that so many were content with their mess of pottage.

CHAPTER TEN

The Breaking Wave

"THE FINAL GERMAN VICTORY over England is only a question of time. The enemy is no longer capable of offensive operations on a large scale." So wrote Alfred Jodl, Hitler's closest strategic adviser, on June 30, 1940, in a memorandum on "the further conduct of the war against England." [1]

The outcome of the war was, to be sure, a "question of time," though not in the sense of Jodl's complacent comment. The Wehrmacht was to win many more battles and conquer vast reaches in eastern Europe. But the victory in the West was Germany's last in which a major campaign was brought to a triumphant conclusion. Except in secondary theaters of war such as Yugoslavia and Greece, the Wehrmacht never again achieved its goal. The wave was to wash far up the beach, but it had reached its crest and was beginning to curl over.

In the West, Hitler and the generals accomplished precisely what they set out to do. But it was not enough to win the war. Was this failure the result of strategic error, and could the downfall of Britain have been accomplished by a different course of action?

In post mortem, it has been suggested that Hitler should have attempted an invasion of England immediately after Dunkirk. [2] The argument is that the French Army south of the Somme was so enfeebled that it could not possibly threaten the Germans, and that the British were then at their weakest, with a disorganized and ill-equipped army, while the Germans had more divisions than they could possibly use in Europe.

Manstein himself is said to have expressed such views in the summer of 1940. Bernhard von Lossberg, then an *Oberstleutnant* at OKW, has described a visit to Manstein's headquarters at that time, in the course of which the latter declared: "After the victory in the encirclement battle of Flanders-Artois, we should have improvised, by every means, a pursuit of the English, and attempted a landing. The elimination of the remaining French forces was a comparatively unimportant matter. The French forces were not dangerous, as they were hardly capable of attacking. Instead, we wasted time in talk and gave the English time to organize their defenses."

However, the German Army could neither fly nor walk on the water, and in June of 1940 there was no shipping available to transport an assault force of sufficient size or maintain it if an initial landing were successful, nor had any troops been trained for amphibious operations. In July, when the generals began to examine the practical possibility of a cross-Channel operation, Halder recorded [3] the Navy's estimate that it would take two months to assemble the necessary shipping. Thereafter extensive amphibious training exercises were commenced. Lacking the shipping and the training, a German landing in England was simply out of the question at the time of Dunkirk, and there is no record that any such proposal was then made.

To have invaded Britain during the very course of the Battle of France, the venture must have been envisaged beforehand and prepared for as a sequel to the fighting in Flanders. The shipping must have been assembled and the invasion forces earmarked and trained, as an integral part of the operational plan *Gelb,* so that all would be in readiness when Dunkirk or its equivalent opened the door of opportunity.[4]

With sufficient foresight and boldness this could have been done, but only at the expense of preparations for the coming and crucial test of strength with the Allied armies on the continent, the outcome of which no man could foresee with certainty. A substantial force of highly trained and combat-worthy troops with supporting aircraft would have had to be kept out of the Battle of France and reserved for the contingency of a Battle of England. The Reich transportation system, already badly strained, would have had to assume additional and onerous burdens.

No doubt the prospect of decisive victory over Britain was worth all this and more. But to envision and start preparing for the opportunity of invading England, while the Allied armies were still deployed in full strength in northern France, would have required a very daring strategy. Certainly neither Manstein nor any of the other principal architects of the German victory advanced such a plan when *Gelb* was being formulated.

Raeder, it is true, had directed his staff as early as November 15, 1939, to prepare plans for a landing in England.[5] But this was undertaken not because Raeder then expected or favored such an operation but rather as a measure of prudence in case Hitler's thoughts should turn in that direction, so as not to be caught unprepared. And Raeder, after all, was the chief sponsor of operation *Weseruebung* in Scandinavia, which, whatever its military justification,[6] ruled out all possibility of a contemporaneous cross-Channel invasion and left the German Navy critically depleted for a subsequent attempt.

Winston Churchill has posed an interesting variant of the problem: [7]

If Hitler had been gifted with supernatural wisdom, he would have slowed down the attack on the French front, making a pause of three or four weeks after Dunkirk on the line of the Seine, and meanwhile developing his preparations to invade England. Thus he would have had a deadly option, and could have tortured us with the hooks of either deserting France in her agony or squandering the last resources for our future existence. The more we urged the French to fight on, the greater was our obligation to aid them, and the more difficult it would have become to make any preparations for defense in England, and above all to keep in reserve the twenty-five squadrons of fighter aircraft on which all depended. On this point we should never have given way, but the refusal would have been bitterly resented by our struggling ally, and would have poisoned all our relations.

But Mr. Churchill does not say how, from Hitler's standpoint, the "deadly option" should have been exercised. To torture the British with a dilemma no doubt would have been gratifying to the Fuehrer, but sooner or later he would have had to resolve his own. If the decision was to eliminate France from the war, what was to be gained by waiting for three or four weeks? Indeed, by beating down the French, Hitler achieved the "poisoned" Anglo-French relations of which Churchill speaks, as Oran was soon to demonstrate. If the decision was to invade England, then the only questions are whether the necessary preparations could have been begun sooner or been more effective than they in fact were, and whether a necessary consequence was abandonment of the Somme-Aisne offensive. These are in fact the questions which are basic to a strategic evaluation of Germany's victory in the Battle of France, and which no doubt were in Manstein's mind if he spoke as reported by Lossberg.[8]

Britain, after all, could only be brought to terms by a successful invasion or by such pressure—the threat of invasion, blockade, and the elimination of potential allies—as would convince her that the military situation was hopeless. To achieve either circumstance, and whether or not an invasion was ever attempted, it should from the outset have been the primary aim of German strategy to follow up any advantage and deal Britain the most punishing blows of which the Wehrmacht was capable. This is what Hitler and the generals failed to grasp.

But was not Hitler well within the realm of reasonable probability in relying on the British to yield in the event the French were knocked out of the war? Despite the British moral and the French treaty commitments to Czechoslovakia, Chamberlain had come with his umbrella to Berchtesgaden and Bad Godesberg, and at Munich Chamberlain and Daladier had sacrificed the Czechs and given way to Hitler's demands. In the spring of 1939 Hitler had destroyed the rump Czech state and suffered nothing more than angry mutterings in London and Paris. Daladier was Premier until March 21, 1940, and Chamberlain Prime Minister until May 10, the very day the German attack in the West was launched. In planning that campaign, was Hitler not justified in assuming that these were hardly the men to persist in a desperate struggle after a sharp defeat?

Such a viewpoint is plausible, but as applied to Britain it does not stand analysis. Whatever Hitler's opinion of Chamberlain, there had been abundant evidence of a hardening British attitude, especially after the Germans marched into Prague. In May 1939, when announcing to the generals his decision to attack Poland,[9] Hitler had referred to the coming conflict with England as "a life-and-death struggle," had described her as "the driving force against Germany," and pictured the British as "proud, courageous, tenacious, firm in resistance, and gifted as organizers." Again in November 1939, when Hitler delivered his "pep talk" to the generals,[10] he referred to the English as a "tough enemy," steadily growing stronger. If the account by an SS intelligence officer, the late Walter Schellenberg, may be believed, in private conversation Hitler readily acknowledged the depth of the British will to resist.[11]

All this did not, of course, make it unreasonable for Hitler to *hope* that the British would tire after the French were beaten, and would decide to make the best of what was bound to be, for them, a bad peace. But it was quite another thing to *rely* on such a development, and indeed it is plain that Hitler did not do so. From time to time he spoke optimistically about making the British see reason, but he was never free from the fear that they would not.

Under these circumstances, it was poor strategy to embark on the western offensive without giving careful thought to the contingency—which soon became the actuality—that the Wehrmacht would knock France out of the war, but that the British would fight on alone. This did not entail that amphibious invasion plans should have been laid and the necessary forces and shipping assembled before the offensive was launched. But it did mean that the campaign in the West should at all times have been conducted so as to inflict all possible military harm on the British, and that the leaders of the Wehrmacht should have been alert to exploit every new opportunity to that same end. This principle was valid whether the war proved long or short, but it was doubly important in the light of Hitler's desire to end the fighting as soon as possible, and his refusal to gear the German domestic economy to the harsh requirements of a protracted struggle.[12]

As has been seen, Raeder marked Britain as the main adversary from the outset. Yet the decision to undertake *Weseruebung* shows how far both Raeder and Hitler were from grasping the essence of a concentrated and purposeful anti-British strategy. The danger of a British occupation of Norway had dwindled with the end of the Russo-Finnish War. The defeat of the French would render remote the future possibility of such a move by the British and would likewise provide the German submarine arm with bases on the French coast far more valuable than any that might be gained in Norway. The Scandinavian venture was bound to delay the main offensive in France and Belgium, and if a victory on the mainland led to the opportunity of a following action against Britain, the good weather of the summer months would be invaluable. *Weseruebung* likewise hazarded the entire German Fleet, which, despite its shortcomings, would be sorely needed for any direct action against Britain, whether by invasion or a sustained attack on the shipping that was her lifeblood.

The German Navy suffered shattering losses in Norwegian waters; nevertheless on May 14, the day after the German armored "wedge" broke the French lines on the Meuse, Raeder and his staff laid plans to send the *Scharnhorst* and *Gneisenau* back to the Narvik area.[13] On May 21, the day after Guderian had reached the Channel Coast at Abbéville and cut off the British and French forces in Belgium, Hitler and Raeder privately discussed the possibility of an invasion of Britain. But at the same meeting Hitler approved Raeder's plan to send not only the two battle cruisers but also the *Hipper* and three destroyers toward the Arctic to attack British shipping out of Narvik.[14] Even though encirclement and destruction of the entire B.E.F. was now a possibility, neither the dictator nor the admiral had yet realized that the outcome of the war hung in the balance not at Narvik but by the English Channel.

The same strategic blindness afflicted the generals. When Guderian was halfway across northern France, Halder was still favoring a south-westerly drive to the Somme, instead of cutting off the Allied forces in Belgium.[15] After Guderian reached the coast, he lay idle for a full day for lack of orders telling him where to go next.[16] These bumbles reflected the muddled thinking which led to the two serious errors, of strategic proportions, that the Germans made during the Battle of France. Both occurred during the last week of May, after the victory in Flanders and northern France was assured. One of them—the famous "stop-order" that facilitated the B.E.F.'s withdrawal to Dunkirk for evacuation—has already been fully explored.[17] The other, less apparent at the time, was the unnecessary commitment of the entire German Army and Air Force to the Somme-Aisne offensive, and the failure to commence preparations for an attack on Britain as soon as the victory in northern France and Flanders was assured.

For if one can hardly blame the Wehrmacht leaders for not foresee-ing the rapid and decisive success of *Gelb* before it was begun on May 10, by May 24 the picture was clear. If the French could not launch a counterattack against the southern flank of Kleist's thin armored wedge, they surely could accomplish nothing after the mass of German infantry was deployed along the Somme-Aisne front. With the B.E.F. and the best of the French Army rendered *hors de combat* in May, there was no need in June to throw 136 German divisions against a beaten and demoralized enemy army less than half that size, especially with the overwhelming armored and air superiority which the Germans had achieved. There was absolutely no reason why the assemblage of shipping, and the marshaling and training of an am-phibious assault force,* could not have been begun during the last week of May, or early in June.†

* Subsequent German estimates of the necessary number of divisions for an invasion of Britain varied from thirteen to forty. Of course, not all of the divisions would have been in the first wave. The Germans' problem did not at all lie in numbers but in surmounting the initial obstacles and maintaining the force once it was ashore. By the time of Dunkirk, the Germans could easily have reserved a force of the necessary size, without risk to the success of the Somme-Aisne offen-sive.

† According to Bartz (*Als der Himmel Brante,* p. 25), after Dunkirk both Kesselring and Student put forward the idea of invading Britain, but Goering would not hear of it. Kesselring says nothing of this in his memoirs, although some weeks later he was one of the strongest protagonists of a cross-Channel operation.

Instead, the Germans allowed six weeks to elapse before serious preparations for an invasion were commenced. They had been blind to the possibility of a large-scale evacuation of the B.E.F. by sea and did not soon enough realize that their primary target lay across the water. Hitler and Rundstedt spared the German tanks near Dunkirk, where their expenditure to prevent, or cut the size of, the evacuation would have been strategically invaluable, in order to save them for the Somme-Aisne offensive for which there was already a superabundance of strength.

In short, the Wehrmacht put all of its power into a haymaker directed at the tottering French, vainly hoping that the breeze of the swing would blow down the stubborn British. This was the basic flaw of German strategy in the Battle of France.

On June 4, as the last troops rescued from Dunkirk debarked in England, the *Gneisenau, Scharnhorst, Hipper,* and four destroyers put out from Wilhelmshaven and sailed northward for "Operation Juno." Two weeks had elapsed since Hitler approved Raeder's proposal for this action. Britain's situation, dismal enough then, by now was perilous in the extreme. Yet at this moment of the greatest German opportunity, their fleet was sent off on a dangerous mission of no strategic significance. Several weeks later the two battle cruisers limped back to home ports, damaged beyond hope of repair that year.

It was the last in the succession of the Germans' moves during the western campaign that so clearly demonstrated their lack of coherent strategic objectives. *Weseruebung,* the "stop-order," the wastefully mounted Somme-Aisne offensive and resultant slackening of pressure on the British, and "Juno"—the British cause might ultimately have prevailed even without these strokes of fortune, but surely the Germans' chances of a successful invasion would have been greatly increased. Never was there a better demonstration that wars are more often won and lost by mistakes than by miracles of achievement.

Perhaps the Germans' errors were not irremediable. They had seriously diminished but by no means eliminated the prospects of a successful invasion of Britain. There were other possible courses of action by which the Reich might secure and expand its position on the continent and move toward a successful conclusion of the war.

Was nun? Spoken or unspoken, this ("what now?") was the question uppermost in the minds of all the Reich's military leaders after the Battle of France.[18] The magnitude of the victory they had gained was matched by the difficulty of the riddle they now confronted. Many things might be undertaken, but the Wehrmacht, for all its power in tanks and Stukas, was an unbalanced force, and the national economy had not been geared to a long war against a grand alliance of hostile powers. There was *embarras de choix,* but no *embarras de richesse.*

To be sure, in 1940 there was no grand alliance; there was only Britain. Nevertheless, the possibility that the course of the war might involve Russia or the United States as allies of Britain was the dominant factor in the strategic riddle. The longer the British were able to hold out in their island fortress and maintain the maritime life lines of empire, the more likely they were to attract allies, whether belligerents or benevolent "neutrals," to help them halt the Teutonic march of conquest. The Germans even had a special word—*bundesfaehig* (capable of being an ally)—which they had used in the early days of the Weimar Republic to describe the national status that would have to be regained in order to put an end to Germany's diplomatic isolation following World War I. To avert the strain and danger of a long war against a hostile alliance, it was obviously desirable that Britain be rendered *unbundesfaehig* as soon as possible.

A direct amphibious assault across the Channel, however, posed tactical obstacles which the Wehrmacht had not been designed to surmount, and if it failed, Britain's alliance-worthiness would be greatly increased. Was an indirect strategy therefore preferable? Britain could also be attacked in the Mediterranean and North Africa. But to a considerable degree such a venture presented the same difficulties as did the direct assault on Britain, in that both called for naval power far in excess of Germany's resources.

True, the Italians had a Navy and the French Fleet was now neutralized, so that Axis prospects in the Mediterranean were by no means hopeless. But the German generals were exceedingly reluctant to rely on their Italian brothers-in-arms, and a North African campaign would involve the Wehrmacht in unprecedented tactical problems at the end of long and vulnerable lines of communication. Furthermore, such an expansion of the theater of war and the appearance of German troops on another continent were bound to increase the neutrals' apprehension of the Nazi giant, threaten their economic interests over a broad area, and increase the likelihood of their intervention to restore the balance of power.

One possible course of action would have been for Germany to adopt a passive strategy and leave the next move to the British.[19] This was essentially what Rundstedt and Leeb had advocated before the Battle of France.[20] Man power could have been released from the Army (which was far larger than necessary to garrison Poland and western Europe and guard the Russo-German border) to farm and factory, in order to increase national productivity. Especially if the economy had at once been mobilized for a long war, the Wehrmacht's deficiencies at sea could have been partly eliminated and the Luftwaffe greatly strengthened.

The obvious disadvantage of such a course (which was in fact anticipated by Halder's staff [21] and was hinted by Hitler himself in conference with Raeder just after Dunkirk [22]) was that the British would profit equally and perhaps more from a prolonged opportunity to rest, refit, and build up their arms. With the supporting resources of a friendly America, eventually the Royal Air Force was likely to outstrip the Luftwaffe. If it was hard to envisage that Britain alone could ever marshal an army large enough to land on the continent and defeat the Germans on the ground, it was nevertheless plain that the British Isles could in time be made virtually impregnable. Furthermore, British troops would surely be sent to North Africa and perhaps to Italy to lay Mussolini by the heels.

Accordingly, the passive strategy offered small prospect of inducing the British to make peace. Since Germany's margin of superiority over Britain was bound to dwindle the longer the war lasted, it would be advantageous to strike again at once, while the margin was greatest.

Of course, if a passive military strategy had been coupled with a radical shift in political and economic policies, Germany might have ultimately secured an advantageous peace. The restoration of national sovereignty in Poland and Czechoslovakia even with territorial annexations by the Reich, mild and enlightened occupation policies in the defeated nations of western Europe, abandonment of the Nazi racial policies—these and other like measures would have vastly diminished the chance of Britain's finding allies and might have enabled Hitler to establish a sort of European union dominated by Germany. It is interesting to reflect that the presently unmilitaristic West German Federal Republic may succeed in accomplishing just this. Theoretically, such a course was open to the Germans in 1940, but to follow it the Third Reich would have to have been a government quite different from what it was in fact.

After the fall of France, the Germans had their choice of two basic strategies to defeat Britain and win the war. One was to seek a speedy victory by direct assault—naval and aerial attacks on shipping, Luftwaffe bombardment of the British homeland, and amphibious operations to establish a bridgehead base for an invasion. The other was by force and threats to expand Germany's economic and military basis in Europe, North Africa, and if possible the Middle East, aiming for victory or at worst a stalemate in a long war with Britain and whatever other powers might join with her.

These two alternatives were clearly enough set forth by Jodl, in the memorandum of June 30 quoted at the beginning of this chapter. "If political means do not attain the goal," he wrote, "then English resistance must be broken either (a) by an attack against the English motherland, or (b) by broadening the war to the periphery." The first course of action might be pursued by a sea and air economic blockade together with an assault against the Royal Air Force and the island's industrial resources, by a terror attack on population centers, or by an invasion and occupation. But an invasion could be attempted only when British air power had been destroyed—perhaps by the end of August or early September. The second avenue to victory—a war against the British Empire—could be conducted through countries that would be glad to see the downfall of English world power, such as Italy, Spain, Russia, and perhaps the Arab lands.

The two alternatives posed by Jodl were not absolutely exclusive of each other. If the first was tried and failed, the second would be prejudiced but by no means foreclosed. Furthermore, the long-term, indirect approach admitted of very wide variations in time, place, and scope.

Within this range of flexibility, however, the question "What now?" ought to have been answered, at the latest in June, with a vigorous program of military action shaped and concentrated in pursuance of one strategy or the other. Instead, the leaders of the Wehrmacht fiddled around for a full month with secondary matters of military administration, and plans for victory parades. Keitel opined that, with the defeat of France, "the task of the Army in this war will be essentially fulfilled," and that the Navy and Luftwaffe should take over chief responsibility for further hostilities against England. Two weeks after Dunkirk, the OKW had done no preparatory work for an invasion.[23] The mechanics of demobilizing part of the Army moved to the forefront of the German military mind.[24]

Hitler himself dawdled in the Black Forest and then went to Berlin to prepare his combination peace offer and victory speech at the Kroll Opera House. Perhaps he imagined that he was allowing the British time to adjust their outlook in the direction of peace, but in fact he was giving them an invaluable breathing spell in which to organize and improvise their defenses against invasion. Thus still another strategic error was added to those committed during the Battle of France.

It is a never-ending post mortem to speculate on whether or not *Sea Lion* would have succeeded had it been attempted. In any event, it was not a project of desperation. The army generals, by no means reckless in their appraisals, were prepared to undertake it. Had it succeeded and the British government been driven out of the islands, perhaps, as Churchill vowed,[25] "our Empire beyond the seas . . . would carry on the struggle until, in God's good time, the New World, with all its power and might, steps forth to the rescue and the liberation of the Old." But it may be just as well that the New World was not put to so terrible a test and, if it had been, "God's good time" would certainly not have been brief.

From Hitler's standpoint, the advantages to be gained from a successful invasion of England far outweighed the penalties of failure, painful and embarrassing as they would have been. If *Sea Lion* had failed at an early stage, German losses would hardly have exceeded what the Wehrmacht had been prepared to face in the Battle of France. Since these were in fact so light, Germany had an abundant reserve of trained ground forces, and the Army would have been much less harmed by the sacrifice of a dozen divisions out of 150 than the Luftwaffe was by the losses actually sustained in the Battle of Britain. Furthermore, *Sea Lion* was a venture wholly compatible with the concept of a short war, which certainly could not be said of the Russian venture on which Hitler embarked a year later. And once in command of the British Isles as well as most of Europe, the Axis position would have been so strong that the prospects of its overturn would have appeared remote and desperate.

If, despite these considerations, *Sea Lion* were to be discarded as unpromising of success, there remained the second basic strategy. Hitler and Mussolini could have embarked on a serious and sustained program to gird the Axis for a long war. To enlarge their own resources and pinch the British "life line of Empire," the Axis forces could have embarked on a campaign of conquest in the Balkans, North Africa, and the Middle East. It is altogether possible that such a drive, had it been settled on as the Wehrmacht's prime mission, could not have been stopped much short of Bagdad, the old symbol of German imperial aspirations in the Middle East.

This would scarcely have been to Russia's liking, but even so Soviet intervention would not have been too great a hazard. Russian offensive capabilities were not then formidable, as the Finnish War had shown. A Russian attack on Germany would almost certainly have been unsuccessful and extremely dangerous to the continuance of the Soviet regime, and Germany would have emerged in a very advantageous position. For that very reason such a development was improbable. The denizens of the Kremlin might well have thought it more prudent to throw in their lot with the Axis than with a British Empire so badly mauled.

However that might have turned out, victory in the West opened up to Hitler the prospect—inviting, dangerous, but by no means remote—of extending Germany's dominion over all of southeastern Europe and the Middle East, with Italy as a junior partner in empire. And such a dominion, if not of millennial stability, could have been shattered only after long years of wasting struggle. With the advent of the atomic bomb, the Old World and much of the New might well have been a shambles before the issue was resolved.

If to attack Britain either across the Channel or in the Mediterranean was deemed too hazardous in view of Germany's limited naval power, there still remained another alternative. There were, after all, only two nations—Russia and the United States—sufficiently powerful so that Britain might hope for decisive results from their entry into the war against Germany. If British hopes for ultimate victory depended on eventual alliance with one or both of them, and if Britain herself could not be assaulted, then the solution must be to destroy her prospects of alliance by eliminating her prospective allies! And if the United States lay out of reach across the Atlantic, so much the worse for adjacent Russia, where the all-conquering German Army could again be brought into play.

In fact, this was precisely the way Hitler viewed the strategic situation as soon as it became apparent that the British would fight on despite the fall of France. As early as July 13, 1940, Hitler and the top generals in conference at the Berghof agreed that Britain's "persistent unwillingness to make peace" was only to be explained by her hope of winning Russia to her side.[26] On July 31, 1940, in the same place and circumstances, Hitler put his thesis very explicitly, with the added thought that the destruction of Russia would likewise eliminate the United States as a potential ally of Britain:[27]

Britain's hope lies in Russia and the United States. If Russia drops out of the picture America, too, is lost for Britain, because elimination of Russia would tremendously increase Japan's power in the Far East. . . .

With Russia smashed, Britain's last hope would be shattered. Germany will then be master of Europe and the Balkans.

Decision: Russia's destruction must therefore be made a part of this struggle. Spring '41.

The sooner Russia is crushed the better. Attack achieves its purpose only if Russian State can be shattered to its roots with one blow. . . .

Despite this conclusive language, the decision to invade Russia was not finally reached until some months later. There was a flaw in Hitler's logic which did not escape the attention of Raeder and others who opposed the Russian campaign, and of which, no doubt, Hitler himself was aware. To be sure, the *defeat* of Russia might well have the decisive consequences which he envisaged. But to *attack* Russia was to fulfill the very hope on which Britain was relying, by making Russia willy-nilly Britain's ally.

Furthermore, the immediate result would be a two-front war, against the stupidity of which Hitler had often inveighed. It is hardly surprising, therefore, that he did not finally commit Germany to the Russian venture at once, nor, indeed, until after the Battle of Britain, the abortive preparations for *Sea Lion,* the ill-considered Italian assault on Greece, unsuccessful efforts to persuade Franco to join in capturing Gibraltar, and the emergence of North Africa as a crucial theater of combat with the British.

In July 1940 Hitler and the generals did not, of course, foresee these many developments in the course of the war during the balance of the year. And while these remarkable events were unfolding, the military leaders of the Third Reich were constantly conferring, debating, and preparing memoranda weighing the comparative merits of the possible courses of action that the situation presented.

The invasion of the Soviet Union might have been envisaged as a component or variant of the indirect, long-term strategy of expanding the economic and geographical basis of the Axis. Indeed, the Russian campaign might have had a favorable outcome for Germany had it been geared to sound objectives and coupled with an occupation policy designed to cultivate anti-Bolshevist and Ukrainian separatist sentiments and exploit, without destroying, the resources of the eastern lands overrun by the Wehrmacht.

But that was not at all the way Hitler conceived of *"Barbarossa,"* as the plan of attack on Russia was to be called. As the records of the

July conferences at the Berghof make plain, Hitler regarded *Barbarossa* as an avenue to an early victory over Britain. And in that frame of mind it was to be actually undertaken. The German domestic economy remained under only light restrictions throughout 1940 and 1941, no effort was made to remedy the strategic shortcomings of the Luftwaffe, and the German troops eventually went into Russia with neither the clothing nor the equipment that would be necessary if the fighting lasted into the winter. The Germans' treatment of the Russian population in the occupied areas was both stupid and atrocious. And thus, with full knowledge of Napoleon's experience, and with his own repeated condemnations of a two-front war staring him in the face, Hitler in July of 1940 imagined and planned to bring about Britain's speedy downfall by invading Russia in 1941!

And what about the views of the German generals and admirals in that crucial summer of 1940? There was no unanimity. Raeder strongly urged a campaign in the Mediterranean, and Brauchitsch favored the capture of Gibraltar. By and large, the army generals were optimistic about the prospects of invading Britain, while the admirals were understandably reluctant. Goering puffed the ability of his Luftwaffe to beat the English to their knees. The OKW was quite unable to reconcile or synthesize the conflicting counsels of the three services. The upshot was that the leaders of the Wehrmacht never laid before Hitler a plan of action which commanded their general support.

Thus the Germans staggered, victorious in battle but strategically planless, into this new phase of the war. As a perceptive commentator on those times has written: [28] "The defeat of France completed the easy period of Hitler's war. Thereafter, the position became totally different, the situation far more complex. The problems facing Germany, no less than Great Britain, were problems of a different order from, of vaster dimensions than, those which had been met before. The new situation presented Hitler with almost limitless possibilities. But it also brought him up against hard facts. . . . In comparison with the powers of strategy now demanded, he had so far succeeded by something like rule of thumb."

Difficult and complex alternatives confronted the leaders of the Wehrmacht in June of 1940. Their failure was not that they made wrong choices; even Great Captains make mistakes. The true measure of the Germans' insufficiency as conquerors was that they did not choose decisively, but tardily and inconclusively.

After the Battle of France the same sort of errors that had been made during its course were repeated again and again. Forces were diverted to secondary objectives at the expense of prime ones; too many things were attempted, while nothing was undertaken with sufficient speed and determination.

For example, the Battle of Britain was launched in the hope of knocking out Britain from the air, although the Luftwaffe had been deliberately designed for tactical rather than strategic use. It should never have been undertaken at all except in conjunction with a firmly intended and carefully co-ordinated amphibious assault. The result was that the Luftwaffe was bled white to no purpose. Then it was saddled with new and extensive commitments in the Mediterranean and North Africa at a time when *Barbarossa* was already in an advanced stage of preparation. And just as *Weseruebung* had delayed the major offensive in the West, so the secondary ventures in Yugoslavia and Greece required a costly postponement of the invasion of Russia. Thus the Wehrmacht embarked upon a series of ventures which, so far from comprising a purposeful strategic pattern, were at cross purposes one with another.

And so the leadership of the Wehrmacht let slip the great opportunity that was theirs in the late spring of 1940. They did not settle on either or both of the basic strategic courses that were open to them. They did not press home the direct assault on Britain; neither did they gird themselves for a long war. The Luftwaffe delivered a heavy but costly and indecisive blow against England. The U-boat arm was strengthened, but insufficiently, and the Luftwaffe hardly at all. Rommel was sent to North Africa, where he scored brilliantly, but he was never given enough strength to turn his desert victories into solid strategic gains. Russia was invaded too late, and on the basis of false strategic and logistical premises.

All these things, ultimately fatal to the Wehrmacht and the Third Reich, were the outcome of the failure of basic planning and decision-making after the victory in the West. And that is why the summer of 1940 was, in a strategic sense, the turning point of the war, little though it seemed such at the time. The wave of conquest broke on the shoals of delay and indecision.

What accounted for this failure? Its roots lay deep in Germany's military and political history, beyond the range of full exploration here. Even within the limits of this work, however, the principal causes of the failure are readily discernible.

The crucial strategic decisions were the responsibility of Hitler as

Fuehrer of the Reich and Supreme Commander of the Wehrmacht, and of the military leaders as his professional advisers and field commanders. In immediate terms the failure of German grand strategy was due to Hitler's deficiencies of temperament and education, and the narrow outlook of the German officer corps.

At the moment of decision in 1940, it is probable that the first factor was the more important. To be sure, there was no officer of great strategic gifts at Hitler's elbow. Neither was there any such in the entourages of Frederick the Great or Napoleon. In fact, Hitler was well served tactically by his generals and admirals, and the erratic, stumbling course of German strategy after the Battle of France is directly traceable to his own defects of mind and character.

Hitler was, after all, a demagogue and politician by experience and inclination. In those terms he was a man of extraordinary gifts, but these did not include a Bismarckian mastery of *Grosspolitik*. He had a deep interest in military affairs, as in architecture, but in both fields he was very much an amateur. Fond of poring over detailed information on weapons and order of battle, and phenomenally retentive, Hitler reveled in military discussion and often scored brilliantly. His curiosity and uninhibited approach to military problems sometimes resulted in valuable contributions at the planning sessions.

However, the Fuehrer's phenomenal grasp of military details was insufficient for the solution of strategic problems. Here he was badly handicapped by lack of information and faulty judgment. Hitler was a bit like Sherlock Holmes, who, according to Dr. Watson, was an expert on the varieties of tobacco ash but totally ignorant of the Copernican system. He was in most respects exceedingly provincial. His knowledge of world affairs was superficial, and his mental pictures of foreign lands and peoples were a gallery of stereotypes, titled with clichés. He was erratic and sloppy in his working habits, and these traits reflected a profound instability which precluded steadfastness of purpose and clarity of vision. He wanted to appear hard, cold, and ruthless, and his actions often were governed by that aim. Underneath the overlay, however, Hitler was nervous, indecisive, impulsive, and lacking in self-control.

In the dramatic and critical setting of June 1940, the Fuehrer floundered. Sinister and powerful figure that he was, Hitler was ill-equipped for the Great Captain's role which he now essayed on the stage of history. This was just as well for the world. If patience, tenacity, and strategic vision had been numbered among Hitler's otherwise remarkable and unlovely attributes, the war might have had a far different outcome.

There was, it now appears, a strong ingredient of infantilism in Hitler's make-up. This was why he was never able to choose among the competing strategic alternatives. Like a child, he could not bear to discard any attractive object; no more could he bring himself to give up ground once gained, in the later years of the war.

Insecure and spoiled by adulation and rapid success, Hitler was always shopping at the bargain counter. He hoped to defeat Britain with the Luftwaffe alone, without risking the Army. He tried to master the Mediterranean littoral with the Luftwaffe and a few army corps but drew back from any major commitment. Finally, he undertook to conquer the Russian sub-continent on the wishful assumption that total victory could be achieved within a few months and without rudimentary precautions against the contingency of prolonged resistance.

And so the leaders of the Wehrmacht, like all Germans, paid dearly for the folly of laying their fate in the hands of a tyrant who was neither statesman nor captain. For all his mnemonic and forensic gifts, Hitler was unfitted and unable to meet the epochal challenge of the situation which he and the generals now confronted.

If Hitler bore the main responsibility for leading the Reich to ruin, the generals and admirals must nevertheless share the blame. Much has been written in praise of the sheer professionalism of the German officer corps, and of its rigorous divorcement from politics. In the United States, ever since the Franco-Prussian War the German military system has attracted admiration and inspired emulation in military circles.[29] Yet the collapse of German military professionalism under the pressures of Nazism and the generals' failure to grasp the strategic problems that Germany confronted in 1940 bespeak grave deficiencies in German military practice.

Between 1933 and 1940, Hitler spent many hours in military company. If the leaders of the Wehrmacht had been men of broad strategic vision, some of their outlook and their wisdom might have rubbed off on the Fuehrer. Hitler was often a poor listener and he was usually a difficult and arrogant pupil, but his mind was highly absorbent. If he came ill-equipped to the great strategic crossroads of 1940, that was partly because he had had small opportunity to learn from generals who had so little to impart.

Professional military men do well to eschew partisan politics. But it does not follow that they should neglect the study of political matters, especially those that are closely related to the military field. "Aim to be yourselves statesmen as well as seamen," Admiral Mahan counseled his brother officers.[30]

Perhaps that is an overstatement, and certainly it is an oversimplification. But if, as Clausewitz teaches, war is a continuation of state policy, and strategy is "the use of combats" to attain the state's objectives, then strategy must be a mixture of military and political elements.

The subject matter of strategy, therefore, is as broad as the state's field of foreign policy and range of objectives. Under Hitler, the Third Reich essayed a role as a world power for which the officer corps was almost as poorly prepared as the Fuehrer himself.

These shortcomings surely did not stem from a lack of doctrinal background. "Once the great victory is gained," wrote Clausewitz,[31] "there should be no talk of rest, of getting breath, or of consolidating, etc., but only of pursuit, of fresh blows whenever necessary, of the capture of the enemy's capital, of attacking . . . whatever else appears to be the point of support of the hostile state." Such lessons were repeated from generation to generation of general staff officers.

Shortly before World War II Oberst Hermann Foertsch, a senior instructor at the famous *Kriegsakademie,* published *The Art of War Today and Tomorrow,*[32] a widely read work replete with extracts from Gneisenau, Clausewitz, Moltke, and other demigods of the officer corps. Therein Gneisenau was extolled as a general who never rested but "drove on and on" in pursuance of his maxim that "the destruction of the enemy is always the main object." So, too, Foertsch quoted Gneisenau's apothegm, "Strategy is the science of making use of space and time," and his observation, "I am more jealous of the latter than of the former. We can always recover ground, but never lost time." [33]

Had France been the principal enemy, it could be said that the Wehrmacht followed these teachings to the letter in 1940. But Hitler and the generals realized full well that Britain was the main foe. The classic German military writings did not guide them toward a strategy suitable to the situation they confronted, and of that there is no better illustration than this very book by Foertsch. Written after one world war and on the eve of a second, at a time when the close interrelation of the land, sea, and air arms was already taken for granted in military science, Foertsch's work is avowedly limited to land warfare. Why? Because [34] "it would not be proper for the author, as an officer of the Army, to also consider questions of naval and aerial warfare." In line with this extraordinary notion of "propriety" in a work devoted to the "art of war," Foertsch treated the air arm purely as a tactical adjunct of the Army. The Navy he hardly mentioned, and he refrained from any discussion of amphibious operations or of the tactical or strategic problems that would be faced by Germany or any other nation at war with a transmarine foe.

The limitations of Foertsch's book reflected the narrow range of German military thinking and the compartmentalization of German military organization and training. There was almost no inclination or opportunity for inter-service staff training, and little attention was given to the strategy and tactics of global warfare and combined operations.

Especially revealing are the indifference or outright hostility encountered by the few officers who grasped the need and sought to fill the gap. Upon his retirement in 1927, General Walter Reinhardt (commander of the Army from 1919 to 1920 and thereafter one of the senior troop commanders), with the support of the Minister of Defense, ex-General Wilhelm Groener, conducted a one-year course for twelve selected officers (ten army and two navy) in which lectures at the University of Berlin and foreign travel were mixed with special studies in military history and strategy. After Reinhardt's death the course was continued under Generalleutnant Edmund Wachenfeld, Chief of Staff of the Berlin Group Command, but it was discontinued in 1933.

In 1935, chiefly on Blomberg's initiative, inter-service staff training was for the first and only time made a formal part of the military system. A *Wehrmachtakademie* was established in Berlin,* at which ten officers (six army and two each navy and air force) were immersed in the broad problems of war leadership under the direction of the able and articulate General Wilhelm Adam.[35]

But the *Wehrmachtakademie* lasted less than three years, and was abolished in 1938 when Adam was appointed army group commander on the western frontier. Despite his prestige and seniority, the academy was regarded with indifference by the Army and the Foreign Office, while the Navy and Luftwaffe were suspicious and hostile, as they were to any real or fancied threat to their autonomy and freedom from domination by the Army. All three services were opposed to the concept of a "Wehrmacht General Staff," and the Army General Staff was in a state of constant feud with Blomberg and his subordinates in the Ministry of War, of which the *Wehrmachtakademie* was part.

* In the United States, the inter-service Armed Forces Staff College was established in 1946, and has since graduated some 4,200 officers. See the description by Hanson Baldwin in *The New York Times*, March 18, 1958.

When the German generals spoke of military strategy, they envisaged the European sub-continent as the field of action.* With characteristic German ingenuity and thoroughness, they devised a military machine and a tactical system superior to anything else in their range of observation, while the French generals slumbered in the past. But in strategic and political terms, the German military mind made no such strides. In everything but tactical science and skill in the field, the German officer corps, like the French, was circumscribed by old conceptions. Its leaders had learned little or nothing since World War I, in which they had all fought.

The personal attributes of Hitler and the leading officers, however, furnish the material for only a partial and superficial diagnosis of the German failure of strategy. Even if Hitler had been better informed and the officer corps more enlightened, the course of events might not have been much different. Dictator and generals were part of the Third Reich, and the Wehrmacht itself was the fruit of the relation between the officer corps and the Nazi party—between the sword and the swastika. And it is in that relation that deeper causes of the strategic failure may be perceived.

Surveying the first phase of World War II—from the conquest of Poland to the fall of France and Hitler's peace overtures on July 19, 1940—perhaps its most salient feature is the enormous gap in quality between German tactics and German strategy. From the sphere of field tactics to the higher reaches of grand strategy, there was a constant deterioration.

On land and sea and in the air, the tactical handling of the German forces in Norway, the Low Countries, and France was superb. On a large scale, no such level of performance had previously been achieved in the twentieth century. Not only in the field and in actual combat but in the organizational and planning work of the staffs, the Wehrmacht's accomplishments were extraordinary. The meticulously timed naval assault at ports scattered from end to end of the long Norwegian coast, the novel and imaginative conjunction of airborne and armored operations in Holland, the machinelike redeployment of the Army for the

---

* Hitler's outlook was similarly limited. See Hanfstaengl, *Unheard Witness* (1957) p. 41: "Neither he [Hitler] nor any of his entourage . . . acquired any conception of the strength of the salt-water powers. They thought along purely continental lines. To them international power politics were based on the limitations inherent in land warfare, and in my decade of struggle to influence the workings of Hitler's mind I never really succeeded in bringing home the importance of America as an integral factor in European politics."

Somme-Aisne offensive—example after example of technical military mastery recurs during the ten weeks of the campaign in western Europe.

At the higher level of inter-service plans and operations, where tactics and strategy often overlap, the Wehrmacht's achievements were often remarkable, but serious shortcomings were likewise apparent. Army-Luftwaffe co-operation is a good example. At the field level, Geissler and Falkenhorst in Norway, or Guderian, Stutterheim, and Loerzer at Sedan, were able to team their ground and air forces, and the results were sensationally successful. But between Goering and Brauchitsch there was no trust or common ground, and this circumstance gave rise to disastrous consequences such as the "stop-order" before Dunkirk.

In the uppermost range of grand strategy, the Germans' record was abysmal. Vitally important problems were overlooked or nonchalantly disposed of on the basis of personal penchants. One need only mention the short wind and imbalance of the Luftwaffe; the refusal to mobilize the German economy for a long war; the failure to evaluate the potential gains and losses from *Weseruebung* in relation to the war as a whole; the purblind occupation policies; the easing of pressure on the British at the moment of their greatest weakness. It is hard to believe that such a series of oversights and blunders could have been made in the land of Clausewitz, whose most basic teachings were thus flouted. In the realm of ultimate strategy—waging total war to achieve a victor's peace—the leaders of the Third Reich were miserably incompetent.

Such a contrast between technical military proficiency and strategic incapacity can hardly be explained by the characteristics of individuals, no matter how highly placed. Rather, it is significant of basic flaws in the structure of the Third Reich, of which the Wehrmacht was a part.

Running all through the story of these plans and campaigns, there is a strong current of tension, sporadically erupting into open conflict, in the highest circles of the Reich. Even among the army generals this tension may be felt between the old guard—the Rundstedts, Leebs, and Brauchitschs—and the new school—the Guderians, Mansteins, and Rommels.

Within the Wehrmacht as a whole, the stresses were more numerous and deeper. The strain between Brauchitsch and Goering, for example, was not merely a matter of personal dislike. It had a history that began in February 1938, when Hitler and Goering extracted commitments from Brauchitsch at the time of his appointment as Commander-in-Chief of the Army.[36] Because of its traditional prestige, the officer corps appeared to the Nazis not as an instrument for defense of the Reich but as a rival in the struggle for power to govern the Reich's destinies. When Dunkirk loomed, it was more important to Goering that the Luftwaffe, rather than the Army, get the credit for the final victory, than that the British be struck with the greatest possible force.

Why were the German occupation policies so suicidal from a strategic standpoint? It is easy to answer that those policies were never sufficiently considered in strategic terms, but why were they not? The reason was that those directly concerned did not have the interests of the Reich primarily at heart. Himmler and his henchmen wanted to enlarge the scope and power of the SS "state within a state" and put their racial theories to the test of practice. The Krupps and Flicks and Farben directors were more concerned with the expansion of their industrial empires than with the development of a sound national policy. Some of the army generals like Stuelpnagel saw the occupation from a less selfish point of view, but they were unable to make their views prevail, partly because the Army's influence in the Reich's affairs had declined, and also because most of the senior officers were insensitive to the strategic implications of occupation policy or preferred not to become involved in such matters.

Of course, inter-service rivalries and private self-seeking at the expense of the national interest in wartime are not peculiar to the Third Reich. In the atmosphere of Nazism, however, these diseases of the body politic seem to have run wild, like an uncontrollable cancer. Undeniably, there was much deep and genuine fervor among the German youth that grew to manhood in Hitler's time, and the soldiers, sailors, and airmen of the Wehrmacht fought as bravely as those of the other countries. But standards of leadership in the Third Reich—political, civil, and military—seem to have been distorted, beyond redemption even under the patriotic stimulus of war, by the evil pressures of the Nazi dictatorship.

It is no wonder, therefore, that Hitler and the generals were helpless to cope with the strategic riddles of 1940. Their failure was inevitable, for the Third Reich was not the potent and efficient engine of conquest that it was generally thought to be. And by a strange but appropriate irony, it was especially in the sphere of strategic decision-making, where by common supposition dictatorships are more swift, flexible, and cold-blooded than democracies, that the Reich was found wanting.

So the fruits of conquest in the West rotted in the victors' hands. For all its tactical brilliance, the Battle of France spelled no final victory for the Germans. After the dust of battle had settled and the promotions and decorations were distributed, there still remained the great riddle: how to end the war. *Was nun?*

Notes

In these notes, the following abbreviations are used:

F.C.N.A.—Fuehrer Conferences on Naval Affairs—summary record of the conferences between Hitler and the Commander-in-Chief of the German Navy, Grossadmiral Erich Raeder, during the period covered by this book.

H.D.—Halder Diary—the shorthand daily diary kept by General Franz Halder, Chief of the General Staff of the German Army.

J.D.—Jodl Diary—the diary kept by Generalmajor Alfred Jodl, Chief of the Operations Division of Hitler's military headquarters (OKW).

N.C.A.—Nazi Conspiracy and Aggression—the so-called "Red Book" series of Nuremberg documents, interrogations, etc.

N.D.—Nuremberg Documents—documents introduced at the Nuremberg trials or printed in connection therewith.

T.M.W.C.—Trial of the Major War Criminals—the published transcript of the first Nuremberg trial, before the International Military Tribunal.

T.W.C.—Trials of War Criminals before the Nuremberg military tribunals—the so-called "Green Book" series of testimony and documents from the twelve subsequent Nuremberg trials.

CHAPTER ONE

1. The retrospective material in this chapter is derived from Taylor, *Sword and Swastika* (1952). See also Goerlitz, *The German General Staff* (1953) pp. 273–359; Wheeler-Bennett, *The Nemesis of Power* (1953) pp. 289–455; Hossbach, *Zwischen Wehrmacht und Hitler* (Hanover 1949); Foerster, *Ein General Kaempft gegen den Krieg* (Munich 1949); Kielmansegg, *Der Fritsch-Prozess 1938* (Hamburg 1949).

2. See, for example, the account of the showing in Oslo on April 5, 1940, in Churchill, *The Gathering Storm* (1948) p. 589. These films fell into Allied hands after the war and portions of them were incorporated in the television series entitled *Air Power,* broadcast by the Columbia Broadcasting System during the season 1956–57.

3. Halder Diary (hereafter cited as "H.D."), entry for Sept. 20, 1939.

4. H.D., undated entry on last page of Volume 1.

5. See, e.g., Abshagen, *Canaris* (London 1956); Colvin, *Master Spy* (1951).

6. Taylor, *Sword and Swastika* (1952) pp. 166–74.

7. For an account of the "Paris branch" of the conspiracy, and Stuelpnagel's participation therein as Military Governor of France, see Von Schramm, *Conspiracy Among Generals* (1956).

8. Guderian, *Panzer Leader* (1952) pp. 472–73.

9. For accounts of Kluge's indecisive but compromising involvements with the secret resistance movement, see Von Schramm, *Conspiracy Among Generals* (1956) *passim*; Schacht, *Account Settled* (London 1949) pp. 150 and 253; Gisevius, *To the Bitter End* (1947) pp. 205–10, 303–04, and 557–58.

10. H.D. Dec. 14, 1939, Mar. 6, and Sept. 4, 1940.

11. See Reitlinger, *The SS, Alibi of a Nation* (London 1956) pp. 76–87 and 124–28; Hausser, *Waffen-SS im Einsatz* (Goettingen 1953) pp. 9–41.

12. Heinkel, *Stormy Life* (1956) pp. 130–31 and 190–200; Galland, *The First and the Last* (1954) pp. 14–15.

13. See the testimony of Kesselring and Milch in IX *Trial of the Major War Criminals* (hereinafter cited as T.M.W.C.) pp. 60–61, 175, and 203–06.

14. Letter to the author dated Aug. 11, 1957, from General der Flieger *a.d.* Georg Rieke, formerly Deputy Chief of the OKL personnel department.

15. Heinkel, *op. cit. supra* p. 189; Galland, *op. cit. supra* p. 107; Frischauer, *The Rise and Fall of Hermann Goering* (1951) pp. 231–38.

16. Galland, *op. cit. supra* pp. 14–15; Tippelskirch, *Geschichte des Zweiten Weltkrieges* (Bonn 1951) p. 12. Asher Lee, in *The German Air Force* (1946) p. 236, gives a figure of 800 a month, but this seems improbably high and is in conflict with the German sources. *Cf.* Churchill, *The Gathering Storm* (1948) p. 338.

17. H.D. July 4, 1940. See also Kesselring's testimony in IX T.M.W.C. p. 202. Asher Lee, *op. cit. supra* pp. 53–54, gives a higher total, which may include noncombat types. Galland, *op. cit. supra* p. 216, gives a lower figure.

18. Churchill, *Their Finest Hour* (1949) pp. 715–17.

19. For the source of these figures, see Koch, *Flak* (Bad Nauheim 1954) pp. 28, 39, and 51.

20. Ruge, *Der Seekrieg 1939–1945* (Stuttgart 1954) pp. 26–31; Woodward, *The Tirpitz* (1954) pp. 46–49; Martienssen, *Hitler and His Admirals* (1949) pp. 12–15.

21. *Fuehrer Conferences on Naval Affairs* (translated and distributed by the British Admiralty, 1947, and hereinafter cited as F.C.N.A.) 1939, pp. 7–8 and 14.

22. From captured German naval records.

23. Groener, *Die Schiffe der Deutschen Kriegsmarine und Luftwaffe 1939–45* (Munich 1954) pp. 8–31; F.C.N.A. 1939, p. 12.

24. F.C.N.A. 1939, pp. 12–13; Bekker, *Defeat at Sea* (1955) pp. 17–21; Martienssen, *op. cit. supra* pp. 37–39.

25. F.C.N.A. 1939, pp. 11–13.

26. F.C.N.A. 1939, pp. 20–21, 26–27, 38–39; Ruge, *op. cit. supra* pp. 39–41.

27. Ruge, *op. cit. supra* pp. 36–38.

28. Nuremberg Document (hereinafter cited as N.D.) 2353-PS; Taylor, *Sword and Swastika* pp. 322–23; Klein, "Germany's Preparation for War: A Re-examination," in XXXVIII *The American Economic Review* (Mar. 1948) p. 56.

29. U. S. Strategic Bombing Survey, *The Effects of Strategic Bombing on the German War Economy* (Oct. 31, 1945) pp. 6–7.

30. *Infra* pp. 252–65.

CHAPTER TWO

1. Churchill, *The Gathering Storm* p. 456.

2. H.D. Sept. 10 and 26, 1939; Greiner, *Die Oberste Wehrmachtfuehrung* (Wiesbaden 1951) pp. 58–59. The source of most of the material on pages 42 and 43 is Halder's diary for the indicated dates.

3. N.D. C-62.

4. N.D. L-52, also dated Oct. 9, 1939.

5. Jodl Diary (hereinafter cited as "J.D.") Oct. 15, 1939.

6. Leeb Defense Exhibit 39, printed in X *Trials of War Criminals before the Nuremberg Military Tribunals* (here-

inafter cited as T.W.C.) pp. 864–72. The document is dated Oct. 11, 1939. See also the translation in N.D. NOKW-3433, utilized in the text.

7. H.D. Oct. 14, 1939.

8. H.D. Oct. 15, 1939.

9. Leeb Defense Exhibit 42, printed in X T.W.C. pp. 872–74.

10. A copy of Rundstedt's letter, dated Oct. 31, 1939, is included in the file constituting N.D. NOKW-511. The file contains no proof that the letter reached Brauchitsch, but there is no apparent reason to doubt that it did.

11. H.D. Nov. 5, 1939.

12. An abstract of the conference is part of N.D. NOKW-511.

13. N.D. C-72.

14. For divergent accounts of the Venlo and Elser episodes see Schellenberg, *The Schellenberg Memoirs* (London 1956) pp. 82–110; Colvin, *Master Spy* (1951) pp. 106–20; Reitlinger, *The SS, Alibi of a Nation* (London 1956) pp. 139–43.

15. N.D. 440-PS.

16. See Guderian, *Panzer Leader* p. 85; Paget, *Manstein* p. 21; Westphal, *The German Army in the West* p. 77.

17. N.D. NOKW-2717.

18. Guderian, *op. cit. supra* pp. 85–88.

19. Kesselring, *A Soldier's Record* (1954) p. 49. The account of the forced landing is based on Bartz, *Als der Himmel Brannte* (Hanover 1955) pp. 7–13, and on the documents reproduced in Jacobsen, *Dokumente zur Vorgeschichte des Westfeldzuges 1939–1940* (Goettingen 1956) pp. 161–85.

20. *United States* v. *List*, Nuremberg Case No. 7, mimeographed transcript, pp. 6892–96.

21. H.D. Mar. 27, 1940.

22. H.D. Apr. 14, 1940.

23. N.D. 630-PS and 3816-PS; see also II T.W.C. pp. 196–98, 279–81.

24. XVI T.M.W.C. p. 662.

25. N.D. 739-D.

26. XVI T.M.W.C. p. 664.

27. See *Sword and Swastika* pp. 357–64.

28. Schlabrendorf, *Offiziere gegen Hitler* (Zurich 1946) pp. 34–35; Reitlinger, *op. cit. supra* pp. 124–25.

29. N.D. 3047-PS. The document is quoted in Abshagen, *Canaris* (London 1956) pp. 143–48. See also the testimony of Canaris' subordinate, Lahousen, in II T.M.W.C. pp. 446–48.

30. H.D. Sept. 19, 1939.

31. N.D. 3047-PS.

32. H.D. Sept. 20, 1939.

33. N.D. 3363-PS.

34. H.D. Oct. 18, 1939.

35. N.D. 864-PS.

36. N.D. 2278-PS.

37. N.D. D-419.

38. The *Von Hassell Diaries* (1951) p. 100.

39. H.D. Jan. 18, 1940.

40. H.D. Jan. 19, 1940.

41. J.D. Jan. 29, 1940.

42. H.D. Feb. 5, 1940. In the entry for Feb. 24, Halder notes that Blaskowitz should be consulted on the tank ditch and the situation of the Jews in Poland before making reply to Himmler. The entry for March 18 notes a conference with *Oberost* at which it was suggested that the tank ditch be constructed "by an organization patterned after the Organization Todt."

43. H.D. March 7, 1940.

44. H.D. May 29, 1940; see *infra* pp. 280–81.

45. IV T.W.C. p. 889 (Hans Frank's diary entry for Dec. 8, 1939).

46. N.D. NO-5322, printed in IV T.W.C. p. 855.

47. N.D. 2916-PS.

48. N.D. 2537-PS.

49. N.D. EC-410.

50. VII T.W.C. pp. 178–83; N.D. NI-8457, 2749, 5947, 1149, 15107, 8380, 8396, 2998, 1197, 1146, 1147, 1148, 1164, and 707.

51. N.D. NO-034.

52. N.D. NI-11781, 11783, 11784, 11113, 1240, and 11086.

53. *Ausgewaehlte Briefe von Generalmajor Helmuth Stieff*, in *Vierteljahrshefte fuer Zeitgeschichte* (h. 3, 1954) pp. 298–300.

54. See Taylor, *Sword and Swastika* p. 361.

55. N.D. NOKW-1531. See also N.D. NOKW-3437, of July 23, 1940, wherein General Werner Kienitz, commander of the XVIIth Corps (then subordinated to the 18th Army), passed the gist of Kuechler's order to the 297th and 298th Divisions.

56. Quoted in *Bombing Vindicated*, by J. M. Spaight (London 1944) pp. 66–67.

57. *Nazi Conspiracy and Aggression* (hereinafter cited as N.C.A.), Supp. B, p. 1119.

58. J.D. Nov. 28, 1953.

59. Churchill, *The Gathering Storm* pp. 491–92.

60. Richards, *Royal Air Force, 1939–1945* (London 1953) Vol. I, pp. 38–74.

61. J. M. Spaight, *Bombing Vindicated* pp. 68–69; Sir Arthur Harris, *Bomber Offensive* pp. 37–38; William L. Shirer, *Berlin Diary* pp. 303–04.

62. See Churchill, *The Gathering Storm* pp. 505–10; Harris, *op. cit. supra* pp. 37–38; Hinsley, *Hitler's Strategy* (Cambridge 1951) pp. 54–55.

63. F.C.N.A. 1939, p. 64.

64. Hinsley, *op. cit. supra* p. 53.

65. F.C.N.A. 1939, p. 46.

66. Churchill, *The Gathering Storm* pp. 567, 716; *Their Finest Hour* pp. 713–14; Roskill, *The War at Sea* (London 1954) Vol. I, pp. 615–18.

67. F.C.N.A. 1939, p. 35.

68. See Churchill, *The Gathering Storm* pp. 513–14.

69. On this point the British and German post mortems are in agreement. See Churchill, *The Gathering Storm* p. 520, and Raeder's statement at Nuremberg, set forth in VIII N.C.A. p. 719.

70. The account of *Graf Spee's* engagement and the events in Montevideo harbor are based on Pope, *Graf Spee* (1957); Bekker, *Defeat at Sea* (1955) pp. 55–72; F.C.N.A. 1939, pp. 59–63.

71. F.C.N.A. 1939, p. 67; J.D. Dec. 18, 1939.

72. Ruge, *Der Seekrieg 1939–1945* (Stuttgart 1954) pp. 59–60; I Roskill, *op. cit. supra* p. 102; J.D. Dec. 17, 1939; Shirer, *Berlin Diary* (1941) pp. 265–66.

73. F.C.N.A. 1940, p. 11; SKL War Diary, entry for Mar. 13, 1940.

74. J.D. Feb. 23, 1940.

CHAPTER THREE

1. Wegener, *Die Strategie des Weltkrieges* (Berlin 1929) p. 49, quoted in Derry, *The Campaign in Norway* (London 1952) pp. 16–17; Hubatsch, *Die Deutsche Besetzung von Daenemark und Norwegen* (Goettingen 1952) pp. 21–22.

2. See Possony, *Decision without Battle*, in 72 U.S. Naval Institute Proceedings 761, 762 (June 1946).

3. *Supra* pp. 46–54.

4. Hubatsch, *op. cit. supra* p. 22.

5. Foltmann and Moeller-Witten, *Opfergang der Generale* (Berlin 1952) p. 63.

6. Carls' letter has not come to light. It was sent shortly prior to Oct. 3, 1939, and was referred by Raeder to his chief of staff, Vizeadmiral Schniewind. See N.D. C-66 and 1546-PS; XIV T.M.W.C. pp. 86 and 308; X T.W.C. p. 783.

7. N.D. C-122 and C-170, Oct. 3, 1939.

8. N.D. C-66 and C-5, Oct. 9, 1939; Hubatsch, *op. cit supra* p. 23.

9. N.D. C-66, C-71, C-170, D-879, and 1546–PS; F.C.N.A. 1939, p. 27.

10. Churchill, *The Gathering Storm* (1948) pp. 531–38.

11. Taylor, *Sword and Swastika* pp. 353–57.

12. There is a good account of the events leading up to the Russo-Finnish War in *Finland and World War II*, edited by J. H. Wuorinen (1948).

13. Waite, *Vanguard of Nazism* (1952) pp. 94–139.

14. Quoted in Wuorinen, *supra* p. 67, from Churchill's radio address of Jan. 20, 1940.

15. For the background of the Quisling-Rosenberg relation, see the latter's testimony in XI T.M.W.C. pp. 455–56 and N.D. 003, 004, and 007-PS.

16. F.C.N.A. 1939, p. 51.

17. F.C.N.A. 1939, pp. 55–57.

18. *Id.* pp. 57–59; N.D. C-64 and C-170; J.D. Dec. 12, 1939.

19. XIV T.M.W.C. pp. 93–94; N.D. C-66.

20. J.D. entry for Dec. 13, 1939, which appears to be misdated, and H.D. Dec. 14, 1939.

21. N.D. 004-PS, 007-PS, and 1639-PS.

22. N.D. NG-2585, and 004-PS and 007-PS.

23. J.D. Dec. 18 and 19, 1939; H.D. Jan. 1, 1940.

24. N.D. C-21, in XXXIV T.M.W.C. pp. 181–85; H.D. Jan. 10, 1940.

25. J.D. Jan. 23 and 24, 1940.

26. N.D. C-63.

27. N.D. NOKW-065.

28. J.D. Feb. 3, 1940; N.D. NOKW-3520 and Schniewind Defense Exhibit 55, both printed in X T.W.C. pp. 777–82.

29. See Frischauer and Jackson, *The Altmark Affair* (1955).

30. Hubatsch, *op. cit. supra* p. 34.

31. J.D. Feb. 21, 1940.

32. Falkenhorst described his initial interviews with Hitler in the course of an interrogation at Nuremberg on Oct. 24, 1945, printed in N.C.A., Supp. B, pp. 1534–47.

33. H.D. Feb. 26, 1940.

34. N.D. C-174. Nine copies only were made, five for OKW, one each for Falkenhorst and the three service commanders-in-chief.

35. J.D. Mar. 1, 1940.

36. This note, made on Mar. 2, is appended to Halder's diary entry for Feb. 21.

37. J.D. Mar. 2, 3, and 4, 1940. The change was effected by an OKW directive signed by Keitel on Mar. 4, 1940, and was elaborated in a Hitler order issued Mar. 14, 1940. See Appendix D, *infra* pp. 433–36.

38. J.D. Mar. 7, 1940. I have been unable to examine the revised directive.

39. H.D. Feb. 21, 1940.

40. Wuorinen, *op. cit. supra* pp. 70–71.

41. Churchill, *The Gathering Storm* pp. 573–74.

42. Churchill, *op. cit. supra* p. 574.

43. J.D. Feb. 26 and 28 and Mar. 3, 1940.

44. N.D. NOKW-2265 and L-323.

45. J.D. Mar. 10, 1940.

46. J.D. Mar. 13 and 14, 1940.

47. J.D. Mar. 28, 1940; SKL War Diary, Jan. 13 and Mar. 13, 1940.

48. *Ciano's Diplomatic Papers* (London 1948) pp. 361–65; Ciano, *Diario* (Rizzoli ed.) Vol. I, p. 239; Bullock, *Hitler* (1952) p. 533.

49. F.C.N.A. 1940, pp. 21–23.

50. H.D. Mar. 27, 1940.

51. F.C.N.A. 1940 (Mar. 26 and 29) pp. 23–24; J.D. Mar. 17, 1940; Richards, *Royal Air Force 1939–1945* (London 1953) Vol. I, p. 68. In the raid on Mar. 16, the *Iron Duke* was damaged again, as well as the cruiser *Norfolk*.

52. F.C.N.A. 1940 (Mar. 29) p. 26; J.D. Mar. 28 and Apr. 2, 1940.

53. Churchill, *The Gathering Storm* pp. 575–83.

54. Derry, *The Campaign in Norway* pp. 15–16. This is the official British history of the campaign.

55. In a letter to Admiral Sir Dudley Pound, the First Sea Lord. See Churchill, *The Gathering Storm* p. 600.

56. *Id.* p. 538.

57. *Id.* p. 545; N.D. D-807.

58. *Supra* pp. 94–96.

59. I T.M.W.C. p. 207.

60. Churchill, *The Gathering Storm* p. 536.

61. In addition to the documents cited *supra* pp. 95 and 96, see N.D. D-843, a message dated Mar. 28, 1940, to Berlin from the German Minister in Oslo, Dr. Curt Braeuer, stating: "It definitely appears, as I have frequently pointed out, that the British have no intentions of landing, but that they want to disturb shipping in Norwegian territorial waters, perhaps . . . in order to provoke Germany."

CHAPTER FOUR

1. In his order of the day of Apr. 1, 1940, reproduced in F.C.N.A. 1940, pp. 26–27.

2. For an excellent analysis of the subject, see DeJong, *The German Fifth Column in World War II* (1956) pp. 54–65 and 158–81.

3. N.C.A., Supp. B, p. 1540.

4. Falkenhorst interrogation, N.C.A., Supp. B, p. 1543.

5. N.D. 3596-PS.

6. J.D. Apr. 1, 1940.

7. For the accounts of the invasion of Norway and Denmark see Hubatsch, *op. cit. supra;* Derry, *op. cit. supra;* DeJong, *loc. cit. supra;* Boehm, *Norwegen Zwischen England und Deutschland* (Lippoldsberg 1956).

8. J.D. Apr. 5 and 6, 1940.

9. J.D. Apr. 3. Likewise, the Navy and Foreign Office agreed on what explanations would be given if the Norwegians should examine any of the ships of the *Ausfuhrstaffel* and discover their contents. But what these explanations were to be does not appear.

10. F.C.N.A. 1940, p. 39.

11. Embry, *Mission Completed* (London 1957) pp. 126–32.

12. This information came from a neutral diplomat in Copenhagen, but the report was not credited in London. See Derry, *op. cit. supra* p. 28.

13. Hubatsch, *op. cit. supra* pp. 57–69.

14. Derry, *op. cit. supra* p. 26.

15. *Ibid.* Mr. Churchill is noncom-

mittal on the matter in *The Gathering Storm* p. 592.

16. J.D. Apr. 8, 1940.

17. F.C.N.A. pp. 35 and 39–40; Hubatsch, *op. cit. supra* p. 129.

18. N.D. 3596-PS.

19. *Ibid.*

20. Derry, *op. cit. supra* p. 39; Hubatsch, *op. cit. supra* p. 161.

21. F.C.N.A. 1940, p. 41.

22. Ruge, *Der Seekrieg 1939–45* (Stuttgart 1954) p. 72.

23. Apparently there was confusion in identifying the German ships as the result of an order from Oslo that French and British ships were not to be fired upon. Derry, *op. cit. supra* p. 39.

23a. Hanfstaengl, *Unheard Witness* (1957) p. 99.

24. See Churchill, *The Gathering Storm* p. 591; Derry, *op. cit. supra* p. 41; Hubatsch, *op. cit. supra* pp. 71–73; Frau G.-D. Dietl and Hermann, *General Dietl* (Munich 1951) pp. 55–58.

25. Dietl and Hermann, *op. cit. supra* pp. 64–68.

26. Hubatsch, *op. cit. supra* p. 111, note 9.

27. Pursuant to plan "R.4"; see p. 98, *supra*.

28. *Infra* pp. 141–47.

29. Lee, *The German Air Force* (London 1948) pp. 47–48.

30. At Nuremberg, Milch testified that he flew to Oslo on Apr. 16 and returned to Germany May 7. See the mimeographed transcript of his testimony in Case No. 2, *United States* v. *Milch* pp. 1781 and 2200.

31. Derry, *op. cit. supra* p. 143.

32. Hubatsch, *op. cit. supra* p. 204, note 18.

33. Hubatsch, *op. cit. supra* p. 204.

34. H.D. Apr. 14, 1940.

35. J.D. Apr. 14, 1940.

36. *Id.* Apr. 15 and 16, 1940.

37. Lossberg, *Im Wehrmacht Fuehrungsstab* (Hamburg 1949) pp. 67–69; see also Hubatsch, *op. cit. supra* p. 189. The order is reproduced in Hubatsch, p. 190, and in Dietl and Hermann, *op. cit. supra* p. 107.

38. J.D. Apr. 19, 1940.

39. Lemkin, *Axis Rule in Occupied Europe* (1944) pp. 498–99.

40. J.D. Apr. 21 and 22, 1940; F.C.N.A. 1940, p. 36.

41. J.D. Apr. 30, 1940.

42. Hengl's report, quoted in Hubatsch, *op. cit. supra* p. 218.

43. *Infra* p. 348.

44. Busch, *Holocaust at Sea* (1956) pp. 27–31.

45. *Supra* p. 82.

46. Derry, *op. cit. supra* p. 60.

47. See the author's foreword to and the last chapter of Foley, *Commando Extraordinary* (1955).

48. Roskill, *The War at Sea* (London 1956) Vol. II, p. 123; Woodward, *The Tirpitz* (1953) p. 105.

49. Derry, *op. cit. supra* p. 231, gives the figure of 242, and Hubatsch, *op. cit. supra* p. 257, the figure of 117. Hubatsch states the total deaths in the campaign at 8942, comprising 3692 Germans, 3349 British, 1355 Norwegians, 530 French and Poles, and 26 Danes.

50. H.D. Apr. 14, 1940.

51. Churchill, *The Gathering Storm* p. 657.

52. See Possony, *Decision Without Battle,* 72 U.S. Naval Institute Proceedings (June 1946) p. 764: "From the tactical point of view, the Norwegian campaign was a remarkable piece of work. Yet, it was also a grave strategic error."

CHAPTER FIVE

1. See Halder's diary for the period and his *Hitler As War Lord* (London 1950) pp. 28–30; Manstein, *Verlorene Siege* (Bonn 1955), pp. 61–124; Guderian, *Panzer Leader* (London 1952) pp. 89–98; Blumentritt, *Von Rundstedt* (London 1952) pp. 55–65; Liddell Hart, *The German Generals Talk* (1948) pp. 63–64 and 107–14; J. F. C. Fuller, *The Second World War* (1949) p. 63; Goerlitz, *Der Zweite Weltkrieg* (Stuttgart 1951) Vol. 1, pp. 82–96.

2. Taylor, *Sword and Swastika* pp. 12–13.

3. N.D. 2329-PS.

4. *Supra* pp. 44–46.

5. N.D. 1796-PS.

6. See, e.g., H.D. Oct. 7, 1939, and N.D. C-62 and L-52 (Oct. 9), as well as N.D. 1796-PS, entry for Dec. 11, 1939.

7. J.D. Oct. 25, 1939.

8. N.D. C-62.

9. H.D. Oct. 17, 1939.

10. It is reproduced in Manstein, *op. cit. supra* pp. 620–23, and in Jacobsen, *Dokumente zur Vorgeschichte des Westfeldzuges 1939–1940* (Goettingen 1956) pp. 41–46, and is briefly discussed in Ellis, *The War in France and Flanders* (London 1953), with a helpful map, p. 342.

11. N.D. 1796-PS, consisting of extracts from the OKW War Diary.

12. J.D. Oct. 15, 1939.

13. N.D. NOKW-2586. The directive is reproduced in part in Manstein, *op. cit. supra* pp. 623–25, in full in Jacobsen, *op. cit. supra* pp. 46–53, and a map is in Ellis, *op. cit. supra* p. 343.

14. The Eighteenth Army was officially established on Nov. 5, 1939.

15. Guderian, *op. cit. supra* p. 89.

16. Halder, *op. cit. supra* p. 28.

17. Blumentritt, *op. cit. supra* p. 59 ("enlarged Schlieffen Plan"); Westphal, *The German Army in the West* (London 1951) p. 77 ("repetition of 1914").

18. Hart, *op. cit. supra* p. 112; Galland, *The First and the Last* (1954) p. 5; Paget, *Manstein* (London 1951) pp. 21–22; Shulman, *Defeat in the West* (1948) p. 39; Wilmot, *The Struggle for Europe* (1952) p. 87; Bullock, *Hitler* (1952) p. 535; Goerlitz, *The German General Staff* (1953) pp. 362–63; Goerlitz, *Der Zweite Weltkrieg* Vol. I, p. 77; Goutard, *1940 La Guerre des Occasions Perdues* (1956) p. 156.

19. Manstein, *op. cit. supra* pp. 96–97. See also the remark of Hoth in N.D. NOKW-2717.

20. For analyses of the Schlieffen plan see Holborn, *Moltke and Schlieffen*, in *Makers of Modern Strategy* (Earle ed. 1948) pp. 186–205; Goerlitz, *History of the German General Staff*, pp. 130–42; Craig, *The Politics of the Prussian Army* (1955) pp. 277–86; Rosinski, *The German Army* (1944 ed.) pp. 84–86.

21. N.D. 1796-PS.

22. J.D. Oct. 31, 1939.

23. F.C.N.A. 1939, p. 41. Rundstedt had already made the same point in his letter to Brauchitsch on Oct. 31, 1939, *supra* p. 52, and Raeder was merely repeating what he had told Hitler on Oct. 10. F.C.N.A. 1939, p. 24.

24. J.D. Nov. 11, 1939.

25. The order is summarized in N.D. 2329-PS and NOKW-2078, and is quoted in Jacobsen, *op. cit. supra* pp. 55–57.

26. *Supra* p. 94.

27. N.D. C-62, 2329-PS, NOKW-2078, NOKW-568, and NOKW-2586.

28. H.D. Nov. 15, 1939.

29. N.D. 440-PS and NOKW-2586.

30. The directives of Jan. 30, 1940, are printed in Jacobsen, *op. cit. supra* pp. 59–64.

31. Manstein, *op. cit. supra* pp. 67–68 and 98.

32. *Id.* pp. 96–100.

33. *Supra* pp. 52–53.

34. N.D. NOKW-511 (6).

35. H.D. Nov. 1, 1939.

36. *Infra* pp. 178–80.

37. *Supra* pp. 53–54.

38. H.D. Nov. 9, 1939.

39. N.D. 2329-PS, in XXX T.M.W.C. pp. 226–29, and in Jacobsen, *op. cit. supra* pp. 53–55.

40. *Supra* pp. 163–64 (N.D. 440-PS).

41. See Manstein, *op. cit. supra* pp. 106–07 and Guderian, *op. cit. supra* pp. 89–90.

42. N.D. NOKW-511 (9).

43. Manstein, *op. cit. supra* pp. 108–90; J.D. Nov. 27, 1939.

44. *Supra* p. 59.

45. N.D. NOKW-511 (10).

46. N.D. NOKW-511 (11). Both (10) and (11) are reproduced in Manstein, *op. cit. supra* pp. 631–37.

47. N.D. NOKW-511 (12) Halder to Manstein, Dec. 5, 1939; H.D. Dec. 7; Manstein, *op. cit. supra* pp. 110–12.

48. H.D. Dec. 22, 1939. Rundstedt was equipped with a detailed memorandum from Manstein dated Dec. 18, 1939. N.D. NOKW-511 (15) and Manstein, *op. cit. supra* pp. 637–41.

49. J.D. Dec. 18 and 19, 1939.

50. H.D. Dec. 25 and 27, 1939.

51. *Supra* pp. 61–64.

52. N.D. NOKW-511 (21) and Manstein, *op. cit. supra* pp. 641–48.

53. N.D. NOKW-511 (22).

54. N.D. NOKW-511 (23), dated Jan. 16, 1940.

55. See N.D. NOKW-511 (25) (26) and (30), dated respectively Jan. 23 and 24 and Feb. 1, 1940, and the references to the conferences on Jan. 25 at Coblenz and Bad Godesberg, between OKH and the army group and army

commanders in Army Groups A and B, in Halder's Diary for those dates and in Manstein, *op. cit. supra* p. 117.

56. See H.D. Feb. 7, 1940; N.D. NOKW-621; Manstein, *op. cit. supra* p. 117; Guderian, *op. cit. supra* p. 90.

57. Manstein, *op. cit. supra* p. 118; *infra* pp. 172 and 179.

58. H.D. Feb. 14, 1940.

59. Guderian, *op. cit. supra* p. 91.

60. J.D. Feb. 13, 1940.

61. J.D. Feb. 17, 1940; Manstein, *op. cit. supra* pp. 118–20.

62. N.D. NOKW-511 (32).

63. See, e.g., Ellis, *op. cit. supra* p. 341; Goerlitz, *The German General Staff* p. 368; Paget, *Manstein* p. 22.

64. J.D. and H.D. Feb. 18, 1940.

65. *Supra* pp. 91–94, and H.D. Feb. 21 and 23, 1940.

66. H.D. Feb. 24, 1940; Ellis, *op. cit. supra* pp. 341–44. The directive is set forth in Jacobsen, *op. cit. supra* pp. 64–68.

67. N.D. NOKW-511 (31); Jacobsen, *op. cit. supra* pp. 68–71, 153–55, and 157–61.

68. For the background material on Wietersheim and Kleist see *Sword and Swastika* pp. 170–71 and 203. On Kleist's selection, see H.D. Feb. 24, 25, 26, 27, and 29, 1940, and Goerlitz, *Der Zweite Weltkrieg* Vol. I, p. 95.

69. H.D. Mar. 13, 15, and 16, 1940, and J.D. Mar. 15 and 16, 1940.

70. H.D. Mar. 17, 1940.

71. Guderian, *op. cit. supra* p. 92.

72. H.D. Mar. 17, 1940.

73. *Infra* pp. 229–31.

74. H.D. Mar. 27, 1940.

75. H.D. Mar. 21, 1940.

76. J.D. Mar. 19, 1940; H.D. Mar. 22, 23, and 26, 1940.

77. H.D. and J.D. Mar. 27, 1940.

78. H.D. Mar. 31 to May 9, 1940, *passim.*

79. H.D. May 4, 1940.

80. H.D. Apr. 29, 1940.

80a. Manstein, *op. cit. supra* p. 98.

81. Halder, *Hitler As War Lord* pp. 28–29.

82. Based on my own notes of my interrogation of Halder on Dec. 12, 13, 15, 16, and 17, 1947.

83. Goerlitz, *The German General Staff* pp. 363 and 367.

84. Heusinger, *Befehl im Widerstreit* (1950) pp. 84–86.

85. See, e.g., Goerlitz, *op. cit. supra* p. 368; Guderian, *op. cit. supra* p. 90; Liddell Hart, *op. cit. supra* p. 64; Blumentritt, *op. cit. supra* pp. 63–64; Paget, *Manstein* p. 22; Bullock, *Hitler* pp. 535–36.

86. Otto Dietrich, *Hitler* (1955) pp. 82–83.

87. *Supra* pp. 163–64.

88. Lee, *The German Air Force* p. 53.

89. See Goering's interrogation in N.C.A., Supp. B, p. 1115; N.D. C-10; H.D. Dec. 7, 1939, and Jan. 10, 1940; J.D. Dec. 1 and 29, 1939.

90. Taylor, *Sword and Swastika* p. 15.

91. F.C.N.A. 1940, pp. 46–48.

CHAPTER SIX

1. DeJong, *The German Fifth Column in World War II* (1956) pp. 66–77 and 182–96.

2. See Doorman, *Military Operations in the Netherlands* (London 1944) *passim;* Van Kleffens, *Juggernaut over Holland* (1941) pp. 69–78.

3. Kesselring, *A Soldier's Record* (1954) pp. 57–58.

4. See Van Kleffens, *op. cit. supra* pp. 82–100.

5. Ellis, *op. cit. supra* pp. 49–50.

6. See, e.g., Van Kleffens, *op. cit. supra* pp. 103–04 and 128; Van Blokland, "The Five Days of Holland," in *The Fortnightly* (London) for Oct. 1940, p. 331; Netherlands Ministry of Defense, *Short Account of Military Operations in the Netherlands from 10th–14th May, 1940* p. 4; Draper, *The Six Weeks' War* (1944) p. 126.

7. Kesselring, *op. cit. supra* p. 54.

8. Richards, *Royal Air Force 1939–1945* Vol. I, p. 114.

9. See Overstraeten, *Albert I–Leopold III* (Bruges 1946) pp. 563–73; Michiels, *18 Jours de Guerre en Belgique* (Paris 1947) p. 62; Doorman, *op. cit. supra* p. 44; *Belgium—The Official Account of What Happened 1939–40* (London 1941) pp. 26–27; *Onderdrukking en Verzet* Vol. 3, pp. 158–60; Van Kleffens *op. cit. supra* pp. 79–81.

10. Schmidt's corps was not formally subordinated to the Eighteenth Army until the second day of the fighting, May 11. H.D. May 11, 1940.

11. Joachim von Kuerenberg, *The Kaiser* (1955) pp. 425–26.

12. See the report of the Dutch postwar Commission of Inquiry, *Enquetecommissie Regeringsbeleid 1940–45* ('s Gravenhage 1949) Vol. IA, pp. 145 and 179–82.

13. Choltitz, *Soldat unter Soldaten* p. 66.

14. Photostatic reproductions of the communications exchanged between the Dutch and Germans are given in 4 *Onderdrukking en Verzet* p. 226. See also VI T.M.W.C. pp. 396–97.

15. It is widely believed that the loss of life was much heavier than as stated in the text. The *Encyclopaedia Britannica* (1953 ed.) Vol. 19, p. 579, states that an estimated 25,000–30,000 persons were killed in the raid. But the official reports of the Netherlands Government submitted to the International Military Tribunal state that 814 persons died. N.D. 224-F, printed in XXXVI T.M.W.C. p. 656. The official British history, however, states that "the total civilian death toll was about 980." Butler, *Grand Strategy*, Vol. II, p. 570.

16. See IX T.M.W.C. pp. 175–77, 213–18, and 338–40; Kesselring, *op. cit. supra* pp. 55–57; Butler, *op. cit. supra* pp. 569–70; OKW Directive No. 11, May 14, 1940, *infra* p. 435.

17. Kesselring, *op. cit. supra* p. 56.

18. 4 *Onderdrukking en Verzet* p. 227.

19. The proclamation is reprinted in English in Ashton, *The Netherlands at War* (London 1941) pp. 24–25.

20. *Supra* pp. 187–88.

21. Churchill, *Their Finest Hour* p. 34.

CHAPTER SEVEN

1. Churchill, *The Gathering Storm* pp. 381 and 472–73, and *Their Finest Hour* pp. 34–35; see also Van Kleffens, *op. cit. supra* pp. 21–22; *Belgium—The Official Account of What Happened 1939–40* (London 1941) pp. 22–23.

2. For the foregoing, see Churchill, *The Gathering Storm* pp. 480–83, and Ellis, *The War in France and Flanders 1939–40* (London 1953) pp. 22–24.

3. *Supra* p. 195.

4. Van Overstraeten, *Albert I–Leopold III* (Bruges 1946) pp. 568–70.

5. Ellis, *op. cit. supra* p. 35. There is no suggestion of advance notice of the attack in Churchill's writings.

6. For accounts of the airborne assault on Fort Eben Emael and the adjacent bridges over the Albert Canal, see Melzer, *Albert-Kanal und Eben-Emael* (Heidelberg 1957); Franz-Joseph Bach, *Aus der Luft Erobert*, in *Die Deutsche Soldaten-Zeitung* for Sept. 10, 17, 24, 1953; Fouillien et Bouhon, *Mai 1940* (Bruxelles 1945) pp. 35–40; *Belgium—The Official Account of What Happened 1939–40* pp. 33–36; Van Overstraeten, *op. cit. supra* pp. 574 and 736–39.

7. *Lastensegler* of Type DFS-230.

8. Kesselring, *A Soldier's Record* (1954) p. 54.

9. Richards, *Royal Air Force 1939–1945* (1953) Vol. I, pp. 116–18.

10. Richards, *supra* p. 119.

11. H.D. May 13, 1940.

12. H.D. May 15, 16, and 17, 1940.

13. *The Rommel Papers*, edited by B. H. Liddell Hart (1953) pp. 3–28.

14. See, e.g., Blumentritt's contribution to *The Fatal Decisions* (Freidin and Richardson ed. 1946) pp. 51–52.

15. *The Rommel Papers* p. 13.

16. Guderian, *Panzer Leader* p. 98.

17. Fouillien and Bouhon, *Mai 1940* p. 44.

18. Guderian, *Panzer Leader* pp. 97–102. See also pp. 476–87, where the corps and divisional orders for the attack across the Meuse are printed.

19. *The Rommel Papers* pp. 13–14; Reinhardt, *Im Schatten Guderians*, in *Wehrkunde* (Oct. 1954).

20. Fouillien and Bouhon, *supra* p. 82. The line to which Corap endeavored to fall back ran from Mettet on the north through Couvin and Rocroi.

21. *The New York Times*, Aug. 18, 1953.

22. H.D. May 14, 1940.

23. Churchill, *Their Finest Hour*, p. 42.

24. Both of these were components of Beyer's XVIIIth Corps, which had to march from thirty miles behind the German frontier and overtake the infantry that started from the border.

25. Guderian, *Panzer Leader* p. 107.

26. H.D. May 17, 1956.

27. Blumentritt, *Von Rundstedt* (1952) pp. 69–71.

28. *Supra* p. 175.

29. H.D. May 17, 1940.

30. H.D. May 15, 1940.

31. H.D. May 18, 1940.

32. J.D. May 18, 1940.

33. Tolstoy, *War and Peace*, Book Ten, Chapter 28.

34. Guderian, *Panzer Leader*, Appendix XI, p. 493, where the XIXth Corps order for May 19 is reproduced.

35. Guderian, *op. cit. supra* p. 113.

36. J.D. May 19–20, 1940.

37. H.D. May 20, 1940.

38. *Supra* pp. 218–19.

39. Kennedy and Landis, *The Surrender of King Leopold* (1950), based on Gort's account in *The London Gazette*, Oct. 10, 1940; Lyet, *La Bataille de France* (Paris 1948) p. 93.

40. *The Rommel Papers* p. 29.

41. The account of the engagement on May 21 is derived chiefly from *The Rommel Papers* pp. 29–34, and Ellis, *The War in France and Flanders 1939–1940* pp. 87–97.

42. H.D. May 21, 1940.

43. Churchill, *Their Finest Hour* pp. 62–73.

44. Ellis, *op. cit. supra* pp. 127–28.

45. Lanz, *Gebirgsjaeger* (Bad Nauheim 1954) pp. 74–82.

46. H.D. May 14 and 16, 1940.

47. H.D. May 14, 1940.

48. Manstein, *Verlorene Siege* pp. 125–33; H.D. May 24 and 30, 1940.

49. H.D. May 23, 1940.

50. H.D. May 14, 15, and 16, 1940. The idea of shifting strength from Bock to Rundstedt after the initial stages of the offensive is found in the OKW planning directive of Nov. 20, 1939, N.D. 440-PS, discussed *supra* p. 168.

51. Guderian, *Panzer Leader* p. 114; Ellis, *The War in France and Flanders* pp. 96 and 379.

52. H.D. May 22, 1956.

53. Teske, *Bewegungskrieg* (Heidelberg 1955) pp. 29–37.

54. Ellis, *op. cit. supra* pp. 130–33; Teske, *op. cit. supra* pp. 44–53.

55. Shirer, *Berlin Diary* p. 386.

56. *Supra* pp. 218–19.

57. H.D. May 21, 1940.

58. *Supra* p. 242.

59. Ellis, *op. cit. supra* pp. 101 and 379, quoting the War Diary of Bock's Army Group A.

60. H.D. May 23, 1940.

61. Accounts of the Ypres conference of May 21 are given in Churchill, *Their Finest Hour* p. 61; Ellis, *op. cit. supra* pp. 107–11; Fouillien and Bouhon, *Mai 1940* pp. 146–49; Kennedy and Landis, *The Surrender of King Leopold* pp. 15–19.

62. Ellis, *op. cit. supra* pp. 114–15.

63. Fouillien and Bouhon, *op. cit. supra* pp. 151–58.

64. Ellis, *op. cit. supra* p. 148.

65. *Infra* pp. 265–66.

66. *Belgium—The Official Account of What Happened 1939–1940* pp. 46–48.

67. H.D. May 27, 1940; *Belgium—The Official Account of What Happened* pp. 49–51.

68. Fouillien and Bouhon, *op. cit. supra* p. 234; Delandsheere and Ooms, *La Belgique sous les Nazis* Vol. II, p. 23.

69. Churchill, *Their Finest Hour* p. 91; Kennedy and Landis, *op. cit. supra* pp. 60–61.

70. See *Belgium—The Official Account of What Happened* pp. 50–52; *The Belgian Campaign and the Surrender of the Belgian Army* (N.Y. 1940) pp. 24–27 and 65–67.

71. Churchill, *Their Finest Hour* pp. 95–96. For a summary of the various comments at the time, see Kennedy and Landis, *op. cit. supra* pp. 1–2. Despite its obvious purpose as an apologia for Leopold, this is a very well documented and useful piece of work.

72. *The Belgian Campaign and the Surrender of the Belgian Army, supra* pp. 25–26.

73. *Belgium—The Official Account of What Happened* p. 47.

74. Ellis, *op. cit. supra* p. 197.

75. Bryant, *The Turn of the Tide* (1957).

76. *Id.* pp. 69–88.

77. Westphal, *The German Army in the West* (1951) p. 82; see also *The Von Hassell Diaries* (1947) p. 142; Shirer, *Berlin Diary* p. 53.

78. Ellis, *op. cit. supra* pp. 69, 83–84; Churchill, *Their Finest Hour* p. 100.

79. Ellis, *op. cit. supra* pp. 154, 178–80.

80. *Supra* pp. 248–49.

81. Churchill, *op. cit. supra* pp. 75–76.

82. Spears, *Prelude to Dunkirk* (1954) pp. 191–92.

83. Ellis, *op. cit. supra* pp. 172–74; Churchill, *op. cit. supra* p. 84.

84. Ellis, *op. cit. supra* pp. 173–74.

85. Churchill, *op. cit. supra* p. 86.

86. Churchill, *op. cit. supra* p. 100; Ellis, *op. cit. supra* p. 182.

87. Ellis, *op. cit. supra* p. 181. These "useless mouths" are *not* included in the Dunkirk evacuation totals given at pp. 271–72, *infra*.

88. In 1948, Rundstedt's attribution to Hitler of responsibility for the stop-order was reported by Milton Shulman in *Defeat in the West* pp. 42–43, and B. H. Liddell Hart, *The German Generals Talk* pp. 132–36. Liddell Hart's work also quotes Kleist and Thoma to the same effect. In 1949, Halder published his booklet *Hitler als Feldherr*, in which he declared (pp. 29–30) that Goering had persuaded Hitler that it would dangerously increase the prestige of the generals if they were allowed to complete their victory at Dunkirk, and therefore the task should be left to the Luftwaffe. See also the English version, *Hitler As War Lord* (1950) p. 30. At the Nuremberg trials, Brauchitsch, Reinhardt, and Salmuth (Bock's chief of staff during the Battle of France) testified that the responsibility was Hitler's. T.M.W.C. Vol. XX, p. 575; mimeographed transcript of record in *United States. v. Leeb*, pp. 3350–53 and 3931–32. The same version is given in the narrative statement (N.D. 3798-PS, p. 39) dated Nov. 19, 1945, prepared and signed at Nuremberg by Brauchitsch, Manstein, Halder, Warlimont, and Westphal. See also Rundstedt's testimony before a Commission of the International Military Tribunal at Nuremberg on June 20, 1946 (mimeographed transcript, p. 1490): ". . . during the western campaign in France, Hitler stopped the armored component of my army group and the result was that the British were able to escape from Dunkirk. That was a very big mistake of a commander. He stated that the reason for this was that in the second phase of the French campaign . . . that he did not want to wreck those armored divisions needlessly. How angry we leaders were at that time is indescribable." In a paper on Hitler, which Rundstedt prepared at Nuremberg, he wrote: "A big mistake was the halting of two armored divisions just before Dunkirk, which enabled the English to escape over the Channel. *He was already thinking of the second part of the*

campaign against France. That is no considered strategy, but the sheer dilettantism of a layman." Gilbert, *The Psychology of Dictatorship* (1950) p. 223.

89. Churchill, *Their Finest Hour* pp. 76–78.

90. E.g., Von Mellenthin, *Panzer Battles* (1955) pp. 18–19; Blumentritt, *Von Rundstedt* (1952) pp. 74–78; Westphal, *The Year of Destiny 1939–1940*, in *The Fatal Decisions* (Freidin and Richardson, edit. 1956) p. 5; *The Rommel Papers* (Liddell Hart, edit. 1953) p. 35; Desmond Young, *Rommel –The Desert Fox* (1950) p. 53; Westphal, *The German Army in the West* (1951) pp. 86–88; Heusinger, *Befehl im Widerstreit* (1950) pp. 91–93; Paget, *Manstein* (1951) p. 25; Kesselring, *A Soldier's Record* (1954) pp. 58–59; Lossberg, *Im Wehrmacht Fuehrungsstab* (1950) pp. 80–82; Greiner, *Die Oberste Wehrmachtfuehrung* (1951) pp. 104–05; Assmann, *Deutsche Schicksalsjahre* (1950) pp. 167–70; Tippelskirch, *Geschichte des Zweiten Weltkriegs* (1951) pp. 94–95; Goerlitz, *History of the German General Staff* (1953) pp. 375–76; Goerlitz, *Der Zweite Weltkrieg* (1951) Vol. I, pp. 131–32; Guderian, *Panzer Leader* (1952) pp. 117–19; Galland, *The First and the Last* (1954) pp. 6–7; Bullock, *Hitler* (1952) pp. 537–38.

91. H.D. May 23, 1940.

92. *Supra* pp. 239–42.

93. *Supra* pp. 247–48.

94. J.D. May 24, 1940.

95. H.D. May 24, 1940.

96. J.D. May 24, 1940.

97. H.D. May 23, 1940; Guderian, *Panzer Leader* p. 114.

98. Ellis, *The War in France and Flanders* pp. 348 and 398.

99. Ellis, *op. cit. supra* pp. 138–39, 383, and 398.

100. Ellis, *op. cit. supra* p. 139.

101. Ellis, *op. cit. supra* pp. 136–37; Guderian, *op. cit. supra* pp. 116–17.

102. Ellis, *op. cit. supra* pp. 138–39 and 383.

103. J.D. May 24, 1940.

104. *Infra* p. 263.

105. H.D. May 25, 1940.

106. Ellis, *op. cit. supra* pp. 150 and 384.

107. Ellis, *op. cit. supra* pp. 151 and 384.

108. *Supra* p. 256 and footnote 90. Blumentritt's account in his biography

of Rundstedt (pp. 74–78) is especially disingenuous.

109. H.D. May 26, 1940.

110. H.D. May 26, 1940.

111. *Supra* pp. 244–52.

112. J.D. May 26, 1940.

113. *Cf.* Guderian, *Panzer Leader* p. 91.

114. Ellis, *op. cit. supra* pp. 151 and 384; H.D. May 23, 1940.

115. Kesselring, *A Soldier's Record* (1953) pp. 58–59; Galland, *The First and the Last* (1954) pp. 6–7.

116. *Supra* p. 256, note 88; letter of July 19, 1957, from Franz Halder to William L. Shirer.

117. Guderian, *Panzer Leader* p. 120; Liddell Hart, *The German Generals Talk* pp. 134–36, and numerous other works cited *supra* p. 256, note 90.

118. Letter of July 19, 1957, from Franz Halder to William L. Shirer.

119. Churchill, *The Gathering Storm* p. 100; Ellis, *op. cit. supra* p. 183.

120. Spears, *Prelude to Dunkirk* p. 192, relating his conference with Reynaud, Weygand, and others on May 25, 1940.

121. Churchill, *op. cit. supra* p. 92; compare Ellis, *op. cit. supra* pp. 208–10.

122. *Infra* p. 266.

123. H.D. May 30, 1940.

124. Churchill, *op. cit. supra* Book One, Chap. 5.

125. Ellis, *op. cit. supra* p. 192; Russell, *The Scourge of the Swastika* (1954) pp. 23–26.

126. Accounts of this conference are given in Churchill, *op. cit. supra* pp. 92–94, and Ellis, *op. cit. supra* pp. 208–10.

127. Ellis, *op. cit. supra* pp. 208 and 288–89.

128. Guderian, *op. cit. supra* pp. 119 and 511–12.

129. Ellis, *op. cit. supra* pp. 214 and 389.

130. H.D. May 31, 1940.

131. Ellis, *op. cit. supra* pp. 226–27 and 390.

132. Manstein, *Verlorene Siege* pp. 130–32; Ellis, *op. cit. supra* pp. 259–61.

133. Ellis, *op. cit. supra* pp. 129 and 391.

134. H.D. May 31, 1940.

135. Richards, *Royal Air Force 1939–1945* Vol. I, p. 136; Ellis, *op. cit. supra* pp. 185–86.

136. Ellis, *op. cit. supra* pp. 212–13 and 389; Richards, *op. cit. supra* pp. 137–38; Galland, *The First and the Last* p. 8.

137. Ellis, *op. cit. supra* pp. 220 and 390.

138. Churchill, *op. cit. supra* p. 105.

139. Ellis, *op. cit. supra* pp. 243 and 391.

140. Churchill, *op. cit. supra* p. 104.

141. Galland, *op. cit. supra* p. 7.

142. Churchill, *op. cit. supra* p. 101.

143. *Supra* pp. 147–49.

144. F.C.N.A. 1940, pp. 51–52.

145. F.C.N.A. 1940, p. 53–56.

CHAPTER EIGHT

1. *Supra* pp. 176–77.

2. J.D. May 20, 1940; H.D. May 21, 1940.

3. H.D. May 20, 1940; J.D. May 21, 1940.

4. H.D. and J.D. May 21, 1940.

5. J.D. May 20, 1940.

6. J.D. May 26, 1940; H.D. May 25 and 26, 1940.

7. H.D. May 28, 1940.

8. *Supra* p. 240.

9. Taylor, *Sword and Swastika* p. 334.

10. *Supra* pp. 69–71.

11. H.D. May 29 and 31, 1940.

12. H.D. May 20, 1940.

13. The plan was distributed by OKH's orders to the field armies, dated May 31, 1940. Ellis, *op. cit. supra* pp. 274 and 392.

14. Guderian, *op. cit. supra* p. 122.

15. *The Rommel Papers* p. 43.

16. Kesselring, *A Soldier's Record* p. 60.

17. See Von Seemen, *Die Ritterkreutztraeger* (Bad Nauheim 1955).

18. H.D. June 1, 1940.

19. *The Rommel Papers* p. 43.

20. H.D. June 4, 1940.

21. Kesselring, *A Soldier's Record* p. 61; H.D. June 4, 1940; Galland, *The First and the Last* p. 9.

22. The French IXth Corps included the one remaining British infantry division in France (the 51st) and the 31st and 40th French infantry divisions.

23. *The Rommel Papers* pp. 44–48.

24. Manstein, *Verlorene Siege* pp. 132–36.

25. *The Rommel Papers* pp. 50–57.
26. Young, *Rommel the Desert Fox* (1950) pp. 53–54.
27. *The Rommel Papers* pp. 55–57.
28. Paget, *Manstein* p. 26; Hart, *The German Generals Talk* (1948) p. 64.
29. Churchill, *Their Finest Hour* pp. 149–50. See also Spears, *The Fall of France* (1955) pp. 123–24; Ellis, *op. cit. supra* p. 276.
30. H.D. June 7, 8, and 9, 1940.
31. In Young, *Rommel the Desert Fox* it is stated (pp. 53–54) that Rommel's mission from the beginning was to prevent the embarkation of the 51st British Division at St. Valéry-en-Caux, which, after Dunkirk, was "about to take ship." Of course this is ridiculous. There was no intention of evacuating the 51st Division until Hoth reached the Seine, and none of using St. Valéry for an evacuation until Rommel's arrival at the coast left the British no alternative.
32. *The Rommel Papers* p. 66.
33. H.D. June 6, 1940.
34. H.D. June 7, 1940.
35. H.D. June 8, 1940.
36. Lanz, *Gebirgsjaeger* (Bad Nauheim 1954) pp. 78–82.
37. Hart, *The German Generals Talk* p. 140.
38. *Supra* pp. 239–40.
39. For these locations and details see *Feldzug in Frankreich*, situation maps for June 7–10, 1940; Hart, *op. cit. supra* pp. 140–41; H.D. June 7–10, 1940.
40. Mellenthin, *Panzer Battles* (1956) pp. 20–21.
41. *Infra* p. 296.
42. Guderian, *Panzer Leader* pp. 123–25.
43. *Supra* pp. 222 and 226.
44. Spears, *The Fall of France* pp. 62–65, 92–95, 109, and 114; Draper, *The Six Weeks' War* (1954) pp. 239–43.
45. *Supra* pp. 227–28 and 287; *The Rommel Papers* pp. 46–53.
46. H.D. June 7, 1940.
47. H.D. June 9, 1940.
48. Guderian, *Panzer Leader* p. 123.
49. Guderian, *op. cit. supra* pp. 121–24.
50. Guderian, *op. cit. supra* pp. 126–27.
51. H.D. June 14, 1940.
52. Churchill, *Their Finest Hour* pp. 192–93; Spears, *The Fall of France* pp. 255–56; Bryant, *The Turn of the Tide* (1957) pp. 135–37.
53. *Feldzug in Frankreich* June 14, 1940.
54. H.D. June 4, 5, 6, 7, 10, 13, and 14, 1940.
55. Ellis, *op. cit. supra* p. 303.
56. *The Rommel Papers* pp. 68–84.
57. Lanz, *Gebirgsjaeger* (1954) p. 87.
58. Spears, *The Fall of France* (1955) pp. 182–84 and 198–99; Bryant, *The Turn of the Tide* pp. 130–34.
59. Westphal, *The German Army in the West* (London 1951) p. 83.
60. Churchill, *Their Finest Hour* pp. 154–55; Shirer, *Berlin Diary* p. 417.
61. Hart, *The German Generals Talk* p. 93.
62. H.D. June 18, 1940.
63. Westphal, *op. cit. supra* p. 83.
64. H.D. June 11, 1940.
65. *Deutsche Soldaten Zeitung*, Aug. 20, 1953, p. 9.
66. H.D. June 14, 1940.
67. Churchill, *Their Finest Hour* p. 191.
68. *Supra* pp. 214–15.
69. H.D. June 15, 1940; Draper, *The Six Weeks' War* pp. 277–81.
70. Mellenthin, *op. cit. supra* pp. 22–23.
71. H.D. June 19, 1940.
72. H.D. June 1, 1940.
73. H.D. June 13, 1940.
74. Draper, *The Six Weeks' War* p. 267; Ciano, *Diario* (pub. 1946) entry for June 15, 1940.
75. Richards, *Royal Air Force* Vol. I, pp. 146–48; Spears, *The Fall of France* pp. 163–68.
76. *Ciano's Diplomatic Papers* (London 1948) pp. 372–75; Ciano, *Diario*, entry for June 18–19, 1940.
77. H.D. June 19 and 20, 1940.
78. H.D. June 20, 1940.
79. Ciano, *Diario*, entry for June 21, 1940.
80. H.D. June 21, 1940.
81. H.D. June 22, 1940.
82. H.D. June 23, 1940; Lanz, *Gebirgsjaeger* p. 89.
83. Churchill, *op. cit. supra* p. 130; Draper, *op. cit. supra* pp. 309–10.
84. Ciano, *Diario*, June 25, 1940.

85. See also Blumentritt, *Rundstedt* p. 82.

86. Fuller, *The Second World War* (1949) p. 65.

87. See, e.g., Churchill, *op. cit. supra* pp. 31, 36, 46–57, 59, 75, and 153; Spears, *The Fall of France, passim;* Draper, *The Six Weeks' War* pp. 313–22; Mellenthin, *Panzer Battles* pp. 23–25; Lyet, *La Bataille de France* (Paris 1947) *passim.*

88. DeJong, *The German Fifth Column* (1956) pp. 202–06.

89. Saint-Exupéry, *Flight to Arras* (1942) pp. 98–100.

90. Shirer, *Berlin Diary* (1941) p. 434.

91. Fuller, *The Second World War* (1949) pp. 63–64.

92. De Guingand, *Operation Victory* (1947) pp. 28–30.

93. Churchill, *op. cit. supra* pp. 46–49.

94. Spears, *The Fall of France* p. 212.

95. Churchill, *op. cit. supra* p. 49.

96. Goerlitz, *Die Zweite Weltkrieg* Vol. I, p. 140; Tippelskirch, *Geschichte des Zweiten Weltkriegs* p. 109; Fuller, *The Second World War* p. 79; Ellis, *The War in France and Flanders* p. 353.

97. *The Rommel Papers* p. 84.

98. *Geschichte der 7 Panzerdivision —Der Kampf im Westen* (1940); Teske, *Bewegungskrieg* (Heidelberg 1955) p. 118.

99. *Supra* p. 303. There were also battle wounds among the generals. For example, Generalleutnant Max Dennerlein, commander of the 290th Division (in the XVIIIth Corps), was severely wounded by a grenade while leading his troops across the Aisne near Soissons. *Deutsche Soldaten Zeitung,* Nov. 1957, p. 9.

100. See *Deutsche Soldaten Zeitung,* Jan. 1, 1954, p. 10; Folttmann and Moeller-Witten, *Opfergang der Generale* (Berlin 1952), p. 55.

101. Churchill, *op. cit. supra* p. 256; Ellis, *op. cit. supra* pp. 326–27.

CHAPTER NINE

1. The account of this episode is based on information furnished to the author by Mme. Schuler-Wagner's

daughter, Mrs. Loul McIntosh, now of New York City. Mme. Schuler-Wagner remembers the Rittmeister's name as "von und zu Otto," but there is no such name in the regular German Army lists, which do, however, show a Rittmeister von und zu Aufsess.

2. See, e.g., Shirer, *Berlin Diary* pp. 413, 441; Pitt, *The Courage of Fear* (1957), p. 84.

3. Lemkin, *Axis Rule in Occupied Europe* (1944) pp. 193–97 and 419–43; *Hitler's Europe*, edit. by Arnold and Veronica Toynbee (Royal Institute of International Affairs, London 1954) pp. 509–19.

4. Trevor-Roper, "The Mind of Adolf Hitler," introductory essay to *Hitler's Secret Conversations* (1953) p. x; Hoffmann, *Hitler Was My Friend* (1955) pp. 216–17.

5. H.D. June 16 and 17, 1940.

6. *Ciano's Diplomatic Papers* (London (1948) pp. 322–75; Ciano, *Diario* pp. 279–80.

7. *Supra* p. 305.

8. H.D. June 20 and 21, 1940.

9. Shirer, *Berlin Diary* (1941) p. 422.

10. H.D. June 21, 1940.

11. See the accounts of the negotiations in Draper, *The Six Weeks' War* pp. 310–13; Schmidt, *Hitler's Interpreter* (1931) pp. 181–84.

12. Ciano, *Diario* pp. 282–83.

13. The texts are given in Draper, *op. cit. supra* pp. 324–30.

14. Schmidt, *op. cit. supra* p. 183.

15. See, e.g., Blumentritt, *Von Rundstedt* pp. 87–91.

16. Hoffmann, *Hitler Was My Friend* (1955) pp. 122–23; Dietrich, *Hitler* (1955) p. 83; Bullock, *Hitler* (1952) pp. 542–43.

17. Taylor, *Sword and Swastika* pp. 354–57.

18. *Supra* p. 34.

19. N.D. EC-606.

20. N.D. EC-21, EC-69, EC-155, EC-618, 1161-PS, 2353-PS, 183-RF, and Keitel 11.

21. N.D. EC-155, EC-618 and 183-RF.

22. N.D. 1161-PS.

23. N.D. NI-048.

24. N.D. 1155-PS.

25. N.D. EC-137.

26. N.D. NI-3513.

27. For all this see, e.g., N.D. NID-1558, NI-3516, NI-3513, NI-3522, NI-3518, NI-3529, and NI-3548.

28. See *Hitler's Europe, supra* pp. 47–59 and 165–71.

29. H.D. May 8 and 9, 1940.

30. The directive of May 15, 1940 is set forth in 5 *Onderdrukking in Verzet* pp. 264–70.

31. H.D. May 16 and 17, 1940.

32. Vagts, *Defense and Diplomacy* (1956) pp. 206–07; Liu, *A Military History of Modern China* (1956) pp. 84, 98, 100, 162–66.

33. H.D. May 17, 1940.

34. *Supra* pp. 91–93.

35. H.D. May 17, 1940.

36. The decree is given in Lemkin, *op. cit. supra* pp. 446–47.

37. *Id.* pp. 447–50.

38. Heinkel, *Stormy Life* (1956) pp. 54–56, 66, 69, and 72; *Who's Who in Germany and Austria* (London 1945) Part II, p. 23.

39. *Supra* pp. 163–64.

40. N.D. 997-PS, 2921-PS, 3333-PS, and 224-F; *Hitler's Europe, loc. cit. supra;* Lemkin, *op. cit. supra* pp. 200–07 and 446–97.

41. N.D. 997-PS; *Hitler's Europe, supra* pp. 497–502.

42. See N.D. 079-UK; *Hitler's Europe, supra* pp. 534–41; Lemkin, *op. cit. supra* pp. 208–20 and 498–505.

43. Lemkin, *op. cit. supra* pp. 125 and 313.

44. N.D. 3604–09-PS, EC-34, EC-41, EC-155, and ECH-2; *Hitler's Europe, supra* pp. 130, 475–94; Lemkin, *op. cit. supra* pp. 125–29 and 313–40.

45. *Supra* pp. 280–81.

46. H.D. June 5, 1940; *Die Hoeheren Dienststellen der Deutschen Wehrmacht* (Munich 1953) p. 63.

47. Dirksen, *Moscow, Tokyo, London* (London 1951) p. 123.

48. N.D. EC-113.

49. N.D. Keitel-13.

50. Westphal, *The German Army in the West* (1951) p. 91.

51. N.D. EC-113.

52. H.D. Sept. 23, 1940.

53. N.D. 1155-PS.

54. T.M.W.C. Vol. VI, p. 437; *Hitler's Europe, supra* pp. 92 and 368.

55. N.D. R-114.

56. Lemkin, *op. cit. supra* p. 171; *Hitler's Europe, supra* p. 368.

57. T.M.W.C. Vol. VI, p. 439.

58. T.M.W.C. Vol. VI, p. 436.

59. H.D. Aug. 22 and 26, 1940.

60. Taylor, *Sword and Swastika* pp. 175–238.

61. Churchill, *Their Finest Hour* p. 100.

62. *Id.* pp. 225–26.

63. H.D. July 13, 1940.

64. See Westphal, *The German Army in the West* p. 92; H.D. July 30, 1940.

65. See, e.g., pp. 82–84 *supra.*

66. N.D. C-41.

67. T.M.W.C. Vol. XIII, p. 477–78.

68. Foltmann and Moeller-Witten, *Opfergang der Generale* (1952) pp. 66, 117, and 129.

69. F.C.N.A. June 20, 1940, p. 58.

70. *Id.* July 11, 1940, pp. 63–66.

71. N.D. 1155-PS.

72. H.D. July 30, Aug. 9 and 10, 1940.

73. F.C.N.A. 1940, pp. 95–96.

74. H.D. Sept. 16, 1940.

75. H.D. Sept. 30, 1940.

76. H.D. Oct. 3, 1940. Halder states that the remark was made by either Hitler or Ribbentrop, and it is definitely characteristic of the former.

77. H.D. Oct. 15, 1940.

78. *Ciano's Diplomatic Papers* (London 1948) pp. 395–98.

79. See the account in Schmidt, *Hitler's Interpreter* (1951) pp. 192–99.

80. *Hitler's Europe, supra* p. 4.

81. H.D. June 23 and 24, 1940; see also the OKW directive of June 19, 1940, summarized in Appendix D, *infra,* p. 436.

82. Lossberg, *Im Wehrmacht Fuehrungsstab* (1949) pp. 85–86.

83. The Black Forest headquarters *Tannenberg* was closed July 6, 1940. See *Die Hoeheren Dienststellen der Deutschen Wehrmacht* (1953) p. 109.

84. Schacht, *Confessions of "The Old Wizard"* (1955) pp. 367–68.

85. H.D. July 5 and 8, 1940.

86. H.D. July 14, 1940.

87. *Id.* July 16 and 20, 1940. In Blumentritt, *Von Rundstedt* (1952) p. 83 it is stated that "a grand Peace Parade took place on the Champs-Élysées," but surely this is erroneous. Guderian, in his *Panzer Leader,* states categorically (pp. 136–37) that the parade did not take place, and there is no mention of

such an affair in the contemporaneous newspaper reports from Paris. See also *Paris-Soir*, July 19, 1940; Meyer, *Grenadiere* (Munich 1957) p. 38.

88. *Voelkischer Beobachter*, July 19, 1940; Shirer, *Berlin Diary* (1941) pp. 451–52.

89. Shirer, *op. cit. supra* pp. 452–57.

90. Hoffmann, *Hitler Was My Friend* (1955) p. 121.

91. *The New York Times*, July 20, 1940, p. 5.

92. This inference was emphatically confirmed by Halder when interrogated by the author on Dec. 16, 1947. See also Manstein, *Verlorene Siege* pp. 149–50.

93. Shirer, *op. cit. supra* p. 456.

94. Frischauer, *The Rise and Fall of Hermann Goering* (1951) p. 193.

95. Seemen, *Die Ritterkreuztraeger* pp. 9 and 296–97.

96. *Supra* p. 304.

97. *Supra* p. 174, and Taylor, *Sword and Swastika* p. 203.

98. *Supra* pp. 83–84.

99. Kesselring, *Soldat bis zum Letzten Tag* (1953) p. 86.

100. *Hitler's Secret Conversations* (1953) p. 66.

101. Gisevius, *To the Bitter End* (1947) p. 456.

102. *The Von Hassell Diaries* (1946), entry for Aug. 10, 1940, p. 147.

103. *Supra* pp. 8–9 and 42–54; Taylor, *Sword and Swastika* pp. 208–28.

104. H.D. Aug. 13, 1940.

105. *Id.* Sept. 3, 1940.

106. *Id.* Aug. 21, 1940.

107. *The Von Hassell Diaries* (1946) p. 139, entry for May 24–27, 1940.

108. Taylor, *Sword and Swastika* pp. 118–238.

CHAPTER TEN

1. N.D. 1776–PS, in XXVIII T.M. W.C., pp. 301–03.

2. See, e.g., Von Lossberg, *Im Wehrmachtfuehrungsstab* (Hamburg 1949) p. 94; Blumentritt, *Von Rundstedt* p. 85.

3. H.D. July 16, 1940.

4. Blumentritt, *op. cit. supra* pp. 84–85.

5. F.C.N.A. 1940, p. 57.

6. *Supra* pp. 84–88.

7. Churchill, *Their Finest Hour* pp. 257–58.

8. *Supra* pp. 352–53.

9. Taylor, *Sword and Swastika* pp. 274–75.

10. *Supra* pp. 56–58.

11. *The Schellenberg Memoirs* (1956) pp. 105–07.

12. *Supra* p. 34.

13. Derry, *The Campaign in Norway* p. 222.

14. F.C.N.A. 1940, p. 49.

15. *Supra* pp. 230–31.

16. *Supra* p. 233.

17. *Supra* pp. 252–65.

18. *Cf.* Manstein, *Verlorene Siege* pp. 152–54.

19. *Fleming*, Operation *Sea Lion* (1957) pp. 305–09.

20. *Supra* pp. 46–53.

21. H.D., e.g., June 17, 18, and 19, and July 14, 1940.

22. F.C.N.A. 1940, entry for June 4, 1940.

23. J. R. M. Butler, *Grand Strategy* (H. M. Stationery Office 1957) p. 270.

24. *Id* pp. 265–66; H.D. entries in June and July 1940.

25. In his great speech in the House of Commons on June 4, 1940. See *Their Finest Hour* p. 118.

26. H.D. July 13 and 22, 1940.

27. *Id.* July 31, 1940.

28. Hinsley, *Hitler's Strategy* (1951) p. 63.

29. See, e.g., Huntington, *The Soldier and the State* (1957) pp. 235–36.

30. *Id.* p. 277.

31. Clausewitz, *On War* (Jolles translation, Infantry Journal Press 1950) p. 618.

32. Published in Germany as *Kriegskunst Heute und Morgen*, and in the United States under the title *The Art of Modern Warfare* (1940) with an introduction by George Fielding Eliot, in a translation by Theodore W. Knauth.

33. Foertsch, *op. cit. supra* p. 74.

34. *Id.* p. 12.

35. For further details on the *Wehrmachtakademie* and its predecessors, see Erfurth, *Die Geschichte des Deutschen Generalstabes 1918–1945* pp. 176–79; Taylor, *Sword and Swastika* pp. 102, 205, 251.

36. *Supra* p. 15; Taylor, *Sword and Swastika* pp. 166–74.

Index to Appendices

GLOSSARY OF GERMAN MILITARY TERMS, COVER-NAMES, AND ABBREVIATIONS

Abwehr	Abw.	Intelligence dept. of OKW
Armee	Arm.	An army (field formation; *cf. Heer)*
Armee Abteilung	Arm. Abt.	The cadre for an army headquarters in process of formation
Armeekorps	AK	Army corps
Armeeoberkommando	AOK	An army headquarters
ausser Dienst	a. D.	Out of service—retired
Barbarossa	——	Cover-name for attack on Soviet Union
Befehlshaber	Befh.	Commander
Braun	——	Cover-name for projected Italo-German offensive across upper Rhine
Chef des Generalstabs des Heeres	C.G.S.	Chief of the General Staff of the Army
Division	Div.	Division
Eisernes Kreuz	E.K.	Iron Cross
Ersatzheer	Ersh.	Home army (replacement and training)
Fall Gelb	——	Cover-name for attack on France and Low Countries, May 1940
Fall Rot	——	Cover-name for second phase of Battle of France, June 1940
Fallschirm	Fallsch.	Parachute
Fallschirmtruppen	F.S. Tr.	Parachute troops
Felsennest	——	Hitler's headquarters in the Eifel, May 10–June 6, 1940
Festung	Fest.	Fortress
Fliegerkorps	Fl. K.	Air corps
Flottenchef	——	Commander of the Fleet
Flugabwehrkanonen	Flak	Antiaircraft artillery
Gebirgstruppen	Geb. Tr.	Mountain troops
Generalkommando	GKdo	Army corps headquarters

Generalquartiermeister	Gen. Qu.	Principal staff officer for supply and administration at OKH
Generalstab des Heeres	Gen St d H	General Staff of the Army
Gruppe	Gr.	Group; in Luftwaffe, about 30 aircraft in 3 Staffeln
Heer	H.	The Army
Heeresgruppe	H. Gr.	An Army group
Hoeheres Kommando z.b.V.	Hoeh. Kdo.	Administrative or second-line headquarters at corps level
Jagdgeschwader	J.G.	Fighter squadron of 3 Gruppen
Junkers 87	Ju 87	Junkers single-engine dive bomber (*Stuka*).
Junkers 88	Ju 88	Junkers twin-engine medium bomber
Juno	—	Cover-name for fleet sortie off Norway in June 1940
Kampfgeschwader	K.G.	Bomber squadron
Kommandeur	Kdr.	Commander (in the Army, of a division, regiment, or battalion)
Kommandierender General	Kom. Gen.	Commanding general of a corps or its equivalent
Kriegsmarine	M.	The Navy
Landwehr	Landw.	Reserve formations of men between 35 and 45 years old
Luftflotte	Lfl.	Air fleet
Luftlandetruppen	L. L. Tr.	Air-landing (airborne) troops
Luftwaffe	Lw.	The Air Force
Marinegruppenkommando	Mar. GrKdo.	Highest naval sector headquarters
Messerschmitt 109	Me 109	Messerschmitt single-engine fighter
Messerschmitt 110	Me 110	Messerschmitt twin-engine fighter
Militaerbefehlshaber	Mil. Bef.	Military Commander in occupied territory, responsible to OKH
Oberbefehlshaber	Ob.	Commander-in-Chief (of army groups, armies, air fleets, naval group commands, and a few other headquarters immediately under OKW, OKH, OKL, or OKM)
Oberbefehlshaber des Heeres	ObdH	Commander-in-Chief of the Army
Oberbefehlshaber der Kriegsmarine	ObdM	Commander-in-Chief of the Navy

Oberbefehlshaber der Luftwaffe	ObdL	Commander-in-Chief of the Air Force
Oberbefehlshaber Ost	Oberost	Commander-in-Chief East
Oberfeldkommandantur	OberfeldKdr.	Military occupation area headquarters
Oberkommando des Heeres	OKH	Headquarters of the Army
Oberkommando der Kriegsmarine	OKM	Headquarters of the Navy
Oberkommando der Luftwaffe	OKL	Headquarters of the Air Force
Oberkommando der Wehrmacht	OKW	Headquarters of the Armed Forces
Oberquartiermeister (I, IV, etc.)	O Qu	Principal OKH staff officer for operations (I) or intelligence (IV), etc.
Oberster Befehlshaber	Oberst. Bef.	Supreme Commander of the Armed Forces (Hitler)
Panzer	Pz.	Armor
Reichsfuehrer SS	RFSS	Leader of the SS (Himmler)
Reichsluftminister	RLM	Reich Air Minister (Goering)
Reichswehr	Rw	The armed forces from 1920 to 1935
Ritterkreuz	Ritt.	Knight's Cross of the Iron Cross
Schutzstaffel der NSDAP	SS	Protection squads; Himmler's components of the Nazi party
Schwerpunkt	—	Point of main effort
Seekriegsleitung	SKL	Naval War Staff
Seeloewe	—	Sea Lion; cover-name for invasion of Britain
Staffel	St.	Basic Luftwaffe formation of about 10 aircraft
Sturzkampfgeschwader	Stuka	Dive-bomber squadron
Tannenberg	—	Hitler's headquarters in the Black Forest, June 28–July 6, 1940
Unterseeboot	U-Boat	Submarine
Waffen-SS	W-SS	Armed and militarized components of the SS
Waffenstillstand	—	Armistice
Wehrkreis	Wkr.	German army district, in peacetime equivalent to corps area
Wehrmacht	Wehrm.	The Armed Forces (from 1935)
Wehrmachtbefehlshaber	W. Bef.	Armed forces commander in occupied territory, responsible to OKW
Wehrmachtfuehrungsstab	WFst.	Operational staff of OKW

Wehrwirtschaft	Wehrwirt.	Military Economy
Weseruebung	W.	Cover-name for invasion of Norway and Denmark
Westfeldzug	—	Campaign in the West (France and Low Countries)
Wolfsschlucht	—	Hitler's headquarters at Brûly-de-Pesche, June 6–25, 1940
Zeppelin	—	OKH headquarters at Zossen
Zerstoerer	Z.	A destroyer (naval)
Zerstoerergeschwader	Z.G.	Twin-engined fighter squadron
zur besonderer Verwendung	z.b.V.	For special employment
zur Verfuegung	z.V.	At disposal; retired officer available for duty

APPENDIX B

GERMAN MILITARY RANKS AND RANK LISTS

MOST GERMAN MILITARY RANKS can be translated accurately by their English equivalents, but for precision the German titles of rank are used in the text. By and large, the German officer ranks follow the pattern common to the military in all countries. The army rank of captain is *Hauptmann* except in the cavalry, where it is *Rittmeister*. The army rank of *General* (equivalent to our rank of lieutenant general) is formally given with the bearer's branch of service—*General der Infanterie, General der Artillerie,* or *General der Flieger* (in the Luftwaffe) as the case may be. An entirely new set of titles was established for the ranks in the SS.

From time to time, often but not always on retirement from active duty, officers of the Wehrmacht were given a sort of brevet rank, in which case their titles of rank were preceded by the word *charakterisiert* (literally "in the character of"), commonly abbreviated as *char*. These officers wore the insignia of their *charakterisiert* rank, but remained junior on the rank list to all those who held the same rank without the prefix.

When officers were retired from the regular active-duty roster, they were either declared unavailable for further duty, in which case they were listed as *a.D.* (*ausser Dienst*, out of service) or, if subject to recall to duty, as *z.V.* (*zur Verfuegung*, at disposal).

In the German Army at the beginning of World War II there were no *Generalfeldmarschaelle*. The commanders-in-chief of the army groups were *Generalobersten,* and of the armies *Generalobersten* or *Generale.* Corps commanders were *Generale* or *Generalleutnante,* and divisional commanders (except in the special case of General Volkmann)* were *Generalleutnante* or *Generalmajore.*

* *Supra,* p. 26.

TABLE 1

COMPARATIVE TABLE OF GERMAN AND AMERICAN
MILITARY RANKS

German Army and Air Force	U. S. Army	SS
Generalfeldmarschall	General of the Army	Reichsfuehrer SS
Generaloberst	General	Oberstgruppenfuehrer
General (der Inf., etc.)	Lt. General	Obergruppenfuehrer
Generalleutnant	Major General	Gruppenfuehrer
Generalmajor	Brig. General	Brigadefuehrer
—	—	Oberfuehrer
Oberst	Colonel	Standartenfuehrer
Oberstleutnant	Lt. Colonel	Obersturmbannfuehrer
Major	Major	Sturmbannfuehrer
Hauptmann Rittmeister	Captain	Hauptsturmfuehrer
Oberleutnant	Lieutenant	Obersturmfuehrer
Leutnant	Second Lieutenant	Untersturmfuehrer

German Navy	U. S. Navy
Grossadmiral	Admiral of the Fleet
Generaladmiral	—
Admiral	Admiral
Vizeadmiral	Vice Admiral
Konteradmiral	Rear Admiral
Kommodore *	Commodore *
Kapitaen zur See	Captain
Fregattenkapitaen	Commander
Korvettenkapitaen	Lt. Commander
Kapitaenleutnant	Lieutenant
Oberleutnant zur See	Lieutenant (j.g.)
Leutnant zur See	Ensign

* *Kommodore* was not one of the regular ranks. A few officers with the rank of *Kapitaen zur See* who were given command of a large number of small ships, such as destroyers or submarines, were given the title *Kapitaen zur See und Kommodore*—for example, Bonte when he commanded the ten destroyers that carried Dietl's troops to Narvik (p. 124, *supra*). The American rank of Commodore was revived during World War II but has since been discontinued.

TABLE 2

ARMY RANK AND ASSIGNMENT LIST: MAY 1940

Name	Seniority	Assignment †
GENERALOBERSTEN		
1. v. Brauchitsch	4.2.38	C.-in-C. Army
2. v. Rundstedt *	1.3.38(1)	Army Group A
3. v. Bock	1.3.38(2)	Army Group B
4. v. Leeb *	1.3.38(3)	Army Group C
5. Keitel, Wilhelm	1.11.38	Chief, OKW
6. List	1.4.39	12th Army
7. Blaskowitz	1.10.39(1)	9th Army [1]
8. v. Kluge	1.10.39(2)	4th Army
9. v. Witzleben	1.10.39(2a)	1st Army
10. v. Reichenau	1.10.39(3)	6th Army
GENERALE		
11. Dollmann	1.4.36(2)	7th Army
12. v. Weichs	1.10.36(3)	2nd Army
13. Heitz	1.4.37(1)	VIIIth Corps
14. v. Kuechler	1.4.37(3)	18th Army
15. v. Wietersheim	1.2.38(2)	XIVth Corps
16. Schroth	1.2.38(3)	XIIth Corps
17. Kuntze	1.2.38(4)	XLIInd Corps [2]
18. Halder	1.2.38(5)	Chief, General Staff, OKH
19. v. Schwedler	1.2.38(6)	IVth Corps
20. v. Schobert	1.2.38(7)	VIIth Corps
21. Busch	1.2.38(8)	16th Army
22. Kienitz	1.4.38(1)	XVIIth Corps
23. Foerster	1.4.38(2)	VIth Corps
24. Beyer	1.4.38(3)	XVIIIth Corps
25. Waeger	1.11.38(1)	XXVIIth Corps [3]
26. Guderian	1.11.38(1a)	XIXth Corps
27. Hoth	1.11.38(2)	XVth Corps

* Officers listed with asterisk were so listed in the official German *Rangliste*, indicating that active rank was held only for the duration of the war. These officers had been temporarily restored to the active list, after a prewar retirement from active duty.

† Unless otherwise indicated, the officer commanded the unit listed in this column. Important changes in assignment between October 1939 and May 1940 are indicated in the numbered notes at the end of the table.

ARMY RANK AND ASSIGNMENT LIST: MAY 1940
[CONTINUED]

Name	Seniority	Assignment
	GENERALE (*continued*)	
28. Strauss	1.11.38(3)	IInd Corps
29. Haase, Curt	1.11.38(4)	IIIrd Corps
30. Volkmann °	1.1.39(1)	94th Division [4]
31. Raschick	1.4.39(1)	No assignment [5]
32. Leeb, Emil	1.4.39(3)	Chief of Ordnance, OKH [6]
33. Friderici	1.4.39(4)	Military Plenipotentiary, Bohemia and Moravia
34. v. Stuelpnagel, Karl-Heinrich	1.4.39(5)	O.Qu.I, OKH
35. Fromm	1.4.39(6)	Home Army
36. Hoepner	1.4.39(7)	XVIth Corps
37. Ruoff	1.5.39	Vth Corps
38. Wodrig	1.10.39(1)	XXVIth Corps
39. v. Falkenhorst	1.10.39(2)	Group XXI [7]
40. Petzel	1.10.39(3)	Wehrkreis XXI
41. v. Erfurth	1.4.40(1)	O.Qu.V, OKH
42. Geyr v. Schweppenburg	1.4.40(2)	XXIVth Corps [8]
43. Hartmann	1.4.40(3)	XXXth Corps
44. v. Boetticher	1.4.40(4)	Mil. Attaché United States
45. v. Cochenhausen, Friedrich °	*Char.* 1.3.38	Wehrkreis XIII
46. Muff	*Char.* 25.3.38	Wehrkreis XI
	GENERALLEUTNANTE	
47. v. Dalwigk zu Lichtenfels	1.10.34(2)	Wehrkreis III
48. Schwandner	1.5.35	Wehrkreis X [9]
49. v. Wilmowsky	1.8.35(1)	Insp. Recruiting Potsdam
50. Luedke	1.11.35(1)	German Troops, Denmark [9]
	——— ‡	
51. Osswald	1.4.36(1)	Wehrkreis V
52. Glokke	1.10.36(4)	Wehrkreis VI
53. v. Rabenau	1.1.37(2)	Chief, Army Archives
54. Otto, Paul	1.1.37(3)	Chief, Army Mission to Slovakia

‡ Below are listed only those *Generalleutnante* and *Generalmajore* who are mentioned in the text, or held important commands in the field, or were *Wehrkreis* commanders, or held important staff assignments. There were 155 *Generalleutnante* and 207 *Generalmajore*, and 408 in all with general officer rank.

ARMY RANK AND ASSIGNMENT LIST: MAY 1940
[CONTINUED]

Name	Seniority	Assignment
	‡ (continued)	
55. Koch-Erpach	1.4.37(2)	8th Division
56. Schaller-Kallide	1.4.37(4)	Wehrkreis XVIII
57. v. Biegeleben	1.8.37(1)	6th Division
58. Weyer	1.8.37(2)	14th Division
59. Koestring	1.8.37(6)	Mil. Attaché Moscow
62. v. Viebahn	1.1.38(5)	257th Division
64. Bock	1.2.38(1)	Wehrkreis XX
65. v. Obstfelder	1.2.38(3)	28th Division
68. Heinrici	1.3.38(1)	16th Division
70. Jacob	1.3.38(3)	Insp. Engineers, OKH
72. Hansen, Christian	1.3.38(6)	Xth Corps [10]
73. Schubert, Albrecht	1.3.38(7)	XXIIIrd Corps [11]
74. v. Vietinghoff	1.3.38(8)	XIIIth Corps
77. Lindemann	1.4.38(1)	36th Division
78. Stumme	1.4.38(2)	XLth Corps [12]
81. v. Manstein	1.4.38(5)	XXXVIIIth Corps [13]
83. Wiktorin	1.4.38(7)	20th Mot. Div.
84. Schmidt, Rudolf	1.6.38(1)	XXXIXth Corps [14]
89. v. Both	1.10.38(1)	Ist Corps
90. Veiel	1.10.38(2)	2nd Pz. Div.
91. v. Cochenhausen, Conrad	1.10.38(3)	10th Division
95. Olbricht	1.1.39(2)	Chief, General Office, OKH
96. Reinhardt	1.1.39(3)	XLIst Corps [15]
97. v. Brockdorff-Ahlefeldt	1.3.39	23rd Division
98. v. Faber du Faur	1.4.39(1)	Attached to 18th Army as a rear area commandant
99. Lemelsen	1.4.39(2)	29th Mot. Div.
100. v. Speck	1.6.39(1)	XLIIIrd Corps [16]
102. v. Kortzfleisch	1.6.39(3)	XIth Corps [17]
104. Feuerstein	1.6.39(5)	2nd Mt. Div.
106. Boehme	1.6.39(7)	32nd Division
107. v. Briesen	1.8.39(1)	30th Division
108. v. Salmuth	1.8.39(2)	Ch. of Staff, A.Gr.B
109. Hansen, Erik	1.8.39(3)	4th Division
110. Brand, Fritz	1.8.39(4)	Insp. War Schools
111. v. Walsporn	1.8.39(5)	5th Pz. Div.
114. Bertram	1.8.39(8)	Pres., Military Court
124. Felber	1.10.39(10)	Ch. of Staff, A.Gr.C [18]

ARMY RANK AND ASSIGNMENT LIST: MAY 1940
[CONTINUED]

Name	Seniority	Assignment
	‡ (continued)	
130. v. Tiedemann	1.11.39(4)	207th Division
131. Groppe	1.11.39(5)	No assignment [18a]
133. v. Arnim	1.12.39(2)	52nd Division
134. Kuebler, Ludwig	1.12.39(3)	1st Mt. Div.
135. Schaal	1.12.39(4)	10th Pz. Div.
137. Thomas, Georg	1.1.40(2)	Chief, Economics, OKW
140. v. Mackensen	1.1.40(5)	Ch. of Staff, 12th Army
141. v. Chappuis	1.1.40(6)	Ch. of Staff, XIVth Corps
143. Fellgiebel	1.2.40(2)	Chief Signal Officer, OKW and OKH
147. v. Sodenstern	1.2.40(6)	Ch. of Staff, A.Gr.A [18]
148. v. Sponeck	1.2.40(7)	22nd Division
149. Sixt v. Armin	1.3.40(1)	95th Division
151. Loch	1.3.40(3)	17th Division
152. Ott, Eugen	1.3.40(4)	Insp. Infantry
153. Dennerlein	1.3.40(5)	290th Division
154. Keitel, Bodewin	1.3.40(6)	Chief of Personnel, OKH
155. Mieth	1.3.40(7)	Acting O.Qu.I, OKH [19]
156. Metz *	1.3.40(8)	XXXIVth Corps Command
157. Model	1.4.40(1)	Ch. of Staff, 16th Army
159. Kuntzen	1.4.40(3)	8th Pz. Div.
161. Kirchner	1.4.40(5)	1st Pz. Div.
162. Fischer v. Weikersthal	1.4.40(6)	Ch. of Staff, 7th Army
163. Hollidt	1.4.40(7)	Ch. of Staff, 9th Army [20]
164. Dietl	1.4.40(8)	3rd Mt. Div.
175. Pellengahr	Char. 1.4.38	196th Division
GENERALMAJORE		
206. v. Tippelskirch, Kurt	1.4.38(13)	O.Qu. IV, OKH
219. v. Hanneken	1.6.38(7)	In Min. of Economics
224. Kempf	1.8.38(3a)	6th Pz. Div.
226. Brennecke	1.8.38(5)	Ch. of Staff, 4th Army
243. Hubicki	1.10.38(12)	9th Pz. Div.
245. Engelbrecht	1.1.39(2)	163rd Division
249. Hilpert	1.1.39(7a)	Ch. of Staff, 1st Army [21]
250. Reinecke	1.1.39(8)	Ch. General Dept., OKW
251. Paulus	1.1.39(9)	Ch. of Staff, 6th Army
253. v. Knobelsdorff	1.1.39(11)	19th Division

ARMY RANK AND ASSIGNMENT LIST: MAY 1940
[CONTINUED]

Name	Seniority	Assignment
	GENERALMAJORE (continued)	
264. v. der Chevallerie	1.3.39(6)	83rd Division
267. Stumpff	1.3.39(9)	3rd Pz. Div.
271. Eberhardt	1.4.39(1)	60th Division
274. Mueller, Eugen	1.4.39(4)	Gen. Qu., OKH [22]
276. Stapf	1.4.39(6)	OKH Liaison to OKL
277. Konrad	1.4.39(7)	Ch. of Staff, 2nd Army [23]
280. Jodl, Alfred	1.4.39(10)	Ch. of Ops., OKW
284. Marcks	1.4.39(14)	Ch. of Staff, 18th Army
293. Stever	1.6.39(1)	4th Pz. Div.
297. Roettig	1.6.39(5)	198th Division
300. Kleffel	1.6.39(8)	1st Division
301. v. Rintelen	1.6.39(9)	Mil. Attaché, Rome
307. Rommel	1.6.39(16)	7th Pz. Div.
313. Wittke	1.8.39(6)	170th Division
314. v. Rothkirch und Panthen	1.8.39(8)	13th Division
318. v. Uthmann	1.10.39(4)	Mil. Attaché, Scandinavia
321. Tittel	1.10.39(7)	69th Division
329. Himer	1.10.39(15)	Ch. of Staff, H.K. XXXI
330. Horn	1.10.39(16)	214th Division
334. Zickwolff	1.10.39(20)	227th Division
335. Gercke	1.10.39(21)	Ch. of Transport, OKH
338. Meyer-Rabingen	1.11.39(3)	197th Division
343. v. Seydlitz-Kurzbach	1.12.39(4)	12th Division
345. Rendulic	1.12.39(6)	14th Division [24]
348. Sintzenich	1.12.39(9)	33rd Division [16]
361. Feldt	1.2.40(7)	1st Cavalry Division
362. v. Langermann und Erlencamp	1.3.40(1)	29th Mot. Division [25]
395. Gullmann	Char. 1.6.39	Cmdt. Muenster [26]

Notes

[1] *Blaskowitz:* Commander-in-Chief East (*Oberost*) in Poland from October 1939 to May 1940. The 9th Army was not formally constituted until May 14, 1940.

[2] *Kuntze:* Commander of the XXIVth Corps until the early spring of 1940, when he was replaced by Geyr v. Schweppenburg.

[3] *Waeger:* Commander of the XXVth Corps in October 1940; subsequently exchanged posts with Ritter v. Prager (see Table 4), then commander of the XXVIIth Corps.

[4] *Volkmann:* Formerly *General der Flieger* and commander of the Air Force War College (*Luftkriegsakademie*). Returned to the Army on the outbreak of war,

with rank and assignment as above. Killed in an automobile accident on August 21, 1940.

[5] *Raschick:* Commander of the XXIIIrd Corps in October 1939, and of the XXXVIIth Corps Command until March 1940. Replaced by Boehm-Tettelbach (see Table 4). Had suffered an accident and was without an assignment until May 1941, when he was appointed commander of Wehrkreis X.

[6] *Leeb, Emil:* Commander of the XIth Corps October to April 1940, and then replaced General Becker, who had committed suicide, as Chief of Ordnance.

[7] *v. Falkenhorst:* Commander of the XXIst Corps, redesignated Group XXI in March 1940, when *Weseruebung* was undertaken.

[8] *Geyr v. Schweppenburg:* Commander of the 3rd Panzer Division until he replaced Kuntze, *supra,* note 2.

[9] *Luedke:* Commander of Wehrkreis X until May 1940, when he was relieved by Schwandner and replaced Kaupisch (see Table 4) in Denmark.

[10] *Hansen, Christian:* Commander of the 25th Division from the outbreak of the war, but after the Polish campaign replaced Ulex (see Table 4) as shown above.

[11] *Schubert, Albrecht:* Commander of the 44th Division until the winter of 1939–40, when he replaced Raschick (*supra,* note 5) as commander of the XXIIIrd Corps.

[12] *Stumme:* Commander of the 2nd Light (converted to the 7th Panzer) Division until he took command of the new XLth Corps and was replaced by Rommel.

[13] *v. Manstein:* Chief of Staff of Army Group A until February 1940, when he was replaced by Sodenstern (*infra,* note 18) and took command of the new XXXVIIIth Corps.

[14] *Schmidt:* Commander of the 1st Panzer Division until February 1940, when he was replaced by Kirchner and took command of the new XXXIXth Corps.

[15] *Reinhardt:* Commander of the 4th Panzer Division until February 1940, when he was replaced by Stever and took command of the new XLIst Corps.

[16] *v. Speck:* Commander of the 33rd Division until the spring of 1940, when he was replaced by Sintzenich and took command of the new XLIIIrd Corps.

[17] *v. Kortzfleisch:* Commander of the 1st Division until April 1940, when he was replaced by Kleffel and himself replaced Emil Leeb (*supra,* note 6).

[18] *Felber and Sodenstern:* Felber was Chief of Staff of the 2nd Army until February 1940, when he replaced Sodenstern as Chief of Staff of Army Group C, and Sodenstern replaced Manstein (*supra,* note 13) in that capacity at Army Group A.

[18a] *Groppe:* Commander of the 214th Division until the spring of 1940, when he was relieved from active duty because of his outspoken opposition to Himmler's social and anti-religious policies.

[19] *Mieth:* Chief of Staff 1st Army until the spring of 1940, when he was assigned as O.Qu. I of OKH in an acting capacity *vice* Karl-Heinrich von Stuelpnagel, who was ill and who, after his recovery, conducted negotiations with the Italians for the proposed Operation *Braun* (*supra,* pp. 176–77).

[20] *Hollidt:* Chief of Staff to Blaskowitz (*supra,* note 1), Commander-in-Chief East (Oberost) from October 1939 to May 1940, when the 9th Army was constituted.

[21] *Hilpert:* Chief of Staff IXth Corps until February 1940, when he replaced Mieth (*supra,* note 19) as Chief of Staff, 1st Army.

[22] *Mueller, Eugen:* Commandant of War Academy at outbreak of war. Appointed *Generalquartiermeister* of OKH in September. Early in 1940 relieved by Eduard Wagner and appointed General z.b.V. (general for special assignments) at OKH.

[23] *Konrad:* Chief of Staff XVIIIth Corps until February 1940, when he replaced Felber as Chief of Staff, 2nd Army.

[24] *Rendulic:* Ill at outbreak of campaign in the West. Took command of the 14th Division in June 1940, succeeding Weyer.

[25] *v. Langermann und Erlencamp:* Inspector of Vehicles and Horses (OKH) at the outbreak of war and succeeded Lemelsen as commander of the 29th Motorized Division in the spring of 1940.

[26] *Gullmann:* Appointed *Oberfeldkommandant* in Luxembourg in May 1940.

TABLE 3

ARMY RANK AND ASSIGNMENT LIST: AUGUST 1940

Name	Seniority	Assignment †
GENERALFELDMARSCHAELLE		
1. v. Brauchitsch	19.7.40(1)	C.-in-C. Army
2. Keitel, Wilhelm	19.7.40(2)	Chief, OKW
3. v. Rundstedt *	19.7.40(3)	Army Group A
4. v. Bock	19.7.40(4)	Army Group B
5. v. Leeb *	19.7.40(5)	Army Group C
6. List	19.7.40(6)	12th Army
7. v. Kluge	19.7.40(7)	4th Army
8. v. Witzleben	19.7.40(8)	1st Army
9. v. Reichenau	19.7.40(9)	6th Army
GENERALOBERSTEN		
10. Blaskowitz	1.10.39(1)	Fuehrer Reserve [1]
11. Halder	19.7.40(1)	Chief, General Staff, OKH
12. Dollmann	19.7.40(2)	7th Army
13. v. Kleist *	19.7.40(3)	Panzer Group Kleist [2]
14. v. Weichs	19.7.40(4)	2nd Army
15. v. Kuechler	19.7.40(5)	18th Army
16. v. Schobert	19.7.40(6)	VIIth Corps
17. Busch	19.7.40(7)	16th Army
18. Guderian	19.7.40(8)	Panzer Group Guderian [2]
19. Hoth	19.7.40(9)	XVth Corps [2]
20. Strauss	19.7.40(10)	9th Army [3]
21. Haase, Curt	19.7.40(11)	IIIrd Corps
22. v. Falkenhorst	19.7.40(12)	Group XXI
23. Hoepner	19.7.40(13)	XVIth Corps
24. Fromm	19.7.40(14)	Home Army

* Officers listed with asterisk were so listed in the official German *Rangliste*, indicating that active rank was held only for the duration of the war. These officers had been temporarily restored to the active list, after a prewar retirement from active duty.

† Unless otherwise indicated, the officer commanded the field unit listed in this column. Important changes in assignment from May through August 1940 are indicated in the numbered notes at the end of the table.

ARMY RANK AND ASSIGNMENT LIST: AUGUST 1940
[CONTINUED]

Name	Seniority	Assignment
	GENERALE ‡	
25. Heitz	1.4.37(1)	VIIIth Corps
26. v. Wietersheim	1.2.38(2)	XIVth Corps
27. Schroth	1.2.38(3)	XIIth Corps
28. Kuntze	1.2.38(4)	XLIInd Corps
29. v. Schwedler	1.2.38(6)	IVth Corps
30. Kienitz	1.4.38(1)	XVIIth Corps
31. Foerster	1.4.38(2)	VIth Corps
32. Waeger	1.11.38(1)	XXVIIth Corps
33. Raschick	1.4.39(1)	No Assignment
34. Leeb, Emil	1.4.39(3)	Chief of Ordance, OKH
35. Friderici	1.4.39(4)	Military Plenipotentiary, Bohemia and Moravia
36. v. Stuelpnagel, K.-H.	1.4.39(5)	Pres., Armistice Comm'n [4]
37. Ruoff	1.5.39	Vth Corps
38. Wodrig	1.10.39(1)	XXVIth Corps
39. Petzel	1.10.39(3)	Wehrkreis XXI
40. v. Erfurth	1.4.40(1)	O.Qu.V, OKH
41. Geyr v. Schweppenburg	1.4.40(2)	XXIVth Corps
42. Hartmann	1.4.40(3)	XXXth Corps
43. v. Boetticher	1.4.40(4)	Mil. Attaché, United States
44. v. Obstfelder	1.6.40(1)	XXIXth Corps [5]
45. Heinrici	1.6.40(1a)	XLIIIrd Corps [6]
46. Jacob	1.6.40(2)	Insp. Engineers, OKH
47. Hansen, Christian	1.6.40(3)	Xth Corps
48. Schubert, Albrecht	1.6.40(4)	XXIIIrd Corps
49. v. Vietinghoff	1.6.40(5)	XLVIth Corps [7]
50. Stumme	1.6.40(6)	XLth Corps
51. v. Manstein	1.6.40(7)	XXXVIIIth Corps
52. Schmidt, Rudolf	1.6.40(8)	XLIst Corps
53. v. Both	1.6.40(9)	Ist Corps
54. Olbricht	1.6.40(10)	Chief, General Office, OKH
55. Reinhardt	1.6.40(11)	XLIst Corps
56. Dietl	1.7.40(1)	Mt. Corps of Norway [8]
57. Jodl	1.7.40(2)	Ch. of Operations, OKW
58. v. Brockdorff-Ahlefeldt	1.8.40(1)	IInd Corps [9]
59. Lemelsen	1.8.40(2)	XLVIIth Corps [10]

‡ Gone from the list of *Generale* are von Speck, killed in action in June 1940; Beyer, taken fatally ill in June 1940; and Volkmann, killed in an automobile accident in August 1940.

ARMY RANK AND ASSIGNMENT LIST: AUGUST 1940
[CONTINUED]

Name	Seniority	Assignment
	GENERALE (*continued*)	
60. v. Kortzfleisch	1.8.40(3)	XIth Corps
61. Boehme	1.8.40(4)	XVIIIth Corps [11]
62. v. Briesen	1.8.40(5)	Commandant, Paris [12]
63. v. Salmuth	1.8.40(6)	Ch. of Staff, Army Group B
64. Hansen, Erik	1.8.40(6a)	4th Division
65. Brand, Fritz	1.8.40(7)	Insp. War Schools
66. Felber	1.8.40(8)	Ch. of Staff, Army Group C [13]
67. Kuebler, Ludwig	1.8.40(9)	1st Mt. Div.
68. Thomas, Georg	1.8.40(10)	Ch. of Economics, OKW
69. v. Sodenstern	1.8.40(11)	Ch. of Staff, Army Group A
70. v. Mackensen	1.8.40(12)	Ch. of Staff, 12th Army
71. Fellgiebel	1.8.40(13)	Chief Signal Officer, OKW and OKH
72. v. Cochenhausen, Friedrich *	*Char.* 1.3.38	Wehrkreis XIII
73. Muff	*Char.* 25.3.38	Wehrkreis XI

GENERALLEUTNANTE

The following *Generalmajore* from Table 2 were promoted to *Generalleutnant*, with seniority as follows:

Hubicki	1.4.40(12)	Mueller, Eugen	1.8.40(8)
Pellengahr	1.6.40(1)	Reinecke	1.8.40(9)
v. Tippelskirch	1.6.40(5)	Paulus	1.8.40(10)
v. Hanneken	1.7.40(5)	v. Rothkirch und	
Kempf	1.8.40(3)	Panthen	1.8.40(12)
Brennecke	1.8.40(5)	Gercke	1.8.40(13)

The following officers were among those promoted to *Generalmajor* in August 1940:

Wagner, Eduard	1.8.40(7)	Generalquartiermeister, OKH
Warlimont	1.8.40(8)	Dep. Ch. of Ops., OKW
v. Greiffenberg	1.8.40(9)	Ch. Operations Sec., OKH
Schoerner	*ern.* 1.8.40	6th Mt. Div.[14]

In all, 39 *Obersten* (including the four listed above) were promoted to *Generalmajor* during June, July, and August 1940, and 35 *Generalmajore* were promoted to *Generalleutnant* during the same period. By August there were approximately 210 *Generalmajore*, and in all 450 officers of general officer rank.

Notes

[1] *Blaskowitz:* Relieved as Commander-in-Chief of the 9th Army at the end of May 1940, and then served as Military Commander for Northern France until the end of June, when he was again relieved. He was without an assignment until the end of October 1940, when he succeeded Witzleben as Commander-in-Chief of the 1st Army.

[2] *v. Kleist, Guderian, and Hoth:* Kleist was commander of the XXIInd Corps, which in March 1940 was upgraded to a "Panzer Group" headquarters, with command of two armored corps. Guderian's XIXth corps was similarly upgraded for the second phase of the Battle of France. So was Hoth's XVth Corps during the latter part of May, but after Dunkirk it reverted to corps status.

[3] *Strauss:* Commander of the IInd Corps until about June 1, 1940, when he succeeded Blaskowitz as Commander-in-Chief of the 9th Army.

[4] *v. Stuelpnagel, Karl-Heinrich:* Oberquartiermeister I of OKH until early June 1940, when he succeeded Strauss as commander of the IInd Corps. Appointed President of the Armistice Commission at the end of June.

[5] *v. Obstfelder:* Commander of the 28th Division until the spring of 1940, when he was given command of the new XXIXth Corps.

[6] *Heinrici:* Commander of the 16th Division until the spring of 1940, when he was appointed acting commander of the XIIth Corps *vice* Schroth, who was ill. In June he was designated commander of the XLIIIrd Corps, succeeding Von Speck, who had been killed in action.

[7] *v. Vietinghoff:* Commander of the XIIIth Corps until the summer of 1940, when he was transferred to the new XLVIth Corps.

[8] *Dietl:* Commander of the 3rd Mountain Division until June 15, 1940, when his headquarters was upgraded to corps status, with command of the 2nd and 3rd Mountain Divisions in northern Norway. His successor as commander of the 3rd Mountain Division was Oberst Julius Ringel.

[9] *v. Brockdorff-Ahlefeldt:* Commander of the 23rd Division until the spring of 1940, when he was given command of the new XXVIIIth Corps. Late in June he was replaced by Weyer and succeeded Karl-Heinrich von Stuelpnagel as commander of the IInd Corps.

[10] *Lemelsen:* Commander of the 29th Motorized Division until the spring of 1940, when he was given command of the new XLVIIth Corps.

[11] *Boehme:* Commander of the 32nd Division until early June 1940, when he was designated acting commander of the XLIIIrd Corps *vice* Von Speck, who was transferred to the XVIIIth Corps *vice* Beyer, taken fatally ill. On June 15 von Speck was killed in action, and Boehme was appointed commander of the XVIIIth Corps.

[12] *von Briesen:* Commander of the 30th Division until after the Armistice, when he was appointed Commandant of Paris.

[13] *Felber:* Remained Chief of Staff of Army Group C until October 1940, when he succeeded Vietinghoff as Commander of the XIIIth Corps.

[14] *Schoerner:* A regimental commander in the 1st Mountain Division until May 1940, when he was given command of the newly constituted 6th Mountain Division.

TABLE 4

RETIRED ARMY GENERALS RECALLED
TO WARTIME DUTY *

1. *von Hammerstein-Equord, Kurt:* Generaloberst–31.3.34. Commander of Wehrkreis IV during the first few days of September 1939, and for the balance of the month commanded Army Cadre A, at the northern end of the western front, opposite Belgium and Holland. Returned to inactive status early in October 1939, and served no more.
2. *von Vollard Bockelberg, Alfred:* General der Artillerie–1.10.33. Commander of Wehrkreis I from October 1939 to May 1940. Military Commander in Paris in June 1940, then returned to inactive status and served no more.
3. *Liebmann, Curt:* General der Infanterie–1.4.35(1). Commander of the 5th Army on the western front from the outbreak of the war to October 10, 1939. Designated for an occupational command in Poland, but returned to inactive status later in October and served no more.
4. *Halm, Hans:* General der Infanterie–1935. Commanded Wehrkreis VIII during early years of the war.
5. *Wachenfeld, Edmund:* General der Artillerie–1.10.35(1). Commanded Wehrkreis VII during early years of the war.
6. *Lutz, Oswald:* General der Panzertruppen–1.11.35. Chief of Liaison Staff Transnistria during 1941.
7. *Kaupisch, Leonhard:* General der Artillerie–1.12.35. Held a border command during the Polish campaign. Commander of the XXXIst Corps Command, 1939–42.
8. *Geyer, Hermann:* General der Infanterie–1.8.36(3). Commander of the IXth Corps, 1939–42.

* No such list was ever published by the Army. This one has been compiled from a variety of sources, as of the summer of 1940. It is incomplete and, no doubt, contains some inaccuracies. Forty or more retired generals, in addition to those here listed, held minor posts during the war.

A few retired officers were temporarily restored to the regular list. These—including Rundstedt, Leeb, Kleist (after his promotion to *Generaloberst* in July 1940), Volkmann, Friedrich von Cochenhausen, and Metz—appear in the preceding rank lists (Tables 2 and 3). The generals in Table 4 were designated *z.V.* (*zur Verfuegung*, at disposal) to distinguish them from those on the regular list.

This list does not include the few leading officers who were not recalled to duty, or whose recall was promptly canceled for political reasons. Among these were Blomberg (stricken from the list in 1938), Heye, Beck, Adam, Joachim von Stuelpnagel, Seutter von Loetzen, von dem Bussche Ippenburg, Franz Kress von Kressenstein, Liese, and Ritter von Mittelberger. Nor does it include Paul Hausser and Ernst Sachs, the only retired generals who transferred to the Waffen-SS.

RETIRED ARMY GENERALS RECALLED
TO WARTIME DUTY

[CONTINUED]

9. *Gruen, Otto:* General der Artillerie—1.8.36(4). Inspector of Artillery, OKH, 1939–44.

10. *von Pogrell, Guenther:* General der Kavallerie—1.10.36(5). Commander of XXXIInd Corps Command, 1940–41.

11. *von Stuelpnagel, Otto:* General der Flieger—1.10.36(1), General der Infanterie early in the war. Commander of Wehrkreis XVII until October 1940. Military Commander in France, October 1940 to February 1942.

12. *Ulex, Wilhelm:* General der Artillerie—1.10.36(6). Commander of the Xth Corps during the Polish campaign. Held an occupational command in Poland until May 1940, when he succeeded Bockelberg in Wehrkreis I. Returned to inactive status about 1942.

13. *von Gienanth, Kurt Freiherr:* General der Kavallerie—1.4.40. Held a border command during the Polish campaign. Commander of XXXVIth Corps Command until May 1940, when he succeeded Blaskowitz as Military Commander in occupied Poland.

14. *Woellwarth, Erich: Char.* General der Infanterie—1.1.29. Succeeded Falkenhausen as Commander of Wehrkreis IV in May 1940, and served there until 1941 or 1942.

15. *von Prager, Karl Ritter: Char.* General der Infanterie—1.2.31. Commander of the XXVIIth Corps during the early months of the war, and then of the XXVth Corps.

16. *Foehrenbach, Max: Char.* General der Artillerie—1.5.31. Commander of Wehrkreis II from May 1940 to 1942, when he died.

17. *Schniewindt, Rudolf: Char.* General der Infanterie—1.10.31. Commander of Wehrkreis IX, 1939 to 1942.

18. *von Falkenhausen, Alexander: Char.* General der Infanterie—8.3.34. Commander of Wehrkreis IV, September 1939 to May 1940. Military Commander of Belgium and northern France from May 1940 to July 1944.

19. *Fessmann, Ernst: Char.* General der Panzertruppen—30.9.37. Commander of the 267th Division, 1939 to 1942.

20. *von Niebelschuetz, Guenther: Char.* General der Infanterie—28.2.38. Rear area commander for the 3rd Army in Poland (?).

21. *Eberth, Karl: Char.* General der Flieger—1.7.38. An artillery commander, 1940–42.

22. *von Greiff, Kurt: Char.* General der Infanterie—27.8.39. Commander of XLVth Corps Command, 1939 to 1942.

23. *Steppuhn, Albrecht: Char.* General der Infanterie—27.8.39. Commander of Wehrkreis XII, 1939 to 1943.

24. *von Roques, Karl: Char.* General der Infanterie—22.4.40. Commanded a training division during the early part of the war, and thereafter commanded the rear area of an army group in Russia.

25. *Streccius, Alfred: Char.* General der Infanterie—27.6.40. Commander

RETIRED ARMY GENERALS RECALLED
TO WARTIME DUTY
[CONTINUED]

of occupation troops in the Netherlands, May to June 1940. Chief of Military Administration in France, June to October 1940. Commander of Wehrkreis XVII (succeeding Otto von Stuelpnagel), until 1943.

26. *Brandt, Georg:* Generalleutnant–1.2.30(1). Commander of XXXIInd Corps Command, 1939 to 1942.

27. *von Schenckendorff, Max:* Generalleutnant–1930. Commander of XXXVth Corps Command, and thereafter of an army group rear area in Russia.

28. *Schmidt, Hans:* Generalleutnant–1931. Commander of the 260th Division until 1942, and then succeeded Geyer as Commander of the IXth Corps.

29. *Vogl, Oskar:* Generalleutnant–1932. Commander of the 167th Division until September 1940. President of the Armistice Commission (succeeding Karl-Heinrich von Stuelpnagel) until 1943.

30. *Boehm-Tettelbach, Alfred:* Generalleutnant–1.10.32(2). Commander of XXXVIIth Corps command, 1940 to 1943.

31. *von Roques, Franz:* Generalleutnant–1.1.33. Training and regional defense 1939–41, and commander of an army group rear area in Russia.

32. *Feige, Hans:* Generalleutnant–1.10.33(5). Commander of Wehrkreis II until May 1940, and thereafter Commander of the XXXVIth Corps Command (upgraded to Corps in 1941) until January 1942.

33. *Heinemann, Erich:* Generalleutnant–1.9.35(1). An artillery commander, 1939–42. Commander of Special Corps LXV (for V-weapons), 1943–44.

34. *Braemer, Walter:* Retired as Generalmajor 1932. Became Brigadefuehrer in the SS. Recalled as Generalleutnant early in the war, and later *Wehrmachtbefehlshaber Ostland* in occupied Russia.

35. *Von Boehm-Bezing, Diether:* Generalleutnant–1.9.35(2). Commander of the 252nd Division early in the war.

36. *Haenicke, Siegfried:* Generalleutnant–1.11.39. Commander of the 61st Division during the early part of the war, and thereafter a corps commander. Occupational commander in Poland from October 1942 until the end of the occupation early in 1945.

37. *Koch, Friedrich: Char.* Generalleutnant–30.9.31. Commander of the 254th Division until the middle of May 1940, and then Commander of the XLIVth Corps until 1942.

38. *Endres, Theodor: Char.* Generalleutnant–30.9.31. Commander of the 212th Division early in the war.

39. *Niehoff, Heinrich: Char.* Generalleutnant–4.2.38. In command of Military District 670, Lille.

40. *von Beneckendorff und von Hindenburg, Oskar: Char.* Generalmajor– 1934. Commander of Wehrkreis I during September 1939, and subsequently in charge of prisoner-of-war camps in Wehrkreis I.

TABLE 5

NAVY RANK AND ASSIGNMENT LIST: MAY 1940

Name	Seniority	Assignment
	GROSSADMIRAL	
1. Raeder	1.4.39	C.-in-C. Navy
	GENERALADMIRAL	
2. Saalwaechter	1.1.40	Western Group Command
	ADMIRAELE	
3. Carls	1.6.37(2) *	Eastern Group Command
4. Witzell	1.11.37	Chief of Ordnance, OKM
5. Bastian	1.4.38(1)	President, Military Court
6. Boehm	1.4.38(2)	Naval Forces in Norway
7. Marschall	1.12.39	*Flottenchef*
8. v. Nordeck	1.1.40(1)	Wilhelmshaven Shipyards
9. Guse	1.1.40(2)	Naval Station, Baltic, and Insp. of Communications
10. Canaris	1.1.40(3)	Chief of Intelligence, OKW
11. Schuster	1.1.40(4)	Economic Warfare, OKW
12. Densch	1.1.40(5)	Naval Station, North Sea
	VIZEADMIRAELE	
13. Goetting	1.10.37(2)	Chief of Torpedoes in Ordnance, OKM
14. Stobwasser	1.10.37(4)	Submarine and Torpedo-boat Maintenance
15. Witthoeft-Emden	1.11.37(1)	Naval Attaché, Washington
16. v. Fischel	1.4.38(3)	Testing of New Ships
17. Rother	1.11.39(1)	Inspector, Blocking Weapons (e.g., mines)
18. Mewis	1.11.39(2)	Naval Forces in Denmark
19. v. Schrader	1.11.39(3)	Norwegian West Coast
20. Mootz	1.1.39(4)	Naval Defense, Baltic
21. Grassmann	1.1.40(1)	Quartermaster, OKM †

* Carls was promoted to *Generaladmiral* on July 19, 1940.

NAVY RANK AND ASSIGNMENT LIST: MAY 1940
[CONTINUED]

Name	Seniority	Assignment
	VIZEADMIRAELE (*continued*)	
22. Luetjens	1.1.40(2)	Commander Reconnaissance Forces and Acting *Flottenchef*
23. Schniewind	1.1.40(3)	Chief of Staff, SKL
24. Patzig	1.1.40(4)	Chief of Personnel, OKM
25. Hormel	1.1.40(5)	Kiel Shipyards
26. Assman	*Char.* 25.1.37	Naval Science, OKM
	KONTERADMIRAELE ‡	
27. Schmundt	1.4.38(3)	Insp. of Training and Acting Commander, Reconnaissance Forces
28. Fanger	1.10.38(1)	Chief of Artillery, Ordnance, OKM
29. Fuchs	1.10.38(2)	Ship-building Dep't, OKM
30. v. Seebach	1.10.38(3)	Insp. Naval Artillery
31. Warzecha	1.11.38	Defense Dep't, OKM
32. Fleischer	1.4.39(3)	Coastal Defense, Friesland
33. Bachmann	1.4.39(4)	Ch. of Staff, North Sea Station
34. Doenitz	1.10.39(3)	Commander U-boats
35. Ciliax	1.11.39(5)	Ch. of Staff, Group West
36. Fricke	1.11.39(8)	Chief of Operations, SKL
37. Kummetz	1.1.40(4)	Insp. Torpedoes and Commander, Oslo Task Torce

† Entitled *Chef, Marinekommandoamt* in 1940, but thereafter renamed *Quartiermeister.*

‡ Below are listed only the *Konteradmiraele* holding positions of special importance or mentioned in the text.

TABLE 6

AIR FORCE RANK AND ASSIGNMENT LIST: AUGUST 1940

Name	Seniority	Assignment
REICHSMARSCHALL		
1. Goering	19.7.40	C.-in-C. Luftwaffe
GENERALFELDMARSCHAELLE		
2. Milch	19.7.40	Inspector-General
3. Sperrle	19.7.40	Luftflotte 3
4. Kesselring	19.7.40	Luftflotte 2
GENERALOBERSTEN		
5. Stumpff	19.7.40(1)	Luftflotte 5
6. Keller	19.7.40(2)	Fliegerkorps IV
7. Weise	19.7.40(3)	Flakkorps I
8. Grauert	19.7.40(4)	Fliegerkorps I
9. Udet	19.7.40(5)	*Generalluftzeugmeister*
GENERALE		
10. Ruedel	1.10.37(1)	Air Defense
11. Klepke †	1.1.39(2)	Insp. of Reconnaissance, RLM
12. Christiansen	1.1.39(3)	*Wehrmachtbefehlshaber*, Netherlands
13. v. Witzendorf	1.2.39(1)	Administration, RLM
14. Loehr	1.3.39(1)	Luftflotte 4
15. v. Schroeder	1.4.39(1)	Civil Air Defense
16. Kuehl	1.4.39(3)	Training, RLM
17. Hirschauer	1.8.39(1)	Air District XVII
18. v. d. Lieth-Thomsen	1.8.39(2)	Science Section, RLM
19. Kitzinger	1.10.39(1)	Western Air Defense
20. Wimmer	1.10.39(4)	Acting C.O., Luftflotte 1
21. Student	22.5.40	Fliegerdivision 7
22. Geissler	19.7.40(1)	Fliegerkorps X
23. v. Greim	19.7.40(2)	Fliegerkorps V

AIR FORCE RANK AND ASSIGNMENT LIST: AUGUST 1940

[CONTINUED]

Name	Seniority	Assignment
	GENERALE (*continued*)	
24. Loerzer	19.7.40(3)	Fliegerkorps II
25. v. Richthofen	19.7.40(4)	Fliegerkorps VIII
26. Jeschonnek	19.7.40(5)	Chief, General Staff OKL
27. Wilberg †	Char. 31.3.38	Training command
28. Quade †	Char. 31.3.38	Training command
29. Dransfeld †	Char. 31.3.39	Insp. Mot. Transp., RLM
	GENERALLEUTNANTE *	
Wenninger	1.3.38(1)	Air Attaché, Brussels
Bogatsch	1.1.40(2)	Liaison with OKH
Kastner-Kirdorff	8.1.40	Personnel, RLM
Bodenschatz	1.1.40(6)	Personal Assistant to Goering
Martini	1.4.40(3)	Chief Signal Officer
Coeler	19.7.40(1)	Fliegerkorps IX
Dessloch	19.7.40(2)	Flakkorps II
Speidel, Wilhelm	19.7.40(3)	Ch. of Staff, Luftflotte 2
v. Seidel	19.7.40(4)	Gen. Qu. OKL
	GENERALMAJORE	
Ritter	1.1.39(7)	Liaison with OKM
Putzier	1.2.39(4)	Special Operations, Luftflotte 2
v. Wuelisch	1.4.40(3)	Air War Academy and Bomber Squadron (K.G.) 77
v. Doering	4.7.40	C.O. Fighters, Luftflotte 2
Korten	19.7.40(1)	Ch. of Staff, Luftflotte 3
Hoffman v. Waldau	19.7.40(2)	Ch. of Ops., Gen. Staff OKL
Osterkamp	19.7.40(3)	Fighter Squadron (J.G.) 51
Knauss	1.8.40(1)	Ch. of Staff, Luftflotte 1
v. Stutterheim	Char. 27.8.39	Close Support Command, Luftflotte 3

† Officers marked with dagger had been recalled from retirement to active duty and were designated "z.V." as in the Army.

* The balance of this table lists only officers holding important posts, or mentioned in the text. There were about 28 *Generalleutnante* and 93 *Generalmajore*, making 150 general officers in all.

TABLE 7

WAFFEN-SS RANK AND ASSIGNMENT LIST: JUNE 1940

Name	*Rank*	*Assignment*
OBERGRUPPENFUEHRER		
1. Dietrich, Josef "Sepp"	7.1.34	SS-Regiment *LAH*
GRUPPENFUEHRER		
2. Eicke, Theodor	7.11.34	SS-*Totenkopf-Division*
3. Hausser, Paul *	6.1.39	SS-*Verfuegungsdivision*
4. Sachs, Ernst *	6.1.39	Chief, SS Communications
5. von Pfeffer-Wildenbruch, Karl	4.20.40	SS-*Polizeidivision*
OBERFUEHRER		
6. Steiner, Felix	12.1.39	SS-Regiment *Deutschland*
7. Kreuger, Walter	1.1.40	Staff, SS-*Polizeidivision*
8. Demelhuber, Karl Maria	1.30.40	SS-Regiment *Germania*
9. Keppler, Georg	5.13.40	SS-Regiment *Der Fuehrer*
STANDARTENFUEHRER		
10. Bittrich, Willi	6.1.39	Inspector, SS military training
11. Wuennenberg, Alfred	1.1.40	Rifle Reg't 3 in SS-*Polizeidiv.*
12. Kleinheisterkamp	5.18.40	Inf. Reg't 3 in SS-*Totenkopf-Div.*

* Hausser and Sachs were the only former army generals in the Waffen-SS. Steiner, Bittrich, and Keppler had been army officers.

APPENDIX C

___

WEHRMACHT ORGANIZATION AND ORDER
OF BATTLE

In this appendix, Charts 1 through 6 are intended to show the structure of and chain of command within the Wehrmacht in the spring of 1940. Chart 12 serves the same purpose for the military and civil administrations established in the countries occupied by the Wehrmacht during the first year of World War II.

No effort has been made to make the charts complete in every detail. In the interests of simplicity, numerous sections and subsections of secondary importance have been omitted, or indicated only sketchily and without the names of the officers who headed them.

For the most part, the names of the various offices have been rendered in English. German has been used when translation would be cumbersome or unclear. In German administrative terminology, the more important units are usually designated by the word *Amt* (department or office), and the subordinate units by the word *Abteilung* (section).

Charts 7 through 11 portray the chain of command and order of battle of the German forces during the campaigns in Norway, Denmark, France, and the Low Countries. By "order of battle" (*Kriegsgliederung*) is meant the identity and subordination of the major tactical units and headquarters. During the course of the fighting, the location and subordination of individual units were frequently shifted according to the requirements of the battle. It has been impossible, of course, to indicate every such shift; nevertheless, the charts should be of assistance to the reader as ready reference in following the story told in the text.

CHART 1
High Command of the Wehrmacht: April 1940

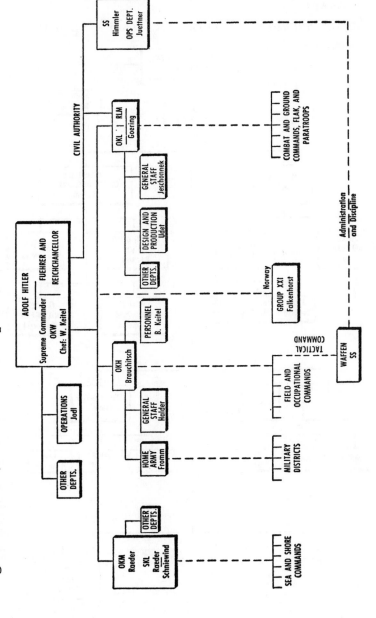

CHART 2

Oberkommando der Wehrmacht (OKW): April 1940

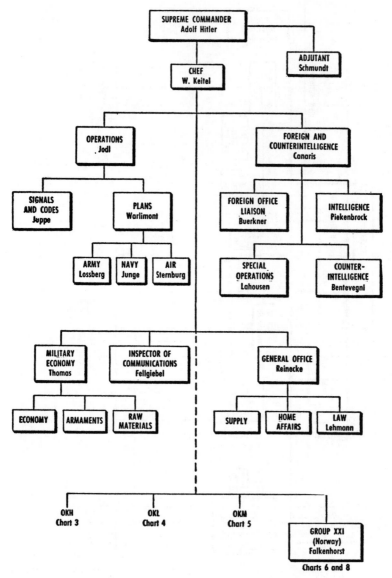

CHART 3

Oberkommando des Heeres (OKH): April 1940

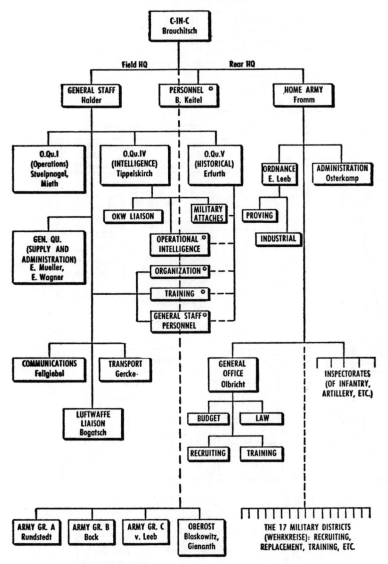

* The Personnel Department and the indicated branches of the General Staff were divided between the field and rear headquarters. The O.Qu.V exercised administrative command of the rear components of the General Staff. The positions of O.Qu.II (training) and O.Qu.III (organization) lapsed upon the outbreak of war; these functions were largely assumed by the Commander of the Home Army and his staff, but the General Staff retained small sections to handle the operational aspects.

CHART 4

Oberkommando der Luftwaffe (OKL): April 1940

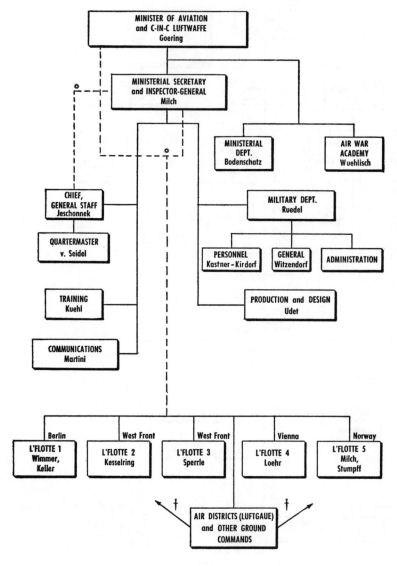

* The Chief of the General Staff and the operational commands were directly subordinate to the Commander-in-Chief in operational matters, but administratively subordinate to the Inspector-General.

† The *Luftgaue* and other ground commands were directly subordinate to OKL, or subordinate to a *Luftflotte*, depending upon their location and the exigencies of the situation.

CHART 5

Oberkommando der Kriegsmarine (OKM): April 1940

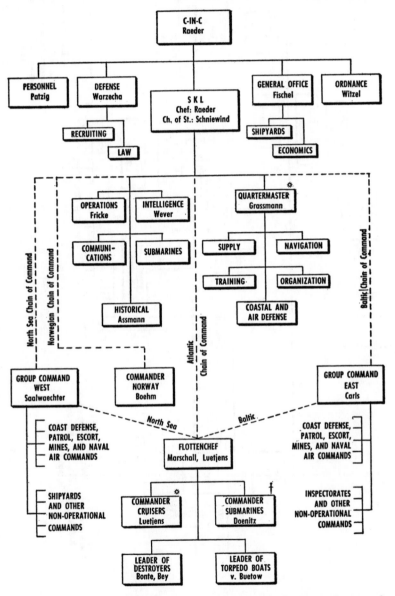

* In 1940, the Quartermaster was called Chief of the *Marinekommandoamt,* and the Commander of Cruisers the Commander *Aufklaerungsstreitkraefte* (Reconnaissance Forces). Their titles later were changed, as given above.

† Doenitz was administratively subordinate to the *Flottenchef* until 1942, but operationally he reported directly to SKL. When the *Flottenchef* took to sea, he commanded only the units in his battle fleet, and other surface units were directed by SKL or one of the Group Commands, according to location.

CHART 6
Chain of Command for Weseruebung: April 1940

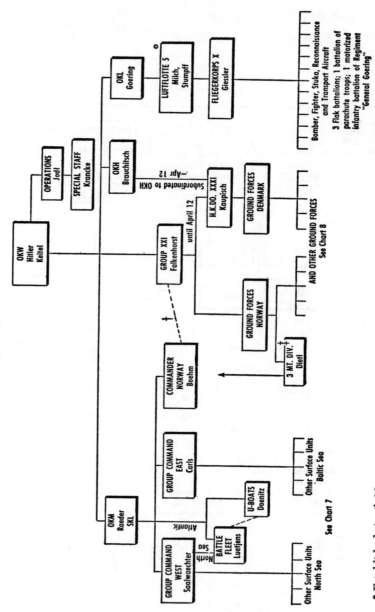

* Established April 12.
† Within Norway, Boehm was subordinate to Falken-horst, but for naval operations he was subordinate to SKL.

‡ Dietl and the Narvik regiment of the 3rd Mountain Division were directly subordinate to OKW from April 15 to May 5.

CHART 7

Naval Order of Battle for Weseruebung: April 1940

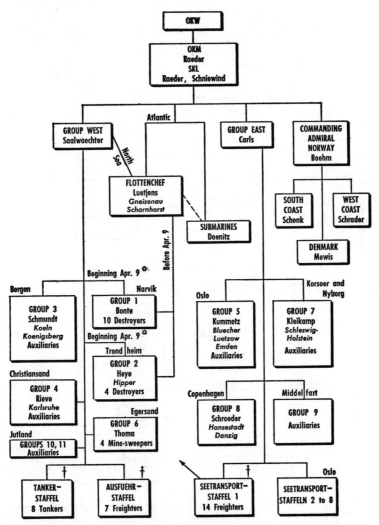

* Groups 1 and 2 sailed with the *Gneisenau* and *Scharnhorst*, and were under the *Flottenchef*'s command until the Groups approached their destinations.

† Of the *Ausfuehrstaffel*, three ships each for Narvik and Trondheim and one for Stavanger. Of the *Tankerstaffel*, two ships each for Narvik, Trondheim, and Oslo, and one each for Bergen and Stavanger. Of the fourteen ships of Seetransport Staffel 1, four were for Oslo and ten for Christiansand, Stavanger, and Bergen. These ten came under command of Group West when they passed out of the Cattegat into the Skagerrak.

CHART 8

Army Order of Battle for Weseruebung: April 1940

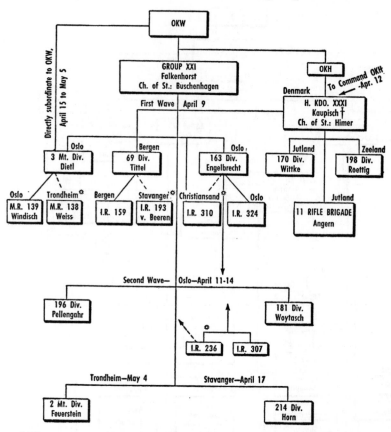

* The regiments landed at Trondheim, Stavanger, and Christiansand operated independently until their own or another divisional headquarters was able to exercise effective command. Infantry Regiments 236 of the 69th Division and 307 of the 163rd Division, landed at Oslo in the second wave, were both subordinated to the 163rd Division.

† Kaupisch's forces also included an *ad hoc* formation of three companies of light tanks (*Panzer Abteilung* 40), and three motorized machine-gun battalions. These, as well as the battalion of the "General Goering" Regiment (a Luftwaffe formation, under the Army's tactical command), were transported to Norway about the middle of April, to reinforce the 163rd and 196th Divisions for their campaign in central Norway.

CHART 9

Chain of Command for the Battle of France: May 1940

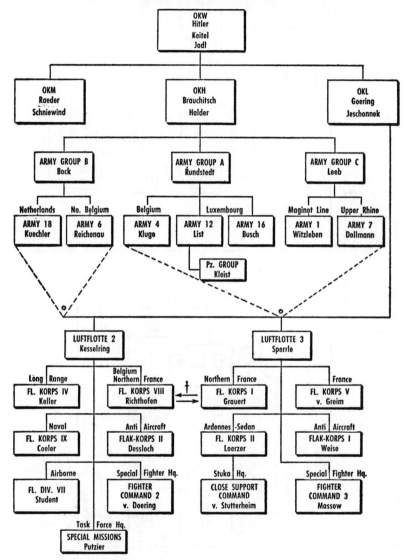

* Luftflotte 2 worked in co-operation with Army Group B, and Luftflotte 3 with Army Groups A and C.

† Fliegerkorps VIII was transferred to Luftflotte 3 on May 15, after the breakthrough on the Meuse. Fliegerkorps I was transferred to Luftflotte 2 on May 23 to support Bock's drive in northern Belgium.

CHART 10
Army Order of Battle in the West: May 10, 1940

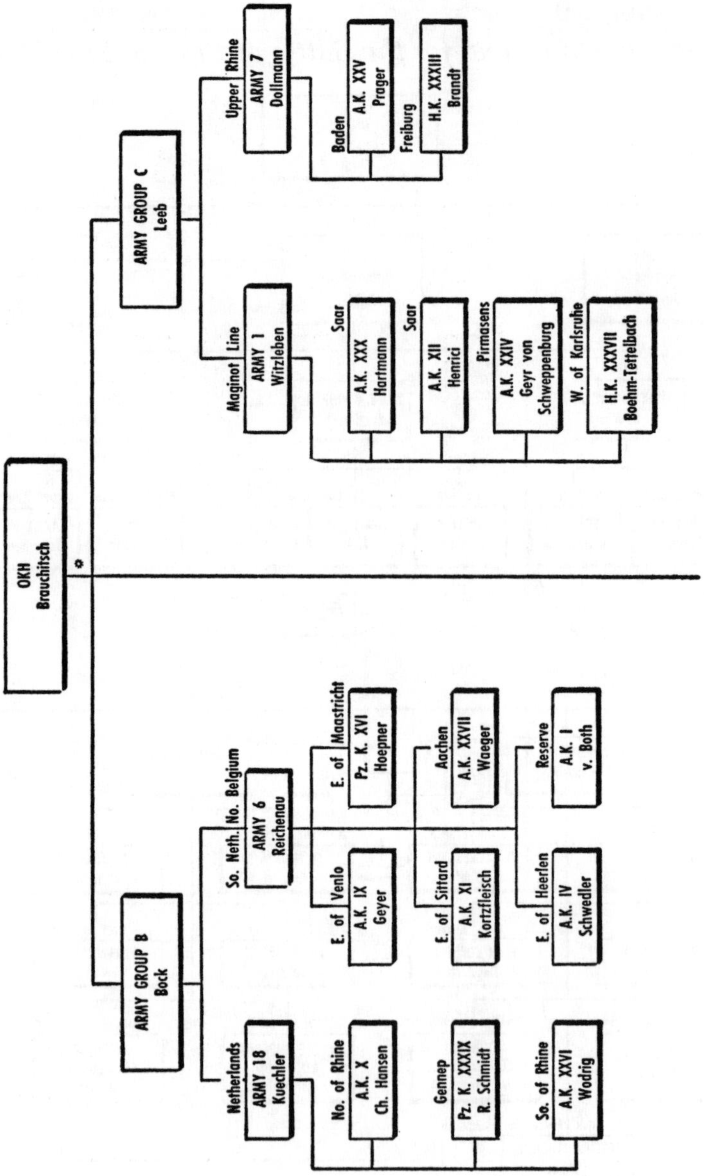

OKH
Brauchitsch

ARMY GROUP C — Leeb

- Upper Rhine: ARMY 7 Dollmann
  - Baden: A.K. XXV Prager
  - Freiburg: H.K. XXXIII Brandt
- Maginot Line: ARMY 1 Witzleben
  - Saar: A.K. XXX Hartmann
  - Saar: A.K. XII Henrici
  - Pirmasens: A.K. XXIV Geyr von Schweppenburg
  - W. of Karlsruhe: H.K. XXXVII Boehm-Tettelbach

ARMY GROUP B — Bock

- So. Neth., No. Belgium: ARMY 6 Reichenau
  - E. of Maastricht: Pz. K. XVI Hoepner
  - Aachen: A.K. XXVII Waeger
  - Reserve: A.K. I v. Both
  - E. of Venlo: A.K. IX Geyer
  - E. of Sittard: A.K. XI Kortzfleisch
  - E. of Heerlen: A.K. IV Schwedler
- Netherlands: ARMY 18 Kuechler
  - No. of Rhine: A.K. X Ch. Hansen
  - Gennep: Pz. K. XXXIX R. Schmidt
  - So. of Rhine: A.K. XXVI Wodrig

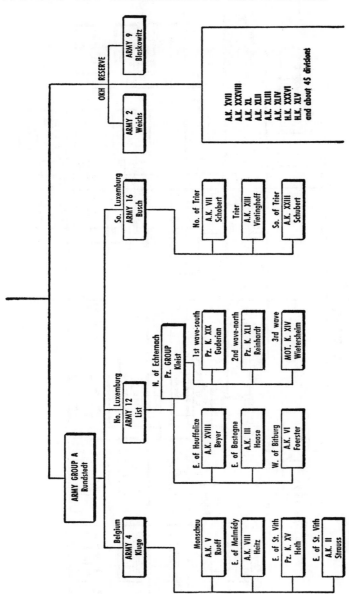

* Within the Army Groups, the Armies and Corps are placed from left to right and top to bottom in order generally corresponding to their actual location from west to east (or north to south, in Army 7 along the Rhine).

CHART 11
Army Order of Battle in the West: June 6, 1940

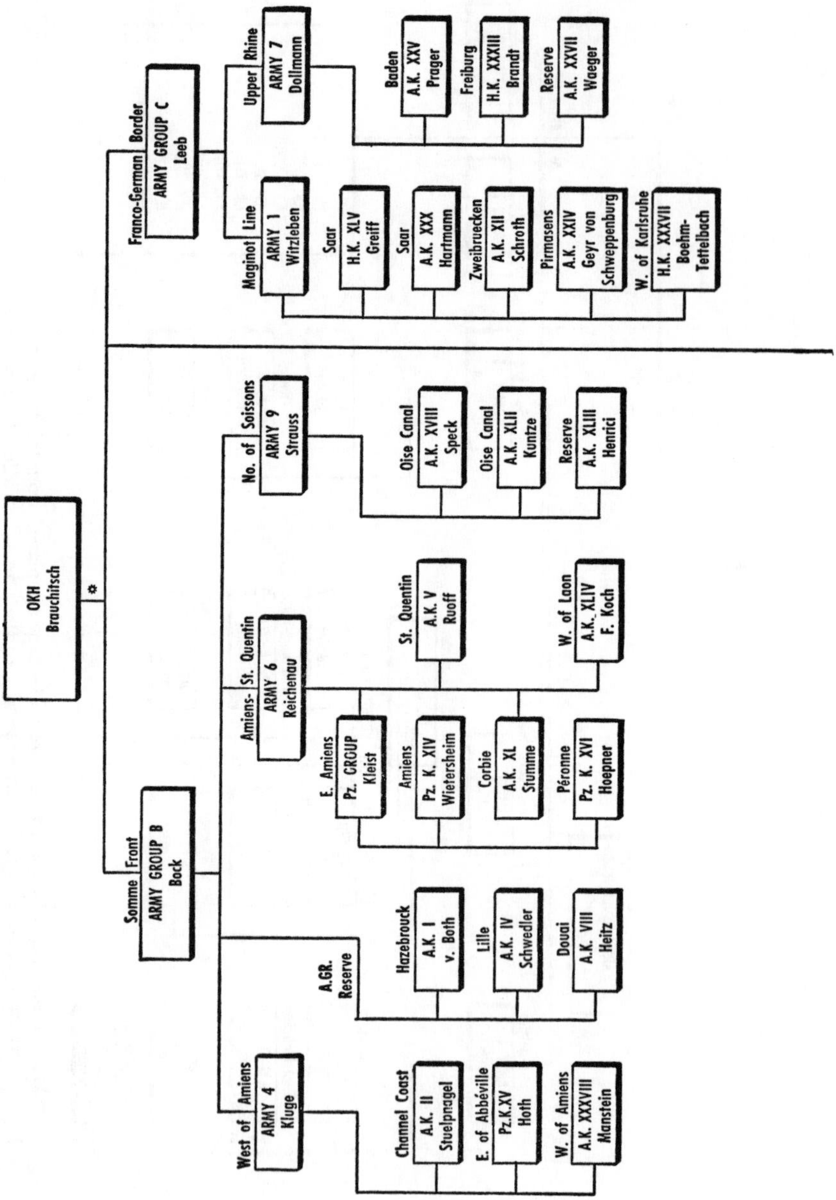

OKH
Brauchitsch

Franco-German Border
ARMY GROUP C
Leeb

Upper Rhine
ARMY 7
Dollmann

Baden
A.K. XXV
Prager

Freiburg
H.K. XXXIII
Brandt

Reserve
A.K. XXVII
Woeger

Maginot Line
ARMY 1
Witzleben

Saar
H.K. XLV
Greiff

Saar
A.K. XXX
Hartmann

Zweibruecken
A.K. XII
Schroth

Pirmasens
A.K. XXIV
Geyr von Schweppenburg

W. of Karlsruhe
H.K. XXXVII
Boehm-Tettelbach

Somme Front
ARMY GROUP B
Bock

No. of Soissons
ARMY 9
Strauss

Oise Canal
A.K. XVIII
Speck

Oise Canal
A.K. XLII
Kuntze

Reserve
A.K. XLIII
Henrici

Amiens-St. Quentin
ARMY 6
Reichenau

St. Quentin
A.K.V
Ruoff

W. of Laon
A.K. XLIV
F. Koch

E. Amiens
Pz. GROUP
Kleist

Amiens
Pz. K. XIV
Wietersheim

Corbie
A.K. XL
Stumme

Péronne
Pz. K. XVI
Hoepner

A.GR.
Reserve

Hazebrouck
A.K. I
v. Both

Lille
A.K. IV
Schwedler

Douai
A.K. VIII
Heitz

West of Amiens
ARMY 4
Kluge

Channel Coast
A.K. II
Stuelpnagel

E. of Abbéville
Pz.K.XV
Hoth

W. of Amiens
A.K. XXXVIII
Manstein

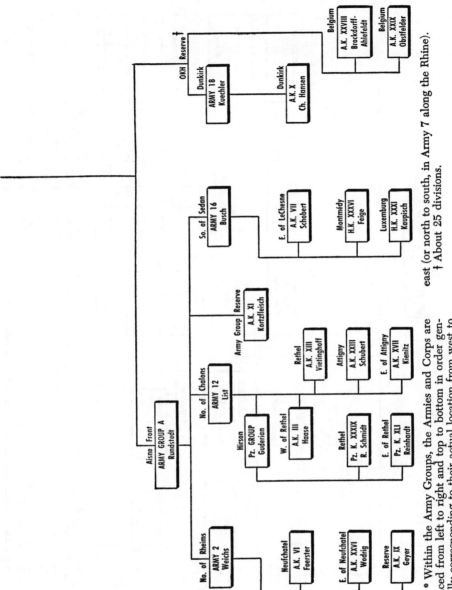

* Within the Army Groups, the Armies and Corps are placed from left to right and top to bottom in order generally corresponding to their actual location from west to east (or north to south, in Army 7 along the Rhine).
† About 25 divisions.

CHART 12

German Occupational Administration: August 1940

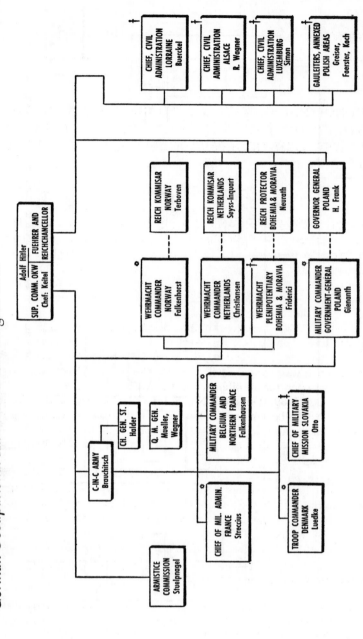

* In occupied France, the Netherlands, Belgium, Norway, Denmark, and the Government General the military administration was divided into area, subarea and district headquarters.

† In Luxemburg, Alsace, Lorraine, and the annexed areas of Poland the military administration was exercised by the expansion of the adjacent *Wehrkreise* and, in Poland, by the creation of the new Wehrkreis XX (Danzig) and Wehrkreis XXI (Posen). The Protectorate of Bohemia and Moravia was administered as a *Wehrkreis*, though not so denominated.

‡ Slovakia was nominally independent, but was garrisoned with German troops.

CHRONOLOGICAL LIST OF "DIRECTIVES FOR THE
CONDUCT OF THE WAR" AND OTHER IMPORTANT
OKW AND OKH ORDERS, AUGUST 31, 1939–AUGUST 1,
1940 *

1. *August 31, 1939:* Directive No. 1 for the Conduct of the War. Poland to be attacked on September 1, 1939. Defensive operations only
in the West, in the event that England and France declare war.
2. *September 3, 1939:* Directive No. 2 for the Conduct of the War.
Since England has declared war, the Navy may now take offensive
action. But the Army and Luftwaffe are to await the opening of actual
hostilities by the British.
3. *September 9, 1939:* Directive No. 3 for the Conduct of the War. After
the Polish forces are beaten, the Western front is to be reinforced.
4. *September 25, 1939:* Directive No. 4 for the Conduct of the War.
Decisions on future strategy will soon be made, and "The possibility
must be kept open for an offensive in the West at any time."
5. *September 30, 1939:* Directive No. 5 for the Conduct of the War.
Polish territory to be governed pursuant to Boundary and Friendship
Treaty of September 28, 1939, with Soviet Union. Commander-in-
Chief of the Army to control the Military Government,† and submit
proposed policies for pacification.
6. *October 9, 1939:* Directive No. 6 for the Conduct of the War. If
England and France will not agree to end the war, there will be an
offensive in the West in the near future. Attack through the Low Countries. Supporting "Memorandum and Guiding Principles for the War in
the West" by Hitler.
7. *October 18, 1939:* Directive No. 7 for the Conduct of the War. Restrictions on air and naval warfare relaxed; concealment of preparations for the coming offensive in the West.

---

* "The Directives for the Conduct of the War" (*Weisungen für die Kriegsfüh-
rung*) were issued by OKW by authority of the Supreme Commander of the Armed
Forces (*Der Oberste Befehlshaber der Wehrmacht*) and were generally signed by
Hitler, but sometimes by Keitel. The numbered series summarized herein lacks
numbers 10 and 12, but there must have been a number 10, since it is referred to
in number 11. Certain other OKW and OKH orders of comparable importance are
included in the table.
† The Army's civil authority in Poland lasted only until Hans Frank's appointment as Governor General, late in October 1939.

8. *October 19, 1939:* OKH deployment directive (*Aufmarschanweisung*) *Gelb* for the Western offensive.

9. *October 29, 1939:* Revised OKH deployment directive *Gelb*.

10. *November 11, 1939:* OKH order to Army Groups A and B, based on Hitler's decision to establish a third mechanized force under the XIXth Corps, in the area of the 12th or 16th Army, to strike through Sedan.

11. *November 14, 1939:* OKW directive signed by Keitel, based on Hitler's decisions (a) to be prepared to occupy Holland in order to forestall British occupation, and (b) that armed enemy passenger vessels can now be sunk without warning.

12. *November 15, 1939:* OKW directive signed by Keitel, specifying that the Army must be prepared to occupy the Netherlands up to the Grebbe line.

13. *November 20, 1939:* Directive No. 8 for the Conduct of the War. The Wehrmacht must be prepared to begin the offensive at any time, so as to take advantage of favorable weather. The Netherlands to be occupied up to the Grebbe line. Be prepared to shift *Schwerpunkt* to Army Group A if opportunity for greater success by A than by B arises, "which seems likely, with the present distribution of enemy forces."

14. *November 29, 1939:* Directive No. 9 for the Conduct of the War. Entitled "Principles for the Conduct of the War against the Enemy's Economy." Great Britain is the "driving spirit" among our enemies; her defeat is "the prerequisite for final victory"; this can best be accomplished by economic means. After victory over Anglo-French field army, "the task of the Navy and Air Force of carrying on warfare against the economic structure of Britain will become of prime importance."

15. *December 13, 1939:* OKW directive by Keitel, based on Hitler's decision to use airborne troops (22nd Division) at Ghent and the Meuse crossings at Namur and Dinant.*

16. *January 11, 1940:* "Basic Order" by Hitler restricting access to operational information; prompted by the loss of documents in the forced landing of an aircraft in Belgium the previous day.

17. *January 23, 1940:* OKW directive based on Hitler's decision that all of the Netherlands is to be occupied, and that the deployment system for *Gelb* must be altered in order to gain the benefits of surprise.

18. *January 30, 1940:* Revised OKH deployment directive *Gelb*, calling for occupation of all of the Netherlands (by the 18th Army, together with airborne troops), and for an armored attack by the XIXth Corps through Sedan.

19. *February 24, 1940:* Revised OKH deployment directive *Gelb*, embodying changed plan based on Manstein and OKH staff recommendations, shifting *Schwerpunkt* to Army Group A in area Sedan-Dinant.

---

* This plan was later altered, and the airborne troops were used in the Netherlands and on the Albert Canal in Belgium.

20. *March 1, 1940:* Hitler's directive for *Weseruebung,* with provision that air components will be under tactical command of Group XXI.

21. *March 4, 1940:* OKW directive by Keitel modifying the *Weseruebung* order by providing that the naval and air components remain under their respective Commanders-in-Chief, but work in close co-operation.

22. *March 14, 1940:* Hitler's directive "clarifying" command questions for *Weseruebung.* In transit, senior officer of Navy or Luftwaffe (as case may be) to be in command. During occupation and land operations, senior army officer to command.

23. *May 14, 1940:* Directive No. 11 for the Conduct of the War. The enemy still fails to recognize the nature of our offensive, and throws his strength into Belgium, neglecting the front opposite Army Group A. Thus there is a great opportunity to exploit the Meuse crossings by a push from north of the Aisne to the northwest, "as set forth in Directive No. 10."

    The Dutch Army "has shown greater power of resistance than was expected. Political as well as military considerations require that this resistance be speedily broken. It is the Army's task to bring about the quick collapse of 'Fortress Holland' by a sufficiently strong offensive from the south in conjunction with the attack from the east."

    The mechanized forces of Army Group B are to be disengaged as soon as possible and moved to the "left attacking wing" in Army Group A.

    The Luftwaffe is to support the focal point of Army Group A's attack, and is also to "facilitate the quick conquest of 'Fortress Holland,'" utilizing the forces that up to now have been supporting the 6th Army in Belgium.

24. *May 24, 1940:* Directive No. 13 for the Conduct of the War. The encircled Allied Forces are to be destroyed by "concentric attack by our northern wing [i.e., Army Group B]." The mission of the Luftwaffe is "to break down all resistance of the surrounded enemy forces, to prevent the escape of the British forces across the Channel, and to secure the southern flank of Army Group A."

    A new offensive is to be launched as soon as possible to destroy the remaining French forces, by attacking to the lower Seine and into the "Belfort-Metz-Paris triangle," with a secondary offensive against the Maginot Line. As soon as forces are available, the Luftwaffe will have the independent mission of attacking the British homeland, the targets to be selected according to the principles of Directive No. 9.

25. *May 26, 1940:* Supplement to Directive No. 9, specifying the British aircraft industry as the most important target.

26. *June 5, 1940:* Hitler directive for the relief of Narvik by a landing east of Tromsoe, to take the British in the rear. OKH to prepare two mixed forces of 3,000 men each, to be transported on the *Bremen* and *Europa.* *

---

* The British evacuation of Narvik rendered this fantastic plan academic.

27. *June 8, 1940:* Directive No. 14 for the Conduct of the War. Because of stubborn resistance on the right of 6th Army front, approval is given of Army Group B's intention to move the XIVth Corps to the left wing of the 4th Army.* 6th Army with XVIth Corps to strike toward the Marne. Army Group A offensive to commence June 9.

28. *June 14, 1940:* Directive No. 15 for the Conduct of the War. The enemy is crumbling. Our two objectives are to prevent the formation of a new front south of Paris, and to penetrate the Maginot Line. The assault at Saarbrücken to commence June 14.

29. *June 19, 1940:* OKW directive signed by Keitel, dispatching part of Kleist's armored group (XVIth Corps) to Lyon, and part (XIVth Corps) to the Spanish border on the Bay of Biscay. The former is to assist the incipient Italian attack at the Little St. Bernard Pass, by advancing to Grenoble-Chambéry. "The Fuehrer intends to stage a big parade in Paris. The time has not yet been set. Troop concentration for this parade must not . . . hamper fast occupation. . . ."

30. *July 2, 1940:* OKW directive by Keitel, reporting Hitler's conclusion that a landing in England is possible, once air superiority is attained. Army, Navy and Luftwaffe to study and report.

31. *July 16, 1940:* Directive No. 16 for the Conduct of the War. Preparations to be made for a landing operation in Britain.

32. *August 1, 1940:* Directive No. 17 for the Conduct of the War. Operations aimed at the destruction of the British Air Force may be begun on August 5.

* This was not done; the XIVth and XVIth Groups were both moved east to the 9th Army area.

Sources,
Acknowledgments
and Bibliography

SINCE THE PUBLICATION in 1952 of *Sword and Swastika,* which the present work follows chronologically, the documentation and literature of the Second World War have grown beyond all possibility of total coverage even by the professional historian. Tons of captured documents have been available for private research, though these are but a small fraction of what remains inaccessible in governmental archives. There has been a flood of official military and diplomatic publications, individual memoirs and biographies, unit histories, and historical narratives ranging from the sensational to the scholarly. Especially in West Germany, the output of books, monographs, and articles has been little short of staggering.

Needless to say, the quality of this vast agglomeration varies widely in accuracy, completeness, and insight. Military directives, orders, reports, and memoranda written during the course of these campaigns are generally authentic portrayals of what was then in the authors' minds. But many orders were not carried out, and many reports embodied inaccurate or incomplete information. Postwar memoirs and testimony are likely to be flawed by lapse of memory or colored by self-justification. The historian of the war years is at once overwhelmed by the sheer volume of his material, frustrated by its incompleteness, and shaken by its frequent personal bias.

The early months of the war, with which this book is concerned, present additional difficulties. On the Allied side comparatively little has been published, and this is hardly surprising. Defeat followed defeat in such rapid and crushing succession that, at the time, the Allied protagonists hardly knew what was happening to them. For many Frenchmen the war was over almost as soon as it began, and for most Americans it did not really begin until Pearl Harbor. Since then, the memory of subsequent victories has dulled that of earlier catastrophes. Finally, as the Wehrmacht then held the initiative, and the decisions of its leaders determined the course of the war, most of the crucial documentation is German.

Therefore, the story of these German conquests must be based principally, though by no means exclusively, on German source materials. Only rarely is there opportunity to verify or supplement them from the "other side of the hill." Fortunately, the German records are numerous and sufficiently varied so that internal cross-checking is frequently possible.

Of first importance are the records of the German high command—the OKW, OKH, OKM, and OKL—and the subordinate headquarters. The Russians are said to have seized most of the OKL files; however that may be, very few high-level Luftwaffe documents are available or known to the western scholar. With this exception, the most significant top-level military directives have been published.

Many of these, as well as reports, studies, and other enlightening military documents, are printed in the published records of the Nuremberg trials. The complete record of testimony at the first Nuremberg trial, and reproductions of all documents introduced before the International Military Tribunal, are available in the forty-two volume *Trial of the Major War Criminals,* published at Nuremberg (1947–49). Additional documents, affidavits, and interrogatories collected for that trial are printed in the series *Nazi Conspiracy and Aggression,* published by the U.S. Government Printing Office. Furthermore, there is additional testimony given before Commissioners of the International Military Tribunal which was, unhappily, omitted from the forty-two-volume record, and is available only in mimeographed form. Finally, selections from the testimony offered and documents submitted during the twelve subsequent Nuremberg trials are to be found in the fifteen-volume series *Trials of Major War Criminals before the Nuremberg Military Tribunals* (U.S. Government Printing Office, 1949–52).

But in the Nuremberg collections there are many other records that have never been published, and must be painfully exhumed from the cellars or attics of the few leading libraries where sets of copies are on deposit. Still, these comprise only documents that were thought informative or significant for war-crimes-trial purposes. The great mass of German military records is in the Departmental Records Branch at Alexandria, Virginia. It has not yet been thoroughly screened, and only a small part has been declassified and made accessible to the public. Among those recently released, however, is a most important document—*Der Feldzug in Frankreich*—containing maps showing the disposition of the German ground forces in the West (down to divisions) on each day from May 10 to June 25, 1940. Based upon the OKH daily situation maps, this collection was made in the summer of 1940 (in twenty copies) by Oberst Hans von Greiffenberg, Chief of the Operations Section of the General Staff, as a souvenir for Hitler and his immediate military entourage.

Among the unofficial contemporaneous records, by far the most informative is the shorthand diary kept by General (later Generaloberst) Franz Halder. How this seven-volume document reached Nuremberg, I do not know. It lay neglected on the shelves, mislabeled as the diary of General Thomas, until early in 1947. When the true authorship of the diary was discovered, arrangements were made to transcribe it from the Gabelsberger shorthand notes made by Halder. To correct inaccuracies and clarify ambiguities, Halder was extensively interrogated. Annotated transcriptions in

German and English were produced and mimeographed, and are presently on deposit in major libraries here and in Europe. The diary begins on August 14, 1939, and runs until September 1942, when Halder was dismissed as Chief of the General Staff. Some entries consist only of working notes; others are reflective or emotional. As a whole, the diary furnishes a reliable and often vivid record of the principal events at OKH, but it is unsystematic and there are many lacunae.

Jodl's diary is also useful, but it comes to an end on May 26, 1940, just before Dunkirk. On the naval side, the most enlightening documents are the minutes of the wartime conferences between Hitler and the Commander-in-Chief of the Navy. Entitled *Fuehrer Conferences on Naval Affairs,* these have been circulated in photo-offset by the British Admiralty.

Some of the postwar German memoirs and biographies are almost valueless; others, even though highly personal, are indispensable. In the latter category must be included the autobiographies of Guderian, Manstein, and Kesselring and, in a more limited sphere, those of Galland and Heinkel. Liddell Hart's collection of the Rommel papers is likewise invaluable.

The most exhaustive bibliography of the Nazi years that I have seen is annexed to the *Vierteljahrshefte fuer Zeitgeschichte,* published in Munich under the auspices of the Institut fuer Zeitgeschichte. The bibliography appended hereto is selective; other sources are given in the notes.

Over the course of the last fifteen years many individuals have participated in amassing the information and developing the viewpoints of which this book is the product. Among those who have been especially generous of their time and attention are Herr Rudolf Absolon, of the West German State Archives (Bundesarchiv), Mr. Philip Brower, and Master Specialist John H. Vought of the Departmental Records Branch, who have responded with great care and courtesy to numerous and detailed inquiries. I am deeply indebted to Hedy Clark for assistance and guidance in matters of translation, and to Zelda Golden, who typed the manuscript. My wife has interrupted her own studies to edit the text, and whether good or bad the book is much the better for her thoughtful criticism.

Bibliography

I. GERMAN ARMED FORCES

FOLTTMANN, JOSEF, AND MOELLER-WITTEN, HANNS: *Opfergang der Generale.* Berlin: Bernard & Graefe, 1952.

GREINER, HELMUTH: *Die Oberste Wehrmachtfuehrung 1939–1943.* Wiesbaden: Limes, 1951.

LOSSBERG, BERNHARD VON: *Im Wehrmacht Fuehrungsstab.* Hamburg: H. H. Noelke, 1950.

SEEMEN, GERHARD VON: *Die Ritterkreuztraeger 1939–1945.* Bad Nauheim: Podzun, 1955.

SIEGLER, FRITZ FRHR. VON: *Die Hoeheren Dienststellen der Deutschen Wehrmacht.* Munich, 1953.

TAYLOR, TELFORD: *Sword and Swastika.* New York: Simon and Schuster, 1952.

A. German Army

BLUMENTRITT, GUENTHER: *Von Rundstedt.* London: Odhams, 1952.

BUCHNER, ALEX: *Gebirgsjaeger an allen Fronten.* Hanover: Sponholtz, 1954.

CHOLTITZ, DIETRICH VON: *Soldat unter Soldaten—Die Deutschen Armee im Frieden und im Krieg.* Zurich: Europa, 1951.

CRAIG, GORDON A.: *The Politics of the Prussian Army 1640–1945.* Oxford: Clarendon, 1955.

Das Deutsche Heer 1939—Gliederung, Standorte, Stellenbesetzung und Verzeichnis sämtlichen Offiziere am 3. 1. 1939. Bad Nauheim: Podzun, 1953.

DIETL, FRAU GERDA-LUISE, AND HERMANN, KURT: *General Dietl.* Munich: Muenchener Buchverlag, 1951.

ERFURTH, WALDEMAR: *Die Geschichte des Deutschen Generalstabes von 1918 bis 1945.* Goettingen: Muesterschmidt, 1957.

GOERLITZ, WALTER: *History of the German General Staff 1657–1945.* Praeger, 1953.

GUDERIAN, GENERAL HEINZ: *Panzer Leader.* London: Michael Joseph, 1952.

HEUSINGER, ADOLF: *Befehl im Widerstreit—Schicksalstunden der Deutschen Armee 1923–1945.* Stuttgart: Rainer Wunderlich, 1950.

LANZ, HUBERT: *Gebirgsjaeger—Die I. Gebirgsdivision 1935–1945.* Bad Nauheim: Podzun, 1954.

MANSTEIN, ERICH VON: *Verlorene Siege.* Bonn: Athenaeum, 1955.

MELLENTHIN, MAJ. GEN. F. W. VON: *Panzer Battles.* University of Oklahoma Press, 1956.

MUELLER-HILLEBRAND, BURKHART: *Das Heer 1933–1945.* Darmstadt: Mittler, 1954–56.

PAGET, R. T.: *Manstein—His Campaigns and His Trial.* London: Collins, 1951.

ROMMEL, ERWIN: *The Rommel Papers.* B. H. Liddell Hart, ed. New York: Harcourt, Brace, 1953.

ROSINSKI, HERBERT: *The German Army. The Infantry Journal,* 1944.

SCHLABRENDORF, FABIAN VON: *Offiziere gegen Hitler.* Zurich: Europa, 1946.

SCHRAMM, WILHELM VON: *Conspiracy among Generals.* New York: Scribner, 1956.

STAHL, GENERALLEUTNANT A. D. FRIEDRICH: *Heeresinteilung 1939.* Bad Nauheim: Podzun, 1954.

TESKE, HERMANN: *Bewegungskrieg—Fuehrungsprobleme einer Infanterie-Division im Westfeldzug 1940.* Heidelberg: Vowinckel, 1955.

WESTPHAL, GENERAL SIEGFRIED: *The German Army in the West.* London: Cassell, 1951.

WHEELER-BENNETT, JOHN W.: *The Nemesis of Power—The German Army in Politics 1918–1945.* London: Macmillan; New York: St. Martin's, 1953.

YOUNG, DESMOND: *Rommel, the Desert Fox.* New York: Harper, 1950.

B. German Air Force

BARTZ, KARL: *Als der Himmel Brannte.* Hanover: Sponholtz, 1955.

BAUMBACH, WERNER: *Zu Spät?* Munich: Pflaum, 1949.

GALLAND, ADOLF: *The First and the Last—The Rise and Fall of the German Fighter Forces, 1938–1945.* New York: Henry Holt, 1954.

HEINKEL, ERNST: *Stormy Life—Memoirs of a Pioneer of the Air Age.* New York: E. P. Dutton, 1956.

KOCH, HORST-ADALBERT: *Flak—Die Geschichte der Deutschen Flakartillerie 1935–1945.* Bad Nauheim: Podzun, 1954.

LEE, ASHER: *The German Air Force.* London: Duckworth, 1946.

OSTERKAMP, THEO: *Durch Hoehen und Tiefen Jagt ein Herz.* Heidelberg: Vowinckel, 1952.

C. German Navy

BEKKER, C. D.: *Defeat at Sea.* New York: Henry Holt, 1955.

BUSCH, FRITZ-OTTO: *Holocaust at Sea—The Drama of the Scharnhorst.* New York: Rinehart, 1956.

FRISCHAUER, WILLI, AND JACKSON, ROBERT: *The Altmark Affair.* New York: Macmillan, 1955.

GROENER, ERICH: *Die Schiffe der Deutschen Kriegsmarine und Luftwaffe.* Munich: Lehmanns, 1954.

LOHMANN, WALTER, AND HILDEBRAND, HANS H.: *Die Deutsche Kriegsmarine 1939–1945.* Bad Nauheim: Podzun, 1956.

MARTIENSSEN, ANTHONY: *Hitler and His Admirals.* New York: E. P. Dutton, 1949.

POPE, DUDLEY: *Graf Spee—The Life and Death of a Raider.* New York: J. B. Lippincott, 1957.

PUTTKAMMER, KARL-JESKO VON: *Die Unheimliche See—Hitler und die Kriegsmarine.* Munich: Kuehne, 1952.

RUGE, FRIEDRICH: *Der Seekrieg 1939–1945.* Stuttgart: K. F. Koehler, 1954.

WOODWARD, DAVID: *The Tirpitz and the Battle for the North Atlantic.* New York: W. W. Norton, 1954.

D. Waffen-SS

HAUSSER, PAUL: *Waffen-SS im Einsatz.* Goettingen: Plesse, 1953.

KRAETSCHMER, E. G.: *Die Ritterkreuztraeger der Waffen-SS.* Goettingen: Plesse, 1955.

REITLINGER, GERALD: *The SS, Alibi of a Nation.* London: Heinemann, 1956.

II. MILITARY OPERATIONS

ASSMANN, KURT: *Deutsche Schicksaljahre.* Wiesbaden: Eberhard Brockhaus, 1950.

BRYANT, SIR ARTHUR: *The Turn of the Tide—A History of the War Years Based on the Diaries of Field-Marshal Lord Alanbrooke, Chief of the Imperial General Staff.* New York: Doubleday, 1957.

FLEMING, PETER: *Operation Sea Lion.* New York: Simon and Schuster, 1957.

GOERLITZ, WALTER: *Der Zweite Weltkrieg 1939–1945.* 2 vol. Stuttgart: Steingrueben, 1951.

HALDER, FRANZ: *Hitler As War Lord.* London: Putnam, 1950.

HART, B. H. LIDDELL: *The German Generals Talk.* New York: William Morrow, 1948.

HINSLEY, F. H.: *Hitler's Strategy.* Cambridge: University Press, 1951.

JACOBSEN, HANS-ADOLF: *Dokumente zur Vorgeschichte des Westfeldzuges 1939–1940.* Goettingen: Musterschmidt, 1956.

KESSELRING, ALBERT: *A Soldier's Record.* New York: William Morrow, 1954.

POSSONY, STEFAN: *Decision Without Battle,* in 72 U.S. Naval Institute Proceedings, 1946.

RICHARDS, DENIS: *Royal Air Force 1939–1945.* London: H. M. Stationery Office, 1953.

ROSKILL, CAPTAIN S. W.: *The War at Sea 1939–1945.* London: H. M. Stationery Office, 1954.

SHULMAN, MILTON: *Defeat in the West.* New York: E. P. Dutton, 1948.

TIPPELSKIRCH, KURT VON: *Geschichte des Zweiten Weltkrieges.* Bonn: Athenaeum, 1951.

WESTPHAL, KREIPE, *et al.: The Fatal Decisions.* Freidin and Richardson, ed. New York: William Sloane, 1956.

A.   Conquest of Norway and Denmark

BOEHM, GENERALADMIRAL A. D. HERMANN: *Norwegen Zwischen England und Deutschland.* Lippoldsberg: Klosterhaus, 1956.

DERRY, T. K.: *The Campaign in Norway.* London: H. M. Stationery Office, 1952.

HUBATSCH, WALTHER: *Die Deutsche Besetzung von Daenemark und Norwegen.* Goettingen: Musterschmidt, 1952.

B.   Conquest of the Netherlands

ASHTON: *The Netherlands at War.* London, 1941.

BLOKLAND, VAN: "The Five Days of Holland." London: *The Fortnightly,* October 1940.

DOORMAN, P. L. G.: *Military Operations in the Netherlands from 10th–17th May, 1940.* London: Allen & Unwin, 1944.

DUTCH COMMISSION OF INQUIRY: *Enquetecomissie Regeringsbeleid 1940–45.* The Hague, 1949.

DUTCH MINISTRY OF WAR: *De Strijd op Nederlands Grond Gebied Tijdens de Wereloorlog II.* The Hague, 1953.

KLEFFENS, EELCO VAN: *Juggernaut over Holland.* 1941.

NETHERLANDS MINISTRY OF DEFENSE: *Short Account of Military Operations in the Netherlands from 10th–14th May, 1940.*

C. Conquest of Belgium

BACH, FRANZ-JOSEPH: *Aus der Luft Erobert. Die Deutsche Soldaten-Zeitung*, September 10, 17 and 24, 1953.

The Belgian Campaign and the Surrender of the Belgian Army. New York: Belgian-American Educational Foundation, 1940.

BELGIAN MINISTRY OF FOREIGN AFFAIRS: *Belgium—The Official Account of What Happened 1939–1940.* London, 1941.

DELANDSHEERE AND OOMS: *La Belgique sous les Nazis.*

FOUILLIEN, M., AND BOUHON, J.: *Mai 1940.* Brussels: L'Edition Universelle, 1945.

KENNEDY, JOSEPH P., AND LANDIS, JAMES M.: *The Surrender of King Leopold.* Joseph P. Kennedy Memorial Foundation, 1950.

MELZER, WALTHER: *Albert-Kanal und Eben-Emael.* Heidelberg: Vowinckel, 1957.

MICHIELS, LT. GEN. OSCAR: *18 Jours de Guerre en Belgique.* Paris: 1947.

OVERSTRAETEN, GENERAL VAN: *Albert I–Leopold III.* Brussels, 1946.

SCHACHT, GERHARD: *Eben Emael–10 May 1940. Wehrwissenschaftliche Rundschau,* May 1954.

WITZIG, RUDOLF: *Die Einnahme von Eben-Emael. Wehrkunde,* May 1954.

D. The Battle of France

DRAPER, THEODORE: *The Six Weeks' War: May 10–June 25, 1940.* New York: Viking, 1944.

ELLIS, MAJOR L. F.: *The War in France and Flanders 1939–1940.* London: H. M. Stationery Office, 1953.

GOUTARD, A.: *1940 La Guerre des Occasions Perdues.* Paris: Hachette, 1956.

LYET, CDT. PIERRE: *La Bataille de France.* Paris: Payot, 1947.

MEIER-WELCKER, HANS: *Der Entschluss zum Anhalten der Deutschen Panzertruppen in Flandern.* Munich: *Vierteljahrshefte fuer Zeitgeschichte,* heft 1, 1954.

MORDAL, JACQUES: *Guderian sur l'Aa ou le Véritable Miracle de Dunkerque. Revue de Défense Nationale,* August-September 1955.

REINHARDT, HANS: *Im Schatten Guderians. Wehrkunde,* October 1954.

III. GENERAL

ABSHAGEN, KARL HEINZ: *Canaris.* London: Hutchinson, 1956.

BULLOCK, ALAN: *Hitler.* New York: Harper, 1952.

BUTLER, J. R. M.: *Grand Strategy—History of the Second World War September 1939–June 1941,* Vol. II. London: H. M. Stationery Office, 1957.

CHURCHILL, WINSTON S.: *The Second World War—The Gathering Storm.* New York: Houghton Mifflin, 1948.

———: *The Second World War—Their Finest Hour.* New York: Houghton Mifflin, 1949.

CIANO, GALEAZZO: *Ciano's Diplomatic Papers*. Malcolm Muggeridge, ed. London: Odhams, 1948.

CIANO, GALEAZZO: *Diario*. Rizolli, 1946.

COLVIN, IAN: *Master Spy—The Incredible Story of Admiral Wilhelm Canaris*. New York: McGraw-Hill, 1951.

DEJONG, LOUIS: *The German Fifth Column in World War II*. Chicago: University of Chicago Press, 1956.

DIETRICH, OTTO: *Hitler*. Regnery, 1955.

FABER DU FAUR, GENLT. A. D. MORIZ VON: *Macht und Ohnmacht—Erinnerungen eines Alten Offiziers*. Stuttgart, 1953.

FOERTSCH, HERMANN: *The Art of Modern Warfare*. Veritas, 1940.

FRISCHAUER, WILLI: *The Rise and Fall of Hermann Goering*. New York: Houghton Mifflin, 1951.

————: *Himmler*. Boston: Beacon, 1953.

FULLER, MAJOR-GENERAL J. F. C.: *The Second World War 1939–1945*. New York: Duell, Sloane & Pearce, 1949.

GISEVIUS, HANS BERND: *To the Bitter End*. New York: Houghton Mifflin, 1947.

HANFSTAENGL, ERNST: *Unheard Witness*. Lippincott, 1957.

HASSELL, ULRICH VON: *The Von Hassell Diaries 1938–1944*. New York: Doubleday, 1947.

LEMKIN, RAPHAEL: *Axis Rule in Occupied Europe*. Carnegie Endowment for International Peace, 1944.

NEUMANN, FRANZ: *Behemoth*. Oxford University Press, 1944.

ROYAL INSTITUTE OF INTERNATIONAL AFFAIRS: *Hitler's Europe*. Arnold and V. M. Toynbee, ed. Oxford University Press, 1954.

SCHELLENBERG, WALTER: *The Schellenberg Memoirs*. New York: Harper, 1957.

SHIRER, WILLIAM L.: *Berlin Diary*. New York: Knopf, 1941.

SPEARS, SIR EDWARD L.: *Assignment to Catastrophe—Vol. I, Prelude to Dunkirk July 1939–May 1940*. New York: A. A. Wyn, 1954.

————: *Assignment to Catastrophe—Vol. II, The Fall of France June 1940*. New York: A. A. Wyn, 1955.

VUORINEN, JOHN H.: *Finland and World War II 1939–1944*. Ronald Press, 1948.

WAITE, ROBERT G. L.: *Vanguard of Nazism—The Free Corps Movement in Postwar Germany 1918–1923*. Cambridge: Harvard University Press, 1952.

WEINBERG, GERALD L.: *Guide to Captured German Documents*. USAF, Maxwell Air Force Base, 1952.

WILMOT, CHESTER: *The Struggle for Europe*. New York: Harper, 1952.

Index

About the Author

In Sword and Swastika, *published in 1952, Telford Taylor described the remarkable conjunction of generals and Nazis in Hitler's Germany up to the fall of 1939. That book and this one were both written from his war and postwar experience as an officer in the Army intelligence service and as chief counsel for the prosecution, with the rank of brigadier general, at the Nuremberg war crimes trials.*

Mr. Taylor, who served in various official capacities during the Roosevelt and Truman Administrations, now practices law in New York City. He is also a visiting lecturer at the Yale Law School and is the author of Grand Inquest: The Story of Congressional Investigations, *published in 1955.*